Modern Labor Economics

100736364045

Modern Labor Economics
Theory and Public Policy

Global Edition
Twelfth Edition

Ronald G. Ehrenberg
School of Industrial and Labor Relations
Cornell University

Robert S. Smith
School of Industrial and Labor Relations
Cornell University

PEARSON

Boston   Columbus   Indianapolis   New York   San Francisco   Upper Saddle River
Amsterdam   Cape Town   Dubai   London   Madrid   Milan   Munich   Paris   Montréal   Toronto
Delhi   Mexico City   São Paulo   Sydney   Hong Kong   Seoul   Singapore   Taipei   Tokyo

Editor-in-Chief: Donna Battista
Head of Learning Asset Acquisition, Global Edition: Laura Dent
Executive Acquisitions Editor: Adrienne D'Ambrosio
Editorial Project Manager: Sarah Dumouchelle
Executive Marketing Manager: Lori DeShazo
Managing Editor: Jeff Holcomb
Senior Production Project Manager: Nancy Freihofer
Acquisitions Editor, Global Edition: Toril Cooper
Project Editor, Global Edition: Daniel Luiz
Media Producer, Global Edition: M. Vikram Kumar
Senior Manufacturing Controller, Production, Global Edition: Trudy Kimber
Permissions Coordinator: Michael Joyce
Art Director: Jonathon Boylan
Cover Design: PreMediaGlobal
Cover Image: © GrandeDuc / Shutterstock
Full-Service Project Management: GEX Publishing Services
Cover Printer: Courier Westford

Credits and acknowledgments borrowed from other sources and reproduced, with permission, in this textbook appear on the appropriate page within text.

Pearson Education Limited
Edinburgh Gate
Harlow
Essex CM20 2JE
England

100736³045

and Associated Companies throughout the world

Visit us on the World Wide Web at:
www.pearsonglobaleditions.com

The rights of Ronald G. Ehrenberg and Robert S. Smith to be identified as the authors of this work have been asserted by them in accordance with the Copyright, Designs and Patents Act 1988.

Authorized adaptation from the United States edition, entitled Modern Labor Economics: Theory and Public Policy, 12th edition, ISBN 978-0-133-46278-4, by Ronald G. Ehrenberg and Robert S. Smith, published by Pearson Education © 2015.

ISBN-10: 1-292-06047-6
ISBN-13: 978-1-292-06047-7

British Library Cataloguing-in-Publication Data
A catalogue record for this book is available from the British Library

14
10 9 8 7 6 5 4 3 2 1

Typeset in Palatino 10/12 by GEX Publishing Services.

Printed and bound by Courier Westford in The United States of America.

Brief Contents

Contents 6

Preface 18

CHAPTER 1 INTRODUCTION 23

CHAPTER 2 OVERVIEW OF THE LABOR MARKET 47

CHAPTER 3 THE DEMAND FOR LABOR 81

CHAPTER 4 LABOR DEMAND ELASTICITIES 117

CHAPTER 5 FRICTIONS IN THE LABOR MARKET 152

CHAPTER 6 SUPPLY OF LABOR TO THE ECONOMY: THE DECISION TO WORK 190

CHAPTER 7 LABOR SUPPLY: HOUSEHOLD PRODUCTION, THE FAMILY, AND THE LIFE CYCLE 233

CHAPTER 8 COMPENSATING WAGE DIFFERENTIALS AND LABOR MARKETS 267

CHAPTER 9 INVESTMENTS IN HUMAN CAPITAL: EDUCATION AND TRAINING 304

CHAPTER 10 WORKER MOBILITY: MIGRATION, IMMIGRATION, AND TURNOVER 349

CHAPTER 11 PAY AND PRODUCTIVITY: WAGE DETERMINATION WITHIN THE FIRM 383

CHAPTER 12 GENDER, RACE, AND ETHNICITY IN THE LABOR MARKET 421

CHAPTER 13 UNIONS AND THE LABOR MARKET 472

CHAPTER 14 UNEMPLOYMENT 524

CHAPTER 15 INEQUALITY IN EARNINGS 561

CHAPTER 16 THE LABOR-MARKET EFFECTS OF INTERNATIONAL TRADE AND PRODUCTION SHARING 589

Answers to Odd-Numbered Review Questions and Problems 617

Name Index 667

Subject Index 673

Contents

Preface   18

CHAPTER 1   **INTRODUCTION**   **23**

The Labor Market   24

Labor Economics: Some Basic Concepts   24
Positive Economics   25
The Models and Predictions of Positive Economics   26
Normative Economics   29
Normative Economics and Government Policy   32
Efficiency versus Equity   33

Plan of the Text   34

Example 1.1   Positive Economics: What Does It Mean to "Understand" Behavior?   27

Review Questions   35

Problems   36

Selected Readings   37

Appendix 1A   Statistical Testing of Labor Market Hypotheses   38

CHAPTER 2   **OVERVIEW OF THE LABOR MARKET**   **47**

The Labor Market: Definitions, Facts, and Trends   48
The Labor Force and Unemployment   49
Industries and Occupations: Adapting to Change   52
The Earnings of Labor   53

How the Labor Market Works   58
The Demand for Labor   59
The Supply of Labor   63
The Determination of the Wage   65

Applications of the Theory   70
Who Is Underpaid and Who Is Overpaid?   71
Unemployment and Responses to Technological Change across Countries   74

Example 2.1   Real Wages across Countries and Time: Big Macs per Hour Worked   56

Example 2.2   The Black Death and the Wages of Labor   69

Example 2.3   Forced Labor in Colonial Mozambique   73

Empirical Study   Pay Levels and the Supply of Military Officers: Obtaining
Sample Variation from Cross-Section Data   76

Review Questions   77

Problems   79

Selected Readings   80

CHAPTER 3   THE DEMAND FOR LABOR   81

Profit Maximization   82
    Marginal Income from an Additional Unit of Input   83
    Marginal Expense of an Added Input   84

The Short-Run Demand for Labor When Both Product and
Labor Markets Are Competitive   85
    A Critical Assumption: Declining MP_L 86
    From Profit Maximization to Labor Demand   87

The Demand for Labor in Competitive Markets When Other Inputs
Can Be Varied   92
    Labor Demand in the Long Run   92
    More Than Two Inputs   95

Labor Demand When the Product Market Is Not Competitive   96
    Maximizing Monopoly Profits   96
    Do Monopolies Pay Higher Wages?   97

Policy Application: The Labor Market Effects of Employer Payroll Taxes
and Wage Subsidies   98
    Who Bears the Burden of a Payroll Tax?   98
    Employment Subsidies as a Device to Help the Poor   100

Example 3.1   The Marginal Revenue Product of College Football Stars   85

Example 3.2   Coal Mining Wages and Capital Substitution   94

Empirical Study   Do Women Pay for Employer-Funded Maternity Benefits? Using
Cross-Section Data Over Time to Analyze "Differences in
Differences"   102

Review Questions   105

Problems   106

Selected Readings   107

Appendix 3A   Graphical Derivation of a Firm's Labor Demand Curve   108

CHAPTER 4   LABOR DEMAND ELASTICITIES   117

The Own-Wage Elasticity of Demand   118
    The Hicks-Marshall Laws of Derived Demand   120
    Estimates of Own-Wage Labor Demand Elasticities   123
    Applying the Laws of Derived Demand: Inferential Analysis   125

The Cross-Wage Elasticity of Demand   127
    Can the Laws of Derived Demand Be Applied to Cross-Elasticities?   128
    Estimates Relating to Cross-Elasticities   130

Policy Application: Effects of Minimum Wage Laws   131
    History and Description   131
    Employment Effects: Theoretical Analysis   132
    Employment Effects: Empirical Estimates   136
    Does the Minimum Wage Fight Poverty?   138
    "Living Wage" Laws   139

Applying Concepts of Labor Demand Elasticity to the Issue of
Technological Change   140

Example 4.1   Why Are Union Wages So Different in Two Parts of the Trucking
                 Industry?   126

Example 4.2   The Employment Effects of the First Federal Minimum Wage   137

Example 4.3   Gross Complementarity in the 19th Century Apparel Industry   142

Empirical Study   Estimating the Labor Demand Curve: Time Series Data and
                      Coping with "Simultaneity"   146

Review Questions   149

Problems   150

Selected Readings   151

CHAPTER 5   FRICTIONS IN THE LABOR MARKET   152

Frictions on the Employee Side of the Market   153
    The Law of One Price   153
    Monopsonistic Labor Markets: A Definition   156
    Profit Maximization under Monopsonistic Conditions   157
    How Do Monopsonistic Firms Respond to Shifts in the Supply Curve?   161
    Monopsonistic Conditions and the Employment Response to Minimum
        Wage Legislation   164
    Job Search Costs and Other Labor Market Outcomes   165
    Monopsonistic Conditions and the Relevance of the Competitive
        Model   167

Frictions on the Employer Side of the Market   168
    Categories of Quasi-Fixed Costs   168
    The Employment/Hours Trade-Off   172

Training Investments   176
    The Training Decision by Employers   176
    The Types of Training   177
    Training and Post-Training Wage Increases   178
    Employer Training Investments and Recessionary Layoffs   180

Hiring Investments   181
    The Use of Credentials   181
    Internal Labor Markets   183
    How Can the Employer Recoup Its Hiring Investments?   185

Example 5.1   Does Employment Protection Legislation Protect Workers?   169

Example 5.2   "Renting" Workers as a Way of Coping with Hiring Costs   174

Example 5.3   Why Do Temporary-Help Firms Provide Free General Skills Training?   182

Empirical Study   What Explains Wage Differences for Workers Who Appear Similar? Using Panel Data to Deal with Unobserved Heterogeneity   184

Review Questions   186

Problems   187

Selected Readings   189

CHAPTER 6   **SUPPLY OF LABOR TO THE ECONOMY: THE DECISION TO WORK**   **190**

Trends in Labor Force Participation and Hours of Work   190
    Labor Force Participation Rates   191
    Hours of Work   193

A Theory of the Decision to Work   195
    Some Basic Concepts   195
    Analysis of the Labor/Leisure Choice   199
    Empirical Findings on the Income and Substitution Effects   214

Policy Applications   217
    Budget Constraints with "Spikes"   217
    Programs with Net Wage Rates of Zero   220
    Subsidy Programs with Positive Net Wage Rates   224

Example 6.1   The Labor Supply of New York City Taxi Drivers   199

Example 6.2   Do Large Inheritances Induce Labor Force Withdrawal?   209

Example 6.3   Daily Labor Supply at the Ballpark   215

Example 6.4   Labor Supply Effects of Income Tax Cuts   216

Example 6.5   Staying Around One's Kentucky Home: Workers' Compensation Benefits and the Return to Work   220

Example 6.6   Wartime Food Requisitions and Agricultural Work Incentives   227

Empirical Study   Estimating the Income Effect Among Lottery Winners: The Search for "Exogeneity"   228

Review Questions   229

Problems   231

Selected Readings   232

CHAPTER 7   **LABOR SUPPLY: HOUSEHOLD PRODUCTION, THE FAMILY, AND THE LIFE CYCLE   233**

A Labor Supply Model That Incorporates Household Production   233
   The Basic Model for an Individual: Similarities with the Labor-Leisure
      Model   234
   The Basic Model for an Individual: Some New Implications   236

Joint Labor Supply Decisions within the Household   239
   Specialization of Function   240
   Do Both Partners Work for Pay?   241
   The Joint Decision and Interdependent Productivity at Home   243
   Labor Supply in Recessions: The "Discouraged" versus the
      "Added" Worker   243

Life Cycle Aspects of Labor Supply   247
   The Substitution Effect and When to Work over a Lifetime   247
   The Choice of Retirement Age   249

Policy Application: Child Care and Labor Supply   254
   Child-Care Subsidies   254
   Child Support Assurance   257

Example 7.1   Obesity and the Household Production Model   237
Example 7.2   Child Labor in Poor Countries   245
Example 7.3   How Does Labor Supply Respond to Housing Subsidies?   249
Empirical Study   The Effects of Wage Increases on Labor Supply (and Sleep):
   Time-Use Diary Data and Sample Selection Bias   260

Review Questions   262
Problems   264
Selected Readings   266

CHAPTER 8   **COMPENSATING WAGE DIFFERENTIALS AND LABOR MARKETS   267**

Job Matching: The Role of Worker Preferences
and Information   267
   Individual Choice and Its Outcomes   268
   Assumptions and Predictions   270
   Empirical Tests for Compensating Wage Differentials   273

Hedonic Wage Theory and the Risk of Injury   274
   Employee Considerations   275
   Employer Considerations   277
   The Matching of Employers and Employees   279
   Normative Analysis: Occupational Safety and Health Regulation   283

Hedonic Wage Theory and Employee Benefits   288
   Employee Preferences   288

Employer Preferences   290
The Joint Determination of Wages and Benefits   292

Example 8.1   Working on the Railroad: Making a Bad Job Good   274

Example 8.2   Parenthood, Occupational Choice, and Risk   281

Example 8.3   Indentured Servitude and Compensating Differentials   283

Empirical Study   How Risky are Estimates of Compensating Wage Differentials for Risk? The "Errors in Variables" Problem   294

Review Questions   296

Problems   297

Selected Readings   298

Appendix 8A   Compensating Wage Differentials and Layoffs   299

CHAPTER 9   **INVESTMENTS IN HUMAN CAPITAL: EDUCATION AND TRAINING   304**

Human Capital Investments: The Basic Model   306
The Concept of Present Value   306
Modeling the Human Capital Investment Decision   308

The Demand for a College Education   310
Weighing the Costs and Benefits of College   310
Predictions of the Theory   311
Market Responses to Changes in College Attendance   317

Education, Earnings, and Post-Schooling Investments in Human Capital   318
Average Earnings and Educational Level   318
On-the-Job Training and the Concavity of Age/Earnings Profiles   321
The Fanning Out of Age/Earnings Profiles   323
Women and the Acquisition of Human Capital   323

Is Education a Good Investment?   328
Is Education a Good Investment for Individuals?   328
Is Education a Good Social Investment?   331
Is Public Sector Training a Good Social Investment?   339

Example 9.1   War and Human Capital   305

Example 9.2   Can Language Affect Investment Behavior?   313

Example 9.3   Did the G.I. Bill Increase Educational Attainment for Returning World War II Vets?   315

Example 9.4   Valuing a Human Asset: The Case of the Divorcing Doctor   329

Example 9.5   The Socially Optimal Level of Educational Investment   337

Empirical Study   Estimating the Returns to Education Using a Sample of Twins: Coping with the Problem of Unobserved Differences in Ability   340

Review Questions   342

Problems   343

Selected Readings   344

Appendix 9A   A "Cobweb" Model of Labor Market Adjustment   345

CHAPTER 10   WORKER MOBILITY: MIGRATION, IMMIGRATION, AND TURNOVER   349

The Determinants of Worker Mobility   350

Geographic Mobility   351

The Direction of Migratory Flows   351

Personal Characteristics of Movers   352

The Role of Distance   354

The Earnings Distribution in Sending Countries and International
Migration   354

The Returns to International and Domestic Migration   356

Policy Application: Restricting Immigration   359

U.S. Immigration History   360

Naive Views of Immigration   363

An Analysis of the Gainers and Losers   365

Do the Overall Gains from Immigration Exceed the Losses?   371

Employee Turnover   374

Wage Effects   374

Effects of Employer Size   375

Gender Differences   376

Cyclical Effects   376

Employer Location   377

Is More Mobility Better?   377

Example 10.1   The Great Migration: Southern Blacks Move North   353

Example 10.2   Migration and One's Time Horizon   355

Example 10.3   The Mariel Boatlift and Its Effects on Miami's Wage
and Unemployment Rates   370

Example 10.4   Illegal Immigrants, Personal Discount Rates, and Crime   373

Empirical Study   Do Political Refugees Invest More in Human Capital than
Economic Immigrants? The Use of Synthetic Cohorts   378

Review Questions   380

Problems   381

Selected Readings   382

CHAPTER 11   PAY AND PRODUCTIVITY: WAGE DETERMINATION WITHIN THE FIRM   383

Motivating Workers: An Overview of the Fundamentals   385

The Employment Contract   385

Coping with Information Asymmetries   386
Motivating Workers   389
Motivating the Individual in a Group   391
Compensation Plans: Overview and Guide to the Rest of
the Chapter   393

Productivity and the Basis of Yearly Pay   393
Employee Preferences   393
Employer Considerations   395

Productivity and the Level of Pay   401
Why Higher Pay Might Increase Worker Productivity   401
Efficiency Wages   403

Productivity and the Sequencing of Pay   404
Underpayment Followed by Overpayment   404
Promotion Tournaments   408
Career Concerns and Productivity   410

Applications of the Theory: Explaining Two Puzzles   412
Why Do Earnings Increase with Job Tenure?   412
Why Do Large Firms Pay More?   414

Example 11.1   The Wide Range of Possible Productivities: The Case of the Factory
That Could Not Cut Output   384

Example 11.2   Calorie Consumption and the Type of Pay   390

Example 11.3   The Effects of Low Relative Pay on Worker Satisfaction   392

Example 11.4   Poor Group Incentives Doom the Shakers   397

Example 11.5   Did Henry Ford Pay Efficiency Wages?   402

Example 11.6   The "Rat Race" in Law Firms   410

Empirical Study   Are Workers Willing to Pay for Fairness? Using Laboratory
Experiments to Study Economic Behavior   416

Review Questions   418

Problems   419

Selected Readings   420

CHAPTER 12   GENDER, RACE, AND ETHNICITY IN THE LABOR MARKET   421

Measured and Unmeasured Sources of Earnings
Differences   422
Earnings Differences by Gender   423
Earnings Differences between Black
and White Americans   432
Earnings Differences by Ethnicity   438

Theories of Market Discrimination   440
Personal-Prejudice Models: Employer Discrimination   441

Personal-Prejudice Models: Customer Discrimination   446
Personal-Prejudice Models: Employee Discrimination   446
Statistical Discrimination   447
Noncompetitive Models of Discrimination   450
A Final Word on the Theories of Discrimination   454

Federal Programs to End Discrimination   454
Equal Pay Act of 1963   454
Title VII of the Civil Rights Act   455
The Federal Contract Compliance Program   459
Effectiveness of Federal Antidiscrimination Programs   461

Example 12.1   Bias in the Selection of Musicians by Symphony Orchestras   427

Example 12.2   Race Discrimination May "Strike" When Few Are Looking: The Case of Umpires in Major League Baseball   437

Example 12.3   Fear and Lathing in the Michigan Furniture Industry   448

Example 12.4   Comparable Worth and the University   458

Empirical Study   Can We Catch Discriminators in the Act? The Use of Field Experiments in Identifying Labor Market Discrimination   462

Review Questions   465

Problems   466

Selected Readings   467

Appendix 12A   Estimating Comparable-Worth Earnings Gaps: An Application of Regression Analysis   468

CHAPTER 13   UNIONS AND THE LABOR MARKET   472

Union Structure and Membership   473
International Comparisons of Unionism   473
The Legal Structure of Unions in the United States   475
Constraints on the Achievement of Union Objectives   479
The Monopoly-Union Model   481
The Efficient-Contracts Model   483

The Activities and Tools of Collective Bargaining   487
Union Membership: An Analysis of Demand and Supply   487
Union Actions to Alter the Labor Demand Curve   492
Bargaining and the Threat of Strikes   494
Bargaining in the Public Sector: The Threat of Arbitration   499

The Effects of Unions   502
The Theory of Union Wage Effects   503
Evidence of Union Wage Effects   506
Evidence of Union Total Compensation Effects   508
The Effects of Unions on Employment   509

The Effects of Unions on Productivity and Profits   510
Normative Analyses of Unions   511

Example 13.1   A Downward Sloping Demand Curve for Football Players?   480

Example 13.2   The Effects of Deregulation on Trucking and Airlines   491

Example 13.3   Permanent Replacement of Strikers   497

Empirical Study   What Is the Gap Between Union and Nonunion Pay? The Importance of Replication in Producing Credible Estimates   514

Review Questions   516

Problems   517

Selected Readings   518

Appendix 13A   Arbitration and the Bargaining Contract Zone   519

CHAPTER 14   UNEMPLOYMENT   524

A Stock-Flow Model of the Labor Market   526
Sources of Unemployment   527
Rates of Flow Affect Unemployment Levels   528

Frictional Unemployment   531
The Theory of Job Search   532
Effects of Unemployment Insurance Benefits   535

Structural Unemployment   539
Occupational and Regional Unemployment Rate Differences   539
International Differences in Long-Term Unemployment   541
Do Efficiency Wages Cause Structural Unemployment?   542

Demand-Deficient (Cyclical) Unemployment   545
Downward Wage Rigidity   545
Financing U.S. Unemployment Compensation   549

Seasonal Unemployment   551

When Do We Have Full Employment?   553
Defining the Natural Rate of Unemployment   553
Unemployment and Demographic Characteristics   554
What Is the Natural Rate?   555

Example 14.1   Is Unemployment Self-Perpetuating?   534

Example 14.2   Unemployment Insurance and Seasonal Unemployment: A Historical Perspective   552

Empirical Study   Do Reemployment Bonuses Reduce Unemployment? The Results of Social Experiments   556

Review Questions   558

Problems   559

Selected Readings   560

CHAPTER 15   **INEQUALITY IN EARNINGS**   **561**

Measuring Inequality   562

Earnings Inequality Since 1980: Some Descriptive Data   565
  The Increased Returns to Higher Education   569
  Growth of Earnings Dispersion within Human-Capital Groups   570

The Underlying Causes of Growing Inequality   572
  Changes in Supply   573
  Changes in Demand: Technological Change   575
  Changes in Demand: Earnings Instability   578
  Changes in Institutional Forces   579

  Example 15.1   Differences in Earnings Inequality across Developed
                     Countries   569

  Example 15.2   Changes in the Premium to Education at the Beginning of the
                     Twentieth Century   571

  Empirical Study   Do Parents' Earnings Determine the Earnings of Their Children?
                        The Use of Intergenerational Data in Studying Economic
                        Mobility   580

Review Questions   581

Problems   583

Selected Readings   584

  Appendix 15A   Lorenz Curves and Gini Coefficients   585

CHAPTER 16   **THE LABOR-MARKET EFFECTS OF INTERNATIONAL TRADE AND PRODUCTION
                 SHARING**   **589**

Why Does Trade Take Place?   590
  Trade between Individuals and the Principle of Comparative
    Advantage   590
  The Incentives for Trade across Different Countries   592

Effects of Trade on the Demand for Labor   596
  Product Demand Shifts   597
  Shifts in the Supply of Alternative Factors of Production   599
  The Net Effect on Labor Demand   601

Will Wages Converge across Countries?   605

Policy Issues   607
  Subsidizing Human-Capital Investments   608
  Income Support Programs   609
  Subsidized Employment   610
  How Narrowly Should We Target Compensation?   611
  Summary   614

`Example 16.1`   The Growth Effects of the Openness to Trade: Japan's Sudden Move to Openness in 1859   597

`Example 16.2`   Could a Quarter of American Jobs Be Offshored? Might Your Future Job Be among Them?   603

Empirical Study   Evaluating European Active Labor Market Policies: The Use of Meta-Analysis   612

Review Questions   614

Problems   615

Selected Readings   616

Answers to Odd-Numbered Review Questions and Problems   617

Name Index   667

Subject Index   673

Preface

Modern Labor Economics: Theory and Public Policy has grown out of our experiences over the last four decades in teaching labor market economics and conducting research aimed at influencing public policy. Our text develops the modern theory of labor market behavior, summarizes empirical evidence that supports or contradicts each hypothesis, and illustrates in detail the usefulness of the theory for public policy analysis. We believe that showing students the social implications of concepts enhances the motivation to learn them, and that using the concepts of each chapter in an analytic setting allows students to see the concepts in action. The extensive use of detailed policy applications constitutes a major contribution of this text.

If, as economists believe, passing "the market test" is the ultimate criterion for judging the success of an innovation, launching this twelfth edition of *Modern Labor Economics* is an endeavor that we have approached with both satisfaction and enthusiasm. We believe that economic analysis has become more widely accepted and valued in the area of policy analysis and evaluation, and that labor economics has become an ever-more vibrant and vigorous field within economics. *Modern Labor Economics* was first published about a decade after neoclassical analysis of the labor market replaced institutional treatment as the dominant paradigm, and in the intervening decades, this paradigm has grown increasingly sophisticated in its treatment of labor-market issues and the institutions that affect them. This period has been a very exciting and rewarding time to be a labor economist, and our enthusiasm for bringing this field to the student remains unabated.

New to This Edition

- This twelfth edition of *Modern Labor Economics* has been thoroughly updated to include the latest descriptive data pertaining to the labor market and the latest references to professional literature. Through these updates our goal is to make our textbook a comprehensive reference for critical factual information about the labor market *and* to the professional literature in labor economics.
- We analyze the effects of the Great Recession of 2008 on retirement ages (Chapter 7), on immigration (Chapter 10), on international differences in unemployment (Chapter 14), and on earnings inequality (Chapter 15). We have also added a section (in Chapter 3) analyzing the efficacy of cutting payroll taxes as a means of stimulating employment during a recession.
- In light of the growing debate on unauthorized immigration, we have expanded our treatment of the labor-market effects of immigration (Chapter 10) to

include analyses of the elasticity of the labor demand curve and the economic effects of low-skilled immigration on higher-skilled workers.

- Our discussion of human capital investments in Chapter 9 has been enhanced to include a more detailed analysis of how "behavioral skills," psychic costs of learning, and personal discount rates affect the returns to education.
- Boxed examples, which illustrate the applicability of economic concepts to the understanding of both daily life and historical developments, have been a key characteristic of *Modern Labor Economics* in its previous eleven editions. In this twelfth edition, we have added eight new boxed examples, ranging from the "Big Mac" real-wage index and how housing subsidies affect labor supply, to the effects of linguistics on personal discount rates and the effects of race on called strikes in baseball.

Overview of the Text

Modern Labor Economics is designed for one-semester or one-quarter courses in labor economics at the undergraduate or graduate level for students who may not have extensive backgrounds in economics. Since 1974, we have taught such courses at the School of Industrial and Labor Relations at Cornell University. The under-graduate course requires only principles of economics as a prerequisite, and the graduate course (for students in a professional program akin to an MBA program) has no prerequisites. We have found that it is not necessary to be highly technical in one's presentation in order to convey important concepts and that students with limited backgrounds in economics can comprehend a great deal of material in a sin-gle course. However, for students who have had intermediate microeconomics, we have included seven chapter appendixes that discuss more advanced material or develop technical concepts in much greater detail than the text discussion permits.

Labor economics has always been an "applied" branch of study, and a thor-ough grounding in the field requires at least an acquaintance with basic meth-odological techniques and problems. The appendix to Chapter 1 presents a brief overview of regression analysis. Then, each succeeding chapter ends with an "empirical study"—relevant to that chapter's content—that introduces students to different *methodological* issues faced by economists doing applied research. It is our hope that this unique feature of the textbook will both enlighten students about, and interest them in, the challenges of empirical research.

After an introduction to basic economic concepts in Chapter 1, Chapter 2 presents a quick overview of demand and supply in labor markets so that stu-dents will see from the outset the interrelationship of the major forces at work shaping labor market behavior. This chapter can be skipped or skimmed by students with strong backgrounds in economics or by students in one-quarter courses. Chapters 3–5 are concerned primarily with the demand for labor, while Chapters 6–10 focus on labor supply issues.

Beginning with Chapter 11, the concepts of economics are used to analyze sev-eral topics of special interest to students of labor markets. The relationship between pay and productivity is analyzed in Chapter 11, and the earnings of women and minorities—encompassing issues of discrimination—are the subjects of Chapter 12. Chapter 13 uses economic concepts to analyze collective bargaining in the private and public sectors, and Chapter 14 discusses the issue of unemployment.

Chapters 15 and 16 offer analyses of two issues of major policy importance in the last two or three decades: the growth in earnings inequality (Chapter 15) and the effects of greater international trade and production sharing (Chapter 16). Both chapters serve a dual role: analyzing important policy issues while *reviewing and utilizing key concepts presented in earlier chapters.*

In addition to the use of public policy examples, the inclusion of technical appendixes, and our end-of-chapter discussions of methodological issues, the text has a number of other important pedagogical features. First, each chapter contains boxed examples that illustrate an application of that chapter's theory in a nontraditional, historical, business, or cross-cultural setting. Second, each chapter contains a number of discussion or review questions that allow students to apply what they have learned to specific policy issues. To enhance student mastery, we provide answers to the odd-numbered questions at the back of the book. Third, lists of selected readings at the ends of chapters refer students to more advanced sources of study. Fourth, the footnotes in the text have been updated to cite the most recent literature on each given topic; they are intended as a reference for students and professors alike who may want to delve more deeply into a given topic.

Accompanying Supplements

Supplements enrich the twelfth edition of *Modern Labor Economics* for both students and instructors.

Students receive a cohesive set of online study tools that are available on the **Companion Web site**, www.pearsonglobaleditions.com/ehrenberg. For each chapter, students will find a chapter summary, review questions, problems, and applications written by Léonie Stone at the State University of New York at Geneseo, a multiple-choice quiz revised by Kevin J. Murphy of Oakland University, econometric and quantitative problems revised by Elizabeth Wheaton of Southern Methodist University, case studies compiled by Lawrence Wohl of Gustavus Adolphus College that illustrate concepts central to the chapters, Web links to labor data sources, and PowerPoint presentations containing all numbered figures and tables from the text. In addition, students can also access Web Appendix 9B: A Hedonic Model of Earnings and Educational Level.

For instructors, an extensive set of online course materials is available for download at the Instructor Resource Center (www.pearsonglobaleditions.com/ehrenberg) on the catalog page for *Modern Labor Economics*. All resources are password-protected for instructor use only. An **Online Test Bank** consists of approximately 600 multiple-choice and short-answer questions that can be downloaded and edited for use in problem sets and exams. The Test Bank has been thoroughly revised and updated by Kevin J. Murphy and is also available as an **Online Computerized Test Bank** in TestGen format.

Also available is the **Online Instructor's Manual**, written by co-author Robert Smith. The Online Instructor's Manual presents answers to the even-numbered review questions and problems in the text, outlines the major concepts in each chapter, and contains two suggested essay questions per chapter (with answers).

Finally, an **Online PowerPoint presentation** is available for each chapter. The slides consist of all numbered figures and tables from the text. New to the twelfth edition are accompanying lecture notes, written by Oluwole Owoye of Western Connecticut State University.

Acknowledgments

Enormous debts are owed to three groups of people. First are those instrumental in teaching us the concepts and social relevance of labor economics when we were students or young professionals: Orley Ashenfelter, Frank Brechling, George Delehanty, Dale Mortensen, John Pencavel, Orme Phelps, and Mel Reder. Second are the generations of undergraduate and graduate students who sat through the lectures that preceded the publication of each new edition of *Modern Labor Economics* and, by their questions and responses, forced us to make ourselves clear.

Third, several colleagues have contributed, both formally and informally, to this twelfth edition. We appreciate the suggestions of the following people:

Casey Abington
Northwest Missouri State University

John Abowd
Cornell University

John T. Addison
University of South Carolina

Sherrilyn M. Billger
Illinois State University

Francine Blau
Cornell University

George Boyer
Cornell University

Robert Chirinko
University of Illinois, Chicago

Gary Fields
Cornell University

Matthew Freedman
Cornell University

Kevin Hallock
Cornell University

Robert Hutchens
Cornell University

George Jakubson
Cornell University

Lawrence Kahn
Cornell University

Richard Mansfield
Cornell University

Brian McCall
University of Michigan

Kevin J. Murphy
Oakland University

Walter Oi
University of Rochester

Victoria Prowse
Cornell University

Silvio Rendon
Stony Brook University

Teresa Riley
Youngstown State University

Tim Schmidle
Workers' Compensation Board, New York State

Douglas Webber
Temple University

Ronald G. Ehrenberg
Robert S. Smith

Pearson wishes to thank the following people for their work on the content of the Global Edition:

Contributors:

Jaya Anita Abraham
Abu Dhabi University
David Kiss
Leibniz University Hanover
Stefania Paladini
Coventry University

Reviewers:

Petr Sedlacek
University of Bonn
Erik Johansson
National Institute of Economic Research, Sweden

CHAPTER 1

Introduction

Economic theory provides powerful, and surprising, insights into individual and social behavior. These insights are interesting because they help us understand important aspects of our lives. Beyond this, however, government, industry, labor, and other groups have increasingly come to understand the usefulness of the concepts and thought processes of economists in formulating social policy.

This book presents an application of economic analysis to the behavior of, and relationship between, employers and employees. The aggregate compensation received by U.S. employees from their employers was $8.6 trillion in the year 2012, while all *other* forms of personal income for that year—from investments, self-employment, pensions, and various government welfare programs—amounted to $5.3 trillion. The *employment* relationship, then, is one of the most fundamental relationships in our lives, and as such, it attracts a good deal of legislative attention. Knowing the fundamentals of labor economics is thus essential to an understanding of a huge array of social problems and programs, both in the United States and elsewhere.

As economists who have been actively involved in the analysis and evaluation of public policies, we obviously believe labor economics is useful in understanding the effects of these programs. Perhaps more importantly, we also believe policy analysis can be useful in teaching the fundamentals of labor economics. We have therefore incorporated such analyses into each chapter, with two purposes in mind. First, we believe that seeing the relevance and social implications of concepts studied enhances the student's motivation to learn. Second, using the concepts of each chapter in an analytical setting serves to reinforce understanding by helping the student to see them "in action."

The Labor Market

There is a rumor that a former U.S. Secretary of Labor attempted to abolish the term *labor market* from departmental publications. He believed that it demeaned workers to regard labor as being bought and sold like so much grain, oil, or steel. True, labor is unique in several ways. Labor services can only be rented; workers themselves cannot be bought and sold. Further, because labor services cannot be separated from workers, the conditions under which such services are rented are often as important as the price. Indeed, *nonpecuniary factors*—such as work environment, risk of injury, personalities of managers, perceptions of fair treatment, and flexibility of work hours—loom larger in employment transactions than they do in markets for commodities. Finally, a host of institutions and pieces of legislation that influence the employment relationship do not exist in other markets.

Nevertheless, the circumstances under which employers and employees rent labor services clearly constitute a market, for several reasons. First, institutions such as want ads and employment agencies have been developed to facilitate contact between buyers and sellers of labor services. Second, once contact is arranged, information about price and quality is exchanged in employment applications and interviews. Third, when agreement is reached, some kind of *contract*, whether formal or informal, is executed, covering compensation, conditions of work, job security, and even the duration of the job. These contracts typically call for employers to compensate employees for their *time* and not for what they produce. This form of compensation requires that employers give careful attention to worker motivation and dependability in the selection and employment process.

The end result of employer–employee transactions in the labor market is, of course, the placement of people in jobs at certain rates of pay. This allocation of labor serves not only the personal needs of individuals but the needs of the larger society as well. Through the labor market, our most important national resource—labor—is allocated to firms, industries, occupations, and regions.[1]

Labor Economics: Some Basic Concepts

Labor economics is the study of the workings and outcomes of the market for labor. More specifically, labor economics is primarily concerned with the behavior of employers and employees in response to the general incentives of wages,

---

[1]For an article that examines work from a philosophical perspective, see Yoram Weiss, "Work and Leisure: A History of Ideas," *Journal of Labor Economics* 27 (January 2009): 1–20.

prices, profits, and nonpecuniary aspects of the employment relationship, such as working conditions. These incentives serve both to motivate and to limit individual choice. The focus in economics is on inducements for behavior that are impersonal and apply to a wide range of people.

In this book, we shall examine, for example, the relationship between wages and employment opportunities; the interaction among wages, income, and the decision to work; the way general market incentives affect occupational choice; the relationship between wages and undesirable job characteristics; the incentives for and effects of educational and training investments; and the effects of unions on wages, productivity, and turnover. In the process, we shall analyze the employment and wage effects of such social policies as the minimum wage, overtime legislation, safety and health regulations, welfare reform, payroll taxes, unemployment insurance, immigration policies, and antidiscrimination laws.

Our study of labor economics will be conducted on two levels. Most of the time, we shall use economic theory to analyze "what is"; that is, we shall explain people's behavior using a mode of analysis called *positive economics*. Less commonly, we shall use *normative* economic analysis to judge "what should be."

Positive Economics

Positive economics is a theory of behavior in which people are typically assumed to respond favorably to benefits and negatively to costs. In this regard, positive economics closely resembles Skinnerian psychology, which views behavior as shaped by rewards and punishments. The rewards in economic theory are pecuniary and nonpecuniary gains (benefits), while the punishments are forgone opportunities (costs). For example, a person motivated to become a surgeon because of the earnings and status surgeons command must give up the opportunity to become a lawyer and must be available for emergency work around the clock. Both the benefits and the costs must be considered in making this career choice.

Scarcity   The pervasive assumption underlying economic theory is that of resource *scarcity*. According to this assumption, individuals and society alike do not have the resources to meet all of their wants. Thus, any resource devoted to satisfying one set of desires could have been used to satisfy another set, which means that there is a cost to any decision or action. The real cost of using labor hired by a government contractor to build a road, for example, is the production lost by not devoting this labor to the production of some other good or service. Thus, in popular terms, "There is no such thing as a free lunch," and we must always make choices and live with the rewards and costs these choices bring us. Moreover, we are always constrained in our choices by the resources available to us.

Rationality   A second basic assumption of positive economics is that people are *rational*—they have an objective and pursue it in a reasonably consistent fashion. When considering *persons*, economists assume that the objective being pursued is *utility maximization;* that is, people are assumed to strive toward the goal of making themselves as happy as they can (given their limited resources). Utility, of course, is generated by both pecuniary and nonpecuniary dimensions of employment.

When considering the behavior of *firms,* which are inherently nonpersonal entities, economists assume that the goal of behavior is *profit maximization.* Profit maximization is really just a special case of utility maximization in which pecuniary gain is emphasized and nonpecuniary factors are ignored.

The assumption of rationality implies a *consistency* of response to general economic incentives and an *adaptability* of behavior when those incentives change. These two characteristics of behavior underlie predictions about how workers and firms will respond to various incentives.[2]

The Models and Predictions of Positive Economics

Behavioral predictions in economics flow more or less directly from the two fundamental assumptions of scarcity and rationality. Workers must continually make choices, such as whether to look for other jobs, accept overtime, move to another area, or acquire more education. Employers must also make choices concerning, for example, the level of output and the mix of machines and labor to use in production. Economists usually assume that when making these choices, employees and employers are guided by their desires to maximize utility or profit, respectively. However, what is more important to the economic theory of behavior is not the *particular* goal of either employees or employers; rather, it is that economic actors weigh the costs and benefits of various alternative transactions in the context of achieving *some* goal or other.

One may object that these assumptions are unrealistic and that people are not nearly as calculating, as well informed about alternatives, or as amply endowed with choices as economists assume. Economists are likely to reply that if people are not calculating, are totally uninformed, or do not have any choices, then most predictions suggested by economic theory will not be supported by real-world evidence. They thus argue that the theory underlying positive economics should be judged on the basis of its *predictions,* not its assumptions.

The reason we need to make assumptions and create a relatively simple theory of behavior is that the actual workings of the labor market are almost inconceivably complex. Millions of workers and employers interact daily, all with their own sets of motivations, preferences, information, and perceptions of self-interest. What we need to discover are general principles that provide useful

---

[2]For articles on rationality and the related issue of preferences, see Gary Becker, "Irrational Behavior and Economic Theory," *Journal of Political Economy* 70 (February 1962): 1–13; Richard H. Thaler, "From Homo Economicus to Homo Sapiens," *Journal of Economic Perspectives* 14 (Winter 2000): 133–141; Stefano DellaVigna, "Psychology and Economics: Evidence from the Field," *Journal of Economic Literature* 47 (June 2009): 315–372; and Andrei Schleifer, "Psychologists at the Gate: A Review of Daniel Kahneman's *Thinking Fast and Slow,*" *Journal of Economic Literature* 50 (December 2012): 1080–1091.

EXAMPLE 1.1

Positive Economics: What Does It Mean to "Understand" Behavior?

The purpose of positive economic analysis is to analyze, or understand, the behavior of people as they respond to market incentives. But in a world that is extremely complex, just what does it mean to "understand" behavior? One theoretical physicist put it this way:

> We can imagine that this complicated array of moving things which constitutes "the world" is something like a great chess game being played by the gods, and we are observers of the game. We do not know what the rules of the game are; all we are allowed to do is to watch the playing. Of course, if we watch long enough, we may eventually catch on to a few of the rules. The rules of the game are what we mean by fundamental physics. Even if we know every rule, however . . . what we really can explain in terms of those rules is very limited, because almost all

situations are so enormously complicated that we cannot follow the plays of the game using the rules, much less tell what is going to happen next. We must, therefore, limit ourselves to the more basic question of the rules of the game. If we know the rules, we consider that we "understand" the world.[a]

If the behavior of nature, which does not have a will, is so difficult to analyze, understanding the behavior of people is even more of a challenge. Since people's behavior does not mechanistically follow a set of rules, the goal of positive economics is most realistically stated as trying to discover their behavioral tendencies.

---

[a]Richard T. Feynman, The Feynman Lectures on Physics, vol. 1, 1963, by Addison-Wesley.

insights into the labor market. We hope to show in this text that a few forces are so basic to labor market behavior that they alone can predict or explain many of the outcomes and behaviors observed in the labor market.

Anytime we attempt to explain a complex set of behaviors and outcomes using a few fundamental influences, we have created a *model*. Models are not intended to capture every complexity of behavior; instead, they are created to strip away random and idiosyncratic factors so that the focus is on general principles. An analogy from the physical sciences may make the nature of models and their relationship to actual behavior clearer.

A Physical Model   Using simple calculations of velocity and gravitational pull, physicists can predict where a ball will land if it is kicked with a certain force at a given angle to the ground. The actual point of landing may vary from the predicted point because of wind currents and any spin the ball might have—factors ignored in the calculations. If 100 balls are kicked, none may ever land exactly on the predicted spot, although they will tend to cluster around it. The accuracy of the model, while not perfect, may be good enough to enable a football coach to decide whether to attempt a field goal. The point is that we usually just need to know the *average tendencies* of outcomes for policy purposes. To estimate these tendencies, we need to know the important forces at work, but we must confine ourselves to few enough influences so that calculating estimates remains feasible. (A further comparison of physics and positive economics is in Example 1.1.)

An Economic Model   To really grasp the assumptions and predictions of economic models, we consider a concrete example. Suppose we begin by asserting that being subject to resource scarcity, workers will prefer high-paying jobs to low-paying ones *if* all other job characteristics are the same in each job. Thus, they will quit low-paying jobs to take better-paying ones if they believe sufficient improvement is likely. This principle does not imply that workers care only about wages or that all are equally likely to quit. Workers obviously care about a number of employment characteristics, and improvement in any of these on their current job makes turnover less likely. Likewise, some workers are more receptive to change than others. Nevertheless, if we hold other factors constant and increase only wages, we should clearly observe that the probability of quitting will fall.

On the employer side of the market, we can consider a similar prediction. Firms need to make a profit to survive. If they have high turnover, their costs will be higher than otherwise because of the need to hire and train replacements. With high turnover, they could not, therefore, afford to pay high wages. However, if they could reduce turnover enough by paying higher wages, it might well be worth incurring the added wage costs. Thus, both the utility-maximizing behavior of employees and the profit-maximizing behavior of firms lead us to expect low turnover to be associated with high wages and high turnover with low wages, other things equal.

We note several important things about the above predictions:

1. The predictions emerge directly from the twin assumptions of scarcity and rationality. Employees and employers, both mindful of their scarce resources, are assumed to be on the lookout for chances to improve their well-being. The predictions are also based on the assumptions that employees are aware of, or can learn about, alternative jobs and that these alternatives are open to them.

2. We made the prediction of a negative relationship between wages and voluntary turnover by holding other things equal. The theory does not deny that job characteristics other than wages matter to employees or that employers can lower turnover by varying policies other than the wage rate. However, keeping these other factors constant, our model predicts a negative relationship if the basic assumptions are valid.

3. The *assumptions* of the theory concern individual behavior of employers and employees, but the *predictions* are about an aggregate relationship between wages and turnover. The prediction is *not* that all employees will remain in their jobs if their wages are increased but that *enough* will remain for turnover to be cut by raising wages. The test of the prediction thus lies in finding out if the predicted relationship between wages and turnover exists using aggregate data from firms or industries.

Careful statistical studies suggest support for the hypothesis that higher pay reduces voluntary turnover. One study, for example, estimated that a 10 percent increase in wages, holding worker characteristics constant, reduced the quit rate by one percentage point.[3] (The statistical technique commonly used by economists to test hypotheses is introduced in Appendix 1A.)

Normative Economics

Understanding normative economics begins with the realization that there are two kinds of economic transactions. One kind is entered into voluntarily because all parties to the transaction gain. If Sally is willing to create blueprints for $20 per hour, for example, and Ace Engineering Services is willing to pay someone up to $22 per hour to do the job, both gain by agreeing to Sally's appointment at an hourly wage between $20 and $22; such a transaction is mutually beneficial. The role of the labor market is to facilitate these voluntary, mutually advantageous transactions. If the market is successful in facilitating *all* possible mutually beneficial transactions, it can be said to have produced a condition economists call *Pareto* (or "economic") *efficiency*.[4] (The word *efficiency* is used by economists in a very specialized sense to denote a condition in which all mutually beneficial transactions have been concluded. This definition of the word is more comprehensive than its normal connotation of cost minimization.) If Pareto efficiency were actually attained, no more transactions would be undertaken voluntarily because they would not be *mutually* advantageous.

The second kind of transaction is one in which one or more parties *lose*. These transactions often involve the redistribution of income, from which some gain at the expense of others. Transactions that are explicitly redistributional, for example, are not entered into voluntarily unless motivated by charity (in which case the donors gain nonpecuniary satisfaction); otherwise, redistributional transactions are mandated by government through tax and expenditure policies. Thus, while markets facilitate *voluntary* transactions, the government's job is often to make certain transactions *mandatory*.

Any normative statement—a statement about what *ought* to exist—is based on some underlying value. Government policies affecting the labor market are often based on the widely shared, but not universally agreed upon, value that society should try to make the distribution of income more equal. Welfare

---

[3] V. Bhaskar, Alan Manning, and Ted To, "Oligopsony and Monopsonistic Competition in Labor Markets," *Journal of Economic Perspectives* 16 (Spring 2002): 158.

[4] Pareto efficiency gets its name from the Italian economist Vilfredo Pareto, who, around 1900, insisted that economic science should make normative pronouncements only about unambiguous changes in social welfare. Rejecting the notion that utility can be measured (and, therefore, compared across individuals), Pareto argued that we can only know whether a transaction improves social welfare from the testimony or behavior of the affected parties themselves. If they as individuals regard themselves as better off, then the transaction is unambiguously good—even though we are unable to measure how much better off they feel.

programs, minimum wage laws, and restrictions on immigration are examples of policies based on *distributional* considerations. Other labor market policies are intended either to change or to overrule the choices workers make in maximizing their utility. The underlying value in these cases is frequently that workers should not be allowed to place themselves or their families at risk of physical or financial harm. The wearing of such personal protective devices as hard hats and earplugs, for example, is seen as so *meritorious* in certain settings that it is required of workers even if they would choose otherwise.

Policies seeking to redistribute income or force the consumption of meritorious goods are often controversial because some workers will feel worse off when the policies are adopted. These transactions must be governmentally mandated because they will not be entered into voluntarily.

Markets and Values   Economic theory, however, reminds us that there is a class of transactions wherein there are no losers. Policies or transactions from which all affected parties gain can be said to be *Pareto-improving* because they promote Pareto efficiency. These policies or transactions can be justified on the grounds that they unambiguously enhance social welfare; therefore, they can be unanimously supported. Policies with this justification are of special interest to economists because economics is largely the study of market behavior—voluntary transactions in the pursuit of self-interest.

A transaction can be unanimously supported when one of the following occurs:

a. All parties who are affected by the transaction gain.
b. Some parties gain and no one else loses.
c. Some parties gain and some lose from the transaction, but the gainers fully compensate the losers.

When the compensation in *c* takes place, case *c* is converted to case *b*. In practice, economists often judge a transaction by whether the gains of the beneficiaries exceed the costs borne by the losers, thus making it *possible* that there would be no losers. However, when the compensation of losers is *possible* but does *not* take place, there are, in fact, losers! Many economists, therefore, argue that compensation *must* take place for a government policy to be justified on the grounds that it promotes Pareto efficiency.

As noted above, the role of the labor market is to facilitate voluntary, mutually advantageous transactions. Hardly anyone would argue against at least some kind of government intervention in the labor market if the market is failing to promote such transactions. Why do markets fail?

Market Failure: Ignorance   First, people may be ignorant of some important facts, thus led to make decisions that are not in their self-interest. For example, a worker who smokes may take a job in an asbestos-processing plant not knowing that the combination of smoking and inhaling asbestos dust substantially increases the risk of disease. Had the worker known this, he or she would probably have stopped smoking or changed jobs, but both transactions were blocked by ignorance.

Market Failure: Transaction Barriers   Second, there may be some barrier to the completion of a transaction that could be mutually beneficial. Often, such a barrier is created by laws that prohibit certain transactions. For example, as recently as three or four decades ago, many states prohibited employers from hiring women to work more than 40 hours-a-week. As a consequence, firms that wanted to hire workers for more than 40 hours-a-week could not transact with those women who wanted to work overtime—to the detriment of both parties. Society as a whole thus suffers losses when transactions that are mutually beneficial are prohibited by government.

Another barrier to mutually beneficial transactions may be the expense of completing the transactions. Unskilled workers facing very limited opportunities in one region might desire to move to take better jobs. Alternatively, they might want to enter job-training programs. In either case, they might lack the funds to finance the desired transactions.

Market Failure: Externalities   Market failure can also arise when a buyer and a seller agree to a transaction that imposes costs or benefits on people who were *not party to their decision*; in other words, some decisions have costs or benefits that are "external" to the decision makers. Why do these externalities cause market failure?

When buyers and sellers make their decisions, they generally weigh the costs and benefits only to themselves—and, of course, decide to complete a transaction when the benefits outweigh the costs. If *all* transaction costs and benefits fall to the decision makers, then society can be assured that the transaction represents a step toward Pareto efficiency. However, if there are costs or benefits to people who were *not* able to influence the decision, then the transaction may not have positive net benefits to society.

For us to have confidence that a particular transaction is a step toward Pareto efficiency, the decision must be *voluntarily* accepted by all who are affected by it. If there are externalities to a transaction, people who are affected by it—but cannot influence the ultimate decision—are being *forced* into a transaction that they may not have been willing to make. If so, it may well be that the costs of the transaction are greater than the benefits, once *all* the costs and benefits (and not just those of the decision makers) are counted.

Child labor offers a stark example of externalities, because children do not have the competence or the power to make many important decisions affecting their lives. If parents are selfish and ignore the interests of their children in making decisions about sending them to work or to school, then society cannot trust their decisions as advancing economic efficiency (because the costs and benefits to the children have been ignored in making work–school decisions).

Externalities would also exist if, say, workers have no mechanism to transfer *their* costs of being injured at work to their *employers*, who are the ones making the decisions about how much to spend to reduce workplace risk. If such a mechanism does not exist (a question we will explore in chapter 8), then our workplaces will be less safe than they should be, because employers are ignoring at least some costs (the ones borne by workers) in making their decisions about risk reduction.

Market Failure: Public Goods   A special kind of externality is sometimes called the "free rider problem." For example, suppose that a union representing workers in the noisy sawmill industry intends to sponsor research on the effects of excessive noise on workers' hearing loss. This research is expensive, but because it would be useful to unions or individual workers in other noisy industries, the sawmill-workers union considers whether it could defray its expenses by selling its findings to other interested parties. The union would quickly realize, however, that once its findings are known to its members or its first "customers," the results would quickly become available to all—through word-of-mouth, newspaper, or Internet sources—even to those "free riders" who do not pay.

Such research findings are an example of what is called a *public good*—a good that can be consumed by any number of people at the same time, including those who do not pay. Because nonpayers cannot be excluded from consuming the good, no potential customer will have an incentive to pay. Knowing this, the potential provider of the good or service (the sawmill-workers union in our example) will probably decide not to produce it.

In the case of public goods, private decision makers ignore the benefits to others when making their decisions because they have no mechanism to "capture" these benefits. As a result, society will under-invest in such goods unless the government, which can *compel* payments through its tax system, steps in to produce the public goods.

Market Failure: Price Distortion   A special barrier to transaction is caused by taxes, subsidies, or other forces that create "incorrect" prices. Prices powerfully influence the incentives to transact, and the prices asked or received in a transaction should reflect the true preferences of the parties to it. When prices become decoupled from preferences, parties may be led to make transactions that are not socially beneficial or to avoid others that would be advantageous. If plumbers charge $25 per hour, but their customers must pay an additional tax of $5 to the government, customers who are willing to pay between $25 and $30 per hour and would hire plumbers in the absence of the tax are discouraged from doing so—to the detriment of both parties.

Normative Economics and Government Policy

Solutions to problems that prevent the completion of socially beneficial transactions frequently involve governmental intervention. If the problem is a lack of information about health risks, say, one obvious solution is for the government to take steps to ensure workers are informed about such risks. If the problem is that some law prevents women, say, from working the hours they want, an obvious solution is to repeal the law.

For other types of transaction barriers, the needed intervention is for the government to either compel or actively promote transactions different from the ones that would be made by "the market" (that is, those made by private decision makers). When the government decides to "replace" a market decision by one of its own, the policy prescription is complicated by the need to guess just what the appropriate transaction is. In the following text, we discuss government interventions to deal with two examples of transaction barriers.

Capital Market Imperfections   Workers find it difficult to obtain loans that would allow them to obtain job training or finance a cross-country move to obtain a better job because usually all they can offer to secure the loan is their promise to pay it back. The government, however, might make such loans even if it faced the same risk of default, because enabling workers to acquire new skills or move to where workers are needed would strengthen the overall economy. Of course, if the government did decide to make these loans, it would have to decide on the appropriate circumstances for approving such loans, including how much money to loan.

Externalities   Earlier, we argued that parents may not take the welfare of their children into account when making decisions about whether to send them to work or to school. A solution to this problem that most societies have undertaken is to require children to stay in school until they reach a certain age and to provide at least that level of schooling for free. Ideally, of course, deciding on the mandatory school-leaving age would require the government to look carefully at the *lifetime benefits* of various schooling levels (see chapter 9) and comparing them to both the direct costs of education and the opportunity costs of the children's lost production. Performing the benefit–cost analyses needed to intelligently address the problem of externalities requires a solid grasp of economic theory (as we will discuss in chapter 8).

Efficiency versus Equity

The social goal of a more equitable distribution of income is often of paramount importance to political decision makers, and disputes can arise over whether equity or economic efficiency should be the prime consideration in setting policy. One source of dispute is rooted in the problem that there is not a unique set of transactions that are Pareto efficient. There are, in fact, a *number* of different sets of transactions that can satisfy our definition of economic efficiency, and questions can arise as to which set is the most equitable.

   To understand the multiple sets of efficient transactions that are possible, we return to our example of the woman willing to create blueprints for $20 per hour. If Ace Engineering Services is willing to pay up to $22 per hour for blueprints, and Sally is willing to work for $20, their agreement on her employment at an hourly wage of, say, $21 would be beneficial to both parties. However, the same can be said for an agreement on wages of either $20.25 or $21.75 per hour. We can objectively judge any of these potential agreements as *efficient* because both parties are better off than they would be if they did not transact. But it is not clear which of the potential agreements are more *equitable* unless we define a subjective standard for "fairness."

   The second source of dispute over equity and efficiency is rooted in the problem that to achieve more equity, steps *away* from Pareto efficiency must often be taken.[5] Minimum wage laws, for example, block transactions that parties might be willing to make at a lower wage; thus, some who would have accepted jobs at less than the legislated minimum are not offered any at all because their services are "priced out of the market." Similarly, welfare programs have often been structured so that recipients who find paid work receive, in effect, a zero wage—a price distortion of major proportions, but one that is neither easily nor cheaply avoided (as we will see in chapter 6).

Normative economics tends to stress efficiency over equity considerations, not because it is more important but because it can be analyzed more scientifically. For a transaction to be mutually beneficial, all that is required is for each party to individually feel better off. Thus, studying voluntary transactions (that is, market behavior) is useful when taking economic efficiency into account. Equity considerations, however, always involve comparing the welfare lost by some against the utility gained by others—which, given the impossibility of measuring happiness, cannot be scientifically done. For policy decisions based on considerations of equity, society usually turns to guidance from the political system, not from markets.

Plan of the Text

The study of labor economics is mainly a study of the interplay between employers and employees—or between demand and supply. Chapter 2 presents a quick overview of demand and supply in the labor market, allowing students to see from the outset the interrelationship of the major forces at work shaping labor market behavior. Chapters 3–5 are primarily concerned with the demand for labor. As such, they are devoted to an analysis of employers' incentives and behavior.

Chapters 6–10 contain analyses of various aspects of workers' labor supply behavior. They address issues of whether to work for pay (as opposed to consuming leisure or working at home without pay), the choice of occupations or jobs with very different characteristics, and decisions workers must make about educational and other investments designed to improve their earning capacities. Like the earlier "demand" chapters, these "supply" chapters necessarily incorporate aspects of behavior on the other (here, employer) side of the labor market.

Chapters 11–16 address special topics of interest to labor economists, including the effects of institutional forces in the labor market. Chapter 11 analyzes how the compensation of workers can be structured to create incentives for greater productivity. Chapter 12 analyzes wage differentials associated with race, gender, and ethnicity. Chapter 13 deals with the labor market effects of unions. Chapter 14 focuses on an analysis of unemployment. The final two chapters discuss the phenomena of inequality (chapter 15) and globalization (chapter 16) while also reviewing most of the major concepts introduced earlier in the text.

---

[5]See Arthur Okun, *Equality and Efficiency: The Big Trade-Off* (Washington, D.C.: Brookings Institution, 1975), for a lucid discussion of the trade-offs between efficiency and equity.

At the end of each chapter are several features that are designed to enhance understanding. First, starting with chapter 2, readers will find a summary of an empirical study related to concepts introduced in the text. These summaries are designed to convey, in a nontechnical way, how researchers can creatively confront the challenges of testing the predictions of economic theory in the "real world." Because the summaries often assume a very basic familiarity with regression analysis (the basic empirical tool in economics), we introduce this statistical technique in Appendix A1.

The end-of-chapter materials also include a set of review questions that are designed to test understanding of the chapter's concepts and how these concepts can be applied to policy issues. The questions are ordered by level of difficulty (the more difficult ones come later), and answers to the odd-numbered questions are in a separate section at the end of the textbook. Some numerically based problems follow the review questions, again with answers to the odd-numbered problems at the end of the textbook.

For students who want to go more deeply into the concepts introduced in the text of each chapter, we provide extensive footnotes designed to provide references to seminal works and the most recent literature. We also provide selected readings at the very end of each chapter that go more deeply into the material. Many chapters also have an appendix that delves deeper into a specialized topic that may be of interest to some readers.

Review Questions

1. Using the concepts of normative economics, when would the labor market be judged to be at a point of optimality? What imperfections might prevent the market from achieving this point?

2. Are the following statements "positive" or "normative"? Why?
   a. Employers should not be required to offer pensions to their employees.
   b. Employers offering pension benefits will pay lower wages than they would if they did not offer a pension program.
   c. If further immigration of unskilled foreigners is prevented, the wages of unskilled immigrants already here will rise.
   d. The military draft compels people to engage in a transaction they would not voluntarily enter into; it should therefore be avoided as a way of recruiting military personnel.
   e. If the military draft were reinstituted, military salaries would probably fall.

3. Consider two scenarios. In the first scenario, a fixed number of workers is compelled to work for a wage rate w. In the second scenario, the same number of workers is hired by firms who also offer the wage rate w. Under which conditions are both scenarios identical from the view of normative economics?

4. What are the functions and limitations of an economic model?

5. In this chapter, a simple model was developed in which it was predicted that workers employed in jobs paying wages

less than they could get in comparable jobs elsewhere would tend to quit to seek higher-paying jobs. Suppose we observe a worker who, after repeated harassment or criticism from her boss, quits an $8-per-hour job to take another job paying $7.50. Answer the three questions below:

a. Is this woman's behavior consistent with the economic model of job quitting outlined in the text?

b. Can we test to see whether this woman's behavior is consistent with the assumption of rationality?

c. Suppose the boss in question had harassed other employees, but this woman was the only one who quit. Can we conclude that economic theory applies to the behavior of some people but not to others?

6. Since the 1950s, trade barriers were reduced all around the world (e.g., establishment of free trade areas). Did this development lead to Pareto-improvements?

7. Child labor laws generally prohibit children from working until age 14 and restrict younger teenagers to certain kinds of work that are not considered dangerous. Reconcile the prohibitions of child labor legislation with the principles underlying normative economic analysis.

8. Consider a small autarkical town with many firms. One firm hires a large number of workers with two consequences. First, the air becomes more polluted because of the firm's increased output level. Second, the remaining firms are concerned about shortages in the supply of labor, which induces them to offer higher wages to applicants. Do you consider both consequences as external effects?

9. Suppose that workers who lose their jobs receive unemployment benefits for up to six months. Thereafter unemployed persons are not eligible for any further payments. The government now decides to pay unemployment benefits for up to nine months. Analyze this reform from the view of both positive and normative economics if unemployment benefits are tax funded and governmental spending is fixed over time.

Problems

1. (Appendix) You have collected the following data (see the following table) on 13 randomly selected teenage workers in the fast-food industry. What is the general relationship between age and wage? Plot the data and then construct a linear equation for this relationship.

Age (years)	Wage (dollars per hour)	Age (years)	Wage (dollars per hour)
16	$7.25	18	$ 8.00
16	$8.00	18	$ 8.50
17	$7.50	18	$ 9.50
17	$8.00	19	$ 8.50
17	$8.25	19	$ 8.75
18	$7.25	19	$10.00
18	$7.75		

2. (Appendix) Suppose that a least squares regression yields the following estimate:

$$W_i = -1 + 0.3A_i$$

where W is the hourly wage rate (in dollars) and A is the age (in years).

   A second regression from another group of workers yields this estimate:

$$W_i = 3 + 0.3A_i - 0.01(A_i)^2$$

   a. How much is a 20-year-old predicted to earn based on the first estimate?
   b. How much is a 20-year-old predicted to earn based on the second estimate?

3. (Appendix) Suppose you estimate the following relationship between wages and age:

$$W_i = -1 + 0.3A_i$$
$$(0.1)$$

(the standard error is in parentheses). Are you confident that wages actually rise with age?

4. (Appendix) Suppose you have information on which of the 13 randomly selected teenage workers in the fast-food industry worked part time and which worked full time. Variable F_i is equal to 1 if the worker is employed full time, and it is equal to zero otherwise. With this information, you estimate the following relationship between wages, age, and full-time employment:

$$W_i = -0.5 + 0.25A_i + 0.75F_i$$
$$(.10) \qquad (.20)$$

(the standard errors are in parentheses).
   a. How much is a 20-year-old who works full time predicted to earn based on this estimate?
   b. How much is a 20-year-old who works part time predicted to earn based on this estimate?

5. (Appendix) Based on the regression estimate in Problem 4, evaluate the statistical significance of the estimated coefficients in the regression.

6. (Appendix) Compare the first regression estimate in Problem 2 with the regression estimate in Problem 4.
   a. Is there an omitted variable bias when the full-time variable is not included? Explain.
   b. What can be said about the correlation between age and full-time employment? Explain.

Selected Readings

Boyer, George R., and Robert S. Smith. "The Development of the Neoclassical Tradition in Labor Economics." *Industrial and Labor Relations Review* 54 (January 2001): 199–223.

Friedman, Milton. *Essays in Positive Economics.* Chicago: University of Chicago Press, 1953.

Hausman, Daniel M. "Economic Methodology in a Nutshell." *Journal of Economic Perspectives* 3 (Spring 1989): 115–128.

McCloskey, Donald. "The Rhetoric of Economics." *Journal of Economic Literature* 21 (June 1983): 481–517.

Statistical Testing of Labor Market Hypotheses

his appendix provides a brief introduction to how labor economists test hypotheses. We will discuss how one might attempt to test the hypothesis presented in this chapter that other things equal, one should expect to observe that the higher the wage a firm pays, the lower the voluntary labor turnover among its employees will be. Put another way, if we define a firm's quit rate as the proportion of its workers who voluntarily quit in a given time period (say, a year), we expect to observe that the higher a firm's wages, the lower its quit rate will be, holding *other* factors affecting quit rates constant.

A Univariate Test

An obvious first step is to collect data on the quit rates experienced by a set of firms during a given year and match these data with the firms' wage rates. This type of analysis is called *univariate* because we are analyzing the effects on quit rates of just one other variable (the wage rate). The data are called *cross-sectional* because they provide observations across behavioral units at a point in time.[1] Table 1A.1 contains such information for a hypothetical set of 10 firms located in a single labor market in, say, 1993. For example, firm A is assumed to have paid an average hourly wage of $4 and to have experienced a quit rate of 40 percent in 1993.

The data on wages and quit rates are presented graphically in Figure 1A.1. Each dot in this figure represents a quit-rate/hourly wage combination for one of the firms in Table 1A.1. Firm A, for example, is represented in the figure by point A, which shows a quit rate of 40 percent and an hourly wage of $4, while point B

---

[1]Several other types of data are also used frequently by labor economists. One could look, for example, at how a given firm's quit rate and wage rate vary over time. Observations that provide information on a single behavioral unit over a number of time periods are called *time-series* data. Sometimes, labor economists have data on the behavior of a number of observational units (e.g., employers) for a number of time periods; combinations of cross-sectional and time-series data are called *panel* data.

Figure 1A.1

Figure 1A.1

Estimated Relationship
between Wages and Quit
Rates Using Data from
Table 1A.1

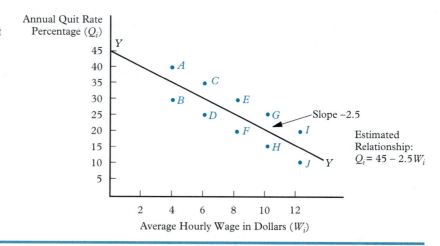

shows comparable data for firm B. From a visual inspection of all 10 data points, it appears from this figure that firms paying higher wages in our hypothetical sample do indeed have lower quit rates. Although the data points in Figure 1A.1 obviously do not lie on a single straight line, their pattern suggests that on average, there is a linear (straight-line) relationship between a firm's quit rate and its wage rate.

Any straight line can be represented by the general equation

$$Y = a + bX \tag{1A.1}$$

Variable Y is the *dependent variable*, and it is generally shown on the vertical axis of the graph depicting the line. Variable X is the *independent*, or *explanatory*, variable,

Table 1A.1

Average-Wage and Quit-Rate Data for a Set of 10 Hypothetical Firms in a Single Labor Market in 1993

Firm	Average Hourly Wage Paid ($)	Quit Rate (%)	Firm	Average Hourly Wage Paid ($)	Quit Rate (%)
A	4	40	F	8	20
B	4	30	G	10	25
C	6	35	H	10	15
D	6	25	I	12	20
E	8	30	J	12	10

which is usually shown on the horizontal axis.[2] The letters "a" and "b" are the *parameters* (the fixed coefficients) of the equation, with "a" representing the intercept and "b" the slope of the line. Put differently, "a" is the value of Y when the line intersects the vertical axis ($X = 0$). The slope, "b," indicates the vertical distance the line travels for each one-unit increase in the horizontal distance. If "b" is a positive number, the line slopes upward (going from left to right); if "b" is a negative number, the line slopes downward.

If one were to try to draw the straight line that best fits the points in Figure 1A.1, it is clear that the line would slope downward and that it would not go through all 10 points. It would lie above some points and below others; thus it would "fit" the points only with some error. We could model the relationship between the data points on the graph, then, as follows:

$$Q_i = \alpha_0 + \alpha_1 W_i + \varepsilon_i \tag{1A.2}$$

Here, Q_i represents the quit rate for firm i, and it is the dependent variable. The independent variable is W_i, firm i's wage rate. α_0 and α_1 are the parameters of the line, with α_0 the intercept and α_1 the slope. The term ε_1 is a random *error term*; it is included in the model because we do not expect that the line (given by $Q_i = \alpha_0 + \alpha_1 W_i$) will connect all the data points perfectly. Behaviorally, we are assuming the presence of random factors unrelated to wage rates that also cause the quit rate to vary across firms.

We seek to estimate what the true values of α_0 and α_1 are. Each pair of values of α_0 and α_1 defines a different straight line, and an infinite number of lines can be drawn that "fit" points A–J. It is natural for us to ask, "Which of these straight lines fits the data the best?" Some precise criterion must be used to decide which line fits the best, and the procedure typically used by statisticians and economists is to choose that line for which the sum (in our example, across all firms) of the squared vertical distances between the line and the individual data points is minimized. The line estimated from the data using this method, which is called *least squares regression analysis*, has a number of desirable properties.[3]

Application of this method to the data found in Table 1A.1 yields the following estimated line:

$$Q_i = 45 - 2.5W_i \tag{1A.3}$$
$$(5.3) \ (0.625)$$

---

[2]An exception occurs in the supply and demand curves facing firms, in which the independent variable, price, is typically shown on the vertical axis.

[3]These properties include that on average, the correct answer for α_1 is obtained; the estimates are the most precise possible among a certain class of estimators; and the sum of the positive and negative vertical deviations of the data points from the estimated line will be zero. For a more formal treatment of the method of least squares, see any statistics or econometrics text. A good introduction for a reader with no statistical background is Larry D. Schroeder, David L. Sjoquist, and Paula E. Stephan, *Understanding Regression Analysis: An Introductory Guide* (Beverly Hills, Calif.: Sage, 1986).

The estimate of α_0 is 45, and the estimate of α_1 is –2.5.[4] Thus, if a firm had a wage rate of $4/hour in 1993, we would predict that its annual quit rate would have been $45 - 2.5(4)$, or 35 percent. This estimated quit/wage relationship is drawn in Figure 1A.1 as the line YY. (The numbers in parentheses below the equation will be discussed later.)

Several things should be noted about this relationship. First, taken at face value, this estimated relationship implies that firms paying their workers *nothing* (a wage of zero) would have been projected to have *only* 45 percent of their workers quit each year ($45 - 2.5(0) = 45$), while firms paying their workers more than $18 an hour would have had negative quit rates.[5] The former result is nonsensical (why would any workers stay if they are paid nothing?), and the latter result is logically impossible (the quit rate cannot be less than zero). As these extreme examples suggest, it is dangerous to use linear models to make predictions that take one outside the range of observations used in the estimation (in the example, wages from $4 to $12). The relationship between wages and quit rates cannot be assumed to be linear (represented by a straight line) for very low and very high values of wages. Fortunately, the linear regression model used in the example can be easily generalized to allow for nonlinear relationships.

Second, the estimated intercept (45) and slope (22.5) that we obtained are only estimates of the "true" relationship, and there is uncertainty associated with these estimates. The uncertainty arises partly from the fact that we are trying to infer the true values of α_0 and α_1—that is, the values that characterize the wage/quit relationship in the entire population of firms—from a sample of just 10 firms. The uncertainty about each estimated coefficient is measured by its *standard error*, or the estimated standard deviation of the coefficient. These standard errors are reported in parentheses under the estimated coefficients in equation (1A.3); for example, given our data, the estimated standard error of the wage coefficient is 0.625, and that of the intercept term is 5.3. The larger the standard error, the greater the uncertainty about our estimated coefficient's value.

Under suitable assumptions about the distribution of ε, the random error term in equation (1A.2), we can use these standard errors to test hypotheses about the estimated coefficients.[6] In our example, we would like to test the hypothesis that α_1 is negative (which implies, as suggested by theory, that higher wages reduce quits) against the *null hypothesis* that α_1 is zero and there is thus no relationship between wages and quits. One common test involves computing for each coefficient a *t statistic*, which is the ratio of the coefficient to its standard error. A heuristic rule, which can be made precise, is that if the absolute value of the t statistic is greater than 2, the hypothesis that the true value of the coefficient equals zero can

---

[4]Students with access to computer software for estimating regression models can easily verify this result.

[5]For example, at a wage of $20/hour, the estimated quit rate would be $45 - 2.5(20)$, or –5 percent per year.

[6]These assumptions are discussed in any econometrics text.

be rejected. Put another way, if the absolute value of a coefficient is at least twice the size of its standard error, one can be fairly confident that the true value of the coefficient is a number other than zero; in this case, we say that the estimated coefficient is *statistically significant* (a shorthand way of saying that it is significantly different from zero in a statistical sense). In our example, the *t* statistic for the wage coefficient is $-2.5/0.625$, or 24.0, which leaves us very confident that the true relationship between wage levels and quit rates is negative.

Multiple Regression Analysis

The preceding discussion has assumed that the only variable influencing quit rates, other than random (unexplained) factors, is a firm's wage rate. The discussion of positive economics in this chapter stresses, however, that the prediction of a negative relationship between wages and quit rates is made holding all other factors constant. As we will discuss in chapter 10, economic theory suggests that there are many factors besides wages that systematically influence quit rates. These include characteristics both of firms (e.g., employee benefits offered, working conditions, and firm size) and of their workers (e.g., age and level of training). If any of these other variables that we have omitted from our analysis tend to vary across firms systematically with the wage rates that the firms offer, the resulting estimated relationship between wage rates and quit rates will be incorrect. In such cases, we must take these other variables into account by using a model with more than one independent variable. We rely on economic theory to indicate which variables should be included in our statistical analysis and to suggest the direction of causation.

To illustrate this procedure, suppose for simplicity that the only variable affecting a firm's quit rate besides its wage rate is the average age of its workforce. With other factors kept constant, older workers are less likely to quit their jobs for a number of reasons (as workers grow older, ties to friends, neighbors, and coworkers become stronger, and the psychological costs involved in changing jobs—which often requires a geographic move—grow larger). To capture the effects of both wage rates and age, we assume that a firm's quit rate is given by

$$Q_i = \alpha'_0 + \alpha'_1 W_i + \alpha'_2 A_i + \varepsilon_i \tag{1A.4}$$

A_i is a variable representing the age of firm i's workers. Although A_i could be measured as the average age of the workforce, or as the percentage of the firm's workers older than some age level, for expositional convenience, we have defined it as a *dichotomous* variable. A_i is equal to 1 if the average age of firm i's workforce is greater than 40, and it is equal to zero otherwise. Clearly, theory suggests that α'_2 is negative, which means that whatever values of α'_0, α'_1, and W_i pertain (that is, keeping all else constant), firms with workforces having an average age above 40 years should have lower quit rates than firms with workforces having an average age equal to or below age 40.

The parameters of equation (1A.4)—that is, the values of α'_0, α'_1, and α'_2 — can be estimated using *multiple regression analysis*, a method that is analogous to the one described earlier. This method finds the values of the parameters that define the best straight-line relationship between the dependent variable and the set of independent variables. Each parameter tells us the effect on the dependent variable of a one-unit change in the corresponding independent variable, *holding the other independent variables constant*. Thus, the estimate of α'_1 tells us the estimated effect on the quit rate (Q) of a one-unit change in the wage rate (W), holding the age of a firm's workforce (A) constant.

The Problem of Omitted Variables

If we use a univariate regression model in a situation calling for a multiple regression model—that is, if we leave out an important independent variable—our results may suffer from *omitted variables bias*. We illustrate this bias because it is an important pitfall in hypothesis testing, and because it illustrates the need to use economic theory to guide empirical testing.

To simplify our example, we assume that we know the true values of α'_0, α'_1, and α'_2 in equation (1A.4) and that there is no random error term in this model (each ε_i is zero). Specifically, we assume that

$$Q_i = 50 - 2.5W_i - 10A_i \qquad (1A.5)$$

Thus, at any level of wages, a firm's quit rate will be 10 percentage points lower if the average age of its workforce exceeds 40 than it will be if the average age is less than or equal to 40.

Figure 1A.2 graphically illustrates this assumed relationship between quit rates, wage rates, and workforce average age. For all firms that employ workers whose average age is less than or equal to 40, A_i equals zero and thus their quit rates are given by the line Z_0Z_0. For all firms that employ workers whose average age is greater than 40, A_i equals 1 and thus their quit rates are given by the line Z_1Z_1. The quit-rate schedule for the latter set of firms is 10 percentage points below the one for the former set. Both schedules indicate, however, that a $1 increase in a firm's average hourly wage will reduce its annual quit rate by 2.5 percentage points (that is, both lines have the same slope).

Now, suppose a researcher were to estimate the relationship between quit rates and wage rates, but ignored the fact that the average age of a firm's workers also affects the quit rate. That is, suppose one were to omit a measure of age and estimate the following equation:

$$Q_i = a_0 + \alpha_1 W_i + \varepsilon_i \qquad (1A.6)$$

Of crucial importance to us is how the estimated value of α_1 will correspond to the true slope of the quit/wage schedule, which we have *assumed* to be –2.5.

Figure 1A.2

True Relationships between Wages and Quit Rates (Equation 1A.5)

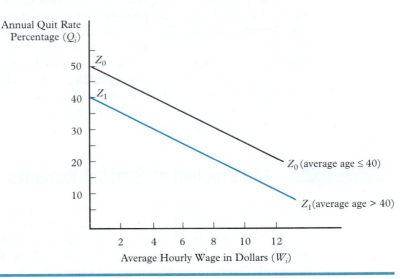

The answer depends heavily on how average wages and the average age of employees vary across firms. Table 1A.2 lists combinations of quit rates and wages for three hypothetical firms that employed older workers (average age greater than 40) and three hypothetical firms that employed younger workers. Given the wage each firm paid, the values of its quit rate can be derived directly from equation (1A.5).

It is a well-established fact that earnings of workers tend to increase as they age.[7] On average, then, firms employing older workers are assumed in the table to have higher wages than firms employing younger workers. The wage/quit-rate

Table 1A.2

Hypothetical Average-Wage and Quit-Rate Data for Three Firms That Employed Older Workers and Three That Employed Younger Workers

| | Employ Older Workers ($A_i = 1$) | | | Employ Younger Workers ($A_i = 0$) | |
Firm	Average Hourly Wage Paid ($)	Quit Rate (%)	Firm	Average Hourly Wage Paid ($)	Quit Rate (%)
k	8	20	p	4	40
l	10	15	q	6	35
m	12	10	r	8	30

[7]Reasons why this occurs will be discussed in chapters 5, 9, and 11.

combinations for these six firms are indicated by the dots on the lines Z_0Z_0 and Z_1Z_1 in Figure 1A.3,[8] which reproduce the lines in Figure 1A.2.

When we estimate equation (1A.6) using these six data points, we obtain the following straight line:

$$Q_i = 57 - 4W_i \tag{1A.7}$$
$$(5.1) \quad (0.612)$$

This estimated relationship is denoted by the line XX in Figure 1A.3. The estimate of α_1, which equals 24, implies that every dollar increase in wages reduces the quit rate by four percentage points, yet we know (by assumption) that the actual reduction is 2.5 percentage points. Our estimated response overstates the sensitivity of the quit rate to wages because the estimated equation ignored the effect that age has on quits.

Put differently, quit rates are lower in high-wage firms *both* because the wages they pay are higher *and* because high-wage firms tend to employ older workers, who are less likely to quit. By ignoring age in the analysis, we mistakenly conclude that quit rates are more sensitive to wage changes than they actually are. Therefore, by omitting from our model an important explanatory variable (age) that both affects quit rates and is associated with wage levels, we have obtained a wrong estimate of the effect of wages on quit rates.

Figure 1A.3

Estimated Relationships between Wages and Quit Rates Using Data from Table 1A.2

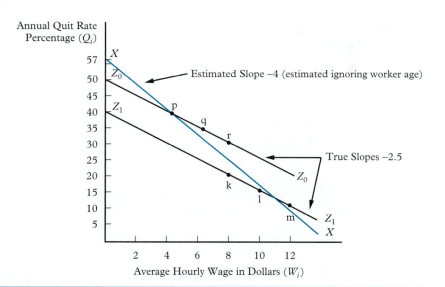

Annual Quit Rate Percentage (Q_i)

Average Hourly Wage in Dollars (W_i)

---

[8]The fact that the dots fall exactly on a straight line is a graphic representation of the assumption in equation (1A.5) that there is no random error term. If random error is present, the dots would fall around, but not all on, a straight line.

This discussion highlights the "other things held equal" nature of most hypotheses in labor economics. In testing hypotheses, we must control for other factors that are expected to influence the variable of interest. Typically, this is done by specifying that the dependent variable is a function of a *set* of variables. This specification must be guided by economic theory, and one reason for learning economic theory is that it can guide us in testing hypotheses about human behavior. Without a firm grounding in theory, analyses of behavior can easily fall victim to omitted variables bias.

Having said this, we must point out that it is neither possible nor crucial to have data on all variables that could conceivably influence what is being examined. As emphasized in this chapter, testing economic models involves looking for *average* relationships and ignoring idiosyncratic factors. Two workers with the same age and the same wage rate may exhibit different quit behaviors because, for example, one wants to leave town to get away from a dreadful father-in-law. This idiosyncratic factor is not important for the testing of an economic model of quit rates because having a father-in-law has neither a predictable effect on quits (some fathers-in-law are desirable to be around) nor any correlation with one's wage rate. To repeat, omitted variables bias is a problem only if the omitted variable has an effect on the dependent variable (quit rate) *and* is correlated with an independent variable of interest (wages).

CHAPTER 2

Overview of the Labor Market

E very society—regardless of its wealth, its form of government, or the organization of its economy—must make basic decisions. It must decide what and how much to produce, how to produce it, and how the output shall be distributed. These decisions require finding out what consumers want, what technologies for production are available, and what the skills and preferences of workers are; deciding where to produce; and coordinating all such decisions so that, for example, the millions of people in New York City and the isolated few in an Alaskan fishing village can all buy the milk, bread, meat, vanilla extract, mosquito repellent, and brown shoe polish they desire at the grocery store. The process of coordination involves creating incentives so that the right amount of labor and capital will be employed at the right place at the required time.

These decisions can, of course, be made by administrators employed by a centralized bureaucracy. The amount of information this bureaucracy must obtain and process to make the millions of needed decisions wisely, and the number of incentives it must create to ensure that these decisions are coordinated, are truly mind-boggling. It boggles the mind even more to consider the major alternative to centralized decision making—the decentralized marketplace. Millions of producers striving to make a profit observe the prices millions of consumers are willing to pay for products and the wages millions of workers are willing to accept for work. Combining these pieces of information with data on various technologies, they decide where to produce, what to produce, whom to hire, and how much to produce. No one is in charge, and while market imperfections impede progress toward achieving the best allocation of resources, millions of people find jobs that enable them to purchase the items they desire each year. The production, employment, and consumption decisions are all made and coordinated by price signals arising through the marketplace.

The market that allocates workers to jobs and coordinates employment decisions is the *labor market*. With roughly 150 million workers and roughly 7 million employers in the United States, thousands of decisions about career choice, hiring, quitting, compensation, and technology must be made and coordinated every day.

Because we believe that it is essential for students to understand the "big picture" at the outset, this chapter presents an overview of what the labor market does and how it works. After seeing how the buying and selling sides of the labor market are coordinated at an overall (or "market") level, we then turn to more detailed analyses of individual behavior on each side in subsequent chapters.

The Labor Market: Definitions, Facts, and Trends

Every market has buyers and sellers, and the labor market is no exception: the buyers are employers, and the sellers are workers. Some of these participants may not be active at any given moment in the sense of seeking new employees or new jobs, but on any given day, thousands of firms and workers will be "in the market" trying to transact. If, as in the case of doctors or mechanical engineers, buyers and sellers are searching throughout the entire nation for each other, we would describe the market as a *national labor market*. If buyers and sellers search only locally, as in the case of data entry clerks or automobile mechanics, the labor market is a *local* one.

When we speak of a particular "labor market"—for taxi drivers, say— we are using the term *loosely* to refer to the companies trying to hire people to drive their cabs and the people seeking employment as cabdrivers. The efforts of these buyers and sellers of labor to transact and establish an employment relationship constitute the market for cabdrivers. However, neither the employers nor the drivers are confined to this market; both could simultaneously be in other markets as well. An entrepreneur with $100,000 to invest might be thinking of operating either a taxi company or a car wash, depending on the projected revenues and costs of each. A person seeking a cab-driving job might also be trying to find work as an actor. Thus, all the various labor markets that we can define on the basis of industry, occupation, geography, transaction rules, or job character are interrelated to some degree. We speak of these narrowly defined labor markets for the sake of convenience.

Some labor markets, particularly those in which the sellers of labor are represented by a union, operate under a very formal set of rules that partly govern buyer–seller transactions. In the unionized construction trades, for example, employers must hire at the union hiring hall from a list of eligible union members.

In other unionized markets, the employer has discretion over who gets hired but is constrained by a union–management agreement in such matters as the order in which employees may be laid off, procedures regarding employee complaints, and promotions. The markets for government jobs and jobs with large nonunion employers also tend to operate under rules that constrain the authority of management and ensure fair treatment of employees. When a formal set of rules and procedures guides and constrains the employment relationship *within* a firm, an *internal labor market* is said to exist.[1]

The Labor Force and Unemployment

Figure 2.1 highlights some basic definitions concerning labor market status. The term *labor force* refers to all those over 16 years of age who are employed, actively seeking work, or expecting recall from a layoff. Those in the labor force who are not employed for pay are the *unemployed*.[2] People who are not employed and are neither looking for work nor waiting to be recalled from layoff by their

Figure 2.1

Labor Force Status of the U.S. Adult Civilian Population, April 2013 (seasonally adjusted)

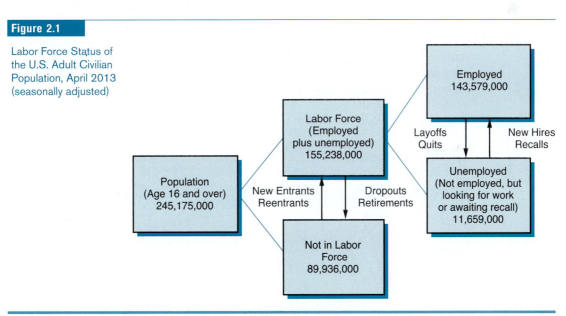

---

[1]An analysis of internal labor markets can be found in Michael L. Wachter and Randall Wright, "The Economics of Internal Labor Markets," *University of Pennsylvania Law Review* 29 (Spring 1990): 240–262.

[2]The official definition of unemployment for purposes of government statistics includes those who have been laid off by their employers, those who have been fired or have quit and are looking for other work, and those who are just entering or reentering the labor force but have not found a job as yet. The extent of unemployment is estimated from a monthly survey of some 50,000 households called the Current Population Survey (CPS). Interviewers ascertain whether household members are employed, whether they meet one of the aforementioned conditions (in which case they are considered "unemployed"), or whether they are out of the labor force.

employers are not counted as part of the labor force. The total labor force thus consists of the employed and the unemployed.

The number and identities of people in each labor market category are always changing, and as we shall see in chapter 14, the flows of people from one category to another are sizable. As Figure 2.1 suggests, there are four major flows between labor market states:

1. Employed workers become unemployed by *quitting* voluntarily or *being laid off* (being involuntarily separated from the firm, either temporarily or permanently).
2. Unemployed workers obtain employment by *being newly hired or being recalled* to a job from which they were temporarily laid off.
3. Those in the labor force, whether employed or unemployed, can leave the labor force by *retiring* or otherwise deciding against taking or seeking work for pay (*dropping out*).
4. Those who have never worked or looked for a job expand the labor force by *entering* it, while those who have dropped out do so by *reentering* the labor force.

In April 2013, there were over 155 million people in the labor force, representing about 63 percent of the entire population over 16 years of age. An overall *labor force participation rate* (labor force divided by population) of 63 percent is higher than the rates of about 60 percent that prevailed prior to the 1980s but—as is shown in Table 2.1—lower than the rate in 2000. Underlying changes over time in the overall labor force participation rate are a continued decline in the

Table 2.1

Labor Force Participation Rates by Gender, 1950–2013

Year	Total (%)	Men (%)	Women (%)
1950	59.9	86.8	33.9
1960	60.2	84.0	37.8
1970	61.3	80.6	43.4
1980	64.2	77.9	51.6
1990	66.5	76.4	57.5
2000	67.2	74.7	60.2
2010 (April)	65.2	71.8	59.0
2013 (April)	63.3	69.8	57.2

Sources: 1950–1980: U.S. President, *Employment and Training Report of the President* (Washington, D.C.: U.S. Government Printing Office), transmitted to the Congress 1981, Table A-1.

1990: U.S. Bureau of Labor Statistics, *Employment and Earnings* 45 (February 1998), Tables A-1 and A-2.

2000: U.S. Bureau of Labor Statistics, *Employment Situation* (News Release, October 2001), Table A-1.

2010: U.S. Bureau of Labor Statistics, *Employment Situation* (Economic News Release, May 2010), Table A-1.

2013: U.S. Bureau of Labor Statistics, *Employment Situation* (Economic News Release, May 2013), Table A-1.

Data and news releases are available online at http://www.bls.gov.

participation rate for men and a dramatic rise in the participation rate for women prior to 2000, with a decline since then. These trends and their causes will be discussed in detail in chapters 6 and 7.

The ratio of those unemployed to those in the labor force is the *unemployment rate*. While this rate is crude and has several imperfections, it is the most widely cited measure of labor market conditions. When the unemployment rate is around 5 percent in the United States, the labor market is considered *tight*, indicating that jobs in general are plentiful and hard for employers to fill and that most of those who are unemployed will find other work quickly. When the unemployment rate is higher—say, 7 percent or above—the labor market is described as *loose*, in the sense that workers are abundant and jobs are relatively easy for employers to fill. To say that the labor market as a whole is loose, however, does not imply that no shortages can be found anywhere; to say it is tight can still mean that in some occupations or places the number of those seeking work exceeds the number of jobs available at the prevailing wage.

Figure 2.2 shows the overall unemployment in the six decades since the end of World War II (data displayed graphically in Figure 2.2 are contained in a table inside the front cover). The data indicate that through the 1960s, the unemployment rate was usually in the range of 3.5 percent to 5.5 percent, twice going up to around 6.8 percent. In the 1970s, 1980s, and early 1990s, the unemployment rate almost never went below 5.5 percent and went to over 9.5 percent in the

---

Figure 2.2

Unemployment Rates for the Civilian Labor Force, 1947–2012 (detailed data in table inside front cover)

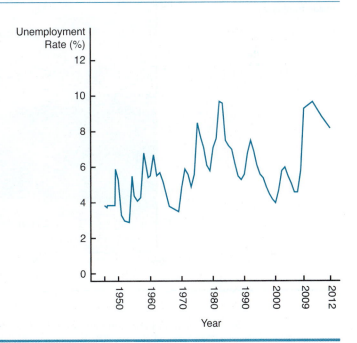

early 1980s. The rate was below 5 percent in 7 of the 11 years from 1997 through 2007, before rising to over 9 percent during the latest recession. We will discuss various issues related to unemployment and its measurement in chapter 14.

Industries and Occupations: Adapting to Change

As we pointed out earlier, the labor market is the mechanism through which workers and jobs are matched. Over the last half-century, the number of some kinds of jobs has expanded and the number of others has contracted. Both workers and employers have had to adapt to these changes in response to signals provided by the labor market. The labor-market changes occurring in a dynamic economy are sizable; for example, during mid-2007 (before the start of the latest recession), one in every 15 jobs in the United States ended, and about the same fraction was newly created—in just a typical *three-month* period![3]

An examination of the industrial distribution of employment from 1954 to 2013 reveals the kinds of changes the labor market has had to facilitate. Figure 2.3,

---

Figure 2.3

Employment Distribution by Major Nonfarm Sector, 1954–2013 (detailed data in table inside front cover)

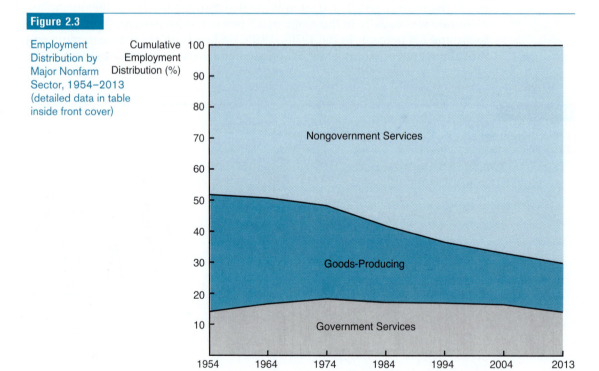

---

[3]U.S. Department of Labor, Bureau of Labor Statistics, "Business Employment Dynamics: Third Quarter 2007," News Release USDL 08-0686 (May 21, 2008), at http://www.bls.gov.

which graphs data presented in a table inside the front cover, discloses a major shift: employment in goods-producing industries (largely manufacturing) has fallen as a share of total nonfarm employment, while private-sector services have experienced dramatic growth. Thus, while a smaller share of the American labor force is working in factories, job opportunities with private employers have expanded in wholesale and retail trade, education and health care, professional and business services, leisure and hospitality activities, finance, and information services. Government employment as a share of the total has fluctuated in a relatively narrow range over the period.

The combination of shifts in the industrial distribution of jobs and changes in the production technology within each sector has also required that workers acquire new skills and work in new jobs. Since 1983, for example, the share of American workers in managerial and professional jobs rose from 23 percent to 38 percent, the share in lower-level service jobs rose from 14 percent to almost 18 percent, while the share in administrative-support, sales, and factory jobs fell from 63 percent to 44 percent.[4]

The Earnings of Labor

The actions of buyers and sellers in the labor market serve both to allocate and to set prices for various kinds of labor. From a social perspective, these prices act as signals or incentives in the allocation process—a process that relies primarily on individual and voluntary decisions. From the workers' point of view, the price of labor is important in determining income—and, hence, purchasing power.

Nominal and Real Wages
The *wage rate* is the price of labor per working hour.[5] The *nominal wage* is what workers get paid per hour in current dollars; nominal wages are most useful in comparing the pay of various workers at a given time. *Real wages*, nominal wages divided by some measure of prices, suggest how much can be purchased with workers' nominal wages. For example, if a worker earns $64 a day and a pair of shoes cost $32, we could say the worker earns the equivalent of two pairs of shoes a day (real wage = $64/$32 = 2).

---

[4]U.S. Department of Labor, Bureau of Labor Statistics, *Employment and Earnings*: 31 (January 1984), Table 20; *Employment and Earnings Online* (January 2013), Table 10 (at http://www.bls.gov).

[5]In this book, we define the hourly wage in the way most workers would if asked to state their "straight-time" wage. It is the money a worker would lose per hour if he or she had an unauthorized absence. When wages are defined in this way, a paid holiday becomes an "employee benefit," as we note in the following, because leisure time is granted while pay continues. Thus, a worker paid $100 for 25 hours—20 of which are working hours and 5 of which are time off—will be said to earn a wage of $4 per hour and receive time off worth $20. An alternative is to define the wage in terms of actual hours worked—or as $5 per hour in the above example. We prefer our definition, because if the worker seizes an opportunity to work one less hour in a particular week, his or her earnings would fall by $4, not $5 (as long as the reduction in hours does not affect the hours of paid holiday or vacation time for which the worker is eligible).

Calculations of real wages are especially useful in comparing the purchasing power of workers' earnings over a period of time when both nominal wages and product prices are changing. For example, suppose we were interested in trying to determine what happened to the real wages of American nonsupervisory workers over the period from 1980 to 2012. We can note from Table 2.2 that the average hourly earnings of these workers in the private sector were $6.85 in 1980, $10.20 in 1990, and $19.77 in 2012; thus, nominal wage rates were clearly rising over this period. However, the prices such workers had to pay for the items they bought were also rising over this period, so a method of accounting for price inflation must be used in calculating real wages.

The most widely used measure for comparing the prices consumers face over several years is the Consumer Price Index (CPI). Generally speaking, this index is derived by determining what a fixed bundle of consumer goods and services (including food, housing, clothing, transportation, medical care, and entertainment) costs each year. The cost of this bundle in the base period is then set to equal 100, and the index numbers for all other years are set proportionately to this base period. For example, if the bundle's average cost over the 1982–1984 period is considered the base (the average value of the index over this period is set to 100), and if the bundle were to cost twice as much in 2012, then the index for 2012 would be set to 200. From the second line in Table 2.2, we can see that with a 1982–1984 base, the CPI was 82.4 in 1980 and 229.6 in 2012—implying that prices had almost tripled (229.6/82.4 = 2.79) over that period. Put differently, a dollar in 2012 appears to have bought about one-third as much as a 1980 dollar.

There are several alternative ways to calculate real wages from the information given in the first two rows of Table 2.2. The most straightforward way is to divide the nominal wage by the CPI for each year and multiply by 100. Doing this converts the nominal wage for each year into 1982–1984 dollars; thus, workers paid $6.85 in 1980 could have bought $8.31 worth of goods and services in 1982–1984. Alternatively, we could use the table's information to put average

Table 2.2

Nominal and Real Hourly Earnings, U.S. Nonsupervisory Workers in the Private Sector, 1980–2012

	1980	1990	2012
Average hourly earnings	$ 6.85	$10.20	$19.77
Consumer Price Index (CPI) using 1982–1984 as a base	82.4	130.7	229.6
Average hourly earnings, 1982–1984 dollars (using CPI)	$ 8.31	$ 7.80	$ 8.61
Average hourly earnings, 2012 dollars (using CPI)	$19.09	$17.92	$19.77
Average hourly earnings, 2012 dollars (using CPI inflation less 1 percent per year)	$13.96	$14.48	$19.77

Source: U.S. President, *Economic Report of the President* (Washington, D.C.: U.S. Government Printing Office, 2013), Tables B-47 and B-60.

hourly earnings into 2012 dollars by multiplying each year's nominal wage rate by the price increase between that year and 2012. Because prices rose 2.79 times between 1980 and 2012, $6.85 in 1980 was equivalent to $19.09 in 2012.

The CPI   Our calculations in Table 2.2 suggest that real wages for American non-supervisory workers were only slightly higher in 2012 than they were in 1980 (and actually fell during the 1980s). A lively debate exists, however, about whether real-wage calculations based on the CPI are accurate indicators of changes in the purchasing power of an hour of work for the ordinary American. The issues are technical and beyond the scope of this text, but they center on two problems associated with using a fixed bundle of goods and services to compare prices from year to year.

One problem is that consumers *change* the bundle of goods and services they actually buy over time, partly in response to changes in prices. If the price of beef rises, for example, consumers may eat more chicken; pricing a fixed bundle may thus understate the purchasing power of current dollars, because it assumes that consumers still purchase the former quantities of beef. For this reason, the bundles used for pricing purposes are updated periodically.

The more difficult issue has to do with the *quality* of goods and services. Suppose that hospital costs rise by 50 percent over a five-year period, but at the same time, new diagnostic equipment and surgical techniques are perfected. Some of the increased price of hospitalization, then, reflects the availability of new services—or quality improvements in previously provided ones—rather than reductions in the purchasing power of a dollar. The problem is that we have not yet found a satisfactory method for feasibly separating the effects of changes in quality.

After considering these problems, some economists believe that the CPI has overstated inflation by as much as one percentage point per year.[6] While not everyone agrees that inflation is overstated by this much, it is instructive to recalculate real-wage changes by supposing that it is. Inflation, as measured by the CPI, averaged 2.6 percent per year from 1990 to 2012, and in Table 2.2, we therefore estimated that it would take $17.92 in 2012 to buy what $10.20 could purchase 22 years earlier. Comparing $17.92 with what was actually paid in 2012—$19.77—we would conclude that real wages had risen by 10 percent from 1990 to 2012. If the true decline in purchasing power were instead only 1.6 percent per year during that period, then it would have taken a wage of only $14.48 in 2012 to match the purchasing power of $10.20 in 1990. Because workers were actually paid $19.77 in 2012, assuming that true inflation was one percentage point below that indicated by the CPI, this results in the conclusion that real wages rose by 36 percent (not just 10 percent) over that period! When we make a similar adjustment in the calculation of real wages for 1980, we estimate that—instead of falling during

---

[6]For a review of studies on this topic, see David E. Lebow and Jeremy B. Rudd, "Measurement Error in the Consumer Price Index: Where Do We Stand?" *Journal of Economic Literature* 41 (March 2003): 159–201. These authors place the upward bias in the CPI at between 0.3 percentage points and 1.4 percentage points per year, with the most likely bias being 0.9 percentage points.

EXAMPLE 2.1

Real Wages across Countries and Time: Big Macs per Hour Worked

"Real wage rates" are calculated by dividing the nominal wage rate by some measure of consumer prices. Because measures of the real wage are intended to indicate how many goods or services can be purchased by working one hour, such measures are relied upon to reflect differences in living standards across countries or across time. There are three major difficulties, however, in generating useful measures of the real wage.

First, we want to measure nominal wages (the numerator) to reflect the wages of workers with comparable skill levels. It is of little use to compare real wages of auto mechanics with bicycle repairers. Second, the prices used in the denominator of our real wage calculation should relate to goods or services of comparable quality. For example, if we are trying to compare, across countries, how many pairs of shoes an hour of work will buy, we would be faced with the problem that shoes in Italy and shoes in Afghanistan could be of very different quality.

Third, if we use a price index (such as the CPI) in our denominator, we are confronted with the fact that the basket of goods and services on which the index is measured will vary over time and across countries. For example, when the basket of goods (starches, meats, tea, sugar, cloth, and so forth) purchased by the typical Londoner in 1704 was used to compare real wages in London and Canton, China, the real wage was higher in London; however, when the basket of the same goods purchased by the Cantonese was used, the real wage was higher in Canton!

A clever measure of real wages that avoids the problems noted above is the "Big Mac per Hour of Work" (BMPH) index – or how many Big Macs a crew member at a McDonald's restaurant can purchase with an hour of work. The numerator of BMPH contains the wages for jobs that are completely comparable across time and place; operations at McDonald's restaurants are standardized through a lengthy operating manual that covers all aspects of food preparation and delivery. The denominator of the index contains the price of a product (a Big Mac) that is also standardized across countries and time. Thus, BMPH offers a true comparison of purchasing power (albeit of a limited good) across time and place.

What does the BMPH tell us? In the United States, for example, BMPH was 2.41 in 2007; that is, a McDonald's crew member was able to purchase 2.41 Big Macs through an hour of work. In contrast, BMPH was 3.09 in Japan, 2.23 in Western Europe, 2.19 in Canada, 1.19 in Russia, 0.57 in China and 0.35 in India. Comparing BMPH over time, however, indicates that from 2000 to 2007, the index fell 7–9% in the United States and Canada, while rising 50–60% in China and India, and by 150% in Russia. From 2007 to 2011, BMPH continued to rise in Russia and China, while it fell in the other places.

Source: Orley Ashenfelter, "Comparing Real Wage Rates," *American Economic Review* 102 (April 2012): 617–642.

the 1980s—real wages rose 3.7 percent from 1980 to 1990. Thus, estimated changes in real wage rates are very sensitive to the magnitude of adjustments in the CPI that many economists think should be made. (Example 2.1 provides a discussion of related problems in calculating real wages, and a clever solution to them.)

Wages, Earnings, Compensation, and Income   We often apply the term *wages* to payments received by workers who are paid on a salaried basis (monthly, for example) rather than on an hourly basis. The term is used this way merely for convenience and is of no consequence for most purposes. It is important, however, to distinguish among wages, earnings, and income, as we do schematically in Figure 2.4. The term *wages* refers to the payment for a *unit* of time, whereas *earnings* refers to wages multiplied by the number of time units (typically hours) worked. Thus, earnings depend on both wages and the length of time the employee works.

Both wages and earnings are normally defined and measured in terms of direct monetary payments to employees (before taxes for which the employee is liable). *Total compensation*, on the other hand, consists of earnings plus *employee benefits*—benefits that are either payments in kind or deferred. Examples of *payments in kind* are employer-provided health care and health insurance, wherein the employee receives a service or an insurance policy rather than money. Paid vacation time is also in this category, since employees are given days off instead of cash.

Deferred payments can take the form of employer-financed retirement benefits, including Social Security taxes, for which employers set aside money now that enables their employees to receive pensions later.

Income—the total command over resources of a person or family during some time period (usually a year)—includes earnings, benefits, and *unearned income*, which includes dividends or interest received on investments and transfer payments received from the government in the form of food stamps, welfare payments, unemployment compensation, and the like.

Figure 2.4

Relationship among Wages, Earnings, Compensation, and Income

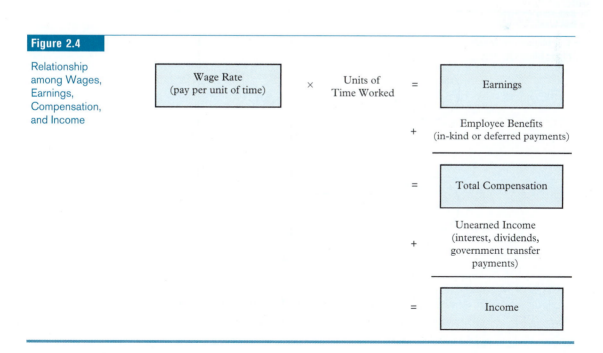

How the Labor Market Works

As shown diagrammatically in Figure 2.5, the labor market is one of three markets in which firms must successfully operate if they are to survive; the other two are the capital market and the product market. The labor and capital markets are the major ones in which firms' inputs are purchased, and the product market is the one in which output is sold. In reality, of course, a firm may deal in many different labor, capital, or product markets simultaneously.

Study of the labor market begins and ends with an analysis of the demand for and supply of labor. On the demand side of the labor market are employers, whose decisions about the hiring of labor are influenced by conditions in all three markets. On the supply side of the labor market are workers and potential workers, whose decisions about where (and whether) to work must take into account their other options for how to spend time.

It is useful to remember that the major labor market outcomes are related to (a) the *terms of employment* (wages, compensation levels, working conditions) and (b) the *levels of employment.* In analyzing both these outcomes, one must usually differentiate among the various occupational, skill, or demographic groups that make up the overall labor market. Any labor market outcome is always affected, to one degree or another, by the forces of both demand and supply. To paraphrase economist Alfred Marshall, it takes both demand and supply to determine economic outcomes, just as it takes both blades of a pair of scissors to cut cloth.

Figure 2.5

The Markets in Which
Firms Must Operate

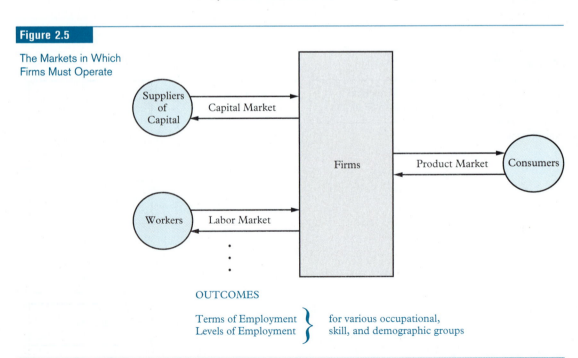

OUTCOMES

Terms of Employment   for various occupational,
Levels of Employment   skill, and demographic groups

In this chapter, we present the basic outlines and broadest implications of the simplest economic model of the labor market. In later chapters, we shall add some complexities to this basic model and explain assumptions and implications more fully. However, the simple model of demand and supply presented here offers some insights into labor market behavior that can be very useful in the formulation of social policy. Every piece of analysis in this text is an extension or modification of the basic model presented in this chapter.

The Demand for Labor

Firms combine various factors of production—mainly capital and labor—to produce goods or services that are sold in a product market. Their total output and the way in which they combine labor and capital depend on three forces: product demand, the amount of labor and capital they can acquire at given prices, and the choice of technologies available to them. When we study the demand for labor, we are interested in finding out how the number of workers employed by a firm or set of firms is affected by changes in one or more of these three forces. To simplify the discussion, we shall study one change at a time while holding other forces constant.

Wage Changes   How does the number of employees (or total labor hours) demanded vary when wages change? Suppose, for example, that we could vary the wages facing a certain industry over a long period of time but keep the technology available, the conditions under which capital is supplied, and the relationship between product price and product demand unchanged. What would happen to the quantity of labor demanded if the wage rate were *increased*?

First, higher wages imply higher costs and, usually, higher product prices. Because consumers respond to higher prices by buying less, employers would tend to reduce their levels of output and employment (other things being equal). This decline in employment is called a *scale effect*—the effect on desired employment of a smaller scale of production.

Second, as wages increase (assuming the price of capital does not change, at least initially), employers have incentives to cut costs by adopting a technology that relies more on capital and less on labor. Desired employment would fall because of a shift toward a more *capital-intensive* mode of production. This second effect is termed a *substitution effect*, because as wages rise, capital is *substituted* for labor in the production process.

The effects of various wages on employment levels might be summarized in a table showing the labor demanded at each wage level. Table 2.3 illustrates such a *demand schedule*. The relationship between wages and employment tabulated in Table 2.3 could be graphed as a *demand curve*. Figure 2.6 shows the demand curve generated by the data in Table 2.3. Note that the curve has a negative slope, indicating that as wages rise, less labor is demanded. (Note also that we follow convention in economics by placing the wage rate on the *vertical* axis despite its being an *independent* variable in the context of labor demand by a firm.) A demand

Table 2.3

Labor Demand Schedule for a Hypothetical Industry

Wage Rate ($)	Desired Employment Level
3.00	250
4.00	190
5.00	160
6.00	130
7.00	100
8.00	70

Note: Employment levels can be measured in number of employees or number of labor hours demanded. We have chosen here to use number of employees.

curve for labor tells us how the desired level of employment, measured in either labor hours or number of employees, varies with changes in the price of labor when the other forces affecting demand are held constant.

Changes in Other Forces Affecting Demand   What happens to labor demand when one of the forces other than the wage rate changes?

First, suppose that *demand for the product* of a particular industry were to increase, so that at any output price, more of the goods or services in question could be sold. Suppose in this case that technology and the conditions under which capital and labor are made available to the industry do not change. Output levels would clearly rise as firms in the industry sought to maximize profits, and this *scale* (or *output*) *effect* would increase the demand for labor at any given wage rate. (As long as the relative prices of capital and labor remain unchanged, there is no *substitution effect.*)

Figure 2.6

Labor Demand Curve (based on data in Table 2.3)

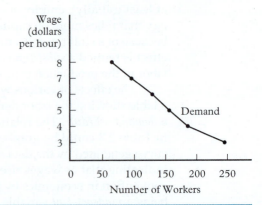

How would this change in the demand for labor be illustrated using a demand curve? Since the technology available and the conditions under which capital and labor are supplied have remained constant, this change in product demand would increase the labor desired at any wage level that might prevail. In other words, the entire labor demand curve *shifts* to the right. This rightward shift, shown as a movement from D to D' in Figure 2.7, indicates that at every possible wage rate, the number of workers demanded has increased.

Second, consider what would happen if the product demand schedule, technology, and labor supply conditions were to remain unchanged, but *the supply of capital* changed so that capital prices fell to 50 percent of their prior level. How would this change affect the demand for labor?

Our method of analyzing the effects on labor demand of a change in the price of *another* productive input is familiar: we must consider the scale and substitution effects. First, when capital prices decline, the costs of producing tend to decline. Reduced costs stimulate increases in production, and these increases tend to raise the level of desired employment at any given wage. The scale effect of a fall in capital prices thus tends to increase the demand for labor at each wage level.

The second effect of a fall in capital prices would be a substitution effect, whereby firms adopt more capital-intensive technologies in response to cheaper capital. Such firms would substitute capital for labor and would use less labor to produce a given amount of output than before. With less labor being desired at each wage rate and output level, the labor demand curve tends to shift to the left.

A fall in capital prices, then, generates *two opposite effects* on the demand for labor. The scale effect will push the labor demand curve rightward, while the substitution effect will push it to the left. As emphasized by Figure 2.8, either effect could dominate. Thus, economic theory does not yield a clear-cut prediction about how a fall in capital prices will affect the demand for labor. (A *rise* in capital prices would generate the same overall ambiguity of effect on the demand

---

Figure 2.7

Shift in Demand for Labor Due to Increase in Product Demand

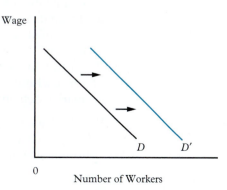

Figure 2.8

Possible Shifts in Demand for Labor Due to Fall in Capital Prices

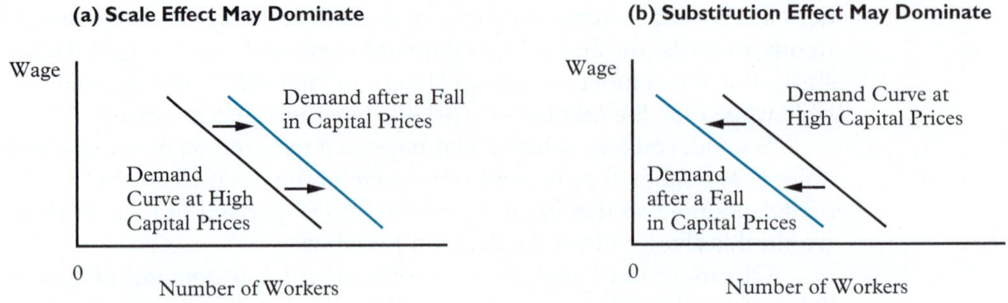

(a) Scale Effect May Dominate

(b) Substitution Effect May Dominate

for labor, with the scale effect pushing the labor demand curve leftward and the substitution effect pushing it to the right.)

The hypothesized changes in product demand and capital supply just discussed have tended to *shift* the demand curve for labor. It is important to distinguish between a *shift* in a demand curve and *movement along* a curve. A labor demand curve graphically shows the *labor desired* as a function of the *wage rate.* When the *wage* changes and other forces are held unchanged, one *moves along* the curve. However, when one of the *other forces* changes, the labor demand curve *shifts.* Unlike wages, these forces are not directly shown when the demand curve for labor is drawn. Thus, when *they* change, a different relationship between wages and desired employment prevails, and this shows up as a shift of the demand curve.

Market, Industry, and Firm Demand   The demand for labor can be analyzed on three levels:

1. To analyze the demand for labor *by a particular firm,* we would examine how an increase in the wage of machinists, say, would affect their employment by a particular aircraft manufacturer.
2. To analyze the effects of this wage increase on the employment of machinists *in the entire aircraft industry,* we would utilize an industry demand curve.
3. Finally, to see how the wage increase would affect the *entire labor market* for machinists in all industries in which they are used, we would use a market demand curve.

We shall see in chapters 3 and 4 that firm, industry, and market labor demand curves vary in *shape* to some extent because *scale* and *substitution effects* have different strengths at each level. However, it is important to remember that the scale and substitution effects of a wage change work in the same direction at each level, so that firm, industry, and market demand curves *all slope downward.*

Long Run versus Short Run   We can also distinguish between *long-run* and *short-run* labor demand curves. Over very short periods of time, employers find it difficult to substitute capital for labor (or vice versa), and customers may not change their product demand very much in response to a price increase. It takes *time* to fully adjust consumption and production behavior. Over longer periods of time, of course, responses to changes in wages or other forces affecting the demand for labor are larger and more complete.

The Supply of Labor

Having looked at a simple model of behavior on the buyer (or demand) side of the labor market, we now turn to the seller (or supply) side of the market. For the purposes of this chapter, we shall assume that workers have already decided to work and that the question facing them is what occupation and what employer to choose.

Market Supply   To first consider the supply of labor to the entire market (as opposed to the supply to a particular firm), suppose that the market we are considering is the one for legal assistants (or "paralegals"). How will supply respond to changes in the wages paralegals might receive?

If the salaries and wages in *other* occupations are held constant and the wages of paralegals rise, we would expect to find more people wanting to become paralegals. For example, suppose that each of 100 people in a high school graduating class has the option of becoming an insurance agent or a paralegal. Some of these 100 people will prefer to be insurance agents even if paralegals are better paid, because they like the challenge and sociability of selling. Some would want to be paralegals even if the pay were comparatively poor, because they hate the pressures of selling. Many, however, could see themselves doing either job; for them, the compensation in each occupation would be a major factor in their decision.

Thus, the supply of labor to a particular market is positively related to the wage rate prevailing in that market, holding other wages constant. That is, if the wages of insurance agents are held constant and the paralegal wage rises, more people will want to become paralegals because of the relative improvement in compensation (as shown graphically in Figure 2.9).

As with demand curves, each supply curve is drawn holding other prices and wages constant. If one or more of these other prices or wages were to change, it would cause the supply curve to *shift*. As the salaries of insurance agents *rise*, some people will change their minds about becoming paralegals and choose to become

Market Supply Curve for Paralegals

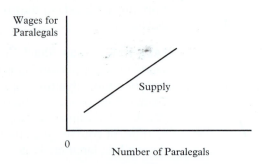

insurance agents. In graphical terms (see Figure 2.10), increases in the salaries of insurance agents would cause the supply curve of paralegals to shift to the left.

Supply to Firms   Having decided to become a paralegal, an individual would then have to decide which offer of employment to accept. If all employers were offering paralegal jobs that were more or less alike, the choice would be based entirely on compensation. Any firm unwise enough to attempt paying a wage below what others are paying would find it could not attract any employees (or at least none of the caliber it wanted). Conversely, no firm would be foolish enough to pay more than the going wage, because it would be paying more than it would have to pay to attract a suitable number and quality of employees. Supply curves to a *firm*, then, are *horizontal*, as shown in Figure 2.11, indicating that at the going wage, a firm could get all the paralegals it needs. If the paralegal wage paid by others in the market is W_0, then the firm's labor supply curve is S_0; if the wage falls to W_1, the firm's labor supply curve becomes S_1.

The difference in slope between the market supply curve and the supply curve to a firm is directly related to the type of choice facing workers. In deciding whether to *enter* the paralegal labor market, workers must weigh both the compensation *and* the job requirements of alternative options (such as being an

Shift in Market Supply Curve for Paralegals as Salaries
of Insurance Agents Rise

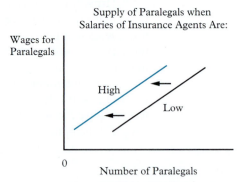

Figure 2.11

Figure 2.11

Supply of Paralegals to a Firm at Alternative Market Wages

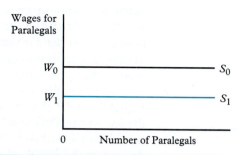

insurance agent). If wages for paralegals were to fall, not everyone would withdraw from that market, because the jobs of insurance agent and paralegal are not perfect substitutes. Some people would remain paralegals after a wage decline because they dislike the job requirements of insurance agents.

Once the decision to become a paralegal had been made, however, the choice of *which employer* to work for would be a choice among alternatives in which the job requirements were nearly the *same*. Thus, the choice would have to be made on the basis of compensation alone. If a firm were to lower its wage offers below those of other firms, it would lose all its applicants. The horizontal supply curve is, therefore, a reflection of supply decisions made among alternatives that are perfect substitutes for each other.

We have argued that firms wishing to hire paralegals must pay the going wage or lose all applicants. While this may seem unrealistic, it is not a bad proposition with which to start our analysis. If a firm offers jobs *comparable* to those offered by other firms but at a lower level of pay, it might be able to attract a few applicants of the quality it desires because a few people will be unaware of compensation elsewhere. Over time, however, knowledge of the firm's poor pay would become more widespread, and the firm would have to rely solely on less-qualified people to fill its jobs. It could secure quality employees at below-average pay only if it offered *noncomparable* jobs (more pleasant working conditions, longer paid vacations, and so forth). This factor in labor supply will be discussed in chapter 8. For now, we will assume that individual firms, like individual workers, are *wage takers;* that is, the wages they pay to their workers must be pretty close to the going wage if they face competition in the labor market. Neither individual workers nor firms can set a wage much different from the going wage and still hope to transact. (Exceptions to this elementary proposition will be analyzed in chapter 5.)

The Determination of the Wage

The wage that prevails in a particular labor market is heavily influenced by labor supply and demand, regardless of whether the market involves a labor union or other nonmarket forces. In this section, we analyze how the interplay of supply and demand in the labor market affects wages.

The Market-Clearing Wage

Recall that the market demand curve indicates how many workers employers would want at each wage rate, holding capital prices and the product demand schedule constant. The market supply curve indicates how many workers would enter the market at each wage level, holding the wages in other occupations constant. These curves can be placed on the same graph to reveal some interesting information, as shown in Figure 2.12.

For example, suppose the market wage were set at W_1. At this low wage, Figure 2.12 indicates that demand *exceeds* supply. Employers will be competing for the few workers in the market, and a shortage of workers would exist. The desire of firms to attract more employees would lead them to increase their wage offers, thus driving up the overall level of wage offers in the market. As wages rose, two things would happen. First, more workers would choose to enter the market and look for jobs (a movement along the supply curve); second, increasing wages would induce employers to seek fewer workers (a movement along the demand curve).

If wages were to rise to W_2, supply would exceed demand. Employers would desire fewer workers than the number available, and not all those desiring employment would be able to find jobs, resulting in a surplus of workers. Employers would have long lines of eager applicants for any opening and would find that they could fill their openings with qualified applicants even if they offered lower wages. Furthermore, if they could pay lower wages, they would want to hire more employees. Some employees would be more than happy to accept lower wages if they could just find a job. Others would leave the market and look for work elsewhere as wages fell. Thus, supply and demand would become more equal as wages fell from the level of W_2.

The wage rate at which demand equals supply is the *market-clearing* wage. At W_e in Figure 2.12, employers can fill the number of openings they have, and all employees who want jobs in this market can find them. At W_e there is no surplus and no shortage. All parties are satisfied, and no forces exist that would alter the wage. The market is in equilibrium in the sense that the wage will remain at W_e.

The market-clearing wage, W_e, thus becomes the *going wage* that individual employers and employees must face. In other words, wage rates are determined

---

Figure 2.12

Market Demand and Supply

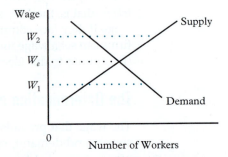

Figure 2.13

Demand and Supply at the "Market" and "Firm" Levels

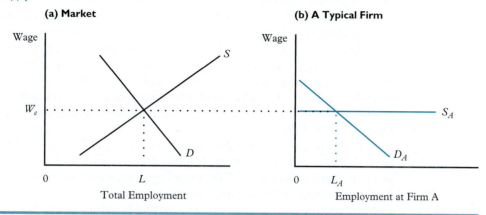

(a) Market **(b) A Typical Firm**

by the market and "announced" to individual market participants. Figure 2.13 graphically depicts *market* supply and demand in panel (a), along with the supply and demand curves for a typical *firm* (firm A) in that market in panel (b). All firms in the market pay a wage of W_e' and total employment of L equals the sum of employment in each firm.

Disturbing the Equilibrium   What could happen to change the market-clearing wage once it has been reached? Changes could arise from shifts in either the demand or the supply curve. Suppose, for example, that the increase in paperwork accompanying greater government regulation of industry caused firms to demand more paralegal help (at any given wage rate) than before. Graphically, as in Figure 2.14, this greater demand would be represented as a rightward shift of the labor demand curve. If W_e were to persist, there would be a labor shortage in the paralegal market (because demand would exceed supply). This shortage

Figure 2.14

New Labor Market Equilibrium after Demand Shifts Right

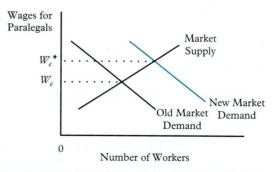

would induce employers to improve their wage offers. Eventually, the paralegal wage would be driven up to W'_e. Notice that in this case, the equilibrium level of *employment* will also rise.

The market wage can also increase if the labor supply curve shifts to the left. As shown in Figure 2.15, such a shift creates a labor shortage at the old equilibrium wage of W_e, and as employers scramble to fill their job openings, the market wage is bid up to W'_e. In the case of a leftward-shifting labor supply curve, however, the increased market wage is accompanied by a decrease in the equilibrium level of employment. (See Example 2.2 for an analysis of the labor market effects of the leftward shift in labor supply accompanying the Black Death in 1348–1351.)

If a leftward shift in labor supply is accompanied by a rightward shift in labor demand, the market wage can rise dramatically. Such a condition occurred in Egypt during the early 1970s. Lured by wages over six times higher in Saudi Arabia and other oil-rich Arab countries, roughly half of Egypt's construction workers left the country just as a residential building boom in Egypt got under way. The combination of a leftward-shifting labor supply curve and a rightward-shifting labor demand curve drove the real wages of Egyptian construction workers up by over 100 percent in just five years![7] (This notable wage increase was accompanied by a net employment *increase* in Egypt's construction industry. The student will be asked in the first review question on page 77 to analyze these events graphically.)

A fall in the market-clearing wage rate would occur if there were increased supply or reduced demand. An increase in supply would be represented by a rightward shift of the supply curve, as more people entered the market at each

---

Figure 2.15

New Labor Market Equilibrium after Supply Shifts Left

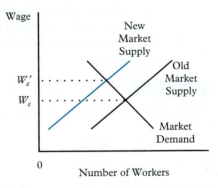

---

[7]Bent Hansen and Samir Radwan, *Employment Opportunities and Equity in Egypt* (Geneva: International Labour Office, 1982): 74. For a book on labor shortages, see Burt S. Barnow, John Trutko, and Jaclyn Schede Piatak, *Occupational Shortages: Concepts, Causes, Consequences, and Cures* (Kalamazoo, MI: W.E. Upjohn Institute for Employment Research), 2013.

EXAMPLE 2.2

The Black Death and the Wages of Labor

An example of what happens to wages when the supply of labor suddenly shifts occurred when plague—the Black Death—struck England (among other European countries) in 1348–1351. Estimates vary, but it is generally agreed that plague killed between 17 percent and 40 percent of the English population in that short period of time. This shocking loss of life had the immediate effect of raising the wages of laborers. As the supply curve shifted to the left, a shortage of workers was created at the old wage levels, and competition among employers for the surviving workers drove the wage level dramatically upward.

Reliable figures are hard to come by, but many believe wages rose by 50–100 percent over the four-year period. A thresher, for example, earning 2½ pence per day in 1348 earned 4½ pence in 1350, and mowers receiving 5 pence per acre in 1348 were receiving 9 pence in 1350. Whether the overall rise in wages was this large or not, there was clearly a labor shortage and an unprecedented increase in wages. A royal proclamation commanding landlords to share their scarce workers with neighbors and threatening workers with imprisonment if they refused work at the pre-plague wage was issued to deal with this shortage, but it was ignored. The shortage was too severe and market forces were simply too strong for the rise in wages to be thwarted.

The discerning student might wonder at this point about the demand curve for labor. Did it not also shift to the left as the population—and the number of consumers—declined? It did, but this leftward shift was not as pronounced as the leftward shift in supply. While there were fewer customers for labor's output, the customers who remained consumed greater amounts of goods and services per capita than before. The money, gold and silver, and durable goods that had existed prior to 1348 were divided among many fewer people by 1350, and this rise in per capita wealth was associated with a widespread and dramatic increase in the level of consumption, especially of luxury goods. Thus, the leftward shift in labor demand was dominated by the leftward shift in supply, and the predictable result was a large increase in wages.

Data from: Harry A. Miskimin, *The Economy of Early Renaissance Europe, 1300–1460* (Englewood Cliffs, N.J.: Prentice-Hall, 1969); George M. Modlin and Frank T. deVyver, *Development of Economic Society* (Boston: D.C. Heath, 1946); Douglass C. North and Robert Paul Thomas, *The Rise of the Western World* (Cambridge: Cambridge University Press, 1973); Philip Ziegler, *The Black Death* (New York: Harper and Row, 1969).

wage (see Figure 2.16). This rightward shift would cause a surplus to exist at the old equilibrium wage (W_e) and lead to behavior that reduced the wage to W''_e in Figure 2.16. Note that the equilibrium employment level has increased. A decrease (leftward shift) in labor demand would also cause a decrease in the market-clearing wage, although such a shift would be accompanied by a *fall* in employment.

Disequilibrium and Nonmarket Influences   That a market-clearing wage exists in theory does not imply that it is reached—or reached quickly—in practice. Because labor services cannot be separated from the worker, and because labor income is by far the most important source of spending power for ordinary people, the labor market is subject to forces that impede the adjustment of both wages and employment to changes in supply or demand. Some of these barriers

Figure 2.16

New Labor Market Equilibrium after Supply Shifts Right

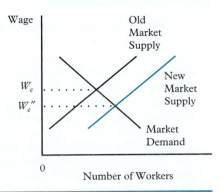

to adjustment are themselves the result of economic forces that will be discussed later in the text. For example, changing jobs often requires an employee to invest in new skills (see chapter 9) or bear costs of moving (chapter 10). On the employer side of the market, hiring workers can involve an initial investment in search and training (chapter 5), while firing them or cutting their wages can be perceived as unfair and therefore have consequences for the productivity of those who remain (chapter 11).

Other barriers to adjustment are rooted in *nonmarket* forces: laws, customs, or institutions constraining the choices of individuals and firms. Although forces keeping wages *below* their market-clearing levels are not unknown, nonmarket forces usually serve to keep wages *above* market levels. Minimum wage laws (discussed in chapter 4) and unions (chapter 13) are examples of influences explicitly designed to raise wages beyond those dictated by the market. Likewise, if there is a widespread belief that cutting wages is unfair, laws or customs may arise that prevent wages from falling in markets experiencing leftward shifts in demand or rightward shifts in supply.

It is commonly believed that labor markets adjust more quickly when market forces are calling for wages to rise as opposed to pressuring them to fall. If this is so, then those markets observed to be in disequilibrium for long periods will tend to be ones with above-market wages. The existence of above-market wages implies that the supply of labor exceeds the number of jobs being offered (refer to the relative demand and supply at wage W_2 in Figure 2.12); therefore, if enough markets are experiencing above-market wages, the result will be widespread *unemployment*.

Applications of the Theory

Although this simple model of how a labor market functions will be refined and elaborated upon in the following chapters, it can explain many important phenomena, including the issues of when workers are overpaid or underpaid and what explains international differences in unemployment.

Who Is Underpaid and Who Is Overpaid?

We pointed out in chapter 1 that a fundamental value of normative economics is that, as a society, we should strive to complete all those transactions that are mutually beneficial. Another way of stating this value is to say that we must strive to use our scarce resources as effectively as possible, which implies that output should be produced in the least-costly manner so that the most can be obtained from such resources. This goal, combined with the labor market model outlined in this chapter, suggests how we can define what it means to be overpaid.

Above-Market Wages   We shall define workers as *overpaid* if their wages are higher than the market-clearing wage for their job. Because a labor surplus exists for jobs that are overpaid, a wage above market has two implications (see Figure 2.17). First, employers are paying more than necessary to produce their output (they pay W_H instead of W_e); they could cut wages and still find enough qualified workers for their job openings. In fact, if they did cut wages, they could expand output and make their product cheaper and more accessible to consumers. Second, more workers want jobs than can find them (Y workers want jobs, but only V openings are available). If wages were reduced a little, more of these disappointed workers could find work. A wage above market thus causes consumer prices to be higher and output to be smaller than is possible, and it creates a situation in which not all workers who want the jobs in question can get them.

An interesting example of above-market wages was seen in Houston's labor market in 1988. Bus cleaners working for the Houston Metropolitan Transit Authority received $10.08 per hour, or 70 percent more than the $5.94 received by cleaners working for private bus companies in Houston. One (predictable) result of this overpayment is that the quit rate among Houston's Transit Authority cleaners was only *one-seventh* as great as the average for cleaners nationwide.[8]

Figure 2.17

Effects of an Above-Market Wage

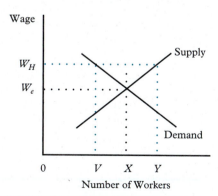

[8]William J. Moore and Robert J. Newman, "Government Wage Differentials in a Municipal Labor Market: The Case of Houston Metropolitan Transit Workers," *Industrial and Labor Relations Review* 45 (October 1991): 145–153.

To better understand the social losses attendant on overpayment, let us return to the principles of normative economics. Can reducing overpayment create a situation in which the gainers gain more than the losers lose? Suppose in the case of Houston's Transit Authority cleaners that the wage of only *newly hired* cleaners was reduced—to $6.40, say. Current cleaners thus would not lose, but many others who were working elsewhere at $5.94 would jump at the chance to earn a higher wage. Taxpayers, realizing that transit services could now be expanded at lower cost than before, would increase their demand for such services, thus creating jobs for these additional workers. Some workers would gain, while no one lost—and social well-being would clearly be enhanced.[9] The wage reduction, in short, would be *Pareto-improving* (see chapter 1).

Below-Market Wages   Employees can be defined as *underpaid* if their wages are below market-clearing levels. At below-market wages, employers have difficulty finding workers to meet the demands of consumers, and a labor shortage thus exists. They also have trouble keeping the workers they do find. If wages were increased, output would rise and more workers would be attracted to the market. Thus, an increase would benefit the people in society in *both* their consumer and their worker roles. Figure 2.18 shows how a wage increase from W_L to W_e would increase employment from V to X (at the same time wages were rising).

Wages in the U.S. Army illustrate how the market adjusts to below-market wages. Prior to 1973, when the military draft was eliminated, the government could pursue a policy of paying below-market wages to military recruits, because the resultant gap between supply and demand could be filled by conscription. Not surprisingly, when comparing wages in the late 1970s with those in the last decade of the military draft, we find that the average military cash wages paid to

---

Figure 2.18

Effects of a Below-Equilibrium Wage

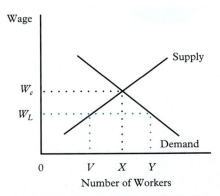

---

[9]If the workers who switched jobs were getting paid approximately what they were worth to their former employers, these employers would lose $5.94 in output but save $5.94 in costs—and their welfare would thus not be affected. The presumption that employees are paid what they are worth to the employer is discussed at length in chapter 3.

EXAMPLE 2.3

Forced Labor in Colonial Mozambique

Two ways to address a labor shortage are to raise wages by enough to attract workers voluntarily into the job or to force workers (by drafting them) into the job. While forced labor may seem to be the cheaper alternative, the resentful workforce that accompanies compulsion carries with it opportunity costs that outweigh the wage savings. An early example can be found in colonial Mozambique.

In the late nineteenth century, Mozambique—which was ruled by Portugal—was divided into several large estates for administrative purposes. The local estate holders owed the colonial administration rent and taxes, but they had the right to collect (and keep) a "head tax" of 800 *reis* per year from each African living within their boundaries. The low wages and harsh working conditions on sugar plantations created a labor shortage on many estates, and in 1880, many estate holders decided to collect the head tax by *forcing Africans to work on their plantation (without pay) for two weeks per year*.

The implied wage rate for these two weeks was 400 *reis* per week, which compares to wages

of 500–750 *reis* per week in areas where plantation labor was recruited through voluntary means. Not surprisingly, estate holders who used forced labor had to contend with a very dissatisfied, resentful group of workers. Their workforce turned over every two weeks, motivation was a problem (causing them to resort to beatings), and they had to employ private police to track down runaways who were seeking to avoid the low implicit pay and harsh methods of motivation.

In 1894, the Mozambique Sugar Company abandoned the use of forced labor, which it found to have very high opportunity costs, and raised wages by enough that workers voluntarily returned to their estates. In essence, then, the estate holders in Mozambique came to the conclusion that it was more profitable to pay the wages they needed to attract a voluntary workforce than to make use of forced labor.

Source: Leroy Vail and Landeg White, *Capitalism and Colonialism in Mozambique: A Study of the Quelimane District* (Minneapolis: University of Minnesota Press, 1980): 77, 120–25, 134.

enlisted personnel rose 19 percent more than those of comparable civilian workers. (See Example 2.3 for other labor market effects of relying on forced labor.)

Economic Rents   The concepts of underpayment and overpayment have to do with the *social* issue of producing desired goods and services in the least-costly way; therefore, we compared wages paid with the *market-clearing wage*. At the level of *individuals*, however, it is often useful to compare the wage received in a job with one's *reservation wage*, the wage below which the worker would refuse (or quit) the job in question. The amount by which one's wage exceeds one's reservation wage in a particular job is the amount of his or her *economic rent*.

Consider the labor supply curve to, say, the military. As shown in Figure 2.19, if the military is to hire L_1 people, it must pay W_1 in wages. These relatively low wages will attract to the military those who most enjoy the military culture and are least averse to the risks of combat. If the military is to be somewhat larger and to employ L_2 people, then it must pay a wage of W_2. This higher wage is required to attract those who would have found a military career unattractive at the lower wage. If W_2 turns out to be the wage that equates supply and demand,

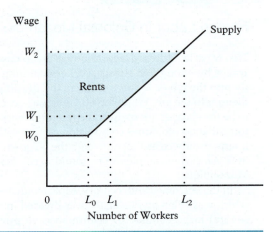

Figure 2.19

Labor Supply to the Military: Different Preferences Imply Different "Rents"

and if the military pays that wage, everyone who would have joined up for less would be receiving an economic rent!

Put differently, the supply curve to an occupation or industry is a schedule of reservation wages that indicates the labor forthcoming at each wage level. The difference between the wage actually paid and workers' reservation wages—the shaded area in Figure 2.19—is the amount of the rent. Since each worker potentially has a different reservation wage, rents may well differ for each worker in the market. In Figure 2.19, the greatest rents are received by those L_0 individuals who would have joined the military even if the wage were only W_0. They collect an economic rent of $W_2 - W_0$.

Why don't employers reduce the wage of each employee down to his or her reservation level? While capturing employee rents would seem to be lucrative, since by definition it could be done without the workers' quitting, attempting to do so would create resentment, and such a policy would be extremely costly, if not impossible, to implement. Employers do not know the true reservation wages of each employee or applicant, and finding it would involve experiments in which the wage offers to each worker either started high and were cut or started low and were raised. This would be costly, and if workers realized the firm was *experimenting*, they would attempt to disguise their true reservation wages and adopt the strategic behavior associated with bargaining (bluffing, for example). Therefore, firms usually pay according to the job, one's level of experience or longevity with the employer, and considerations of merit—but not according to preferences.

Unemployment and Responses to Technological Change across Countries

We noted earlier that labor markets are often influenced by nonmarket forces that keep wages above market-clearing levels. Because these nonmarket forces generally take the form of laws, government programs, customs, or institutions (labor unions, for example), their strength typically varies across countries. Can we form some conclusions about the countries in which they are most pronounced?

Theory presented in this chapter suggests that if wages are above market-clearing levels, unemployment will result (the number of people seeking work will exceed the number of available jobs). Furthermore, if wages are held above market-clearing levels and the labor demand curve *shifts to the left*, unemployment will rise to even higher levels (you should be able to show this by drawing a graph with an unchanging supply curve, a fixed wage rate, and a leftward-shifting demand curve). Moreover, above-market wages deter the growth of *new* jobs, so wages "stuck" above market-clearing levels also can cause those who suffer a spell of unemployment to remain in that status for a long time. Thus, measures of the incidence and duration of unemployment—which, fortunately, are comparably defined and estimated in several advanced economies—can sometimes be used to infer the relative strength of nonmarket forces across countries. Consider, for example, what happened to unemployment rates in Europe and North America in the 1980s and 1990s.

One phenomenon characterizing the 1980s was an acceleration of technological change, associated primarily with computerization, in the advanced economies of the world. These changes led to a fall in the demand for less-skilled, less-educated, lower-paid workers. In Canada and the United States the decline in demand for low-skilled workers led to a fall in their real wages throughout the 1980s; despite that, the unemployment rate for less-educated workers rose over that decade—from 7.2 percent to 8.5 percent in the United States and from 6.3 percent to 9.3 percent in Canada.

In the two European countries for which we have data on wages and unemployment by skill level, however, nonmarket forces caused the real wages of low-paid workers to *rise* over the decade, with the consequence that increases in unemployment for the less educated were much more pronounced. In France, real wages among the lowest-paid workers rose 1 percent per year, and their unemployment rate increased from 4.6 percent to 10.7 percent over the decade. In Germany, where the pay of low-wage workers rose an average of 5 percent per year, unemployment rates among these workers went from 4.4 percent to 13.5 percent.[10]

---

[10]Earnings data for all four countries are for workers in the lowest decile (lowest 10 percent) of their country's earnings distribution. These data are found in Organisation for Economic Co-operation and Development (OECD), *Employment Outlook: July 1993* (Paris: OECD, 1993), Table 5.3. Data on unemployment rates are from Federal Reserve Bank of Kansas City, *Reducing Unemployment: Current Issues and Policy Options* (Kansas City, Mo.: Federal Reserve Bank of Kansas City, 1994): 25. For analyses of the relative performance of labor markets in Europe and the United States, see Francine D. Blau and Lawrence M. Kahn, *At Home and Abroad: U.S. Labor-Market Performance in International Perspective* (New York: Russell Sage Foundation, 2002); Gilles Saint-Paul, "Why Are European Countries Diverging in Their Unemployment Experience?" *Journal of Economic Perspectives* 18 (Fall 2004): 49–68; Richard Freeman, *America Works: The Exceptional U.S. Labor Market* (New York: Russell Sage Foundation, 2007); and Stephen Nickell, "Is the U.S. Labor Market Really that Exceptional? A Review of Richard Freeman's *America Works: The Exceptional U.S. Labor Market*," *Journal of Economic Literature* 46 (June 2008): 384–395.

EMPIRICAL STUDY

PAY LEVELS AND THE SUPPLY OF MILITARY OFFICERS: OBTAINING SAMPLE VARIATION FROM CROSS-SECTION DATA

Economic theory predicts that the supply to a particular occupation is expected to increase when the pay for that occupation increases or when the pay in alternative occupations falls. In the late 1960s, the U.S. government was considering a policy change that eventually resulted in the elimination of the military draft, and it needed to estimate how much military pay would have to rise—relative to civilian pay—to attract the needed number of officers and enlisted personnel without the presence of a draft. Estimating the labor supply curve of, say, officers depends on whether we can obtain an appropriate data set.

Any study of how (independent) variable X affects (dependent) variable Y requires that the researcher have access to a data set in which both X and Y show considerable *variation*. Put differently, scientific research into cause and effect requires that we observe how *different* causes produce *different* effects! Researchers who are able to conduct laboratory experiments expose their subjects to different "treatments" and then look for differences in outcomes. Economists are rarely able to conduct experiments, so they must look for data sets in which X and Y naturally differ across the observations in a sample. If the ratio of military pay to civilian pay is our independent variable (X), and the

number of people who decide to join the military as officers is our dependent variable (Y), how can we generate a sample in which both variables display enough variation to estimate a relationship?

One way is to use data over a period of 20–30 years ("time series" data), with each year's relative wage and number of new officers representing one observation in the sample. The problem with a time series is that samples are necessarily small (there are not that many years for which we have good data). Behavior can also be affected by all kinds of changing conditions or preferences over time (for example, wars, new occupations both in and out of the military, and changing attitudes of the labor force toward risk), so that with time series data, we also need to control for these time-related changes to be confident we have isolated the effects of *pay* on labor supply decisions.

Another way to study the effects of relative pay on labor supply is to use "cross-section" data, which involves collecting observations on pay and labor supply for different people at one point in time. This usually allows for a much larger data set, but it requires that those in the data set be operating in sufficiently different environments that X and Y will actually vary. Within any year, for example, military pay for entry-level officers is the same for every-one, so we can use cross-section data to study military supply decisions only if the *civilian wages* facing sample members can be accurately measured and turn out to vary significantly.

One study done in the late 1960s analyzed enrollment data from 82 Reserve Officer Training Corps (ROTC) programs offered by universities in 1963. The supply variable (Y) in this study was measured as the percentage of men at each of the 82 universities enrolled in an Army, Navy, or Air Force ROTC program (the military was virtually all male at that time). Because military pay facing ROTC graduates at each of the 82 institutions was the same, differences in civilian pay opportunities for recent graduates represented the only pay variable that could be used. It turned out that the average earnings of recent male college graduates from each of the 82 universities were both available and varied enough across the universities to be useful; thus, the variable measuring pay (X) was the average earnings in 1963 of men who graduated from each of the universities in 1958.

Theory leads us to expect that the higher civilian pay was for the graduates of a university, the lower would be its ROTC enrollments. The results estimated that there was indeed a negative and statistically significant relationship between civilian pay and ROTC enrollments.[a] The size of the estimated relationship suggested that where civilian pay was 10 percent higher, ROTC enrollments were 20 percent lower. This finding implies that if military pay were to have risen by 10 percent, holding civilian pay constant, ROTC enrollments would have risen by 20 percent. Clearly, ROTC enrollments were very responsive to civilian salaries!

---

[a] Other independent variables were added to the estimating equation to account for the fact that the universities sampled offered different mixes of Army, Navy, and Air Force ROTC programs. Furthermore, because students in the South may have had a greater preference for military service at any pay level, the list of independent variables also included a variable indicating if the university was located in the South.

Source: Stuart H. Altman and Alan E. Fechter, "The Supply of Military Personnel in the Absence of a Draft," *American Economic Review* 57 (May 1967): 19–31.

Review Questions

1. As discussed on page 68, in the early 1970s, Egypt experienced a dramatic outflow of construction workers seeking higher wages in Saudi Arabia at the same time that the demand for their services rose within Egypt. Graphically represent these two shifts of supply and demand, and then use the graph to predict the direction of change in wages and employment within Egypt's construction sector during that period.

2. Analyze the impact of the following changes on wages and employment in a given occupation:
   a. A decrease in the danger of the occupation.

b. An increase in product demand.

c. Increased wages in alternative occupations.

3. What would happen to the wages and employment levels of engineers if government expenditures on research and development programs were to fall? Show the effect graphically.

4. Suppose a particular labor market were in market-clearing equilibrium. What could happen to cause the equilibrium wage to fall? Suppose price levels were rising each year, but money wages were "sticky downward" and never fell; how would real wages in this market adjust?

5. Assume that you have been hired by a company to do a salary survey of its arc welders, whom the company suspects are overpaid. Given the company's expressed desire to maximize profits, what definition of *overpaid* would you apply in this situation, and how would you identify whether arc welders are, in fact, overpaid?

6. Ecuador is the world's leading exporter of bananas, which are grown and harvested by a large labor force that includes many children. Assume Ecuador now outlaws the use of child labor on banana plantations. Using economic theory in its positive mode, analyze what would happen to employment and wages in the banana farming industry in Ecuador. Use supply and demand curves in your analysis.

7. Unions can raise wages paid to their members in two ways. (i) Unions can negotiate a wage rate that lies above the market-clearing wage. While management cannot pay below that rate, management does have the right to decide how many workers to hire. (ii) Construction unions often have agreements that require management to hire only union members, but they also have the power to control entry into the union. Hence, they can raise wages by restricting labor supply.

a. Graphically depict method (i) above using a labor supply and a labor demand curve. Show the market-clearing wage as W_e, the market-clearing employment level as L_e, the (higher) negotiated wage as W_u, the level of employment associated with W_u as L_u, and the number of workers wanting to work at W_u as L_s.

b. Graphically depict method (ii) above using a labor supply and a labor demand curve. Show the market-clearing wage as W_e, the market-clearing employment level as L_e, the number of members the union decides to have as L_u (which is less than L_e), and the wage associated with L_u as W_u.

8. American students have organized opposition to the sale by their campus stores of university apparel made for American retailers by workers in foreign countries who work in sweatshop conditions (long hours at low pay in bad working conditions). Assume this movement takes the form of boycotting items made under sweatshop conditions.

a. Analyze the immediate labor market outcomes for sweatshop workers in these countries using supply and demand curves to illustrate the mechanisms driving the outcomes.

b. Assuming that actions by American students are the only force driving the improvement of wages and working conditions in foreign countries, what must these actions include to ensure that the workers they are seeking to help are unambiguously better off?

9. Suppose the Occupational Safety and Health Administration were to mandate that all punch presses be fitted with a very expensive device to prevent injuries to workers. This device does not improve the efficiency with which punch presses operate. What does this requirement do to the demand curve for labor? Explain.

10. Suppose we observe that employment levels in a certain region suddenly decline as a result of (i) a fall in the region's demand for labor and (ii) wages that are fixed in the short run. If the *new* labor demand curve remains unchanged for a long period and the region's labor supply curve does not shift, is it likely that employment in the region will recover? Explain.

11. In the economic recovery of 2003–2004, job growth in Canada was much faster than job growth in the United States. Please answer the following questions: (a) Generally speaking, how does economic growth affect the demand curve for labor? (b) Assume that growth does not affect the labor supply curve in either country, and suppose that the faster job growth in Canada was accompanied by slower (but positive) wage growth there than in the United States. What would this fact tell us about the reasons for the relatively faster job growth in Canada?

12. The government of Qatar is to host the 2022 FIFA World Cup. There is increased demand for construction workers in the economy to prepare the infrastructure for the event. Analyze how this affects the labor demand curve. Use this analysis to predict the effect on wages and number of jobs in the construction sector in Qatar.

Problems

1. In a particular country in the year 2010, the adult population is 250 million and there are 120.5 million employed and 6.5 million unemployed people. Calculate the unemployment rate and the labor participation rate.

2. In an economy, the demand for workers is given by the equation $L_D = 200{,}000 - 150W$, and the supply is $L_S = 14{,}000 + 250W$, where L = number of workers and W = the daily wage.
   a. What are the equilibrium wage and number of workers in this market?
   b. If 15,000 more workers immigrate into this economy, find the new labor supply and new wage. Comment on the impact of immigration on the equilibrium wage.

3. Have the real average hourly earnings for production and nonsupervisory workers in the United States risen during the past 12 months? Go to the Bureau of Labor Statistics Web site (http://stats.bls.gov) to find the numbers needed to answer the question.

4. In an economy, the CPI (with a base of 100 in 2007) rose from 118.96 in January 2013 to 119.12 in January 2014. If the nominal wage for household maids increased from $13.7 to $16.5 in the same period, calculate the real wage for the two periods. Is there an increase in the real wage from 2013 to 2014?

5. From Table 2.2, the CPI (with a base of 100 in 1982–1984) rose from 130.7 in 1990 to 201.6 in 2006. The federal minimum wage (nominal hourly wage) in 1990 was $3.80, and it was $5.15 in 2006. Calculate the minimum wage in real (1982–1984) dollars. Did the federal minimum wage increase or decrease in real dollars from 1990 to 2006?

6. The following table carries the demand and supply information for X-ray technicians in a town.

Wage Rate ($/day)	Number of Technicians Demanded (D)	Number of Technicians Supplied (S)
15	120	40
20	100	50
25	80	60
30	70	70
35	60	90
40	50	100
45	30	120

a. Plot the demand and supply curves
b. Identify the equilibrium wage and employment levels.
c. If the demand for X-ray technicians decreases by 20 at all wage levels, what will be the new demand and the new equilibrium wage?

7. From the original demand function in Problem 6 (see table), how many cashiers would have jobs if the wage paid were $8.00 per hour? Discuss the implications of an $8 wage in the market for cashiers.

Selected Readings

Blau, Francine D., and Lawrence M. Kahn. *At Home and Abroad: U.S. Labor-Market Performance in International Perspective.* New York: Russell Sage Foundation, 2002.

Freeman, Richard. *America Works: The Exceptional U.S. Labor Market.* New York: Russell Sage Foundation, 2007.

Nickell, Stephen. "Is the U.S. Labor Market Really That Exceptional? A Review of Richard Freeman's *America Works: The Exceptional U.S. Labor Market.*" *Journal of Economic Literature* 46 (June 2008): 384–395.

President's Commission on an All-Volunteer Armed Force. *Report of the President's Commission on an All-Volunteer Armed Force.* Chapter 3, "Conscription Is a Tax," 23–33. Washington, D.C.: U.S. Government Printing Office, February 1970.

Rottenberg, Simon. "On Choice in Labor Markets." *Industrial and Labor Relations Review* 9 (January 1956): 183–199. [Robert J. Lampman. "On Choice in Labor Markets: Comment." *Industrial and Labor Relations Review* 9 (July 1956): 636–641.]

Saint-Paul, Gilles. "Why Are European Countries Diverging in Their Unemployment Experience?" *Journal of Economic Perspectives* 18 (Fall 2004): 49–68.

CHAPTER 3

The Demand for Labor

The demand for labor is a derived demand, in that workers are hired for the contribution they can make toward producing some good or service for sale. However, the wages workers receive, the employee benefits they qualify for, and even their working conditions are all influenced, to one degree or another, by the government. There are minimum wage laws, pension regulations, restrictions on firing workers, safety requirements, immigration controls, and government-provided pension and unemployment benefits that are financed through employer payroll taxes. All these requirements and regulations have one thing in common: they increase employers' costs of hiring workers.

We explained in chapter 2 that both the scale and the substitution effects accompanying a wage change suggest that the demand curve for labor is a *downward-sloping function of the wage rate*. If this rather simple proposition is true, then policies that mandate increases in the costs of employing workers will have the undesirable side effect of reducing their employment opportunities. If the reduction is large enough, lost job opportunities could actually undo any help provided to workers by the regulations. Understanding the characteristics of labor demand curves, then, is absolutely crucial to anyone interested in public policy. To a great extent, how one feels about many labor market regulatory programs is a function of one's beliefs about labor demand curves.

This chapter will identify *assumptions* underlying the proposition that labor demand is a downward-sloping function of the wage rate. Chapter 4 will take the downward-sloping nature of labor demand curves as given, addressing instead why, in the face of a given wage increase, declines in demand might be large in some cases and barely perceptible in others.

Profit Maximization

The fundamental assumption of labor demand theory is that firms—the employers of labor—seek to maximize profits. In doing so, firms are assumed to continually ask, "Can we make changes that will improve profits?" Two things should be noted about this constant search for enhanced profits. First, a firm can make changes only in variables that are within its control. Because the price a firm can charge for its product and the prices it must pay for its inputs are largely determined by others (the "market"), profit-maximizing decisions by a firm mainly involve the question of *whether, and how, to increase or decrease output*.

Second, because the firm is assumed to constantly search for profit-improving possibilities, our theory must address the *small* ("marginal") changes that must be made almost daily. Major decisions of whether to open a new plant or introduce a new product line, for example, are relatively rare; once having made them, the employer must approach profit maximization incrementally through the trial-and-error process of small changes. We therefore need to understand the basis for these incremental decisions, paying particular attention to when an employer *stops* making changes in output levels or in its mix of inputs.

(With respect to the employment of inputs, it is important to recognize that analyzing marginal changes implies considering a small change in one input *while holding employment of other inputs constant*. Thus, when analyzing the effects of adjusting the labor input by one unit, for example, we will do so on the assumption that capital is held constant. Likewise, marginal changes in capital will be considered assuming the labor input is held constant.)

In incrementally deciding on its optimal level of *output*, the profit-maximizing firm will want to expand output by one unit if the added revenue from selling that unit is greater than the added cost of producing it. As long as the marginal revenue from an added unit of output exceeds its marginal cost, the firm will continue to expand output. Likewise, the firm will want to contract output whenever the marginal cost of production exceeds marginal revenue. Profits are maximized (and the firm stops making changes) when output is such that marginal revenue equals marginal cost.

A firm can expand or contract output, of course, only by altering its use of *inputs*. In the most general sense, we will assume that a firm produces its output by combining two types of inputs, or *factors of production*: *labor and capital*. Thus, the rules stated earlier for deciding whether to marginally increase or reduce output have important corollaries with respect to the employment of labor and capital:

    a. If the income generated by employing one more unit of an input exceeds the additional expense, then add a unit of that input.

    b. If the income generated by one more unit of input is less than the additional expense, reduce employment of that input.

    c. If the income generated by one more unit of input is equal to the additional expense, no further changes in that input are desirable.

Decision rules (a) through (c) state the profit-maximizing criterion in terms of *inputs* rather than output; as we will see, these rules are useful guides to deciding *how*—as well as *whether*—to marginally increase or decrease output. Let us define and examine the components of these decision rules more closely.

Marginal Income from an Additional Unit of Input

Employing one more unit of either labor or capital generates additional income for the firm because of the added output that is produced and sold. Similarly, reducing the employment of labor or capital reduces a firm's income flow because the output available for sale is reduced. Thus, the marginal income associated with a unit of input is found by multiplying two quantities: the change in physical output produced (called the input's *marginal product*) and the MR generated per unit of physical output. We will therefore call the marginal income produced by a unit of input the input's *marginal revenue product*. For example, if the presence of a tennis star increases attendance at a tournament by 20,000 spectators, and the organizers net $25 from each additional fan, the marginal income produced by this star is equal to her marginal product (20,000 fans) times the marginal revenue of $25 per fan. Thus, her marginal revenue product equals $500,000. (For an actual calculation of marginal revenue product in college football, see Example 3.1.)

Marginal Product   Formally, we will define the *marginal product of labor*, or MP_L, as the change in physical output (ΔQ) produced by a change in the units of labor (ΔL), holding capital constant:[1]

$$MP_L = \Delta Q/\Delta L \quad \text{(holding capital constant)} \qquad (3.1)$$

Likewise, the marginal product of capital (MP_K) will be defined as the change in output associated with a one-unit change in the stock of capital (ΔK), holding labor constant:

$$MP_K = \Delta Q/\Delta K \quad (\text{holding labor constant}) \qquad (3.2)$$

---

[1]The symbol Δ (the uppercase Greek letter delta) is used to signify "a change in."

Marginal Revenue   The definitions in equations (3.1) and (3.2) reflect the fact that a firm can expand or contract its output only by increasing or decreasing its use of either labor or capital. The marginal revenue that is generated by an extra unit of output depends on the characteristics of the product market in which that output is sold. If the firm operates in a purely competitive product market, and therefore has many competitors and no control over product price, the marginal revenue per unit of output sold is equal to product price (P). If the firm has a differentiated product, and thus has some degree of monopoly power in its product market, extra units of output can be sold only if product price is reduced (because the firm faces the *market* demand curve for its particular product); students will recall from introductory economics that in this case, marginal revenue is less than price ($MR < P$).[2]

Marginal Revenue Product   Combining the definitions presented in this section, the firm's marginal revenue product of labor, or MRP_L, can be represented as

$$MRP_L = MP_L \cdot MR \quad \text{(in the general case)} \tag{3.3a}$$

or as

$$MRP_L = MP_L \cdot P \quad \text{(if the product market is competitive)} \tag{3.3b}$$

Likewise, the firm's marginal revenue product of capital (MRP_K) can be represented as $MP_K \cdot MR$ in the general case or as $MP_K \cdot P$ if the product market is competitive.

Marginal Expense of an Added Input

Changing the levels of labor or capital employed, of course, will add to or subtract from the firm's total costs. The marginal expense of labor (ME_L) that is incurred by hiring more labor is affected by the nature of competition in the labor market. If the firm operates in a competitive labor market and has no control over the wages that must be paid (it is a "wage taker"), then ME_L is simply equal to the market wage. Put differently, firms in competitive labor markets have labor supply curves that are horizontal at the going wage (refer back to Figure 2.11); if they hire an additional hour of labor, their costs increase by an amount equal to the wage rate, W.

In this chapter, we will maintain the assumption that the labor market is competitive and that the labor supply curve to firms is therefore *horizontal* at the going wage. In chapter 5, we will relax this assumption and analyze how upward-sloping labor supply curves to individual employers alter the marginal expense of labor.

---

[2]A competitive firm can sell added units of output at the market price because it is so small relative to the entire market that its output does not affect price. A monopolist, however, *is* the supply side of the product market, so to sell extra output, it must lower price. Because it must lower price on *all* units of output, and not just on the extra units to be sold, the MR associated with an additional unit is below price.

EXAMPLE 3.1

The Marginal Revenue Product of College Football Stars

Calculating a worker's marginal revenue product is often very complicated due to lack of data and the difficulty of making sure that everything else is being held constant and only *additions* to revenue are counted. Perhaps for this reason, economists have been attracted to the sports industry, which generates so many statistics on player productivity and team revenues.

Football is a big-time concern on many campuses, and some star athletes generate huge revenues for their colleges, even though they are not paid—except by receiving a free education. Robert Brown collected revenue statistics for 47 Division I-A college football programs for the 1988–1989 season—including revenues retained by the school from ticket sales, donations to the athletic department, and television and radio payments. (Unfortunately, this leaves out some other potentially important revenue sources, such as parking and concessions at games and donations to the general fund.)

Next, he examined variation in revenues due to market size, strength of opponents, national ranking, and the number of players on the team who were so good that they were drafted into professional football (the National Football League [NFL]). Brown found that each additional player drafted into the NFL was worth about $540,000 ($999,000 in 2012 dollars) in extra revenue to his team. Over a four-year college career, a premium player could therefore generate about $4 million in revenues for the university.

Data from: Robert W. Brown, "An Estimate of the Rent Generated by a Premium College Football Player," *Economic Inquiry* 31 (October 1993), 671–684.

In the analysis that follows, the marginal expense of adding a unit of capital will be represented as C, which can be thought of as the expense of renting a unit of capital for one time period. The specific calculation of C need not concern us here, but it clearly depends on the purchase price of the capital asset, its expected useful life, the rate of interest on borrowed funds, and even special tax provisions regarding capital.

The Short-Run Demand for Labor When Both Product and Labor Markets Are Competitive

The simplest way to understand how the profit-maximizing behavior of firms generates a labor demand curve is to analyze the firm's behavior over a period of time so short that the firm cannot vary its stock of capital. This period is what we will call the *short run*, and, of course, the time period involved will vary from firm to firm (an accounting service might be able to order and install a new computing system for the preparation of tax returns within three months, whereas it may take an oil refinery five years to install a new production process). What is simplifying about the short run is that, with capital fixed, a firm's choice of output level and its choice of employment level are two aspects of the very same decision. Put differently, in the short run, the firm needs only to decide *whether* to alter its output level; *how* to increase or decrease output is not an issue, because only the employment of labor can be adjusted.

Table 3.1

The Marginal Product of Labor in a Hypothetical Car Dealership (Capital Held Constant)

Number of Salespersons	Total Cars Sold	Marginal Product of Labor
0	0	
1	10	10
2	21	11
3	26	5
4	29	3

A Critical Assumption: Declining MP_L

We defined the marginal product of labor MP_L as the change in the (physical) output of a firm when it changes its employment of labor by one unit, holding capital constant. Since the firm can vary its employment of labor, we must consider how increasing or reducing labor will affect labor's marginal product. Consider Table 3.1, which illustrates a hypothetical car dealership with sales personnel who are all equally hardworking and persuasive. With no sales staff, the dealership is assumed to sell zero cars, but with one salesperson, it will sell 10 cars per month. Thus, the marginal product of the first salesperson hired is 10. If a second person is hired, total output is assumed to rise from 10 to 21, implying that the marginal product of a second salesperson is 11. If a third equally persuasive salesperson is hired, sales rise from 21 to 26 ($MP_L = 5$), and if a fourth is hired, sales rise from 26 to 29 ($MP_L = 3$).

Table 3.1 assumes that adding an extra salesperson increases output (cars sold) in each case. As long as output *increases* as labor is added, labor's marginal product is *positive*. In our example, however, MP_L increased at first (from 10 to 11) but then fell (to 5 and eventually to 3). Why?

The initial rise in marginal product occurs *not* because the second salesperson is better than the first; we ruled out this possibility by our assumption that the salespeople were equally capable. Rather, the rise could be the result of cooperation between the two in generating promotional ideas or helping each other out in some way. Eventually, however, as more salespeople are hired, MP_L must fall. A fixed building (remember that capital is held constant) can contain only so many cars and customers; thus, each additional increment of labor must eventually produce progressively smaller increments of output. This law of *diminishing marginal returns* is an empirical proposition that derives from the fact that as employment expands, each additional worker has a progressively smaller share of the capital stock to work with. For expository convenience, we shall assume that MP_L is always decreasing.[3]

---

[3]We lose nothing by this assumption because we show later in this section that a firm will never be operated at a point where its MP_L is increasing.

From Profit Maximization to Labor Demand

From the profit-maximizing decision rules discussed earlier, it is clear that the firm should keep increasing its employment of labor as long as labor's marginal revenue product exceeds its marginal expense. Conversely, it should keep reducing its employment of labor as long as the expense saved is greater than the income lost. *Profits are maximized, then, only when employment is such that any further one-unit change in labor would have a marginal revenue product equal to marginal expense*:

$$MRP_L = ME_L \qquad (3.4)$$

Under our current assumptions of competitive product and labor markets, we can symbolically represent the profit-maximizing level of labor input as that level at which

$$MP_L \cdot P = W \qquad (3.5)$$

Clearly, equation (3.5) is stated in terms of some *monetary* unit (dollars, for example).

Alternatively, however, we can divide both sides of equation (3.5) by product price, P, and state the profit-maximizing condition for hiring labor in terms of *physical quantities*:

$$MP_L = W/P \qquad (3.6)$$

We defined MP_L as the change in physical output associated with a one-unit change in labor, so it is obvious that the left-hand side of equation (3.6) is in physical quantities. To understand that the right-hand side is also in physical quantities, note that the numerator (W) is the dollars per unit of labor, and the denominator (P) is the dollars per unit of output. Thus, the ratio W/P has the dimension of physical units. For example, if a woman is paid $10 per hour and the output she produces sells for $2 per unit, from the firm's viewpoint, she is paid five units of output per hour (10 ÷ 2). From the perspective of the firm, these five units represent her "real wage."

Labor Demand in Terms of Real Wages   The demand for labor can be analyzed in terms of either *real* or *money* wages. Which version of demand analysis is used is a matter of convenience only. In this and the following section, we give examples of both.

Figure 3.1 shows a marginal product of labor (MP_L) schedule for a representative firm. In this figure, the MP_L is tabulated on the vertical axis and the number of units of labor employed on the horizontal axis. The negative slope of the schedule indicates that each additional unit of labor employed produces a progressively smaller (but still positive) increment in output. Because the real wage and MP_L are both measured in the same dimension (units of output), we can also plot the real wage on the vertical axis of Figure 3.1.

Figure 3.1

Demand for Labor in the Short Run
(Real Wage)

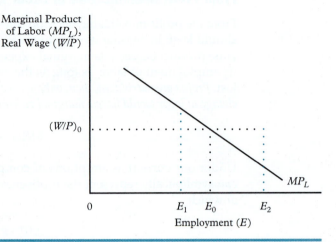

Given any real wage (by the market), the firm should thus employ labor to the point at which MP_L just equals the real wage (equation (3.6)). In other words, *the firm's demand for labor in the short run is equivalent to the downward-sloping segment of its MP_L schedule.*[4]

To see that this is true, pick any real wage—for example, the real wage denoted by $(W/P)_0$ in Figure 3.1. We have asserted that the firm's demand for labor is equal to its MP_L schedule and, consequently, that the firm would employ E_0 employees. Now, suppose that a firm initially employed E_2 workers as indicated in Figure 3.1, where E_2 is *any* employment level greater than E_0. At the employment level E_2, the MP_L is less than the real wage rate; the marginal real cost of the last unit of labor hired is therefore greater than its marginal product. As a result, profit could be increased by reducing the level of employment. Similarly, suppose instead that a firm initially employed E_1 employees, where E_1 is *any* employment level less than E_0. Given the specified real wage $(W/P)_0$, the MP_L is greater than the real wage rate at E_1—and, consequently, the marginal additions to output of an extra unit of labor exceed its marginal real cost. As a result, a firm could increase its profit level by expanding its level of employment.

Hence, to maximize profits, given any real wage rate, a firm should stop employing labor at the point at which any additional labor would cost more than it would produce. This profit-maximization rule implies two things. First, the firm should employ labor up to the point at which its real wage equals MP_L—but not beyond that point.

[4]We should add here, "provided that the firm's revenue exceeds its labor costs." Above some real wage level, this may fail to occur, and the firm will go out of business (employment will drop to zero).

Second, its profit-maximizing level of employment lies in the range where its MP_L is *declining*. If $W/P = MP_L$, but MP_L is *increasing*, then adding another unit of labor will create a situation in which marginal product *exceeds* W/P. As long as adding labor causes MP_L to exceed W/P, the profit-maximizing firm will continue to hire labor. It will stop hiring only when an extra unit of labor would reduce MP_L below W/P, which will happen only when MP_L is declining. Thus, the only employment levels that could possibly be consistent with profit maximization are those in the range where MP_L is decreasing.

Labor Demand In Terms of Money Wages   In some circumstances, labor demand curves are more readily conceptualized as downward-sloping functions of *money* wages. To make the analysis as concrete as possible, in this section, we analyze the demand for department store detectives.

At a business conference one day, a department store executive boasted that his store had reduced theft to 1 percent of total sales. A colleague shook her head and said, "I think that's too low. I figure it should be about 2 percent of sales." How can more shoplifting be better than less? The answer is based on the fact that reducing theft is costly in itself. A profit-maximizing firm will not want to take steps to reduce shoplifting if the added costs it must bear in so doing exceed the value of the savings such steps will generate.

Table 3.2 shows a hypothetical marginal revenue product of labor MRP_L schedule for department store detectives. Hiring one detective would, in this example, save $50 worth of thefts per hour. Two detectives could save $90 worth of thefts each hour, or $40 more than hiring just one. The MRP_L of hiring a second detective is thus $40. A third detective would add $20 more to thefts prevented each hour.

The MRP_L does *not* decline from $40 to $20 because the added detectives are incompetent; in fact, we shall assume that all are equally alert and well trained. MRP_L declines, in part, because surveillance equipment (capital) is fixed; with each added detective, there is less equipment per person. However, the MRP_L also declines because it becomes progressively harder to generate savings. With just a few detectives, the only thieves caught will be the more-obvious, less-experienced

Table 3.2

Hypothetical Schedule of Marginal Revenue Productivity of Labor for Store Detectives

Number of Detectives on Duty during Each Hour Store Is Open	Total Value of Thefts Prevented per Hour	Marginal Value of Thefts Prevented per Hour (MRP_L)
0	$ 0	$—
1	$ 50	$50
2	$ 90	$40
3	$110	$20
4	$115	$ 5
5	$117	$ 2

shoplifters. As more detectives are hired, it becomes possible to prevent theft by the more-expert shoplifters, but they are harder to detect and fewer in number. Thus, MRP_L falls because theft prevention becomes more difficult once all those who are easy to catch have been apprehended.

To draw the demand curve for labor, we need to determine how many detectives the store will want to hire at any given wage rate, keeping in mind that employers—through part-time employment—are able to hire fractional workers. For example, at a wage of $50 per hour, how many detectives will the store want? Using the $MRP_L = W$ criterion (equation (3.5)), the answer is "up to one." At $40 per hour, the store would want to stop hiring at two, and at $20 per hour, it would stop at three. The labor demand curve that summarizes the store's profit-maximizing employment of detectives is shown in Figure 3.2.

Figure 3.2 illustrates a fundamental point: the labor demand curve in the short run slopes downward because it *is* the MRP_L curve—and the MRP_L curve slopes downward because of labor's diminishing marginal product. The demand curve and the MRP_L curve coincide; this could be demonstrated by graphing the MRP_L schedule in Table 3.2, which would yield exactly the same curve as in Figure 3.2. When one detective is hired, MRP_L is $50; when two are hired, MRP_L is $40; and so forth. Since MRP_L always equals W for a profit maximizer who takes wages as given, the MRP_L curve and labor demand curve (expressed as a function of the money wage) must be the same.

An implication of our example is that there is some level of shoplifting the store finds more profitable to tolerate than to eliminate. This level will be higher at high wages for store detectives than at lower wages. To say the theft rate is

---

Figure 3.2

Demand for Labor in the Short Run (Money Wage)

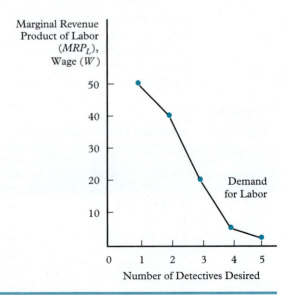

"too low" thus implies that the marginal costs of crime reduction exceed the marginal savings generated, and the firm is therefore failing to maximize profits.

Finally, we must emphasize that the marginal product of an individual is *not* a function solely of his or her personal characteristics. As stressed earlier, the marginal product of a worker depends upon the number of similar employees the firm has already hired. An individual's marginal product also depends upon the size of the firm's capital stock; increases in the firm's capital stock shift the entire MP_L schedule up. It is therefore incorrect to speak of an individual's productivity as an immutable factor that is associated only with his or her characteristics, independent of the characteristics of the other inputs he or she has to work with.

Market Demand Curves   The demand curve (or schedule) for an individual firm indicates how much labor that firm will want to employ at each wage level. A *market demand curve* (or schedule) is just the *summation* of the labor demanded by all firms in a particular labor market at each level of the *real* wage.[5] If there are three firms in a certain labor market, and if at a *given* real wage firm A wants 12 workers, firm B wants 6, and firm C wants 20, then the market demand at that real wage is 38 employees. More important, because market demand curves are so closely derived from firm demand curves, they too will *slope downward* as a function of the real wage. When the real wage falls, the number of workers that existing firms want to employ increases. In addition, the lower real wage may make it profitable for new firms to enter the market. Conversely, when the real wage increases, the number of workers that existing firms want to employ decreases, and some firms may be forced to cease operations completely.

Objections to the Marginal Productivity Theory of Demand   Two kinds of objections are sometimes raised to the theory of labor demand introduced in this section. The first is that almost no employer can ever be heard uttering the words "marginal revenue product of labor" and that the theory assumes a degree of sophistication that most employers do not have. Employers, it is also argued, are unable in many situations to accurately measure the output of individual workers.

These first objections can be answered as follows: Whether employers can verbalize the profit-maximizing conditions or whether they can explicitly measure the MRP_L, they must at least *intuit* them to survive in a competitive environment. Competition will "weed out" employers who are not good at generating profits, just as competition will weed out pool players who do not understand the intricacies of how speed, angles, and spin affect the motion of bodies through space. Yet, one could canvass the pool halls of America and probably find few who could verbalize Newton's laws of motion! The point is

---

[5]If firms' demand curves are drawn as a function of the money wage, they represent the downward-sloping portion of the firms' MRP_L curves. In a competitive industry, the price of the product is given to the firm by the market; thus, at the firm level, the MRP_L has imbedded in it a given product price. When aggregating labor demand to the *market* level, product price can no longer be taken as given, and the aggregation is no longer a simple summation.

that employers can *know* concepts without being able to verbalize them. Those that are not good at maximizing profits will not last very long in competitive markets.

The second objection is that in many cases, it seems that adding labor while holding capital constant would not add to output at all. For example, one secretary and one computer can produce output, but it might seem that adding a second secretary while holding the number of computers constant could produce nothing extra, since that secretary would have no machine on which to work.

The answer to this second objection is that the two secretaries could take turns using the computer so that neither became fatigued to the extent that mistakes increased and typing speeds slowed down. The second secretary could also answer the telephone and expedite work in other ways. Thus, even with technologies that seem to require one machine per person, labor will generally have a marginal product greater than zero if capital is held constant.

The Demand for Labor in Competitive Markets When Other Inputs Can Be Varied

An implication of our theory of labor demand is that, because labor can be varied in the short run—that is, at any time—the profit-maximizing firm will always operate so that labor's marginal revenue product equals the wage rate (which is labor's marginal expense in a competitive labor market). What we must now consider is how the firm's ability to adjust *other* inputs affects the demand for labor. We first analyze the implications of being able to adjust capital in the long run, and we then turn our attention to the case of more than two inputs.

Labor Demand in the Long Run

To maximize profits in the long run, the firm must adjust both labor and capital so that the marginal revenue product of each equals its marginal expense. Using the definitions discussed earlier in this chapter, profit maximization requires that the following two equalities be satisfied:

$$MP_L \cdot P = W \quad \text{(a restatement of equation 3.5)} \tag{3.7a}$$

$$MP_K \cdot P = C \quad \text{(the profit-maximizing condition for capital)} \tag{3.7b}$$

Equations (3.7a) and (3.7b) can be rearranged to isolate P, so these two profit-maximizing conditions can also be expressed as

$$P = W/MP_L \quad \text{(a rearrangement of equation 3.7a)} \tag{3.8a}$$

$$P = C/MP_K \quad \text{(a rearrangement of equation 3.7b)} \tag{3.8b}$$

Furthermore, because the right-hand sides of equations (3.8a) and (3.8b) equal the same quantity, P, profit maximization therefore requires that

$$W/MP_L = C/MP_K \tag{3.8c}$$

The economic meaning of equation (3.8c) is key to understanding how the ability to adjust capital affects the firm's demand for labor. Consider the left-hand side of equation (3.8c): the numerator is the cost of a unit of labor, while the denominator is the extra output produced by an added unit of labor. Therefore, the ratio W/MP_L turns out to be the added cost of producing an added unit of output when using labor to generate the increase in output.[6] Analogously, the right-hand side is the marginal cost of producing an extra unit of output using capital. What equation (3.8c) suggests is that to maximize profits, *the firm must adjust its labor and capital inputs so that the marginal cost of producing an added unit of output using labor is equal to the marginal cost of producing an added unit of output using capital.* Why is this condition a requirement for maximizing profits?

To maximize profits, a firm must be producing its chosen level of output in the least-cost manner. Logic suggests that as long as the firm can expand output more cheaply using one input than the other, it cannot be producing in the least-cost way. For example, if the marginal cost of expanding output by one unit using labor were $10, and the marginal cost using capital were $12, the firm could keep output constant and lower its costs of production! How? It could reduce its capital by enough to cut output by one unit (saving $12) and then add enough labor to restore the one-unit cut (costing $10). Output would be the same, but costs would have fallen by $2. Thus, for the firm to be maximizing profits, it must be operating at the point such that further marginal changes in both labor and capital would neither lower costs nor add to profits.

With equations (3.8a) to (3.8c) in mind, what would happen to the demand for labor in the long run if the wage rate (W) facing a profit-maximizing firm were to rise? First, as we discussed in the section on the "The Short-Run Demand for Labor When Both Product and Labor Markets Are Competitive," the rise in W disturbs the equality in equation (3.8a), and the firm will want to cut back on its use of labor even before it can adjust capital. Because the MP_L is assumed to rise as employment is reduced, any cuts in labor will raise MP_L.

Second, because each unit of capital now has less labor working with it, the MP_K falls, disturbing the equality in equation (3.8b). By itself, this latter inequality will cause the firm to want to reduce its stock of capital.

Third, the rise in W will initially end the equality in equation (3.8c), meaning that the marginal cost of production using labor now exceeds the marginal cost using capital. If the above cuts in labor are made in the short run, the associated

---

[6]Because $MP_L = \Delta Q/\Delta L$, the expression W/MP_L can be rewritten as $W \cdot \Delta L/\Delta Q$. Since $W\Delta L$ represents the added cost from employing one more unit of labor, the expression $W\Delta L/\Delta Q$ equals the cost of an added unit of output when that unit is produced by adding labor.

EXAMPLE 3.2

Coal Mining Wages and Capital Substitution

That wage increases have both a *scale effect* and a *substitution effect*, both of which tend to reduce employment, is widely known—even by many of those pushing for higher wages. John L. Lewis was president of the United Mine Workers from the 1920s through the 1940s, when wages for miners were increased considerably with full knowledge that this would induce the substitution of capital for labor. According to Lewis:

> Primarily the United Mine Workers of America insists upon the maintenance of the wage standards guaranteed by the existing contractual relations in the industry, in the interests of its own membership. . . . But in insisting on the maintenance of an American wage standard in the coal fields the United Mine Workers is also

doing its part, probably more than its part, to force a reorganization of the basic industry of the country upon scientific and efficient lines. The maintenance of these rates will accelerate the operation of natural economic laws, which will in time eliminate uneconomic mines, obsolete equipment, and incompetent management.

The policy of the United Mine Workers of America will inevitably bring about the utmost employment of machinery of which coal mining is physically capable. . . . Fair wages and American standards of living are inextricably bound up with the progressive substitution of mechanical for human power. It is no accident that fair wages and machinery will walk hand-in-hand.

Source: John L. Lewis, *The Miners' Fight for American Standards* (Indianapolis: Bell, 1925): 40, 41, 108.

increase in MP_L and decrease in MP_K will work toward restoring equality in equation (3.8c); however, if it remains more costly to produce an extra unit of output using labor than using capital, the firm will want to substitute capital for labor in the long run. Substituting capital for labor means that the firm will produce its profit-maximizing level of output (which is clearly reduced by the rise in W) in a more capital-intensive way. The act of substituting capital for labor also will serve to increase MP_L and reduce MP_K, thereby reinforcing the return to equality in equation (3.8c).

In the end, the increase in W will cause the firm to reduce its desired employment level for two reasons. The firm's profit-maximizing level of output will fall, and the associated reduction in required inputs (both capital and labor) is an example of the *scale effect*. The rise in W also causes the firm to substitute capital for labor so that it can again produce in the least-cost manner; changing the mix of capital and labor in the production process is an example of the *substitution effect*. The scale and substitution effects of a wage increase will have an ambiguous effect on the firm's desired stock of *capital*, but both effects serve to reduce the demand for *labor*. Thus, as illustrated in Example 3.2, the long-run ability to adjust capital lends further theoretical support to the proposition that the labor demand curve is a downward-sloping function of the wage rate.

More Than Two Inputs

Thus far, we have assumed that there are only two inputs in the production process: capital and labor. In fact, labor can be subdivided into many categories; for example, labor can be categorized by age, educational level, and occupation. Other inputs that are used in the production process include materials and energy. If a firm is seeking to minimize costs, in the long run, it should employ all inputs up until the point that the marginal cost of producing an added unit of output is the same regardless of which input is increased. This generalization of equation (3.8c) leads to the somewhat obvious result that the demand for *any* category of labor will be a function of its own wage rate *and* (through the scale and substitution effects) the wage or prices of all other categories of labor, capital, and supplies.

If Inputs are Substitutes in Production
The demand curve for each category of labor will be a downward-sloping function of the wage rate paid to workers in that category for the reasons discussed earlier, but how is it affected by wage or price changes for *other* inputs? If two inputs are *substitutes in production* (that is, if the greater use of one in producing output can compensate for reduced use of the other), then increases in the price of the *other* input may shift the entire demand curve for a *given* category of labor either to the right or to the left, depending on the relative strength of the substitution and scale effects. If an increase in the price of one input shifts the demand for *another* input to the left, as in panel (a) of Figure 3.3, the scale effect has dominated the substitution effect, and the two inputs are said to be *gross complements*; if the increase shifts the demand for the other input to the right, as in panel (b) of Figure 3.3, the substitution effect has dominated, and the two inputs are *gross substitutes*.

Figure 3.3

Effect of Increase in the Price of One Input (*k*) on Demand for Another Input (*j*), Where Inputs Are Substitutes in Production

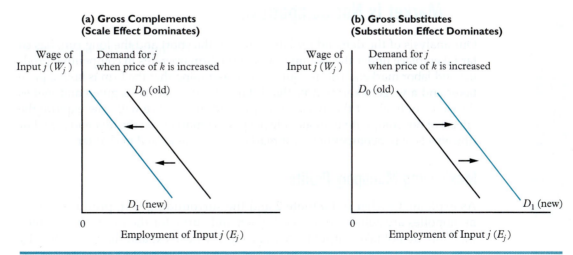

(a) Gross Complements (Scale Effect Dominates)

Wage of Input j (W_j)

Demand for j when price of k is increased

D_0 (old)

D_1 (new)

0

Employment of Input j (E_j)

(b) Gross Substitutes (Substitution Effect Dominates)

Wage of Input j (W_j)

Demand for j when price of k is increased

D_0 (old)

D_1 (new)

0

Employment of Input j (E_j)

consumers in the form of higher prices. The ability to pay high wages makes a manager's life more pleasant by making it possible to hire people who might be more attractive or personable or have other characteristics managers find desirable.

The evidence on monopoly wages, however, is not very clear as yet. Some studies suggest that firms in industries with relatively few sellers *do* pay higher wages than competitive firms for workers with the same education and experience. Other studies of regulated monopolies, however, have obtained mixed results on whether wages tend to be higher for comparable workers in these industries.[8]

Policy Application: The Labor Market Effects of Employer Payroll Taxes and Wage Subsidies

We now apply labor demand theory to the phenomena of employer payroll taxes and wage subsidies. Governments widely finance certain social programs through taxes that require *employers* to remit payments based on their total payroll costs. As we will see, new or increased payroll taxes levied on the employer raise the cost of hiring labor, and they might therefore be expected to reduce the demand for labor. Conversely, it can be argued that if the government were to subsidize the wages paid by employers, the demand for labor would increase; indeed, wage subsidies for particular disadvantaged groups in society are sometimes proposed as a way to increase their employment. In this section, we will analyze the effects of payroll taxes and subsidies.

Who Bears the Burden of a Payroll Tax?

Payroll taxes require employers to pay the government a certain percentage of their employees' earnings, often up to some maximum amount. Unemployment insurance as well as Social Security retirement, disability, and Medicare programs are prominent examples. Does taxing employers to generate revenues for these programs relieve *employees* of a financial burden that would otherwise fall on them?

Suppose that only the employer is required to make payments and that the tax is a fixed amount (X) per labor hour rather than a percentage of payroll. Now, consider the market demand curve D_0 in Figure 3.4, which is drawn in such a way that desired employment is plotted against the wage *employees receive*. Prior to the imposition of the tax, the wage employees receive is the same as the wage employers pay. Thus, if D_0 were the demand curve before the tax was imposed, it would have the conventional interpretation of indicating how much labor firms

[8]Ronald Ehrenberg, *The Regulatory Process and Labor Earnings* (New York: Academic Press, 1979); Barry T. Hirsch, "Trucking Regulation, Unionization, and Labor Earnings," *Journal of Human Resources* 23 (Summer 1988): 296–319; S. Nickell, J. Vainiomaki, and S. Wadhwani, "Wages and Product Market Power," *Economica* 61 (November 1994): 457–473; and Marianne Bertrand and Sendhil Mullainathan, "Is There Discretion in Wage Setting? A Test Using Takeover Legislation," *RAND Journal of Economics* 30 (Autumn 1999): 535–554.

would be willing to hire at any given wage. However, after imposition of the tax, employer wage costs would be X above what employees received.

Shifting the Demand Curve
If employees received W_0, employers would now face costs of $W_0 + X$. They would no longer demand E_0 workers; rather, because their costs were $W_0 + X$, they would be at point C on the original demand curve, and would want E_2 workers. Point A (where W_0 and E_2 intersect) would lie on a *new* market demand curve, formed when demand shifted down because of the tax (remember, the wage on the vertical axis of Figure 3.4 is the wage *employees receive,* not the wage employers pay). Only if employee wages fell to $W_0 - X$ would firms want to continue hiring E_0 workers, for *employer* costs would then be the same as before the tax. Thus, point B would also be on the new, shifted demand curve. Note that with a tax of X, the new demand curve (D_1) is parallel to the old one, and the vertical distance between the two is X.

Now, the tax-related shift in the market demand curve to D_1 implies that there would be an excess supply of labor at the previous equilibrium wage of W_0. This surplus of labor would create downward pressure on the *employee* wage, and this downward pressure would continue to be exerted until the employee wage fell to W_1, the point at which the quantity of labor supplied just equaled the quantity demanded. At this point, (G), employment would have also fallen to E_1. Thus, *employees* bear a burden in the form of *lower wage rates and lower employment levels.* The lesson is clear: *employees* are not exempted from bearing costs when the government chooses to generate revenues through a payroll tax on *employers.*

Figure 3.4 does suggest, however, that employers may bear at least *some* of the tax, because the wages received by employees do not fall by the full amount of the tax ($W_0 - W_1$ is smaller than X, which is the vertical distance between the two demand curves). This occurs because, with an upward-sloping labor market supply curve, employees withdraw labor as their wages fall, and it becomes more

Figure 3.4

The Market Demand Curve and Effects of an Employer-Financed Payroll Tax

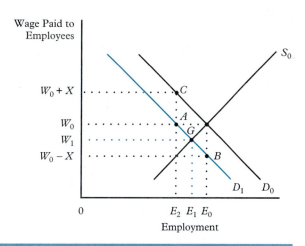

difficult for firms to find workers. If wages fell to $W_0 - X$, the withdrawal of workers would create a labor shortage that would drive wages to some point (W_1 in our example) between W_0 and $W_0 - X$. Only if the labor market supply curve were *vertical*—meaning that lower wages have no effect on labor supply—would the *entire amount of the tax* be shifted to workers in the form of a decrease in their wages by the amount of X (see Figure 3.5).

Effects of Labor Supply Curves   The extent to which the labor market *supply* curve is sensitive to wages affects the proportion of the employer payroll tax that gets shifted to employees' wages. The less responsive labor supply is to changes in wages, the fewer the employees who withdraw from the market and the higher the proportion of the tax that gets shifted to workers in the form of a wage decrease (compare the outcomes in Figures 3.4 and 3.5). It must also be pointed out, however, that to the degree employee wages do *not* fall, employment levels *will;* when employee wages do not fall much in the face of an employer payroll-tax increase, employer labor costs are increased—and this increase reduces the quantity of labor employers demand.

A number of empirical studies have sought to ascertain what fraction of employers' payroll-tax costs are actually passed on to employees in the form of lower wages (or lower wage increases). Although the evidence is somewhat ambiguous, a comprehensive review of these studies led to at least a tentative conclusion that most of a payroll tax is eventually shifted to wages, with little long-run effect on employment.[9]

Employment Subsidies as a Device to Help the Poor

The opposite of a payroll tax on employers is a government subsidy of employers' payrolls. In Figure 3.4, for example, if instead of *taxing* each hour of labor by X the government *paid* the employer X, the market labor demand curve would

---

Figure 3.5

Payroll Tax with a Vertical Supply Curve

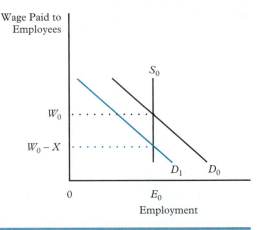

shift *upward* by a vertical distance of X. This upward movement of the demand curve would create pressures to increase employment and the wages received by employees; as with a payroll tax, whether the eventual effects would be felt more on employment or on wage rates depends on the shape of the labor market supply curve.

(Students should test their understanding in this area by drawing labor demand curves that reflect a new payroll subsidy of X per hour and then analyzing the effects on employment and employee wages with market supply curves that are, alternatively, upward-sloping and vertical. *Hint:* The outcomes should be those that would be obtained if demand curve D_1 in Figures 3.4 and 3.5 were shifted by the subsidy to curve D_0.)

Payroll subsidies to employers can take many forms. They can be in the form of cash payments, as implied by the above hypothetical example, or they can be in the form of tax credits. These credits might directly reduce a firm's payroll-tax rate or they might reduce some other tax by an amount proportional to the number of labor hours hired; in either case, the credit has the effect of reducing the cost of hiring labor. Below, we first discuss programs that directly subsidize hiring, and then turn to the potential employment effects of cutting employers' payroll taxes.

Hiring Subsidy Programs   Programs that subsidize hiring can apply to a firm's employment *level*, to any *new* employees hired after a certain date (even if they just replace workers who have left), or only to new hires that serve to *increase* the firm's level of employment. Finally, subsidies can be either *general* or *selective*. A general subsidy is not conditional on the characteristics of the people hired, whereas a selective, or *targeted*, plan makes the subsidy conditional on hiring people from certain target groups (such as the disadvantaged).

Experience in the United States with targeted wage subsidies has been modest. The Targeted Jobs Tax Credit (TJTC) program, which began in 1979 and was changed slightly over the years until it was finally discontinued in 1995, targeted disadvantaged youth, the handicapped, and welfare recipients, providing their employers with a tax credit that lasted for one year. In practice, the average duration of jobs under this program was six months, and the subsidy reduced employer wage costs by about 15 percent for jobs of this duration.

---

[9]Daniel S. Hamermesh, *Labor Demand* (Princeton, N.J.: Princeton University Press, 1993), 169–173. Also see Patricia M. Anderson and Bruce D. Meyer, "The Effects of the Unemployment Insurance Payroll Tax on Wages, Employment, Claims and Denials," *Journal of Public Economics* 78 (October 2000): 81–106; and Kevin Lang, "The Effect of the Payroll Tax on Earnings: A Test of Competing Models of Wage Determination," National Bureau of Economic Research Working Paper No. 9537, February 2003. Less wage and more job loss is reported in Adriana Kugler and Maurice Kugler, "Labor Market Effects of Payroll Taxes in Developing Countries: Evidence from Colombia," *Economic Development and Cultural Change* 57 (January 2009): 335–358. For a study that raises some interesting theoretical and empirical questions about the effects of employer payroll taxes, see Emmanuel Saez, Manos Matsaganis and Panos Tsakloglou, "Earnings Determination and Taxes: Evidence from a Cohort Based Payroll Tax Reform in Greece," *Quarterly Journal of Economics* 127 (February 2012): 493–533.

EMPIRICAL STUDY

Do Women Pay for Employer-Funded Maternity Benefits? Using Cross-Section Data over Time to Analyze "Differences in Differences"

During the last half of 1976, Illinois, New Jersey, and New York passed laws requiring that employer-provided health insurance plans treat pregnancy the same as illness (that is, coverage of doctor's bills and hospital costs had to be the same for pregnancy as for illnesses or injuries). These mandates increased the cost of health insurance for women of childbearing age by an amount that was equal to about 4 percent of their earnings. Were these increases in employer costs borne by employers or did they reduce the wages of women by an equivalent amount?

A problem confronting researchers on this topic is that the adopting states are all states with high incomes and that are likely to have state legislation encouraging the expansion of employment opportunities for women. Thus, comparing wage *levels* across states would require that we statistically control for all the factors, besides the maternity-benefit mandate, that affect wages. Because we can never be sure that we have adequate controls for the economic, social, and legal factors that affect wage levels by state, we need to find another way to perform the analysis.

Fortunately, answering the research question is facilitated by several factors: (a) some states adopted these laws and some did not; (b) even in states

that adopted these laws, the insurance cost increases applied only to women (and their husbands) of childbearing age and not to single men or older workers; and (c) the adopting states passed these laws during the same time period, so variables affecting women's wages that change over time (such as recessions or the rising presence of women in the labor force) do not cloud the analysis.

Factors (a) and (c) above allow the conduct of what economists call a "differences-in-differences" analysis. Specifically, these factors allow us to compare wage *changes*, from the pre-adoption years to the post-adoption ones, among women of childbearing age in adopting states (the "experimental group") to wage changes over the same period for women of the same age in states that did not adopt (a "comparison group"). By comparing within-state *changes* in wages, we avoid the need to find measures that would control for the economic, social, and public-policy forces that make the initial wage *level* in one state differ from that in another; whatever the factors are that raise wage levels in New Jersey, for example, they were there both before and after the adoption of mandated maternity benefits.

One might argue, of course, that the adopting and nonadopting states were subject to *other* forces (unrelated to maternity benefits) that led to different degrees of wage change over this period. For example, the economy of New Jersey might have been booming during the period when maternity benefits were adopted, while economies elsewhere might not have been. However, if an adopting state is experiencing unique wage pressures in addition to those imposed by maternity benefits, the effects of these other pressures should show up in the wage changes experienced by single men or older women—groups in the adopting states that were not affected by the mandate. Thus, we can exploit factor (b) above by also comparing the wage changes for women of childbearing age in adopting states to those for single men or older women in the same states.

The three factors above enabled one researcher to measure how the wages of married women, aged 20–40, changed from 1974–1975 to 1977–1978 in the three adopting states. These changes were then compared to changes in wages for married women of the same age in nonadopting (but economically similar) states.

To account for forces *other than changing maternity benefits* that could affect wage changes across states during this period, the researcher also measured changes in wages for unmarried men and workers over 40 years of age. This study concluded that in the states adopting mandated maternity benefits, the post-adoption wages of women in the 20–40 age group were about 4 percent lower than they would have been without adoption. This finding suggests that the entire cost of maternity benefits was quickly shifted to women of childbearing age.

Source: Jonathan Gruber, "The Incidence of Mandated Maternity Benefits," *American Economic Review* 84 (June 1994): 622–641. For a study that did not find measureable effects of mandated health benefits on *wages*, but did find that mandates were accompanied by increased reliance on part-time workers (for whom the provision of health insurance was not required), see Thomas C. Buchmueller, John DiNardo, and Robert G. Valletta, "The Effect of an Employer Health Insurance Mandate on Health Insurance Coverage and the Demand for Labor: Evidence from Hawaii," *American Economic Journal: Economic Policy* 3 (November 2011): 25–51.

One problem that limited the effectiveness of the TJTC program was that the eligibility requirements for many of its participants were stigmatizing; that is, being eligible (on welfare, for example) was often seen by employers as a negative indicator of productivity. Nevertheless, one evaluation found that the employment of disadvantaged youth was enhanced by the TJTC. Specifically, it found that when 23- to 24-year-olds were removed from eligibility for the TJTC by changes in 1989, employment of disadvantaged youths of that age fell by over 7 percent.[10] A more recent study found that the immediate employment and wage effects of a payroll subsidy were positive, but relatively small and not sustained.[11]

Payroll Tax Cuts Cutting the payroll taxes that employers must pay is an alternative policy that could be used to stimulate hiring. We noted when discussing Figure 3.5, however, that if employer payroll taxes are increased or decreased when the labor supply curve is *vertical,* the effects of the demand-curve shifts will be felt only on the wages employees receive, not on employment. But there are reasons to believe that cutting payroll taxes *during a period when unemployment is widespread* could have the effect of increasing employment.

Suppose that, in Figure 3.6, the demand curve for labor—reflecting an existing employer payroll tax—is D_1. The labor supply curve is S_1, but for some reason the wage rate employers pay is stuck at W', which is above the market-clearing level (of W^*). At W', only E_1 workers can find employment; however, there are E' workers who are willing to work at that wage. Thus, if wages are indeed stuck at W', society will experience unemployment (in this case of $E'-E_1$ workers). Would unemployment be reduced if the government were to cut the employer payroll tax?

If the government were to reduce the employer payroll tax, the labor demand curve would be shifted *right* – to, say, D_2 in Figure 3.6. With employee wages at W', employment would grow to E_2, and unemployment would be reduced to $E'-E_2$. Put differently, when unemployment is associated with wages above market-clearing levels, cutting employer payroll taxes can have the effect of increasing employment, not wages.[12]

Figure 3.6

Payroll Tax Reductions in a Period of Widespread Unemployment

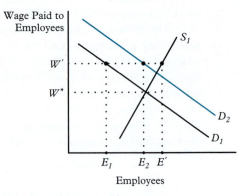

---

[10]Lawrence F. Katz, "Wage Subsidies for the Disadvantaged," in *Generating Jobs: How to Increase Demand for Less-Skilled Workers*, eds. Richard B. Freeman and Peter Gottschalk (New York: Russell Sage Foundation, 1998): 21–53.

[11]Sasrah Hamersma, "The Effects of an Employer Subsidy on Employment Outcomes: A Study of the Work Opportunity and Welfare-to-Work Tax Credits," *Journal of Policy Analysis and Management* 27 (Summer 2008): 498–520. A more positive view of the potential for payroll subsidies to increase employment can be found in Timothy J. Bartik and John H. Bishop, "The Job Creation Tax Credit," Economic Policy Institute Briefing Paper No. 248 (Washington, D.C.: October 20, 2009).

[12]For a more detailed analysis, see David Neumark, "Spurring Job Creation in Response to Severe Recessions: Reconsidering Hiring Credits," working paper no. 16866, National Bureau of Economic Research (Cambridge, Mass., March 2011).

Review Questions

1. In a statement during the 1992 presidential campaign, one organization attempting to influence the political parties argued that the wages paid by U.S. firms in their Mexican plants were so low that they "have no relationship with worker productivity." Comment on this statement using the principles of profit maximization.

2. Assume that wages for keyboarders (data entry clerks) are lower in India than in the United States. Does this mean that keyboarding jobs in the United States will be lost to India? Explain.

3. The Occupational Safety and Health Administration promulgates safety and health standards. These standards typically apply to machinery (capital), which is required to be equipped with guards, shields, and the like. An alternative to these standards is to require the employer to furnish personal protective devices to employees (labor)—such as earplugs, hard hats, and safety shoes. *Disregarding* the issue of which alternative approach offers greater protection from injury, what aspects of each alternative must be taken into account when analyzing the possible *employment* effects of the two approaches to safety?

4. Suppose that prisons historically have required inmates to perform, *without pay*, various cleaning and food preparation jobs within the prison. Now, suppose that prisoners are offered paid work in factory jobs within the prison walls and that the cleaning and food preparation tasks are now performed by nonprisoners hired to do them. Would you expect to see any differences in the *technologies* used to perform these tasks? Explain.

5. Years ago, Great Britain adopted a program that placed a tax—to be collected from employers—on wages in *service* industries. Wages in manufacturing industries were not taxed. Discuss the wage and employment effects of this tax policy.

6. To create a Medicare program for women industrial workers, the government wants to put a payroll tax of 50 cents per hour on the factories. What will be the effect of the payroll tax on the wage received by the women? What will be the effect on the wage costs the employers pay?

7. In the last two decades, the United States has been subject to huge increases in the illegal immigration of workers from Mexico, most of them unskilled, and the government has considered ways to reduce the flow. One policy is to impose larger financial penalties on employers who are discovered to have hired illegal immigrants. What effect would this policy have on the employment of unskilled illegal immigrants? What effect would it have on the demand for skilled "native" labor?

8. If anti-sweatshop movements are successful in raising pay and improving working conditions for apparel workers in foreign countries, how will these changes abroad affect labor market outcomes for workers in the apparel and retailing industries in the United States? Explain.

9. The unemployment rate in Country X is currently over 10 percent, and the youth (under age 25) unemployment rate is about 22 percent. Over the next few years, one million people on the unemployment

rolls will be offered subsidized jobs (the government subsidy will go to employers who create new jobs, and the subsidy will be X euros per hour per employee hired). Use the theory studied in this course to analyze how wage subsidies to employers are likely to affect employment levels in Country X.

10. Suppose that all employers in the internet industry currently allow their programmers and web designers to work from home, which appeals to those with childcare or other responsibilities that can be accomplished at less cost than if they had to leave home and commute to work. Now suppose that these employers become convinced that they can increase the productivity of their programmers and designers by requiring them to work together in company offices. That is, the internet employers come to believe that both creativity and a more positive company culture will be stimulated among their workers if working from home is no longer allowed. Use concepts covered in chapters 2 and 3 to analyze the likely labor-market effects of this new policy on the internet industry.

Problems

1. An experiment conducted in Tennessee found that the scores of second-graders and third-graders on standardized tests for reading, math, listening, and word study skills were the same in small classrooms (13 to 17 students) as in regular classrooms (22 to 25 students). Suppose that there is a school that had 90 third-graders taught by four teachers that added two additional teachers to reduce class sizes. If the Tennessee study can be generalized, what is the marginal product of labor (MP_L) of these two additional teachers?

2. Daron has a chocolate chip-making unit and finds that the marginal productivity of labor is $MP_L = 15 - 0.4L$, where L is the number of labor hours. If chocolate chips are sold at $2 per kilogram and the prevailing wage rate is $15 per hour, calculate the profit-maximizing number of hours of labor in the factory.

3. Suppose that the supply curve for lifeguards is $L_S = 20$, and the demand curve for lifeguards is $L_D = 100 - 20W$, where L = the number of lifeguards and W = the hourly wage. Graph both the demand and supply curves. Now, suppose that the government imposes a tax of $1 per hour per worker on companies hiring lifeguards. Draw the new (after-tax) demand curve in terms of the employee wage. How will this tax affect the wage of lifeguards and the number employed as lifeguards?

4. The following table carries information on the output from a fertilizer manufacturing unit. The factory currently employs 6 daily laborers.

Number of Workers	Output (in Tons)
1	8
2	12.2
3	14.8
4	16.9
5	18.3
6	19.5
7	20.5

a. If the daily wage is $5, is the firm employing the optimum number of workers?

b. Is the firm following the law of diminishing marginal product? Explain.

5. A video game manufacturing unit faces the production function $Q = 25K^{0.2}L^{0.8}$, where Q = number of video games produced, K = capital equipment, and L = labor hours used. It is assumed that both capital and labor markets are competitive. The wages are $5 per hour. The rent for the capital equipment is $10 per hour. The $MP_L = 20K^{0.2}L^{-0.2}$ and $MP_K = 5K^{-0.8}L^{0.8}$. Calculate the profit maximizing labor–capital ratio for the company.

6. The following table shows the number of cakes that could be baked daily at a local bakery, depending on the number of bakers.

Number of Bakers	Number of Cakes
0	0
1	10
2	18
3	23
4	27

a. Calculate the MP_L.
b. Do you observe the law of diminishing marginal returns? Explain.
c. Suppose each cake sells for $10. Calculate the MRP_L.
d. Draw the MRP_L curve, which is the demand curve for bakers.
e. If each baker is paid $80 per day, how many bakers will the bakery owner hire, given that the goal is to maximize profits? How many cakes will be baked and sold each day?

7. (Appendix) Creative Dangles is an earring design and manufacturing company. The production function for earrings is $Q = 25KL$, where Q = pairs of earrings per week, K = hours of equipment used, and L = hours of labor. Workers are paid $8 per hour, and the equipment rents for $8 per hour.
a. Determine the cost-minimizing capital-labor ratio at this firm.
b. How much does it cost to produce 10,000 pairs of earrings?
c. Suppose the rental cost of equipment decreases to $6 per hour. What is the new cost-minimizing capital-labor ratio?

8. In a town the demand for math tutors is given by the equation $L_D = 65 - W$, where D = number of math tutors and W = hourly wage. The supply curve $L_S = 5 + 2W$.
a. Calculate the equilibrium wage and number of math tutors in the town and graph the demand and supply curve.
b. If the town mayor imposes a payroll tax of $5 on the employers, how will it affect the equilibrium wage and equilibrium number? How much revenue will the government get through this?

Selected Readings

Blank, Rebecca M., ed. *Social Protection Versus Economic Flexibility: Is There a Trade-Off?* Chicago: University of Chicago Press, 1994.

Hamermesh, Daniel S. *Labor Demand*. Princeton, N.J.: Princeton University Press, 1993.

Katz, Lawrence F. "Wage Subsidies for the Disadvantaged." In *Generating Jobs: How to Increase Demand for Less-Skilled Workers*, eds. Richard B. Freeman and Peter Gottschalk, 21–53. New York: Russell Sage Foundation, 1998.

Graphical Derivation of a Firm's Labor Demand Curve

T his chapter describes verbally the derivation of a firm's labor demand curve. This appendix will present the *same* derivation graphically. This graphical representation permits a more rigorous derivation, but our conclusion that demand curves slope downward in both the short and the long run will remain unchanged.

The Production Function

Output can generally be viewed as being produced by combining capital and labor. Figure 3A.1 illustrates this production function graphically and depicts several aspects of the production process.

Consider the convex curve labeled $Q = 100$. Along this line, every combination of labor (L) and capital (K) produces 100 units of output (Q). That is, the combination of labor and capital at point A (L_a, K_a) generates the same 100 units of output as the combinations at points B and C. Because each point along the $Q = 100$ curve generates the same output, that curve is called an *isoquant* (*iso* = "equal"; *quant* = "quantity").

Two other isoquants are shown in Figure 3A.1 ($Q = 150, Q = 200$). These isoquants represent higher levels of output than the $Q = 200$ curve. The fact that these isoquants indicate higher output levels can be seen by holding labor constant at L_b (say) and then observing the different levels of capital. If L_b is combined with K_b in capital, 100 units of Q are produced. If L_b is combined with K'_b, 150 units are produced (K'_b is greater than K_b). If L_b is combined with even more capital (K_b, say), 200 units of Q could be produced.

Note that the isoquants in Figure 3A.1 have *negative* slopes, reflecting an assumption that labor and capital are substitutes. If, for example, we cut capital from K_a to K_b, we could keep output constant (at 100) by increasing labor from L_a to L_b. Labor, in other words, could be substituted for capital to maintain a given production level.

Figure 3A.1

A Production Function

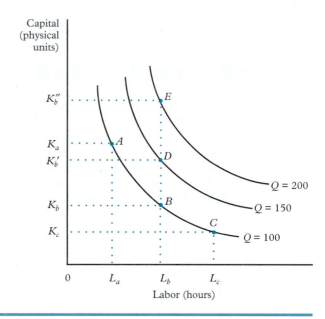

Finally, note the *convexity* of the isoquants. At point A, the $Q = 100$ isoquant has a steep slope, suggesting that to keep Q constant at 100, a given decrease in capital could be accompanied by a *modest* increase in labor. At point C, however, the slope of the isoquant is relatively flat. This flatter slope means that the same given decrease in capital would require a much *larger* increase in labor for output to be held constant. The decrease in capital permitted by a given increase in labor while output is being held constant is called the *marginal rate of technical substitution (MRTS)* between capital and labor. Symbolically, the *MRTS* can be written as

$$MRTS = \frac{\Delta K}{\Delta L} | \overline{Q} \qquad (3.A1)$$

where Δ means "change in" and $\overline{Q}$ means "holding output constant." The *MRTS* is negative because if L is increased, K must be reduced to keep Q constant.

Why does the absolute value of the *MRTS* diminish as labor increases? When labor is highly used in the production process and capital is not very prevalent (point C in Figure 3A.1), there are many jobs that capital can do. Labor is easy to replace; if capital is increased, it will be used as a substitute for labor in parts of the production process where it will have the highest payoff. As capital becomes progressively more utilized and labor less so, the few remaining workers will be doing jobs that are hardest for a machine to do, at which point it will take a lot of capital to substitute for a worker.[1]

Demand for Labor in the Short Run

This chapter argues that firms will maximize profits in the short run (K fixed) by hiring labor until labor's marginal product (MP_L) is equal to the real wage (W/P). The reason for this decision rule is that the real wage represents the *cost* of an added unit of labor (in terms of output), while the marginal product is the *output* added by the extra unit of labor. As long as the firm, by increasing labor (K fixed), gains more in output than it loses in costs, it will continue to hire employees. The firm will stop hiring when the marginal cost of added labor exceeds MP_L.

The requirement that $MP_L = W/P$ in order for profits to be maximized means that the firm's labor demand curve in the short run (in terms of the *real* wage) is identical to its MP_L schedule (refer to Figure 3.1). Remembering that the MP_L is the extra output produced by one-unit increases in the amount of labor employed, holding capital constant, consider the production function displayed in Figure 3A.2. Holding capital constant at K_a, the firm can produce 100 units of Q if it employs labor equal to L_a. If labor is increased to L_a', the firm can produce 50 more units of Q; if labor is increased from L_a' to L_a'', the firm can produce an additional 50 units. Notice, however, that the required increase in labor to get the latter 50 units of added output, $L_a'' - L_a'$, is larger than the extra labor required to produce the first 50-unit increment ($L_a' - L_a$). This difference can only mean that as labor is increased when K is held constant, each successive labor hour hired generates progressively smaller increments in output. Put differently, Figure 3A.2 graphically illustrates the diminishing marginal productivity of labor.

Why does labor's marginal productivity decline? This chapter explains that labor's marginal productivity declines because, with K fixed, each added worker has less capital (per capita) with which to work. Is this explanation proven in Figure 3A.2? The answer is, regrettably, no. Figure 3A.2 is drawn *assuming* diminishing marginal productivity. Renumbering the isoquants could produce a different set of marginal productivities. (To see this, change $Q = 150$ to $Q = 200$, and change $Q = 200$ to $Q = 500$. Labor's marginal productivity would then rise.) However, the logic that labor's marginal product must eventually fall as labor is increased, holding buildings, machines, and tools constant, is compelling. Further, as this chapter points out, even if MP_L rises initially, the firm will stop hiring labor only in the range where MP_L is declining; as long as MP_L is above W/P and *rising*, it will pay to continue hiring.

---

[1]Here is one example. Over time, telephone operators (who used to place long-distance calls) were replaced by a very capital-intensive direct-dialing system. Those operators who remain employed, however, perform tasks that are the most difficult for a machine to perform—handling collect calls, dispensing directory assistance, and acting as troubleshooters when problems arise.

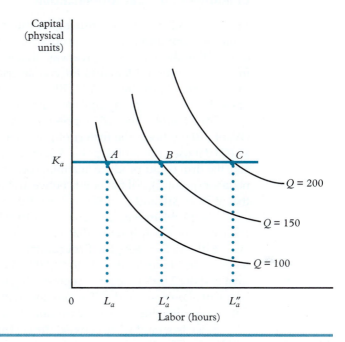

Figure 3A.2

The Declining Marginal Productivity of Labor

The assumptions that MP_L declines eventually and that firms hire until $MP_L = W/P$ are the bases for the assertion that a firm's short-run demand curve for labor slopes downward. The graphical, more rigorous derivation of the demand curve in this appendix confirms and supports the verbal analysis in the chapter. However, it also emphasizes more clearly than a verbal analysis can that the downward-sloping nature of the short-run labor demand curve is based on an *assumption*—however reasonable—that MP_L declines as employment is increased.

Demand for Labor in the Long Run

Recall that a firm maximizes its profits by producing at a level of output (Q^*) where marginal cost equals MR. That is, the firm will keep increasing output until the addition to its revenues generated by an extra unit of output just equals the marginal cost of producing that extra unit of output. Because MR, which is equal to output *price* for a competitive firm, is not shown in our graph of the production function, the profit-maximizing level of output cannot be determined. However, continuing our analysis of the production function can illustrate some important aspects of the demand for labor in the long run.

Conditions for Cost Minimization

In Figure 3A.3, profit-maximizing output is assumed to be Q^*. How will the firm combine labor and capital to produce Q^*? It can maximize profits only if it produces Q^* in the least expensive way; that is, it must minimize the costs of producing Q^*. To better understand the characteristics of cost minimization, refer to the three *isoexpenditure* lines—AA', BB', DD'—in Figure 3A.3. Along any one of these lines, the costs of employing labor and capital are equal.

For example, line AA' represents total costs of $1,000. Given an hourly wage (W) of $10 per hour, the firm could hire 100 hours of labor and incur total costs of $1,000 if it used no capital (point A'). In contrast, if the price of a unit of capital (C) is $20, the firm could produce at a total cost of $1,000 by using 50 units of capital and no labor (point A). All the points between A and $A9$ *represent combinations of L and K* that at $W = $10 and $C = $20, cost $1,000 as well.

The problem with the isoexpenditure line of AA' is that it does not intersect the isoquant Q^*, implying that Q^* cannot be produced for $1,000. At prices of $W = $10 and $C = $20, the firm cannot buy enough resources to produce output level Q^* and hold total costs to $1,000. The firm can, however, produce Q^* for a total cost of $2,000. Line DD', representing expenditures of $2,000, intersects the Q^* isoquant at points X and Y. The problem with these points, however, is that they are not cost-minimizing; Q^* can be produced for less than $2,000.

Since isoquant Q^* is convex, the cost-minimizing combination of L and K in producing Q^* will come at a point where an isoexpenditure line is *tangent* to the isoquant (that is, just barely touches isoquant Q^* at only one place). Point Z, where labor equals L_Z and capital equals K_Z, is where Q^* can be produced at minimal cost, *given* that $W = $10 and $C = $20. No lower isoexpenditure curve touches the isoquant, meaning that Q^* cannot be produced for less than $1,500.

Figure 3A.3

Cost Minimization in the Production of Q^*
(Wage = $10 per Hour; Price of a Unit of
Capital = $20)

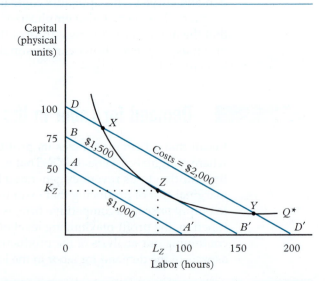

An important characteristic of point Z is that the slope of the isoquant at point Z and the slope of the isoexpenditure line are the same (the slope of a curve at a given point is the slope of a line tangent to the curve at that point). The slope of the isoquant at any given point is the $MRTS$ as defined in equation (3A.1). Another way of expressing equation (3A.1) is

$$MRTS = \frac{-\Delta K/\Delta Q}{\Delta L/\Delta Q} \tag{3A.2}$$

Equation (3A.2) directly indicates that the $MRTS$ is a ratio reflecting the reduction of capital required to decrease output by one unit if enough extra labor is hired so that output is tending to increase by one unit. (The ΔQs in equation (3A.2) cancel each other and keep output constant.) Pursuing equation (3A.2) one step further, the numerator and denominator can be rearranged to obtain the following:[2]

$$MRTS = \frac{-\Delta K/\Delta Q}{\Delta L/\Delta Q} = \frac{-\Delta Q/\Delta L}{\Delta Q/\Delta K} = -\frac{MP_L}{MP_K} \tag{3A.3}$$

where MP_L and MP_K are the marginal productivities of labor and capital, respectively.

The slope of the *isoexpenditure line* is equal to the negative of the ratio W/C (in Figure 3A.3, W/C equals 10/20, or 0.5).[3] Thus, at point Z, where Q^* is produced in the minimum-cost fashion, the following equality holds:

$$MRTS = -\frac{MP_L}{MP_K} = -\frac{W}{C} \tag{3A.4}$$

Equation (3A.4) is simply a rearranged version of equation (3.8c).[4]

The economic meaning, or logic, behind the characteristics of cost minimization can most easily be seen by stating the $MRTS$ as $-\dfrac{\Delta K/\Delta Q}{\Delta L/\Delta Q}$ (see equation 3A.2) and equating this version of the $MRTS$ to $-\dfrac{W}{C}$:

$$\frac{\Delta K/\Delta Q}{\Delta L/\Delta Q} = -\frac{W}{C} \tag{3A.5}$$

or

$$\frac{\Delta K}{\Delta Q} \cdot C = \frac{\Delta L}{\Delta Q} \cdot W \tag{3A.6}$$

---

[2]This is done by making use of the fact that dividing one number by a second one is equivalent to *multiplying* the first by the *inverse* of the second.

[3]Note that $10/20 = 75/150$, or $0B/0B'$.

[4]The negative signs on each side of equation (3A.4) cancel each other and can therefore be ignored.

Equation (3A.6) makes it plain that to be minimizing costs, the cost of producing an extra unit of output by adding only labor must equal the cost of producing that extra unit by employing only additional capital. If these costs differed, the company could reduce total costs by expanding its use of the factor with which output can be increased more cheaply and cutting back on its use of the other factor. Any point where costs can still be reduced while Q is held constant is obviously not a point of cost minimization.

The Substitution Effect

If the wage rate, which was assumed to be $10 per hour in Figure 3A.3, goes up to $20 per hour (holding C constant), what will happen to the cost-minimizing way of producing output of Q^*? Figure 3A.4 illustrates the answer that common sense would suggest: total costs rise, and more capital and less labor are used to produce Q^*. At $W = \$20$, 150 units of labor can no longer be purchased if total costs are to be held to $1,500; in fact, if costs are to equal $1,500, only 75 units of labor can be hired. Thus, the isoexpenditure curve for $1,500 in costs shifts from BB' to BB'' and is no longer tangent to isoquant Q^*. Q^* can no longer be produced for $1,500, and the cost of producing Q^* will rise. In Figure 3A.4, we assume the least-cost expenditure rises to $2,250 (isoexpenditure line EE' is the one tangent to isoquant Q^*).

Figure 3A.4

Cost Minimization in the Production of Q^*
(Wage = $20 per Hour; Price of a
Unit of Capital = $20)

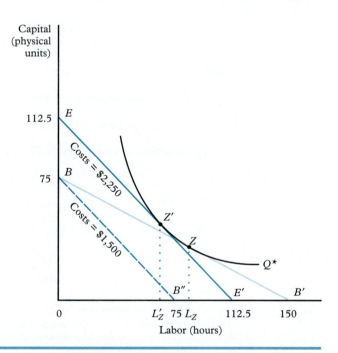

Moreover, the increase in the cost of labor relative to capital induces the firm to use more capital and less labor. Graphically, the old tangency point of Z is replaced by a new one (Z'), where the marginal productivity of labor is higher relative to MP_K, as our discussions of equations (3.8c) and equation (3A.4) explained. Point Z' is reached (from Z) by adding more capital and reducing employment of labor. The movement from L_Z to L'_z is the *substitution effect* generated by the wage increase.

The Scale Effect

The fact that Q^* can no longer be produced for $1,500, but instead involves at least $2,250 in costs, will generally mean that it is no longer the profit-maximizing level of production. The new profit-maximizing level of production will be less than Q^* (how much less cannot be determined unless we know something about the product demand curve).

Suppose that the profit-maximizing level of output falls from Q^* to Q^{**}, as shown in Figure 3A.5. Since all isoexpenditure lines have the new slope of 21 when $W = 20$ and $C = 20$, the cost-minimizing way to produce Q^{**} will lie on an isoexpenditure line parallel to EE'. We find this cost-minimizing way to produce Q^{**} at point Z', where an isoexpenditure line (FF') is tangent to the Q^{**} isoquant.

Figure 3A.5

The Substitution and Scale Effects of a Wage Increase

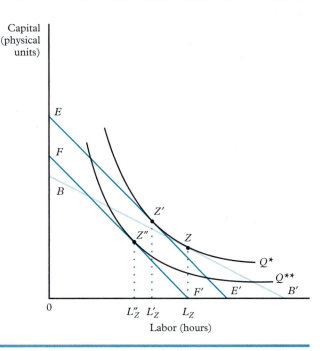

The *overall* response in the employment of labor to an increase in the wage rate has been a fall in labor usage from L_z to L''_z. The decline from L_z to L'_z is called the substitution effect, as we have noted. It results because the *proportions* of K and L used in production change when the ratio of wages to capital prices (W/C) changes. The *scale effect* can be seen as the reduction in employment from L'_z to L''_z, wherein the usage of both K and L is cut back solely because of the reduced *scale* of production. Both effects are simultaneously present when wages increase and capital prices remain constant, but as Figure 3A.5 emphasizes, the effects are conceptually distinct and occur for different reasons. Together, these effects lead us to assert that the long-run labor demand curve slopes downward.

CHAPTER 4

Labor Demand Elasticities

I n 1995, a heated debate broke out among economists and policymakers about the employment effects of minimum wage laws. Clearly, the standard theory developed in chapter 3 predicts that if wages are raised above their market level by a minimum wage law, employment opportunities will be reduced as firms move up (and to the left) along their labor demand curves. Two prominent labor economists, however, after reviewing previous work on the subject and doing new studies of their own, published a 1995 book in which they concluded that the predicted job losses associated with increases in the minimum wage simply could not be observed to occur, at least with any regularity.[1]

The book triggered a highly charged discussion of a long-standing question: just how responsive is employment demand to given changes in wages?[2] Hardly anyone doubts that jobs would be lost if mandated wage increases were huge, but how many are lost with modest increases?

---

[1]David Card and Alan B. Krueger, *Myth and Measurement: The New Economics of the Minimum Wage* (Princeton, N.J.: Princeton University Press, 1995).

[2]Six reviews of Card and Krueger, *Myth and Measurement*, appear in the book review section of the July 1995 issue of *Industrial and Labor Relations Review* 48, no. 4. More recent reviews of findings can be found in Richard V. Burkhauser, Kenneth A. Couch, and David C. Wittenburg, "A Reassessment of the New Economics of the Minimum Wage Literature with Monthly Data from the Current Population Survey,"*Journal of Labor Economics* 18 (October 2000): 653–680; and David Neumark and William Wascher, "Minimum Wages and Employment: A Review of Evidence from the New Minimum Wage Research," working paper no. 12663, National Bureau of Economic Research (Cambridge, Mass., January 2007).

The focus of this chapter is on the degree to which employment responds to changes in wages. The responsiveness of labor demand to a change in wage rates is normally measured as an *elasticity*, which in the case of labor demand is the percentage change in employment brought about by a 1 percent change in wages. We begin our analysis by defining, analyzing, and measuring *own-wage* and *cross-wage* elasticities. We then apply these concepts to analyses of minimum wage laws and the employment effects of technological innovations.

The Own-Wage Elasticity of Demand

The *own-wage elasticity of demand* for a category of labor is defined as the percentage change in its employment (E) induced by a 1 percent increase in its wage rate (W):

$$\eta_{ii} = \frac{\%\Delta E_i}{\%\Delta W_i} \tag{4.1}$$

In equation (4.1), we have used the subscript i to denote category of labor i, the Greek letter η(eta) to represent elasticity, and the notation %Δ to represent "percentage change in." Since the previous chapter showed that labor demand curves slope downward, an increase in the wage rate will cause employment to decrease; the own-wage elasticity of demand is therefore a negative number. What is at issue is its magnitude. The larger its *absolute value* (its magnitude, ignoring its sign), the larger the percentage decline in employment associated with any given percentage increase in wages.

Labor economists often focus on whether the absolute value of the elasticity of demand for labor is greater than or less than 1. If it is greater than 1, a 1 percent increase in wages will lead to an employment decline of greater than 1 percent; this situation is referred to as an *elastic* demand curve. In contrast, if the absolute value is less than 1, the demand curve is said to be *inelastic*: a 1 percent increase in wages will lead to a proportionately smaller decline in employment. If demand is elastic, aggregate earnings (defined here as the wage rate times the employment level) of individuals in the category will decline when the wage rate increases, because employment falls at a faster rate than wages rise. Conversely, if demand is inelastic, aggregate earnings will increase when the wage rate is increased. If the elasticity just equals -1, the demand curve is said to be *unitary elastic*, and aggregate earnings will remain unchanged if wages increase.

Figure 4.1 shows that the flatter of the two demand curves graphed (D_1) has greater elasticity than the steeper (D_2). Beginning with any wage (W, for example), a given wage change (to W', say) will yield greater responses in employment with demand curve D_1 than with D_2. To judge the different elasticities of response brought about by the same percentage wage increase, compare $(E_1 - E'_1)/E_1$ with $(E_2 - E'_2)/E_2$. Clearly, the more elastic response occurs along D_1.

To speak of a demand curve as having "an" elasticity, however, is technically incorrect. Given demand curves will generally have elastic and inelastic

Figure 4.1

Relative Demand Elasticities

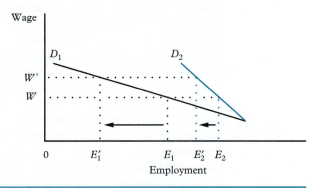

ranges, and while we are usually interested only in the elasticity of demand in the range around the current wage rate in any market, we cannot fully understand elasticity without comprehending that it can vary along a given demand curve.

   To illustrate, suppose we examine the typical straight-line demand curve that we have used so often in chapters 2 and 3 (see Figure 4.2). One feature of a straight-line demand curve is that at *each* point along the curve, a unit change in wages induces the *same* response in terms of units of employment. For example, at any point along the demand curve shown in Figure 4.2, a $2 decrease in wages will increase employment by 10 workers.

Figure 4.2

Different Elasticities along a Demand Curve

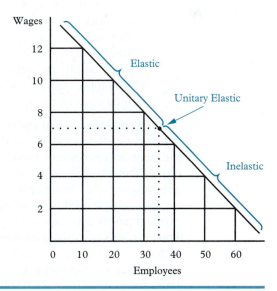

However, the same responses in terms of *unit* changes along the demand curve do *not* imply equal *percentage* changes. To see this point, look first at the upper end of the demand curve in Figure 4.2 (the end where wages are high and employment is low). A $2 decrease in wages when the base is $12 represents a 17 percent reduction in wages, while an addition of 10 workers when the starting point is also 10 represents a 100 percent increase in demand. Demand at this point is clearly *elastic*. However, if we look at the same unit changes in the lower region of the demand curve (low wages, high employment), demand there is inelastic. A $2 reduction in wages from a $4 base is a 50 percent reduction, while an increase of 10 workers from a base of 50 is only a 20 percent increase. Since the percentage increase in employment is smaller than the percentage decrease in wages, demand is seen to be inelastic at this end of the curve.

Thus, the upper end of a straight-line demand curve will exhibit greater elasticity than the lower end. Moreover, a straight-line demand curve will actually be elastic in some ranges and inelastic in others (as shown in Figure 4.2).

The Hicks–Marshall Laws of Derived Demand

The factors that influence own-wage elasticity can be summarized by the Hicks–Marshall laws of derived demand—four laws named after two distinguished British economists, John Hicks and Alfred Marshall, who are closely associated with their development.[3] These laws assert that, other things equal, the own-wage elasticity of demand for a category of labor is generally higher under the following conditions:

1. When the price elasticity of demand for the product being produced is higher.
2. When other factors of production can be more easily substituted for the category of labor.
3. When the supply of other factors of production is more highly elastic (that is, usage of other factors of production can be increased without substantially increasing their prices).
4. When the cost of employing the category of labor is a larger share of the total costs of production.

In seeking to explain why these laws generally hold, it is useful to act as if we could divide the process by which an increase in the wage rate affects the demand for labor into two steps. First, an increase in the wage rate increases the relative cost of the category of labor in question and induces employers to use less of it and more of other inputs (the *substitution effect*). Second, when the wage increase causes the marginal costs of production to rise, there are pressures to increase product prices and reduce output, causing a fall in employment (the *scale effect*). The four laws of derived demand each deal with substitution or scale effects.

---

[3]John R. Hicks, *The Theory of Wages*, 2nd ed. (New York: St. Martin's Press, 1966): 241–247; and Alfred Marshall, *Principles of Economics*, 8th ed. (London: Macmillan, 1923): 518–538.

Demand for the Final Product   We noted above that wage increases cause production costs to rise and tend to result in product price increases. The greater the price elasticity of demand for the final product, the larger the percentage decline in output associated with a given percentage increase in price—and the greater the percentage decrease in output, the greater the percentage loss in employment (other things equal). Thus, *the greater the elasticity of demand for the product, the greater the elasticity of demand for labor.*

One implication of this first law is that, other things equal, the demand for labor at the *firm* level will be more elastic than the demand for labor at the *industry*, or market, level. For example, the product demand curves facing *individual* carpet-manufacturing companies are highly elastic because the carpet of company X is a very close substitute for the carpet of company Y. Compared with price increases at the *firm* level, however, price increases at the *industry* level will not have as large an effect on demand because the closest substitutes for carpeting are hardwood, ceramic, or some kind of vinyl floor covering—none a very close substitute for carpeting. (For the same reasons, the labor demand curve for a monopolist is less elastic than for an individual *firm* in a competitive industry. Monopolists, after all, face *market* demand curves for their product because they are the only seller in the particular market.)

Another implication of this first law is that *wage elasticities will be higher in the long run than in the short run.* The reason for this is that price elasticities of demand in product markets are higher in the long run. In the short run, there may be no good substitutes for a product or consumers may be locked into their current stock of consumer durables. After a period of time, however, new products that are substitutes may be introduced, and consumers will begin to replace durables that have worn out.

Substitutability of Other Factors   As the wage rate of a category of labor increases, firms have an incentive to try to substitute other, now relatively cheaper, inputs for the category. Suppose, however, that there were no substitution possibilities; a given number of units of the type of labor *must* be used to produce one unit of output. In this case, there is no reduction in employment due to the substitution effect. In contrast, when substitution possibilities do present themselves, a reduction in employment owing to the substitution effect will accompany whatever reductions are caused by the scale effect. Hence, other things equal, *the easier it is to substitute other factors of production, the greater the wage elasticity of labor demand.*[4]

Limitations on substitution possibilities need not be solely technical ones. For example, as we shall see in chapter 13, unions often try to limit substitution possibilities by including specific work rules in their contracts (e.g., minimum crew size for railroad locomotives). Alternatively, the government may legislate

---

[4]There are certain conditions under which greater substitutability may not lead to a more elastic labor demand; see Robert S. Chirinko and Debdulal Mallick, "The Elasticity of Derived Demand, Factor Substitution, and Product Demand: Corrections to Hicks' Formula and Marshall's Four Rules," *Labour Economics* 18 (2011): 708–711.

limitations by specifying minimum employment levels for safety reasons (e.g., each public swimming pool in New York State must always have a lifeguard present). Such restrictions make the demand for labor less elastic, but substitution possibilities that are not feasible in the short run may well become feasible over longer periods of time. For example, if the wages of railroad workers went up, companies could buy more powerful locomotives and operate with larger trains and fewer locomotives. Likewise, if the wages of lifeguards rose, cities might build larger, but fewer, swimming pools. Both adjustments would occur only in the long run, which is another reason the demand for labor is more elastic in the long run than in the short run.

The Supply of Other Factors   Suppose that, as the wage rate increased and employers attempted to substitute other factors of production for labor, the prices of these other factors were bid up. This situation might occur, for example, if we were trying to substitute capital equipment for labor. If producers of capital equipment were already operating their plants near capacity, so that taking on new orders would cause them substantial increases in costs because they would have to work their employees overtime and pay them a wage premium, they would accept new orders only if they could charge a higher price for their equipment. Such a price increase would dampen firms' "appetites" for capital and thus limit the substitution of capital for labor.

For another example, suppose an increase in the wages of unskilled workers caused employers to attempt to substitute skilled employees for unskilled employees. If there were only a fixed number of skilled workers in an area, their wages would be bid up by employers. As in the prior example, the incentive to substitute alternative factors would be reduced, and the reduction in unskilled employment due to the substitution effect would be smaller. In contrast, if the prices of other inputs did not increase when employers attempted to increase their use, other things equal, the substitution effect—and thus the wage elasticity of labor demand—would be larger.

Note again that prices of other inputs are less likely to be bid up in the long run than in the short run. In the long run, existing producers of capital equipment can expand their capacity and new producers can enter the market. Similarly, in the long run, more skilled workers can be trained. This observation is an additional reason the demand for labor will be more elastic in the long run.

The Share of Labor in Total Costs   Finally, the share of the category of labor in total costs is crucial to the size of the elasticity of labor demand. If the category's initial share were 20 percent, a 10 percent increase in the wage rate, other things equal, would raise total costs by 2 percent. In contrast, if its initial share were 80 percent, a 10 percent increase in the wage rate would increase total costs by 8 percent. Since employers would have to increase their product prices by more in the latter case, output and employment would fall more in that case. *Thus, the greater the category's share in total costs, the greater the wage elasticity of demand.*[5]

Estimates of Own-Wage Labor Demand Elasticities

We now turn to the results of studies that estimate own-wage demand elasticities for labor as a generic input (that is, labor undifferentiated by skill level). The estimates we discuss are based on studies that utilize wage, output, and employment data from firms or narrowly defined industries. Thus, the employment responses being estimated approximate those that would be expected to occur in a firm that had to raise wages to remain competitive in the labor market. These estimates are suggestive of what might be a "typical" response but, of course, are not indicative of what would happen with any particular firm.

As our analysis has indicated, employers' labor demand responses to a wage change can be broken down into two components: a scale effect and a substitution effect. These two effects can themselves be expressed as elasticities, and their sum is the own-wage labor demand elasticity. In Table 4.1, we display the results of estimates of (a) the short-run scale effect, (b) the substitution effect, and (c) the overall elasticity of demand for labor in the long run.

The scale effect (expressed as an elasticity) is defined as the percentage change in employment associated with a given percentage change in the wage, *holding production technology constant*; that is, it is the employment response that occurs without a substitution effect. By definition, the *short-run* labor demand elasticity includes *only* the scale effect, although we noted earlier that the scale effect is likely to be greater in the long run than it is in the short run (owing to greater possibilities for *product market* substitutions in the long run). Therefore, estimates of short-run labor demand elasticities will be synonymous with the short-run scale effect, which may approximate the long-run scale effect if product market substitutions are relatively swift. A study using data from British manufacturing plants estimated the short-run, own-wage labor demand elasticity to be −0.53 (see Table 4.1). The short-run labor demand curve for a typical firm or narrowly defined sector, therefore, would appear to be inelastic.

The substitution effect, when expressed as an elasticity, is the percentage change in employment associated with a given percentage change in the

---

[5]An exception to the law occurs when it is easier for employers to substitute other factors of production for the category of labor than it is for customers to substitute other products for the product being produced; in this case, the law is reversed. Suppose, for example, that the elasticity of product demand among a firm's customers were zero; in this case, a rising wage rate would create only a substitution effect. With a larger labor share, and thus a higher ratio of labor to capital, the *percentage* fall in labor usage as wages rise will tend to be smaller, thus causing the elasticity of demand for labor to be smaller. For more on the effects of labor's share on the elasticity of demand, see Saul D. Hoffman, "Revisiting Marshall's Third Law: Why Does Labor's Share Interact with the Elasticity of Substitution to Decrease the Elasticity of Labor Demand?" *Journal of Economic Education* 40 (Fall 2009): 437–445.

Table 4.1

Components of the Own-Wage Elasticity of Demand for Labor: Empirical Estimates Using Plant-Level Data

	Estimated Elasticity
Short-Run Scale Effect	
British manufacturing firms, 1974–1982	−0.53
Substitution Effect	
32 studies using plant or narrowly defined industry data	Average: −0.45 (typical range: −0.15 to −0.75)
Overall Labor Demand Elasticity	
British plants, 1984	−0.93
British coal mines, 1950–1980	−1.0 to −1.4

Source: Daniel S. Hamermesh, *Labor Demand* (Princeton, N.J.: Princeton University Press, 1993): 94–104.

wage rate, *holding output constant*. That is, it is a measure of how employers change their production techniques in response to wage changes, even if output does not change (that is, even if the scale effect is absent). It happens that substitution effects are easier to credibly estimate, so there are many more studies of these effects. One careful summary of 32 studies estimating substitution-effect elasticities placed the average estimated elasticity at −0.45 (which is what is displayed in Table 4.1), with most estimates falling into the range of −0.15 to −0.75.[6]

With the short-run scale elasticity and the substitution elasticity each very close to −0.5, it is not surprising that estimates of the long-run overall elasticity of demand for labor are close to unitary in magnitude. Table 4.1 indicates that a study of plants across several British industries estimated an own-wage elasticity of −0.93, whereas another of British coal mines placed the elasticity of demand for labor in the range of −1.0 to −1.4.[7] Thus, these estimates suggest that if the wages a firm must pay rise by 10 percent, the firm's employment will shrink by close to 10 percent in the long run, other things being equal (that is, unless something else occurs that also affects the demand for labor).

[6]Daniel S. Hamermesh, *Labor Demand* (Princeton, N.J.: Princeton University Press, 1993): 103.

[7]A more recent analysis of the wages and employment of American women in the period following World War II estimates that the overall elasticity of demand for their labor was very similar—in the range of -1.0 to -1.5. See Daron Acemoglu, David H. Autor, and David Lyle, "Women, War and Wages: The Effect of Female Labor Supply on the Wage Structure at Midcentury," *Journal of Political Economy* 112 (June 2004): 497–551. Estimates of the own-wage elasticity of demand for skilled and unskilled manufacturing labor in Germany are somewhat lower (–0.6 to –1.3); see John T. Addison, Lutz Bellmann, Thorsten Schank, and Paulino Teixeira, "The Demand for Labor: An Analysis Using Matched Employer–Employee Data from the German LIAB. Will the High Unskilled Worker Own-Wage Elasticity Please Stand Up?" *Journal of Labor Research*, 29 (June 2008): 114–137.

Applying the Laws of Derived Demand: Inferential Analysis

Because empirical estimates of demand elasticities that may be required for making particular decisions are often lacking, it is frequently necessary to guess what these elasticities are likely to be. In making these guesses, we can apply the laws of derived demand to predict at least relative magnitudes for various types of labor. Consider first the demand for unionized New York City garment workers. As we shall discuss in chapter 13, because unions are complex organizations, it is not always possible to specify what their goals are. Nevertheless, it is clear that most unions value both wage *and* employment opportunities for their members. This observation leads to the simple prediction that, other things equal, the more elastic the demand for labor, the smaller the wage gain that a union will succeed in winning for its members. The reason for this prediction is that the more elastic the demand curve, the greater the percentage employment decline associated with any given percentage increase in wages. As a result, we can expect the following:

1. Unions would win larger wage gains for their members in markets with inelastic labor demand curves.
2. Unions would strive to take actions that reduce the wage elasticity of demand for their members' services.
3. Unions might first seek to organize workers in markets in which labor demand curves are inelastic (because the potential gains to unionization are higher in these markets).

Because of foreign competition, the price elasticity of demand for the clothing produced by New York City garment workers is extremely high. Furthermore, employers can easily find other inputs to substitute for these workers—namely, lower-paid nonunion garment workers in the South or in other countries. These facts lead one to predict that the wage elasticity of demand for New York City unionized garment workers is very high. Consequently, union wage demands have historically been moderate. The union has also sought to reduce the elasticity of product demand by supporting policies that reduce foreign competition, and it has pushed for higher federal minimum wages to reduce employers' incentives to move their plants to the South. (For another illustration of how an elastic *product* demand inhibits union wage increases, see Example 4.1.)

Next, consider the wage elasticity of demand for unionized airplane pilots in the United States. Only a small share of the costs of operating large airplanes goes to pay pilots' salaries; such salaries are dwarfed by fuel and capital costs. Furthermore, substitution possibilities are limited; there is little room to substitute unskilled labor for skilled labor (although airlines can substitute capital for labor by reducing the number of flights they offer while increasing the size of airplanes). In addition, before the deregulation of the airline industry in 1978, many airlines faced no competition on many of their routes or were prohibited from reducing their prices to compete with other airlines that flew the same routes. These factors all suggest that the wage elasticity of demand for airline pilots was

EXAMPLE 4.1

Why Are Union Wages So Different in Two Parts of the Trucking Industry?

The trucking industry's "general freight" sector, made up of motor carriers that handle nonspecialized freight requiring no special handling or equipment, is split into two distinct segments. One type of general freight carrier exclusively handles full truckloads (TLs), taking them directly from a shipper to a destination. The other type of carrier handles less-than-truckload (LTL) shipments, which involve multiple shipments on each truck and an intricate coordination of pickups and deliveries. These two segments of the general freight industry have vastly different *elasticities of product demand*; thus, the union that represents truck drivers has a very different ability to raise wages (without suffering unacceptable losses of employment) in each segment.

The TL part of the industry has a product market that is very competitive, because it is relatively easy for firms or individuals to enter the market; one needs only a truck, the proper driver's license, and access to a telephone (to call a freight broker, who matches available drivers with shipments needing delivery). Because this part of the industry has many competing firms, with the threat of even more if prices rise, each firm faces a relatively elastic product demand curve.

Firms specializing in LTL shipments must have a complex system of coordinated routes running between and within cities, and they must therefore be large enough to support their own terminals for storing and transferring shipments from one route to another. The LTL segment of the industry is not easily entered and thus is partially monopolized. From 1980 to 1995—a time period over which the number of TL carriers tripled—virtually the only new entrants into the LTL market were regional subsidiaries of pre-existing national carriers! To contrast competition in the two product markets somewhat differently, in 1987, the four largest LTL carriers accounted for 37 percent of total LTL revenues, while the four largest TL carriers accounted for only 11 percent of TL revenues.

The greater extent of competition in the TL part of the industry implies that at the firm level, *product* demand is more elastic there than in the LTL sector; other things being equal, then, we would expect the *labor* demand curve to also be more elastic in the TL sector. Because unions worry about potential job losses when negotiating with carriers about wages, we would expect to find that union wages are lower in the TL than in the LTL part of the industry. In fact, a 1991 survey revealed that the union mileage rates (drivers are typically compensated on a cents-per-mile basis) were dramatically different in the two sectors:

TL sector

Average union rate: 28.4 cents per mile Ratio, union to nonunion rate: 1.23

LTL sector

Average union rate: 35.8 cents per mile Ratio, union to nonunion rate: 1.34

The above data support the theoretical implication that a union's power to raise wages is greater when product (and therefore labor) demand is relatively inelastic. In the less-competitive LTL segment of the trucking industry, union drivers' wages are higher, both absolutely and relative to nonunion wages, than they are in the more competitive TL sector.

Data from: Michael H. Belzer, "Collective Bargaining after Deregulation: Do the Teamsters Still Count?" *Industrial and Labor Relations Review* 48 (July 1995): 636–655; and Michael H. Belzer, *Paying the Toll: Economic Deregulation of the Trucking Industry* (Washington, D.C.: Economic Policy Institute, 1994).

quite low (inelastic). As one might expect, pilots' wages were also quite high because their union could push for large wage increases without fear that these increases would substantially reduce pilots' employment levels. However, after airline deregulation, competition among airline carriers increased substantially, leading to a more elastic labor demand for pilots. As a result, many airlines "requested," and won, reduced wages from their pilots.

The Cross-Wage Elasticity of Demand

Because firms may employ several categories of labor and capital, the demand for any one category can be affected by price changes in the others. For example, if the wages of carpenters rose, more people might build brick homes and the demand for *masons* might increase. An increase in carpenters' wages might decrease the overall level of home building in the economy, however, which would decrease the demand for *plumbers*. Finally, changes in the price of *capital* could increase or decrease the demand for workers in all three trades.

The direction and magnitude of the above effects can be summarized by examining the elasticities of demand for inputs with respect to the prices of *other* inputs. The *elasticity of demand for input j with respect to the price of input k* is the percentage change in the demand for input *j* induced by a 1 percent change in the price of input *k*. If the two inputs are both categories of labor, these *cross-wage elasticities of demand* are given by

$$\eta_{jk} = \frac{\%\Delta E_j}{\%\Delta W_k} \tag{4.2}$$

and

$$\eta_{kj} = \frac{\%\Delta E_k}{\%\Delta W_j}$$

where, again, the Greek letter h is used to represent the elasticity. If the cross-elasticities are positive (with an increase in the price of one "category" increasing the demand for the other), the two are said to be *gross substitutes*. If these cross-elasticities are negative (and an increase in the price of one "category" reduces the demand for the other), the two are said to be *gross complements* (refer back to Figure 3.3).

It is worth reiterating that whether two inputs are gross substitutes or gross complements depends on the relative sizes of the scale and substitution effects. To see this, suppose we assume that adults and teenagers are substitutes in production. A decrease in the teenage wage will thus have opposing effects on adult employment. On the one hand, there is a substitution effect: for a given level of output, employers will now have an incentive to substitute teens for adults in the production process and reduce adult employment. On the other hand, there is a scale effect: a lower teenage wage reduces costs and provides employers with an incentive to increase employment of all inputs, including adults.

If the scale effect proves to be smaller than the substitution effect, adult employment will move in the same direction as teenage wages, and the two groups will be gross substitutes. In contrast, if the scale effect is larger than the substitution effect, adult employment and teenage wages will move in opposite directions, and the two groups will be gross complements. Knowing that two groups are substitutes in production, then, is not sufficient to tell us whether they are gross substitutes or gross complements.[8]

Because economic theory cannot indicate in advance whether two given inputs will be gross substitutes or gross complements, the major policy questions about cross-wage elasticities of demand relate to the issue of their *sign*; that is, we often want most to know whether a particular cross-elasticity is positive or negative. Before turning to a review of actual findings, we analyze underlying forces that determine the signs of cross-elasticities.

Can the Laws of Derived Demand Be Applied to Cross-Elasticities?

The Hicks–Marshall laws of derived demand are based on four technological or market conditions that determine the size of *own-wage* elasticities. Each of the four conditions influences the substitution or the scale effect, and as noted above, the relative strengths of these two effects are also what determine the sign of *cross-elasticities*. The laws that apply to own-wage elasticities cannot be applied directly to cross-elasticities because with cross-elasticities, the substitution effect (if there is one) and the scale effect work in opposite directions. The same underlying considerations, however, are basic to an analysis of cross-elasticities.

As we discuss these four considerations in the context of cross-elasticities, it will be helpful to have an example in mind. Let us return, then, to the question of what might happen to the demand for adult workers if the wages of teenage workers were to fall. As noted above, the answer depends on the relative strengths of the scale and substitution effects. What determines the strength of each?

The Scale Effect   The most immediate effect of a fall in the wages of teenagers would be reduced production costs for those firms that employ them. Competition in the product market would ensure that lower costs are followed by price reductions, which should stimulate increases in both product demand and the level of output. Increased levels of output will tend to cause increases in employment of all kinds of workers, including adults. This chain of events obviously describes

---

[8]As noted in chapter 3, if two groups are complements in production, a decrease in the price of one should lead to increased employment of the other. Complements in production are always gross complements.

behavior underlying the scale effect, and we now investigate what conditions are likely to make for a strong (or weak) scale effect.

The initial cost (and price) reductions would be greater among those employers for whom teenage wages constituted a higher proportion of total costs. Other things equal, greater price reductions would result in greater increases in both product demand and overall employment. Thus, *the share of total costs devoted to the productive factor whose price is changing* will influence the size of the scale effect. The larger this share, other things equal, the greater the scale effect (and the more likely it is that gross complementarity will exist). This tendency is analogous to the fourth Hicks–Marshall law discussed earlier; the difference is that with cross-elasticities, the factor whose *price* is changing is not the same as the one for which *employment* changes are being analyzed.

The other condition that greatly influences the size of the scale effect is product demand elasticity. In the earlier case of teenage wage reductions, the greater the increase in product demand when firms reduce their prices, the greater the tendency for employment of all workers, including adults, to increase. More generally, *the greater the price elasticity of product demand, other things equal, the greater the scale effect (and thus the greater the likelihood of gross complementarity)*. The effects of product demand elasticity are thus similar for both own-wage and cross-wage elasticities.

The Substitution Effect

After teenage wages fall, firms will also have incentives to alter their production techniques so that teenagers are more heavily used. Whether the greater use of teenagers causes an increase or some loss of adult jobs partially depends on a technological question: are teenagers and adults substitutes or complements in production? If they are complements in production, the effect on adults of changing productive techniques will reinforce the scale effect and serve to unambiguously increase adult employment (meaning, of course, that adults and teenagers would be gross complements). If they are substitutes in production, however, then changing productive techniques involves using a higher ratio of teenagers to adults, and the question then becomes whether this substitution effect is large or small relative to the scale effect.

A technological condition affecting the size of the substitution effect is a direct carryover from the second Hicks–Marshall law discussed previously: *the substitution effect will be greater when the category of labor whose price has changed is easily substituted for other factors of production*. When analyzing the effects on adult employment of a decline in the teenage wage, it is evident that when teenagers are more easily substituted for adults, the substitution effect (and therefore the chances of gross substitutability between the two categories of labor) will be greater.

Another condition influencing the size of the substitution effect associated with a reduction in the teenage wage relates to the labor supply curve of adults. If the adult labor supply curve were upward-sloping and rather steep, then adult wages would tend to fall as teenagers were substituted for adults and the demand curve for adults shifted left. This fall would blunt the substitution effect because adults would also become cheaper to hire. Conversely, if the adult labor supply curve were relatively flat, adult wages would be less affected by reduced demand and the substitution effect would be less blunted. As in the case of own-wage elasticities, *more-elastic supply curves of substitute inputs also lead to a greater substitution effect, other things equal, in the case of cross-wage elasticities.*[9]

Estimates Relating to Cross-Elasticities

Estimating at least the *sign* of cross-wage labor demand elasticities is useful for answering many public-policy questions. For example, if we were to reduce the *teenage* minimum wage, how would this affect the demand for *adult* labor? If *capital* were to be subsidized, how would this affect the demand for *labor?* Or, to take a hotly debated issue in recent years (and one we will return to in chapter 10), when *immigrant* labor becomes cheaper and more available, what are the likely effects on the demand for various grades of *native* labor? These questions, of course, are really asking whether the pairs of inputs italicized in each sentence are gross complements or gross substitutes.

While the major policy interest is whether two inputs are *gross* complements or *gross* substitutes, obtaining credible estimates is challenging (because it is difficult to estimate scale effects). Therefore, most of the cross-wage empirical studies to date focus on whether two factors are substitutes or complements *in production*. These studies estimate the employment response for one category of labor to a wage or price change elsewhere, *holding output constant* (which in effect allows us to focus just on changes in the *mix* of factors used in production). The factors of production paired together for analysis in these studies are numerous, and the results are not always clear-cut; nevertheless, the findings taken as a whole offer at least a few generalizations:[10]

1. Labor and energy are clearly substitutes in production, although their degree of substitutability is small. Labor and materials are probably substitutes in production, with the degree of substitutability again being small.

2. Skilled labor and unskilled labor are substitutes in production.[11]

---

[9]The share of the teenage wage bill in total costs influences the substitution effect as well as the scale effect in the example we are analyzing. For example, if teenage labor costs were a very large fraction of total costs, the possibilities for further substitution of teenagers for adults would be rather limited (this can be easily seen by considering an example in which teenagers constituted 100 percent of all production costs). Thus, while a larger share of teenagers in total cost would make for a relatively large scale effect, it also could reflect a situation in which the possibilities of substituting teenagers for adults are smaller than they would otherwise be.

[10]Hamermesh, *Labor Demand*, 105–127.

[11]James D. Adams, "The Structure of Firm R&D, the Factor Intensity of Production, and Skill Bias," *Review of Economics and Statistics* 81 (August 1999): 499–510; and Antonio Ciccone and Giovanni Peri, "Long-Run Substitutability between More and Less Educated Workers: Evidence from U.S. States, 1950–1990," *Review of Economics and Statistics* 87 (November 2005): 652–663.

3. We are not certain whether either skilled or unskilled labor is a substitute for or a complement with capital in the production process. What does appear to be true is that skilled (or well-educated) labor is more likely to be complementary with capital than is unskilled labor—and that if they are both substitutes for capital, the degree of substitutability is smaller for skilled labor.[12]

4. The finding summarized in 3 above suggests that skilled labor is more likely than unskilled labor to be a *gross* complement with capital. This finding is important to our understanding of recent trends in the earnings of skilled and unskilled workers (see chapter 15), because the prices of computers and other high-tech capital goods have fallen dramatically in the past decade or so.

5. The finding in 3 above also implies that if the wages of both skilled and unskilled labor were to rise by the same percentage, the magnitude of any employment loss associated with the substitution effect (as capital is substituted for labor) will be greater for the unskilled. Thus, we expect that, other things equal, *own-wage* labor demand elasticities will be larger in magnitude for unskilled than for skilled workers.

Policy Application: Effects of Minimum Wage Laws

History and Description

The Fair Labor Standards Act of 1938 was the first major piece of protective labor legislation adopted at the national level in the United States. Among its provisions were a minimum wage rate, below which hourly wages could not be reduced, an overtime-pay premium for workers who worked long workweeks, and restrictions on the use of child labor. When initially adopted, the minimum wage was set at $0.25 an hour and covered roughly 43 percent of all nonsupervisory wage and salary workers—primarily those employed in larger firms involved in interstate commerce (manufacturing, mining, and construction). Both the basic minimum wage and coverage under the minimum wage have expanded over time. Indeed, as of 2009, the minimum wage was set at $7.25 an hour and roughly 90 percent of all nonsupervisory workers were covered by its provisions.

It is important to emphasize that the minimum wage rate is specified in *nominal* terms and not in terms *relative* to some other wage or price index. As illustrated in Figure 4.3, the nominal wage rate has usually been raised only once every few years. Until the early 1980s, newly legislated minimum wage rates were typically at least 45 percent of the average hourly wage in manufacturing.

---

[12]See Claudia Goldin and Lawrence Katz, "The Origins of Technology-Skill Complementarity," *Quarterly Journal of Economics* 113 (May 1998): 693–732, for citations to the literature.

Figure 4.3

Federal Minimum Wage Relative to Wages in Manufacturing, 1938–2012

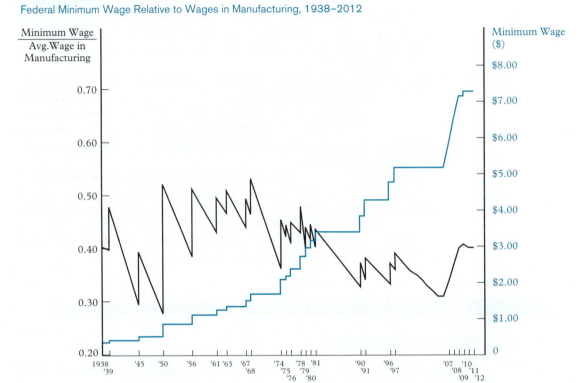

During the years between legislation, productivity growth and inflation caused manufacturing wages to rise, with the result that the minimum wage has often fallen by 10 or more percentage points relative to the manufacturing wage before being raised again. In the last two decades, even the newly legislated minimums were below 40 percent of the average manufacturing wage. Under a law passed by Congress in 2007, which set the minimum wage at $5.85 and called for it to rise to $7.25 over a two-year period, the minimum wage in 2009 was again about 40 percent of the average manufacturing wage. With slow wage growth in manufacturing, the ratio remained at 40 percent into 2013.

Employment Effects: Theoretical Analysis

Since the minimum wage was first legislated, a concern has been that it will reduce employment, especially among the groups it is intended to benefit. In the face of downward-sloping labor demand curves, a policy that compels firms to raise the wages paid to all low-wage workers can be expected to *reduce employment opportunities* for the least skilled or least experienced. Furthermore, if the percentage loss of employment among low-wage workers is greater than the percentage increase in their wages—that is, if the demand curve for low-wage workers is *elastic*—then the *aggregate* earnings of low-wage workers could be made smaller by an increase in the minimum wage.

In evaluating the findings of research on the employment effects of minimum wages, we must keep in mind that good research must be guided by good theory. Theory provides us with a road map that directs our explorations into the real world, and it suggests several issues that must be addressed by any research study of the minimum wage.

Nominal Versus Real Wages

Minimum wage levels in the United States have been set in nominal terms and adjusted by Congress only sporadically. The result is that general price inflation gradually lowers the real minimum wage during the years between congressional action, so what appears to be a fixed minimum wage turns out to have constantly changing incentives for employment.

Also, the federal minimum wage in the United States is uniformly applied to a large country characterized by regional differences in prices. Taking account of regional differences in prices or wages, we find that the real minimum wage in Alaska (where wages and prices are very high) is lower than it is in Mississippi. Recognizing that there are regional differences in the real minimum wage leads to the prediction that employment effects of a uniformly applied minimum wage law generally will be most adverse in regions with the lowest costs of living. (Researchers must also take into account the fact that many states have their own minimum wage laws, many having minimums that exceed the federal minimum.)

Holding Other Things Constant

Predictions of job loss associated with higher minimum wages are made *holding other things constant*. In particular, the prediction grows out of what is expected to happen to employment as one moves up and to the left along a *fixed* labor demand curve. If the labor demand curve were to shift at the same time that a new minimum becomes effective, the employment effects of the shift could be confounded with those of the new minimum.

Consider, for example, Figure 4.4, in which, for simplicity, we have omitted the labor supply curve and focused on only the demand side of the market. Suppose that D_0 is the demand curve for low-skilled labor in year 0, in which year the real wage is W_0/P_0 and the employment level is E_0. Further assume that in the absence of any change in the minimum wage, the money wage and the price level would both increase by the same percentage over the next year, so that the real wage in year 1 (W_1/P_1) would be the same as that in year 0.

Now, suppose that in year 1, two things happen. First, the minimum wage rate is raised to W_2, which is greater than W_1, so that the real wage increases to W_2/P_1. Second, because the economy is expanding, the demand for low-skilled labor shifts out to D_1. The result of these two changes is that employment increases from E_0 to E_1.

Minimum Wage Effects: Growing Demand
Obscures Job Loss

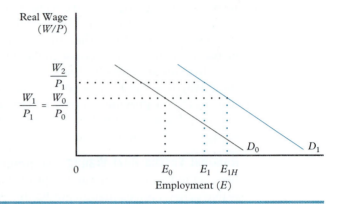

Comparisons of observed employment levels at two points of time have led some investigators to conclude that minimum wage increases had no adverse employment effects. However, this simple before/after comparison is *not* the correct one if labor demand has shifted, as in Figure 4.4. Rather, we should ask, "How did the actual employment level in period 1 compare with the level that *would have prevailed* in the absence of the increase in the minimum wage?" Since demand grew between the two periods, this hypothetical employment level would have been E_{1H}. Because E_{1H} is greater than E_1, the actual level of employment in period 1, there is a loss of jobs $(E_{1H} - E_1)$ caused by the minimum wage. In a growing economy, then, the expected effect of a one-time increase in the minimum wage is to *reduce the rate of growth of employment*. Controlling for all the "other things" besides wages that affect labor demand turns out to be the major difficulty in measuring employment changes caused by the minimum wage.

Effects of Uncovered Sectors   The federal minimum wage law, like many government regulations, has an *uncovered* sector. Coverage has increased over the years, but the law still does not apply to some nonsupervisory workers (mainly those in small firms in the retail trade and service industries). Also, with millions of employers and limited resources for governmental enforcement, *noncompliance* with the law may be widespread, creating another kind of noncoverage.[13] The existence of uncovered sectors significantly affects how the overall employment of low-wage workers will respond to increases in the minimum wage.

Consider the labor market for unskilled, low-wage workers that is depicted in Figure 4.5. The market has two sectors. In one, employers must pay wages

---

[13]Orley Ashenfelter and Robert Smith, "Compliance with the Minimum Wage Law," *Journal of Political Economy* 87 (April 1979): 335–350. A more recent study of noncompliance (among apparel contractors) can be found in David Weil, "Public Enforcement/Private Monitoring: Evaluating a New Approach to Regulating the Minimum Wage," *Industrial and Labor Relations Review* 58 (January 2005): 238–257.

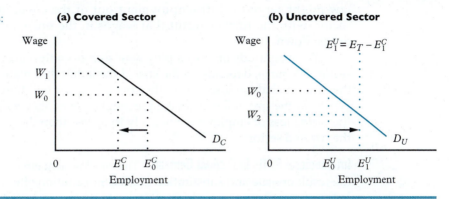

Figure 4.5

Minimum Wage Effects:
Incomplete Coverage
Causes Employment
Shifts

equal to at least the minimum wage of W_1; wages in the uncovered sector are free to vary with market conditions. While the total labor supply to both markets taken as a whole is fixed at E_T (that is, the total labor supply curve is vertical), workers can freely move from one sector to the other seeking better job offers. Free movement between sectors suggests that in the absence of minimum wage regulations, the wage in each sector will be the same. Referring to Figure 4.5, let us assume that this "pre-minimum" wage is W_0 and that total employment of E_T is broken down into E_0^c in the covered sector plus E_0^u in the uncovered sector.

If a minimum wage of W_1 is imposed on the covered sector, all unskilled workers will prefer to work there. However, the increase in wages in that sector, from W_0 to W_1, reduces demand, and covered-sector employment will fall from E_0^c to E_1^c. Some workers who previously had, or would have found, jobs in the covered sector must now seek work in the uncovered sector. Thus, to the E_0^u workers formerly working in the uncovered sector are added $E_0^c - E_1^c$ other workers seeking jobs there. Hence, all unskilled workers in the market who are not lucky enough to find "covered jobs" at W_1 must now look for work in the uncovered sector,[14] and the (vertical) supply curve to that sector becomes $E_1^u = E_0^u + (E_0^c - E_1^c) = E_T - E_1^c$. The increased supply of workers to that sector drives down the wage there from W_0 to W_2.

The presence of an uncovered sector thus suggests the possibility that employment among unskilled workers will be rearranged, but not reduced, by an increase in the minimum wage. In the above example, all E_T workers remained employed after the minimum was imposed. Rather than reducing

---

[14]Under some circumstances, it may be rational for these unemployed workers to remain unemployed for a while and to search for jobs in the covered sector. We shall explore this possibility of "wait unemployment"—which is discussed by Jacob Mincer in "Unemployment Effects of Minimum Wage Changes," *Journal of Political Economy* 84 (August 1976): S87–S104—in chapter 13. At this point, we simply note that if it occurs, unemployment will result.

overall employment of the unskilled, then, a partially covering minimum wage law might serve to shift employment out of the covered to the uncovered sector, with the further result that wages in the uncovered sector would be driven down.

The magnitude of any employment shift from the covered to the uncovered sector, of course, depends on the size of the latter; the smaller it is, the lower are the chances that job losers from the covered sector will find employment there. Whatever the size of the uncovered sector, however, its very presence means that the *overall* loss of employment is likely to be less than the loss of employment in the covered sector.

Intersectoral Shifts in Product Demand   The employment effects of a wage change are the result of scale and substitution effects. Substitution effects stem from changes in how firms choose to produce, while scale effects are rooted in consumer adjustments to changes in product prices. Recall that faced with a given increase (say) in the minimum wage, firms' increases in costs will generally be greater when the share of low-wage labor in total costs is greater; thus, the same increase in the minimum wage can lead to rather different effects on product prices among different parts of the covered sector. Furthermore, if these subsectors compete with each other for customers, it is possible that scale effects of the increased wage will serve to *increase* employment among some firms in the covered sector.

Suppose, for example, that convenience stores sell items that supermarkets also carry and that a minimum wage law raises the wages paid to low-skilled workers in both kinds of stores. If low-skilled labor costs are a higher fraction of total costs in convenience stores than they are in supermarkets, then, other things equal, the minimum wage law would raise costs in convenience stores by a greater percentage. With prices of items increasing more in convenience stores than in supermarkets, consumers would tend to shift some of their convenience store purchases to supermarkets. Thus, the minimum wage increase could have an ambiguous effect on employment in supermarkets. On the one hand, increased costs of unskilled workers in supermarkets would create scale and substitution effects that cause employment to decline. On the other hand, because they may pick up business formerly going to convenience stores, supermarkets may experience a scale effect that could work to increase their demand for labor.

Employment Effects: Empirical Estimates

While the initial employment effects of adopting a minimum wage in the United States were readily observed (see Example 4.2), the effects of more recent increases are not as obvious—and must therefore be studied using sophisticated statistical techniques. The demographic group for which the effects of minimum wages are expected to be most visible is composed of teenagers—a notoriously low-paid group!—but studies of how mandated wage increases have affected their employment have produced no consensus.

EXAMPLE 4.2

The Employment Effects of the First Federal Minimum Wage

When the federal minimum wage first went into effect, on October 24, 1938, it was expected to have a substantial impact on the economy of the South, where wages were much lower than in the rest of the country. An examination of one of the largest manufacturing industries in the South, seamless hosiery, verifies these predictions.

It is readily apparent that the new minimum wage was binding in the seamless hosiery industry. By 1940, nearly one-third of the labor force earned within 2.5 cents per hour of the minimum wage (which was then 32.5 cents per hour). A longitudinal survey of 87 firms shows that employment, which had been rising, reversed course and started to fall, even though overall demand for the product and production levels were rising. Employment fell by 5.5 percent in southern mills but rose by 4.9 percent in northern mills. Even more strikingly, employment fell by 17 percent in mills that had previously paid less than the new minimum wage, while it stayed virtually the same at higher-wage mills.

Before the passage of the minimum wage, there had been a slow movement from the use of hand-transfer to converted-transfer knitting machines. (A converted-transfer machine had an attachment to enable automated production for certain types of work.) The minimum wage seems to have accelerated this trend. In the first two years of the law's existence, there was a 23 percent decrease in the number of hand-transfer machines, a 69 percent increase in converted-transfer machines, and a 10 percent increase in fully automatic machines. In addition, the machines were used more intensively than before. A night shift was added at many mills, and these workers did not receive extra pay for working this undesirable shift. Finally, total imports of seamless hosiery surged by about 27 percent within two years of the minimum wage's enactment.

Data from: Andrew J. Seltzer, "The Effects of the Fair Labor Standards Act of 1938 on the Southern Seamless Hosiery and Lumber Industries," *Journal of Economic History* 57 (June 1997): 396–415.

Widely reviewed and replicated studies of employment changes in the fast-food industry, for example, disagree on whether employment was affected at all by minimum wage increases in the early 1990s.[15] A study that reviewed and updated prior estimates of how *overall* teenage employment has responded to increases in the minimum wage, however, found negative effects on employment. Once account is taken of the extent to which minimum wage increases raised

---

[15]See David Neumark and William Wascher, "Minimum Wages and Employment: A Case Study of the Fast-Food Industry in New Jersey and Pennsylvania: Comment,"and David Card and Alan B. Krueger, "Minimum Wages and Employment: A Case Study of the Fast-Food Industry in New Jersey and Pennsylvania: Reply," both in *American Economic Review* 90 (December 2000): 1362–1420. A more recent study is by Arindrajit Dube, T. William Lester, and Michael Reich, "Minimum Wage Effects Across State Borders: Estimates Using Contiguous Counties," *Review of Economics and Statistics* 92 (November 2010): 945–964. These studies contain references to earlier studies and reviews on this topic.

the average wage of teenagers, the implications of this latter study are that the elasticity of demand for teenagers is in the range of −0.4 to −1.9.[16]

A recent estimate of how increases in the minimum wage affects employment for *all* low-wage workers, not just teenagers, suggests an own-wage labor demand elasticity that is considerably lower. This study looked at the employment status of those who were at or near the minimum wage right before it increased and then looked at their employment status a year later. The estimated decline in the probability of employment implied that the labor demand curve facing these workers has an own-wage elasticity of roughly −0.15.[17]

With some studies estimating no effect on employment, and with many of those that do estimating an own-wage labor demand elasticity well below unity (the average we saw in Table 4.1), we remain notably uncertain about how employment among low-wage workers responds to increases in the minimum wage. We will come back to this issue in chapter 5 and offer a possible reason for why *mandated* wage increases might have a smaller and more uncertain effect on labor demand than wage increases generated by market forces.

Does the Minimum Wage Fight Poverty?

Aside from the potentially adverse effects on employment opportunities for low-wage workers, two other reasons suggest that the minimum wage is a relatively ineffective instrument to reduce poverty. First, many who live in poverty are not affected by the minimum wage, either because they are not employed or because their wages, while low, are already above the minimum. For example, one study of the minimum wage increases in 1990–1991 divided the distribution of family

---

[16]The reviews cited in footnote 2 suggest that the elasticity of teenage employment with respect to changes in the minimum wage generally falls into the range of −0.2 to −0.6. Dividing these elasticities by the estimated elasticity of response in the average teen wage to changes in the minimum wage (the percentage change in the average teen wage divided by the percentage change in the minimum wage was in the range of 0.32 to 0.48) yields estimates of the elasticity of the labor demand curve for teenagers. A recent study suggests that most of the effects of minimum wages on teenage employment are observed in temporary jobs or new hires; see Jeffrey P. Thompson, "Using Local Labor Market Data to Re-Examine the Employment Effects of the Minimum Wage,"*Industrial and Labor Relations Review* 62 (April 2009): 343–366.

[17]David Neumark, Mark Schweitzer, and William Wascher, "The Effects of Minimum Wages Throughout the Wage Distribution," *Journal of Human Resources* 39 (Spring 2004): 425–450. This study finds that the elasticity of employment with respect to changes in the minimum wage for those at the minimum is –0.12, while the elasticity of their wages to changes in the minimum is +0.8; dividing −0.12 by 0.8 equals the estimated demand elasticity of –0.15. Similar findings when the focus is on adult women can be found in John T. Addison and Orgul Demet Ozturk, "Minimum Wages, Labor Market Institutions, and Female Employment: A Cross-Country Analysis," *Industrial and Labor Relations Review* 65 (October 2012): 779–809; more elastic responses of employment to minimum-wage changes are found by Joseph J. Sabia, Richard V. Burkhauser and Benjamin Hansen, "Are the Effects of Minimum Wage Increases Always Small? New Evidence from a Case Study of New York State," *Industrial and Labor Relations Review* 65 (April 2012): 350–376.

incomes into 10 equally sized groups (deciles). Among adults in the lowest decile, 80 percent were below the poverty line (given the size of their families), yet only about one-quarter of them worked; of those who did work, less than one-third earned wages that were less than the new minimum![18] Thus, even without any loss of employment opportunities, less than 10 percent of those in the lowest income decile stood to benefit from the 1990–1991 increases in the minimum wage.

Second, many of those most affected by the minimum wage are teenagers, who may not reside in poor families. The study cited earlier found that only 19 percent of the estimated earnings increases generated by the higher minimum wage went to families with incomes below the poverty line, while over 50 percent of the increases went to families whose incomes were at least twice the poverty level.

"Living Wage" Laws

Perhaps because the federal minimum wage is relatively low and has not been changed very often, roughly 100 cities, counties, and school districts in the United States have adopted "living wage" ordinances. These ordinances apply to a subset of employers within their jurisdictions and impose wage floors that are higher than either federal or state minimum wages on these employers. The affected employers are generally those performing contracts with the local government, although in some cases, the ordinances also apply to employers receiving business assistance from the city or county. Living wage levels usually relate to the federal poverty guidelines, which in 2007 were $17,170 for a family of three and $20,650 for a family of four in the continental United States (it takes wages of $8.50 to $10 per hour to reach these poverty lines). In 2007, typical wage levels specified by living wage laws were in the range of $8 to $12 per hour.

The potentially beneficial effects of living wage ordinances for low-wage workers are obviously limited by the rather narrow group of employers to which they apply. The benefits are also reduced, of course, if these laws cause the affected employers to either reduce their employment levels or move their operations to cities that do not have living wage regulations.

---

[18]Richard V. Burkhauser, Kenneth A. Couch, and David C. Wittenburg, "'Who Gets What' from Minimum Wage Hikes: A Re-Estimation of Card and Krueger's Distributional Analysis in *Myth and Measurement: The New Economics of the Minimum Wage*," *Industrial and Labor Relations Review* 49 (April 1996): 547–552. For a summary of studies on how minimum-wage laws (and other social policies) affect poverty, see David Neumark, "Alternative Labor Market Policies to Increase Economic Self-Sufficiency: Mandating Higher Wages, Subsidizing Employment, and Increasing Productivity," working paper no. 14807, National Bureau of Economic Research (Cambridge, Mass., March 2009); also see Joseph J. Sabia and Richard V. Burkhauser, "Minimum Wages and Poverty: Will a $9.50 Federal Minimum Wage Really Help the Working Poor?" *Southern Economic Journal* 76 (January 2010): 592–623. For a different view of minimum-wage laws, see Bruce E. Kaufman, "Institutional Economics and the Minimum Wage: Broadening the Theoretical and Policy Debate," *Industrial and Labor Relations Review* 63 (April 2010): 427–453.

Estimating the employment effects of adopting living wage laws, however, requires more than merely comparing employment changes in cities with and without such regulations, because the two groups of cities may have fundamentally different employment or wage trends. Cities with rapidly expanding employment opportunities, for example, may decide differently about adopting a living wage law than cities with stagnant or declining opportunities. Because these laws are relatively new, and because the best way to evaluate their employment effects is subject to debate, there is currently no consensus about how living wage ordinances affect employment.[19]

Applying Concepts of Labor Demand Elasticity to the Issue of Technological Change

Technological change, which can encompass the introduction of new products and production techniques as well as changes in technology that serve to reduce the cost of capital (for example, increases in the speed of computers), is frequently viewed as a blessing by some and a curse by others. Those who view it positively point to the enormous gains in the standard of living made possible by new technology, while those who see technological change as a threat often stress its adverse consequences for workers. Are the concepts underlying the elasticity of demand for labor useful in making judgments about the effects of technological change?

Product Demand Shifts   There are two aspects of technological change that affect the demand for labor. One is product demand. *Shifts* in product demand curves will tend to shift labor demand curves in the same direction, and changes in the *elasticity* of product demand with respect to product price will tend to cause qualitatively similar changes in the own-wage elasticity of labor demand. The invention of new products (personal computers, for example) that serve as substitutes for old ones (typewriters) will tend to shift the labor demand curve in the older sector to the left, causing loss of employment in that sector. If greater product substitution possibilities are also created by these new inventions, the introduction of new products can increase the *elasticity* of product—and labor—demand. This increases the amount of job loss associated with collectively bargained wage increases, and it reduces the

---

[19]One promising way to estimate the employment effects is to compare employment changes in cities that implemented living wage laws with those in cities that passed such laws but saw them derailed by some outside force (the state legislature or a court decision). This approach is included in Scott Adams and David Neumark, "The Effects of Living Wage Laws: Evidence from Failed and Derailed Living Wage Campaigns," *Journal of Urban Economics* 58 (September 2005): 177–202. For estimated employment effects of a *city* minimum wage, see Arindrajit Dube, Suresh Naidu, and Michael Reich, "The Economic Effects of a Citywide Minimum Wage," *Industrial and Labor Relations Review* 60 (July 2007): 522–543.

power of unions to secure large wage increases in the older sector. While benefiting consumers and providing jobs in the new sectors, the introduction of new products does necessitate some painful changes in established industries, as workers, unions, and employers must all adjust to a new environment.

Capital-Labor Substitution   A second aspect of technological change is often associated with automation, or the substitution of capital for labor. For purposes of analyzing its effects on labor demand, this second aspect of technological change should be thought of as reducing the cost of capital. In some cases—the mass production of personal computers is one example—a fall in capital prices is what literally occurs. In other cases of technological change—the miniaturization of computer components, for example, which has made possible new production techniques—an invention makes completely new technologies available. When something is unavailable, it can be thought of as having an infinite price (it is not available at any price); therefore, the availability of a new technique is equivalent to observing a decline in its price to some finite number. In either case, with a decline in its cost, capital tends to be substituted for labor in the production process.

The *sign* of the cross-elasticity of demand for a given category of labor with respect to a fall in the price of capital depends on whether capital and the category of labor are gross substitutes or gross complements. If a particular category of labor is a substitute in production for capital, *and* if the scale effect of the reduced capital price is relatively weak, then capital and the category of labor are gross substitutes and automation reduces demand for workers in this category. As is illustrated in Example 4.3, however, for categories of labor that are not close substitutes for the new technology, however, the scale effect may dominate, and the two can be gross complements. Thus, the effect of automation on the demand for *particular* categories of labor can be either positive or negative.

Clearly, whether capital and a given type of labor are gross substitutes depends on several factors, all of which are highly specific to particular industries and production processes. Perhaps the most that can be said generally is that unskilled labor and capital are more likely to be substitutes in production than are skilled labor and capital, which some studies have identified as complements in production. Because factors of production that are complementary must be gross complements, technological change is more likely to increase the demand for skilled than for unskilled labor.[20]

---

[20]See David Autor, Lawrence Katz, and Alan Krueger, "Computing Inequality: Have Computers Changed the Labor Market?" *Quarterly Journal of Economics* 113 (November 1998): 1169–1213. For a study indicating that capital and labor exhibit gross complementarity in the manufacturing sector of developing countries, but that this complementarity is probably larger for skilled workers, see Anusha Chari, Peter Blair Henry and Diego Sasson, "Capital Market Integration and Wages," *American Economic Journal: Macroeconomics* 4 (April 2012): 102–132.

EXAMPLE 4.3

Gross Complementarity in the 19th Century Apparel Industry

In 1820, there were some 200,000 handloom weavers in England's Lancashire region, where most of English cotton manufacturing took place. Most of the handloom weavers worked at home as self-employed subcontractors. Another 85,000 workers were employed in the cotton mills of Lancashire.

In the 1820s, however, the powerloom had been improved to the point that it began to substitute for the handloom in weaving cotton cloth. Powerloom weaving had to be done in the cotton mills, not at home, and the substitution of mechanized weaving for the handloom meant that by 1850 only 40,000 handloom weavers were left in Lancashire.

The reduced cost of weaving using the powerloom, however, led to a marked increase in the demand for cotton goods. By 1850, the employment in Lancashire cotton mills had grown from 85,000 to 275,000. Thus, while 160,000 jobs (mostly at home) were lost, 190,000 factory jobs were added—and for the industry as a whole, the scale effect dominated the substitution effect.

While employment in cotton manufacturing grew, and consumers benefited from the cost savings of the powerloom, it is important to acknowledge that this economic change forced the handloom weavers to change their lifestyle, move into urban areas, and acquire new skills. Their experience serves as a reminder that the changes that accompany economic growth are often painful for many workers.

Source: Duncan Bythell, *The Handloom Weavers* (Cambridge: Cambridge University Press, 1969).

Before concluding that technological change is a threat to the unskilled, however, we must keep three things in mind. First, even factors that are substitutes in production can be gross complements (if scale effects are large enough). Second, substitution of capital for labor can destroy some jobs, but accompanying scale effects can create others, sometimes in the same industry.

Finally, although the fraction of all workers who are unskilled laborers has declined over the course of the last 100 years, this decline is not in itself convincing evidence of gross substitutability between capital and unskilled labor. The concepts of elasticity and cross-elasticity refer to changes in labor demand caused by changes in wages or capital prices, *holding all else constant*. That is, labor demand elasticities focus on the labor demand curve at a particular point in time. Actual employment outcomes over time are also influenced by labor *supply* behavior of workers. Thus, from simple observations of employment levels over time, it is impossible to tell anything about own-wage demand elasticities or about the signs or magnitudes of cross-elasticities of labor demand.

Overall Effects of Technological Change   From the analysis above, it is clear that technological innovations affect the demand for labor through both the scale and substitution effects. In many public discussions of technological change, however, scale effects are overlooked, and the focus is placed on the substitution effect—sometimes in frightening words. For example, in a book titled *The Collapse of Work*, published in 1979, the authors referred to technological change as creating a "jobs holocaust" and called for policies designed to cope with "ever-increasing unemployment."[21] Because of the fears created by technological change, we need to pause and use economic analysis to consider whether technological change creates, *for an entire society*, more harm than good.

Fortunately, the fear that technological change creates a "jobs holocaust" has proven groundless. When *The Collapse of Work* was published, for example, 60 percent of adults in the United States were working, and among all those who wanted to work, 5.8 percent were unemployed. In 2008, after three decades of rapid technological innovation, the unemployment rate also stood at 5.8 percent (a bit above the average for the years 2000–2009), but 62 percent of American adults were working!

Technological change, however, does impose costs on *some* workers—those who face decreased demand for their services and must therefore bear the costs of changing jobs. These costs may involve wage loss, temporary unemployment, or the need to invest in learning new skills. But because technological innovation also enhances the demand for *other* workers and results in lower costs or greater product variety for *consumers*, it is natural to ask if there is a way to analyze whether the *overall net effects* of technological change are positive or negative. Put differently (and in the context of the normative principles outlined in chapter 1), can economic theory be used to tell us whether, within a society, the gainers gain more from technological change than the losers lose?

To begin our analysis, let us consider a society that has a fixed amount of labor and capital resources, and for the sake of simplicity, let us assume that these resources can be used to produce two goods: food and clothing. Figure 4.6 summarizes the production possibilities we assume for this simple society. If all labor and capital inputs were devoted to the production of food, 200 million units of food (and no clothing) could be produced (see point Y). Similarly, if all resources were devoted to the production of clothing, 100 million units of clothing (and no food) could be produced (point X). If, say, 50 percent of the resources were devoted to food and 50 percent to clothing, the society could produce 100 million units of food and 50 million units of clothing (point A). Limits on the combinations of food and clothing this society could produce are displayed in Figure 4.6 along line XY, which is called a "production possibilities curve."[22] All combinations along or below (southwest of) XY are possible; combinations above XY (to the northeast of it) cannot be produced.

---

[21]Clive Jenkins and Barrie Sherman, *The Collapse of Work* (Fakenham, England: Eyre Methuen, 1979), chapter 20.

[22]The production possibilities "curve" in Figure 4.6 is a straight line, which reflects the simplifying assumption that the ratio at which food can be "transformed" into clothing, and vice versa, never changes. This assumption is not necessary to the argument but does make it a bit easier to grasp initially.

Figure 4.6

The Production Possibilities for a Hypothetical Society

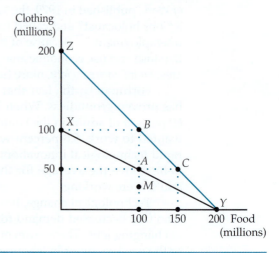

In complex, modern societies, the *actual* mix of food and clothing produced can be decided by the government, by the market, or by some combination of the two. At one extreme, a centralized governmental bureaucracy could mandate how much food and clothing are to be produced; at the other, the decision could arise from the market interactions between consumers (demand) and producers (supply). Of course, even in a market setting, government could influence the mix of food and clothing produced—through taxes, subsidies, or regulations that alter the cost or methods of producing food and/or clothing.

Whatever the decision-making process, we normally assume that a society would want to choose a mix of food and clothing that lies *on* the production possibilities curve rather than a mix that lies *below* the curve. If, for example, a society were to choose the combination of food and clothing represented by point *M* in Figure 4.6, it would not be producing as much food or clothing as it could, given its technology and resources. In short, its resources would be under-utilized, and its consumers would not have available to them all the goods these resources would allow. Let us start our analysis, then, by supposing that the society depicted in Figure 4.6 chooses point *A* along *XY* and produces 100 million units of food and 50 million of clothing.

Now, imagine that someone invents a device that doubles the speed of the sewing process, making it possible to produce twice as much clothing with any level of inputs. Thus, if all resources were devoted to the production of clothing, this new device would permit the production of 200 million units of clothing (point *Z*)—a large increase over the old level of 100 million units. However, the new device does nothing to enhance the production of food, so if all resources were devoted to the production of food, this society could still produce only 200 million units of food. The new set of production possibilities is depicted by the blue line (ZY) in Figure 4.6.

Looking at Figure 4.6, it is obvious that the new technological invention expands the consumption possibilities for those in this society. They might choose to keep half of their resources allocated to food production and half to clothing production; if so, they could consume the same 100 million units of food but increase their clothing consumption from 50 to 100 million units (see point B in Figure 4.6). Alternatively, they could choose to keep clothing consumption at 50 million units, which with the new device now would require only 25 percent of society's resources to produce, and devote 75 percent of their inputs to food; food production would then increase from 100 to 150 million units (see point C in the figure). Finally, instead of keeping the production of one good constant and increasing the other, they could choose to allocate inputs so that *more of both goods are produced* (see all the points between B and C).

Obviously, choosing any point other than B involves a reallocation of labor and capital between the food and clothing industries. Even if society were to continue allocating half of its resources to each industry, however, the new sewing technology might change the occupational requirements in the clothing industry—requiring that workers in that industry learn new skills or accept different employment conditions. The faster and more smoothly these inter- and intraindustry changes occur, the faster the move from the initial point on XY to a new point on ZY. For a society to *actually* obtain the increased production made possible by technological change, then, it must have policies or institutions that promote (or at least permit) the mobility of capital and labor.

To this point, our analysis of the effects of technological change has demonstrated that such change makes it possible for society to obtain more goods and services from its limited resources, thus potentially increasing average consumption per capita.[23] But would greater *average* consumption levels be enough to guarantee that society *as a whole* gains from technological change? To answer this question, we must return to some principles of both positive and normative analysis introduced in chapter 1.

Economic theory assumes that individuals, as both workers and consumers, are attempting to maximize their utility. Furthermore, we usually assume utility is enhanced when individuals are able to consume more goods or services (including leisure; see footnote 22). Thus, one might think that when technological change increases the *average* consumption per capita, economic theory leads us to say that society has been made better off—but this is not completely correct.

---

[23]For ease of illustration, we have confined our analysis to the two goods of food and clothing—but the analysis and its conclusions are unaffected if we consider a society in which people can consume many goods or services, including *leisure* (see chapter 6).

EMPIRICAL STUDY

ESTIMATING THE LABOR DEMAND CURVE: TIME SERIES DATA AND COPING WITH "SIMULTANEITY"

When a proposed labor market policy increases the cost of labor, we frequently want economists to tell us more than "It will reduce employment." We want to know *how much* employment will be affected! Thus, for practical purposes, it is very helpful to have estimates of the elasticity of demand for labor.

Estimating the elasticity of demand for labor is actually very difficult, which helps account for how few studies of demand elasticity were cited in Table 4.1. First, we can obtain credible estimates only if we have data on wages and employment for groups of workers who are reasonably homogeneous in terms of their job requirements, their substitutability with capital, and the characteristics of product demand facing their employers. Given the diversity of firms that hire workers in a given occupation (security guards, for example, are hired by retailers, schools, and movie stars), homogeneity often requires analyzing groups so narrow that data are very difficult to obtain.

A second problem in estimating labor demand curves is that wages and employment are determined *simultaneously* by the interaction of supply and demand curves, and both curves show a (different) relationship between wages and employment. If we gather data just on wage and employment levels, we will not be able to tell whether we

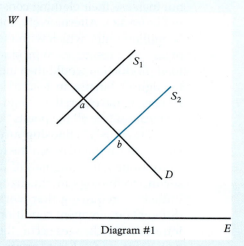

Diagram #1

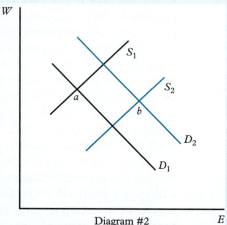

Diagram #2

are estimating a demand curve, a supply curve, or neither! Consider Diagrams #1 and #2, which show wage (*W*) and employment (*E*) outcomes in the market for an occupation.

What we hope to do is illustrated in Diagram #1. There, the labor demand curve remains unchanged, but the supply curve shifts for some reason. All that is observed by the researcher are points *a* and *b*, but connecting them traces out the demand curve (of course, credible estimates would require many more than two observations).

Thus, if the demand curve is not shifting, we can "identify" it if we can observe a shifting supply curve. In reality, however, both supply and demand curves can shift over time (see Diagram #2). When both shift, drawing a line between points *a* and *b* traces out neither a supply nor a demand curve. How can we identify the demand curve when both are likely to be shifting?

First, we must have access to variables that cause the demand curve to shift; if we can *control* for factors that shift the demand curve over time, we—in a statistical sense—can shift it back to its original position and create a situation like that in Diagram #1.

Second, for the condition in Diagram #1 to be met, we must also find at least one variable that *shifts the supply curve but does not affect demand*. (Some variables, like real income levels, can theoretically affect both labor demand *and* labor supply curves. If all our "shift" variables are expected to affect both curves, we are back in the situation depicted by Diagram #2, where we cannot distinguish between the two curves!)

A study of the demand for coal miners in Britain (cited at the bottom of Table 4.1) offers an example of how to estimate a labor demand curve for a specific occupation. The occupation is found in one industry, which is very homogeneous in terms of product demand and employer technology, and time-series data on wages and employment were available for several years (the study used data from the 1950–1980 period). The researchers were able to gather data on factors that were expected to shift the labor demand curve (the price of oil, for example, which is a substitute for coal in generating electricity). They also had access to data on variables that were expected to shift the supply curve—including those (such as wages in alternative jobs miners might choose) that were expected to shift *only* the supply curve. The researchers were thus able to identify the labor demand function, and their use of regression analyses suggested that the labor demand elasticity (of employment changes with respect to wage changes) in British coal mining was −1.0 to −1.4.

Source: Alan A. Carruth and Andrew J. Oswald, "Miners' Wages in Post-War Britain: An Application of a Model of Trade Union Behaviour,"*Economic Journal* 95 (December 1985): 1003–1020.

Consider an (admittedly extreme) case in which the sole beneficiary of technological change is society's richest person, who makes $100 billion per year, and the costs fall on one million low-wage workers, who each make $16,000 per year. If the rich person gains $5 billion from technological change, while costs of $4,000 fall on each of the one million low-wage workers (for a total of $4 billion in costs), society as a whole gains $1 billion in overall consumption. However, as explained below, this $1 billion gain could be associated with *a loss in overall utility* in society.[24]

The gain to the rich person in our example represents 5 percent of his or her annual income, and with such a huge income to begin with, the addition of $5 billion may not add much to this person's utility. The loss of $4,000 per worker for each of one million workers is equal to 25 percent of their annual income, and the associated loss of utility may—in the aggregate—be larger than the relatively small gains to the rich person. The only way to ensure that society as a whole gains (in terms of *utility*) in this case is to require the gainer to compensate all the losers. If the person who gained were required to distribute $4 billion of the gains to those who bore the costs of change, the workers would end up being no worse off, and the gainer would still be ahead because of the $1 billion he or she gets to keep. Thus, after the compensation of losers takes place, a normative condition put forth in chapter 1 would hold: some would gain from technological change, and no one would lose.

To restate the normative principle outlined in chapter 1, *we can be sure that society gains from any economic transaction—technological change in this case—only when all those who lose from it are fully compensated.* Because most technological change occurs through decisions made by the millions of firms in the marketplace, what is needed to compensate those who lose jobs as a result of these decisions is a broad set of social insurance policies that can assist displaced workers. Unemployment insurance, for example, can support workers during their search for new jobs, and wage supplements of one form or another can minimize their loss of income if they have to take a lower-wage job; training programs can assist with the acquisition of new skills; government employment centers or online "job banks" can help the workers locate job openings; public wage subsidies can be paid to firms that add new workers; and in some countries, the government operates as the "employer of last resort"—putting to work those who cannot find new jobs. While we analyzed wage subsidies to employers in chapter 3, we will analyze the effects of many of these other programs later in this text.

---

[24]See Richard Layard, "Happiness and Public Policy: A Challenge to the Profession," *Economic Journal* 116 (March 2006): C24–33, for a discussion of psychologically based findings that people in wealthy economies are *loss-averse*; that is, their gains in utility from increases in income are smaller than their losses in utility from reduced income.

Review Questions

1. Suppose that the government raises the minimum wage by 20 percent. Thinking of the four Hicks–Marshall laws of derived demand as they apply to a particular industry, analyze the conditions under which job loss among teenage workers in that industry would be smallest.

2. California employers of more than 50 workers are now required to offer paid family leave for workers with newborn children. Under this law, businesses with more than 50 workers are required to hold a job for a worker who goes on paid leave for up to six weeks. When on leave, workers receive 55 percent of their normal pay. What are the likely responses on the demand (employer) side of the labor market? Include in your analysis a consideration of factors that would affect the *size* of these responses.

3. The federal government, in an effort to stimulate job growth, passes a law that gives a tax credit to employers who invest in new machinery and other capital goods. Applying the concepts underlying cross-elasticities, discuss the conditions under which employment gains in a particular industry will be largest.

4. The public utilities commission in a state lifts price controls on the sale of natural gas to manufacturing plants and allows utilities to charge market prices (which are 30 percent higher). What conditions would minimize the extent of manufacturing job loss associated with this price increase?

5. Many employers provide health insurance for their employees, but others—primarily small employers—do not. Suppose that the government wants to ensure that all employees are provided with health insurance coverage that meets or exceeds some standard. Suppose also that the government wants employers to pay for this coverage and is considering two options:

   Option A: An employer not voluntarily offering its employees acceptable coverage would be required to pay a tax of X cents per hour for each labor hour employed. The funds collected would support government-provided health coverage.

   Option B: Same as option A, except that the government-provided coverage would be financed by a tax collected as a fraction of the employer's total revenues.

   Compare and contrast the labor market effects of each of the two options.

6. In 1942, the government promulgated regulations that prohibited the manufacture of many types of garments by workers who did the sewing, stitching, and knitting in their homes. If these prohibitions are repealed so that clothing items may now be made either by workers in factories or by independent contractors doing work in their homes, what effect will this have on the labor demand curve for *factory workers* in the garment industry?

7. Briefly explain how the following programs would affect the elasticity of demand for labor in the steel industry:
   a. An increased tariff on steel imports.
   b. A law making it illegal to lay off workers for economic reasons.
   c. A boom in the machinery industry (which uses steel as an input)—causing production in that industry to rise.
   d. A decision by the owners of steel mills to operate each mill longer than has been the practice in the past.
   e. An increase in the wages paid by employers in the steel industry.
   f. A tax on each ton of steel produced.

8. In 2012, a group in Germany proposed a "wealth tax"—on buildings, machinery and equipment—that would be levied on all employers having at least $1.4 million invested in such assets. Use theory learned in this chapter to analyze the labor-market effects on employees in large German firms, and explain under what conditions German workers would be *worse* off.

Problems

1. The labor demand for math tutors is given by $L_D = 2000 - 5W$. If wages change from $100 to $200, calculate the own-wage elasticity. Is the demand curve elastic, inelastic, or unit elastic at this point?

2. Professor Pessimist argues before Congress that reducing the size of the military will have grave consequences for the typical American worker. He argues that if 1 million individuals were released from the military and were instead employed in the civilian labor market, average wages in the civilian labor market would fall dramatically. Assume that the demand curve for civilian labor does not shift when workers are released from the military. *First*, draw a simple diagram depicting the effect of this influx of workers from the military. *Next*, using your knowledge of (i) the definition of the own-wage elasticity of labor demand, (ii) the magnitude of this elasticity for the economy as a whole, and (iii) the size of civilian employment in comparison with this flood from the military, graph these events and estimate the magnitude of the reduction in wages for civilian workers as a whole. Do you concur with Professor Pessimist?

3. Suppose that the demand for burger flippers at fast-food restaurants in a small city is $L_D = 300 - 20W$, where $L=$ the number of burger flippers and $W=$ the wage in dollars per hour. The equilibrium wage is $4 per hour, but the government puts in place a minimum wage of $5 per hour.
   a. How does the minimum wage affect employment in these fast-food restaurants? Draw a graph to show what has happened, and estimate the effects on employment in the fast-food sector.
   b. Suppose that in the city above, there is an uncovered sector where $L_S = -100 + 80W$ and $L_D = 300 - 20W$, before the minimum wage is put in place. Suppose that all the workers who lose their jobs as burger flippers due to the introduction of the minimum wage seek work in the uncovered sector. What happens to wages and employment in that sector? Draw a graph to show what happens, and analyze the effects on both wages and employment in the uncovered sector.

4. The following table gives the demand for florists at a local flower-selling company.

Points	Wage ($)	Number of Hours
A	20	5
B	15	8
C	10	10
D	8	12
E	5	14

a. Draw the labor demand curve.

b. Calculate the wage elasticity at the given points and indicate whether the curve is elastic, inelastic, or unit elastic.

c. Comment on the change in elasticity along the demand curve.

5. Union A faces a demand curve in which a wage of $4 per hour leads to demand for 20,000 person-hours, and a wage of $5 per hour leads to demand for 10,000 person-hours. Union B faces a demand curve in which a wage of $6 per hour leads to demand for 30,000 person-hours, whereas a wage of $5 per hour leads to demand for 33,000 person-hours.

a. Which union faces the *more* elastic demand curve?

b. Which union will be more successful in increasing the total income (wages times person-hours) of its membership?

6. Calculate the own-wage elasticity of demand for occupations a, b, and c below. E_D and W are the original employment and wage. E'_D and W' are the new employment and wage. State whether the demand is elastic, inelastic, or unitary elastic.

a. $\%\Delta E_D = 5$, $\%\Delta W = -10$

b. $E_D = 50$, $W = 7$
$E'_D = 40$, $W' = 8$

c. $E_D = 80$, $W = 8$
$E'_D = 100$, $W' = 6$

7. When the cost of coffee-making machines fell by 15%, the demand for coffee brewers fell by 8%. Calculate the cross-wage elasticity of demand for coffee brewers in this case. Are they gross substitutes or gross complements?

Selected Readings

Card, David, and Alan B. Krueger. *Myth and Measurement: The New Economics of the Minimum Wage*. Princeton: N.J.: Princeton University Press, 1995.

Cunningham, Wendy. *Minimum Wages and Social Policy: Lessons from Developing Countries*. Washington, D.C.: World Bank, 2007.

Hamermesh, Daniel S. *Labor Demand*. Princeton, N.J.: Princeton University Press, 1993.

Kennan, John. "The Elusive Effects of Minimum Wages." *Journal of Economic Literature* 33 (December 1995): 1950–1965.

Neumark, David, and William L. Wascher. *Minimum Wages*. Cambridge, Mass.: MIT Press, 2010.

"Review Symposium: *Myth and Measurement: The New Economics of the Minimum Wage*, by David Card and Alan B. Krueger." *Industrial and Labor Relations Review* 48 (July 1995).

CHAPTER 5

Frictions in the Labor Market

To this point in our analysis of the labor market, we have treated the cost of labor to employers as having two characteristics. First, we have assumed that the wage rate employers must pay is *given* to them by the market; that is, the supply of labor curve *to a firm* has been assumed to be horizontal (at the market wage). An employer cannot pay less than the going wage because, if it did so, *its workers would instantly quit and go to firms paying the going wage*. Likewise, it can acquire all the labor it wants at the market wage, so paying more would only raise its costs and reduce its ability to compete in the product market (as noted in chapter 3, only firms with product-market monopolies could pay more than they have to and still survive). Individual employers in competitive product markets, then, have been seen as wage takers (not wage makers), and their labor market decisions have involved only *how much* labor and capital to employ.

Second, we have treated all labor costs as *variable*—that is, as being strictly proportional to the length of time the employee works. Variable labor costs, such as the hourly wage rate, recur every period and, of course, can be reduced if the hours of work are reduced. By assuming that all labor costs are variable, we have in effect assumed that firms can instantaneously adjust their labor input and associated costs as market conditions change.

The purpose of this chapter is to consider how the demand for labor is affected when we assume that both workers and firms find it *costly to make changes* to their behavior when demand or supply conditions are altered.

Because higher costs of change, generally speaking, will cause workers and firms to display more resistance to change, economists borrow (loosely) a concept from physics and talk about these costs as causing labor market "frictions." In this chapter, we will analyze the implications of frictions in the labor market. That is, we will explore the implications of assuming that workers find it costly to change employers and that firms find it costly to hire or fire workers.

In the first section, we look at frictions on the *employee* side of the market, analyzing the labor market effects of employee costs when moving among employers. We will see that as the costs to workers of changing employers rise, the hiring decisions *firms* make differ from predictions of the competitive model—especially in the presence of government-mandated wages. We will also briefly investigate the implications of workers' mobility costs for the observed correlations between wages and labor market experience, tenure with one's employer, and unemployment.

In the final three sections of this chapter, we turn to an analysis of costs that *employers* bear when changing the level of employment. We will distinguish between variable labor costs, which are hourly in nature, and "quasi-fixed" costs that are associated only with the *number* of workers hired (including investments that firms make in hiring and training workers). The presence of quasi-fixed costs on the employer side of the market raises interesting questions we will address concerning firms' use of overtime, their decisions to train some workers but not others, who is laid off during business downturns, the relationship between pay and productivity, and the effects on job growth of employment-protection laws.

Frictions on the Employee Side of the Market

In this section, we first analyze a major implication of assuming employees can move among employers in a costless way and the evidence *against* this implication. We then build a model of wage and employment decisions based on the assumption that employee mobility is costly, and we explore the labor market predictions of this model.

The Law of One Price

The simple model of the labor market based on the assumption of costless employee mobility among employers has a powerful, and testable, prediction: *workers who are of equal skills within occupations will receive the same wage.*[1] This implication is known as the "law of one price," and it rests squarely on the assumption that workers can move from employer to employer without delay

---

[1]This prediction should be qualified by adding "if they are working in similar environments." As we will discuss in chapter 8, we do expect that similar workers will be paid differently if they are working in cities with different costs of living, say, or if some work in more dangerous or unpleasant settings than others.

and without cost. If a firm currently paying the market wage were to attempt to pay even a penny less per hour, this model assumes that it would instantly lose all its workers to firms paying the going wage. Furthermore, because an employer can obtain all the labor it wants at the going wage, none would get any advantage from paying more than the market. Thus, the market will assure that all workers with the same skill set will receive the same wages.

The problem with this prediction is that it does not seem to be supported by the facts. For example, how are we to explain that registered nurses in Albany, Madison, and Sacramento—all medium-sized state capitals with very comparable costs of living—received, on average, hourly wages of $27.98, $33.93, and $53.37 (respectively) in 2012?[2] We may also question how the market could permit the wages of payroll and timekeeping clerks in *employment services firms* to average, at $17.05 per hour, 14 percent less than their counterparts working for *insurance carriers*.[3]

If workers were completely mobile across employers, these geographic, inter-firm, or cross-industry wage differentials within occupations could not be maintained (unless, as we note in footnote 1, the working conditions at high-paying and low-paying firms are very different). Workers in these occupations who found themselves in low-wage firms would quit and move to the higher-wage firms, even if it meant changing the area in which they live or the industry in which they work. The fact that these wage differences are observed suggests that *worker mobility is costly* and, therefore, limited in some way.

It takes time and effort for nurses in Albany, for example, to find out that wages are higher in Sacramento—and once having found out, they will find it costly to apply, interview, move across country, and leave their friends and relatives in Albany. Similar costs will be borne by workers who may be candidates to move within the area in which they live to firms or industries paying higher wages; they must first go to the trouble of acquiring information and then bear the costs of applying and moving to a new employer.

Some of these mobility costs are monetary in nature (printing résumés, buying clothes for interviewing, hiring movers), but all employment changes also involve nonmonetary costs: the expenditure of time for completing applications

---

[2]U.S. Department of Labor, Bureau of Labor Statistics, *Occupational Employment Statistics*, http://www.bls.gov/oes/current/oessrcma.htm.

[3]U.S. Department of Labor, Bureau of Labor Statistics, *Occupational Employment Statistics*, http://www.bls.gov/oes/current/oessrci.htm. For more careful studies of intra-occupational wage differences and the law of one price, see Stephen Machin and Alan Manning, "A Test of Competitive Labor Market Theory: The Wage Structure among Care Assistants in the South of England," *Industrial and Labor Relations Review* 57 (April 2004): 371–385; V. Bhaskar, Alan Manning, and Ted To, "Oligopsony and Monopsonistic Competition in Labor Markets," *Journal of Economic Perspectives* 16 (Spring 2002): 155–174; Dale T. Mortensen, *Wage Dispersion: Why Are Similar Workers Paid Differently?* (Cambridge, Mass.: Massachusetts Institute of Technology, 2003); and Samuel Berlinski, "Wages and Contracting Out: Does the Law of One Price Hold?" *British Journal of Industrial Relations* 46 (March 2008): 59–75.

and interviews, giving up valued nonwage benefits on one's current job (flexible scheduling, specific job duties, employer location, opportunities to socialize with colleagues),[4] and the stress of leaving the "known" for a new place of employment. It is important to note that workers are likely to differ in how they evaluate these nonmonetary costs, so some will find moving more aggravating (costly) than others.

Assuming that worker mobility is costly has profound theoretical implications rooted in the shape of the labor supply curve to individual employers. Instead of being horizontal, as assumed earlier, *the supply of labor curve to firms becomes upward sloping when employee mobility is assumed to be costly.* Consider the relationship shown by the solid line in Figure 5.1. If Firm A is paying, say, $9.25 per hour and decides to raise its wage to $9.50, it could increase the number of workers willing to work for it from E_0 to E_H. The higher wage would attract workers from other firms whose costs of moving are relatively low, and it would reduce the chances that any of its current employees will leave; however, this wage increase is unlikely to attract *all* the other workers in the market because some would find it too costly to change employers for this modest pay increase. Likewise, if Firm A were to reduce its wage to $9.00, the number of workers it can attract might go down to E_L, as it is probable that it would lose some of its current workers but unlikely (because of mobility costs) that it would lose them all. The supply curve traced out by these responses to Firm A's wage changes would look like the solid line in Figure 5.1.

Figure 5.1

The Supply of Labor to Firm A: Worker-Mobility Costs Increase the Slope of the Labor Supply Curve Facing Individual Employers

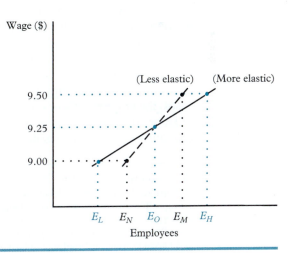

---

[4]For a theory of monopsonistic competition based on different preferences among employees for nonwage benefits, see V. Bhaskar and Ted To, "Minimum Wages for Ronald McDonald Monopsonies: A Theory of Monopsonistic Competition," *Economic Journal* 109 (April 1999): 190–203.

How would *increased* costs of mobility affect the labor supply curve facing Firm A? With higher mobility costs, wage increases would yield *smaller* increases in labor supply, and wage decreases would result in *smaller* reductions in labor supply. To fix ideas, let us return to Figure 5.1. Suppose that a wage increase to $9.50 had increased supply to the firm only to E_M and that a decrease to $9.00 would reduce labor supply only to E_N. The labor supply curve these responses would generate is shown by the dashed-line curve in Figure 5.1, which is steeper—or less elastic—than the solid one (the elasticity of a labor supply curve is defined as the percentage change in labor supplied divided by the percentage change in the wage offered).

Thus, the higher workers' mobility costs are, the steeper the labor supply curve facing a firm will tend to be. Conversely, as mobility costs fall, other things equal, the labor supply curve to firms will flatten and become more elastic. It is in the special case of zero mobility costs that the labor supply curve to individual firms becomes horizontal—and thus infinitely elastic—at the market wage. Interestingly, several recent studies of how the wage paid by a firm affects its employees' likelihood of quitting, as well as its ability to recruit new applicants, suggest labor supply elasticities to individual employers that are far from infinite in magnitude.[5]

Monopsonistic Labor Markets: A Definition

Economists describe the presence of upward-sloping labor supply curves to *individual employers* as creating *monopsonistic* conditions in the labor market. Explaining why we use this terminology takes us back to chapter 2 and the distinction between supply of labor curves to a *market* as opposed to individual firms in the market.

A labor market monopsonist is, strictly speaking, a firm that is the only buyer of labor in its labor market: a coal mine in an isolated small town in West Virginia, for example, or a pineapple plantation on a tiny Hawaiian island. In both these cases, the employer faces (as the only employer in the market) the *market* supply of labor curve, which we noted in chapter 2 is upward-sloping. For example, if a coal mine operator in an isolated town wants to expand its labor supply, it cannot

---

[5]An entire issue of the *Journal of Labor Economics* 28 (April 2010) was devoted to articles on monopsonistic conditions in labor markets. Especially relevant to estimates of the labor supply curve facing employers are the articles by Douglas O. Staiger, Joanne Spetz, and Ciaran S. Phibbs, "Is There Monopsony in the Labor Market? Evidence from a Natural Experiment" (pp. 211–236); Torberg Falch, "The Elasticity of Labor Supply at the Establishment Level" (pp. 237–266); and Michael R. Ransom and David P. Sims, "Estimating the Firm's Labor Supply Curve in a 'New Monopsony' Framework: Schoolteachers in Missouri" (pp. 331–356). The introduction to the issue by Orley C. Ashenfelter, Henry Farber, and Michael R. Ransom, "Modern Models of Monopsony in Labor Markets: A Brief Survey" (pp. 203–210) provides an excellent synopsis of the papers. For a more recent test of monopsonistic conditions in a particular labor market, see Jordan Matsudaira, "Monopsony in the Low-Wage Labor Market? Evidence from Minimum Nurse Staffing Regulations,"*Review of Economics and Statistics* (forthcoming).

simply get workers at the going wage from competing mines in the local area (there are none). Instead, it will have to increase wages to (a) attract miners who must move in from out of town; (b) attract workers from other occupations whose preferences were such that, at the old, lower mining wage, they preferred to work at a job that was less dangerous or dusty; or (c) induce people currently out of the labor force to seek paid employment.

In chapter 3, we first developed the labor demand curve under the twin assumptions that both product and labor markets were competitive. Toward the end of the chapter, we briefly analyzed how *product-market* monopolies (only one *seller* of a product) affect the demand for labor, but we deferred the analysis of conditions under which the *labor market* is not competitive. We now return to our analysis of labor demand and consider the implications when the labor market is not completely competitive—that is, when mobility costs impede workers' entry to, and exit from, various places of employment. We call such labor markets *monopsonistic*.

Before proceeding, however, we must emphasize that when we describe a labor market as monopsonistic, we are not thinking exclusively of the rather rare case of pure monopsony (single employers in isolated places). Indeed, our analysis of monopsonistic labor markets rests *only* on the assumption that *the labor supply curves facing individual employers slope upward* (and are not horizontal). In this analysis, it does not matter *why* these curves slope upward! Being the only employer in town is clearly one cause, but in the prior section, we argued that these curves slope upward because employees find it costly to change jobs—even when there are several potential employers for them in their labor market. Thus, despite the term *monopsonistic*, the analysis that follows applies to labor markets that have many employers in them.

Profit Maximization under Monopsonistic Conditions

Recall from chapter 3 that profit-maximizing firms will hire labor as long as an added worker's marginal revenue product is greater than his or her marginal expense. Hiring will stop when marginal revenue product equals marginal expense. When it is assumed that extra workers can be attracted to the firm at the going wage rate (that is, when labor supply curves to firms are horizontal), then the marginal expense is simply equal to the wage rate. When firms face upward-sloping labor supply curves, however, the marginal expense of hiring labor *exceeds* the wage. Our purpose now is to analyze how both wages and employment are affected when the marginal expense of labor exceeds the wage rate.

Why the Marginal Expense of Labor Exceeds the Wage Rate   We start by considering why an upward-sloping labor supply curve causes the marginal expense of labor to exceed the wage rate. To see this, take the hypothetical example of a start-up firm that must attract employees from other employers. Its potential employees find it costly to change jobs, and for some, the costs are higher than for others. Therefore, the start-up firm faces an upward-sloping labor supply schedule like that represented in Table 5.1. If the firm wants to operate with 10 employees,

Table 5.1

Labor Supply Schedule for a Hypothetical Firm Operating in a Monopsonistic Market

Offered Wage ($)	Supply of Labor	Total Hourly Labor Cost ($)	Marginal Expense of Labor ($)
8	10	80	
9	11	99	19
10	12	120	21
11	13	143	23

it would have to pay $8 per hour, but if it wants to attract 11 employees, it must pay $9—and if it wants 12 workers, it must pay $10 per hour.

Simple multiplication indicates that its hourly labor costs with 10 employees would be $80, but with 11 employees, it would be $99; thus, the *marginal* expense of adding the eleventh worker is $19. If the firm were to operate with 12 workers instead of 11, its hourly costs would rise from $99 to $120, for a marginal expense equal to $21. One can immediately see that the marginal expenses of $19 and $21 are far greater than the wages paid (of $10 and $11).

Why is the marginal expense in this case so much greater than the wage? In moving from 10 to 11 workers, for example, the firm would have to pay one dollar more per hour to each of the 10 it originally planned to hire and then pay $9 to the added worker—for a total of $19 in extra costs. The marginal expense, then, includes the wages paid to the extra worker (as was the case in chapter 3) plus the additional cost of raising the wage for all other workers.[6]

The hypothetical data in Table 5.1 are graphed in Figure 5.2. The (solid) supply curve in Figure 5.2 indicates, of course, the number of employees attracted to the firm at each wage level. In short, it represents, for the firm in question, the *wage it must pay* to get to each of the employment levels it is considering. The dashed line represents the *marginal expense*—the added cost of increasing the employment level by one worker. The marginal expense curve both *lies above* the supply curve and is *steeper in slope* (that is, goes up at a faster rate).[7]

---

[6]We are assuming here that the firm plans to offer its prospective workers the same wage and does not have the ability to find out which of its applicants would work for less. For a fuller discussion of this issue, with some empirical results that support this assumption, see Alan Manning, *Monopsony in Motion: Imperfect Competition in Labor Markets* (Princeton, N.J.: Princeton University Press, 2003), chapter 5.

[7]In the hypothetical example outlined in Table 5.1 and Figure 5.2, the slope of the supply curve is 1; to obtain one more worker, the firm must raise its wage by $1. The slope of the marginal expense curve, however, is 2 (in going from 11 to 12 workers, for example, the marginal expense rises from $19 to $21). In general, it is easy to show (if one knows a bit of calculus) that if the supply curve to a firm is a straight line, the marginal expense curve associated with that supply curve will have a slope that is *twice as steep.*

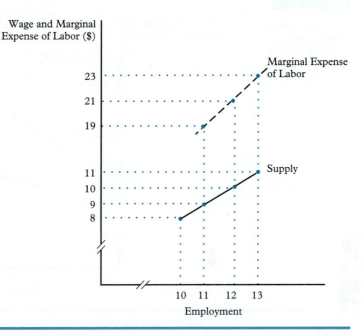

Figure 5.2

A Graph of the Firm-Level
Data in Table 5.1

The Firm's Choice of Wage and Employment Levels

What are the labor market effects caused by having the marginal expense of labor lie above the wage rate? To maximize profits, we know that any firm—including those in monopsonistic markets—should hire labor until the point at which the marginal revenue product of labor (MRP_L) equals labor's marginal expense (ME_L):

$$MRP_L = ME_L \qquad\qquad (5.1)$$

To illustrate the effects of having ME_L exceed the wage (W), we turn to Figure 5.3, which displays, for a given employer, its labor supply curve, the associated marginal expense of labor curve, and the downward-sloping curve depicting the firm's MRP_L.

Any firm in a monopsonistic labor market must make two decisions about hiring. First, like firms in competitive labor markets, it must decide *how much labor to hire*. This decision, consistent with the profit-maximizing criterion in equation (5.1), is made by finding the employment level at which $MRP_L = ME_L$. In Figure 5.3, the profit-maximizing level of employment for the firm shown is E^* because it is at E^* that $MRP_L = ME_L$ (note the intersection of the relevant curves at point X).

Second, the firm must find the *wage rate necessary* to generate E^* employees. In Figure 5.3, the wage rate that will attract E^* workers is W^* (note point Y on the labor supply curve). The firm's labor supply curve represents the relationship between its potential wage rates and the number of workers interested in working

Figure 5.3

Profit-Maximizing
Employment and Wage
Levels in a Firm Facing
a Monopsonistic Labor
Market

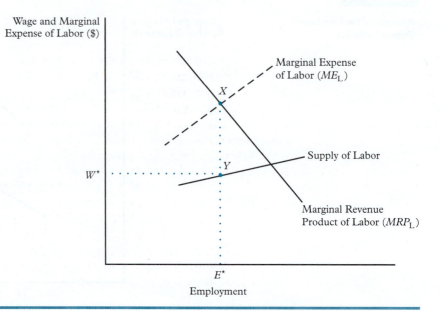

there. Thus, this second decision (about wages) is shown graphically by reading from the labor supply curve the wage needed to attract the profit-maximizing number of workers.

Monopsonistic Conditions and Firms' Wage Policies

A difference between competitive and monopsonistic labor markets that immediately stands out concerns the wage policies of employers. With a competitive labor market, where individual firms are wage takers and can hire all the labor they want at the going wage, employers decide only on the number of workers they want to hire; the wage they pay is given to them by the market. We have seen, however, that firms facing monopsonistic conditions have a second decision to make: they must decide on the wage to pay as well. Further, while firms in competitive labor markets hire until the MRP_L equals the (given) wage, firms in monopsonized markets pay workers a wage less than their marginal revenue product.

The implication that firms in monopsonistic labor markets must have their own wage policies does not suggest, of course, that they set wages without constraints. We saw in the model depicted in Figure 5.3 that the wages they pay are determined both by their MRP_L curve and the labor supply curve they face, and in our simple model, both curves were given to the firm and thus were outside its control. Furthermore (and not illustrated by the figure), firms must make labor market decisions that allow them to remain competitive in their product markets. Thus, monopsonistic conditions do not give firms a completely free hand in deciding on their wages; they must still face constraints imposed by both labor and product markets.

Within the product and labor market constraints facing them, however, different firms in monopsonistic labor markets may well offer different wages to equivalent workers. It is unlikely that the labor supply and MRP_L curves would be exactly the same for different firms in the same labor market; thus, we should not be surprised if exactly comparable workers were to have different marginal productivities and receive different wages at different firms. Thus, a firm employing older equipment and having a lower MRP_L could coexist with one having new equipment and a higher MRP_L by paying a lower wage to the same kind of worker. Indeed, a careful summary of studies on wage differences and the law of one price found strong evidence suggesting that the same worker would receive different pay if he or she worked for different employers.[8]

How Do Monopsonistic Firms Respond to Shifts in the Supply Curve?

In a monopsonistic labor market, the firm does not really have a labor demand curve! Labor demand curves for a firm are essentially derived from sequentially asking, "If the market wage were at some level (say, $5), what would be the firm's profit-maximizing level of employment? If, instead, the wage were $6, what would be the firm's desired level of employment?" Under monopsonistic conditions, the firm is not a wage taker, so asking hypothetical questions about the level of wages facing the firm is meaningless. Given the firm's labor supply curve and its schedule of marginal revenue product (MRP_L at various levels of employment), there is only one profit-maximizing level of employment and only one associated wage rate, both of which are chosen by the firm.

Shifts in Labor Supply That Increase ME_L   Consider the short-run and long-run effects on a monopsonistic firm's desired level of employment if the supply curve facing the firm shifts (but remains upward-sloping). Suppose, for example, that the labor supply curve were to shift to the left, reflecting a situation in which fewer people are willing to work at any given wage level. With the competitive model of labor demand, a leftward shift of a market supply curve would cause the market wage to increase and the level of employment to fall, as employers moved to the left along their labor demand curves. Will these changes in wages and employment occur under monopsonistic conditions?

In Figure 5.4, the MRP_L curve is fixed (we are in the short run), and the leftward shift of the labor supply curve is represented by a movement to curve S' from the original curve S. With a supply curve of S, the firm's marginal expense of labor curve was ME_L, and it chose to hire E workers and pay them a wage of W. When the supply curve shifts to S', the firm's marginal labor expenses shift to a higher curve ME'_L. Therefore, its new profit-maximizing level of employment falls to E', and its new wage rate increases to W'. Thus, with a monopsonistic

---

[8]See Mortensen, *Wage Dispersion*, chapter 1.

Figure 5.4

The Monopsonistic Firm's Short-Run Response to a Leftward Shift in Labor Supply: Employment Falls and Wage Increases

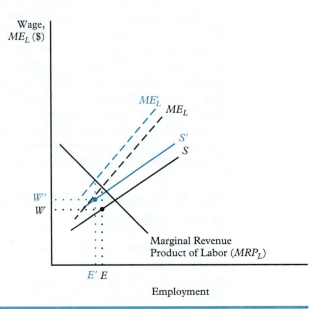

model (just as with the competitive model), a leftward shift in labor supply increases ME_L, raises wages, and reduces firms' desired levels of employment in the short run.

In the long run, labor's increased marginal expense will induce the substitution of capital for labor as firms seek to find the cost-minimizing mix of capital and labor. You will recall that the cost-minimizing conditions for capital and labor under *competitive* conditions were given in equation (3.8c), in which the wage rate was treated as the marginal expense of labor. In a monopsonistic labor market, ME_L exceeds W, so the left-hand side of equation (3.8c) must be written in its general form:

$$ME_L/MP_L = C/MP_K \tag{5.2}$$

Clearly, if a monopsonist is minimizing its costs of production and its ME_L is increased, it will want to restore equality to condition (5.2) by substituting capital for labor. Thus, employment decreases even more in the long run than in the short run.

Effects of a Mandated Wage

Let us next consider what would happen if some nonmarket force were to compel the firm to pay a particular wage rate that was higher than the one it was paying. Would the firm's desired level of employment decline? For a monopsonistic firm's short-run response, refer to Figure 5.5, where the firm initially equates MRP_L and ME_L at point A and chooses to hire E_0 workers, which requires it to pay a wage of W_0.

Figure 5.5

Minimum-Wage Effects under Monopsonistic
Conditions: Both Wages and Employment
Can Increase in the Short Run

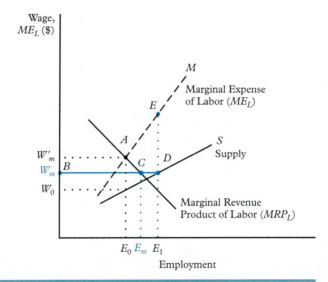

Suppose now that a mandated wage of W_m is set in Figure 5.5. This mandate prevents the firm from paying a wage less than W_m and effectively creates a horizontal portion (BD) in the labor supply curve facing the firm (which is now BDS). The firm's marginal expense of labor curve is now $BDEM$, because up to employment level E_1, the marginal expense of labor is equal to W_m. The firm, which maximizes profits by equating marginal revenue with marginal expense (this equality is now at point C), will hire E_m workers. Even though wages have risen from W_0 to W_m, desired employment rises from E_0 to E_m!

For a monopsonistic firm, then, a mandated wage can simultaneously increase the *average* cost of labor (that is, the wages paid to workers) and reduce ME_L. It is the decrease in *marginal* expense that induces the firm to expand output and employment in the short run. Thus, because an upward-sloping supply curve is converted to one that is horizontal, at least for employment near the current level, it is possible that both wages and employment can increase with the imposition of a mandated wage on a monopsonistic firm. This possibility is subject to two qualifications, however.

First, in the context of Figure 5.5, employment will increase only if the mandated wage is set between W_0 and W'_m. A mandated wage above W'_m would increase ME_L above its current level (W'_m) and cause the profit-maximizing level of employment to fall below E_0. (The student can verify this by drawing a horizontal line from any point above W'_m on the vertical axis and noting that it will intersect the MRP_L curve to the left of E_0.)

Second, Figure 5.5, with its fixed MRP_L curve, depicts only the short-run response to a mandated wage. In the long run, two (opposing) effects on employment are possible. With a mandated wage that is *not too high*, a monopsonistic firm's ME_L is reduced, causing a substitution of labor for capital in the long run. While the monopsonistic firm's *marginal* expense of labor may have fallen, however, labor's *average* cost (the wage) has increased. It is now more expensive to produce the same level of output than before; thus, profits will decline. If it is in a competitive product market, a firm's initial profit level will be normal for that market, so the decline will push its profits below normal. Some owners will get out of the market, putting downward pressure on employment. If this latter (scale) effect is large enough, employment in monopsonistic sectors could fall in the long run if a mandated wage were imposed.

In summary, then, the presence of monopsonistic conditions in the labor market introduces uncertainty into how employment will respond to the imposition of a mandated wage *if* the new wage reduces the firm's marginal expense of labor. Any shift in the supply of labor curve that *increases* the marginal expense of labor, of course, will unambiguously reduce employment.

Monopsonistic Conditions and the Employment Response to Minimum Wage Legislation

At the end of chapter 4, we argued that the estimated responses of employment to increases in the legislated minimum wage presented something of a puzzle. Not all credible empirical studies demonstrate the employment loss predicted by the presence of downward-sloping labor demand curves, and many that do find employment loss tend to show losses that are smaller than we would expect, given the estimates of labor demand elasticities in Table 4.1. Can the presence of monopsonistic conditions in the labor market offer a potential explanation for these findings?

We saw in the previous section that if the labor market is monopsonistic, legislated increases in the minimum wage raise wages but—if modest enough in size—can reduce the marginal expense of labor. Thus, our expectations about the direction of employment changes caused by a higher minimum wage are ambiguous: some firms might experience increases in employment (because ME_L falls), but others might be forced to close because higher total labor costs render their operations nonprofitable.

Our discussion in the previous section might also help explain why the labor demand elasticities presented in Table 4.1 tend to be larger (more elastic) than those implied by many studies of employment responses to minimum-wage changes. The elasticities presented in Table 4.1 were estimated from wage and employment outcomes that were generated by market forces. Graphically, these estimates were derived from analyses like the one presented in Figure 5.4, where a leftward shift in the supply curve unambiguously caused wages to rise and employment to fall. Increases in the minimum wage cause a very different set of responses, as we saw when comparing Figures 5.4 and 5.5. If monopsonistic conditions exist, then theory leads us to expect that employment responses to wage changes generated by *market* forces might be different from employment responses to *legislated* wage increases.

Is it credible to assert that monopsonistic conditions might be what underlie the small or uncertain direction of employment changes we find in minimum wage studies? Most of these studies focus on teenagers, and one might think that teenagers could move almost without cost from one part-time job to another. If mobility is virtually costless for teenagers, they would freely move among employers in response to small wage differentials, the teenage labor market would correspond closely to the competitive model, and we would have to look elsewhere for an explanation of the uncertain estimated effects of minimum wages on teenage employment.

We have argued that mobility is hindered (made more costly) by imperfect information about alternative wage offers and job requirements, by the time and aggravation of applying and being evaluated, and by the necessity of giving up valued nonwage job characteristics that might be difficult to replace in the new job. Teenagers, as well as adults, face these categories of cost. Moreover, teenagers often take jobs with the intent of staying only a short time, and they may perceive the total gains from going to a higher-paying employer as too small to justify the investment of time and effort needed to change employers. Thus, it is not inconceivable that the supply curves to firms that typically employ teenagers (fast-food outlets, for example) are upward-sloping and that monopsonistic conditions prevail even in these places.

Job Search Costs and Other Labor Market Outcomes

The presence of job mobility costs for workers means that they must make decisions about when to search for a new employer (and incur the costs of search) and when to stay put. These decisions about search have some interesting implications that can help explain why wages rise with both labor market experience and the length of time (tenure) with a particular employer. Other reasons why wages rise with experience and tenure will be discussed later in the text; however, our current discussion of job search costs warrants attention to these implications here. We will also discuss how job search costs affect decisions by those who are unemployed.

Wage Levels, Luck, and Search
We have seen that employee mobility costs can create monopsonistic conditions that result in pay differences among workers who have equal productive capabilities. Monopsonistic conditions, however, are not the sole cause of wage differences for workers who appear to be similar. Indeed, we will spend much time later in this text analyzing wage differences associated with job or worker characteristics that are often not easily measured or observed: different working conditions (chapter 8), different on-the-job training requirements or opportunities (chapter 9), and different ways to use pay in creating incentives for productivity (chapter 11). In addition, we will also analyze wage differences related to racial, ethnic, or gender differences that may be unrelated to productive characteristics (chapter 12).

What the theory of monopsonistic labor markets offers to the analysis of wage differences, however, is the implication that to some extent, a worker's wage depends on luck. Some workers will be fortunate enough to obtain a job offer from a high-paying employer, and some will not. Furthermore, given the costs of changing employers, the mobility from low-wage to high-wage firms may never be great or rapid enough to bring wages into equality.

When workers who may think they can get improved job offers face costs in searching for employers, we are naturally drawn to thinking about an employee–employer "matching" process that occurs over a period that may be lengthy. Workers can be viewed as wanting to obtain the best match possible but finding that there is a cost to getting better matches. Those who see their jobs as a poor match (perhaps because of low pay) have more incentives to search for other offers than do workers who are lucky enough to already have good matches (high wages). Over time, as the unlucky workers have more opportunity to acquire offers, matches for them should improve—but, of course, at some wage levels, likely wage increases from a search are so small (or, given the worker's expected stay on the job, so short-lived) that further search is not worth the cost.

Labor-market studies have observed that workers' wages tend to increase both with (1) overall labor market experience *and*, (2) holding labor market experience constant, the length of time with one's employer ("job tenure").[9] Job search considerations may play a role in producing these patterns, and we will briefly discuss them here.

Wages and Labor Market Experience

One of the things that make job searches costly is that it takes time and effort to obtain job offers. Furthermore, job openings occur more or less randomly over time, so that during any one period in which a worker is "in the market," not all potentially attractive openings even exist. As time passes, however, jobs open up and workers have a chance to decide whether to apply. Those who have spent more time in the labor market have had more chances to acquire better offers and thus improve upon their initial job matches. While other explanations are explored in chapter 9, the costs of job searches offer one explanation for why we observe that, in general, *workers' wages improve the longer they are active in the labor market.*

Wages and Job Tenure

With costly job searches, workers who are fortunate enough to find jobs with high-paying employers will have little incentive to continue searching, while those who are less fortunate will want to search again. This means that the workers who have been with their firms the longest will tend to be the ones who got higher wages to begin with, and we should therefore observe a positive correlation between tenure and earnings. Indeed, as noted earlier, empirical studies also find that among workers with the same skills and labor market

---

[9]Manning, *Monopsony in Motion*, chapter 6.

experience, *those who have longer job tenure with their employers also tend to have higher wages.* While there are other potential explanations for this relationship as well (see chapters 9 and 11), the presence of costly job search suggests that it may not simply be longer tenures that cause higher wages; rather, higher wages can also cause longer job tenures!

Job Search Costs and Unemployment   Job search costs can also help to explain the existence (and level) of unemployment. While we analyze unemployment in chapter 14, the relationship between search costs and the phenomenon of unemployment is important to introduce at this point. Briefly put, searching for job offers is something that the unemployed must do, and the search process will take time and effort. The longer it takes for a worker to receive an acceptable offer, the longer the unemployed worker will remain unemployed. Thus, higher job search costs will tend to lengthen the spells of unemployment and hence increase the unemployment rate.[10]

Monopsonistic Conditions and the Relevance of the Competitive Model

If employee mobility costs mean that monopsonistic conditions exist in the typical labor market, does this imply that the competitive model is irrelevant or misleading? While we have seen that the competitive model does indeed offer predictions that are at least partially contradicted by the evidence, it is difficult to believe that it is irrelevant, especially in the long run.

The major difference between the competitive and monopsonistic models, of course, is the assumption about employee mobility costs. When we consider workers as a group, however, mobility costs are likely to be higher in the near term than over the long haul. It is relatively costly, for example, for a registered nurse with a family established in Albany to move herself and her family to Sacramento. Likewise, an established payroll clerk working with an employment agency may find it aggravating or time-consuming to search for, and then move to, a similar job in the furniture industry. It is much less costly, however, for a recent graduate or immigrant who is trying to decide where in the country to locate, or in which industry to work, to "move among" job offers. Recent graduates or immigrants have to search and make a decision anyway (established workers often do not), and when choosing among offers, they have much less to give up in terms of established relationships by taking one offer over the other. As time passes, those established in jobs retire and are replaced by new workers who see the advantages of locating in certain areas or accepting work in certain industries; thus, over time, we would expect wage differences owing to luck to dissipate—even if mobility costs are present in the short term. One study, for

---

[10]See Manning, *Monopsony in Motion*, chapter 9, for a discussion of job search and unemployment.

example, found that new immigrants to the United States are more likely to be clustered in states offering the highest wages for their skill groups and that their presence has helped to narrow regional wage differences.[11]

It is also the case that, monopsonistic conditions notwithstanding, employers cannot deviate too far from the market when setting wages, for if they do, they will encounter problems in attracting, retaining, and motivating their workers (a topic to which we will return in chapter 11). Nobel laureate Paul Samuelson put the issue this way in his bestselling economics textbook:

> Just because competition is not 100 per cent perfect does not mean that it must be zero. The world is a blend of (1) competition and (2) some degree of monopoly power over the wage to be paid. A firm that tries to set its wage too low will soon learn this. At first, nothing much need happen; but eventually, it will find its workers quitting a little more rapidly than would otherwise be the case. Recruitment of new people of the same quality will get harder and harder, and slackening off in the performance and productivity of those who remain on the job will become noticeable.[12]

Frictions on the Employer Side of the Market

Employers also face frictions in searching for and hiring employees. These frictions cause firms to bear costs that are associated with the number of workers hired rather than the hours they work, and they are called "quasi-fixed" costs because they are either difficult or impossible to cut in the short run—unlike variable costs (such as hourly wages), which can be readily cut by reducing the hours of work. The presence of quasi-fixed costs slows the adjustment of employment levels to changing market conditions faced by firms. The types of quasi-fixed costs are first discussed in this section, and we then move to an analysis of their implications for the labor market behavior of firms.

Categories of Quasi-Fixed Costs

Employers often incur substantial quasi-fixed costs in hiring and compensating their employees. In general, these costs fall into two categories: *investments* in their workforce and certain *employee benefits*. We discuss each type of quasi-fixed costs next.

Labor Investments   When an employer has a job vacancy, it must incur certain costs in finding a suitable employee to hire. It has to advertise the position, screen applications, interview potential candidates, and (in the case of highly

---

[11]George Borjas, "Does Immigration Grease the Wheels of the Labor Market?" *Brookings Papers on Economic Activity* (2001): 69–119.

[12]Paul A. Samuelson, *Economics: An Introductory Analysis* (New York: McGraw-Hill, 1951): 554.

EXAMPLE 5.1

Does Employment Protection Legislation Protect Workers?

Many European countries have adopted employment protection policies that make it more costly for employers to dismiss employees. These policies contain provisions for determining when dismissal is "unjustified" or "unfair," and some (as in Greece) go so far as saying that neither lack of business nor lack of competence is a justifiable reason for dismissal. While many countries have policies that do not go that far—requiring only that firms attempt to transfer or retrain candidates for dismissal—the severance pay required when dismissals are considered "unjust" is frequently in the range of 8 to 12 months of pay.

Procedural inconveniences to employers, such as the need to notify or obtain the approval of third parties (labor unions, for example) and the rights of employees to challenge dismissal in a legal setting, are also part of these laws; additional procedures and delays are imposed on employers wanting to make collective layoffs. Finally, these policies also regulate and restrict the use of temporary employees or employees on fixed-length contracts, because use of these employees is seen as a way around the goal of employment protection.

A study that rated the strictness of each country's employment-protection laws found that those with the strictest laws did indeed have lower movements of workers from employment into unemployment. That is, stronger employment protection policies do reduce layoffs. However, the stronger these policies are, the slower the flow out of unemployment, because the costs of these policies also inhibit employers from creating new jobs. While the reduced flows both into and out of unemployment tend to have offsetting effects on the overall unemployment rate, the study did find that stricter employment protection is associated with more *long-term* unemployment and *lower employment levels for women and youth.*

Source: OECD Employment Outlook: 2004 (Paris: Organisation for Economic Co-operation and Development, 2004), chapter 2; and Lawrence M. Kahn, "The Impact of Employment Protection Mandates on Demographic Temporary Employment Patterns: International Microeconomic Evidence," *Economic Journal* 117 (June 2007): F333–F356. For a study finding productive benefits to laws that protect workers' jobs, see Viral Acharya, Ramin Baghai, and Krishnamurthy Subramanian, "Wrongful Discharge Laws and Innovation," *Review of Financial Studies* (forthcoming).

sought applicants) "wine and dine" the worker selected. A 1982 survey, for example, which was weighted toward employers hiring less-skilled workers, found that even for these vacancies, almost 22 person-hours were spent screening and interviewing applicants.[13] Once hired, there are the additional costs of orienting the new worker and getting him or her on the payroll.

A hiring cost not to be overlooked—especially because it has been the subject of public policy debates—is the cost of *terminating* the worker. Every employee a firm hires might also have to be let go if economic circumstances or job performance require it. As we discuss in Example 5.1, policies that require severance pay or otherwise increase the costs of *ending* the employment relationship thus add to the quasi-fixed costs of *hiring* workers.

---

[13]See John Bishop, "Improving Job Matches in the U.S. Labor Market," *Brookings Papers on Economic Activity: Microeconomics* (1993): 379.

Table 5.2

The Marginal Product of Labor in a Hypothetical Car Dealership (Capital Held Constant)

Activity	Average Hours
Hours of formal instruction by training personnel	19
Hours spent by management in orientation, informal training, extra supervision	59
Hours spent by coworkers in informal training	34
Hours spent by new worker watching others do work	41
Total	153

Source: John Bishop, "The Incidence of and Payoff to Employer Training," Cornell University Center for Advanced Human Resource Studies Working Paper 94–17, July 1994, 11.

In addition to the hiring costs, firms typically provide formal or informal training to both their new and continuing workers. The costs of this training generally fall into three classes:

1. The *explicit* monetary costs of formally employing trainers and providing training materials.
2. The *implicit*, or opportunity, costs of lost production incurred when experienced employees take time to demonstrate procedures to trainees in less-formal settings.
3. The *implicit*, or opportunity, costs of the trainee's time.

A survey in the early 1990s found that in the first 3 months (or 520 hours of work) an employee is with a firm, about 30 percent (153 hours) of his or her time is spent in training. The data from this study, summarized in Table 5.2, also suggest that very little of this training was formal classroom-type instruction; most took place informally at the workstation.[14]

Hiring and training costs can be categorized as *investments* because they are incurred in the present and have benefits (in the form of increased productivity) only in the future. Investments are inherently risky because, once made, the costs are "sunk," and there are no guarantees about future returns. We will analyze the effects of these investments on employer behavior later in this chapter.

Employee Benefits   Besides their direct wage and salary earnings, workers also typically receive nonwage compensation in the form of employer-provided medical and life insurance, retirement plans, vacation days, Social Security payments, and other *employee benefits*. Table 5.3 details the employee benefits received by workers in 2013, and it is important to note that many of these benefits represent

---

[14]For other studies and related references, see Harley Frazis, Maury Gittleman, and Mary Joyce, "Correlates of Training: An Analysis Using Both Employer and Employee Characteristics," *Industrial and Labor Relations Review* 53 (April 2000): 443–462.

Table 5.3

Employee Benefits as a Percentage of Total Compensation, 2013 (Average Hourly Cost in Parentheses)

Legally required payments	7.8	($2.41)
Social Security	5.6	($1.74)
Workers' compensation	1.4	($0.42)
ᵃUnemployment insurance and other	0.8	($0.25)
Retirement	4.7	($1.47)
ᵃEmployment costs based on benefit formulas (defined benefit plans)	2.9	($0.90)
Employer costs proportional to earnings (defined contribution plans)	1.8	($0.57)
ᵃ**Insurance** (medical, life)	9.0	($2.81)
ᵃ**Paid vacations, holidays, sick leave**	7.0	($2.17)
Other	2.4	($0.73)
Total	30.9	($9.59)

ᵃCategory of costs believed by authors to be largely quasi-fixed (see discussion in the text).

Source: U.S. Labor Department, Bureau of Labor Statistics, "Employer Costs for Employee Compensation—March 2013," Table 1, news release USDL: 13-1140 (June 12, 2013).

quasi-fixed costs to the employer. That is, many employee benefits are associated with the number of employees but not with the hours they work.

Most life and medical insurance policies have premiums to the employer that are charged on a per-worker basis and are not proportional to the hours worked. Pay for time not worked (vacation, holidays, and sick leave) also tends to be quasi-fixed. Some pension costs are proportional to hours worked because many employers offer *defined contribution* plans and make payments to a retirement fund for each worker that are proportional to wage or salary earnings. However, some employers have *defined benefit* pension plans that promise pension payments to retirees that are a function of years of service, not hours of work; the costs of these plans are thus quasi-fixed in nature.

In the category of legally required benefits, workers' compensation insurance costs are strictly proportional to hours worked because they are levied as a percentage of payroll, and Social Security taxes are proportional for most employees.[15] However, the unemployment insurance payroll-tax liability is specified to be a percentage (the tax rate) of each employee's yearly earnings up to a maximum level (the taxable wage base), which in 2013 was between $7,000 and $15,000 in over two-thirds of all states.[16] Since most employees earn more than $15,000 per year,

[15]The Social Security payroll-tax liability of employers is specified as a percentage of each employee's earnings up to a maximum taxable wage base. In 2010, this tax was 6.20 percent of earnings up to $106,800 for retirement and disability insurance and 1.45 percent on all earnings for Medicare. Because the maximum earnings base exceeded the annual earnings of most workers, the employer's payroll tax liability is increased when a typical employee works an additional hour per week.

[16]U.S. Department of Labor, Employment and Training Administration, *Comparison of State Unemployment Laws,* January 1, 2013 (http://www.unemploymentinsurance.doleta.gov/unemploy/comparison2013.asp).

having an employee work an additional hour per week will *not* cause any increase in the employer's payroll-tax liability. Therefore, unemployment insurance costs are a quasi-fixed cost to most employers.

In Table 5.3, we have indicated (by a superscript *a*) which nonwage costs are usually of a quasi-fixed nature. The data suggest that almost 20 percent of total compensation costs—or about $12,000 per year for the average full-time worker—are quasi-fixed. The quasi-fixed nature of many nonwage labor costs has important effects on employer hiring and overtime decisions. These effects are discussed in the following section.

The Employment/Hours Trade-Off

The simple model of the demand for labor presented in the preceding chapters spoke to the quantity of labor demanded, making no distinction between the number of individuals employed by a firm and the average length of its employees' workweek. Holding all other inputs constant, however, a firm can produce a given level of output with various combinations of the number of employees hired and the number of hours worked per week. Presumably, increases in the number of employees hired will allow for shorter workweeks, whereas longer workweeks will allow for fewer employees, other things equal.

In chapter 3, we defined the marginal product of labor (MP_L) as the change in output generated by an added unit of labor, holding capital constant. Once we distinguish between the *number* of workers hired (which we will denote by M) and the *hours* each works on average (H), we must think of two marginal products of labor. MP_M is the added output associated with an added worker, holding both capital and average hours per worker constant. MP_H is the added output generated by increasing average hours per worker, holding capital and the number of employees constant. As with MP_L, we assume that both MP_M and MP_H are positive but that they decline as M and H (respectively) increase.[17]

How does a firm determine its optimal employment/hours combination? Is it ever rational for a firm to work its existing employees overtime on a regularly scheduled basis, even though it must pay them a wage premium, rather than hiring additional employees?

Determining the Mix of Workers and Hours   The fact that certain labor costs are not hours-related, while others are, will lead employers to think of "workers" and "hours-per-worker" as two substitutable labor inputs. Thus, the profit-maximizing employer will weigh the cost of producing an added unit of output by hiring more workers against the cost of producing an added unit of output by employing its

---

[17]When the number of employees is increased, the decline in MP_M may be due to the reduced quantity of capital now available to each individual employee. When the hours each employee works per week are increased, the decline in MP_H may occur because after some point, fatigue sets in.

Figure 5.6

The Predicted Relationship between ME_M/ME_H and Overtime Hours

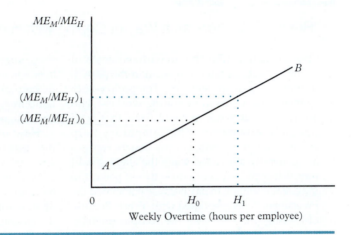

current workers for more hours. Recalling our discussion of equation 3.8c, profit maximization can only be achieved when these two costs are equal. Thus, if the marginal expense of hiring an added worker is ME_M, and the marginal expense of hiring current workers for an extra hour is ME_H, then for profits to be maximized, the following condition must hold:

$$\frac{ME_M}{MP_M} = \frac{ME_H}{MP_H} \tag{5.3}$$

The left-hand side of equation (5.3) is the cost of an added unit of output produced by hiring more workers, and the right-hand side is the cost of an added unit of output produced by hiring workers for more hours.

One implication of equation (5.3) is that if for some reason ME_M rises relative to ME_H, firms will want to substitute hours for workers by hiring fewer employees but having each work more hours. (An alternative to hiring more workers or increasing hours is to "rent" workers; see Example 5.2.) Conversely, if ME_H rises relative to ME_M, the employer will want to produce its profit-maximizing level of output with a higher ratio of workers to average hours per worker. The relationship between ME_M/ME_H and hours of work is graphed in Figure 5.6, which indicates that as ME_M rises relative to ME_H, other things equal, hours of work per employee tend to rise.

Policy Analysis: The Overtime Pay Premium   In the United States, the Fair Labor Standards Act requires that employees covered by the act (generally, hourly paid, nonsupervisory workers) receive an overtime pay premium of at least 50 percent of their regular hourly wage for each hour worked in excess of 40 per week. Many overtime hours are worked because of unusual circumstances that are difficult or impossible to meet by hiring more workers: rush orders,

EXAMPLE 5.2

"Renting" Workers as a Way of Coping with Hiring Costs

One indication that the quasi-fixed costs of hiring are substantial can be seen in the growth of temporary-help agencies. Temporary-help agencies specialize in recruiting workers who are then put to work in client firms that need temporary workers. The temporary-help agency bills its clients, and its hourly charges are generally above the wage the client would pay if it hired workers directly—a premium the client is willing to pay because it is spared the investment costs associated with hiring. Because obtaining jobs through the temporary-help agency also saves employees repeated investment costs associated with searching and applying for available temporary openings, its employees are willing to take a wage less than

they otherwise would receive. The difference between what its clients are charged and what its employees are paid permits the successful temporary-help agency to cover its recruiting and assignment costs.

How anxious are firms and workers to avoid the costs of search and hiring? Some 2 million workers were employed by temporary-help services in 1995, and growth in this industry has been so rapid that it accounted for one-fourth of all employment growth in the United States during the mid-1990s.

Data from: Lewis M. Segal and Daniel G. Sullivan, "The Growth of Temporary Services Work," *Journal of Economic Perspectives* 11 (Spring 1997): 117–136.

absent workers, and mechanical failures are all examples of these emergency situations. However, some overtime is regularly scheduled; for example, over 20 percent of men who are skilled craft workers or technicians usually work more than 44 hours per week.[18]

Given the "time-and-one-half" premium that must be paid for overtime work, we can conclude that employers who regularly schedule overtime do so because it is cheaper than incurring the quasi-fixed costs of employing more workers. Indeed, the production workers most likely to work long hours on a regular basis are those for which hiring and training costs are higher. For example, while over 20 percent of male craft workers are scheduled for more than 44 hours each week, only 12 percent of unskilled males usually work more than 44 hours.[19]

In the fall of 2004, the U.S. Department of Labor introduced several controversial revisions to federal overtime regulations that redefined which jobs are exempt from coverage. Generally speaking, for a job to be exempt from the requirements of overtime pay, the employee must be paid on a salaried basis (not by the hour) and perform administrative, professional, or executive

---

[18]Daniel Hecker, "How Hours of Work Affect Occupational Earnings," *Monthly Labor Review* 121 (October 1998): 8–18.

[19]Dora L. Costa, "Hours of Work and the Fair Labor Standards Act: A Study of Retail and Wholesale Trade, 1938–1950," *Industrial and Labor Relations Review* 53 (July 2000): 648–664, references empirical work on the use of overtime. Also see Hecker, "How Hours of Work Affect Occupational Earnings," 10.

duties. The regulations introduced in 2004 disallowed exemptions for low-paying salaried jobs (paying less than $455 per week), regardless of duties—thus adding overtime coverage to an estimated 1.3 million workers. The new regulations, however, revised the definitions of "administrative," "professional," and "executive" duties and added many computer and outside sales jobs to the list of those exempt from overtime regulations. Also made exempt were jobs in which total pay exceeds $100,000 per year.[20]

These revisions created a storm of public comment and criticism. While they were lauded for giving "greater protection" to low-paid hourly employment, the revisions were also criticized for making it easier to exempt jobs, thus "making it likely that millions of [workers] will work longer hours at reduced pay."[21] We will briefly analyze these two claims using economic theory.

Overtime and Spreading the Work   It is often argued that the time-and-one-half requirement for overtime protects workers by "spreading the work" (creating more job openings) through reduced usage of overtime. One reason to be cautious in our expectations that increased coverage will create more jobs is that applying the overtime premium increases the average cost of labor even if a firm *eliminates* its prior use of overtime! Firms using overtime before *could* have increased their workforce and reduced the use of overtime earlier; the fact that they did not suggests that the quasi-fixed costs of hiring made that a more costly option. If they now eliminate overtime and hire more workers at the same base wage rate, their labor costs will clearly rise. Increased labor costs will tend to reduce both the scale of output and increase firms' incentives to substitute capital for labor, thereby reducing the total labor hours demanded by affected firms. Thus, even if base wages are not changed, it is unlikely that all the reduced overtime hours will be replaced by hiring more workers.

Overtime and Total Pay   Will newly covered workers experience an increase in earnings, and will those in newly exempt jobs experience an earnings decrease as a result of the revisions? It is possible that they will not, because the base wage rate may change in response to changes in overtime coverage.

We have seen that many overtime hours are regularly scheduled, and in these cases, it is possible that employers and employees mutually agree (informally, at least) on a "package" of weekly hours and total compensation. If so, firms that regularly schedule overtime hours might respond to a legislated increase in coverage by reducing the straight-time salary in a way that, after taking the newly required overtime payments into account, would leave total compensation per

---

[20]U.S. Department of Labor, Wage and Hour Division, "Defining and Delimiting the Exemptions for Executive, Administrative, Professional, Outside Sales and Computer Employees: Economic Report," *Federal Register* 69, no. 79, part 2 (April 23, 2004): 22191.

[21]Ross Eisenbrey and Jared Bernstein, "Eliminating the Right to Overtime Pay: Department of Labor Proposal Means Lower Pay, Longer Hours for Millions of Workers," *Economic Policy Institute Briefing Paper* (June 26, 2003): 1.

worker unchanged. Similarly, employees who lose coverage under overtime laws and are asked to work more hours may be unwilling to stay in those jobs—unless, of course, their pay is increased accordingly.

Indeed, one study of wages in the United States found that when mandated overtime premiums rose, base wages tended to fall, most notably in firms that regularly scheduled the most overtime.[22] Another study of the effects of overtime premiums in the United States also found evidence that base wages adjust to mandated changes in these premiums in a way that suggests employers and employees regard hours and pay as a package; this study found that legislated expansions in overtime coverage have had no measurable effect on overtime hours worked.[23]

Training Investments

We have identified employer-provided training as an important investment that can increase the quasi-fixed costs of hiring workers. The costs of training, even if provided by the employer, are often at least partly paid by workers themselves in one way or another, so training investments represent a rather unique friction in the labor market. This section explores the implications of this friction for both employer behavior and employee behavior.

The Training Decision by Employers

Consider an employer who has just hired a new employee. If the employer decides to bear the cost of training this worker, it will incur the explicit and implicit training costs discussed earlier—including, of course, the forgone output of the worker being trained. Thus, in the training period, the employer is likely to be bearing costs on behalf of this new worker that are greater than the worker's marginal revenue product. Under what conditions would an employer be willing to undertake this kind of investment?

As with any investment, an employer that bears net costs during the training period would only do so if it believes that it can collect returns on that investment *after training*. It is the prospect of increased employee productivity that motivates an employer to offer training, but the only way the employer can make a return on its investment is to "keep" some of that added post-training revenue by not giving all of it to the worker in the form of a wage increase.

Put succinctly, for a firm to invest in training, two conditions must be met. First, the training that employees receive must increase their marginal revenue productivity more than it increases their wage. Second, the employees must stay with the employer long enough for the employer to receive the required returns

[22]Anthony Barkume, "The Structure of Labor Costs with Overtime Work in U.S. Jobs," *Industrial and Labor Relations Review* 64 (October 2010): 128–142.

[23]Stephen J. Trejo, "Does the Statutory Overtime Premium Discourage Long Workweeks?" *Industrial and Labor Relations Review* 56 (April 2003): 530–551.

(obviously, the longer the employees stay with the firm, other things equal, the more profitable the investment will be).

The Types of Training

At the extremes, there are two types of training that employers can provide. *General training* teaches workers skills that can be used to enhance their productivity with many employers; learning how to speak English, use a word-processing program, drive a truck, or create Web sites are examples of general training. At the other end of the spectrum is *specific training*, which teaches workers skills that increase their productivity only with the employer providing the training. Examples of specific training include teaching workers how to use a machine unique to their workplace or orienting them to particular procedures and people they will need to deal with in various circumstances they will encounter at work.

General Training   Paying for general training can be a rather risky investment for an employer, for if the employer tries to keep post-training wage increases below increases in marginal revenue productivity, trained workers might leave. Because general training can raise productivity with other employers too, trained workers may have incentives to look for higher wage offers from employers that have no training costs to recoup!

Thus, theory suggests that if employee mobility costs are not very great, employers will be deterred from investing in general training. The likelihood of making back their required returns is low, because the gap between marginal revenue product and the post-training wage might not be sufficiently great, or the expected tenure of the trained workers with the firms sufficiently long, to recoup their investment costs. When worker-mobility costs are low, firms either will not provide the training or will require the employees to pay for it by offering a very low (or, in the case of some interns, a zero) wage rate during the training period.

Recent work, however, finds that firms often *do* invest in general training, a fact that suggests worker mobility among firms is costly—and that the labor market is therefore characterized by monopsonistic conditions. A related possibility is that, while the skills taught to employees are general in nature, the *combinations* of general skills required by particular employers vary markedly, and this variability reduces the transferability of skills among employers.[24]

[24]Edward P. Lazear, "Firm-Specific Human Capital: A Skill-Weights Approach," *Journal of Political Economy* 117 (October 2009): 914–940; Daron Acemoglu and Jörn-Steffen Pischke, "Beyond Becker: Training in Imperfect Labour Markets," *Economic Journal* 109 (February 1999): F112–F142; Mark A. Loewenstein and James R. Spletzer, "General and Specific Training: Evidence and Implications," *Journal of Human Resources* 34 (Fall 1999): 710–733; Laurie J. Bassi and Jens Ludwig, "School-to-Work Programs in the United States: A Multi-Firm Case Study of Training, Benefits, and Costs," *Industrial and Labor Relations Review* 53 (January 2000): 219–239; Edwin Leuven, Hessel Oosterbeek, Randolph Sloof, and Chris van Klaveren, "Worker Reciprocity and Employer Investment in Training," *Economica* 72 (February 2005): 137–149; and Colleen Flaherty Manchester, "General Human Capital and Employee Mobility: How Tuition Reimbursement Increases Retention through Sorting and Participation," *Industrial and Labor Relations Review* 65 (October 2012): 951–974.

Specific Training Employers have stronger incentives to invest in specific training, because such training does not raise the worker's productivity with other firms, and it therefore does not make the worker more attractive to competing employers. While the training itself does not increase the outside offers an employee might be able to receive, a firm undertaking investments in specific training must nevertheless take precautions to keep the trained employee from quitting, because once the employee quits, the employer's investment is destroyed (that is, returns on the investment cannot be realized). Thus, concerns about the possibility that trained employees will quit before the employer can receive its required investment returns exist relative to specific, as well as general, training. These concerns lead us to a discussion of (a) who bears the costs of training and (b) the size of post-training wage increases.

Training and Post-Training Wage Increases

Consider a situation in which worker-mobility costs are relatively low, and the *employer* is considering bearing all the costs of training. With investment costs to recoup, the employer would be unable to raise wages very much after training and still have incentives to invest. We know that higher wages reduce the probability of a worker quitting, so by failing to increase the wage much after training, the employer would put its investment at risk. Trained workers might decide to quit at even a small provocation (the boss is in a bad mood one day, for example, or they are asked to work overtime for a while), and without some assurance that trained employees will stay, the firm would be reluctant to make a training investment for which it bore all the costs.

Conversely, if a firm's *employees* paid for their own training by taking a lower wage than they could get elsewhere during the training period, they would require the benefits of a much higher post-training wage to make employment at the firm attractive. If they were to get all of their improved marginal revenue product in the form of a wage increase, however, an employer that finds it relatively inexpensive to hire and fire workers would have little to lose by firing *them* at the smallest provocation—and if they get fired, *their* investment is destroyed!

Thus, if labor market frictions are otherwise small, the best way to provide incentives for on-the-job training is for employers and employees to *share* the costs and returns of the investment. If *employees* pay part of these costs, the post-training wage can be increased more than if employers bear all the training costs—and the increased post-training wage protects *firms'* investments by reducing the chances trained workers will quit. The training costs borne by *employers* must be recouped by not raising the post-training wage very much, but this condition helps protect *workers'* investments by making it attractive for firms to retain them unless the provocation is major (we discuss the issue of layoffs in more detail a bit later in this chapter). Put differently, if both employers and employees share in the costs of training, and thus share in the returns, they both have something to lose if the employment relationship is ended in the post-training period.

Figure 5.7

Productivity and Wage Growth, First Two Years on Job, by Occupation and Initial Hours of Employer Training

Percentage Increase, Productivity and Wages

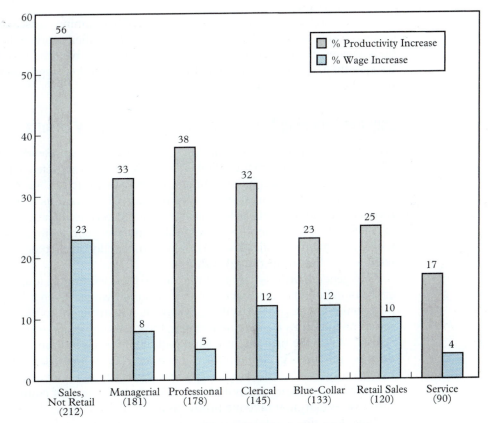

Occupation (Hours of Training in First 3 Months)

Source: John Bishop, "The Incidence of and Payoff to Employer Training," Cornell University Center for Advanced Human Resource Studies, working paper 94–17, July 1994, Table 1.

Empirical studies measuring the wage profiles associated with on-the-job training in the United States, however, suggest that *employers bear much of the costs and reap most of the returns associated with training*. Wages apparently are not depressed enough during the training period to offset the employer's direct costs of training, so subsequent wages increases are much smaller than productivity increases.[25] A survey of employers, summarized in Figure 5.7, estimated that productivity

[25]John Bishop, "The Incidence of and Payoff to Employer Training," Cornell University Center for Advanced Human Resource Studies Working Paper 94–17, July 1994; and Margaret Stevens, "An Investment Model for the Supply of General Training by Employers," *Economic Journal* 104 (May 1994): 556–570.

increases, which generally rose with the hours of initial on-the-job training, were far larger than wage increases over a worker's first two years with an employer. Other studies that directly link the wage profiles of American workers with the amount of training they have received find that post-training wage increases are relatively modest.[26]

The evidence that employers bear much of the training costs, and reap much of the returns, suggests that these employers believe their workers face relatively high worker-mobility costs. These firms are willing to bear the investment costs because they do not feel the need to raise the post-training wage much in order to retain their trained employees.

Employer Training Investments and Recessionary Layoffs

We have seen that employers will have incentives to invest in worker training only when the post-training marginal revenue productivity is expected to be sufficiently above the wage so that the investment returns are attractive. Suppose a firm has made the investment but at some point thereafter finds that its workers' marginal revenue productivity falls below what it expected because of a business downturn (a "recession"). If it cannot lower wages for one reason or another (we will discuss why wages might be inflexible in a downward direction in chapter 14), will the firm want to lay off its trained workers?

In general, firms will not want to lay off their workers as long as the workers are bringing in revenues that are in excess of their wages. Even if the gap between marginal revenue productivity and wage is not sufficient to yield an attractive return on the firm's training investment, those training costs—once incurred—are "sunk." While the firm might wish it had not invested in training, the best it can do after training is get what returns it can. Workers who are laid off clearly bring in no returns to the employer, so its incentives are to retain any worker whose marginal revenue productivity exceeds his or her wage. Of course, if the downturn causes marginal revenue productivity to still fall below the wage rate, firms do have incentives to lay off trained workers (unless they believe the downturn will be very short and do not want to take the risk that the laid-off workers will search for other employment).

The presence of employer training investments, then, offers an explanation for two phenomena we observe in the labor market. *First, as a general rule, we observe that workers who are least susceptible to being laid off during recessions are the*

---

[26]David Blanchflower and Lisa Lynch, "Training at Work: A Comparison of U.S. and British Youths," in *Training and the Private Sector: International Comparisons,* ed. Lisa Lynch (Chicago: University of Chicago Press for the National Bureau of Economic Research, 1994): 233–260; Jonathan R. Veum, "Sources of Training and Their Impact on Wages," *Industrial and Labor Relations Review* 48 (July 1995): 812–826; Alan Krueger and Cecilia Rouse, "The Effect of Workplace Education on Earnings, Turnover, and Job Performance," *Journal of Labor Economics* 16 (January 1998): 61–94; and Judith K. Hellerstein and David Neumark," Are Earnings Profiles Steeper than Productivity Profiles? Evidence from Israeli Firm-Level Data," *Journal of Human Resources* 30 (Winter 1995): 89–112.

most skilled and those with the longest job tenures.[27] Older and more skilled workers are those most likely to have been the objects of past employer training investments, and they therefore tend to enter recessions with larger gaps between marginal revenue product and wage. These gaps cushion any fall in marginal revenue product and provide their employers with stronger incentives to keep on employing them during the downturn. Workers who enter the recession with wages closer to marginal revenue productivity are more likely to find that the downturn causes their marginal revenue product to fall below their wage, and when this occurs, employers may find it profitable to lay them off.

Second, we observe that average labor productivity—output per labor hour—falls in the early stages of a recession and rises during the early stages of recovery. As demand and output start to fall, firms that have invested in worker training respond by keeping their trained workers on the payroll even though their marginal productivity falls. Such "labor hoarding" causes output per worker to fall. Of course, when demand picks up again, firms can increase output without proportionately increasing their employment because, in effect, they have maintained an inventory of trained labor. In the latter situation, output per worker rises.

Hiring Investments

In addition to training employees, firms must also evaluate them when making hiring, placement, and promotion decisions. They may therefore find that training programs—even ones with a "general" component—can be used to help them discover the learning abilities, work habits, and motivation levels of new employees (see Example 5.3).[28] Thus, some of what appears to be general training may actually represent an investment in firm-specific information about employees that will be useful later on in making assignments and deciding on promotions. We conclude this chapter with a section that analyzes hiring and screening investments in greater detail.

The Use of Credentials

Since firms often bear the costs of hiring and training workers, it is in their interest to make these costs as low as possible. Other things equal, firms should prefer to obtain a workforce of a given quality at the least possible cost. Similarly, they should prefer to hire workers who are fast learners, because such workers could be trained at less cost. Unfortunately, it may prove expensive for firms to

---

[27]See Hilary Hoynes, "The Employment, Earnings and Income of Less Skilled Workers over the Business Cycle," in *Finding Jobs: Work and Welfare Reform*, eds. Rebecca Blank and David Card (New York: Russell Sage Foundation, 2000): 23–71.

[28]Margaret Stevens, "An Investment Model for the Supply of General Training by Employers." Also see W. R. Bowman and Stephen L. Mehay, "Graduate Education and Employee Performance: Evidence from Military Personnel," *Economics of Education Review* 18 (October 1999): 453–463.

EXAMPLE 5.3

Why Do Temporary-Help Firms Provide Free General Skills Training?

Temporary-help agencies employ about 3 percent of American workers. They hire workers who are, in effect, "rented out" to client firms, and they make their money by charging clients an hourly fee that exceeds what they pay their employees by 35 percent to 65 percent. Most provide their employees with nominally free training (temp workers are paid during training days), which is given "up front" with no requirement of continued employment. The training is general, focusing on word-processing and other computer skills. Training periods average only 11 hours, but the skills are clearly valuable—one leading company charges $150 per worker per day to provide similar training to its clients' non-temporary workers. Why do these temp agencies give valuable general training to workers who could take their new skills and run?

One economist explains this phenomenon by noting that providing training allows the temp agencies to find lower-paid workers who may lack certain skills but have an aptitude for, and place a value on, learning. The training allows temp agencies to screen such workers and learn about their abilities. How can these agencies capitalize on the information they generate about their trainees?

Many client firms use temp agencies to acquire information on applicants for permanent jobs without having to put much into the quasi-fixed costs of hiring and firing—and, of course, many temp workers are looking for permanent jobs. Indeed, about 15 percent of temporary-help workers are hired for permanent jobs by client firms each month. Temp agencies have thus become a means of providing and auditioning potential permanent workers to their clients, and they are paid primarily as information brokers. Client firms are willing to pay a premium for this information without themselves having to risk an investment, temp workers are willing to take a lower wage for the opportunity to audition for permanent work, and the audition period is long enough for temp agencies to recoup training costs because it takes some time for client firms to make their own evaluations.

Source: David Autor, "Why Do Temporary Help Firms Provide Free General Skills Training?" *Quarterly Journal of Economics* 116 (November 2001): 1409–1448.

extensively investigate the background of every individual who applies for a job to ascertain his or her skill level and ability to undertake training.

One way to reduce these costs is to rely on *credentials*, or *signals*, in the hiring process rather than intensively investigating the qualities of individual applicants.[29] For example, if, *on average*, college graduates are more productive than high school graduates, an employer might specify that a college degree is a requirement for the job. Rather than interviewing and testing all applicants to try to ascertain the productivity of each, the firm may simply select its new employees from the pool of applicants who meet this educational standard.

Such forms of *statistical discrimination*, judging individuals by *group* characteristics, have obvious costs. On the one hand, for example, some high school graduates may be fully qualified to work for a firm that insists on college graduates.

---

[29]See Michael Spence, "Job Market Signaling," *Quarterly Journal of Economics* 87 (August 1973): 355–374. Refer to chapter 9 for a more detailed discussion of signaling.

Excluding them from the pool of potential applicants imposes costs on them (they do not get the job); however, it also imposes costs on the employer *if* other qualified applicants cannot be readily found. On the other hand, there may be some unproductive workers among the group of college graduates, and an employer who hires them may well suffer losses while they are employed. However, if the reduction in hiring costs that arises when *signals* (such as educational credentials, marital status, or age) are used is large, it may prove profitable for an employer to use them even if an occasional unsatisfactory worker sneaks through.

Internal Labor Markets

One of the difficulties in hiring employees is that such personal attributes as dependability, motivation, honesty, and flexibility are difficult to judge from interviews, employment tests, or even the recommendations of former employers. This difficulty has led many larger firms to create an *internal labor market*, in which workers are hired into relatively low-level jobs and higher-level jobs are filled only from within the firm. This policy gives employers a chance to observe *actual* productive characteristics of the employees hired, and this information is then used to determine who stays with the firm and how fast and how high employees are promoted.

The *benefits* of using an internal labor market to fill vacancies are that the firm knows a lot about the people working for it. Hiring decisions for upper-level jobs in either the blue-collar or the white-collar workforces will thus offer few surprises to the firm. The *costs* of using the internal labor market are associated with the restriction of competition for the upper-level jobs to those in the firm. Those in the firm may not be the best employees available, but they are the only ones the firm considers for these jobs. Firms most likely to decide that the benefits of using an internal labor market outweigh the costs are those whose upper-level workers must have a lot of firm-specific knowledge and training that can best be attained by on-the-job learning over the years.[30]

As noted earlier, firms that pay for *training* will want to ensure that they obtain employees who can learn quickly and will remain with them long enough for the training costs to be recouped through the post-training surplus. For these firms, the internal labor market offers two attractions. First, it allows the firm to observe workers on the job and thus make better decisions about which workers will be the recipients of later, perhaps very expensive, training. Second, the internal labor market tends to foster an attachment to the firm by its employees. They know that they have an inside track on upper-level vacancies because outsiders will not be considered. If they quit the firm, they would lose this privileged position. They are thus motivated to become long-term employees of the firm. The full implications of internal labor markets for wage policies within the firm will be discussed in chapter 11.

---

[30]For a detailed discussion of internal labor markets, see Paul Osterman, ed., *Internal Labor Markets* (Cambridge, Mass.: MIT Press, 1984); and George Baker and Bengt Holmstrom, "Internal Labor Markets: Too Many Theories, Too Few Facts," *American Economic Review* 85 (May 1995): 255–259.

EMPIRICAL STUDY

WHAT EXPLAINS WAGE DIFFERENCES FOR WORKERS WHO APPEAR SIMILAR? USING PANEL DATA TO DEAL WITH UNOBSERVED HETEROGENEITY

To test whether the law of one price holds in the labor market, we must test to see if workers who are productively equivalent receive different wages. If we try to use cross-sectional data at one point in time to perform our test, however, we run up against a huge problem: researchers cannot observe all the characteristics that affect worker productivity. For example, we cannot measure how willing a worker is to work overtime with little notice, how pleasant the worker is to customers or coworkers, or whether he or she is a "team player" or has a sunny personality. Without some way to account for worker differences in these characteristics that are important but not directly observed (what economists have come to call "unmeasured worker heterogeneity"), we cannot credibly test to see if the law of one price holds.

To better understand the problem, suppose that we estimate the average relationship between wages employees receive and their measured characteristics by using a sample of cross-section data. We can then use this relationship to derive an expected wage for a particular woman, say, given her age, education, occupation, and other observed qualities. If her actual wage exceeds her expected wage, we do not know if she is merely lucky (and the law of one price does not hold) or if she has unobserved qualities that employers value (and is therefore more productive than average, given her measured characteristics).

Fortunately, there is a way to deal with the problem of unobserved heterogeneity, but it requires undertaking the expense of gathering "panel data"—data that allow for observations on the same individual in two or more years. If we can follow individuals through time, we can analyze how their wages *change* as they move from job to job, employer to employer, or from one educational level to another. If the woman in our example who received a higher-than-expected wage with her first employer now changes jobs and receives an above-expected wage with the next, the likelihood is that she is an above-average producer and did not merely get lucky twice.

Thus, if we can follow individual workers through time, we can control for their unobserved personal productive characteristics ("person effects") by focusing on how the same person's wage varies when some measurable condition (education, occupation, or employer, for example) changes. To understand how the ability to control for person effects influences conclusions about how closely labor market outcomes correspond to predictions concerning the law of one price, consider findings from a 1999 study using panel data from France.

When the relationships between wages and measured worker productive characteristics were analyzed in a cross-section of several million French workers, the researchers found that these measured characteristics could explain only about 30 percent of the variation in wages across the population. This finding seems to suggest that the predictions of the law of one price are badly off! Once person effects (in addition to the measured characteristics) were accounted for using panel data,

however, the researchers were able to account for 77 percent of the variation in French wages. While there is still variation in wages that apparently cannot be explained by employee characteristics (observed and unobserved), the use of panel data permits a more valid test of the law of one price. The findings from using panel data suggest that there may be less variation due to luck than meets the eye.

Source: John M. Abowd, Francis Kramarz, and David N. Margolis, "High Wage Workers and High Wage Firms," *Econometrica* 67 (March 1999): 251–333.

How Can the Employer Recoup Its Hiring Investments?

Whether a firm invests in training its workers or in selecting them, it will do so only if it believes it can generate an acceptable rate of return on its investment. For a labor investment to be worthwhile, an employer must be able to benefit from a situation in which workers are paid less than their marginal value to the firm in the post-investment period. How can employers generate a post-investment surplus from their *hiring* investments?

Suppose that applicants for a job vacancy have average, below-average, or above-average productivity, but the employer cannot tell which without making some kind of investment in acquiring that information. If the firm does not make this investment, it must assume that any particular applicant is of average ability and pay accordingly. If the firm makes an investment in acquiring information about its applicants, however, it could then hire *only* those whose productivity is above average. The surplus required to pay back its investment costs would then be created by paying these above-average workers a wage less than their true productivity.

Would the firm pay its new workers the average wage even though they are above average in productivity, thereby obtaining the full surplus? As with the case of training, the firm would probably decide to pay a wage greater than the average, but still below workers' actual productivity, to increase the likelihood that the workers in whom it has invested will remain. If its workers quit, the firm would have to invest in acquiring information about their replacements.

While the self-interest of employers would drive them to pay an above-average wage to above-average workers, two things could allow the screening firm to pay a wage that is still lower than workers' full productivity. One is the presence of mobility costs among employees. The other is that information one employer finds out through a costly screening process may not be observable by other employers without an investment of their own. Either of these conditions would inhibit employees from obtaining wage offers from competing firms that could afford to pay full-productivity wages because they had no screening expenses to recoup.

Review Questions

1. How do worker-mobility costs affect the slope of labor supply curves to individual firms?

2. Why do upward-sloping labor supply curves to firms cause the marginal expense of labor to exceed the wage rate?

3. Suppose an author argues that output per worker usually grows during the first year of an expansion because firms are slow to hire new labor. Is this argument supported by the theory learned in this chapter?

4. "Minimum wage laws help low-wage workers because they simultaneously increase wages and reduce the marginal expense of labor." Analyze this statement.

5. An author recently asserted that low-wage jobs provide fewer hours of work than high-wage jobs. According to economic theory, is this statement likely to be correct? Why?

6. Workers in a certain job are trained by the company, and the company calculates that to recoup its investment costs, the workers' wages must be $5 per hour below their marginal productivity. Suppose that after training, wages are set at $5 below marginal productivity but that developments in the product market quickly (and permanently) reduce marginal productivity by $2 per hour. If the company does not believe it can lower wages or employee benefits, how will its employment level be affected in the short run? How will its employment level be affected in the long run? Explain, being sure to define what you mean by the short run and the long run!

7. For decades, most large employers bought group health insurance from insurers who charged them premiums on a *per-worker* basis. In 1993, a proposal for a national health insurance plan contained a provision requiring group health insurers to charge premiums based on *payroll* (in effect, financing health insurance by a payroll "tax"). Assuming the *total* premiums paid by employers remain the same, what are the labor market implications of this proposed change in the way in which health insurance is financed?

8. The manager of a major league baseball team argues, "Even if I thought Player X was washed up, I couldn't get rid of him. He's in the third year of a four-year, $24-million deal. Our team is in no position financially to eat the rest of his contract." Analyze the manager's reasoning by using economic theory.

9. The president of France has announced that his government is considering abandoning its 2002 law that placed a cap on the hours that French employees could work each week (French workers were not allowed to work more than 35 hours per week). The reasons for eliminating the cap on weekly hours were listed as "unanticipated adverse consequences" in the areas of skill formation and employment levels. Use economic theory learned in this course to analyze the effects of the hours cap on skill formation and employment levels.

10. The State of North Carolina has a program for state-subsidized training of disadvantaged workers at its community colleges. Employers adding at least 12 jobs can arrange for a community college to provide a program tailored to the individual firm. The college places ads for new hires and screens the applicants, the firms choose whom they want trained from the list supplied by the college, and the college provides the training (using equipment supplied by the firm). Finally, the firm selects employees from among those who successfully complete the training. Trainees are not paid during the training period. Analyze the likely effects on wages, employment, and hours of work associated with adopting this program.

Problems

1. Suppose a firm's labor supply curve is $E = 5W$, where W is the hourly wage.
   a. Solve for the hourly wage that must be paid to attract a given number of workers (E) to the firm.
   b. Express the total hourly labor cost associated with any given level of employment.
   c. Express the marginal expense of labor (ME_L) incurred when hiring an additional worker.

2. Assume that the labor supply curve to a firm is the one given in Problem 1. If the firm's marginal revenue product (MRP_L) $= 240 - 2E$, what is the profit-maximizing level of employment (E^*), and what is the wage level (W^*) the firm would have to pay to obtain E^* workers?

3. A firm is considering hiring a worker and providing the worker with general training. The training costs $1,000, and the worker's MRP_L during the training period is $3,000. If the worker can costlessly move to another employer in the post-training period and that employer will pay a wage equaling the new MRP_L, how much will the training firm pay the worker in the training period?

4. As with the own-wage elasticity of demand for labor, the elasticity of supply of labor can be similarly classified. The elasticity of supply of labor is *elastic* if elasticity is greater than 1. It is *inelastic* if the elasticity is less than 1, and it is *unitary elastic* if the elasticity of supply equals 1. For each of the following occupations, calculate the elasticity of supply, and state whether the supply of labor is elastic, inelastic, or unitary elastic. E_S and W are the original supply of workers and wage. E'_S and W' are the new supply of workers and wage.
   a. $\%\Delta E_S = 7, \%\Delta W = 3$
   b. $E_S = 120, W = \$8$
      $E'_S = 90, W' = \$6$
   c. $E_S = 100, W = \$5$
      $E'_S = 120, W' = \$7$

5. The supply of labor is given in the following table for Teddy's Treats, a dog biscuit company, which is a profit-maximizing monopsonist.

Offered Wage ($)	Supply of Labor (Number of Hours)
4	18
5	19
6	20
7	21
8	22

   a. Calculate the total labor cost and the marginal expense of labor for each level of employment.
   b. Draw the supply of labor curve and the marginal expense of labor curve.

6. Teddy's Treats, the dog biscuit company in Problem 5, has the following MRP_L:

Number of Hours	MRP_L
18	29
19	27
20	25
21	23
22	21

a. Add the marginal revenue product curve to the drawing in Problem 5.
b. If Teddy's Treats is maximizing profits, how many hours of labor will be hired? What wage will be offered?

7. Suppose the workers at Teddy's Treats increase the number of hours they are willing to work at each wage rate. The new supply is as follows:

Offered Wage ($)	Supply of Labor (Number of Hours)
4	19
5	20
6	21
7	22
8	23

a. Calculate the total labor cost and the marginal expense of labor associated with each employment level.
b. Draw the new supply and marginal expense curves.
c. Compare the supply of labor and marginal expense of labor curves with the corresponding curves in Problem 5. What changes occurred?
d. Assuming MRP_L is unchanged, how many hours of labor will now be hired? What wage will be offered?

8. Suppose the marginal expense of hiring another worker is $150, and the marginal expense of hiring current workers for an extra hour is $10. The added output associated with an added worker, holding both capital and average hours per worker constant, is 120. The added output generated by increasing average hours per worker, holding capital and the number of employees constant, is 7. If the firm is interested in maximizing profits, what should it do?

9. The following table gives the quantity of labor, the offered wage, and the MRP_L at Toasty Tasties, a restaurant that specializes in breakfast and lunch.

Quantity of Labor (Number of Hours)	Offered Wage ($)	MRP_L
5	6	–
6	8	50
7	10	38
8	12	26
9	14	14
10	16	2
11	18	1

a. Calculate the marginal expense of labor.
b. Draw the supply of labor, the marginal expense of labor, and the MRP_L curves at Toasty Tasties.
c. To maximize profits, how many hours of labor should be hired? What wage will the employer offer?
d. What would happen if some nonmarket force were to compel the firm to pay its employees $14 per hour?
e. What would happen if some nonmarket force were to compel the firm to pay its employees $26 per hour?
f. What would happen if some nonmarket force were to compel the firm to pay its employees an hourly wage that is larger than $26 per hour?

Selected Readings

Becker, Gary. *Human Capital.* 2nd ed. New York: National Bureau of Economic Research, 1975.

Hart, Robert. *Working Time and Employment.* London: Allen and Unwin, 1986.

Lynch, Lisa, ed. *Training and the Private Sector: International Comparisons.* Chicago: University of Chicago Press, 1994.

Manning, Alan, ed. "Modern Models of Monopsony in Labor Markets: Tests and Papers from a Conference Held in Sundance, Utah, November 2008, Organized by Orley Ashenfelter, Henry Farber, and Michael Ransom," *Journal of Labor Economics* 28 (April 2010): 203–472.

Manning, Alan. *Monopsony in Motion: Imperfect Competition in Labor Markets.* Princeton, N.J.: Princeton University Press, 2003.

Osterman, Paul, ed. *Internal Labor Markets.* Cambridge, Mass.: MIT Press, 1984.

Parsons, Donald. "The Firm's Decision to Train." In *Research in Labor Economics* 11, eds. Lauri J. Bassi and David L. Crawford, 53–75. Greenwich, Conn.: JAI Press, 1990.

Williamson, Oliver, et al. "Understanding the Employment Relation: The Analysis of Idiosyncratic Exchange." *Bell Journal of Economics* 16 (Spring 1975): 250–280.

CHAPTER 6

Supply of Labor to the Economy: The Decision to Work

This and the next four chapters will focus on issues of *worker* behavior. That is, chapters 6–10 will discuss and analyze various aspects of *labor supply* behavior. Labor supply decisions can be roughly divided into two categories. The first, which is addressed in this chapter and the next, includes decisions about whether to work at all and, if so, how long to work. Questions that must be answered include whether to participate in the labor force, whether to seek part-time or full-time work, and how long to work both at home and for pay. The second category of decisions, which is addressed in chapters 8–10, deals with the questions that must be faced by a person who has decided to seek work for pay: the occupation or general class of occupations in which to seek offers (chapters 8 and 9) and the geographical area in which offers should be sought (chapter 10).

This chapter begins with some basic facts concerning labor force participation rates and hours of work. We then develop a theoretical framework that can be used in the analysis of decisions to work for pay. This framework is also useful for analyzing the structure of various income maintenance programs.

Trends in Labor Force Participation and Hours of Work

When a person actively seeks work, he or she is, by definition, in the *labor force*. As pointed out in chapter 2, the *labor force participation rate* is the percentage of a given population that either has a job or is looking for one. Thus, one clear-cut statistic important in measuring people's willingness to work outside the home is the labor force participation rate.

Labor Force Participation Rates

One of the most dramatic changes in the labor market over the past six decades has been the increased labor force participation of women, especially married women. Table 6.1 shows the dimensions of this change. As recently as 1950, less than 25 percent of married women were in the labor force, but by 1980, this percentage had doubled. Recently, the labor force participation rate of married women has reached over 60 percent, although since 2000, the growth for married women seems to have stopped and the rates for single women have fallen.[1] One interest of this chapter is in understanding the forces underlying these changes.

Table 6.1

Labor Force Participation Rates of Females in the United States over 16 Years of Age, by Marital Status, 1900–2011 (Percentage)

Year	All Females	Single	Widowed, Divorced	Married
1900	20.6	45.9	32.5	5.6
1910	25.5	54.0	34.1	10.7
1920	24.0			9.0
1930	25.3	55.2	34.4	11.7
1940	26.7	53.1	33.7	13.8
1950	29.7	53.6	35.5	21.6
1960	37.7	58.6	41.6	31.9
1970	43.3	56.8	40.3	40.5
1980	51.5	64.4	43.6	49.8
1990	57.5	66.7	47.2	58.4
2000	59.9	68.9	49.0	61.1
2011	58.1	62.8	48.8	60.2

Sources: 1900–1950: Clarence D. Long, *The Labor Force under Changing Income and Employment* (Princeton, N.J.: Princeton University Press, 1958), Table A–6.

1960–2011: U.S. Department of Labor, Bureau of Labor Statistics, *Handbook of Labor Statistics,* Bulletin 2340 (Washington, D.C.: U.S. Government Printing Office, 1989), Table 6; and U.S. Census Bureau, *2010 Statistical Abstract,* Section 12 (Table 598), http://www.census.gov/compendia/statab/2012/tables//12s0597.pdf; and U.S. Department of Labor, Bureau of Labor Statistics, *Women in the Labor Force: A Databook,* Report 1040 (February 2013), Table 4, http://www.bls.gov/cps/wlf-databook-2012.pdf.

---

[1]Chinhui Juhn and Simon Potter, "Changes in Labor Force Participation in the United States," *Journal of Economic Perspectives* 20 (Summer 2006): 27–46, offers a summary analysis of changes in the participation rates of both women and men.

As can be seen in Table 6.2, a second set of changes in labor force participation is the decrease in the participation rates of men, especially among the young and the old. The most substantial decreases in the United States have been among those 65 and older, from about 42 percent in 1950 to about half that currently—although since 1990 rates have been climbing a bit. Participation rates for men of "prime age" have declined only slightly since 1950, although among 45- to 64-year-olds, there were sharp decreases in the 1930s and 1970s. Clearly, men are starting their work lives later and ending them earlier than they were in 1950.

The trends in American labor force participation rates have also been observed in other industrialized countries. In Table 6.3, we display, for countries with comparable data, the trends in participation rates for women in the 25–54 age group and for men near the age of early retirement (55 to 64 years old). Typically, the fraction of women in the labor force rose from half or less in 1965 to three-quarters or more roughly 5 years later. Among men between the ages of 55 and 64, participation fell markedly in each country, although the declines were

Table 6.2

Labor Force Participation Rates for Males in the United States, by Age, 1900–2011 (percentage)

	Age Groups					
Year	**14–19**	**16–19**	**20–24**	**25–44**	**45–64**	**Over 65**
1900	61.1		91.7	96.3	93.3	68.3
1910	56.2		91.1	96.6	93.6	58.1
1920	52.6		90.9	97.1	93.8	60.1
1930	41.1		89.9	97.5	94.1	58.3
1940	34.4		88.0	95.0	88.7	41.5
1950	39.9	63.2	82.8	92.8	87.9	41.6
1960	38.1	56.1	86.1	95.2	89.0	30.6
1970	35.8	56.1	80.9	94.4	87.3	25.0
1980		60.5	85.9	95.4	82.2	19.0
1990		55.7	84.4	94.8	80.5	16.3
2000		52.8	82.6	93.0	80.4	17.7
2011		33.7	74.7	90.0	78.5	21.3

Sources: 1900–1950: Clarence D. Long, The Labor Force under Changing Income and Employment (Princeton, N.J.: Princeton University Press, 1958), Table A–2.

1960: U.S. Department of Commerce, Bureau of the Census, Census of Population, 1960: Employment Status, Subject Reports PC(2)–6A, Table 1.

1970: U.S. Department of Commerce, Bureau of the Census, Census of Population, 1970: Employment Status and Work Experience, Subject Reports PC(2)–6A, Table 1.

1980–2011: U.S. Census Bureau, 2010 Statistical Abstract, Section 12 (Table 575), http://www.census.gov/compendia/statab/2010edition.html; and U.S. Department of Labor, Bureau of Labor Statistics, *Women in the Labor Force: A Databook*, Report 1040 (February 2013), Table 1, http://www.bls.gov/cps/wlf-databook-2012.pdf.

Table 6.3

Labor Force Participation Rates of Women and Older Men, Selected Countries, 1965–2011 (Percentage)

Country	1965	1973	1983	1993	2011
Women, Age 25 to 54					
Canada	33.9	44.0	65.1	75.6	82.1
France	42.8	54.1	67.0	76.1	83.4
Germany	46.1	50.5	58.3	72.5	82.1
Japan	–	53.0[a]	59.5	65.2	71.6
Sweden	56.0	68.9	87.1	88.2	88.1
United States	45.1	52.0	67.1	74.6	74.7
Men, Age 55 to 64					
Canada	86.4	81.3	72.3	60.4	68.5
France	76.0	72.1	53.6	43.5	47.1
Germany	84.6	73.4	63.1	53.0	71.7
Japan	–	86.3[a]	84.7	85.4	83.1
Sweden	88.3	82.7	77.0	70.9	80.1
United States	82.9	76.9	69.4	66.5	69.3

[a]Data are for 1974 (earlier data not comparable).

Source: Organisation for Economic Co-operation and Development, Labour Force Statistics (Paris: OECD, various dates), http://stats.oecd.org/Index.aspx?DatasetCode=LFS_SEXAGE_I_R

much larger in some countries (France, for example) than others (Japan, Sweden). Furthermore, the downward trends in five of the six countries shown appear to have reversed since the mid-1990s. Thus, while there are some differences in trends across the countries, it is likely that common forces are influencing labor supply trends in the industrialized world.

Hours of Work

Because data on labor force participation include both the employed and those who want a job but do not have one, they are a relatively pure measure of labor supply. In contrast, the weekly or yearly hours of work put in by the typical employee are often thought to be determined only by the demand side of the market. After all, don't employers, in responding to the factors discussed in chapter 5, set the hours of work expected of their employees? They do, of course, but hours worked are also influenced by *employee* preferences on the supply side of the market, especially in the long run.

Even though employers set work schedules, employees can exercise their preferences regarding hours of work through their choice of part-time or full-time work, their decisions to work at more than one job, or their selection of occupations and employers.[2] For example, women managers who work full-time average more hours of work per week than full-time clerical workers, and male sales workers work more hours per week than their full-time counterparts in skilled craft jobs. Moreover, different employers offer different mixes of full-time and part-time work, require different weekly work schedules, and have different policies regarding vacations and paid holidays.

Employer offers regarding both hours and pay are intended to enhance their profits, but they must also satisfy the preferences of current and prospective employees. For example, if employees receiving an hourly wage of $X for 40 hours per week really wanted to work only 30 hours at $X per hour, some enterprising employer (presumably one with relatively lower quasi-fixed costs) would eventually seize on their dissatisfaction and offer jobs with a 30-hour workweek, ending up with a more satisfied, productive workforce in the process.

While the labor supply preferences of employees must be satisfied in the long run, most of the short-run changes in hours of work seem to emanate from the *demand* side of the market.[3] Workweeks typically vary over the course of a business cycle, for example, with longer hours worked in periods of robust demand. In analyzing trends in hours of work, then, we must carefully distinguish between the forces of supply and demand.

In the first part of the twentieth century, workers in U.S. manufacturing plants typically worked 55 hours per week in years with strong economic activity; in the last two decades, American manufacturing workers have worked, on average, less than 40 hours per week during similar periods. For example, in the years 1988, 1995, and 2004—when the unemployment rate was roughly 5.5 percent and falling—manufacturing production workers averaged 38.4, 39.3, and 38.6 hours per week, respectively. In general, the decline in weekly hours of manufacturing

---

[2]At any time, roughly 5 percent of American workers hold more than one job—although many more (20 percent of men and 12 percent of women) hold more than one job *at some point within a year*. See Christina H. Paxson and Nachum Sicherman, "The Dynamics of Dual Job Holding and Job Mobility," *Journal of Labor Economics* 14 (July 1996): 357–393; and Steven F. Hipple, "Multiple Jobholding During the 2000s," *Monthly Labor Review* 133 (July 2010): 21–32. For a study that tests (and finds support for) the assumption that workers are *not* restricted in their choice of work hours, see John C. Ham and Kevin T. Reilly, "Testing Intertemporal Substitution, Implicit Contracts, and Hours Restriction Models of the Labor Market Using Micro Data," *American Economic Review* 92 (September 2002): 905–927.

[3]See, for example, Joseph G. Altonji and Christina H. Paxson, "Job Characteristics and Hours of Work," in *Research in Labor Economics*, vol. 8, ed. Ronald Ehrenberg (Greenwich, Conn.: JAI Press, 1986); Orley Ashenfelter, "Macroeconomic Analyses and Microeconomic Analyses of Labor Supply," *Carnegie-Rochester Conference Series on Public Policy* 21 (1984): 117–156. A more recent study has shown that workers' desired labor supply adjustments come more from changing jobs than from changing hours with the same employer; see Richard Blundell, Mike Brewer, and Marco Francesconi, "Job Changes and Hours Changes: Understanding the Path of Labor Supply Adjustment," *Journal of Labor Economics* 26 (July 2008): 421–454.

work in the United States occurred prior to 1950, and since then, hours of work have shown little tendency to decline.[4]

A Theory of the Decision to Work

Can labor supply theory help us to understand the long-run trends in labor force participation and hours of work noted above? Because labor is the most abundant factor of production, it is fair to say that any country's well-being in the long run depends heavily on the willingness of its people to work. Leisure and other ways of spending time that do not involve work for pay are also important in generating well-being; however, any economy relies heavily on goods and services produced for market transactions. Therefore, it is important to understand the *work-incentive* effects of higher wages and incomes, different kinds of taxes, and various forms of income maintenance programs.

The decision to work is ultimately a decision about how to spend time. One way to use our available time is to spend it in pleasurable leisure activities. The other major way in which people use time is to work. We can work around the home, performing such *household production* as raising children, sewing, building, or even growing food. Alternatively, we can work for pay and use our earnings to purchase food, shelter, clothing, and child care.

Because working for pay and engaging in household production are two ways of getting the same jobs done, we shall initially ignore the distinction between them and treat work activities as working for pay. We shall therefore be characterizing the decision to work as a choice between leisure and working for pay. Most of the crucial factors affecting work incentives can be understood in this context, but insight into labor supply behavior can also be enriched by a consideration of household production; this we do in chapter 7.

If we regard the time spent eating, sleeping, and otherwise maintaining ourselves as more or less fixed by natural laws, then the discretionary time we have (16 hours a day, say) can be allocated to either work or leisure. It is most convenient for us to begin our analysis of the work/leisure choice by analyzing the *demand for leisure hours*.

Some Basic Concepts

Basically, the demand for a good is a function of three factors:

1. The *opportunity cost* of the good (which is often equal to *market price*).
2. One's level of *wealth*.
3. One's set of *preferences*.

---

[4]The averages cited in this paragraph refer to *actual* hours of work (obtained from the *Census of Manufactures*), not the more commonly available "hours paid for," which include paid time off for illness, holidays, and vacations. A relatively recent study found an unexpected *expansion* of work hours among highly educated men during the last two decades of the twentieth century; see Peter Kuhn and Fernando Lozano, "The Expanding Workweek? Understanding Trends in Long Work Hours among U.S. Men, 1979–2006," *Journal of Labor Economics* 26 (April 2008): 311–343.

For example, consumption of heating oil will vary with the *cost* of such oil; as that cost rises, consumption tends to fall unless one of the other two factors intervenes. As *wealth* rises, people generally want larger and warmer houses that obviously require more oil to heat.[5] Even if the price of energy and the level of personal wealth were to remain constant, the demand for energy could rise if a falling birthrate and lengthened life span resulted in a higher proportion of the population being aged and therefore wanting warmer houses. This change in the composition of the population amounts to a shift in the overall *preferences* for warmer houses and thus leads to a change in the demand for heating oil. (Economists usually assume that preferences are given and not subject to immediate change. For policy purposes, changes in prices and wealth are of paramount importance in explaining changes in demand because these variables are more susceptible to change by government or market forces.)

Opportunity Cost of Leisure   To apply this general analysis of demand to the demand for leisure, we must first ask, "What is the opportunity cost of leisure?" The cost of spending an hour watching television is basically what one could earn if one had spent that hour working. Thus, the opportunity cost of an hour of leisure is equal to one's *wage rate*—the *extra earnings* a worker can take home from an *extra hour of work*.[6]

Wealth and Income   Next, we must understand and be able to measure wealth. Naturally, wealth includes a family's holdings of bank accounts, financial investments, and physical property. Workers' skills can also be considered assets, since these skills can be, in effect, rented out to employers for a price. The more one can get in wages, the larger the value of one's human assets. Unfortunately, it is not usually possible to directly measure people's wealth. It is much easier to measure the *returns* from that wealth, because data on total *income* are readily available from government surveys. Economists often use total income as an indicator of total wealth, since the two are conceptually so closely related.[7]

Defining the Income Effect   Theory suggests that if income increases while wages and preferences are held constant, the number of leisure hours demanded will rise. Put differently, *if income increases, holding wages constant, desired hours of work will go down.* (Conversely, if income is reduced while the wage rate is

---

[5]When the demand for a good rises with wealth, economists say the good is a *normal good*. If demand falls as wealth rises, the good is said to be an *inferior good* (traveling or commuting by bus is sometimes cited as an example of an inferior good).

[6]This assumes that individuals can work as many hours as they want at a fixed wage rate. While this assumption may seem overly simplistic, it will not lead to wrong conclusions with respect to the issues analyzed in this chapter. More rigorously, it should be said that leisure's marginal opportunity cost is the marginal wage rate (the wage one could receive for an extra hour of work).

[7]The best indicator of wealth is permanent, or long-run potential, income. Current income may differ from permanent income for a variety of reasons (unemployment, illness, unusually large amounts of overtime work, etc.). For our purposes here, however, the distinction between current income and permanent income is not too important.

held constant, desired hours of work will go up.) Economists call the response of desired hours of leisure to changes in income, with wages held constant, the *income effect*. The income effect is based on the simple notion that as incomes rise, holding leisure's opportunity cost constant, people will want to consume more leisure (which means working less).

Because we have assumed that time is spent either in leisure or in working for pay, the income effect can be expressed in terms of the *supply of working hours* as well as the demand for leisure hours. Because the ultimate focus of this chapter is labor supply, we choose to express this effect in the context of supply.

Using algebraic notation, we define the income effect as the change in hours of work (ΔH) produced by a change in income (ΔY), holding wages constant ($\overline{W}$):

$$\text{Income Effect} = \frac{\Delta H}{\Delta Y}\Big|\overline{W} < 0 \tag{6.1}$$

We say the income effect is *negative* because the *sign* of the *fraction* in equation (6.1) is *negative*. If income goes up (wages held constant), hours of work fall. If income goes down, hours of work increase. The numerator (ΔH) and denominator (ΔY) in equation (6.1) move in opposite directions, giving a negative sign to the income effect.

Defining the Substitution Effect Theory also suggests that *if income is held constant, an increase in the wage rate will raise the price and reduce the demand for leisure, thereby increasing work incentives.* (Likewise, a decrease in the wage rate will reduce leisure's opportunity cost and the incentives to work, holding income constant.) This *substitution effect* occurs because as the cost of leisure changes, income held constant, leisure and work hours are substituted for each other.

In contrast to the income effect, the substitution effect is *positive*. Because this effect is the change in hours of work (ΔH) induced by a change in the wage (ΔW), holding income constant ($\overline{Y}$), the substitution effect can be written as

$$\text{Substitution Effect} = \frac{\Delta H}{\Delta W}\Big|\overline{Y} > 0 \tag{6.2}$$

Because the numerator (ΔH) and denominator (ΔW) always move in the same direction, at least in theory, the substitution effect has a positive sign.

Observing Income and Substitution Effects Separately When wages rise or fall, both income and substitution effects are simultaneously present, often working against each other. At times, however, it is possible to observe situations or programs that create only one effect or the other.

Receiving an inheritance offers an example of the income effect by itself. The bequest enhances wealth (income) *independent* of the hours of work. Thus, income is increased *without* a change in the compensation received from an hour of work. In this case, the income effect induces the person to consume more leisure, thereby reducing the willingness to work. (Some support for this theoretical prediction can be seen later in Example 6.2.)

Observing the substitution effect by itself is rare, but one example comes from the 1980 presidential campaign, when candidate John Anderson proposed a program aimed at conserving gasoline. His plan consisted of raising the gasoline tax but offsetting this increase by a reduced Social Security tax payable by individuals on their earnings. The idea was to raise the price of gasoline without reducing people's overall spendable income.

For our purposes, this plan is interesting because, for the typical worker, it would have created only a substitution effect on labor supply. Social Security revenues are collected by a tax on earnings, so reductions in the tax are, in effect, increases in the wage rate for most workers. For the average person, however, the increased wealth associated with this wage increase would have been exactly offset by increases in the gasoline tax.[8] Hence, wages would have been increased while income was held more or less constant. This program would have created a substitution effect that induced people to work more hours.

Both Effects Occur When Wages Rise   While the above examples illustrate situations in which the income or the substitution effect is present by itself, *normally both effects are present, often working in opposite directions*. The presence of both effects working in opposite directions creates ambiguity in predicting the overall labor supply response in many cases. Consider the case of a person who receives a wage increase.

The labor supply response to a simple wage increase will involve *both* an income effect and a substitution effect. The *income effect* is the result of the worker's enhanced wealth (or potential income) after the increase. For a given level of work effort, he or she now has a greater command over resources than before (because more income is received for any given number of hours of work). The *substitution effect* results from the fact that the wage increase raises the opportunity costs of leisure. Because the actual labor supply response is the *sum* of the income and substitution effects, we cannot predict the response in advance; theory simply does not tell us which effect is stronger.

---

[8]An increase in the price of gasoline will reduce the income people have left for expenditures on nongasoline consumption only if the demand for gasoline is inelastic. In this case, the percentage reduction in gasoline consumption is smaller than the percentage increase in price; total expenditures on gasoline would thus rise. Our analysis assumes this to be the case. For a study of how gasoline taxes affect labor supply, see Sarah West and Roberton Williams, "Empirical Estimates for Environmental Policy Making in a Second-Best Setting," National Bureau of Economic Research, Working Paper No. 10330 (March 2004).

If the *income* effect is stronger, the person will respond to a wage increase by decreasing his or her labor supply. This decrease will be *smaller* than if the same change in wealth were due to an increase in *nonlabor* wealth, because the substitution effect is present and acts as a moderating influence. However, as seen in Example 6.1, when the *income* effect dominates, the substitution effect is not large enough to prevent labor supply from *declining*. It is entirely plausible, of course, that the *substitution* effect will dominate. If so, the actual response to wage increases will be to *increase* labor supply.

Should the substitution effect dominate, the person's labor supply curve—relating, say, his or her desired hours of work to wages—will be *positively sloped*. That is, labor supplied will increase with the wage rate. If, on the other hand, the income effect dominates, the person's labor supply curve will be *negatively sloped*. Economic theory cannot say which effect will dominate, and in fact, individual labor supply curves could be positively sloped in some ranges of the wage and negatively sloped in others. In Figure 6.1, for example, the person's desired hours of work increase (substitution effect dominates) when wages go up as long as wages are low (below W^*). At higher wages, however, further increases result in reduced hours of work (the income effect dominates); economists refer to such a curve as *backward-bending*.

Analysis of the Labor/Leisure Choice

This section introduces indifference curves and budget constraints—visual aids that make the theory of labor supply easier to understand and to apply to complex policy issues. These graphical aids visually depict the basic factors underlying the demand for leisure (supply of labor) discussed earlier.

EXAMPLE 6.1

The Labor Supply of New York City Taxi Drivers

Testing the theory of labor supply is made difficult by the fact that most workers cannot change their hours of work very much without changing jobs. Taxi drivers in New York City, however, do choose their own hours of work, so it is interesting to see how their hours of work—reflected in miles driven—responded to fare increases approved by the city's Taxi and Limousine Commission in 1996 and 2004. These fare increases raised the hourly pay of taxi drivers by an average of 19 percent, and a careful study of how drivers responded found that they *reduced* their miles driven by about 4 percent. Clearly, then, the income effect of their wage increases was stronger than the substitution effect.

Source: Orley Ashenfelter, Kirk Doran, and Bruce Schaller, "A Shred of Credible Evidence on the Long-Run Elasticity of Labor Supply," *Economica* 77 (October, 2010): 637–650. For more analysis on this topic, see Vincent P. Crawford and Juanjuan Meng, "New York City Cab Drivers' Labor Supply Revisited: Reference-Dependent Preferences with Rational-Expectations Targets for Hours and Income," *American Economic Review* 101 (August 2011): 1912–1932.

Figure 6.1

An Individual Labor Supply Curve Can Bend Backward

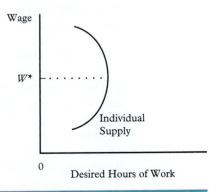

Preferences   Let us assume that there are two major categories of goods that make people happy—leisure time and the goods people can buy with money. If we take the prices of goods as fixed, then they can be compressed into one index that is measured by money income (with prices fixed, more money income means it is possible to consume more goods). Using two categories, leisure and money income, allows our graphs to be drawn in two-dimensional space.

Since both leisure and money can be used to generate satisfaction (or *utility*), these two goods are to some extent substitutes for each other. If forced to give up some money income—by cutting back on hours of work, for example—some increase in leisure time could be substituted for this lost income to keep a person as happy as before.

To understand how preferences can be graphed, suppose a thoughtful consumer/worker were asked to decide how happy he or she would be with a daily income of $64 combined with 8 hours of leisure (point *a* in Figure 6.2). This level of happiness could be called utility level *A*. Our consumer/worker could name *other combinations* of money income and leisure hours that would *also* yield utility level *A*. Assume that our respondent named five other combinations. All six combinations of money income and leisure hours that yield utility level *A* are represented by heavy dots in Figure 6.2. The curve connecting these dots is called an *indifference curve*, which connects the various combinations of money income and leisure that yield equal utility. (The term *indifference curve* is derived from the fact that since each point on the curve yields equal utility, a person is truly indifferent about where on the curve he or she will be.)

Our worker/consumer could no doubt achieve a higher level of happiness if he or she could combine the 8 hours of leisure with an income of $100 per day instead of just $64 a day. This higher satisfaction level could be called utility level *B*. The consumer could name other combinations of money income and leisure that would also yield *this* higher level of utility. These

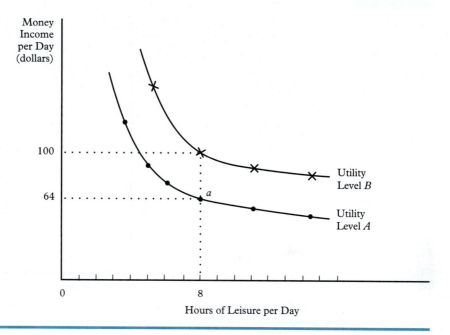

Figure 6.2

Two Indifference Curves for the Same Person

combinations are denoted by the Xs in Figure 6.2 that are connected by a second indifference curve.

Indifference curves have certain specific characteristics that are reflected in the way they are drawn:

1. Utility level *B* represents more happiness than level *A*. Every level of leisure consumption is combined with a higher income on *B* than on *A*. Hence, our respondent prefers all points on indifference curve *B* to any point on curve *A*. A whole *set* of indifference curves could be drawn for this one person, each representing a different utility level. Any such curve that lies to the northeast of another one is preferred to any curve to the southwest because the northeastern curve represents a higher level of utility.

2. Indifference curves *do not intersect*. If they did, the point of intersection would represent one combination of money income and leisure that yielded two different levels of satisfaction. We assume our worker/consumer is not so inconsistent in stating his or her preferences that this could happen.

3. Indifference curves are *negatively sloped* because if either income or leisure hours are increased, the other is reduced in order to preserve the same level of utility. If the slope is steep, as at segment *LK* in Figure 6.3, a given loss of income need not be accompanied by a large

Figure 6.3

An Indifference Curve

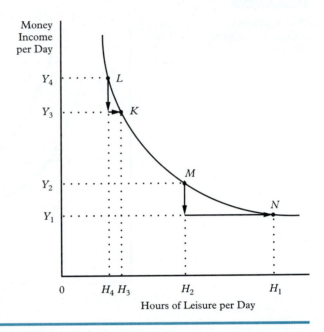

Hours of Leisure per Day

increase in leisure hours to keep utility constant.[9] When the curve is relatively flat, however, as at segment *MN* in Figure 6.3, a given decrease in income must be accompanied by a large increase in the consumption of leisure to hold utility constant. Thus, when indifference curves are relatively steep, people do not value money income as highly as when such curves are relatively flat; when they are flat, a loss of income can only be compensated for by a large increase in leisure if utility is to be kept constant.

4. Indifference curves are *convex*—steeper at the left than at the right. This shape reflects the assumption that when money income is relatively high and leisure hours are relatively few, leisure is more highly valued (and income less valued) than when leisure is abundant and income relatively scarce. At segment *LK* in Figure 6.3, a great loss of income (from Y_4 to Y_3, for example) can be compensated for by just a little increase in leisure,

---

[9]Economists call the change in money income needed to hold utility constant when leisure hours are changed by one unit the *marginal rate of substitution* between leisure and money income. This marginal rate of substitution can be graphically understood as the slope of the indifference curve at any point. At point *L*, for example, the slope is relatively steep, so economists would say that the marginal rate of substitution at point *L* is relatively high.

whereas a little loss of leisure time (from H_3 to H_4, for example) would require a relatively large increase in income to maintain equal utility. What is relatively scarce is more highly valued.

5. Conversely, when income is low and leisure is abundant (segment *MN* in Figure 6.3), income is more highly valued. Losing income (by moving from Y_2 to Y_1, for example) would require a huge increase in leisure for utility to remain constant. To repeat, what is relatively scarce is assumed to be more highly valued.

6. Finally, different people have different sets of indifference curves. The curves drawn in Figures 6.2 and 6.3 were for *one person*. Another person would have a completely different set of curves. People who value leisure more highly, for example, would have had indifference curves that were generally steeper (see Figure 6.4a). People who do not value leisure highly would have relatively flat curves (see Figure 6.4b). Thus, individual preferences can be portrayed graphically.

Income and Wage Constraints   Everyone would like to maximize his or her utility, which would be ideally done by consuming every available hour of leisure combined with the highest conceivable income. Unfortunately, the resources anyone can command are limited. Thus, all that is possible is to do the best one can, given limited resources. To see these resource limitations graphically requires superimposing constraints on one's set of indifference curves to see which combinations of income and leisure are available and which are not.

Suppose the person whose indifference curves are graphed in Figure 6.2 had no source of income other than labor earnings. Suppose, further, that he or she could earn $8 per hour. Figure 6.5 includes the two indifference curves shown in Figure 6.2 as well as a straight line (*ED*) connecting combinations of leisure and income that are possible for a person with an $8 wage and no outside income.

Indifference Curves for Two Different People

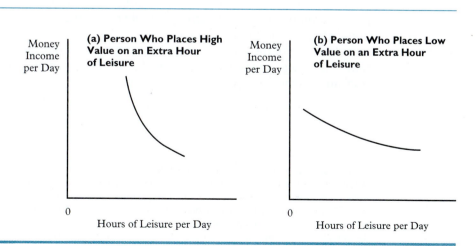

Money Income per Day

(a) Person Who Places High Value on an Extra Hour of Leisure

Money Income per Day

(b) Person Who Places Low Value on an Extra Hour of Leisure

0

Hours of Leisure per Day

0

Hours of Leisure per Day

Figure 6.5

Indifference Curves and
Budget Constraint

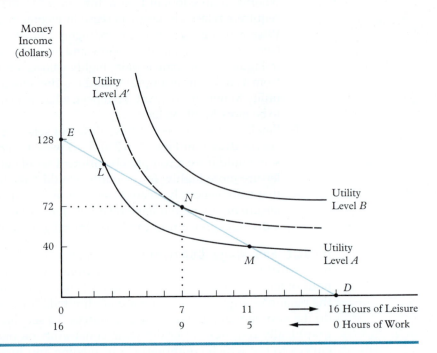

If 16 hours per day are available for work and leisure,[10] and if this person consumes all 16 in leisure, then money income will be zero (point *D* in Figure 6.5).
If 5 hours a day are devoted to work, income will be $40 per day (point *M*), and
if 16 hours a day are worked, income will be $128 per day (point *E*). Other points
on this line—for example, the point of 15 hours of leisure (1 hour of work) and
$8 of income—are also possible. This line, which reflects the combinations of lei-
sure and income that are possible for the individual, is called the *budget constraint*.
Any combination to the right of the budget constraint is not achievable; the
person's command over resources is simply not sufficient to attain these combinations of leisure and money income.

The *slope* of the budget constraint is a graphical representation of the wage
rate. One's wage rate is properly defined as the increment in income (ΔY) derived
from an increment in hours of work (ΔH):

$$\text{Wage Rate} = \frac{\Delta Y}{\Delta H} \tag{6.3}$$

[10]Our assumption that 8 hours per day are required for sleeping and other "maintenance" activities is
purely for ease of exposition. These activities themselves are a matter of economic choice, at least to
some extent; see, for example, Jeff E. Biddle and Daniel S. Hamermesh, "Sleep and the Allocation of
Time," *Journal of Political Economy* 98, no. 5, pt. 1 (October 1990): 922–943. Modeling a three-way choice
between work, leisure, and maintenance activities would complicate our analysis without changing
the essential insights theory can offer about the labor/leisure choice workers must make.

Now $\Delta Y/\Delta H$ is exactly the slope of the budget constraint (in absolute value).[11] Figure 6.5 shows how the constraint rises $8 for every 1-hour increase in work: if the person works 0 hours, income per day is zero; if the person works 1 hour, $8 in income is received; if he or she works 5 hours, $40 in income is achieved. The constraint rises $8 because the wage rate is $8 per hour. If the person could earn $16 per hour, the constraint would rise twice as fast and therefore be twice as steep.

It is clear from Figure 6.5 that our consumer/worker cannot achieve utility level B. He or she can achieve *some* points on the indifference curve representing utility level A—specifically, those points between L and M in Figure 6.5. However, if our consumer/worker is a utility maximizer, he or she will realize that a utility level *above* A is possible. Remembering that an infinite number of indifference curves can be drawn between curves A and B in Figure 6.5, one representing each possible level of satisfaction between A and B, we can draw a curve (A') that is northeast of curve A and just *tangent* to the budget constraint at point N. Any movement along the budget constraint *away* from the tangency point places the person on an indifference curve lying *below A'*.

Workers who face the same budget constraint, but who have different preferences for leisure, will make different choices about hours of work. If the person whose preferences were depicted in Figure 6.5 had placed lower values on leisure time—and therefore had indifference curves that were comparatively flatter, such as the one shown in Figure 6.4b—then the point of tangency with constraint ED would have been to the left of point N (indicating more hours of work). Conversely, if he or she had steeper indifference curves, signifying that leisure time was more valuable (see Figure 6.4a), then the point of tangency in Figure 6.5 would have been to the right of point N, and fewer hours of work would have been desired. Indeed, some people will have indifference curves so steep (that is, preferences for leisure so strong) that there is no point of tangency with ED. For these people, as is illustrated by Figure 6.6, utility is maximized at the "corner" (point D); they desire no work at all and therefore are not in the labor force.

The Income Effect   Suppose now that the person depicted in Figure 6.5 receives a source of income independent of work. Suppose further that this *nonlabor* income amounts to about $36 per day. Thus, even if this person worked 0 hours per day, his or her daily income would be $36. Naturally, if the person worked more than 0 hours, his or her daily income would be equal to $36 plus earnings (the wage multiplied by the hours of work).

---

[11]The vertical change for a one-unit change in horizontal distance is the definition of *slope*. *Absolute value* refers to the magnitude of the slope, disregarding whether it is positive or negative. The budget constraint drawn in Figure 6.5 is a straight line (and thus has a constant slope). In economic terms, a straight-line budget constraint reflects the assumption that the wage rate at which one can work is fixed and that it does not change with the hours of work. However, the major theoretical implications derived from using a straight-line constraint would be unchanged by employing a convex one, so we are using the fixed-wage assumption for ease of exposition.

Figure 6.6

The Decision Not to Work Is a
"Corner Solution"

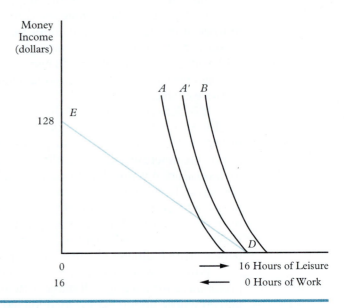

Our person's command over resources has clearly increased, as can be shown by drawing a new budget constraint to reflect the nonlabor income. As shown by the darker blue line in Figure 6.7, the endpoints of the new constraint are point *d* (0 hours of work and $36 of money income) and point *e* (16 hours of work and $164 of income—$36 in nonlabor income plus $128 in earnings). Note that the new constraint is *parallel* to the old one. Parallel lines have the same slope; since the slope of each constraint reflects the wage rate, we can infer that the increase in nonlabor income has not changed the person's wage rate.

We have just described a situation in which a pure *income effect* should be observed. Income (wealth) has been increased, but the wage rate has remained unchanged. The previous section noted that if wealth *increased* and the opportunity cost of leisure remained constant, the person would consume more leisure and work *less*. We thus concluded that the income effect was negative, and this negative relationship is illustrated graphically in Figure 6.7.

When the old budget constraint (*ED*) was in effect, the person's highest level of utility was reached at point *N*, working 9 hours a day. With the new constraint (*ed*), the optimum hours of work are 8 per day (point *P*). The new source of income, because it does not alter the wage, has caused an income effect that results in one less hour of work per day. Statistical analyses of people who received large inheritances (Example 6.2) or who won large lottery prizes[12] support the prediction that labor supply is reduced when unearned income rises.

[12]Guido W. Imbens, Donald B. Rubin, and Bruce I. Sacerdote, "Estimating the Effects of Unearned Income on Labor Earnings, Savings, and Consumption: Evidence from a Survey of Lottery Players," *American Economic Review* 91 (September 2001): 778–794.

Figure 6.7

Indifference Curves
and Budget Constraint
(with an Increase in
Nonlabor Income)

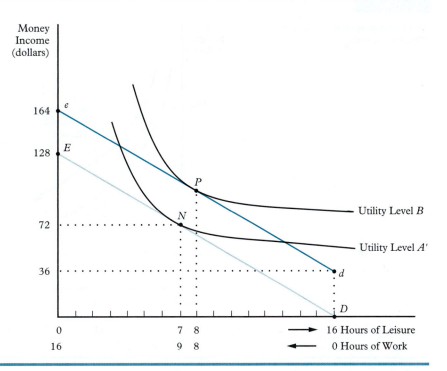

Money
Income
(dollars)

164 — *e*

128 — *E*

P

N

72

Utility Level *B*

Utility Level *A'*

36 ·· *d*

D

| 0 | 7 8 | 16 Hours of Leisure |
| 16 | 9 8 | 0 Hours of Work |

Income and Substitution Effects with a Wage Increase   Suppose that instead
of increasing one's command over resources by receiving a source of nonlabor
income, the wage rate were to be increased from $8 to $12 per hour. This increase,
as noted earlier, would cause *both* an income effect and a substitution effect;
workers would be wealthier *and* face a higher opportunity cost of leisure. Theory
tells us in this case that the substitution effect pushes them toward more hours
of work and the income effect toward fewer, but it cannot tell us which effect
will dominate.

Figures 6.8 and 6.9 illustrate the possible effects of the above wage change
on a person's labor supply, which we now assume is initially 8 hours per day.
Figure 6.8 illustrates the case in which the observed response by a worker is to
increase the hours of work; in this case, the substitution effect is stronger than the
income effect. Figure 6.9 illustrates the case in which the income effect is stronger
and the response to a wage increase is to reduce the hours of work. The difference between the two figures lies *solely* in the shape of the indifference curves
that might describe a person's preferences; the budget constraints, which reflect
wealth and the wage rate, are exactly the same.

Figures 6.8 and 6.9 both show the old constraint, *AB*, the slope of which
reflects the wage of $8 per hour. They also show the new one, *AC*, which reflects

Figure 6.8

Wage Increase with Substitution
Effect Dominating

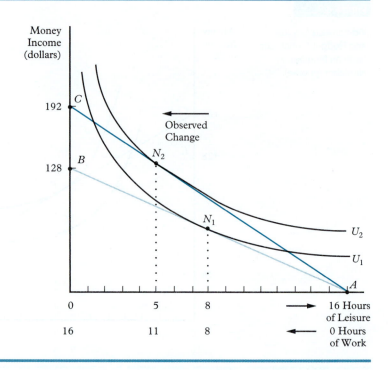

the $12 wage. Because we assume workers have no source of nonlabor income, both constraints are anchored at point A, where income is zero if a person does not work. Point C on the new constraint is now at $192 (16 hours of work times $12 per hour).

With the worker whose preferences are depicted in Figure 6.8, the wage increase makes utility level U_2 the highest that can be reached. The tangency point at N_2 suggests that 11 hours of work is optimum. When the old constraint was in effect, the utility-maximizing hours of work were 8 per day (point N_1). Thus, the wage increase would cause this person's desired hours of work to increase by 3 per day.

With the worker whose preferences are depicted in Figure 6.9, the wage increase would make utility level U'_2 the highest one possible (the prime emphasizes that workers' preferences differ and that utility *levels* in Figures 6.8 and 6.9 cannot be compared). Utility is maximized at N'_2, at 6 hours of work per day. Thus, with preferences like those in Figure 6.9, working hours fall from 8 to 6 as the wage rate increases.

Isolating Income and Substitution Effects   We have graphically depicted the income effect by itself (Figure 6.7) and the two possible outcomes of an increase in wages (Figures 6.8 and 6.9), which combine the income and substitution effects.

Figure 6.9

Wage Increase with
Income Effect Dominating

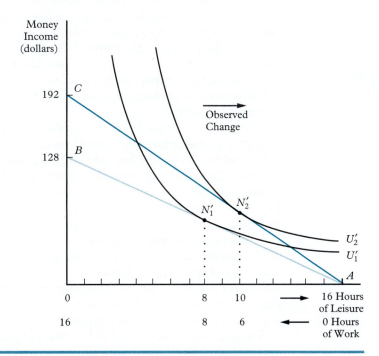

Is it possible to graphically isolate the substitution effect? The answer is yes, and the most meaningful way to do this is to return to the context of a wage change, such as the one depicted in Figures 6.8 and 6.9. We arbitrarily choose to analyze the response shown in Figure 6.8.

EXAMPLE 6.2

Do Large Inheritances Induce Labor Force Withdrawal?

Do large bequests of unearned income reduce people's incentives to work? One study divided people who received inheritances in 1982–1983 into two groups: those who received small bequests (averaging $7,700) and those who received larger ones, averaging $346,200. The study then analyzed changes in the labor force participation behavior of the two groups between 1982 and 1985. Not surprisingly, those who received the larger inheritances were more likely to drop out of the labor force. Specifically, in an environment in which other forces were causing the labor force participation rate among the small-bequest group to rise from 76 percent to 81 percent, the rate in the large-bequest group fell from 70 percent to 65 percent. Somewhat more surprising was the fact that perhaps in anticipation of the large bequest, the labor force participation rate among the people in the latter group was lower to begin with!

Data from: Douglas Holtz-Eakin, David Joulfaian, and Harvey S. Rosen, "The Carnegie Conjecture: Some Empirical Evidence," *Quarterly Journal of Economics* 108, no. 2 (1993): 413–435. The findings reported above hold up even after controlling for such factors as age and earnings.

Figure 6.10 has three panels. Panel (a) repeats Figure 6.8; it shows the final, overall effect of a wage increase on the labor supply of the person whose preferences are depicted. As we saw earlier, the effect of the wage increase in this case is to raise the person's utility from U_1 to U_2 and to induce this worker to increase desired hours of work from 8 to 11 per day. Embedded in this overall effect of the wage increase, however, is an income effect pushing toward less work and a substitution effect pushing toward more. These effects are graphically separated in panels (b) and (c).

Panel (b) of Figure 6.10 shows the income effect that is embedded in the overall response to the wage change. By definition, the income effect is the change in desired hours of work brought on by increased wealth, holding the wage rate constant. To reveal this embedded effect, we ask a hypothetical question: "What would have been the change in labor supply if the person depicted in panel (a) had reached the new indifference curve (U_2) with a change in *nonlabor* income instead of a change in his or her wage rate?"

We begin to answer this question graphically by moving the old constraint to the northeast, which depicts the greater command over leisure time and goods—and hence the higher level of utility—associated with greater wealth. The constraint is shifted outward while maintaining its original slope (reflecting the old $8 wage), which holds the wage constant. The dashed line in panel (b), which is parallel to AB, depicts this hypothetical movement of the old constraint, and it results in a tangency point at N_3. This tangency suggests that had the person received nonlabor income, with no change in the wage, sufficient to reach the new level of utility, he or she would have *reduced* work hours from 8 (N_1) to 7 (N_3) per day. This shift is graphical verification that the income effect is negative, assuming that leisure is a normal good.

The substitution effect is the effect on labor supply of a change in the wage rate, holding wealth constant. It can be seen in panel (c) of Figure 6.10 as the difference between where the person actually ended up on indifference curve U_2 (tangency at N_2) and where he or she would have ended up with a pure income effect (tangency at N_3). Comparing tangency points on the *same* indifference curve is a graphical approximation to holding wealth constant. Thus, *with* the wage change, the person represented in Figure 6.10 ended up at point N_2, working 11 hours a day. *Without* the wage change, the person would have chosen to work 7 hours a day (point N_3). The wage change *by itself*, holding utility (or real wealth) constant, caused work hours to increase by 4 per day.[13] This increase demonstrates that the substitution effect is positive.

To summarize, the observed effect of raising wages from $8 to $12 per hour increased the hours of work in Figure 6.10 from 8 to 11 per day. This observed

---

[13]In our initial definition of the substitution effect, we held *money income* constant, while in the graphical analysis, we held *utility* constant. These slightly different approaches were followed for explanatory convenience, and they represent (respectively) the theoretical analyses suggested by Evgeny Slutsky and John Hicks.

Figure 6.10

Wage Increase with Substitution Effect
Dominating: Isolating Income and Substitution
Effects

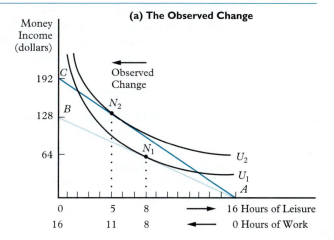

(a) The Observed Change

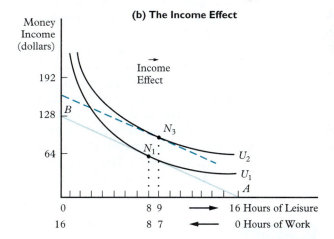

(b) The Income Effect

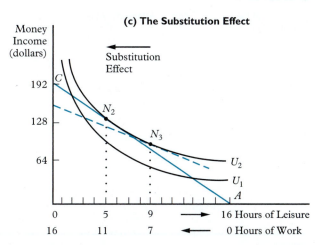

(c) The Substitution Effect

effect, however, is the *sum* of two component effects. The income effect, which operates because a higher wage increases one's real wealth, tended to *reduce* the hours of work from 8 to 7 per day. The substitution effect, which captures the pure effect of the change in leisure's opportunity cost, tended to push the person toward 4 more hours of work per day. The end result was an increase of 3 in the hours worked each day.

Which Effect Is Stronger? Suppose that a wage increase changes the budget constraint facing a worker from *CD* to *CE* in Figure 6.11. If the worker had a relatively flat set of indifference curves, the initial tangency along *CD* might be at point *A*, implying a relatively heavy work schedule. If the person had more steeply sloped indifference curves, the initial tangency might be at point *B*, where hours at work are fewer.

One important influence on the size of the income effect is the extent of the northeast movement of the new constraint: the more the constraint shifts outward, the greater the income effect will tend to be. For a person with an initial tangency at point *A*, for example, the northeast movement is larger than that for a person whose initial tangency is at point *B*. Put in words, the increased command over resources made possible by a wage increase is only attainable if one works, and the more work-oriented the person is, the greater will be his or her increase in resources. Other things equal, people who are working longer hours will exhibit greater income effects when wage rates change.

To take this reasoning to the extreme, suppose a person's indifference curves were so steep that the person was initially out of the labor force (that is, when the budget constraint was *CD* in Figure 6.11, his or her utility was maximized at point *C*). The wage increase and the resultant new constraint, *CE*, can induce only two outcomes: the person will either begin to work for pay or remain

---

Figure 6.11

The Size of the Income Effect Is Affected by the
Initial Hours of Work

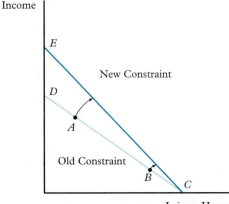

out of the labor force. *Reducing* the hours of paid employment is not possible. For those who are out of the labor force, then, the decision to *participate* as wage offers rise clearly reflects a dominant substitution effect. Conversely, if someone currently working decides to change his or her participation decision and drop out of the labor force when wages fall, the substitution effect has again dominated. Thus, the *labor force participation decisions brought about by wage changes exhibit a dominant substitution effect.* We turn now to a more detailed analysis of the decision whether to join the labor force.

The Reservation Wage   An implication of our labor supply theory is that if people who are not in the labor force place a value of $X on the marginal hour of leisure, then they would be unwilling to take a job unless the offered wages were greater than $X. Because they will "reserve" their labor unless the wage is $X or more (see Example 6.3), economists say that they have a *reservation* wage of $X. The reservation wage, then, is the wage below which a person will not work, and in the labor/leisure context, it represents the value placed on an hour of lost leisure time.[14]

Refer back to Figure 6.6, which graphically depicted a person choosing not to work. The reason there was no tangency between an indifference curve and the budget constraint—and the reason the person remained out of the labor force—was that the wage was everywhere lower than his or her marginal value of leisure time.

Often, people are thought to behave as if they have both a reservation wage *and a certain number of work hours* that must be offered before they will consider taking a job. The reasons are not difficult to understand and are illustrated in Figure 6.12. Suppose that taking a job entails 2 hours of commuting time (round-trip) per day. These hours, of course, are unpaid, so the worker's budget constraint must reflect that if a job is accepted, 2 hours of leisure are given up before there is any increase in income. These fixed costs of working are reflected in Figure 6.12 by segment AB. Segment BC, of course, reflects the earnings that are possible (once at work), and the slope of BC represents the person's wage rate.

Is the wage underlying BC great enough to induce the person to work? Consider indifference curve U_1, which represents the highest level of utility this person can achieve, given budget constraint ABC. Utility is maximized at point A, and the person chooses not to work. It is clear from this choice that the offered wage (given the 2-hour commute) is below the person's reservation wage, but can we show the latter wage graphically?

To take work with a 2-hour commute, the person depicted in Figure 6.12 must find a job able to generate a combination of earnings and leisure time that yields a utility level equal to, or greater than, U_1. This is possible only if the person's budget constraint is equal to (or to the right of) ABD, which is tangent to U_1 at

---

[14]See Hans G. Bloemen and Elena G. F. Stancanelli, "Individual Wealth, Reservation Wages, and Transitions into Employment," *Journal of Labor Economics* 19 (April 2001): 400–439, for a study of reservation wages.

Figure 6.12

Reservation Wage with Fixed Time
Costs of Working

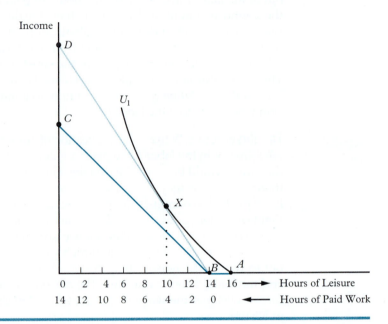

point X. The person's reservation wage, then, is equal to the slope of BD, and you
can readily note that in this case, the slope of BD exceeds the slope of BC, which
represents the currently offered wage. Moreover, to bring utility up to the level of
U_1 (the utility associated with not working), the person shown in Figure 6.12 must
be able to find a job at the reservation wage that offers 4 hours of work per day. Put
differently, at this person's reservation wage, he or she would want to consume
10 hours of leisure daily, and with a 2-hour commute, this implies 4 hours of work.

Empirical Findings on the Income and Substitution Effects

Labor supply theory suggests that the choices workers make concerning their
desired hours of work depend on their wealth and the wage rate they can command, in addition to their preferences. In particular, this theory suggests the
existence of a negative income effect and a positive substitution effect. Empirical
tests of labor supply theory generally attempt to determine if these two effects
can be observed, if they operate in the expected directions, and what their relative
magnitudes are.

Most recent studies of labor supply have used large samples of individuals to
analyze how labor force participation and hours of work are affected by changes in
wage rates and income—often induced by changes in taxes—holding other influences (age, for example) constant. Studies of male and female labor force behavior are done separately because of the different roles men and women typically

EXAMPLE 6.3

Daily Labor Supply at the Ballpark

The theory of labor supply rests in part on the assumption that when workers' offered wages climb above their reservation wages, they will decide to participate in the labor market. An implication of this theory is that in jobs for which hiring is done on a daily basis, and for which wages fluctuate widely from day to day, we should observe daily fluctuations in participation. These expectations are supported by the daily labor supply decisions of vendors at Major League Baseball games.

One such study examined the individual labor supply behavior of vendors in one ballpark over the course of the 1996 major league baseball season. Vendors walk through the stands selling food and drinks, and their earnings are completely determined by the sales they are able to make each day. The vendors studied could freely choose whether to work any given game, and the data collected by this study clearly suggest they made their decisions by weighing their opportunity cost of working against their expected earnings during the

course of the game. (Expected earnings, of course, are related to a number of factors, including how many fans were likely to attend the game.)

The study was able to compare the actual amount earned by each vendor at each game with the number of vendors who had decided to work. The average amount earned by vendors was $43.81, with a low of $26.55 for one game and a high of $73.15 for another—and about 45 vendors worked the typical game at this ballpark. The study found that an increase in average earnings of $10 (which represents about a one standard deviation increase from the mean of $43.81) lured about six extra vendors to the stadium.

Clearly, then, vendors behaved as if they had reservation wages that they compared with expected earnings when deciding whether to work particular games.

Data from: Gerald Oettinger, "An Empirical Analysis of the Daily Labor Supply of Stadium Vendors," *Journal of Political Economy* 107 (April 1999): 360–392.

---

play in performing household work and child-rearing—activities that clearly affect labor supply decisions but about which information is usually very limited.

A comprehensive review of numerous studies of the labor supply behavior of men finds that the sizes of the estimated effects vary with both the data and the statistical methodology used. Taken as a whole, however, the studies find strong evidence that, as theory suggests, observed substitution effects are positive and observed income effects are negative. What is less clear is which effect dominates when wages change; indeed, it appears that the typical study finds the two effects to be roughly similar in magnitude.[15] Studies of the retirement behavior of older men (a topic we will address in chapter 7) find, also as theory suggests, that the substitution effect dominates the decision to withdraw from the labor force.[16]

---

[15]Michael P. Keane, "Labor Supply and Taxes: A Survey," *Journal of Economic Literature* 49 (December 2011): 961–1075.

[16]Franco Peracchi and Finis Welch, "Trends in the Labor Force Transitions of Older Men and Women," *Journal of Labor Economics* 12 (April 1994): 210–242.

Studies of the labor supply behavior of women generally have found a greater responsiveness to wage changes than is found among men. As noted earlier, labor supply can be measured both by labor force participation rates and by hours of work. Historically, women's labor force participation rates have been more responsive than men's to wage changes. (As seen in Example 6.4, the labor force participation rate for married women has also been more responsive to wage changes than have been their hours of work.) There is evidence, however, that in the last two decades, the labor supply behavior of women has become much more similar to that for men—meaning that the labor supply of women is *becoming less*

EXAMPLE 6.4

Labor Supply Effects of Income Tax Cuts

In 1986, Congress changed the personal income tax system in the United States by drastically reducing tax rates on upper levels of income. Before this change, for example, families paid a 50 percent tax rate on taxable incomes over $170,000; after the change, this tax rate was reduced to 28 percent. The tax rate on taxable incomes over $50,000 was also set at 28 percent, down from about 40 percent. Lower income tax rates have the effect of increasing take-home earnings, and they therefore act as an increase in wage rates. Because lower rates generate an income and a substitution effect that work in opposite directions, they have an ambiguous anticipated effect on labor supply. Can we find out which effect is stronger in practice?

The 1986 changes served as a *natural experiment* (abrupt changes in only one variable, the sizes of which vary by group). The changes were sudden, large, and very different for families of different incomes. For married women in families that, without their earnings, had incomes at the 99th percentile of the income distribution (that is, the upper 1 percent), the tax rate cuts meant a 22 percent increase in their take-home wage rates. For women in families with incomes at the 90th percentile, the smaller tax rate cuts meant a 12 percent increase in take-home wages. It turns out that married women at the 99th and 90th percentiles of family income were similar in age, education, and occupation—and increases in

their labor supply had been similar prior to 1986. Therefore, comparing their responses to very different changes in their after-tax wage rates should yield insight into how the labor supply of married women responded to tax rate changes.

One study compared labor supply increases, from 1984 to 1990, for married women in the 99th and 90th percentiles. It found that the labor force participation rate for women in the 99th percentile rose by 19.4 percent and that, if working, their hours of work rose by 12.7 percent during that period. In contrast, both labor force participation and hours of work for women at the 90th percentile rose only by about 6.5 percent. The data from this natural experiment, then, suggest that women who experienced larger increases in their take-home wages desired greater increases in their labor supply—which implies that the substitution effect dominated the income effect for these women. Also, consistent with both theory and the results from other studies (discussed in the text), the dominance of the substitution effect was more pronounced for labor force participation decisions than it was for hours-of-work decisions.

Data from: Nada Eissa, "Taxation and Labor Supply of Married Women: The Tax Reform Act of 1986 as a Natural Experiment," Working Paper No. 5023, National Bureau of Economic Research, Cambridge, Mass., February 1995.

responsive to wage changes than it used to be. The reduced responsiveness has been especially noticeable in women's labor force participation decisions, where the differences between men and women have been greatest.[17] This growing similarity in labor supply behavior may well reflect a growing similarity in the expectations held by women and men concerning work and careers.

Policy Applications

Many income maintenance programs create budget constraints that increase income while reducing the take-home wage rate (thus causing the income and substitution effects to work in the same direction). Therefore, using labor supply theory to analyze the work-incentive effects of various social programs is both instructive and important. We characterize these programs by the budget constraints they create for their recipients.

Budget Constraints with "Spikes"

Some social insurance programs compensate workers who are unable to work because of a temporary work injury, a permanent disability, or a layoff. Workers' compensation insurance replaces most of the earnings lost when workers are hurt on the job, and private or public disability programs do the same for workers who become physically or emotionally unable to work for other reasons. Unemployment compensation is paid to those who have lost a job and have not been able to find another. While exceptions can be found in the occasional jurisdiction,[18] it is generally true that these *income replacement* programs share a common characteristic: they pay benefits only to those who are not working.

To understand the consequences of paying benefits only to those who are not working, let us suppose that a workers' compensation program is structured so that, after injury, workers receive their pre-injury earnings for as long as they are off work. Once they work even one hour, however, they are no longer considered disabled and cannot receive further benefits. The effects of this program on work incentives are analyzed in Figure 6.13, in which it is assumed that the pre-injury budget constraint was AB and pre-injury earnings were $E_0(= AC)$. Furthermore, we assume that the worker's "market" budget constraint (that is, the constraint

---

[17]Keane, "Labor Supply and Taxes: A Survey"; Francine D. Blau and Lawrence M. Kahn, "Changes in the Labor Supply Behavior of Married Women: 1980–2000," *Journal of Labor Economics* 25 (July 2007): 393–438; Bradley T. Heim, "Structural Estimation of Family Labor Supply with Taxes: Estimating a Continuous Hours Model Using a Direct Utility Specification," *Journal of Human Resources* 44 (Spring 2009): 350–385; Kelly Bishop, Bradley Heim, and Kata Mihaly, "Single Women's Labor Supply Elasticities: Trends and Policy Implications," *Industrial and Labor Relations Review* 63 (October 2009): 146–168.

[18]UI and workers' compensation programs in the United States are run at the state level and thus vary in their characteristics to some extent.

Figure 6.13

Budget Constraint with a
Spike

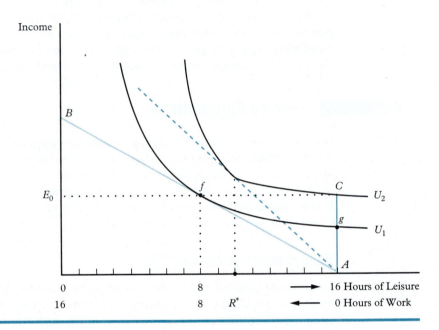

in the absence of a workers' compensation program) is unchanged, so that after recovery, the pre-injury wage can again be earned. Under these conditions, the post-injury budget constraint is *BAC*, and the person maximizes utility at point *C*—a point of no work.

Note that constraint *BAC* contains the segment *AC*, which looks like a spike. It is this spike that creates severe work-incentive problems, for two reasons. First, the returns associated with the first hour of work are *negative*. That is, a person at point *C* who returns to work for 1 hour would find his or her income to be considerably reduced by working. Earnings from this hour of work would be more than offset by the reduction in benefits, which creates a negative "net wage." The substitution effect associated with this program characteristic clearly discourages work.[19]

Second, our assumed no-work benefit of *AC* is equal to E_0, the pre-injury level of earnings. If the worker values leisure at all (as is assumed by

---

[19]In graphical terms, the budget constraint contains a vertical spike, and the slope of this vertical segment is infinitely negative. In economic terms, the implied infinitely negative (net) wage arises from the fact that even 1 minute of work causes a person to lose his or her entire benefit. For empirical evidence, see Susan Chen and Wilbert van der Klaauw, "The Work Disincentive Effects of the Disability Insurance Program in the 1990s," *Journal of Econometrics* 142 (February 2008): 757–784. For an analysis of disability insurance usage, see David H. Autor and Mark G. Duggan, "The Growth in the Social Security Disability Rolls: A Fiscal Crisis Unfolding," *Journal of Economic Perspectives* 20 (Summer 2006): 71–96.

the standard downward slope of indifference curves), being able to receive the old level of earnings while also enjoying more leisure clearly enhances utility. The worker is better off at point C than at point f, the pre-injury combination of earnings and leisure hours, because he or she is on indifference curve U_2 rather than U_1. Allowing workers to reach a higher utility level without working generates an income effect that discourages, or at least slows, the return to work.

Indeed, the program we have assumed raises a worker's reservation wage above his or her pre-injury wage, meaning that a return to work is possible only if the worker qualifies for a higher-paying job. To see this graphically, observe the dashed blue line in Figure 6.13 that begins at point A and is tangent to indifference curve U_2 (the level of utility made possible by the social insurance program). The slope of this line is equal to the person's reservation wage, because if the person can obtain the desired hours of work at this or a greater wage, utility will be at least equal to that associated with point C. Note also that for labor force participation to be induced, the reservation wage must be received for at least R^* hours of work.

Given that the work-incentive aspects of income replacement programs often quite justifiably take a backseat to the goal of making unfortunate workers "whole" in some economic sense, creating programs that avoid work disincentives is not easy. With the preferences of the worker depicted in Figure 6.13, a benefit of slightly less than Ag would ensure minimal loss of utility while still providing incentives to return to work as soon as physically possible (work would allow indifference curve U_1 to be attained—see point f—while not working and receiving a benefit of less than Ag would not). Unfortunately, workers differ in their preferences, so the optimal benefit—one that would provide work incentives yet ensure only minimal loss of utility—differs for each individual.

With programs that create spikes, the best policymakers can do is set a no-work benefit as some fraction of previous earnings and then use administrative means to encourage the return to work among any whose utility is greater when not working. Unemployment insurance (UI), for example, replaces something like half of lost earnings for the typical worker, but the program puts an upper limit on the weeks each unemployed worker can receive benefits. Workers' compensation replaces two-thirds of lost earnings for the average worker but must rely on doctors—and sometimes judicial hearings—to determine whether a worker continues to be eligible for benefits. (For evidence that more-generous workers' compensation benefits do indeed induce longer absences from work, see Example 6.5.)[20]

---

[20]For a summary of evidence on the labor supply effects of UI and workers' compensation, see Alan B. Krueger and Bruce D. Meyer, "Labor Supply Effects of Social Insurance," in *Handbook of Public Economics*, vol. 4, eds. Alan Auerbach and Martin Feldstein (Amsterdam: North Holland, 2002); and Peter Kuhn and Chris Riddell, "The Long-Term Effects of Unemployment Insurance: Evidence from New Brunswick and Maine, 1940–1991," *Industrial and Labor Relations Review* 63 (January 2010): 183–204.

EXAMPLE 6.5

Staying Around One's Kentucky Home: Workers' Compensation Benefits and the Return to Work

Workers injured on the job receive workers' compensation insurance benefits while away from work. These benefits differ across states, but they are calculated for most workers as some fraction (normally two-thirds) of weekly, pre-tax earnings. For high-wage workers, however, weekly benefits are typically capped at a maximum, which again varies by state.

On July 15, 1980, Kentucky raised its maximum weekly benefit by 66 percent. It did not alter benefits in any other way, so this change effectively granted large benefit increases to high-wage workers without awarding them to anyone else. Because those injured before July 15 were ineligible for the increased benefits, even if they remained off work after July 15, this policy change created a nice natural experiment: one group

of injured workers was able to obtain higher benefits, while another group was not. Did the group receiving higher benefits show evidence of reduced labor supply, as suggested by theory?

The effects of increased benefits on labor supply were unmistakable. High-wage workers ineligible for the new benefits typically stayed off the job for four weeks, but those injured after July 15 stayed away for five weeks—25 percent longer! No increases in the typical time away from work were recorded among lower-paid injured workers, who were unaffected by the changes in benefits.

———

Data from: Bruce D. Meyer, W. Kip Viscusi, and David L. Durbin, "Workers' Compensation and Injury Duration: Evidence from a Natural Experiment," *American Economic Review* 85 (June 1995): 322–340.

Programs with Net Wage Rates of Zero

The programs just discussed were intended to confer benefits on those who are unable to work, and the budget-constraint spike was created by the eligibility requirement that to receive benefits, one must not be working. Other social programs, such as welfare, have different eligibility criteria and calculate benefits differently. These programs factor income needs into their eligibility criteria and then pay benefits based on the difference between one's actual earnings and one's needs. We will see that paying people the difference between their earnings and their needs creates a net wage rate of zero; thus, the work-incentive problems associated with these welfare programs result from the fact that they increase the income of program recipients while also drastically reducing the price of leisure.

Nature of Welfare Subsidies   Originally, welfare programs tended to take the form of a guaranteed annual income, under which the welfare agency determined the income needed by an eligible person (Y_n in Figure 6.14) based on family size, area living costs, and local welfare regulations. Actual earnings were then subtracted from this needed level, and a check was issued to the person each month for the difference. If the person did not work, he or she received a subsidy of Y_n. If the person worked, and if earnings caused dollar-for-dollar reductions in welfare benefits, then a budget constraint like $ABCD$ in Figure 6.14 was created. The person's income remained at Y_n as long as he or she was subsidized. If receiving the

forcing recipients off welfare or by inducing them to leave so they can "save" their eligibility in case they need welfare later in life. Thus, in terms of Figure 6.14, the lifetime limit ultimately removes *ABC* from the potential recipient's budget constraint, which then reverts to the market constraint of *AD*.

Clearly, the lifetime limit increases work incentives by ultimately eliminating the income subsidy. However, within the limits of their eligible years, potential welfare recipients must choose when to receive the subsidy and when to "save" their eligibility in the event of a future need. Federal law provides for welfare subsidies only to families with children under the age of 18; consequently, the closer one's youngest child is to 18 (when welfare eligibility ends anyway), the smaller are the incentives of the parent to forgo the welfare subsidy and save eligibility for the future.[25]

Work Requirements   As noted earlier, PRWORA introduced a work requirement into the welfare system, although in some cases, unpaid work or enrolling in education or training programs counts toward that requirement. States differ in how the earnings affect welfare benefits, and many have rules that allow welfare recipients to keep most of what they earn (by not reducing, at least by much, their welfare benefits); we analyze such programs in the next section. For now, we can understand the *basic* effects of a work requirement by maintaining our assumption that earnings reduce welfare benefits dollar for dollar.

Figure 6.16 illustrates the budget constraint associated with a minimum work requirement of 6 hours a day (30 hours per week). If the person fails to work the required 6 hours a day, no welfare benefits are received, and he or she will be along segment *AB* of the constraint. If the work requirement is met, but earnings are less than Y_n, welfare benefits are received (see segment *BCD*). If the work requirement is exceeded, income (earnings plus benefits) remains at Y_n—the person is along *CD*—until earnings rise above needed income and the person is along segment *DE* of the constraint and no longer eligible for welfare benefits.

The work-incentive effects of this *work requirement* can be seen from analyzing Figure 6.16 in the context of people whose skills are such that they are potential welfare recipients. At one extreme, some potential recipients may have such steeply sloped indifferences curves (reflecting a strong preference, or a need, to stay at home) that utility is maximized along segment *AB*, where so little market work is performed that they do not qualify for welfare. At the opposite extreme, others may have such flat indifference curves (reflecting a strong preference for income and a weak preference for leisure) that their utility is maximized along segment *DE*; they work so many hours that their earnings disqualify them for welfare benefits.

In the middle of the above extremes will be those whose preferences lead them to work enough to qualify for welfare benefits. Clearly, if their earnings reduce their benefits dollar for dollar—as shown by the horizontal segment *DC* in Figure 6.16—they will want to work just the *minimum hours* needed to qualify for

---

[25]Jeffrey Grogger, "Time Limits and Welfare Use," *Journal of Human Resources* 39 (Spring 2004): 405–424.

Figure 6.16

The Welfare System with a
Work Requirement

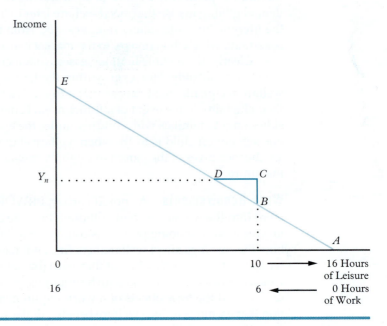

welfare, because their utility will be maximized at point *C* and not along *DC*. (For labor supply responses to different forms of a work requirement—requisitions of food from farmers during wartime—see Example 6.6 on page 227.)

Subsidy Programs with Positive Net Wage Rates

So far, we have analyzed the work-incentive effects of income maintenance programs that create net wage rates for program recipients that are either negative or zero (that is, they create constraints that have either a spike or a horizontal segment). Most current programs, however, including those adopted by states under PRWORA, create positive net wages for recipients. Do these programs offer a solution to the problem of work incentives? We will answer this question by analyzing a relatively recent and rapidly growing program: the Earned Income Tax Credit (EITC).

The EITC program makes income tax credits available to low-income families with at least one worker. A tax credit of $1 reduces a person's income taxes by $1, and in the case of the EITC, if the tax credit for which workers qualify exceeds their total income tax liability, the government will mail them a check for the difference. Thus, the EITC functions as an earnings subsidy, and because the subsidy goes only to those who work, the EITC is seen by many as an income maintenance program that preserves work incentives. This view led Congress to vastly expand the EITC under President Bill Clinton and it is now the largest cash subsidy program directed at low-income households with children.

The tax credits offered by the EITC program vary with one's earnings and the number of dependent children. For purposes of our analysis, which is intended to illustrate the work-incentive effects of the EITC, we will focus on the credits in the year 2012 offered to unmarried workers with two children. Figure 6.17 graphs the relevant program characteristics for a worker with two children who could earn a market (unsubsidized) wage reflected by the slope of AC. As we will see later, for such a worker, the EITC created a budget constraint of ABDEC.

For workers with earnings of $13,090 or less, the tax credit was calculated at 40 percent of earnings. That is, for every dollar earned, a tax credit of 40 cents was also earned; thus, for those with earnings of under $13,090, net wages ($W_n$) were 40 percent higher than market wages (W). Note that this tax credit is represented by segment AB on the EITC constraint in Figure 6.17 and that the slope of AB *exceeds the slope of the market constraint AC.*

The maximum tax credit allowed for a single parent with two children was $5,236 in 2012. Workers who earned between $13,090 and $17,100 per year qualified for this maximum tax credit. Because these workers experienced no increases or reductions in tax credits per added dollar of earnings, their net wage is equal to their market wage. The constraint facing workers with earnings in this range is represented by segment BD in Figure 6.17, which has a slope equal to that of segment AC.

For earnings above $17,100, the tax credit was gradually phased out, so that when earnings reached $41,952, the tax credit was zero. Because after $17,100 each dollar earned reduced the tax credit by 21 cents, the net wage of EITC recipients was only 79 percent of their market wage (note that the slope of segment DE in Figure 6.17 is flatter than the slope of AC).

Figure 6.17

Earned Income Tax Credit
(Unmarried, Two Children),
2012

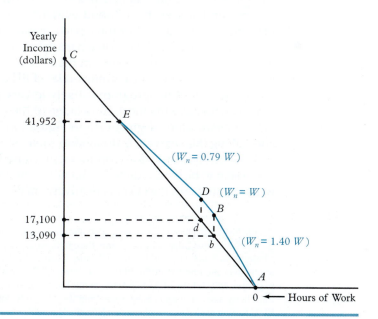

Looking closely at Figure 6.17, we can see that EITC recipients will be in one of three "zones": along *AB*, along *BD*, or along *DE*. The incomes of workers in all three zones are enhanced, which means that all EITC recipients experience an income effect that pushes them in the direction of less work. However, the program creates quite different net wage rates in the zones, and therefore the substitution effect differs across zones.

For workers with earnings below $13,090, the net wage is greater than the market wage (by 40 percent), so along segment *AB*, workers experience an increase in the price of leisure. Workers with earnings below $13,090, then, experience a substitution effect that pushes them in the direction of more work. With an income effect and a substitution effect that push in opposite directions, it is uncertain which effect will dominate. What we can predict, though, is that some of those who would have been out of the labor force in the absence of the EITC program will now decide to seek work (earlier, we discussed the fact that for nonparticipants in the labor force, the substitution effect dominates).

Segments *BD* and *DE* represent two other zones, in which theory predicts that labor supply will *fall*. Along *BD*, the net wage is equal to the market wage, so the price of leisure in this zone is unchanged while income is enhanced. Workers in this zone experience a pure income effect. Along segment *DE*, the net wage is actually below the market wage, so in this zone, *both* the income and the substitution effects push in the direction of reduced labor supply.

Using economic theory to analyze labor supply responses induced by the constraint in Figure 6.17, we can come up with two predictions. First, if an EITC program is started or expanded, we should observe that the labor force participation rate of low-wage workers will increase. Second, a new or expanded EITC program should lead to a reduction in working hours among those along *BD* and *DE* (the effect on hours along *AB* is ambiguous).

Several studies have found evidence consistent with prediction that the EITC should increase labor force participation, with one study finding that over half of the increase in labor force participation among *single mothers* from 1984 to 1996 was caused by expansions in the EITC during that period. As suggested by Figure 6.17, however, the earnings-related EITC are complex to calculate, so that knowledge about the program is likely to vary across individuals. Among individuals who have the most knowledge of the program, it appears that hours of work increase along segment *AB* in Figures 6.17—meaning that the substitution effect along this segment is dominant. Along segment *DE*, where both the income and substitution effects are predicted to cause hours of work to decrease, there does seem to be the predicted reduction in hours worked among knowledgeable workers, although the effect is relatively small.[26]

---

[26]Nada Eissa and Hilary W. Hoynes, "Behavioral Responses to Taxes: Lessons from the EITC and Labor Supply," National Bureau of Economic Research, working paper no. 11729 (November 2005); and Raj Chetty, John Friedman, and Emmanuel Saez, "Using Differences in Knowledge Across Neighborhoods to Uncover the Impacts of the EITC on Earnings," National Bureau of Economic Research, working paper no. 18232 (July 2012). Citations to the literature on the EITC and labor supply can be found in Raj Chetty and Emmanuel Saez, "Teaching the Tax Code: Earnings Responses to an Experiment with EITC Recipients," *American Economic Journal: Applied Economics* 5 (January 2013): 1–31.

EXAMPLE 6.6

Wartime Food Requisitions and Agricultural Work Incentives

Countries at war often adopt "work requirement" policies to obtain needed food supplies involuntarily from their farming populations. Not surprisingly, the way in which these requisitions are carried out can have enormous effects on the work incentives of farmers. Two alternative methods are contrasted in this example: one was used by the Bolshevik government during the civil war that followed the Russian revolution and the other by Japan during World War II.

From 1917 to 1921, the Bolsheviks requisitioned from farmers all food in excess of the amounts needed for the farmers' own subsistence; in effect, the surplus was confiscated and given to soldiers and urban dwellers. Graphically, this policy created a budget constraint for farmers like ACY_s in the following diagram (a). Because farmers could keep their output until they reached the subsistence level of income (Y_s), the market wage prevailed until income of Y_s was reached. After that, their net wage was zero (on segment CY_s), because any extra output went to the government. Thus, a prewar market constraint of AB was converted to ACY_s, with the consequence that most farmers

maximized utility near point C. Acreage planted dropped by 27 percent from 1917 to 1921, while harvested output fell by 50 percent!

Japan during World War II handled its food requisitioning policy completely differently. It required a quota to be delivered by each farmer to the government at very low prices, paying farmers the lump sum of EF in diagram (b). Japan, however, allowed farmers to sell any produce above the quota at higher (market) prices. This policy converted the prewar constraint of AB to one much like EFG in diagram (b). In effect, farmers had to work AE hours for the government, for which they were paid EF, but they were then allowed to earn the market wage after that. This policy preserved farmers' work incentives and apparently created an income effect that increased the total hours of work by Japanese farmers, for despite war-induced shortages of capital and labor, rice production was greater in 1944 than in 1941!

Data from: Jack Hirshleifer, Economic Behavior in Adversity (Chicago: University of Chicago Press, 1987): 16–21, 39–41.

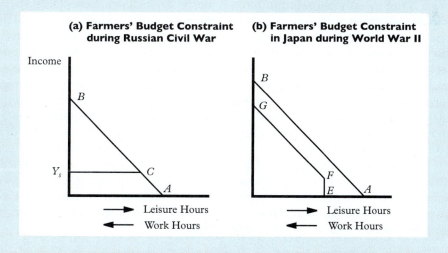

(a) Farmers' Budget Constraint during Russian Civil War

(b) Farmers' Budget Constraint in Japan during World War II

EMPIRICAL STUDY

ESTIMATING THE INCOME EFFECT AMONG LOTTERY WINNERS: THE SEARCH FOR "EXOGENEITY"

Regression analysis, described in Appendix 1A, allows us to analyze the effects of one or more *independent* variables on a *dependent* variable. This statistical procedure is based on an important assumption: that each independent variable is *exogenous* (determined by some outside force and not itself influenced by the dependent variable). That is, we assume that the chain of causation runs from the independent variables to the dependent variable, with no feedback from the dependent variable to those that we assume are independent.

The issue of exogeneity arises when estimating the effects on hours of work caused by a change in income (wages held constant). Theory leads us to predict that desired hours of work are a function of wages, wealth, and preferences. Wealth is not usually observed in most data sets, so *nonlabor* income, such as the returns from financial investments, is used as a proxy for it. Measuring the effect that nonlabor income (an independent, or causal, variable) has on desired hours of work (our dependent variable), holding the wage constant, is intended to capture the income effect predicted by labor supply theory.

The problem is that those who have strong preferences for income and weak preferences for leisure, for example, may tend to accumulate financial assets over time and end up with relatively high levels of nonlabor income later on. Put differently, high levels of work hours (supposedly our dependent variable) may create high levels of nonlabor income (what we hoped would be our independent variable); thus, when we estimate a correlation between work hours and nonlabor income, we cannot be sure whether we are estimating the income effect, some relationship between hard work and savings, or a mix of both (a problem analogous to the one discussed in the empirical study in chapter 4). In estimating the income effect, therefore, researchers must be careful to use measures of nonlabor income that are truly exogenous and not themselves influenced by the desired hours of work.

Are lottery winnings an exogenous source of nonlabor income? Once a person enters a lottery, winning is a completely random event and thus is not affected by work hours; however, entering the lottery may not be so independent. If those who enter the lottery also have the strongest preferences for leisure, for example, then correlating work hours and lottery winnings across different individuals would not necessarily isolate the income effect. Rather, it might just reflect that those with stronger preferences for leisure (and thus lower work hours) were more likely to enter (and thus win) the lottery.

Therefore, if we want to measure the income effect associated with winning the lottery, we need to find a way to hold both wages *and* preferences for leisure constant. One study of how winning the lottery affected labor supply took account of the preferences of lottery players by performing a before-and-after analysis using panel data on winners and nonwinners. That is, for winners—defined as receiving prizes over $20,000, with a median prize of $635,000—the authors compared hours of work for six years before winning to hours of work during the six years after winning. By focusing on each individual's *changes* in hours and lottery winnings over the two periods, the effects of preferences (which are assumed to be unchanging) drop out of the analysis.

"Nonwinners" in the study were defined as lottery players who won only small prizes, ranging from $100 to $5,000. Labor supply changes for them before and after their small winnings were then calculated and compared to the changes observed among the winners. The study found that for every $100,000 in prizes, winners reduced their hours of work such that their earnings went down by roughly $11,000 (that is, winners spent about 11 percent of their prize on "buying" leisure). These findings, of course, are consistent with the predictions concerning the income effect of nonlabor income on labor supply.

Source: Guido W. Imbens, Donald B. Rubin, and Bruce I. Sacerdote, "Estimating the Effect of Unearned Income on Labor Earnings, Savings, and Consumption: Evidence from a Survey of Lottery Players," *American Economic Review* 91 (September 2001): 778–794.

Review Questions

1. Referring to the definitions in footnote 5, is the following statement true, false, or uncertain? "Leisure must be an inferior good for an individual's labor supply curve to be backward-bending." Explain your answer.

2. "A wage increase reduces the demand for leisure hours." Comment on this statement and explain.

3. Suppose a government is considering several options to ensure that legal services are provided to the poor:
   Option A: All lawyers would be required to devote 5 percent of their work time to the poor, free of charge.
   Option B: Lawyers would be required to provide 100 hours of work, free of charge, to the poor.
   Option C: Lawyers who earn over $50,000 in a given year would have to donate $5,000 to a fund that the government would use to help the poor.
   Discuss the likely effects of each option on the hours of work among lawyers. (It would help to *draw* the constraints created by each option.)

4. The way the workers' compensation system works now, employees permanently injured on the job receive a payment of $X each year, whether they work or not. Suppose the government were to implement a new program in which those who did not work at all got $0.5X, but those who did work got $0.5X plus workers' compensation of 50 cents *for every hour worked* (of course, this subsidy would be in addition to the wages paid by their employers). What would be the change in work incentives associated with this change in the way workers' compensation payments were calculated?

5. A firm wants to offer paid sick leave to its workers, but it wants to encourage them not to abuse it by being unnecessarily absent. The firm is considering two options:
   a. Ten days of paid sick leave per year; any unused leave days at the end of the year are converted to cash at the worker's daily wage rate.
   b. Ten days of paid sick leave per year; if no sick days are used for two consecutive years, the company agrees to buy the worker a $100,000 life insurance policy.

   Compare the work-incentive effects of the two options, both immediately and in the long run.

6. In 2002, a French law went into effect that cut the standard workweek from 39 to 35 hours (workers got paid for 39 hours even though they worked 35) while at the same time prohibiting overtime hours from being worked. (Overtime in France is paid at 25 percent above the normal wage rate.)
   a. Draw the old budget constraint, showing the overtime premium after 39 hours of work.
   b. Draw the new budget constraint.

   c. Analyze which workers in France are better off under the 2002 law. Are any worse off? Explain.

7. Suppose there is a proposal to provide poor people with housing subsidies that are tied to their income levels. These subsidies will be in the form of vouchers the poor can turn over to their landlords in full or partial payment of their housing expenses. The yearly subsidy will equal $2,400 as long as earnings do not exceed $8,000 per year. The subsidy is to be reduced 60 cents for every dollar earned in excess of $8,000; that is, when earnings reach $12,000, the person is no longer eligible for rent subsidies.

   Draw an arbitrary budget constraint for a person, assuming that he or she receives no government subsidies. Then draw in the budget constraint that arises from the above housing subsidy proposal. After drawing in the budget constraint associated with the proposal, analyze the effects of this proposed housing subsidy program on the labor supply behavior of various groups in the population.

8. The Tax Reform Act of 1986 was designed to reduce the marginal tax rate (the tax rate on the last dollars earned) while eliminating enough deductions and loopholes so that total revenues collected by the government could remain constant. Analyze the work-incentive effects of tax reforms that lower marginal tax rates while keeping total tax revenues constant.

9. The current UI program in the United States gives workers $X per day if they are unemployed but zero if they take a job for even 1 hour per day. Suppose that the law is changed so that UI beneficiaries can keep getting benefits of $X per day if they work 2 or fewer hours per day, but if they work more than 2 hours per day, their UI benefits end. Draw the old and

new budget constraints (clearly labeled) associated with the UI program, and analyze the work incentives of this proposed change.

10. Assume that the current Disability Insurance (DI) benefit for those who are unable to work is $X per day and that DI benefits go to *zero* if a worker accepts a job for even 1 hour per week. Suppose that the benefit rules are changed so those disabled workers who take jobs that pay less than $X per day receive a benefit that brings *their total daily income* (earnings plus the DI benefit) up to $X. As soon as their labor market earnings rise above $X per day, their disability benefits end. Draw the old and new budget constraints (label each clearly) associated with the DI program, and analyze the work-incentive effects of the change in benefits.

Problems

1. When the Fair Labor Standards Act began to mandate paying 50 percent more for overtime work, many employers tried to avoid it by cutting hourly pay so that total pay and hours remained the same.
   a. Assuming that this 50 percent overtime pay premium is newly required for all work beyond eight hours per day, draw a budget constraint that pictures a strategy of cutting hourly pay so that at the original hours of work, total earnings remain the same.
   b. Suppose that an employer initially paid $11 per hour and had a 10-hour workday. What hourly base wage will the employer offer so that the total pay for a 10-hour workday will stay the same?
   c. Will employees who used to work 10 hours per day want to work more or fewer than 10 hours in the new environment (which includes the new wage rate and the mandated overtime premium)?

2. Deeya, a part-time instructor, is paid $680 for 8 hours of teaching per week. If she teaches overtime, each hour will earn her $90 for a maximum of two hours, but she prefers practicing the piano to teaching overtime. Calculate the opportunity cost of this preference.

3. Suppose you win a lottery, and your after-tax gain is $50,000 per year until you retire. As a result, you decide to work part time at 30 hours per week in your old job instead of the usual 40 hours per week.
   a. Calculate the annual income effect from this lottery gain based on a 50-week year. Interpret the results in light of the theory presented in this chapter.
   b. What is the substitution effect associated with this lottery win? Explain.

4. The federal minimum wage was increased on July 24, 2007, to $5.85 from $5.15. If 16 hours per day are available for work and leisure, draw the daily budget constraint for a worker who was earning the minimum wage rate of $5.15 and the new budget constraint after the increase.

5. Wenshin gets an interest of $40 per day from his personal wealth. His wage rate is $20 per hour. If he can work 16 hours a day, draw his budget constraint.

6. Stella can work up to 16 hours per day at her job. Her wage rate is $8.00 per hour for the first 8 hours. If she works more than 8 hours, her employer pays "time and a half." Draw Stella's daily budget constraint.

7. A worker used to work for 8 hours a day for a wage of $8 per hour. His optimum hour of leisure is indicated by the point *a* in the graph and *BD* represents his initial budget line. When his wage rate is increased to $10, his new optimum is at *b*. Calculate the wage increase that he gets. For this worker, which effect is stronger, the income effect or the substitution effect?

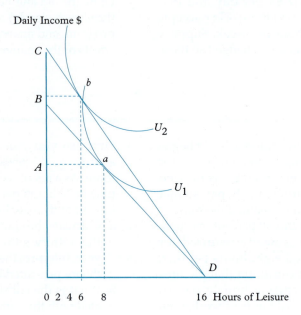

Daily Income $

0 2 4 6   8   16 Hours of Leisure

Selected Readings

Blank, Rebecca M. "Evaluating Welfare Reform in the United States." *Journal of Economic Literature* 40 (December 2002): 1105–1166.

Card, David E., and Rebecca M. Blank, eds. *Finding Jobs: Work and Welfare Reform*. New York: Russell Sage Foundation, 2000.

Hoffman, Saul D., and Laurence S. Seidman. *Helping Working Families: The Earned Income Tax Credit*. Kalamazoo, Mich.: W. E. Upjohn Institute for Employment Research, 2002.

Killingsworth, Mark R. *Labor Supply*. Cambridge, England: Cambridge University Press, 1983.

Linder, Staffan B. *The Harried Leisure Class*. New York: Columbia University Press, 1970.

Moffitt, Robert. "Incentive Effects of the U.S. Welfare System: A Review." *Journal of Economic Literature* 30 (March 1992): 1–62.

Pencavel, John. "Labor Supply of Men: A Survey." In *Handbook of Labor Economics*, eds. Orley Ashenfelter and David Card. Amsterdam, N.Y.: Elsevier, 1999.

CHAPTER 7

Labor Supply: Household Production, the Family, and the Life Cycle

In chapter 6, the theory of labor supply focused on the simple case in which individuals decide how to allocate their time between labor and leisure. This chapter elaborates on this simple labor supply model by taking account of three issues. First, much of the time spent at home is given to work activities (cooking and child care, for example), not leisure. Second, for those who live with partners, decisions about work for pay, household work, and leisure are usually made in a way that takes account of the activities and income of other household members. Third, just as time at paid work is substitutable with time at home, time spent working for pay in one part of the life cycle is substitutable with time later on. These refinements of our simple model do not alter the fundamental considerations or predictions of labor supply theory, but they do add useful richness to it.

A Labor Supply Model That Incorporates Household Production

In chapter 6, we built a model of labor supply on the simple assumption that people have but two ways to spend time: working for pay or consuming leisure. In reality, of course, the choices are more complex—and much of the time spent at home is in activities (cooking, cleaning, child care, etc.) that are closer to work than to leisure. Can we build a model of labor supply that takes account of these other uses of household time?

To get a sense of how potential labor force participants actually allocate their time, consider the data in Table 7.1, which breaks down activities into four

Table 7.1

Weekly Hours Spent in Household Work, Paid Work, and Leisure Activities by Men and Women over Age 18, 2012

	Households with Children < 6		Households with Children 6–17		Households with No Children < 18	
	Women	Men	Women	Men	Women	Men
Paid Work[a]	21	37	24	38	21	28
Household Work[b]	40	23	31	18	23	16
Leisure[c]	30	35	36	39	45	49
Personal Care[d]	75	71	76	72	77	74

[a]Includes commuting time.

[b]Includes time spent purchasing goods/services and caring for others.

[c]Includes time spent in volunteer and educational activities.

[d]Includes time spent sleeping and eating.

Source: U.S. Department of Labor, Bureau of Labor Statistics, "American Time Use Survey—2012 Results," Table 8 at http://www.bls.gov/news.release/atus.t08.htm.

categories (paid work, household work, leisure, and personal care) for three household groupings based on the presence and ages of children. The averages in the table suggest that women with very young children spend more time in household work activities and less time performing paid (or "market") work than women with older children. Women in all three categories of households spend more time in household work and less time in paid work than men do—but these disparities in hours shrink as children grow older and leave home. Time spent in leisure time, which is somewhat greater for men than women, increases for both women and men as children age. Personal care time varies little across groupings.

The Basic Model for an Individual: Similarities with the Labor-Leisure Model

Incorporating household activities other than leisure into our model of labor supply does not require significant changes in the model developed in chapter 6, but it does require us to replace the category of "leisure time" with one we will call "household production time" (or household time, for short). Time spent in household production includes doing chores or relaxing at home, but it also includes time spent on chores or relaxation that take one out of the household, such as shopping or going to a movie.

To illustrate the major effects of including household activities other than leisure into our model, let us consider a hypothetical household with a single decision-maker, Sally, who is the unmarried mother of small children. As we assumed in chapter 6, we will suppose that Sally needs 8 hours a day for personal care, so she therefore has 16 hours per day available for paid work, leisure, or household work. In Figure 7.1, we put Sally's available time on the horizontal axis—with household time running from left to right and market work (paid work) time running from right to left.

As before, we assume that Sally is trying to maximize her utility. She can acquire the commodities that enhance her utility—a clean house, good meals, happy children, relaxation activities—either by spending household time to *make* these commodities herself or by earning income that allows her to *buy* goods or services from others. Taken together, the two axes in Figure 7.1 reflect the two sources of inputs that can be used to produce utility for Sally: household time is on the horizontal axis, and income is on the vertical axis.

Sally's choices about how to use her time, as we discussed in chapter 6, are affected by her preferences, her income, and her wage rate. These influences are discussed in the following sections.

Preferences   As in chapter 6, we will continue to use downward-sloping indifference curves to graphically represent Sally's preferences. Nutritional meals, for example, generate utility for her, and one option she has is to grow her own food and fully prepare her meals at home. Other options, which could yield meals of equal utility, would involve mixing more purchased goods or services with less household preparation time: buying packaged foods to be heated at home, for example, or eating meals in a restaurant. Relaxation also produces utility, and *relaxation generating equal utility* could involve time but not much in the way of purchased goods (a day hiking in a local park) or more purchased goods and less time (an evening at a nightclub).

Because purchased goods and time are substitutes for each other in producing commodities that generate utility, Sally's indifference curves are downward-sloping (as explained in chapter 6). We also continue to draw these

Figure 7.1

Household Time and Income Are
Substitutes in the Production of
Commodities Sally Consumes

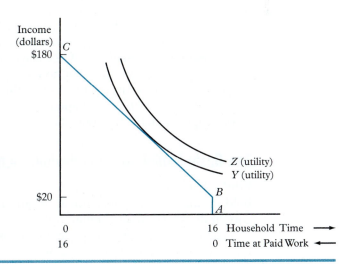

curves as convex for reasons similar to those given in chapter 6; that is, we assume that if Sally were trying to substitute more and more purchased goods for her time in the production of child care, say, she would find it increasingly difficult to do so and keep her utility constant. Finally, our graphical presentation of Sally's preferences assumes that if her ability to command resources were to increase—so that she could move from indifference curve Y in Figure 7.1 to indifference curve Z—her utility would increase. These assumptions lead to indifference curves for Sally that are identical to those presented in chapter 6.

Budget Constraint   Of course, Sally must make her choices about spending time in the context of her income and wage rate, and the budget constraint she faces sets out the limits on those choices. The constraint ABC in Figure 7.1 is drawn on the assumption that Sally can earn $10 per hour and that if she does not work for pay, she would have unearned income of $20 per day.

The constraint ABC, as with those we drew in chapter 6, runs between the two axes. At the lower right, the constraint tells us how much income she can spend if she performs no market work and spends all available time in household production ($20); at the upper left, it tells us how much income she could spend if she allocates all 16 hours to working for pay ($160 + $20 = $180). As before, the slope of the constraint reflects her wage rate, which is also the opportunity cost of household time (that is, if the wage she can earn is $10 per hour, an hour spent in doing household chores or in leisure requires her to forgo $10 of potential earnings). Thus, we draw her budget constraint, ABC in Figure 7.1, just as we drew constraints in chapter 6.

Income and Substitution Effects   With budget constraints and indifference curves shaped in the same way, it is not surprising that the labor-leisure model of chapter 6 and the household production model analyzed here have the same underlying labor supply implications. Specifically, if we assume that Sally's income rises and her wage rate—the opportunity cost of household time—is held constant, the household model predicts that she will spend more time in household production (consuming more commodities that bring her utility) and less time at paid work. Likewise, if her wage rate were to rise, holding her income constant, she would increase her hours of paid work, because the cost of staying at home would have risen while her wealth had not. In short, *the income and substitution effects introduced in* chapter 6 *work in exactly the same way* if we place our labor supply model in the context of household production rather than leisure.

The Basic Model for an Individual: Some New Implications

While changing the focus from leisure time to the broader category of household production time does not alter our labor supply model in a fundamental way, it does lead to additional topics of analysis that will be addressed in this and succeeding sections. One immediate insight is obvious but of critical importance: decisions about labor supply and decisions about how to produce the

EXAMPLE 7.1

Obesity and the Household Production Model

Obesity is a major health problem in the United States. During the period from the late 1970s to the early 1990s, the percentage of adult Americans considered obese rose from 14 percent to almost 22 percent! Obesity is now the second leading cause of early death; 300,000 premature deaths each year are associated with complications from obesity (heart disease, stroke, and diabetes, among others). One estimate indicates that in 1995, the annual costs of obesity (medical treatment plus lost productivity) came to almost $100 billion. Obesity, of course, is related to both genetic and other family influences, but the abrupt increase suggests that other factors may also have come into play. Can economic theory give us insights into this problem?

The model of household production presented in this chapter suggests that time spent in household work, such as meal preparation, will be responsive to changes in *preferences* and to both the *income and substitution effects*. As income grows, holding wages constant, we expect more time to be devoted to producing the goods we consume at home. However, as wages increase, holding income constant, the increase in the opportunity cost of time causes people to allocate *less* time to the household and more time to working for pay. If opportunity costs or changes in preferences have induced more people (women in particular) to seek market work and to spend less time in household work (including food preparation), we would expect the demand for convenience foods to grow.

Indeed, between 1972 and 1997—when the percentage of American women who were employed rose from 44 percent to 60 percent—the number of fast-food restaurants per capita doubled, and the number of full-service restaurants per capita rose by one-third. Fast-food restaurants, in particular, serve foods that are high in caloric content,

and one recent study found that the increase in the availability of these restaurants is strongly associated with increased obesity. That is, holding personal characteristics constant, the study found that the incidence of obesity increased more in areas with greater growth in restaurants per capita.

Moreover, the study also found evidence that both the income and substitution effect influenced obesity in the predicted direction. Within given geographic areas and various demographic groups defined by sex, race, marital status, and education, the study found that individuals with higher family incomes—holding wages for their demographic group constant—were *less* likely to be obese. This finding is consistent with the prediction that the *income effect* induces people to spend more time at home and become less dependent on fattening convenience foods.

However, individuals in areas and groups with higher hourly wages (and hours of market work)—holding income constant—had *increased* probabilities of being obese. The latter finding suggests that as the opportunity costs of time rise, the *substitution effect* may induce people to spend less time at home and be more reliant on convenience foods. Indeed, a recent study finds that as workers' wages (and the cost of time) rise, they spend less time eating meals and more time "grazing" while they work, which also leads to weight gain.

Sources: Shin-Yi Chou, Michael Grossman, and Henry Saffer, "An Economic Analysis of Adult Obesity: Results from the Behavioral Risk Factor Surveillance System," *Journal of Health Economics* 23 (May 2004): 565–587; and Daniel S. Hamermesh, "Grazing, Goods and Girth: Determinants and Effects," NBER Working Paper No. 15277 (Cambridge, Mass.: August 2009).

commodities we consume are jointly made. Thus, the choices made about market work, how many children a family has, how children are raised, how meals are prepared (see Example 7.1), and so forth, are affected by the same set of forces. This insight has spawned an entire subfield within economics: economic analysis of the family, which goes beyond the labor supply issues introduced here to deal with issues of marriage, divorce, fertility, child-rearing practices, and other activities and decisions families undertake.[1]

We must also more carefully consider the indifference curves in Figure 7.1. The slopes of these curves reflect the difficulty Sally faces in replacing her household time with purchased goods or services. If she is particularly gifted as a mother, if she is performing work that is difficult to replace by purchasing goods or services, or if she derives a lot of pleasure from household production, her indifference curves will be steeply drawn—meaning that if she were to reduce her time at home, *she would have to be compensated by a large increase in income* to keep her utility constant. Steeper indifference curves, of course, create tangency points with the budget constraint that are farther to the right in Figure 7.1; thus, the steeper Sally's indifference curves, the more hours she will spend at home and the fewer hours she will supply to the labor market. If her indifference curves are steep enough, she will not even seek market work and therefore not participate in the labor force.

As Sally's children grow older, she might find that it becomes easier to substitute purchased goods or services for her household time; suitable child care may become easier to find, for example, or day-care needs will fall when children enter school. If her indifference curves were to flatten, she would be more likely to join the labor force—and, if working for pay, more likely to work full-time.

The household model, then, predicts that as time at home becomes less necessary or easier to replace with purchased goods and services, labor force participation rates and hours of paid work will rise. Historically, women have borne the primary responsibility for household production, and with inventions such as washing machines and dryers, automatic dishwashers, microwave ovens, online shopping, and electronic banking, it has become easier to substitute purchased goods for household time. The predictable rise in the labor force participation rates of women was seen in Table 6.1.

It is also likely that the ages of children affect the trade-offs parents are willing to make between household time and income. Table 7.2 provides evidence consistent with the assertion that as children grow older, the labor force participation rates of their mothers rise. Married women have a labor force participation rate of 57 percent with an infant in the home, but their participation rate rises to 62 percent, on average, when the child is two. For single mothers, the increase in labor force participation is much more dramatic: the average participation rate increases from

[1]See Francine D. Blau, Marianne A. Ferber, and Anne E. Winkler, *The Economics of Women, Men, and Work*, 6th ed. (Upper Saddle River, NJ: Pearson/Prentice Hall, 2010); and Shelly Lundberg and Robert A. Pollak, "The American Family and Family Economics," *Journal of Economic Perspectives* 21 (Spring 2007): 3–26, for works that summarize economic analyses of fertility, child-rearing, and other important decisions made by households. For studies that analyze the trade-offs between market work and household work, see Alexander M. Gelber and Joshua W. Mitchell, "Taxes and Time Allocation: Evidence from Single Women," National Bureau of Economic Research Working Paper No. 15583 (Cambridge, Mass.: 2009); and Richard Rogerson, "Structural Transformation and the Deterioration of European Labor Market Outcomes," *Journal of Political Economy* 116 (April, 2008): 235–259.

Table 7.2

Labor Force Participation Rates and Full-Time Employment, Mothers of Young Children, by Age of Child, 2012

Age of Youngest Child	Labor Force Participation Rate		Percent Working Full-Time*	
	Married (%)	Single (%)	Married (%)	Single (%)
Under 1 year	57	57	75	61
1 year	62	66	70	67
2 years	62	71	72	69

*Percent of *employed* mothers working full time.

Source: U.S. Department of Labor, Bureau of Labor Statistics, "Employment Characteristics of Families—2012," USDL 13-0730 (Friday, April 26, 2013), Table 6.

57 percent to 71 percent as children grow from infancy to age two. The percentage of employed single mothers who work full-time also rises, while the comparable percentage for married mothers did not show a clear pattern in 2012.

Beyond the implications for a single household decision-maker in a given year, the household production model produces insights about the decisions that must be made by households that have more than one decision-maker. The household production model also has insights for decisions about how to allocate time over an entire lifetime, not just a single year. These implications are analyzed in the following sections.

Joint Labor Supply Decisions within the Household

The models depicted in chapter 6 and so far in this chapter have been for a single decision-maker, who was assumed to be trying to maximize his or her own utility. For those who live with partners, however, some kind of *joint* decision-making process must be used to allocate the time of each and to agree on who does what in the household. This process is complicated by emotional relationships between the partners, and their decisions about market and household work are also heavily influenced by custom.[2] Nevertheless, economic theory may help provide insight into at least some of the forces that shape the decisions all households must make.

Just how to model the different decision-making processes that can be used by households is a question economists have only begun to study. The formal models of decision-making among married couples that have been developed, all of which are based on principles of utility maximization, fall into two general

[2]See Julie A. Nelson, "I, Thou, and Them: Capabilities, Altruism, and Norms in the Economics of Marriage," *American Economic Review* 84 (May 1994): 126–131; and Claire Brown, "An Institutional Model of Wives' Work Decisions," *Industrial Relations* 24 (Spring 1985): 182–204.

categories.[3] The simplest models extend the assumption of a single decision-maker to marriage partners, either by assuming they both have exactly the same preferences or by assuming that one makes all the decisions. These "unitary" models imply that couples should have the same expenditure pattern regardless of which partner receives the income. Empirical work tends to reject this simple view of how household decisions are made.[4]

A second way to model a household's decision-making process is to assume a "collective" model in which the partners have their own utility functions and *bargain* over the allocation of each other's time. The power each has in the bargaining process is seen as related to how well each person would do if the partners were unable to resolve conflict and their relationship was dissolved. This model suggests that partners with greater access to resources carry more influence in family decision making. There is growing evidence in support of the bargaining model, including the sad fact that women with fewer economic resources of their own are more likely to be victims of domestic violence when disputes arise.[5]

Whatever process partners use to decide on the allocation of their time–and it may be different in different households–there are certain issues that nearly all households must face. We turn now to a brief analysis of some joint decisions that affect labor supply.

Specialization of Function

Partners often find it beneficial to specialize to some extent in the work that needs to be done, both in the market and in the household. Often, one or the other partner will bear primary responsibilities for meal planning, shopping, home maintenance, or child-rearing. It may also be the case that when both work for pay, one or the other of the partners will be more available for overtime, for job-related travel, or for cutting short a workday if an emergency arises at home. What factors are weighed in deciding who specializes in what?

Theory   Consider a couple trying to decide which partner, if either, will take primary responsibility for child-rearing by staying at home or by taking a job that has a less-demanding schedule or a shorter commute. Because the person with primary child-care duties will probably end up spending more hours in the household, the couple needs to answer two questions: Who is relatively more productive at home? Who is relatively more productive in market work?

---

[3]See Shelly Lundberg and Robert A. Pollak, "Bargaining and Distribution in Marriage," *Journal of Economic Perspectives* 10 (Fall 1996): 139–158.

[4]Francine D. Blau, Marianne A. Ferber, and Anne E. Winkler, *The Economics of Women, Men, and Work*, 47.

[5]Richard Blundell, Pierre-Andre Chiappori, and Costas Meghir, "Collective Labor Supply with Children," *Journal of Political Economy* 113 (December 2005): 1277–1306; Lauren Cherchye, Bram De Rock, and Frederic Vermeulen, "Married with Children: A Collective Labor Supply Model with Detailed Time Use and Intrahousehold Expenditure Information," *American Economic Review* 102 (December 2012): 3377–3405; and Anna Aizer, "The Gender Wage Gap and Domestic Violence," *American Economic Review* 100 (September 2010): 1847–1859.

For example, a married couple deciding whether one partner should stay home more and perform most of the child-rearing would want to consider what gains and losses are attendant on either the husband or the wife assuming this responsibility. The losses from staying home are related to the market wage of each, while the gains depend on their enjoyment of, and skill at, child-rearing. (Since enjoyment of the parenting process increases utility, we can designate both higher levels of enjoyment *and* higher levels of skill as indicative of greater "productivity" in child-rearing.) Wage rates for women, for reasons discussed in later chapters, typically have been below those for men. It is also likely that because of socialization, wives have been historically more productive than husbands in child-rearing. If a given woman's wage rate is lower than her husband's and the woman is more productive in child-rearing, the family gives up less in market goods and gains more in child-rearing if the wife takes primary responsibility in this area.

Implications for the Future   Modeling the choice of who handles most of some household duty as influenced by relative household and market productivities is not meant to imply that customs are unimportant in shaping preferences or limiting choices concerning household production; clearly, they are. What the theory of household production emphasizes is that the distribution of household work may well change as wages, incomes, and home productivities change. One study has found that when both spouses work outside the home, the weekly hours that each spends in household work are affected by their relative wage rates. That is, as wives' wages and labor-market opportunities rise, the household work done by husbands appears to increase, while the share of household work done by wives decreases.[6]

Do Both Partners Work for Pay?

It is clearly not necessary, of course, that one partner specializes in household production by staying home full-time. Many household chores, from lawn care to child care, can be hired out or done with more purchased goods or services and less household time. Moreover, there is evidence that greater hours of household work actually reduce one's future wage offers, so there are long-term costs associated with specializing in household work.[7]

Generally speaking, as long as an extra hour of market work by both partners creates the ability to buy more goods or services than are required to compensate for the lost hour of household time, both can enhance their resources if

---

[6]Joni Hersch and Leslie S. Stratton, "Housework, Wages, and the Division of Household Time for Employed Spouses," *American Economic Review* 84 (May 1994): 120–125; Marianne Bertrand, Claudia Goldin, and Lawrence F. Katz, "Dynamics of the Gender Gap for Young Professionals in the Financial and Corporate Sectors," *American Economic Journal: Applied Economics* 2 (July 2010): 228–255; and James Feyrer, Bruce Sacerdote, and Ariel Dora Stern, "Will the Stork Return to Europe and Japan? Understanding Fertility within Developed Nations," *Journal of Economic Perspectives* 22 (Summer 2008): 3–22.

[7]Joni Hersch and Leslie S. Stratton, "Housework and Wages," *Journal of Human Resources* 37 (Winter 2002): 217–229; and Elizabeth Ty Wilde, Lily Batchelder, and David T. Ellwood, "The Mommy Track Divides: The Impact of Childbearing on Wages of Women of Differing Skill Levels," National Bureau of Economic Research, working paper no. 16582 (Cambridge, Mass., December 2010).

they work for pay that extra hour. Put in the context of Figure 7.2, if both partners are at a point like A, increasing time in paid work by decreasing time at home from H_0 to H_1 will add more in resources (BD) than is required to compensate for the lost home time (BC).

Clearly, a steeper budget constraint (holding income constant) will tend to increase—through the substitution effect—the desirability of increased hours of market work. However, flatter indifference curves will also have this same effect, because they represent an increased willingness to trade away household hours for income (less income is required to compensate for a lost hour at home). We have already mentioned some forces that could lead to flatter indifference curves: inventions that allow easier substitution of purchased goods for household time, the reduced value of time spent at home as children age, or greater future wage penalties associated with staying at home.

Another force that could flatten the indifference curves of household partners has received some attention recently. Some assert that couples in America are placing a growing value on purchased goods that are *easily observed by others*, such as luxury automobiles or large homes, and less value on the commodities produced in obscurity at home (playing board games or reading with children, for example).[8] If there is a growing emphasis on an individual's or a family's *relative standing* in society, and if status depends on publicly observed consumption, then the increased desire for income would flatten indifference curves and lead to more hours at paid work and fewer hours at home.[9]

Figure 7.2

Home versus Market Productivity for a Partner

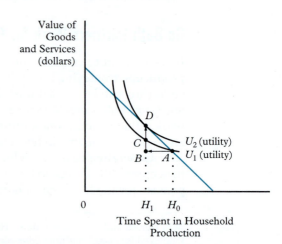

---

[8]Robert H. Frank, *Luxury Fever: Why Money Fails to Satisfy in an Era of Excess* (New York: The Free Press, 1999).

[9]David Neumark and Andrew Postlewaite, "Relative Income Concerns and the Rise in Married Women's Employment," *Journal of Public Economics* 70 (October 1998): 157–183, offers an example of an attempt to analyze whether *status* concerns drive women to increased work for pay.

The Joint Decision and Interdependent Productivity at Home

We have seen that family labor supply decisions are enhanced by considering the household and market productivities of each partner. However, one partner's productivity at home is affected by the *other* partner's labor supply to the market, so that modeling the joint decision is quite complex. On the one hand, if a married woman decides to increase her hours worked outside the home, her husband's marginal productivity at home may *rise* as he takes over chores she once performed. Thus, in terms we have discussed earlier, a wife's increased hours of paid work could serve to make the indifference curves of her husband *steeper*, causing him to reduce his hours of paid work and increase his hours at home.

On the other hand, if the two partners enjoy each other's company, the value a husband places on his time at home could be *reduced* if his wife is home less often, *flattening* his indifference curves and pushing toward an increase in his hours of paid work. Theory cannot predict whether one partner will have steeper or flatter indifference curves if the other partner reduces time at home, and empirical work on this topic has produced no consensus.[10]

Labor Supply in Recessions: The "Discouraged" versus the "Added" Worker

Changes in one partner's productivity, either at home or in market work, can alter the family's basic labor supply decision. Consider, for example, a "traditional" family in which market work is performed by the husband and in which the wife is employed full-time in the home. What will happen if a recession causes the husband to become unemployed?

Added-Worker Effect   The husband's market productivity declines, at least temporarily. The drop in his market productivity relative to his household productivity (which is unaffected by the recession) makes it more likely that the family will find it beneficial for him to engage in household production. If the wage his wife can earn in paid work is not affected, the family *may* decide that to try to maintain the family's prior level of utility (which might be affected by both consumption and *savings* levels), *she* should seek market work and *he* should substitute for her in home production for as long as the recession lasts. He may remain a member of the labor force as an unemployed worker awaiting recall, and as she begins to look for work, she becomes an added member of the labor force. Thus, in the face of falling family income, the number of family members seeking

---

[10]For reviews of these issues, see Mark Killingsworth, *Labor Supply* (Cambridge: Cambridge University Press, 1983); Marjorie B. McElroy, "Appendix: Empirical Results from Estimates of Joint Labor Supply Functions of Husbands and Wives," in *Research in Labor Economics*, vol. 4, ed. Ronald Ehrenberg (Greenwich, Conn.: JAI Press, 1981): 53–64; and, more recently, Daniel S. Hamermesh, "Timing, Togetherness and Time Windfalls," *Journal of Population Economics* 15 (November 2002): 601–623.

market work may increase. This potential response is akin to the income effect, in that as family income falls, fewer commodities are consumed—and less time spent in consumption is matched by more desired hours of work for pay.

Discouraged-Worker Effect   At the same time, however, we must look at the *wage rate* someone without a job can *expect* to receive if he or she looks for work. This expected wage, denoted by $E(W)$, can actually be written as a precise statistical concept:

$$E(W) = \pi W \tag{7.1}$$

where W is the wage rate of people who have the job and π is the probability of obtaining the job if out of work. For someone without a job, the opportunity cost of staying home is $E(W)$. The reduced availability of jobs that occurs when the unemployment rate rises causes the *expected wage of those without jobs to fall* sharply for two reasons. First, an excess of labor supply over demand tends to push down real wages (for those with jobs) during recessionary periods. Second, the chances of getting a job fall in a recession. Thus, both W and π fall in a recession, causing $E(W)$ to decline.

Noting the *substitution effect* that accompanies a falling expected wage, some have argued that people who would otherwise have been looking for work become discouraged in a recession and tend to remain out of the labor market. Looking for work has such a low expected payoff for them that they decide spending time at home is more productive than spending time in job search. The reduction of the labor force associated with discouraged workers in a recession is a force working against the added-worker effect—just as the substitution effect works against the income effect. (As illustrated in Example 7.2, income and substitution effects can also help analyze the issue of child labor.)

Which Effect Dominates?   It is possible, of course, for both the added-worker and the discouraged-worker effects to coexist, because "added" and "discouraged" workers will be different groups of people. Which group predominates, however, is the important question. If the labor force is swollen by added workers during a recession, the published unemployment rate will likewise become swollen (the added workers will increase the number of people looking for work). If workers become discouraged and drop out of the labor market after having been unemployed, the decline in people seeking jobs will depress the unemployment rate. Knowledge of which effect predominates is needed in order to make accurate inferences about the actual state of the labor market from the published unemployment rate.

We know that the added-worker effect does exist, although it tends to be rather small. The added-worker effect is confined to the relatively few families whose sole breadwinner loses a job, and there is some evidence that it may be reduced by the presence of unemployment insurance benefits; furthermore, as

EXAMPLE 7.2

Child Labor in Poor Countries

The International Labour Organization (ILO) estimates that in 2004, 126 million children worldwide—roughly 8 percent of all children—performed work that was hazardous to their physical or educational development. Many fear that child labor is on the rise, driven by an increase in the use of low-wage labor from poor countries in the production of manufactured products sold in rich countries. What are the predictions of economic theory concerning child labor?

Household production theory views choices about household and labor market activities as functions of market wages, household productivity, and family income. One of the labor supply decisions the household must make is whether, and when, to send children into the labor force—and theory suggests there are two conflicting forces created by the recent globalization of production.

On the one hand, the creation of manufacturing jobs in poor countries increases the earnings opportunities for their residents. If such residents choose to leave what they are currently doing and take a manufacturing job, we must assume (if their decision is voluntarily made) that they believe they will be better off. Thus, the new job opportunities represent a wage increase, and the related *substitution effect* would tend to draw them, and possibly their children, into these jobs. While many children in these new jobs will have previously worked at either a lower-paying job or in the household (performing agricultural or craft work), others may have parents who see the higher wages their children can earn as an inducement to send them to work rather than to school. It is this latter group of parents whose decisions would *increase* the use of child labor.

On the other hand, an increase in parental earnings opportunities would create an *income effect* that could reduce the use of child labor within families. Many families are too poor to forgo the income children can provide (the World Bank estimates that in 2001, 1.1 billion people in the world had consumption levels below $1 a day and that 2.7 billion lived on less than $2 a day). If child and adult labor are seen by parents as alternative means of providing family income, when adult earnings rise, an *income effect* is generated that could induce parents to *withdraw* their children from the labor force.

To date, there are two pieces of data suggesting that the income effect dominates the substitution effect—and that as earnings opportunities increase, parents want more leisure (or schooling) for their children. First, child labor is greatest in the poorest parts of the world—highest in Africa and Asia and lowest in Europe and North America. Second, the number of children performing hazardous work fell by 26 percent from 2002 to 2006, with the decline being largest (33 percent) for children under the age of 15. One can thus hope that as incomes grow and schooling becomes more available in poor countries, child labor will one day become a thing of the past.

Sources: Kaushik Basu, "Child Labor: Cause, Consequence, and Cure, with Remarks on International Labor Standards," *Journal of Economic Literature* 37, no. 3 (September 1999): 1083–1119; International Labour Office, Office of the Director-General, *The End of Child Labour: Within Reach*, Report I (B), International Labour Conference, 95th Session (Geneva: International Labour Office, 2006); Shanina Amin, Shakil Quayes, and Janet M. Rives, "Are Children and Parents Substitutes or Complements in the Family Labor Supply Decision in Bangladesh?" *Journal of Developing Areas* 40 (Fall 2006): 15–37. Also see Eric V. Edmonds and Norbert Schady, "Poverty Alleviation and Child Labor," *American Economic Journal: Economic Policy* 4 (November 2012): 100–124.

more and more women become regularly employed for pay, the added-worker effect will tend to both decline and become increasingly confined to teenagers. In contrast, the fall in expected real wages occurs in nearly *every* household, and since the substitution effect is relatively strong for married women, it is not surprising that studies have consistently found the discouraged-worker effect to be dominant—although there is evidence that both the discouraged-worker and added-worker effects are becoming smaller over time.[11] Other things equal, *the labor force tends to shrink during recessions and grow during periods of economic recovery.*

Hidden Unemployment   The dominance of the discouraged-worker effect creates what some call the *hidden* unemployed—people who would like to work but believe jobs are so scarce that looking for work is of no use. Because they are not looking for work, they are not counted as unemployed in government statistics. Focusing on the period from 2007 to 2009, when the overall official unemployment rate rose from 4.6 percent to 9.3 percent, can give some indication of the size of hidden unemployment.

In 2007, an average of 7.1 million people (4.6 percent of the labor force) were counted as unemployed. In addition, 369,000 people indicated that they wanted work but were not seeking it because they believed jobs were unavailable to them; this group constituted 0.5 percent of those adults not in the labor force. By 2009, some 14.3 million people (9.3 percent of the labor force) were officially counted as unemployed, but there were 778,000 others among the group not seeking work because they believed jobs were unavailable. Coincident with reduced job opportunities, the number of "discouraged workers" had grown to 1 percent of those adults not in the labor force. If discouraged workers were counted as unemployed members of the labor force, the unemployment rate would have been 4.9 percent in 2007 and 9.7 percent by 2009; thus, while the official unemployment rate went up 4.7 percentage points, a rate that included discouraged workers would have gone up by 4.8 percentage points.[12]

---

[11]T. Aldrich Finegan, Roberto V. Peñaloza, and Mototsugu Shintani, "Reassessing Cyclical Changes in Workers' Labor Market Status: Gross Flows and the Types of Workers Who Determine Them," *Industrial and Labor Relations Review* 61 (January 2008): 244–257; and Catalina Amuedo-Dorantes and Jean Kimmel, "Moonlighting over the Business Cycle," *Economic Inquiry* 47 (October 2009): 754–765. Also see Melvin Stephens Jr., "Worker Displacement and the Added Worker Effect," *Journal of Labor Economics* 20 (July 2002): 504–537; Paul Bingley and Ian Walker, "Household Unemployment and the Labour Supply of Married Women," *Economica* 68 (May 2001): 157–185; and Hans G. Bloemen, "Job Search, Search Intensity, and Labor Market Transitions: An Empirical Analysis,"*Journal of Human Resources* 40 (Winter 2005): 231–269.

[12]To say that including discouraged workers would change the published unemployment rate does not imply that it *should* be done. For a summary of the arguments for and against counting discouraged workers as unemployed, see the final report of the National Commission on Employment and Unemployment Statistics, *Counting the Labor Force* (Washington, D.C.: NCEUS, 1979): 44–49.

Life Cycle Aspects of Labor Supply

Because market productivity (wages) and household productivity vary over the life cycle, people vary the hours they supply to the labor market over their lives. In the early adult years, relatively fewer hours are devoted to paid work than in later years, and more time is devoted to schooling. In the very late years, people fully or partially retire, although at varying ages. In the middle years (say, 25 to 50), most males are in the labor force continuously, but for married women, labor force participation rates rise with age. While the issue of schooling is dealt with in chapter 9, expanding the model of household production discussed in this chapter to include life-cycle considerations can enrich our understanding of labor supply behavior in several areas, two of which are discussed in the following sections.

The Substitution Effect and When to Work over a Lifetime

Just as joint decisions about market and household work involve comparing market and home productivities of the two partners, deciding *when* to work over the course of one's life involves comparing market and home productivities *over time*. The basic idea here is that people will tend to perform the most market work when their earning capacity is high relative to home productivity. Conversely, they will engage in household production when their earning capacity is relatively low.

Suppose a sales representative working on a commission basis knows that her potential income is around $60,000 in a certain year but that July's income potential will be twice that of November's. Would it be rational for her to schedule her vacation (a time-intensive activity) in November? The answer depends on her market productivity relative to her household productivity for the two months. Obviously, her market productivity (her wage rate) is higher in July than in November, which means that the opportunity costs of a vacation are greater in July. However, if she has children who are free to vacation only in July, she may decide that her household productivity (in terms of utility) is so much greater in July than in November that the benefits of vacationing in July outweigh the costs. If she does not have children of school age, the utility generated by a November vacation may be sufficiently close to that of a July vacation that the smaller opportunity costs make a November vacation preferable.

Similar decisions can be made over longer periods of time, even one's entire life. As chapter 9 will show, market productivity (reflected in the wage) starts low in the young adult years, rises rapidly with age, then levels off and even falls in the later years, as shown in panel (a) of Figure 7.3. This general pattern occurs within each of the broad educational groupings of workers, although the details of the wage trajectories differ. With an *expected* path of wages over their lives, workers can generate rough predictions of two variables critical to labor supply decisions: lifetime wealth and the costs of leisure or household time they

Figure 7.3

Life-Cycle Allocation of Time

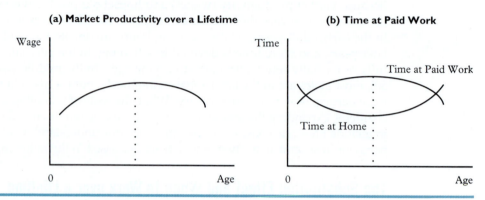

(a) Market Productivity over a Lifetime

Wage

0   Age

(b) Time at Paid Work

Time

Time at Paid Work

Time at Home

0   Age

will face at various ages. Thus, if home productivity is more or less constant as they age, workers who make labor supply decisions by taking expected lifetime wealth into account will react to *expected* (life cycle) wage increases by unambiguously increasing their labor supply. Such wage increases raise the cost of leisure and household time but do not increase expected lifetime wealth; these wage increases, then, are accompanied only by a substitution effect.

Introducing life-cycle considerations into labor supply theory yields a prediction that the profiles of time spent at, and away from, market work will resemble those shown in panel (b) of Figure 7.3; that is, workers will spend more time at paid work activities in their (relatively high-wage) middle years. Similarly, life-cycle considerations suggest that the consumption of very time-intensive leisure activities will occur primarily in one's early and late years. (That travelers abroad are predominantly young adults and the elderly is clearly related to the fact that for these groups, opportunity costs of time are lower.)

If workers make labor supply decisions with the life cycle in mind, they will react differently to expected and unexpected wage changes. Expected wage changes will generate only a substitution effect, because estimates of lifetime wealth will remain unchanged (see Example 7.3). *Unexpected* wage changes, however, will cause them to revise their estimates of lifetime wealth, and these changes will be accompanied by both substitution and income effects. Empirical tests of the life-cycle model of labor supply are relatively recent; to date, they suggest that life-cycle considerations are of modest importance in the labor supply decisions of most workers.[13]

---

[13]For a paper with references to earlier work in this area, see John C. Ham and Kevin T. Reilly, "Testing Intertemporal Substitution, Implicit Contracts, and Hours Restriction Models of the Labor Market Using Micro Data," *American Economic Review* 92 (September 2002): 905–927. Also see Susumu Imai and Michael P. Keane, "Intertemporal Labor Supply and Human Capital Accumulation," *International Economic Review* 45 (May 2004): 601–641.

EXAMPLE 7.3

How Does Labor Supply Respond to Housing Subsidies?

As we saw in chapter 6, Figure 6.17 (on the Earned Income Tax Credit), subsidies to families that become less generous as family income rises create two incentives to reduce work hours. First, the subsidy enhances the consumption possibilities of affected families, and it is thus accompanied by an *income effect* that reduces desired work hours. Second, if the earnings of family members rise, the subsidy is reduced; this reduction acts like a tax that reduces the wage rate, creating a *substitution effect* that also reduces desired hours of work.

In the United States, one of the largest federal subsidies to the poor comes in the form of housing vouchers, which help about 2 million households each year. Eligible families can present vouchers to their landlords to help pay for their rent (the landlords then turn in the vouchers to the government for reimbursement). The value of the vouchers is dependent on family income, with more needy families receiving vouchers of higher value.

Owing to budgetary limits, there are typically many more families applying for vouchers than can receive them. Chicago, for example, opened its housing-voucher waitlist in 1997 for the first time in 12 years, and over 82,000 income-eligible families applied for vouchers. The city randomly assigned the applicants to a waiting list and told the top 35,000 that they could expect to receive a voucher in the near future; the other 47,000 were told they would not receive one.

A study of how these Chicago housing subsidies affected labor supply found two results of interest to us in the context of this chapter. One finding was that, consistent with our analysis of both the income and substitution effects, the hours of work of able-bodied, working-age voucher recipients decreased by 6 percent after they started receiving the vouchers.

The other finding was noted among the fortunate 35,000 applicants who were told they would receive vouchers in the future. The study found that work hours increased in the years *after* families were told they could expect to receive a voucher, but *before* they actually received one. This increase is consistent with the predictions of the life-cycle model of labor supply; namely, given their expected lifetime wealth (which was enhanced by the prospect of a housing voucher), it appears that families wanted to move their labor supply from periods when their take-home wages would be relatively low—after they received vouchers—to a period when wages are higher.

Source: Brian A. Jacob and Jens Ludwig, "The Effects of Housing Assistance on Labor Supply: Evidence from a Voucher Lottery," *American Economic Review* 102 (February 2012): 272–304.

The Choice of Retirement Age

A multiyear perspective is also required to more fully model workers' retirement decisions, because *yearly* retirement benefits, expected *lifetime* benefits, and lifetime *earnings* are all influenced by the date of retirement. Yearly retirement benefits are received by retirees in the form of pension payments, usually in monthly installments; the size of these benefits are directly or indirectly related to a retiree's past earnings per year and the number of years he or she worked. The total value of these promised yearly benefits over the expected remaining lifetime of the retiree is what we mean by "expected lifetime benefits." This value is obviously affected by the size of the yearly benefits and the age (and remaining life expectancy) of the retiree, but finding the value involves more than simply adding up the yearly benefits.

Summing yearly benefits over several future years must take account of the fact that over time, current sums of money can grow "automatically" with interest. For example, if the interest rate is 10 percent per year, an employer promising to pay a worker $1,000 *this* year has undertaken a greater expense (and is thus offering something of greater value) than one who promises to pay a worker $2,000 *in 10 years*. In the former case, the employer needs to have $1,000 on hand right now, whereas in the latter case, the employer needs to set aside only $772 now (at 10 percent interest, $772 will grow into $2,000 in 10 years). Economists therefore say that $772 is the "present value" of the promised $2,000 in 10 years (at a 10 percent interest rate).

We will discuss how to calculate present values in chapter 9; for now, all you need to know is that the present value of a stream of future income is the fund one must possess *today* to guarantee this stream in the future, given an assumed rate of interest at which the money left in the fund can be invested. For example, if a pension system promises to make payments of $10,000 per year for 17 years to a retiree, one might think that it must have funds of $170,000 now to guarantee the promised flow of payments. However, if it can invest its funds at a 2 percent yearly rate of interest, we can use a standard formula to calculate that it must have roughly $143,000 on hand *now* to guarantee the payments. It will draw down the fund by $10,000 per year, but funds that remain can be invested and generate interest of 2 percent per year, which, of course, can be used to help fund future payments. Thus, we can say that the present value of a stream of $10,000 payments for 17 years is $143,000 if the interest rate is 2 percent.

The purpose of this section is to explore some of the economic factors that affect the age of retirement. For the sake of illustration, we discuss the retirement incentives facing a 62-year-old male who earns, and can continue to earn, $40,000 per year as shown in Table 7.3. To further simplify our discussion, we assume this man has no pension other than that provided by Social Security and that, for him, retirement means the cessation of all paid work.

The retirement incentives facing this worker are related to three basic factors: (a) the present value of income available to him over his remaining life expectancy if he retires now, at age 62; (b) the *change* in this sum if retirement is delayed; and (c) preferences regarding household time and the goods one can buy with money. As we will show later, in terms of the labor supply analyses in this chapter and chapter 6, factor (a) is analogous to nonlabor income, and factor (b) is analogous to the wage rate.

Graphing the Budget Constraint

Table 7.3 summarizes the present value now (at age 62) of pension and earned income available to our hypothetical worker at each possible retirement age, up to age 70. If he retires at age 62, the present value of income over his remaining life expectancy is $153,666. If he delays retirement until age 63, the present value of his remaining lifetime income rises by $42,617, to $196,283; most of this increase comes from added earnings (shown in the third column), but note that the present value of his lifetime pension benefits also rises slightly if he delays retirement (see the fourth column). Delaying retirement until age 64 would add an even greater amount to the present value of his future lifetime income—which would rise from $196,283 to $240,642. Because a later

Table 7.3

Estimated Social Security Benefits and Earnings for a Hypothetical Male, Age 62 (Yearly Wage = $40,000; Interest Rate = 2%; Life Expectancy = 17 Years)

Age of Retirement[b]	Yearly Soc. Sec. Benefit ($)	*Present Value[a] of Remaining Lifetime:* Earnings ($)	Soc. Sec. Benefits ($)	Total ($)
62	10,752	0	153,666	153,666
63	11,568	39,216	157,067	196,283
64	12,684	77,662	162,980	240,642
65	13,836	115,355	167,502	282,857
66	15,012	152,309	170,362	322,671
67	16,404	188,538	173,478	362,016
68	17,820	224,057	174,402	398,459
69	19,248	258,880	172,897	431,777
70	20,712	293,019	169,056	462,075

[a]Present values calculated as of age 62. All dollar values are as of the current year.

[b]Yearly Social Security benefits are estimated assuming that such benefits begin *in the year retirement starts*. Thus, the table ignores the fact that after a worker reaches normal retirement age (age 66 for those born between 1943 and 1954), he or she can receive Social Security benefits before retiring; however, delaying receipt of benefits does increase their yearly levels.

retirement age implies fewer years over which benefits will be received, whether lifetime pension benefits rise or fall with retirement age depends on how yearly pension benefits are changed with the age of retirement. In Table 7.3, the lifetime benefits shown in the fourth column increase slightly if retirement is delayed to age 68, but they fall at later ages of retirement.

The data in the last column of Table 7.3 are presented graphically in Figure 7.4 as budget constraint *ABJ*. Segment *AB* represents the present value of lifetime income if our worker retires at age 62 and, as such, represents nonlabor income. The slope of segment *BC* represents the $42,617 increase in lifetime income (to $196,283) if retirement is delayed to age 63, and the slopes of the other segments running from points *B* to *J* similarly reflect the increases in discounted lifetime income associated with delaying retirement by a year. These slopes, therefore, represent the yearly *net wage*.

Changes in the Constraint   Given preferences summarized by curve U_1, the optimum age of retirement for our hypothetical worker is age 64. How would his optimum age of retirement change if Social Security benefits were increased?[14] The answer depends on how the increases are structured. If the benefit increases were such that the same fixed amount was unexpectedly added to lifetime benefits at each retirement age, the

[14]The analysis in this section borrows heavily from Olivia S. Mitchell and Gary S. Fields, "The Effects of Pensions and Earnings on Retirement: A Review Essay," *Research in Labor Economics*, vol. 5, ed. Ronald Ehrenberg (Greenwich, Conn.: JAI Press, 1982): 115–155.

Figure 7.4

Choice of Optimum Retirement Age for Hypothetical Worker (Based on data in Table 7.3)

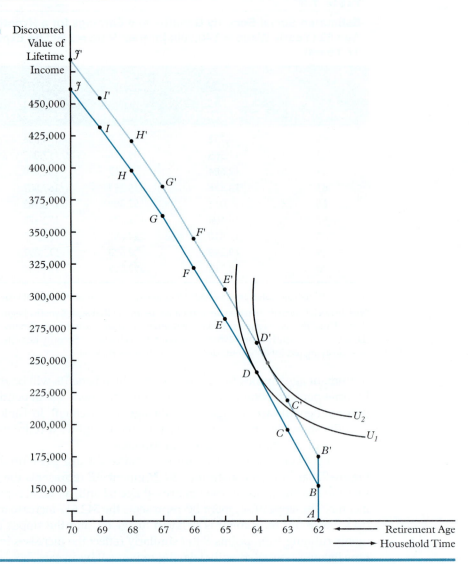

constraint facing our 62-year-old male would shift up (and out) to $AB'J'$. The slopes along the segments between B' and J' would remain parallel to those along BJ; thus, there would be an income effect with no substitution effect (that is, no change in the yearly net wage). The optimum age of retirement would be unambiguously reduced, as shown in Figure 7.4.

Alternatively, if Social Security benefits were adjusted in a way that produced larger increases in the present value of lifetime benefits when retirement is deferred past age 62, point B would be unaffected, but the segments between B and the vertical axis would become more steeply sloped. The increased slope of the constraint would induce the behavior associated with a wage increase; a substitution effect would move our hypothetical worker in the direction of later retirement, but the income effect associated with greater lifetime wealth would push in the direction of earlier retirement. We do not know which effect would dominate.

(It is instructive to note that incentives to retire are also affected by economic conditions. For example, the "Great Recession" of 2008–2009 affected retirement-age workers along two dimensions. First, the decline in stock prices reduced the value of investment funds workers had accumulated to finance their retirement; this reduction in the value of pension assets created an income effect that pushed these workers to delay retirement. Second, however, many older workers lost their jobs and faced lower pay if they continued working—creating a substitution effect that pushed them toward earlier retirement. Both effects have been documented in studies of how retirement ages were affected by the Great Recession.[15])

Our analysis of Figure 7.4 suggests that policies designed to affect the retirement ages of workers in a particular direction would benefit from making sure that both income and substitution effects work in the *same* direction. For example, many private sector pension plans had provisions that induced workers to retire early. They awarded generous benefits to those who retired early and simultaneously *reduced the present value of lifetime pension benefits* that accumulated if retirement were delayed. Perhaps in part because firms now want experienced workers to stay longer, many of these pension plans have been eliminated or changed so that benefits for early retirement have been reduced and the additions to the value of lifetime pension benefits if retirement is delayed have grown larger.

In terms of Figure 7.4, reducing the benefits associated with early retirement cuts the height of AB' to below AB, which tends to move the entire constraint down and to the left; workers' lifetime wealth tends to fall, and an income effect pushes them toward later retirement. Increases in the present value of lifetime pension benefits that are associated with later retirement increases the slope of $B'J'$, creating a substitution effect (by increasing the opportunity cost of retiring a year earlier) that also works in the direction of later retirement.[16]

---

[15]Courtney C. Cole and Phillip B. Levine, "Recessions, Retirement, and Social Security," and Gopi Shah Godi, John B. Shoven, and Sita Nataraj Slavov, "What Explains Changes in Retirement Plans during the Great Recession?" both in *American Economic Review: Papers and Proceedings* 101 (May 2011): 23–34.

[16]Leora Friedberg and Anthony Webb, "Retirement and the Evolution of Pension Structure," *Journal of Human Resources* 40 (Spring 2006): 281–308. The income and substitution effects of the private sector pension changes described clearly work in the same direction for earlier ages of retirement; however, if the increased slope of $B'J'$ is steep enough, the new constraint may cross the old one at later ages of retirement and create a zone in the new constraint that lies to the northeast of the original one. In this new zone, the substitution effect associated with the increased slope of $B'J'$ would be at least partially offset by an income effect that pushes toward earlier retirement—so the ultimate effect on retirement age in this zone is ambiguous. For other economic analyses of retirement, see Richard Disney and Sarah Smith, "The Labour Supply Effect of the Abolition of the Earnings Rule for Older Workers in the United Kingdom," *Economic Journal* 112 (March 2002): 136–152; Jonathan Gruber and David A. Wise, eds., *Social Security Programs and Retirement Around the World: Micro-estimation*, NBER Conference Report Series (Chicago: University of Chicago Press, 2004); and Jeffrey B. Liebman, Erzo F. P. Luttmer, and David G. Seif, "Labor Supply Responses to Marginal Social Security Benefits: Evidence from Discontinuities," *Journal of Public Economics* 93 (December 2009): 1208–1223.

A complete analysis of the retirement decision, of course, must also take account of preferences for household production. A recent study has found, for example, that those who work for pay engage in more household work activities and have fewer hours of leisure than people who do not work for pay. Furthermore, it found that older people engage in both household work and leisure at different times of the day than they did when younger. Taken together, the study suggests that retirement decisions are affected if the demand for leisure rises with age, and that allowing older workers phased retirement (part-time work for a few years) or flexible scheduling may be a better way to increase retirement ages than changing pension formulas.[17]

Policy Application: Child Care and Labor Supply

For many families, a critical element of what we have called household production is the supervision and nurture of children. Most parents are concerned about providing their children with quality care, whether this care is produced mostly in the household or is purchased to a great extent outside the home. Society at large also has a stake in the quality of care parents provide for their children. There are many forms such programs take, from tax credits for child-care services purchased by working parents to governmental subsidies for day care, school lunches, and health care. The purpose of this section is to consider the labor market implications of programs to support the care of children.

Child-Care Subsidies

Roughly 46 percent of American children under age 5 are cared for by paid providers of child care, and on average, these costs represent 10.5% percent of family income—although it approaches 19 percent for families earning less than $36,000 per year.[18] Child-care costs obviously rise with the hours of care, but part of these costs appear to be fixed: one study found that child-care costs per hour of work were three times greater for women who worked fewer than 10 hours per week than for those who worked more.[19] Over the last two decades, however, federal spending on child-care subsidies has more than doubled, and the purpose of this section is to analyze the effects of these greater subsidies on the labor supply of parents.

---

[17]Daniel S. Hamermesh and Stephen Donald, "The Time and Timing Costs of Market Work," National Bureau of Economic Research, working paper no. 13127 (May 2007).

[18]U.S. Census Bureau, "Who's Minding the Kids? Child Care Arrangements: Spring 2011," Table 6, at http://www.census.gov/prod/2013pubs/p70-135.pdf. Also see Patricia M. Anderson and Phillip B. Levine, "Child Care and Mothers' Employment Decisions," in *Finding Jobs: Work and Welfare Reform*, eds. David E. Card and Rebecca M. Blank (New York: Russell Sage Foundation, 2000): 426.

[19]David C. Ribar, "A Structural Model of Child Care and the Labor Supply of Married Women," *Journal of Labor Economics* 13 (July 1995): 558–597.

Reducing the Fixed Costs of Care   Suppose for a moment that child-care costs are purely fixed, so that without a subsidy, working parents must pay a certain amount per day no matter how many hours their children are in care. Figures 7.5 and 7.6 illustrate how a subsidy that covers the entire cost of child care affects the labor supply incentives of a mother who has daily unearned income equal to ab.

Consider first the case of a mother who is not now working (Figure 7.5). If she decides to work, she must choose from points along the line cd, with the distance bc representing the fixed costs of child care. The slope of cd, of course, represents her wage rate. Given her preferences and the constraint depicted in Figure 7.5, this woman receives more utility from not working (at point b) than she would from working (point X). If the fixed cost were reduced to zero by a child-care subsidy, so her constraint were now abe, her utility would be maximized at point Y on curve U_3, and she would now find it beneficial to work. *Thus, child-care subsidies that reduce or remove the fixed cost of child care will encourage work among those previously out of the labor force.* (Such subsidies do not guarantee that all those out of the labor force would now join it, because some people will have such steep indifference curves that work will still not be utility-maximizing.)

Now, consider the case represented in Figure 7.6 of a woman who is already working when the subsidy is adopted. Before the subsidy, her utility was maximized at point X' on indifference curve U'_1, a point at which H'_1 hours are worked. When the subsidy generates the constraint abe, her utility will now be

---

Figure 7.5

Labor Supply and Fixed
Child-Care Costs: A Parent
Initially Out of the Labor
Force

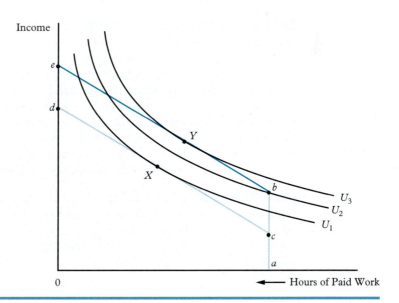

Figure 7.6

Labor Supply and Fixed
Child-Care Costs: A Parent
Initially Working for Pay

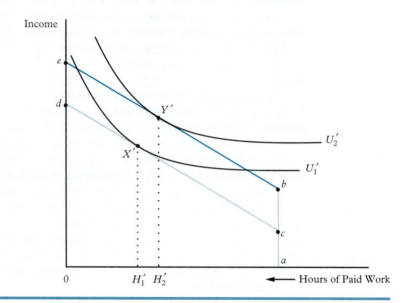

maximized at point Y' (on U'_2), and she will reduce her hours of work to H'_2. *Thus, for those already working, removing the fixed cost of child care has an income effect that pushes them toward fewer hours of work.* (Note, however, that the woman depicted in Figure 7.6 remains in the labor force.)

Reducing the Hourly Costs of Care   Now, let us take a case in which the costs of child care are purely hourly and have no fixed component. If such costs, say, are $3 per hour, they simply reduce the hourly take-home wage rate of a working parent by $3. If a government subsidy were to reduce the child-care costs to zero, the parent would experience an increase in the take-home wage, and the labor supply effects would be those of a wage increase. For those already working, the subsidy would create an income effect and a substitution effect that work in opposite directions on the desired hours of work. For those not in the labor force, the increased take-home wage would make it more likely they would join the labor force (the substitution effect dominates in participation decisions).

Observed Responses to Child-Care Subsidies   Our analysis above suggests that child-care subsidies, which in actuality reduce *both* the fixed and the hourly cost of care, would have a theoretically ambiguous effect on the hours of work among those already in the labor force. The effect on labor force participation, however, is theoretically clear: child-care subsidies should increase the labor force participation rates among parents, especially mothers. Empirical studies of the relationship between child-care costs and labor force participation are consistent with this latter prediction: when costs go down, labor force participation goes up. Furthermore, it appears that the greatest increases are among those with the lowest incomes.[20]

Child Support Assurance

The vast majority of children who live in poor households have an absent parent. The federal government has taken several steps to ensure, for families receiving welfare, that absent parents contribute adequately to their children's upbringing. Greater efforts to collect child support payments are restricted in their effectiveness by the lack of resources among some absent parents, deliberate noncompliance by others, and the lack of court-awarded child support obligations in many more cases of divorce. To enhance the resources of single-parent families, some have proposed the creation of child support assurance programs. The essential feature of these programs is a guaranteed child support benefit that would be paid by the government to the custodial parent in the event the absent parent does not make payments. If the absent parent makes only a portion of the required support payment, the government would make up the remainder.

A critical question to ask about such a program is how it would affect the labor supply of custodial parents. The answer provided by economic theory is not completely straightforward.

Consider a single mother who has two options for supporting herself and her children. One option is to work outside the home with no support from the absent father or from the welfare system. In Figure 7.7, we assume that the budget constraint provided by this option can be graphed as *AB*, which has a slope that represents her wage rate. The mother's other option is to apply for welfare benefits, which we assume would guarantee her an income of *AC*. Recall from chapter 6 that welfare payments are typically calculated by subtracting from a family's "needed" level of income (*AC*) its actual income from other sources, including earnings. Thus, the welfare constraint is *ACDB*, and it can be seen that segment *CD* is reflective of a take-home wage rate equal to zero.

---

[20]See Anderson and Levine, "Child Care and Mothers' Employment Decisions," for a summary of empirical work on how the cost of child care affects mothers' decisions to work. For a more recent publication, see Erdal Tekin, "Childcare Subsidies, Wages, and Employment of Single Mothers," *Journal of Human Resources* 42 (Spring 2007): 453–487; and Pierre Lefebvre and Philip Merrigan, "Child-Care Policy and the Labor Supply of Mothers with Young Children: A Natural Experiment from Canada," *Journal of Labor Economics* 26 (July 2008): 519–548. Francine Blau and Lawrence Kahn, "Female Labor Supply: Why is the U.S. Falling Behind?" National Bureau of Economic Research working paper no. 18702 (Cambridge, Mass.: January 2013) finds that women's labor force participation rates are rising faster in Europe than in the United States because "family-friendly" policies are expanding faster in Europe.

Figure 7.7

Budget Constraints Facing a Single
Parent before and after Child Support
Assurance Program Adopted

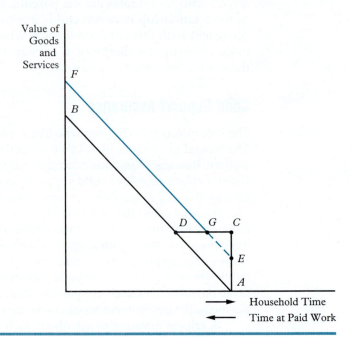

Household Time
Time at Paid Work

If the mother's indifference curves are steeply sloped (meaning, of course, that she is less able or less willing to substitute for her time at home), her utility is maximized at point *C*; she applies for welfare and does not work for pay. If her utility isoquants are relatively flat, her utility will be maximized along segment *DB*, and in this case, she works for pay and does not rely on welfare benefits to supplement her income.

Suppose that a child support assurance program is adopted that guarantees support payments of *AE* to the mother, regardless of her income. If she works, the effect of the new program would be to add the amount *AE* (= *BF*) to her earnings. If she does not work and remains on welfare, her *welfare* benefits are reduced by *AE*; thus, her child support benefits *plus* her welfare benefits continue to equal *AC*. After the child support assurance program is implemented, her budget constraint is *ACGF*.[21]

How will the new child support programs affect the mother's time in the household and her hours of paid work? There are three possibilities. First, some mothers will have isoquants so steeply sloped that they will remain out of

[21]Irwin Garfinkel, Philip K. Robins, Pat Wong, and Daniel R. Meyer, "The Wisconsin Child Support Assurance System: Estimated Effects on Poverty, Labor Supply, Caseloads, and Costs," *Journal of Human Resources* 25 (Winter 1990): 1–31.

Figure 7.8

A Single Parent Who Joins the Labor Force after Child Support Assurance Program Adopted

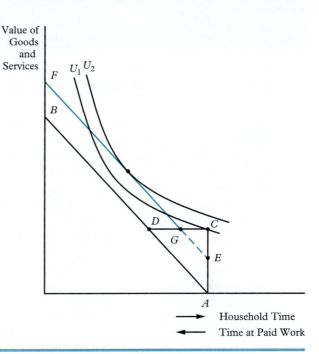

the labor force and spend all their time in the household (they will remain at point C in Figure 7.7). These mothers would receive child support payments of *AE* and welfare benefits equal to *EC*.

Second, for those who worked for pay before and were therefore along segment *DB*, the new program produces a pure income effect. These mothers will continue to work for pay, but their utility is now maximized along *GF*, and they can be expected to reduce their desired hours of work outside the home.

Third, some women, like the one whose isoquants (U_1 and U_2) are shown in Figure 7.8, will move from being on welfare to seeking paid work; for these women, the supply of labor to market work increases. These women formerly maximized utility at point *C*, but the new possibility of working *and* still being able to receive an income subsidy now places their utility-maximizing hours of paid work along segment *GF*.

On balance, then, the hypothetical child support assurance program discussed earlier can be expected to *increase the labor force participation rate* among single mothers (and thus reduce the number on welfare) while *reducing the desired hours of paid work* among those who take jobs. Studies that analyze the labor

EMPIRICAL STUDY

The Effects of Wage Increases on Labor Supply (and Sleep): Time-Use Diary Data and Sample Selection Bias

We have seen that the expected effects of a wage increase on labor supply are theoretically ambiguous; if the substitution effect dominates, the effect will be to increase desired hours of work, but if the income effect dominates, desired hours will decrease. How labor supply would be affected by wage increases associated with, say, income-tax rate reductions is therefore a question that must be answered empirically—and the research in this area must contend with problems of measuring both hours of work and the wage rate.

Hours of work in studies of labor supply are typically measured through household surveys, which ask workers how many hours they worked "last week." The answers given by workers to this question are somewhat suspect. While those who are paid by the hour have reason to keep careful track of their weekly work hours, salaried workers do not, and many are therefore inclined to give the easy answer of "40." Indeed, when work hours derived from these household surveys are compared to work hours derived from *diary* studies (which are more expensive to collect, because they ask workers in detail about how they used time in the past 24 hours), we find substantial differences. For example, while data from household surveys imply that, for men,

weekly hours at work fell by 2.7 percent from 1965 to 1981, diary studies suggest the decline was in fact 13.5 percent.[a]

Measuring wage rates is problematic on two accounts. First, the hourly "wage" for salaried workers is conventionally calculated by dividing their "earnings last week" by their own estimate of how many hours they worked. If they overstate their hours of work, their calculated wage is then understated—and the lower calculated wage is thus associated negatively (and spuriously) with the overstated hours of work. Understating their work hours creates the opposite bias.

Second, those who are not working do not have an observable wage rate. Should we just drop them from the sample and focus our analysis on those for whom a wage is observed? We cannot simply exclude those not in the labor force from our study of labor supply. Theory suggests that potential workers compare their wage offers to their reservation wages, and if offers lie below the reservation wage, they decide not to work. The statistical methods we use to analyze data rely on their being randomly generated, and dropping those who are not working (either because they have unusually high reservation wages or unusually low wage rates) would make the sample nonrandom by introducing the element of what economists call "sample selection bias."

If those not in the labor force must be in our analysis, what is the appropriate wage to use for them? Surely, they could earn *something* if they worked, so their potential wage is not zero—it simply is not observed. Because we do not directly observe reservation wages or wage offers, we must use statistical methods to *impute* a wage for those not in the labor force. Fortunately, techniques for dealing with this imputation problem have been developed, and one is illustrated by the study to be described.

An interesting use of diary-derived data can be seen in a study that analyzed how wages affect sleep, nonmarket (leisure plus household work) time, and labor supply. The diary data address the accuracy problems noted above in estimating hours of work (the dependent variable when analyzing labor supply). *Wages* for the employed were conventionally measured and statistically related to their personal characteristics, such as education, union status, and place of residence; this statistical relationship was then used to *predict* wages for everyone in the sample, including those not in the labor force.

When the researchers used regression techniques to relate hours of work to predicted wages, they found that increased wages *reduced* the labor supply of men—but so slightly that the effect was essentially zero. Thus, for men, the results imply that the income effect and substitution effect are essentially of equal strength and cancel each other out. For women, the substitution effect dominated, with a 10 percent increase in wages being associated with a 2 percent *increase* in hours of work. (Interestingly, higher wages were associated with men spending *more* time in nonmarket activities—presumably leisure—while they led to women spending less time in such activities, probably because they did less household work. Higher wages led to less sleep for both men and women, but these effects were small.)

[a]F. Thomas Juster and Frank P. Stafford, "The Allocation of Time: Empirical Findings, Behavioral Models, and Problems of Measurement," *Journal of Economic Literature* 29 (June 1991): 494.

Source: Jeff E. Biddle and Daniel S. Hamermesh, "Sleep and the Allocation of Time," *Journal of Political Economy* 98, no. 5, pt. 1 (October 1990): 922–943.

market effects of child support payments (from absent fathers) have found that the labor supply responses among single mothers are consistent with theoretical expectations.[22]

[22]John W. Graham and Andrea H. Beller, "The Effect of Child Support Payments on the Labor Supply of Female Family Heads," *Journal of Human Resources* 24 (Fall 1989): 664–688; and Wei-Yin Hu, "Child Support, Welfare Dependency, and Women's Labor Supply," *Journal of Human Resources* 34 (Winter 1999): 71–103.

Review Questions

1. Suppose that 5 percent unemployment is defined as "full employment," but current unemployment is 7 percent. Suppose further that we have the following information:

Unemploy- ment Rate (%)	Labor Force	Unemploy- ment	Employ- ment
5	6,000	300	5,700
7	5,600	392	5,208

    a. What is the amount of "hidden" unemployment when the unemployment rate is 7 percent?
    b. If the population is 10,000, what change occurs in the participation rate as a result of the marginal change in the unemployment rate?
    c. What is the economic significance of hidden unemployment? Should measured and hidden unemployment be added to obtain a "total unemployment" figure?

2. A study of the labor force participation rates of women in the post–World War II period noted:

    > Over the long run, women have joined the paid labor force because of a series of changes affecting the nature of work. Primary among these was the rise of the clerical and professional sectors, the increased education of women, labor-saving advances in households, declining fertility rates, and increased urbanization.

    Relate each of these factors to the household production model of labor supply outlined in this chapter.

3. In a debate in the 1976 U.S. presidential campaign, candidate Jimmy Carter argued, "While it is true that much of the recent rise in employment is due to the entrance of married women and teenagers into the labor force, this influx of people into the labor force is itself a sign of economic decay. The reason these people are now seeking work is because the primary breadwinner in the family is out of work and extra workers are needed to maintain the family income." Comment.

4. Is the following statement true, false, or uncertain? Why? "If a married woman's husband gets a raise, she tends to work less, but if *she* gets a raise, she tends to work more."

5. Suppose day-care centers charge working parents for each hour their children spend at the centers (no fixed costs of care). Suppose, too, that the federal government passes subsidy legislation so that the hourly cost per child now borne by the parents is cut in half. Would this policy cause an increase in the labor supply of parents with small children?

6. Assume that a state government currently provides no child-care subsidies to working single parents, but it now wants to adopt a plan that will encourage labor force participation among single parents. Suppose that child-care costs are hourly, and suppose the government adopts a child-care subsidy that pays $3 per hour for each hour the parent works, up to 8 hours per day. Draw a current budget constraint (net of child-care costs) for an assumed single mother and then draw in the new constraint. Discuss the likely effects on labor force participation and hours of work.

7. Suppose that as the ratio of the working population to the retired population continues to fall, the voters approve a change in the way Social Security benefits are calculated—a way that effectively reduces every retired person's benefits by half. This change affects all those in the population,

no matter what their age or current retirement status, and it is accompanied by a 50 percent reduction in payroll taxes. What would be the labor supply effects on those workers who are very close to the typical age of retirement (62 to 65)? What would be the labor supply effects on those workers just beginning their careers (workers in their twenties, for example)?

8. A state government wants to provide incentives for single parents to enter the labor market and become employed. It is considering a policy of paying single parents of children under age 18 $20 per day if the parent works at least 6 hours a day, 5 days a week. Draw an assumed current daily budget constraint for a single parent and then draw in the constraint that would be created by the $20 subsidy. Discuss the likely effects on (a) labor force participation and (b) hours of work.

9. In this chapter, individuals (our families) allocate their time between two activities: paid work and household production. Alternatively, household production can be introduced directly into the labor supply-leisure model from Chapter 6 by assuming that a person can spend his or her time on either paid work or leisure. Household work H enters this framework as an additional constraint: if, for instance, a person's total available time is 16 hours per day, then he or she can only decide on how to spend the remaining $16 - H$ hours on paid work or leisure. Throughout, assume that leisure L is measured in hours and consumption (value) C is measured in dollars.
   a. Suppose that a person can earn $5 per hour. Sketch that person's budget constraint in a leisure-consumption diagram for $H_1 = 8$. On the same graph, sketch the daily budget constraint for $H_2 = 4$.
   b. What is the maximum attainable amount of leisure and consumption for $H = H_1, H_2$?

10. Assume that a state government currently provides no child-care subsidies to working single parents, but it now wants to adopt a plan that will encourage labor force participation among single parents. Suppose child-care costs are hourly and that the government adopts a child-care subsidy of $4 per hour if the single parent works 4 or more hours per day. Draw the current daily budget constraint (assume a wage that is net of the hourly child-care costs) for a single mother and then draw in the new constraint. Discuss the likely effects on labor force participation and hours of work.

11. Company X has for some time hired skilled technicians on one-year contracts to work at a remote location. It offers a $10,000 signing bonus and an hourly wage rate of $20 per hour. Company Y now enters the market and offers no signing bonus but offers an hourly wage of $25. Both companies want to attract workers who will work longer than 2,000 hours during the year (all hours are paid at the straight-time wage rate given above).
   a. First, suppose that workers receive offers from both companies; on the same graph, draw the income-household time ("budget") constraints for the coming year under both offers. (Clearly label which is Company X and which is Y.)
   b. Second, consider a worker for Company X who chose to work 2,500 hours last year. Suppose that her contract is up and that she now has offers from both Company X and Company Y. Can we tell which offer she will choose, assuming her preferences for income and household time have not changed? Explain (or demonstrate). If she changes companies, will she continue to work 2,500 hours or will she increase hours or reduce them? Explain fully.

Problems

1. The following table gives information for June 2006 and June 2007 on the thousands of people who are in the labor force, the thousands of people who are defined as unemployed, and the thousands of people not in the labor force because they believe that no job is available. The latter group consists of those people who are "discouraged" workers, and some regard them as the *hidden* unemployed (they have searched for work in the past and are available to work, but they believe jobs are so scarce that looking for work is of no use).

Date	Number in Labor Force	Number Unemployed	Number Discouraged
June 2006	152,557	7,341	481
June 2007	154,252	7,295	401

Source: Bureau of Labor Statistics, U.S. Department of Labor, Current Population Survey (CPS), Tables A-1 and A-13.

a. Calculate the officially defined unemployment rates for June 2006 and June 2007. What is the change in the unemployment rate from June 2006 to June 2007?

b. Calculate unofficial unemployment rates that include the hidden unemployed for both dates. What is the change in this unemployment rate from June 2006 to June 2007?

c. If the officially defined unemployment rate is falling, what effect would you expect this to have on the number of discouraged workers? How has the change in the number of discouraged workers affected the change in the officially defined unemployment rate from June 2006 to June 2007?

2. Mary and John live in a small house. Both of them can spend up to 16 hours (per day) in paid work or household production. Their objective is maximization of household utility.

a. Suppose that John's hourly wage exceeds Mary's. Who should go to work first? Sketch the household budget constraint to illustrate your answer. Let the horizontal axis denote "hours spent in household production." The vertical axis should denote "value of consumption (dollars)."

b. How would you construct the joint indifference curve? What implicit assumption do you make when deriving a joint indifference curve?

c. Due to inflation, the average price of consumer goods increased. Provided that wages did not change, how will inflation affect the (i) joint budget constraint, (ii) joint indifference curve, and (iii) the couple's labor supply?

d. How does inflation affect John and Mary's relative labor supply? Let S_1^{John} denote John's labor supply in the past, and S_2^{John} denote his current labor supply. Let $\delta^{John} = \dfrac{S_2^{John} - S_1^{John}}{S_1^{John}}$ denote the relative change in John's labor supply. Do you expect δ^{John} to be greater or smaller than δ^{Mary}?

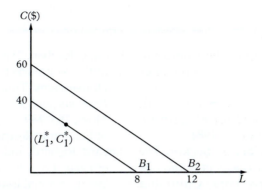

3. This problem builds on Review Question 9. The figure gives Sally's daily budget constraints for $H_1 = 8$ and $H_2 = 4$. Given H_1, suppose that the point (L_1^*, C_1^*) maximizes Sally's utility:

   a. On her birthday, Sally received a microwave oven as a present, which allows her to prepare food in much less time. As a consequence, Sally is required to spend only H_2 on household work. How will this affect her optimal levels of leisure and consumption?

   b. Explain your result in light of this statement: "With inventions such as washing machines and dryers, automatic dishwashers, microwave ovens ... it has become easier to substitute purchased goods for household time." (Chapter 7, page 238).

4. This problem builds on Review Question 9. Sally, a working single mother of a three-year-old child, faces two options. She can raise her child at home, which is associated with $H_1 = 8$ hours homework per day. Alternatively, Sally can purchase daycare services (fixed cost: $40 per day) and reduce homework by 4 hours (i.e., $H_2 = 4$). In any case, Sally receives financial support from her mother ($40 per day). Sally's hourly wage rate is $5.

   a. For each case, draw Sally's budget constraint in one diagram.

   b. Compare Sally's budget constraints. Which choices are attainable in both cases? In addition, highlight Sally's attainable choices that are exclusive to each case.

   c. How will Sally decide (i) if she has a strong preference for leisure? (ii) if daycare services become cheaper?

   d. The government of Sally's country decides to lower trade barriers. As a consequence, Sally can now choose from a much greater number of products. How will this affect Sally's willingness to purchase childcare services?

Selected Readings

Becker, Gary S. "A Theory of the Allocation of Time." *Economic Journal* 75 (September 1965): 493–517.

Fields, Gary S., and Olivia S. Mitchell. *Retirement, Pensions, and Social Security.* Cambridge, Mass.: MIT Press, 1984.

Ghez, Gilbert R., and Gary S. Becker. *The Allocation of Time and Goods over the Life Cycle*, chapter 3. New York: Columbia University Press, 1975.

Gronau, Reuben. "The Measurement of Output of the Nonmarket Sector: The Evaluation of Housewives' Time." In *The Measurement of Economic and Social Performance*, ed. Milton Moss, 163–189. New York: National Bureau of Economic Research, 1973.

Layard, Richard, and Jacob Mincer, eds. *Journal of Labor Economics* 3, no. 1, pt. 2 (January 1985). "Special Issue on Child Care." *Journal of Human Resources* 27 (Winter 1992).

CHAPTER 8

Compensating Wage Differentials and Labor Markets

Chapters 6 and 7 analyzed workers' decisions about *whether to seek employment* and *how long to work*. Chapters 8 and 9 will analyze workers' decisions about the industry, occupation, or firm in which they will work. This chapter will emphasize the influence on job choice of such daily, *recurring* job characteristics as the work environment, the risk of injury, and the generosity of employee benefits. Chapter 9 will analyze the effects of required educational *investments* on occupational choice.

Job Matching: The Role of Worker Preferences and Information

One of the major functions of the labor market is to provide the signals and the mechanisms by which workers seeking to maximize their utility can be matched to employers trying to maximize profits. Matching is a formidable task because workers have varying skills and preferences and because employers offer jobs that differ in requirements and working environment. The process of finding the worker–employer pairings that are best for each is truly one of trial and error, and whether the process is woefully deficient or reasonably satisfactory is an important policy issue that can be analyzed using economic theory in its normative mode.

The assumption that workers are attempting to maximize utility implies that they are interested in both the pecuniary and the nonpecuniary aspects of their jobs. On the one hand, we expect that higher compensation levels in a job (holding job tasks constant) would attract more workers to it. On the other hand, it is clear that pay is not all that matters; occupational tasks and how workers' preferences mesh with those tasks are critical elements in the matching process. The focus of this chapter is on how the labor market accommodates worker preferences.

If all jobs in a labor market were *exactly alike* and located in the *same place*, an individual's decision about where to seek work would be a simple matter of choosing the job with the highest compensation. Any differences in the pay offered by employers would cause movement by workers from low-paying to high-paying firms. If there were no barriers inhibiting this movement, as discussed in chapter 5, the market would force offers of all employers into equality.

All jobs are not the same, however. Some jobs are in clean, modern spaces, and others are in noisy, dusty, or dangerous environments. Some permit employee discretion in regard to the hours or the pace of work, while others allow less flexibility. Some employers offer more generous employee-benefit packages than others, and different *places* of employment involve different commuting distances and neighborhood characteristics. In this chapter we discuss the ways that differences in job characteristics influence individual choice and observable market outcomes.

Individual Choice and Its Outcomes

Suppose several unskilled workers have received offers from two employers. Employer X pays $8 per hour and offers clean, safe working conditions. Employer Y also pays $8 per hour but offers employment in a dirty, noisy factory. Which employer would the workers choose? Most would undoubtedly choose employer X because the pay is the same while the job is performed under more agreeable conditions.

Clearly, however, $8 is not an equilibrium wage in both firms.[1] Because firm X finds it easy to attract applicants at $8, it will hold the line on any future wage increases. Firm Y, however, must clean up the plant, pay higher wages, or do both if it wants to fill its vacancies. Assuming it decides not to alter working conditions, it must pay a wage *above* $8 to be competitive in the labor market. The *extra* wage it must pay to attract workers is called a *compensating wage differential* because the higher wage is paid to compensate workers for the undesirable working conditions. If such a differential did not exist, firm Y could not attract the unskilled workers that firm X can obtain.

An Equilibrium Differential   Suppose that firm Y raises its wage offer to $8.50 while the offer from X remains at $8. Will this 50-cent-per-hour differential—an extra $1,000 per year—attract *all* the workers in our group to firm Y? If it did attract them all, firm X would have an incentive to raise its wages, and firm Y might want to lower its offers a bit; the 50-cent differential in this case would *not* be an equilibrium differential.

More than likely, however, the higher wage in firm Y would attract only *some* of the group to firm Y. Some people are not bothered much by dirt and noise,

---

[1]A few people may be indifferent to noise and dirt in the workplace. We assume here that these people are so rare, or firm Y's demand for workers is so large, that Y cannot fill all its vacancies with just those who are totally insensitive to dirt and noise.

and they may decide to take the extra pay and put up with the poorer working conditions. Those who are very sensitive to noise or dust may decide that they would rather be paid less than expose themselves to such working conditions. If both firms could obtain the quantity and quality of workers they wanted, the 50-cent differential *would* be an equilibrium differential, in the sense that there would be no forces causing the differential to change.

The desire of workers to avoid unpleasantness or risk, then, should force employers offering unpleasant or risky jobs to pay higher wages than they would otherwise have to pay. This wage differential serves two related, socially desirable ends. First, it serves a *social* need by giving people an incentive to voluntarily do dirty, dangerous, or unpleasant work. Second, at an *individual* level, it serves as a reward to workers who accept unpleasant jobs by paying them more than comparable workers in more pleasant jobs.

The Allocation of Labor   A number of jobs are unavoidably nasty or would be very costly to make safe and pleasant (coal-mining, deep-sea diving, and police work are examples). There are essentially two ways to recruit the necessary labor for such jobs. One is to compel people to do these jobs (the military draft is the most obvious contemporary example of forced labor). The second way is to induce people to do the jobs voluntarily.

Most modern societies rely mainly on incentives, compensating wage differentials, to recruit labor to unpleasant jobs voluntarily. Workers will mine coal, bolt steel beams together 50 stories off the ground, or agree to work at night because, compared to alternative jobs for which they could qualify, these jobs pay well. Night work, for example, can be stressful because it disrupts normal patterns of sleep and family interactions; however, employers often find it efficient to keep their plants and machines in operation around the clock. The result is that nonunion employees working night shifts are paid about 4 percent more than they would receive if they worked during the day.[2]

Compensation for Workers   Compensating wage differentials also serve as *individual* rewards by paying those who accept bad or arduous working conditions more than they would otherwise receive. In a parallel fashion, those who opt for more pleasant conditions have to "buy" them by accepting lower pay. For example, if a person takes the $8-per-hour job with firm X, he or she is giving up the $8.50-per-hour job with less pleasant conditions in firm Y. The better conditions are being bought, in a very real sense, for 50 cents per hour.

---

[2]Peter F. Kostiuk, "Compensating Differentials for Shift Work," *Journal of Political Economy* 98, no. 5, pt. 1 (October 1990): 1054–1075. Shift-work differentials are even larger in France; see Joseph Lanfranchi, Henry Ohlsson, and Ali Skalli, "Compensating Wage Differentials and Shift Work Preferences," *Economics Letters* 74 (February 2002): 393–398. Compensating wage differentials of almost 12 percent have been estimated for registered nurses who work at night; see Edward J. Schumacher and Barry T. Hirsch, "Compensating Differentials and Unmeasured Ability in the Labor Market for Nurses: Why Do Hospitals Pay More?" *Industrial and Labor Relations Review* 50 (July 1997): 557–579.

Thus, compensating wage differentials become the prices at which good working conditions can be purchased by, or bad ones sold by, workers. Contrary to what is commonly asserted, a monetary value *can* often be attached to events or conditions whose effects are primarily psychological in nature. Compensating wage differentials provide the key to the valuation of these nonpecuniary aspects of employment.

For example, how much do workers value a work schedule that permits them to enjoy leisure activities and sleep at the usual times? If we know that night-shift workers earn 4 percent—or about $1,000 per year for a typical worker—more than they otherwise would earn, the reasoning needed to answer this question is straightforward. Those who have difficulty sleeping during the day, or whose favorite leisure activities require the companionship of family or friends, are not likely to be attracted to night work for only $1,000 extra per year; they are quite willing to forgo a $1,000 earnings premium to obtain a normal work schedule. Others, however, are less bothered by the unusual sleep and leisure patterns, and they are willing to work at night for the $1,000 premium. While some of these latter workers would be willing to give up a normal work schedule for *less* than $1,000, others find the decision to work at night a close call at the going wage differential. If the differential were to marginally fall, a few working at night would change their minds and refuse to continue, while if the differential rose a bit above $1,000, a few more could be recruited to night work. Thus, the $1,000 yearly premium represents what those *at the margin* (the ones closest to changing their minds) are willing to pay for a normal work schedule.[3]

Assumptions and Predictions

We have seen how a simple theory of job choice by individuals leads to the *prediction* that compensating wage differentials will be associated with various job characteristics. Positive differentials (higher wages) will accompany "bad" characteristics, while negative differentials (lower wages) will be associated with "good" ones. However, it is very important to understand that this prediction can *only* be made *holding other things equal*.

Our prediction about the existence of compensating wage differentials grows out of the reasonable assumption that if an informed worker has a choice between a job with "good" working conditions and a job of equal pay with "bad" working conditions, he or she will choose the "good" job. If the employee is an unskilled laborer, he or she may be choosing between an unpleasant job spreading hot asphalt or a more comfortable job in an air-conditioned warehouse. In either case, he or she is going to receive something close to the wage rate unskilled workers typically receive. However, our theory would predict that this worker would receive *more* from the asphalt-spreading job than from the warehouse job.

---

[3]Daniel S. Hamermesh, "The Timing of Work over Time," *Economic Journal* 109 (January 1999): 37–66, finds evidence that as people become wealthier, they increasingly want to avoid working at night.

Thus, the predicted outcome of our theory of job choice is *not* simply that employees working under "bad" conditions receive more than those working under "good" conditions. The prediction is that, *holding worker characteristics constant*, employees in bad working conditions receive higher wages than those working under more pleasant conditions. The characteristics that must be held constant include all the other things that influence wages: skill level, age, experience, race, gender, union status, region of the country, and so forth. Three assumptions have been used to arrive at this prediction.

Assumption 1: Utility Maximization

Our first assumption is that workers seek to maximize their *utility*, not their income. Compensating wage differentials will arise only if some people do *not* choose the highest-paying job offered, preferring instead a lower-paying but more pleasant job. This behavior allows those employers offering lower-paying, pleasant jobs to be competitive. Wages do not equalize in this case. Rather, the *net advantages*—the overall utility from the pay and the psychic aspects of the job—tend to equalize for the marginal worker.

Assumption 2: Worker Information

The second assumption implicit in our analysis is that workers are aware of the job characteristics of potential importance to them. Whether they know about them before they take the job or find out about them soon after taking it is not too important. In either case, a company offering a "bad" job with no compensating wage differential would have trouble recruiting or retaining workers—trouble that would eventually force it to raise its wage.

It is quite likely, of course, that workers would quickly learn about danger, noise, rigid work discipline, job insecurity, and other obvious bad working conditions. It is equally likely that they would *not* know the *precise* probability of being laid off, say, or of being injured on the job. However, even with respect to these probabilities, their own direct observations or word-of-mouth reports from other employees could give them enough information to evaluate the situation with some accuracy. For example, the proportions of employees considering their work dangerous have been shown to be closely related to the actual injury rates published by the government for the industries in which they work.[4] This finding illustrates that while workers probably cannot state

---

[4]W. Kip Viscusi, "Labor Market Valuations of Life and Limb: Empirical Evidence and Policy Implications," *Public Policy* 26 (Summer 1978): 359–386. W. Kip Viscusi and Michael J. Moore, "Worker Learning and Compensating Differentials," *Industrial and Labor Relations Review* 45 (October 1991): 80–96, suggest that the accuracy of risk perceptions rises with job tenure. For an analysis of how well people estimate their risk of traffic fatality and their overall risk of death, see Henrik Andersson and Petter Lundborg, "Perception of Own Death Risk: An Analysis of Road-Traffic and Overall Mortality Risks," *Journal of Risk and Uncertainty* 34 (February 2007): 67–84. Another study has shown that people do adjust their behavior to even very low probabilities of risk; see Daniel Sutter and Marc Poitras, "Do People Respond to Low Probability Risks? Evidence from Tornado Risk and Manufactured Homes," *Journal of Risk and Uncertainty* 40 (April 2010): 181–196.

the precise probability of being injured, they do form accurate judgments about the relative risks of several jobs.

Where predictions may disappoint us, however, is with respect to *very* obscure characteristics. For example, while we now know that asbestos dust is highly damaging to worker health, this fact was not widely known 50 years ago. One reason information on asbestos dangers in plants was so long in being generated is that it takes more than 20 years for asbestos-related disease to develop. Cause and effect were thus obscured from workers and researchers alike, creating a situation in which job choices were made in ignorance of this risk. Compensating wage differentials for this danger could thus not possibly have arisen at that time. Our predictions about compensating wage differentials, then, hold only for job characteristics that workers know about.

Assumption 3: Worker Mobility   The final assumption implicit in our theory is that workers have a range of job offers from which to choose. Without a range of offers, workers would not be able to select the combination of job characteristics they desire or avoid the ones to which they do not wish exposure. A compensating wage differential for risk of injury, for example, simply could not arise if workers were able to obtain only dangerous jobs. It is the act of choosing safe jobs over dangerous ones that forces employers offering dangerous work to raise wages.

One manner in which this choice can occur is for each job applicant to receive several job offers from which to choose. However, another way in which choice could be exercised is for workers to be (at least potentially) highly mobile. In other words, workers with few concurrent offers could take jobs and continue their search for work if they thought an improvement could be made. Thus, even with few offers at any *one* time, workers could conceivably have relatively wide choice over a *period* of time, which would eventually allow them to select jobs that maximized their utility.

How mobile are workers? As of January 2006, about 22 percent of all American workers who were 20 years of age or older had been with their employers for a year or less, and 3.5 percent started with a new employer each month. For some, finding a new employer was necessary because they were fired or laid off by their prior employer, but roughly 2 percent of workers in the United States *voluntarily* quit their jobs in any given *month*—and roughly 40 percent of those go to jobs paying lower wages (possibly because of more attractive working conditions or benefits).[5]

---

[5]U.S. Department of Labor, Bureau of Labor Statistics, "Employee Tenure Summary," news release USDL 06-1563 (http://www.bls.gov/news.release/tenure.nr0.htm), September 8, 2006, Table 3; U.S. Department of Labor, Bureau of Labor Statistics, "Job Openings and Labor Turnover Survey" (http://data.bls.gov/cgi-bin/surveymost and http://data.bls.gov/cgi-bin/dsrv); and Peter Rupert, "Wage and Employer Changes over the Life Cycle," *Economic Commentary*, Federal Reserve Bank of Cleveland (April 15, 2004).

Empirical Tests for Compensating Wage Differentials

The prediction that there are compensating wage differentials for undesirable job characteristics is over two hundred years old. Adam Smith, in his *Wealth of Nations*, published in 1776, proposed five "principal circumstances which . . . make up for a small pecuniary gain in some employments, and counterbalance a great one in others." Among the circumstances Smith listed were the constancy of employment, the difficulty of learning the job, the probability of success, and the degree of trust placed in the worker. While our discussion in this chapter could focus on any one of these, most of the work to date has focused on his assertion that "the wages of labour vary with the ease or hardship, the cleanliness or dirtiness, the honourableness or dishonourableness of the employment."[6]

There are two difficulties in actually estimating compensating wage differentials. First, we must be able to create data sets that allow us to match, at the level of individual workers, their relevant job characteristics with their personal characteristics (age, education, union status, and so forth) that also influence wages. Second, we must be able to specify in advance those job characteristics that are generally regarded as disagreeable (for example, not everyone may regard outdoor work or repetitive tasks as undesirable).

The most extensive testing for the existence of compensating wage differentials has been done with respect to the risks of injury or death on the job, primarily because higher levels of such risks are unambiguously "bad." These studies generally, but not always, support the prediction that wages will be higher whenever risks on the job are higher. Recent estimates of such compensating differentials for the United States suggest that wages tend to be around 1 percent higher for workers facing three times the average risk of a job-related fatality than for those who face the average yearly level of risk (which is about 1 in 30,000).[7]

Many other studies of compensating wage differentials have been done, but because they are spread thinly across a variety of job characteristics, judging the strength of their support for the theory is problematic. Nonetheless, positive wage premiums have been related, holding other influences constant, to such disagreeable characteristics as night work, an inflexible work schedule, having to stand a lot, working in a noisy or polluted environment, and having an unsteady job (see Example 8.1 for less formal data on another "bad" working condition: working away from home).[8]

---

[6]See Adam Smith, *Wealth of Nations* (New York: Modern Library, 1937), book 1, chapter 10.

[7]Thomas J. Kniesner, W. Kip Viscusi, Christopher Woock, and James P. Ziliak, "The Value of a Statistical Life: Evidence from Panel Data," *Review of Economics and Statistics* 94 (February 2012): 74–87.

[8]Christophe Daniel and Catherine Sofer, "Bargaining, Compensating Wage Differentials, and Dualism of the Labor Market: Theory and Evidence for France," *Journal of Labor Economics* 16 (July 1998): 546–575; Matthew A. Cole, Robert J. R. Elliott, and Joanne K. Lindley, "Dirty Money: Is There a Wage Premium for Working in a Pollution Intensive Industry?" *Journal of Risk and Uncertainty* 39 (October 2009): 161–180; and Emilia Del Bono and Andrea Weber, "Do Wages Compensate for Anticipated Working Time Restrictions? Evidence from Seasonal Employment in Austria," *Journal of Labor Economics* 26 (January 2008): 181–221.

EXAMPLE 8.1

Working on the Railroad: Making a Bad Job Good

While compensating wage differentials are difficult to measure with precision, the theory in this chapter can often find general support in everyday discussions of job choice. This example is based on a newspaper article about the exclusive use of Navajos by the Santa Fe Railway to repair and replace its 9,000 miles of track between Los Angeles and Chicago.

The 220 Navajos were organized into two "steel gangs." Workers did what machines cannot: pull and sort old spikes, weld the rails together, and check the safety of the new rails. The grueling work was intrinsically unappealing: jobs lasted for only 5 to 8 months per year; much of the work was done in sweltering desert heat; workers had to live away from their families and were housed in bunk cars with up to 16 other workers; and the remote locations rendered the off-hours boring and lonely.

Two hypotheses about jobs such as these can be derived from the theory in this chapter. These hypotheses are listed next, along with supporting quotations or facts from the newspaper article.

Hypothesis 1. Companies offering unappealing jobs find it difficult to recruit and retain employees.

Workers who take these jobs are the ones for whom the conditions are least disagreeable.

> They had tried everyone. The Navajos were the only ones willing to be away from home, to do the work, and to do a good job.
>
> [A Santa Fe recruiter]

> Lonely? No, I never get lonely. There is nothing but Navajo here. . . . We speak the same language and understand one another. . . . It's a good job.
>
> [A steel gang worker with 16 years' experience]

Hypothesis 2. The jobs are made appealing to the target group of workers by raising wages well above those of their alternatives.

> I wish I could stay home all the time and be with my family. It's just not possible. Where am I going to find a job that pays $900 every two weeks?
>
> [A steel gang veteran of 11 years]

(Steel gang wages in the early 1990s ranged between $12 and $17 per hour, well above the national average of about $10 per hour for "handlers and laborers.")

Data from: Paula Moñarez, "Navajos Keep Rail Lines Safe," *Long Beach Independent Press-Telegram,* May 14, 1992, D1.

Hedonic Wage Theory and the Risk of Injury

We now turn to a graphic presentation of the theory of compensating wage differentials, which has become known as *hedonic* wage theory.[9] The graphic tools used permit additional insights into the theory and greatly clarify the normative analysis of important regulatory issues. In this section, we analyze the theory of compensating wage differentials for a *negative* job characteristic, the risk of injury, and apply the concepts to a normative analysis of governmental safety regulations.

---

[9]The philosophy of hedonism is usually associated with Jeremy Bentham, a philosopher of the late eighteenth century who believed people always behaved in ways that they thought would maximize their happiness. The analysis that follows is adapted primarily from Sherwin Rosen, "Hedonic Prices and Implicit Markets," *Journal of Political Economy* 82 (January/February 1974): 34–55.

Job injuries are an unfortunate characteristic of the workplace, and injury rates vary considerably across occupations and industries. For example, while we noted that the average yearly rate of fatal injury in the American workplace is about one in 30,000, the rates for truck drivers and roofers are 7 to 10 times higher. Roughly 2 percent of American workers are injured seriously enough each year that they cannot perform their normal duties for at least a day, but even in the manufacturing sector, these rates vary from 1 percent in petroleum manufacturing to 3.5 percent in wood manufacturing.[10]

To simplify our analysis of compensating wage differentials for the risk of injury, we shall assume that compensating differentials for every *other* job characteristic have already been established. This assumption allows us to see more clearly the outcomes of the job selection process, and since the same analysis could be repeated for every other characteristic, our conclusions are not obscured by it. To obtain a complete understanding of the job selection process and the outcomes of that process, it is necessary, as always, to consider both the employer and the employee sides of the market.

Employee Considerations

Employees, it may safely be assumed, dislike the risk of being injured on the job. A worker who is offered a job for $8 per hour in a firm in which 3 percent of the workforce is injured each year would achieve a certain level of utility from that job. If the risk of injury were increased to 4 percent, holding other job characteristics constant, the job would have to pay a higher wage to produce the same level of utility (except in the unlikely event that the costs of wage loss, medical treatment, and suffering caused by the added injuries were *completely* covered by the firm or its insurance company after the fact).[11]

Other combinations of wage rates and risk levels could be devised that would yield the same utility as the $8/hour–3 percent risk offer. These combinations can be connected on a graph to form an indifference curve (for example, the curve U_2 in Figure 8.1). Unlike the indifference curves drawn in chapters 6 and 7, those in Figure 8.1 slope upward because risk of injury is a "bad" job characteristic, not a "good" (such as leisure). In other words, if risk increases, wages must rise if utility is to be held constant.

As in the previous chapters, there is one indifference curve for each possible level of utility. Because a higher wage at a given risk level will generate more utility, indifference curves lying to the northwest represent higher utility.

---

[10]U.S. Bureau of Labor Statistics, "2011 Census of Fatal Occupational Injuries (revised data)", http://www.bls.gov/iif/oshwc/cfoi/cfch0010.pdf; and U.S. Bureau of Labor Statistics, "Workplace Injury and Illness Summary," USDL-12-2121, October 25, 2012, Table 1.

[11]Compensating wage differentials provide for *ex ante*—"before the fact"—compensation related to injury risk. Workers can also be compensated (to keep utility constant) by *ex post*—or after-injury—payments for damages. Workers' compensation insurance provides for *ex post* payments, but these payments typically offer incomplete compensation for all the costs of injury.

Figure 8.1

A Family of Indifference Curves
between Wages and Risk of Injury

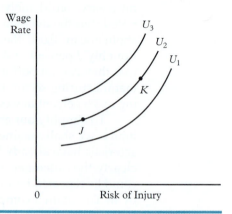

Thus, all points on curve U_3 in Figure 8.1 are preferred to those on U_2, and those on U_2 are preferred to the ones on U_1.[12] The fact that each indifference curve is convex (when viewed from below) reflects the normal assumption of diminishing marginal rates of substitution. At point K of curve U_2, the person receives a relatively high wage and faces a high level of risk. He or she will be willing to give up a lot in wages to achieve a given reduction in risk because risk levels are high enough to place one in imminent danger, and the consumption level of the goods that are bought with wages is already high. However, as risk levels and wage rates fall (to point J, say), the person becomes less willing to give up wages in return for the given reduction in risk; the danger is no longer imminent, and consumption of other goods is not as high.

People differ, of course, in their aversion to the risk of being injured. Those who are very sensitive to this risk will require large wage increases for any increase in risk, while those who are less sensitive will require smaller wage increases to hold utility constant. The more-sensitive workers will have indifference curves that are steeper at any level of risk, as illustrated in Figure 8.2. At risk level R_1, the slope at point C is steeper than at point D. Point C lies on the indifference curve of worker A, who is highly sensitive to risk, while point D lies on an indifference curve of worker B, who is less sensitive. Of course, each person has a whole family of indifference curves that are not shown in Figure 8.2, and each will attempt to achieve the highest level of utility possible.

---

[12]When a "bad" is on the horizontal axis (as in Figure 8.1) and a "good" on the vertical axis, people with more of the "good" and less of the "bad" are unambiguously better off, and this combination is achieved by moving in a northwest direction on the graph.

Figure 8.2

Representative Indifference Curves for Two Workers
Who Differ in Their Aversion to Risk of Injury

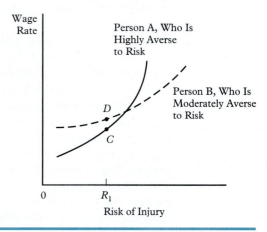

Employer Considerations

Employers are faced with a wage/risk trade-off of their own that derives from three assumptions. First, it is presumably costly to reduce the risk of injury facing employees. Safety equipment must be placed on machines, production time must be sacrificed for safety training sessions, protective clothing must be furnished to workers, and so forth. Second, competitive pressures will presumably force many firms to operate at *zero profit* (that is, at a point at which all costs are covered and the rate of return on capital is about what it is for similar investments).[13] Third, all *other* job characteristics are presumably given or already determined. The consequence of these three assumptions is that if a firm undertakes a program to reduce the risk of injury, it must reduce wages to remain competitive.

Thus, forces on the employer side of the market tend to cause low risk to be associated with low wages and high risk to be associated with high wages, *holding other things constant*. These "other things" may be employee benefits or other job characteristics; assuming they are given will not affect the validity of our analysis (even though it may seem at first unrealistic). The major point is that if a firm spends *more on safety*, it must spend *less on other things* if it is to remain competitive. The term *wages* can thus be thought of as shorthand for "terms of employment" in our theoretical analyses.

---

[13]If returns are permanently below normal, it would benefit the owners to close down the plant and invest their funds elsewhere. If returns are above normal, other investors will be attracted to the industry and profits will eventually be driven down by increased competition.

The employer trade-offs between wages and levels of injury risk can be graphed through the use of *isoprofit curves*, which show the various combinations of risk and wage levels that yield a given level of profits (*iso* means "equal"). Thus, all the points along a given curve, such as those depicted in Figure 8.3, are wage/risk combinations that yield the *same* level of profits. Curves to the southeast represent higher profit levels because with all other items in the employment contract given, each risk level is associated with a *lower* wage level. Curves to the northwest represent, conversely, lower profit levels.

Note that the isoprofit curves in Figure 8.3 are concave (from below). This concavity is a graphic representation of our assumption that there are diminishing marginal returns to safety expenditures. Suppose, for example, that the firm is operating at point *M* in Figure 8.3—a point where the risk of injury is high. The first expenditures by the firm to reduce risk will have a relatively high return because the firm will clearly choose to attack the safety problem by eliminating the most obvious and cheaply eliminated hazards. Because the risk (and accompanying injury cost) reductions are relatively large, the firm need not reduce wages by very much to keep profits constant. Thus, the isoprofit curve at point *M* is relatively flat. At point *N*, however, the curve is steeply sloped, indicating that wages will have to be reduced by quite a bit if the firm is to maintain its profits in the presence of a program to reduce risk. This large wage reduction is required because, at this point, further increases in safety are very costly.

We also assume that employers differ in the ease (cost) with which they can eliminate hazards. We have just indicated that the cost of reducing risk levels is reflected in the *slope* of the isoprofit curve. In firms where injuries are costly to reduce, large wage reductions will be required to keep profits constant in the face of a safety program; the isoprofit curve in this case will be steeply sloped.

Figure 8.3

A Family of Isoprofit
Curves for an Employer

Figure 8.4

Figure 8.4

The Zero-Profit Curves of Two Firms

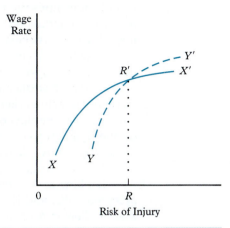

The isoprofit curve of one such firm is shown as the dashed curve YY' in Figure 8.4. The isoprofit curves of firms where injuries are easier to eliminate are flatter. Note that the solid curve XX' in Figure 8.4 is flatter at each level of risk than YY'; this is most easily seen at point R' and indicates that firm X can reduce risk more cheaply than firm Y.

The Matching of Employers and Employees

The aim of employees is to achieve the highest possible utility from their choice of a job. If they receive two offers at the same wage rate, they will choose the lower-risk job. If they receive two offers in which the risk levels are equal, they will accept the offer with the higher wage rate. More generally, they will choose the offer that falls on the highest, or most northwest, indifference curve.

In obtaining jobs, employees are constrained by the offers they receive from employers. Employers, for their part, are constrained by two forces. On the one hand, they cannot make outrageously lucrative offers because they will be driven out of business by firms whose costs are lower. On the other hand, if their offered terms of employment are very low, they will be unable to attract employees (who will choose to work for other firms). These two forces compel firms in competitive markets to operate on their zero-profit isoprofit curves.

To better understand the offers firms make, refer to Figure 8.4, where two different firms are depicted. Firm X, the firm that can cheaply reduce injuries, can make higher wage offers at low levels of risk (left of point R') than can firm Y. Because it can produce safety more cheaply, it can pay higher wages at low levels of risk and still remain competitive. Any offers along segment XR' will be preferred by employees to those along YR' because, for given levels of risk, higher wages are paid.

At higher levels of risk, however, firm Y can outbid firm X for employees. Firm X does not save much money if it permits the risk level to rise above R, because risk reduction is so cheap. Because firm Y *does* save itself a lot by operating at levels of risk beyond R, it is willing to pay relatively high wages at high risk levels. For employees, offers along $R'Y'$ will be preferable to those along $R'X'$, so those employees working at high-risk jobs will work for Y.

Graphing worker indifference curves and employer isoprofit curves together can show which workers choose which offers. Figure 8.5 contains the zero-profit curves of two employers (X and Y) and the indifference curves of two employees (A and B). Employee A maximizes utility (along A_2) by working for employer X at wage W_{AX} and risk level R_{AX}, while employee B maximizes utility by working for employer Y at wage W_{BY} and risk level R_{BY}.

Looking at A's choice more closely, we see that if he or she took the offer B accepted—W_{BY} and R_{BY}—the level of utility achieved would be A_1, which is less than A_2. Person A values safety very highly, and wage W_{BY} is just not high enough to compensate for the high level of risk. Person B, whose indifference curves are flatter (signifying he or she is less averse to risk), finds the offer of W_{BY} and R_{BY} on curve B_2 superior to the offer A accepts. Person B is simply not willing to take a cut in pay to W_{AX} in order to reduce risk from R_{BY} to R_{AX}, because that would place him or her on curve B_1.

Figure 8.5

Matching Employers and Employees

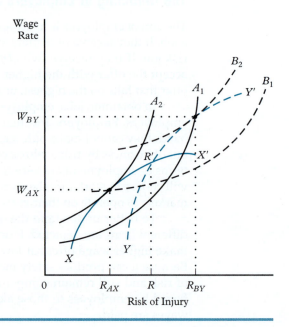

> **EXAMPLE 8.2**
>
> ## Parenthood, Occupational Choice, and Risk
>
> The theory of compensating wage differentials is built on the assumption that among workers in a given labor market, those with the stronger aversions to risk will select themselves into safer (but lower-paying) jobs. It is difficult to test the implications of this assumption because measuring risk aversion is not generally possible. However, one study analyzed workers' choices when the relative strength of aversion to injury risk could be logically inferred.
>
> It is well known that women are found in safer jobs than men. In the mid-1990s, for example, men made up 54 percent of all workers but constituted 92 percent of workers killed on the job! What is not so well known is that among each gender group, there is an equally striking pattern—*men and women who are single parents choose to work in safer jobs.*
>
> This study argues that workers who are raising children feel a greater need to avoid risk on the job because they have loved ones who depend on them, and, of course, this should be especially true for single parents. Indeed, the study found that married women without children worked in jobs with a greater risk of death than married women with children, but that single mothers chose to work in even safer jobs.
>
> It was found that among men, those who were single parents worked in safer jobs than married men, but married men with children apparently did not behave much differently than those without. The study argues that because married men are typically not in the role of caregiver to their children, they may believe they can take higher-paying, riskier jobs but adequately protect their children through buying life insurance. Married women, in contrast, do not find life insurance as effective in protecting children, because it provides only money, which cannot replace the care and nurturing that mothers give.
>
> *Source:* Thomas DeLeire and Helen Levy, "Worker Sorting and the Risk of Death on the Job," *Journal of Labor Economics* 22 (October 2004): 925–953.

The matching of A with firm X and B with firm Y is not accidental or random.[14] Since X can "produce" safety more cheaply than Y, it is logical that X will be a low-risk producer who attracts employees, such as A, who value safety highly. Likewise, employer Y generates a lot of cost savings by operating at high-risk levels and can thus afford to pay high wages and still be competitive. Y attracts people such as B, who have a relatively strong preference for money wages and a relatively weak preference for safety. (For a study of how aversion to risk affects job choice, see Example 8.2.)

The Offer Curve   The job-matching process, of course, can be generalized beyond the case of two employees and two employers. To do this, it is helpful to note that in Figures 8.4 and 8.5, the only offers of jobs to workers with a chance of being accepted lie along $XR'Y'$. The curve $XR'Y'$ can be called an *offer curve* because only along $XR'Y'$ will offers that employers can afford to make be potentially acceptable

---

[14]The theoretical implication that workers sort themselves into jobs based on their preferences is directly tested in Alan B. Krueger and David Schkade, "Sorting in the Labor Market: Do Gregarious Workers Flock to Interactive Jobs?" *Journal of Human Resources* 43 (Fall 2008): 859–883.

Figure 8.6

An Offer Curve

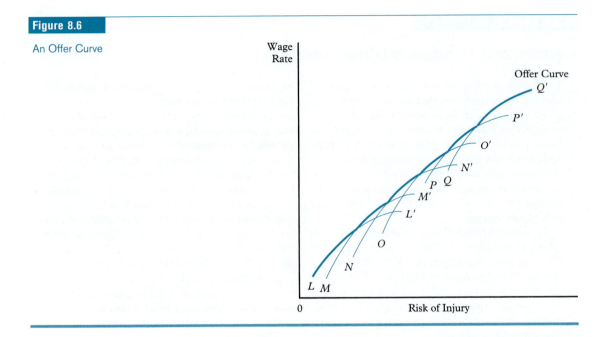

to employees. The concept of an offer curve is useful in generalizing our discussion beyond two firms, because a single offer curve can summarize the potentially acceptable offers any number of firms in a particular labor market can make.

Consider, for example, Figure 8.6, which contains the zero-profit isoprofit curves of firms L through Q. We know from our discussions of Figures 8.4 and 8.5 that employees will accept offers along only the most northwest segments of this set of curves; to do otherwise would be to accept a lower wage at each level of risk. Thus, the potentially acceptable offers will be found along the darkened curve of Figure 8.6, which we shall call the offer curve. The more types of firms there are in a market, the smoother this offer curve will be; however, it will always slope upward because of our twin assumptions that risk is costly to reduce and that employees must be paid higher wages to keep their utility constant if risk is increased. In some of the examples that follow, the offer curve is used to summarize the feasible, potentially acceptable offers employers are making in a labor market, because using an offer curve saves our diagrams from becoming cluttered with the isoprofit curves of many employers.

Major Behavioral Insights   From the perspective of "positive economics," our hedonic model generates two major insights. The first is that wages rise with risk, other things equal. According to this prediction, there will be compensating wage differentials for job characteristics that are viewed as undesirable by workers whom employers must attract (see Example 8.3). Second, workers with strong preferences for safety will tend to take jobs in firms where safety can be

EXAMPLE 8.3

Indentured Servitude and Compensating Differentials

In colonial days, indentured servitude offered a way in which poor immigrants could obtain passage to the New World. Immigrants who did not have the funds to buy ship passage from their countries of origin could sign a contract (an indenture) with a merchant or sea captain in their country of origin, under which the immigrant would be provided passage and in return would promise to work as a servant in the country of destination for a specified number of years. The merchant or sea captain was then responsible for feeding, clothing, and transporting the servants to their destinations. Upon arrival, the merchant or sea captain would sell the indenture to a local farmer or planter, for whom the servant would work during the duration of the indenture.

From the servants' viewpoint, the major characteristics of an indenture were its length and the destination, some of which provided less harsh working conditions or better post-indenture work opportunities. The market for indentures in Britain was apparently competitive, in that there were enough British agents selling these indentures— and the potential servants were well-enough informed about destination characteristics—that a compensating differential arose. For example, indentures of adults to be sold in the West Indies, where sugar-plantation workers toiled in unpleasant conditions and had few post-servitude job opportunities, were about 9 months (or 16 percent) shorter than indentures sold in Maryland!

Source: David Galenson, "Immigration and the Colonial Labor System: An Analysis of the Length of Indenture," *Explorations in Economic History* 14 (November, 1977): 360–377.

generated most cheaply. Workers who are not as averse to accepting risk will seek out and accept the higher-paying, higher-risk jobs offered by firms that find safety costly to "produce."[15] The second insight, then, is that the job-matching process—if it takes place under the conditions of knowledge and choice—is one in which firms and workers offer and accept jobs in a fashion that makes the most of their strengths and preferences.

Normative Analysis: Occupational Safety and Health Regulation

The hedonic analysis of wages in the context of job safety can be normatively applied to government regulation of workplace safety. In particular, we now have the conceptual tools to analyze such questions as the *need* for regulation and, if needed, what the *goals* of the regulation should be.

Are Workers Benefited by the Reduction of Risk?
In 1970, Congress passed the Occupational Safety and Health Act, which directed the U.S. Department of Labor to issue and enforce safety and health standards for all private employers. Safety standards are intended to reduce the risk of traumatic injury, while health

---

[15]There is evidence that workers with fewer concerns about off-the-job risk (smokers, for example) also choose higher-risk jobs; for an analysis of this issue, see W. Kip Viscusi and Joni Hersch, "Cigarette Smokers as Job Risk Takers," *Review of Economics and Statistics* 83 (May 2001): 269–280.

Figure 8.7

The Effects of Government Regulation in a Perfectly Functioning Labor Market

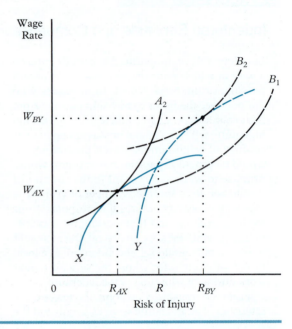

standards address worker exposure to substances thought to cause disease. The stated goal of the act was to ensure the "highest degree of health and safety protection for the employee."

Despite the *ideal* that employees should face the minimum possible risk in the workplace, implementing this ideal as social *policy* is not necessarily in the best interests of workers. Our hedonic model can show that reducing risk in some circumstances will lower the workers' utility levels. Consider Figure 8.7.

Suppose a labor market is functioning about like our textbook models, in that workers are well informed about dangers inherent in any job and are mobile enough to avoid risks they do not wish to take. In these circumstances, wages will be positively related to risk (other things equal), and workers will sort themselves into jobs according to their preferences. This market can be modeled graphically in Figure 8.7, where, for simplicity's sake, we have assumed there are two kinds of workers and two kinds of firms. Person A, who is very averse to the risk of injury, works at wage W_{AX} and risk R_{AX} for employer X. Person B works for employer Y at wage W_{BY} and risk R_{BY}.

Now, suppose the Occupational Safety and Health Administration (OSHA), the Department of Labor agency responsible for implementing the federal safety and health program, promulgates a standard that makes risk levels above R_{AX} illegal. The effects, although unintended and perhaps not immediately obvious, would be detrimental to employees such as B. Reducing risk is costly, and the best wage offer a worker can obtain at risk R_{AX} is W_{AX}. For B, however, wage W_{AX} and risk R_{AX} generate *less utility* than did Y's offer of W_{BY} and R_{BY}.

When the government mandates the reduction of risk in a market where workers are compensated for the risks they take, it penalizes workers such as B, who are not terribly sensitive to risk and appreciate the higher wages associated with higher risk. The critical issue, of course, is whether workers have the knowledge and choice necessary to generate compensating wage differentials. Many people believe that workers are uninformed and unable to comprehend different risk levels or that they are immobile and thus do not choose risky jobs voluntarily. If this belief were true, government regulation *could* make workers better off. Indeed, while the evidence of a positive relationship between wages and risk of fatal injury should challenge the notion that information and mobility are *generally* insufficient to create compensating differentials, there are specific areas in which problems obviously exist. For example, the introduction each year of new workplace chemicals whose health effects on humans may be unknown for two or more decades (owing to the long gestation periods for most cancers and lung diseases) clearly presents substantial informational problems to affected labor market participants.

To say that worker utility *can* be reduced by government regulation does not, then, imply that it *will* be reduced. The outcome depends on how well the unregulated market functions and how careful the government is in setting its standards for risk reduction. The following section will analyze a government program implemented in a market that has *not* generated enough information about risk for employees to make informed job choices.

How Strict Should OSHA Standards Be?

Consider a labor market, like that mentioned previously for asbestos workers, in which ignorance or worker immobility hinders labor market operation. Let us also suppose that the government becomes aware of the health hazard involved and wishes to set a standard regulating worker exposure to this hazard. How stringent should this standard be?

The crux of the problem in standard-setting is that reducing hazards is costly; the greater the reduction, the more it costs. While businesses bear these costs initially, they ultimately respond to them by cutting costs elsewhere and raising prices (to the extent that cutting costs is not possible). Since labor costs constitute the largest cost category for most businesses, it is natural for firms facing large government-mandated hazard reduction costs to hold the line on wage increases or to adopt policies that are the equivalent of reducing wages: speeding up production, being less lenient with absenteeism, reducing employee benefits, and so forth. It is also likely, particularly in view of any price increases (which, of course, tend to reduce product demand), that employment will be cut back. Some of the job loss will be in the form of permanent layoffs that force workers to find other jobs—jobs they presumably could have had before the layoff but chose not to accept. Some of the loss will be in the form of cutting down on hiring new employees who would have regarded the jobs as their best employment option.

Thus, whether in the form of smaller wage increases, more difficult working conditions, or inability to obtain or retain one's first choice in a job, the costs of compliance with health standards will fall on employees. A graphic example can be used to make an educated guess about whether worker utility will be

Figure 8.8

A Worker Accepting Unknown Risk

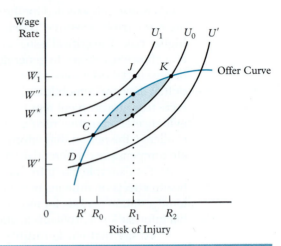

enhanced or not as a result of the increased protection from risk mandated by an OSHA health standard.

Figure 8.8 depicts a worker who believes she has taken a low-risk job when in fact she is exposing herself to a hazard that has a relatively high probability of damaging her health in 20 years. She receives a wage of W_1 and *believes* she is at point J, where the risk level is R_1 and the utility level is U_1. Instead, she is in fact at point K, receiving W_1 for accepting (unknowingly) risk level R_2; she would thus experience lower utility (indifference curve U_0) if she knew the extent of the risk she was taking.

Suppose now that the government discovers that her job is highly hazardous. The government could simply inform the affected workers and let them move to other work. However, if it has little confidence in the ability of workers to understand the information or to find other work, the government could pass a standard that limits employee exposure to this hazard. But what level of protection should this standard offer?

If OSHA forced the risk level down to R', the best wage offer the worker in our example could obtain is W' (at point D on the offer curve). Point D, however, lies on indifference curve U', which represents a lower level of utility than she is in fact getting now (U_0). She would be worse off with the standard. On the other hand, if the government forced risk levels down to a level between R_0 and R_2, she would be better off because she would be able to reach an indifference curve above U_0 (within the shaded area of Figure 8.8). To better understand this last point, we will briefly explain the concepts underlying *benefit-cost analysis*, the technique economists recommend for estimating which government mandates will improve social welfare.

Benefit-Cost Analysis   The purpose of benefit-cost analysis in the labor market is to weigh the likely costs of a government regulation against the value that workers place on its expected benefits (as measured by what workers would be willing to pay for these benefits). In the terms of Figure 8.8, the per-worker *costs* of achieving reduced risk under the OSHA standard are reflected along the offer curve, which indicates the wage cuts that firms would have to make to keep profits constant. For example, if OSHA mandated that risk levels fall from R_2 to R_1, employer costs would require that wage offers fall to W''. The per-worker cost of this standard would therefore be $(W_1 - W'')$.

Conceptually, the *benefits* of the OSHA standard can be measured by the wage reductions that workers would be willing to take if they could get the reduced risk. In Figure 8.8, the worker depicted would be willing to take a wage as low as W^* if risk is cut to R_1, because at that wage and risk level, her utility is the same as it is now (recall she *is actually* at point K on curve U_0). Thus, the *most* she would be willing to pay for this risk reduction is $(W_1 - W^*)$. If wages were forced below W^*, she would be worse off (on a lower indifference curve), and if wages were above W^*, she would be better off than she is now.

In the example graphed by Figure 8.8, a mandated risk level of R_1 would produce benefits that outweigh costs. That is, the amount that workers would be willing to pay $(W_1 - W^*)$ would exceed the costs $(W_1 - W)$. If employers could get the wage down to W^*, they would be more profitable than they are now, and workers would have unchanged utility. If the wage were W'', workers would be better off and employers would have unchanged profits, while a wage between W^* and W'' would make both parties better off. All these possible options would be Pareto-improving (at least one party would be better off and neither would be worse off).

In Figure 8.8, mandated risk levels between R_0 and R_2 would produce benefits greater than costs. These risk levels could be accompanied by wage rates that place the parties in the shaded zone, which illustrates all the Pareto-improving possibilities. Risk levels below R_0 would impose costs on society that would be greater than the benefits.

Moving away from textbook graphs, how can we estimate, in a practical way, the wage reductions workers would be willing to bear in exchange for a reduction in risk? The answer lies in estimating compensating wage differentials in markets that appear to work. Suppose that workers are estimated to accept wage cuts of $700 per year for reductions in the yearly death rate of 1 in 10,000—which is an amount consistent with the most recent analyses of compensating wage differentials.[16] If so, workers apparently believe that, other things equal, they receive about $700 in benefits when the risk of death is reduced by this amount. While estimated values of this willingness to pay are no doubt imprecise,

---

[16]Thomas J. Kniesner, W. Kip Viscusi, Christopher Woock, and James P. Ziliak, "The Value of a Statistical Life: Evidence from Panel Data."

analyzing compensating wage differentials is probably the best way to make an educated guess about what values workers attach to risk reduction.

Even if the estimates of what workers are willing to pay for reduced risk are crude and subject to a degree of error, they can still be used to assess the wisdom of government regulations. If we believe workers are willing to pay in the neighborhood of $700 per year to obtain a 1-in-10,000 reduction in the yearly risk of being killed on the job, then safety or health standards imposed by the government that cost far more than that should be reconsidered. For example, in the 1980s, OSHA adopted three regulations whose per-worker costs for a 1-in-10,000 reduction in fatal risk ranged between $8,000 and $78,000,000![17] Even if we think our willingness-to-pay estimate of $700 is half (or a quarter) of the true willingness to pay for risk reduction, these safety and health standards appear to have mandated a level of risk reduction that reduced workers' utility, not enhanced it.

Hedonic Wage Theory and Employee Benefits

In Table 5.3, we saw that employee benefits are roughly 30 percent of total compensation for the typical worker. Over half of such benefits relate to pensions and medical insurance, both of which have grown in importance over the past 30 years and have attracted the attention of policymakers. In this section, we use hedonic theory to analyze the labor market effects of employee benefits.

Employee Preferences

The distinguishing feature of most employee benefits is that they compensate workers in a form *other* than currently spendable cash. In general, there are two broad categories of such benefits. First are *payments in kind*—that is, compensation in the form of such commodities as employer-provided insurance or paid vacation time.[18] The second general type of employee benefit is *deferred compensation*, which is compensation that is earned now but will be paid in the form of money later on. Employer contributions to employee pension plans make up the largest proportion of these benefits.

---

[17]John Morrall III, "Saving Lives: A Review of the Record," *Journal of Risk and Uncertainty* 27 (December 2003): 221–237.

[18]A woman earning $15,000 per year for 2,000 hours of work can have her hourly wage increased from $7.50 to $8 by either a straightforward increase in current money payments or a reduction in her working hours to 1,875, with no reduction in yearly earnings. If she receives her raise in the form of paid vacation time, she is in fact being paid in the form of a commodity: leisure time.

Payments in Kind   It is a well-established tenet of economic theory that, *other things equal*, people would rather receive $X in cash than a commodity that costs $X. The reason is simple. With $X in cash, the person can choose to buy the particular commodity or choose instead to buy a variety of other things. Cash is thus the form of payment that gives the recipient the most discretion and the most options in maximizing utility.

As might be suspected, however, "other things" are not equal. Specifically, such in-kind payments as employer-provided health insurance offer employees a sizable tax advantage because, for the most part, they are not taxable under current income tax regulations. The absence of a tax on important in-kind payments is a factor that tends to offset their restrictive nature. A worker may prefer $1,000 in cash to $1,000 in some in-kind payment, but if his or her income tax and payroll tax rates total 25 percent, the comparison is really between $750 in cash and $1,000 in the in-kind benefit.

Deferred Compensation   Like payments in kind, deferred compensation schemes are restrictive but enjoy a tax advantage over current cash payments. In the case of pensions, for example, employers currently contribute to a pension fund, but employees do not obtain access to this fund until they retire. However, neither the pension fund *contributions* made on behalf of employees by employers nor the *interest* that compounds when these funds are invested is subject to the personal income tax. Only when the retirement benefits are received does the ex-worker pay taxes.

Indifference Curves   Two opposing forces are therefore at work in shaping workers' preferences for employee benefits. On the one hand, these benefits are accorded special tax treatment, a feature of no small significance when one considers that income and Social Security taxes come to well over 20 percent for most workers. On the other hand, benefits involve a loss of discretionary control over one's total compensation. The result is that if we graph worker preferences regarding cash compensation (the wage rate) and employee benefits, we would come up with indifference curves generally shaped like the one shown in Figure 8.9. When cash earnings are relatively high and employee benefits are small (point *J*), workers are willing to give up a lot in terms of cash earnings to obtain the tax advantages of employee benefits. However, once compensation is heavily weighted toward such benefits (point *K*), further increases in benefits reduce discretionary earnings so much that the tax advantages seem small; at point *K*, then, the indifference curve is flatter. Hence, indifference curves depicting preferences between cash earnings and employee benefits are shaped like those in chapters 6 and 7.[19]

---

[19]As noted in footnote 12, the indifference curves in the prior section were *upward*-sloping because a "bad," not a "good," was on the horizontal axis.

Figure 8.9

An Indifference Curve between
Wages and Employee Benefits

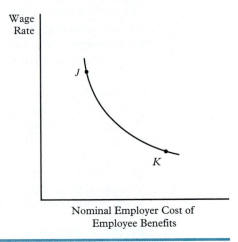

Employer Preferences

Employers also have choices to make in the mix of cash compensation and employee benefits offered to their workers. Their preferences about this mix can be graphically summarized through the use of isoprofit curves.

Isoprofit Curves With a Unitary Slope
The best place to start our analysis of the trade-offs employers are willing to offer workers between cash compensation and employee benefits is to assume they are totally indifferent about whether to spend $X on wages or $X on benefits. Both options cost the same, so why would they prefer one option to the other?

If firms were indifferent about the mix of cash and benefits paid to workers, their only concern would be with the *level* of compensation. If the market requires $X in total compensation to attract workers to a particular job, firms would be willing to pay $X in wages, $X in benefits, or adopt a mix of the two totaling $X in cost. These equally attractive options are summarized along the zero-profit isoprofit curve shown in Figure 8.10. Note that this curve is drawn with a slope of −1, indicating that to keep profits constant, every extra dollar the firm puts into the direct cost of employee benefits must be matched by payroll reductions of a dollar.

Isoprofit Curves with a Flatter Slope
The trade-offs that employers are willing to make between wages and employee benefits are not always one-for-one. Some benefits produce tax savings to employers when compared to paying workers in cash. For example, Social Security taxes that employers must pay are levied on their cash payroll, not on their employee benefits, so compensating workers with in-kind or deferred benefits instead of an equal amount of cash reduces their tax liabilities.

Figure 8.10

An Isoprofit Curve Showing the Wage/Benefit
Offers a Firm Might Be Willing to Make to Its
Employees: A Unitary Trade-Off

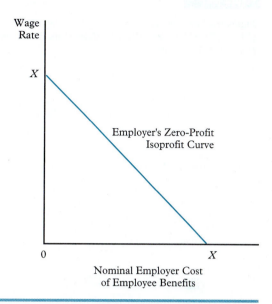

Moreover, offering benefits that are more valued by one group of prospective workers than another can be a clever way to save on the costs of screening applicants. The key here is to offer benefits that will attract applicants with certain characteristics the firm is searching for and will discourage applications from others. For example, deferred compensation will generally be more attractive to workers who are more future-oriented, and offering tuition assistance will be attractive only to those who place a value on continued education. Applicants who are present-oriented or do not expect to continue their schooling will be discouraged from even applying, thus saving employers who offer these two benefits (instead of paying higher wages) the costs of screening applicants they would not hire anyway.

When employee benefits have tax or other advantages to the firm, the isoprofit curve is flattened (see curve A in Figure 8.11). This flatter curve indicates that benefits nominally costing $300, say, might save enough in other ways that only a $280 decrease in wages would be needed to keep profits constant.

Isoprofit Curves With a Steeper Slope   Employee benefits can also increase employer costs in other areas and thus end up being more expensive than paying in cash. The value of life and health insurance provided by employers, for example, is typically unaffected by the hours of work (as long as employees are considered "full time"). Increasing insurance benefits rather than wage rates, then, will produce an *income effect* without a corresponding increase in the price of leisure. Increasing compensation in this way will push workers in the direction of

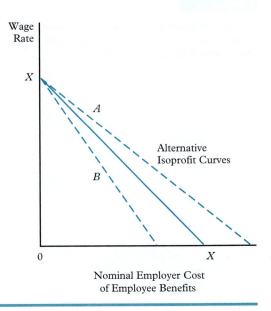

Figure 8.11

Alternative Isoprofit Curves Showing the Wage/Benefit Offers a Firm Might Be Willing to Make to Its Employees: Nonunitary Trade-Offs

reduced work hours, possibly through greater levels of absenteeism.[20] If employee benefits increase costs in other areas, the isoprofit curve will steepen (see curve B in Figure 8.11)—indicating that to keep profits constant, wages would have to drop by more than $300 if benefits nominally costing $300 are offered.

The Joint Determination of Wages and Benefits

The offer curve in a particular labor market can be obtained by connecting the relevant portions of each firm's zero-profit isoprofit curve. When all firms have isoprofit curves with a slope of –1, the offer curve is a straight line with a negative and unitary slope. One such offer curve is illustrated in Figure 8.12, and the only difference between this curve and the zero-profit isoprofit curve in Figure 8.10 is that the latter traced out *hypothetical* offers *one* firm could make, while this one traces out the *actual* offers made by *all* firms in this labor market. Of course, if firms have isoprofit curves whose slopes are different from –1, the offer curve will not look exactly like that depicted in Figure 8.12. Whatever its shape or the absolute value of its slope at any point, it will slope downward.

Employees, then, face a set of wage and employee-benefit offers that imply the necessity for making trade-offs. Those employees (like worker Y in Figure 8.12) who attach relatively great importance to the availability of currently spendable

[20]See Steven G. Allen, "Compensation, Safety, and Absenteeism: Evidence from the Paper Industry," *Industrial and Labor Relations Review* 34 (January 1981): 207–218, and also his "An Empirical Model of Work Attendance," *Review of Economics and Statistics* 63 (February 1981): 77–87.

Figure 8.12

Market Determination of the Mix
of Wages and Benefits

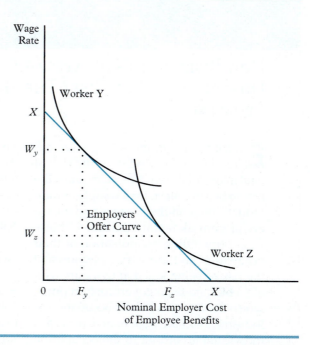

cash will choose to accept offers in which total compensation is largely in the form of wages. Employees who may be less worried about current cash income but more interested in the tax advantages of benefits will accept offers in which employee benefits form a higher proportion of total compensation (see the curve for worker Z in Figure 8.12). Thus, employers will tailor their compensation packages to suit the preferences of the workers they are trying to attract. If their employees tend to be young or poor, for example, their compensation packages may be heavily weighted toward wages and include relatively little in the way of pensions and insurance. Alternatively, if they are trying to attract people in an area where family incomes are high and hence employee benefits offer relatively large tax savings, firms may offer packages in which benefits constitute a large proportion of the total.

Figure 8.12 shows that workers receiving more generous benefits pay for them by receiving lower wages, other things being equal. Furthermore, if employer isoprofit curves have a unitary slope, a benefit that costs the employer $1 to provide will cost workers $1 in wages. In other words, economic theory suggests that workers pay for their own benefits.

Actually observing the trade-off between wages and employee benefits is not easy. Because firms that pay high wages usually also offer very good benefit packages, it often appears to the casual observer that wages and employee benefits are *positively* related. Casual observation in this case is misleading, however, because it does not allow for the influences of *other factors*, such as the demands of the job and the quality of workers involved, that influence total compensation. The other factors are most conveniently controlled for statistically, and the few

EMPIRICAL STUDY

How Risky Are Estimates of Compensating Wage Differentials for Risk? The "Errors in Variables" Problem

Estimating the compensating wage differentials associated with the risk of fatal injury in the workplace requires the researcher to collect, for a sample of individuals, data on their wages and a variety of nonrisk factors that affect these wages (including an indication of their occupation and industry). Measures of the risk of being killed at work are usually obtained from government reports, which tabulate this risk by occupation or industry; risks are then matched to each individual according to the occupation or industry indicated. The objective, of course, is to estimate (using multivariate regression techniques) the effect of risk on wages, after controlling for all other variables that affect wages. How confident can we be in the results obtained?

The two major sources of workplace-death statistics in the United States are the Bureau of Labor Statistics (BLS) and the National Institute for Occupational Safety and Health (NIOSH), but neither source is problem-free. BLS surveys employers about workplace injuries (including fatal injuries), while NIOSH collects its fatality data from an examination of death certificates. It is often difficult, however, to judge how a fatality should be recorded. For example, roughly 25 percent of American fatalities at work occur in highway accidents, and another 12 percent result from homicides.

Thus, it is not surprising that the two sources do not agree exactly on whether a fatality was work-related; in 1995, for example, BLS data placed the number of workplace fatalities at 6,275, while NIOSH counted 5,314.

A second problem in calculating risk faced by individual workers arises from the happy fact that being killed at work is a relatively rare event (roughly, 4 per 100,000 workers each year). Suppose, for example, we wanted to calculate risks for the 500 detailed occupational categories used by the U.S. Census within each of 200 narrowly defined industries. This would require 100,000 occupation-by-industry cells, and with roughly 5,500 deaths each year, most cells would show up as having zero risk. For this reason, fatal injury risk is reported at rather aggregated levels—either by industry *or* by occupation but *not by both together.*

BLS reports risks at the *national* level for industries or occupations, but only for cells that have at least five deaths. Thus, industries or occupations with relatively small numbers of workers or low levels of risk are not represented in their data. NIOSH reports risk measures by *state,* but only for highly aggregated industries and occupations (about 20 of each). Matching risk levels to workers at aggregated levels forces us to assume that all workers in the relevant occupation or industry face the same risk. For example, using NIOSH data for occupations assumes that within each state, police officers and dental assistants face the same risk (both are lumped together in the NIOSH sample as "service workers"). Alternatively, using BLS industry data forces us to assume that bookkeepers and lumberjacks in the logging industry (a narrowly defined industry in the BLS data) face identical risk.

Clearly, then, there are errors in attributing occupational or industry risk levels to individuals. Regression techniques assume that the *dependent* variable (in this case, the wage rate) is measured with error, but it assumes that the *independent* variables, such as risk of death, are not. When there is an "errors in variables" problem with a particular independent variable, the estimated effect of that variable on the dependent variable is biased toward zero—which, of course, reduces our confidence in the results.

One study, for example, compared the different compensating wage differentials estimated by using four alternative risk measures: BLS risk by industry, BLS risk reported by occupation, NIOSH data by industry, and NIOSH data by occupation. In three of the four estimates, compensating differentials for added risk were significantly positive (as expected), although they varied in size—with the largest being over twice the size of the smallest. The fourth estimated wage differential was negative and therefore contrary to the predictions of theory.

Another study compared estimates of compensating wage differentials using injury-risk data at the *industry* level (as done in the studies discussed previously) with estimates using risk data at the *employer* level. While one might expect that data at the employer level would be a more accurate characterization of risk facing an individual worker, it is also possible that—especially with smaller firms—injuries are so relatively rare that firm-level data for any given year are not an accurate depiction of long-run risk facing the employee. Indeed, this study found that the estimated compensating wage differentials for added risk were *smaller* (but still positive) using firm-level data!

Sources: Dan A. Black and Thomas J. Kniesner, "On the Measurement of Job Risk in Hedonic Wage Models," *Journal of Risk and Uncertainty* 27 (December 2003): 205–220; and Rafael Lalive, "Did We Overestimate the Value of Health?" *Journal of Risk and Uncertainty* 27 (October 2003): 171–193.

statistical studies on this subject tend to support the prediction of a negative relationship between wages and benefits.[21] The policy consequences of a negative wage/benefits trade-off are enormously important, because government legislation designed to impose or improve employee benefits might well be paid for by workers in the form of lower future wage increases.

---

[21]Craig A. Olson, "Do Workers Accept Lower Wages in Exchange for Health Benefits?" *Journal of Labor Economics* 20, no. 2, pt. 2 (April 2002): S91–S114; and Scott Adams, "Health Insurance Market Reform and Employee Compensation: The Case of Pure Community Rating in New York," *Journal of Public Economics* 91 (June 2007): 1119–1133. See Edward Montgomery and Kathryn Shaw, "Pensions and Wage Premia," *Economic Inquiry* 35 (July 1997): 510–522, for a paper that references earlier work on compensating wage differentials for pensions.

Review Questions

1. Comment on this quote: "I cannot understand why some university graduates start doing research in the humanities. These persons have above-average skills, however, they voluntarily choose a career characterized by both low wages and job insecurity ... Just imagine the value of forgone lifetime earnings!"

2. Statement 1: "Business executives are greedy profit-maximizers, caring only for themselves." Statement 2: "It has been established that workers doing filthy, dangerous work receive higher wages, other things equal." Can both of these statements be generally true? Why?

3. "There are three methods of allocating labor across a spectrum of jobs that may differ substantially in working conditions. One is the use of force, one is the use of trickery, and one is the use of compensating wage differentials." Comment.

4. Suppose that someone claims that low-wage jobs lack the healthcare and pension benefits enjoyed by higher-wage employees. Assuming this claim to be true, does this fact contradict the theory of compensating wage differentials? Explain.

5. Is the following true, false, or uncertain? "Certain occupations, such as coal mining, are inherently dangerous to workers' health and safety. Therefore, unambiguously, the most appropriate government policy is the establishment and enforcement of rigid safety and health standards." Explain your answer.

6. Consider two labor markets: unlike the "risky" labor market, the "safe" labor market provides safe workplaces. Let Δ denote the compensating wage differential. Demand for workers in the risky sector is $L_D^{risky} = 1000 - \Delta$. The corresponding supply is $L_S^{risky} = \frac{1}{2}\Delta$. For safety reasons, the government restricts the maximum number of workers in the risky sector to 200. How large is the wage differential in equilibrium if (i) many firms compete for workers, (ii) only one firm is operating in the risky sector?

7. In some developing countries, there are two types of jobs in the garment industry. "Regulated" jobs are characterized by both (relatively) high salaries and safety standards. The "informal" jobs are not monitored by any governmental agency, leading to low wages and high health risks. Discuss whether these facts contradict the theory of compensating wage differentials.

8. "The concept of compensating wage premiums for dangerous work does not apply to industries like the coal industry, where the union has forced all wages and other compensation items to be the same. Because all mines must pay the same wage, compensating differentials cannot exist." Is this statement correct? (Assume wages and other forms of pay must be equal for dangerous and nondangerous mines, and consider the implications for individual labor supply behavior.)

9. In 1991, Germany proposed that the European Union countries collectively agree that no one be allowed to work on Sundays (exceptions could be made for Muslims, Jews, and other religious groups celebrating the Sabbath on a day other than Sunday). Use economic theory both *positively* and *normatively* to assess, as completely as you can, the effects of prohibiting work on Sundays.

10. In 2005, a federal court authorized United Airlines (UAL) to terminate its pension plan. The government will take over pension payments to retired UAL employees, but this action means that pension benefits will be less than promised by UAL to both its current retirees and current workers. What *future* labor market effects would you expect to occur from this sudden and unexpected reduction of pension benefits?

Problems

1. A researcher estimates the following wage equation for underwater construction workers: $W_i = 10 + .5D$, where W = the wage in dollars per hour and D = the depth underwater at which workers work, in meters. Based on this information, draw the offer curve and possible indifference curves for workers A and B: A works at a depth of 3 meters, and B works at 5 meters. At their current wages and depths, what is the trade-off (keeping utility constant) between hourly wages and a 1-meter change in depth that each worker is willing to make? Which worker has a greater willingness to pay for reduced depth at 3 meters of depth?

2. (Appendix) A firm uses labor L and capital K to produce output $q = f(L, K) = L \cdot K$. Output is sold for $1 per unit. The firm owns two units of capital and cannot rent additional capital. It has to choose between two options: (i) provide a risky workplace and use both units of capital in production, or (ii) use one unit of capital to make the workplace safe. Express the firm's optimal decision as a function of the prevailing compensating wage differential.

3. (Appendix). Thomas's utility function is $U = \sqrt{Y}$, where Y = annual income. He has two job offers. One is in an industry in which there are no layoffs and the annual pay is $40,000. In the other industry, there is uncertainty about layoffs. Half the years are bad years, and layoffs push Thomas's annual pay down to $22,500. The other years are good years. How much must Thomas earn in the good years in this job to compensate him for the high risk of layoffs?

4. Assume that jobs are identical along all dimensions except risk of injury. The following figures depict indifference curves for two workers A and B:

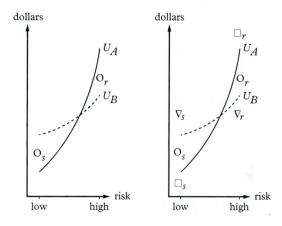

   a. Consider the left figure first. Suppose that workers are free to choose between the two "risk-wage bundles" O_s and O_r. How much labor is supplied to the risky sector? Highlight the compensating wage differential in the figure.

   b. Now consider the second figure: How much labor is supplied to the risky sector if workers can choose between (i) ∇_s and ∇_r, (ii) $\square_s$ and $\square_r$? Explain.

5. Sheldon is indifferent between a combination of 2% risk of injury and a wage rate of $15 per hour and a combination of 3% risk of injury and a wage rate of $18 per hour. Shelby is indifferent between a combination of 2% risk of injury and a wage rate of $16 per hour and a combination of 3% risk of injury and a wage rate of $18 per hour.

   a. Who has a stronger aversion toward risk?

b. Consider a market "offer curve" that is concave. Where along this curve is Sheldon's utility likely to be maximized? Compare this to where Shelby is likely to maximize utility. Explain.

6. The demand for labor in Occupation A is $L_D = 20 - W$, where L_D = number of workers demanded for that occupation, in thousands. The supply of labor for Occupation A is $L_A = -1.25 + .5W$. For Occupation B, the demand for labor is similar, but the supply of labor is $L_B = -.5 + .6W$, which is indicative of a more pleasant environment associated with that occupation in comparison with Occupation A. What is the compensating wage differential between the two occupations?

The zero-profit isoprofit curve for Company ABC is $W = 4 + .5R$, where W = the wage rate that the firm will offer at particular risk levels, R, keeping profits at zero. The zero-profit isoprofit curve for Company XY is $W = 3 + .75R$.

a. Draw the zero-profit isoprofit curves for each firm. What assumption about marginal returns to safety expenditures underlies a linear isoprofit curve?

b. At what risk level will the firms offer the same wage?

c. At low-risk levels, which firm will be preferred by workers? At high-risk levels, which firm will be preferred by workers? Explain.

Selected Readings

Duncan, Greg, and Bertil Holmlund. "Was Adam Smith Right After All? Another Test of the Theory of Compensating Wage Differentials." *Journal of Labor Economics* 1 (October 1983): 366–379.

Fishback, Price V. "Operations of 'Unfettered' Labor Markets: Exit and Voice in American Labor Markets at the Turn of the Century." *Journal of Economic Literature* 36 (June 1998): 722–765.

Rosen, Sherwin. "Hedonic Prices and Implicit Markets." *Journal of Political Economy* 82 (January–February 1974): 34–55.

———. "The Theory of Equalizing Differences." In *Handbook of Labor Economics*, eds. Orley Ashenfelter and Richard Layard, 641–692. New York: North-Holland, 1986.

Smith, Robert S. "Compensating Wage Differentials and Public Policy: A Review." *Industrial and Labor Relations Review* 32 (April 1979): 339–352.

Viscusi, W. Kip, and Joseph E. Aldy. "The Value of a Statistical Life: A Critical Review of Market Estimates Throughout the World." *Journal of Risk and Uncertainty* 27 (August 2003): 5–76.

Viscusi, W. Kip. "The Value of Risks to Life and Health." *Journal of Economic Literature* 31 (December 1993): 1912–1946.

Compensating Wage Differentials and Layoffs

A s mentioned in the chapter text, one of the circumstances identified by Adam Smith under which compensating wage differentials would arise relates to the "constancy or inconstancy of employment." While there is evidence, as we shall see, to support this prediction, the relationship of wages to layoff probabilities is by no means as simple as Smith thought. In particular, there are three issues relevant to the analysis, all of which we shall discuss briefly.[1]

Unconstrained Choice of Work Hours

Suppose that in the spirit of chapters 6 and 7, employees are free to choose their hours of work in a labor market that offers an infinite choice of work hours. Given the wage a particular worker can command and his or her nonwage income, the utility-maximizing choice of working hours would be selected. For the person depicted in Figure 8A.1, the utility-maximizing choice of work hours is H^*, given his or her offered wage rate (W^*) and level of nonwage income (assumed here to be zero).

If H^* is thought of in terms of yearly work hours, it is easy to understand that a worker may *prefer* a job involving layoff! Suppose H^* is 1,500 hours per year, or essentially three-quarters of the typical "full-time" job of 2,000 hours. One could work 6 hours a day, 5 days a week, for 50 weeks a year, or one could work 8 hours a day, 5 days a week, for 9 months and agree to be laid off for 3 months. Which alternative holds more appeal to any given individual depends on his or her preferences with respect to large blocks of leisure or household time, but it is clear that many people value such large blocks. Teachers, for example, typically work full-time during a nine-month school year, and then some of them vacation during the summer. Many other jobs, from the construction trades to work in canning

---

[1]The analysis in this appendix draws heavily on John M. Abowd and Orley Ashenfelter, "Anticipated Unemployment, Temporary Layoffs, and Compensating Wage Differentials," in *Studies in Labor Markets*, ed. Sherwin Rosen (Chicago: University of Chicago Press, 1981): 141–170.

Choice of Hours of Work

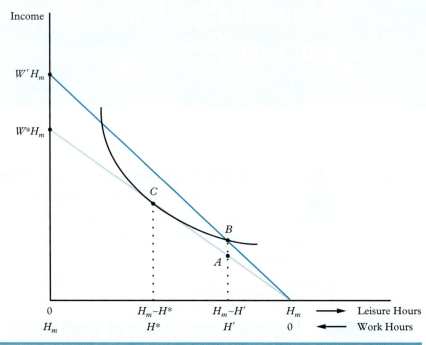

factories, involve predictable seasonal layoffs, and workers in these jobs may have chosen them because they value the leisure or household production time accompanying the layoffs.

Putting the point differently, the theory of compensating wage differentials suggests they will be positive only when a job characteristic is regarded as bad by the marginal worker. Predictable blocks of leisure or household time accompanying seasonal layoffs may not be regarded as bad by the marginal worker. In fact, workers in some markets may see layoffs as a mechanism through which they can best achieve their desired yearly hours of work.

Constrained Hours of Work

Suppose that the worker depicted in Figure 8A.1 is offered a choice between a job offering wage W^* and hours H^* and one offering fewer hours than desired because of a predictable layoff each year that reduces hours of work to H'. Clearly, if the wage for the latter job remains at W^*, the worker's utility will be reduced by taking the job offering H' hours because he or she will be on an indifference curve passing through point A. The job offering W^* and H^* is thus clearly preferred.

However, suppose that H is offered at a wage of W, where W' exceeds W^* by enough so that point B can be reached. Point B, where the wage is W and hours of work are H', is on the *same* indifference curve as point C (the utility-maximizing point when W^* is the offered wage). Point B is not a point of utility maximization at a wage offer of W, but if the worker is offered an unconstrained choice of hours at wage rate W^*, or a wage of W where working hours are *constrained* to equal H, he or she would be indifferent between the two job offers.[2]

In the previous example, $(W' - W^*)$ is the compensating wage differential that would have to arise for the worker to consider a job where hours of work were constrained to lie below those otherwise desired. Many people view a layoff as an event that prevents workers from working the number of hours they would otherwise desire to work. If this is the case, and if these layoffs are predictable and known with certainty, such as layoffs accompanying model changeovers in the auto industry, then compensating wage differentials associated with the predictable, certain layoff rate would arise in a well-functioning labor market (that is, one where workers are informed and mobile).[3]

The Effects of Uncertain Layoffs

In the previous section, we assumed that layoffs were predictable and known with certainty. In most cases, however, they are not. While we might expect layoff rates to be higher in some industries than in others, they are in fact often subject to considerable random fluctuation *within* industries over the years. This *uncertainty* of layoffs is itself another aspect of affected jobs that is usually thought to be a negative feature and for which a compensating wage differential might arise.

Suppose that utility is measurable and is a function only of income, so that it can be graphed against income (Y), as in Figure 8A.2.[4] Suppose also that the person depicted is offered a job for which a wage of W' and yearly hours of H' are known *with certainty*. The utility associated with these H' hours, $U(H')$, is a function of his or her income at H' hours of work: $W'H'$ (again assuming no nonwage income).

Now, suppose there is another job paying W' in which the *average* hours of work per year are H', but half of the time H_h is worked, and half of the time H_l is worked. Although we have assumed that $0.5H_h + 0.5H_l = H'$, so that over the years the person averages H' hours of work, it turns out that with the concave utility function we have drawn, the person's average utility is *below* $U(H')$. To understand this, we must look closely at Figure 8A.2.

---

[2]Point B is not a point of tangency; that is, at a wage of W', the worker depicted in Figure 8A.1 would prefer to work more than H' hours if he or she were free to choose work hours. We have assumed in the discussion that the choice is constrained so that hours cannot exceed H'.

[3]A similar argument can be used to predict that workers will receive compensating wage differentials if they are forced to work longer hours than they would otherwise prefer. For the argument and evidence in support of it, see Ronald G. Ehrenberg and Paul L. Schumann, "Compensating Wage Differentials for Mandatory Overtime," *Economic Inquiry* 22 (December 1984).

[4]Although economists typically work with *ordinal* utility functions, which specify the relative ranking of alternatives without assigning each alternative a numerical value of utility, the analysis of choice under uncertainty requires the use of *cardinal* utility functions (ones in which each alternative is assigned a specific numerical value of utility).

Figure 8A.2

The Choice between H'
Hours with Certainty and
H' Hours on Average

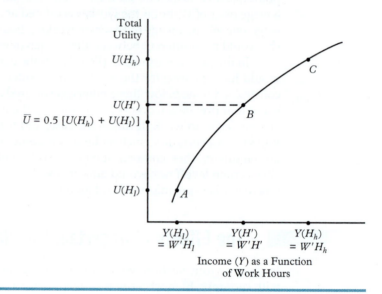

Income (Y) as a Function
of Work Hours

When the person's working hours are H_h, which is half the time, he or she earns $W'H_h$, and this income yields a utility of $U(H_h)$. Thus, half the time, the worker will be at point C enjoying utility level $U(H_h)$. The other half of the time, however, the person will be working H_l hours, earning $W'H_l$ in income, and be at point A enjoying utility of $U(H_l)$. His or her average utility is thus $\overline{U}$, which is $\overline{U} = 0.5\ U(H_h) + 0.5\ U(H_l)$. Note that $\overline{U}$, which is midway between $U(H_h)$ and $U(H_l)$ in our example, lies *below* $U(H')$—the utility derived from a job paying W' and employing the person for H' hours *with certainty* every year.

Why is $\overline{U} < U(H')$ even though H' hours are worked on *average* in both cases? The answer lies in the concavity of the utility function, which economists define as exhibiting *risk aversion*. Moving from $Y(H')$ to $Y(H_h)$ covers the same absolute distance on the horizontal axis as moving from $Y(H')$ to $Y(H_l)$, but the changes in *utility* are not the same in magnitude. In particular, moving from $Y(H')$ to $Y(H_h)$ (points B to C) in the good years adds *less* to utility than moving from $Y(H')$ to $Y(H_l)$ (points B to A) in the bad years takes away. Put differently, the concavity of the total utility curve in Figure 8A.2 implies diminishing marginal utility of income. Thus, in the unlucky years, when hours are below H, there is a relatively big drop in utility (as compared to the utility associated with H hours), while in the lucky years, the added income increases utility by a relatively small amount.

The upshot of this discussion is that when workers are averse to risk—that is, when their utility functions are concave so that they in essence place a larger value on negative changes from a given level of income than they do on positive changes of equal dollar magnitude—they would prefer a job paying W' and offering H' hours with certainty to one paying W' and offering H' hours only on average. Thus, to compensate them for the loss in utility associated with *risk aversion*, they would require a wage above W' for the job offering H' hours only on average.

The Observed Wage/Layoff Relationship

The previous discussion centered on worker preferences regarding layoffs. For compensating wage differentials to arise, of course, employers must be willing to pay them. That is, employers must profit from being able to lay off workers, and if we are to observe firms pursuing a high-wage/high-layoff strategy, their gains from layoff must exceed their costs of higher wages.

The previous discussion also neglected unemployment insurance (UI) payments to laid-off workers. This topic is discussed in some detail in chapter 14. Here, we need note only that if UI payments fully compensate laid-off workers for their lost utility, compensating wage differentials will not arise. Compensating wage differentials will arise only if UI payments do not fully compensate laid-off workers.

One study that looked very carefully at the relationship between wages and layoffs suggests that the compensating wage differential for an average probability of layoff is around 4 percent of wages, with over 80 percent of this differential related to the aversion to risk associated with the variability (uncertainty) in layoff rates facing workers over time. Workers in the high-layoff industries of automobile manufacturing and construction received estimated compensating wage differentials ranging over the early 1970s from 6 percent to 14 percent and 6 percent to 11 percent, respectively.[5] A study of farm workers around 1990 found that those who risked unemployment by working seasonally were paid from 9 percent to 12 percent more per hour than those who held permanent jobs in farming.[6]

---

[5]These estimates are from the Abowd and Ashenfelter article in footnote 1 of this appendix. Similar evidence can be found in Elisabeth Magnani, "Product Market Volatility and the Adjustment of Earnings to Risk," *Industrial Relations* 41 (April 2002): 304–328. For those interested in how UI benefits affect wages, see David A. Anderson, "Compensating Wage Differentials and the Optimal Provision of Unemployment Insurance," *Southern Economic Journal* 60 (January 1994): 644–656.

[6]Enrico Moretti, "Do Wages Compensate for Risk of Unemployment? Parametric and Semiparametric Evidence from Seasonal Jobs," *Journal of Risk and Uncertainty* 20 (January 2000): 45–66.

CHAPTER 9

Investments in Human Capital: Education and Training

Many labor supply choices require a substantial initial *investment* on the part of the worker. Recall that investments, by definition, entail an initial cost that one hopes to recoup over some period of time. Thus, for many labor supply decisions, *current* wages and working conditions are not the only deciding factors. Modeling these decisions requires developing a framework that incorporates investment behavior and a *lifetime* perspective.

Workers undertake three major kinds of labor market investments: education and training, migration, and search for new jobs. All three investments involve an initial cost, and all three are made in the hope and expectation that the investment will pay off well into the future. To emphasize the essential similarity of these investments to other kinds of investments, economists refer to them as investments in *human capital*, a term that conceptualizes workers as embodying a set of skills that can be "rented out" to employers. The knowledge and skills a worker has—which come from education and training, including the learning that experience yields—generate a certain *stock* of productive capital. The *value* of this productive capital is derived from how much these skills can earn in the labor market. Job search and migration are activities that increase the value of one's human capital by increasing the price (wage) received for a given stock of skills.

EXAMPLE 9.1

War and Human Capital

We can illustrate the relative importance of physical and human capital by noting some interesting facts about severely war-damaged cities. The atomic attack on Hiroshima destroyed 70 percent of of the city's buildings and killed about 30 percent of the population. Survivors fled the city in the aftermath of the bombing, but within three months, two-thirds of the city's surviving population had returned. Because the air-burst bomb left the city's underground utility networks intact, power was restored to surviving areas in one day. Through railway service began again in two days, and telephone service was restarted in a week. Plants responsible for three-quarters of the city's industrial production (many were located on the outskirts of the city and were undamaged) could have begun normal operations within 30 days.

In Hamburg, Germany, a city of around 1.5 million in the summer of 1943, Allied bombing raids over a 10-day period in July and August destroyed about half of the buildings in the city and killed about 3 percent of the city's population. Although there was considerable damage to the water supply system, electricity and gas service were adequate within a few days after the last attack, and within four days, the telegraph system was again operating. The central bank was reopened and business had begun to function normally after one week, and postal service was resumed within 12 days of the attack. The Strategic Bombing Survey reported that within 5 months, Hamburg had recovered up to 80 percent of its former productivity.

The speed and success of recovery from these disasters has prompted one economist to offer the following two observations:

(1) the fraction of the community's real wealth represented by visible material capital is small relative to the fraction represented by the accumulated knowledge and talents of the population, and (2) there are enormous reserves of energy and effort in the population not drawn upon in ordinary times but which can be utilized under special circumstances such as those prevailing in the aftermath of disaster.

Data from: Jack Hirshleifer, *Economic Behavior in Adversity* (Chicago: University of Chicago Press, 1987): 12–14, 78–79.

Society's total wealth is a combination of human and nonhuman capital. Human capital includes accumulated investments in such activities as education, job training, and migration, whereas nonhuman capital includes society's stock of natural resources, buildings, and machinery. Total per capita wealth in the United States, for example, was estimated to be roughly $480,000 in 2008, 75 percent of which was in the form of human capital.[1] (Example 9.1 illustrates the overall importance of human capital in another way.)

Investment in the knowledge and skills of workers takes place in three stages. First, in early childhood, the acquisition of human capital is largely determined by the decisions of others. Parental resources and guidance, plus our cultural environment and early schooling experiences, help to influence basic language and mathematical skills, attitudes toward learning, and general health

---

[1]United Nations (UNU-IHDP and UNEP), *Inclusive Wealth Report 2012: Measuring Progress Toward Sustainability* (Cambridge: Cambridge University Press, 2012), Data Annex.

and life expectancy (which themselves affect the ability to work). Second, teenagers and young adults go through a stage in which they acquire knowledge and skills as full-time students in a high school, college, or vocational training program. Finally, after entering the labor market, workers' additions to their human capital generally take place on a part-time basis, through on-the-job training, night school, or participation in relatively short, formal training programs. In this chapter, we focus on the latter two stages.

One of the challenges of any behavioral theory is to explain why people faced with what appears to be the same environment make different choices. We will see in this chapter that individuals' decisions about investing in human capital are affected by the ease and speed with which they learn, their aspirations and expectations about the future, and their access to financial resources.

Human Capital Investments: The Basic Model

Like any other investment, an investment in human capital entails costs that are borne in the near term with the expectation that benefits will accrue in the future. Generally speaking, we can divide the *costs* of adding to human capital into three categories:

1. *Out-of-pocket* or *direct* expenses, including tuition costs and expenditures on books and other supplies.
2. *Forgone earnings* that arise because during the investment period, it is usually impossible to work, at least not full-time.
3. *Psychic losses* that occur because learning is often difficult and tedious.

In the case of educational and training investments by workers, the expected *returns* are in the form of higher future earnings, increased job satisfaction over their lifetime, and a greater appreciation of nonmarket activities and interests. Even if we could quantify all the future benefits, summing them over the relevant years is not a straightforward procedure because of the *delay* involved in receiving these investment returns.

The Concept of Present Value

When an investment decision is made, the investor commits to a *current* outlay of expenses in return for a stream of expected *future* benefits. Investment returns are clearly subject to an element of risk (because no one can predict the future with certainty), but they are also *delayed* in the sense that they typically flow in over what may be a very long period. The investor needs to compare the value of the current investment outlays with the current value of expected returns but in so doing must take into account effects of the delay in returns. We explain how this is done.

Suppose a woman is offered $100 now or $100 in a year. Would she be equally attracted to these two alternatives? No, because if she received the money now, she could either spend (and enjoy) it now or she could invest the $100 and earn interest over the next year. If the interest rate were 5 percent, say, $100 now could grow into $105 in a year's time. Thus, $100 received *now* is worth more than $100 to be received in a year.

With an interest rate of 5 percent, it would take an offer of $105 to be received in a year to match the value of getting $100 now. Because $100 now could be grown into $105 at the end of a year, these two offers have equivalent value. Another way of putting this equivalence is to say that with a 5 percent interest rate, the future value in a year (B_1) of $100 now is $105. This calculation can be shown algebraically by recognizing that after a year, the woman could have her principal (B_0) of $100 plus interest ($r = .05$) on that principal:

$$B_1 = B_0 + B_0(r) = B_0(1 + r) = 100(1.05) = 105 \qquad (9.1)$$

We can also say that the present value (B_0) of $105 to be received *in a year* is (at a 5 percent interest rate) $100. Because $B_1 = B_0(1 + r)$, it is also true that

$$B_0 = \frac{B_1}{(1 + r)} = \frac{105}{1.05} = 100 \qquad (9.2)$$

Thus, receiving $105 in one year is equivalent to receiving $100 in the present and investing it at 5 percent for one year. The procedure for taking a future value and transforming it into its present-value equivalent is called *discounting*. If the future return is only a year away, we discount (divide) it by the factor $(1 + r)$ to calculate its present-value equivalent.

What if the return is two years away? If we were to take a present sum of B_0 and invest it, after one year, it would equal $B_1 = B_0(1 + r)$. At the end of that first year, we could take our new asset (B_1) and invest it for another year at interest rate r. At the end of two years, then, we would have the sum B_2:

$$B_2 = B_1 + B_1(r) = B_1(1 + r) \qquad (9.3)$$

Substituting equation (9.1) into equation (9.3) yields the following:

$$B_2 = B_0(1 + r) + B_0(1 + r)(r) = B_0(1 + r)(1 + r) = B_0(1 + r)^2 \qquad (9.4)$$

(Equation 9.4 illustrates the law of compound interest because in the second period, interest is earned on both the original principal and the interest earned in the first period.)

Now, if $B_2 = B_0(1 + r)^2$, it is also true that

$$B_0 = \frac{B_2}{(1 + r)^2} \qquad (9.5)$$

To find the present value of a benefit to be received in two years, then, requires that we discount the future benefit by $(1 + r)^2$. If the benefit were to be received in three years, we can use the logic underlying equations (9.3) and (9.4) to calculate that the discount factor would be $(1 + r)^3$. Benefits in four years would be discounted to their present values by dividing by $(1 + r)^4$, and so forth. Clearly, the discount factors rise exponentially, reflecting that current funds can earn compound interest if left invested at interest rate r.

If a human capital investment yields returns of B_1 in the first year, B_2 in the second, and so forth for T years, the sum of these benefits has a present value that is calculated as follows:

$$\text{Present Value} = \frac{B_1}{1 + r} + \frac{B_2}{(1 + r)^2} + \frac{B_3}{(1 + r)^3} + \cdots + \frac{B_T}{(1 + r)^T} \tag{9.6}$$

where the interest rate (or discount rate) is r. As long as r is positive, benefits in the future will be progressively discounted. For example, if $r = 0.06$, benefits payable in 30 years would receive a weight that is only 17 percent of the weight placed on benefits payable immediately ($1.06^{30} = 5.74$; $1/5.74 = 0.17$). The smaller r is, the greater the weight placed on future benefits; for example, if $r = 0.02$, a benefit payable in 30 years would receive a weight that is 55 percent of the weight given to an immediate benefit.

Modeling the Human Capital Investment Decision

Our model of human capital investment assumes that people are utility maximizers and take a lifetime perspective when making choices about education and training. They are therefore assumed to compare the near-term investment costs (C) with the present value of expected future benefits when making a decision, say, about additional schooling. Investment in additional schooling is attractive if the present value of future benefits exceeds costs:

$$\frac{B_1}{1 + r} + \frac{B_2}{(1 + r)^2} + \cdots + \frac{B_T}{(1 + r)^T} > C \tag{9.7}$$

Utility maximization, of course, requires that people continue to make additional human capital investments as long as condition (9.7) is met and that they stop only when the benefits of additional investment are equal to or less than the additional costs.

There are two ways we can measure whether the criterion in (9.7) is met. Using the *present-value method*, we can specify a value for the discount rate, r, and then determine how the present value of benefits compares to costs. Alternatively, we can adopt the *internal rate of return method*, which asks, "How large could the discount rate be and still render the investment profitable?" Clearly, if the benefits are so large that even a very high discount rate would render investment profitable, then the project is worthwhile. In practice, we calculate this internal rate of return by setting the present value of benefits equal to costs, solving for r, and then comparing r to the rate of return on other investments.

Some basic implications of the model embedded in expression (9.7) are illustrated graphically in Figure 9.1, which depicts human capital decisions in terms of marginal costs and marginal benefits (focus for now on the black lines in the figure). The marginal costs (MC) of each additional unit of human capital (the tuition, supplies, forgone earnings, and psychic costs of an additional year of schooling, say) are assumed to be constant. The present value of the marginal benefits (MB) is shown as declining, because each added year of schooling means fewer years over which benefits can be collected. The utility-maximizing amount of human capital (HC^*) for any individual is shown as that amount for which $MC = MB$.

Those who find learning to be especially arduous will implicitly attach a higher marginal psychic cost to acquiring human capital. As shown by the blue line, MC', in Figure 9.1a, individuals with higher MC will acquire lower levels of human capital (compare HC' with HC^*). Similarly, those who expect smaller future benefits from additional human capital investments (the blue line, MB', in Figure 9.1b) will acquire less human capital.

This straightforward theory yields some interesting insights about the behavior and earnings of workers. Many of these insights can be discovered by analyzing the decision confronting young adults about whether to invest full-time in college after leaving high school.

Figure 9.1

The Optimum Acquisition of Human Capital

(a)   **(b)**

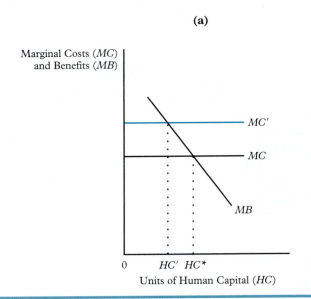
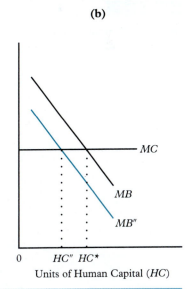

The Demand for a College Education

The demand for a college education, as measured by the percentage of graduating high school seniors who enroll in college, is surprisingly variable. For males, enrollment rates went from 55.2 percent in 1970, down to 46.7 percent in 1980, back to 58 percent in 1990, and reaching almost 63 percent by 2010. The comparable enrollment rates for women started lower, at 48.5 percent in 1970, rose slowly during the 1970s, and then have risen quickly thereafter, reaching 74 percent by 2010. Why have enrollment rates followed these patterns?

Weighing the Costs and Benefits of College

Clearly, people attend college when they believe they will be better off by so doing. For some, at least part of the benefits may be short term—they like the courses or the lifestyle of a student—and to this extent, college is at least partially a *consumption* good. The consumption benefits of college, however, are unlikely to change much over the course of a decade, so changes in college attendance rates over relatively short periods of time probably reflect changes in *MC* or benefits associated with the *investment* aspects of college attendance.

A person considering college has, in some broad sense, a choice between two streams of earnings over his or her lifetime. Stream A begins immediately but does not rise very high; it is the earnings stream of a high school graduate. Stream B (the college graduate) has a negative income for the first four years (owing to college tuition costs), followed by a period when the salary may be less than what the high school graduate makes, but then it takes off and rises above stream A. Both streams are illustrated in Figure 9.2. (Why these streams are

Figure 9.2

Alternative Earnings Streams

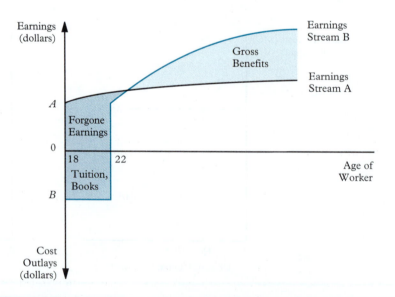

differentially *curved* will be discussed later in this chapter.) The streams shown in the figure are stylized so that we can emphasize some basic points. Actual earnings streams will be shown in Figures 9.3 and 9.4.

Obviously, the earnings of the college graduate would have to rise above those of the high school graduate to induce someone to invest in a college education (unless, of course, the consumption-related returns were large). The gross benefits—the difference in earnings between the two streams—must total much more than the costs because such returns are in the future and are therefore discounted. For example, suppose it costs $25,000 per year to obtain a four-year college education and the real interest rate (the nominal rate less the rate of inflation) is 2 percent. The after-tax returns—if they were the same each year—must be $3,652 in constant-dollar terms (that is, after taking away the effects of inflation) each year for 40 years in order to justify the investment on purely monetary grounds. These returns must be $3,652 because $100,000 invested at a 2 percent interest rate can provide a payment (of interest and principal) totaling $3,652 a year for 40 years.[2]

Predictions of the Theory

In deciding whether to attend college, no doubt few students make the very precise calculations suggested in expression (9.7). Nevertheless, if they make less formal estimates that take into account the same factors, we can make four predictions concerning the demand for college education:

1. Present-oriented people are less likely to go to college than forward-looking people (other things equal).
2. Most college students will be young.
3. College attendance will decrease if the costs of college rise (other things equal).
4. College attendance will increase if the gap between the earnings of college graduates and high school graduates widens (again, other things equal).

Present-Orientedness   Although we all discount the future somewhat with respect to the present, psychologists use the term *present-oriented* to describe people who do not weight future events or outcomes very heavily. In terms of expressions (9.6) and (9.7), a present-oriented person is one who uses a very high discount rate (*r*).

Suppose we were to calculate investment returns using the *present-value method*. If *r* is large, the present value of benefits associated with college will be lower than if *r* is smaller. Thus, a present-oriented person would impute smaller

---

[2]This calculation is made using the annuity formula,

$$Y = X \frac{1 - [1/(1 + r)^n]}{r},$$

where Y = the total investment ($100,000 in our example), X = the yearly payment ($3,652), r = the rate of interest (0.02), and n = the number of years (40). In this example, we treat the costs of a college education as being incurred all in one year rather than being spread out over four, a simplification that does not alter the magnitude of required returns much at all.

benefits to college attendance than one who is less present-oriented, and those who are present-oriented would be less likely to attend college. Using the *internal rate of return method* for evaluating the soundness of a college education, we would arrive at the same result. If a college education earns an 8 percent rate of return, but the individuals in question are so present-oriented that they would insist on a 25 percent rate of return before investing, they would likewise decide not to attend.

The prediction that present-oriented people are less likely to attend college than forward-looking ones is difficult to substantiate because the rates of discount that people use in making investment decisions can rarely be quantified.[3] However, the model does suggest that people who have a high propensity to invest in education will also engage in other forward-looking behavior. Certain medical statistics tend to support this prediction.

In the United States, there is a strong statistical correlation between education and health status.[4] People with more years of schooling have lower mortality rates, fewer symptoms of disease (such as high blood pressure, high cholesterol levels, abnormal X-rays), and a greater tendency to report themselves to be in good health. This effect of education on health is independent of income, which appears to have no effect of its own on health status except at the lowest poverty levels. Is this correlation between education and health a result of better use of medical resources by the well-educated? It appears not. Better-educated people undergoing surgery choose the same doctors, enter the hospital at the same stage of disease, and have the same length of stay as less-educated people of equal income.

What *may* cause this correlation is a more forward-looking attitude among those who have obtained more education. People with lower discount rates will be more likely to attend college, and they will *also* be more likely to adopt forward-looking habits of health. They may choose healthier diets, be more aware of health risks, and make more use of preventive medicine. This explanation for the correlation between education and health is not the only plausible one, but it receives some direct support from American data on cigarette smoking.[5] From 1966 to 1987, the proportion of male college graduates who smoked fell

---

[3]A study that inferred personal discount rates from the choices of separation-pay options made by military retirees found that those officers with graduate degrees had lower discount rates than officers without graduate degrees and that college-educated officers had lower discount rates than enlisted personnel (who generally do not have college educations). See John T. Warner and Saul Pleeter, "The Personal Discount Rate: Evidence from Military Downsizing Programs," *American Economic Review* 91 (March 2001): 33–53.

[4]The analysis of the correlation between education and health status is taken from Victor Fuchs, "The Economics of Health in a Post-Industrial Society," *Public Interest* (Summer 1979): 3–20. For a more recent study, see David Cutler and Adriana Lleras-Muney, "Education and Health: Evaluating Theories and Evidence," National Bureau of Economic Research Working Paper no. 12352 (Cambridge, Mass.: June 2006).

[5]It could be, for example, that healthy people, with longer life spans, are more likely to invest in human capital because they expect to experience a longer payback period. Alternatively, we could argue that the higher incomes of college graduates later in life mean they have more to lose from illness than do noncollege graduates. Data on smoking are from U.S. Department of Health and Human Services, Public Health Service, *Smoking Tobacco and Health*, DHHS publication no. (CDC)87-8397, October 1989, 5. For a study of smoking and wages, see Irina B. Grafova and Frank P. Stafford, "The Wage Effects of Personal Smoking History," *Industrial and Labor Relations Review* 62 (April 2009): 381–393.

by 50 percent, while it was unchanged among male high school dropouts. It is unlikely that the less-educated group was uninformed of smoking dangers; it is more likely that they were less willing to give up a present source of pleasure for a distant benefit. Thus, we have at least some evidence that people who invest in education also engage in *other* forward-looking behavior. (See Example 9.2 for evidence that the way in which languages *grammatically* treat future events affects the investment behaviors of their native speakers.)

Age   Given similar *yearly* benefits of going to college, young people have a larger present value of *total* benefits than older workers simply because they have a longer remaining work life ahead of them. In terms of expression (9.7), T is greater for younger people than for older ones. We would therefore expect younger people to have a greater propensity than older people to obtain a college education or engage in other forms of training activity. This prediction is parallel to the predictions in chapter 5 about which workers employers will decide to invest in when they make decisions about hiring or specific training.

Costs   A third prediction of our model is that human capital investments are more likely when costs are lower. The major monetary costs of college attendance are forgone earnings and the direct costs of tuition, books, and fees. (Food and lodging are not always opportunity costs of going to college because some of these costs would have to be incurred in any event.) Thus, if forgone earnings or tuition costs fall, other things equal, we would expect a rise in college enrollments.

EXAMPLE 9.2

Can Language Affect Investment Behavior?

Languages differ in how future events are framed. In talking about today's weather, English speakers would say, "It is cold today," but in discussing tomorrow's weather, the language requires them to say, "It will be cold tomorrow." In German, however, the equivalent statements would be "It is cold today" and "It is cold tomorrow." Might the fact that German does not require a strong separation of the present from the future cause its speakers to feel the future is less distant, thereby causing them to be more forward-looking in making decisions? Put differently, do those who speak languages that do not grammatically distinguish the future from the present have lower discount rates than those raised to speak languages that require a strong distinction?

As stated in the text, it is difficult to quantify people's discount rates. However, if those speaking languages that do not grammatically separate the present and future have lower discount rates, then we should observe that they are more likely to make investments of one kind or another than those who speak languages, like English, that require a strong separation of future and present. Interestingly, one study did find that in cultures where the present and future are not grammatically separated, people were more likely to engage in such future-oriented behaviors as saving for retirement and investing in their health (exercising, quitting smoking, and dieting)!

Source: M. Keith Chen, "The Effect of Language on Economic Behavior: Evidence from Savings Rates, Health Behaviors, and Retirement Assets," *American Economic Review* 103 (April 2013): 690–731.

Potential college students, however, vary in their access to the funds required to pay for tuition, books, and fees. Some obtain all or part of these funds from the generosity of others (their families or college scholarships), while others must bear the costs of taking out loans or generating their own funds through working. Put differently, there are wide *differences in how costly it is to obtain the funds needed for college*, and those who find it very costly or impossible to obtain such funds are said by economists to be "credit-constrained." Subsidized, low-interest government loans to college students and publicly funded universities are two major ways in which society has tried to deal with credit constraints facing potential college students. Most studies find that relaxing these constraints (making borrowing easier or cheaper) increases college attendance and that the public policies undertaken in the United States to relax the constraints have been largely successful.[6]

The costs of college attendance are an additional reason older people are less likely to attend than younger ones. As workers age, their greater experience and maturity result in higher wages and therefore greater opportunity costs of college attendance. Interestingly, as suggested by Example 9.3, college attendance by military veterans (who are older than the typical college student) has been responsive to the educational subsidies for which they are eligible.[7]

In addition to the financial costs of a college investment, there are the *psychic* costs we mentioned earlier. Our theory predicts that students who have greater aptitudes for the kind of learning college demands are more likely to attend than those for whom learning is more difficult or unpleasant. In fact, there is mounting evidence that the acquisition of human capital is powerfully influenced by family background—that is, by the parental investments and family environments that affect both the *cognitive* and the *behavioral* skills (such as attentiveness, motivation, coping strategies) needed to succeed in high school and beyond. There is evidence, for example, that children from single-parent or low-income households enter kindergarten with fewer of the cognitive *and* social-emotional skills required for success in school; this fact has led to a growing interest among economists in whether, and how, *early childhood* programs improve these skills and thus permanently lower the psychic cost of schooling for the students they target.[8]

---

[6]For a study that refers to prior literature, see Katharine G. Abraham and Melissa A. Clark, "Financial Aid and Students' College Decisions: Evidence from the District of Columbia's Tuition Assistance Grant Program," *Journal of Human Resources* 41 (Summer 2006): 578–610. Articles directly measuring credit constraints include Stephen V. Cameron and Christopher Taber, "Estimation of Educational Borrowing Constraints Using Returns to Schooling," *Journal of Political Economy* 112 (February 2004): 132–183; and Pedro Carneiro and James J. Heckman, "The Evidence on Credit Constraints in Post-Secondary Schooling," *Economic Journal* 112 (October 2002): 705–734. The latter article analyzes reasons why family income and college attendance rates are positively correlated; it concludes that financial credit constraints are much less important in explaining this relationship than are the attitudes and skills children acquire from their parents.

[7]Also see Joshua D. Angrist, "The Effect of Veterans' Benefits on Education and Earnings," *Industrial and Labor Relations Review* 46 (July 1993): 637–652.

[8]For review articles that contain citations to the extensive literature on this topic see Greg J. Duncan and Katherine Magnuson, "Investing in Preschool Programs," *Journal of Economic Perspectives* 27 (Spring 2013): 109–132; and Richard J. Murnane, "U.S. High School Graduation Rates: Patterns and Explanations," *Journal of Economic Literature* 51 (June 2013): 370–422.

EXAMPLE 9.3

Did the G.I. Bill Increase Educational Attainment for Returning World War II Vets?

Veterans returning from service in World War II were eligible to receive unprecedented federal support through the G.I. Bill if they chose to attend college. Benefits under the G.I. Bill substantially subsidized the costs of a college education, covering the tuition charged by almost all private and public universities and providing monthly stipends ranging from roughly 50 percent to 70 percent of the median income in the United States at the time. After the war, many veterans enrolled in college—and total college enrollments jumped by more than 50 percent from their pre-war levels. Over 2.2 million veterans attended college under the bill, accounting for about 70 percent of the male student body at the peak of the bill's usage. Because of these effects, Senator Ralph Yarborough called the World War II G.I. Bill "one of the most beneficial, far-reaching programs ever instituted in American life."

Did the G.I. Bill really have a big effect or did it merely subsidize returning veterans who would have gone to college anyway? A recent article helps to answer this question by comparing the college attendance of male veterans

with otherwise similar individuals. It finds that among high school graduates, World War II veterans completed an average of about 0.3 more years of college than did nonveterans and that they had a 6 percentage-point greater college completion rate. Similar estimates were obtained when comparing those eligible for war service and G.I. Bill subsidies with those born too late to serve in the war.

The conclusions of this study are that the responses of veterans to the G.I. Bill's subsidies were quite similar to the contemporary responses of students to changes in tuition costs. In both cases, a 10 percent reduction in the cost to students of attending college resulted in a 4 or 5 percent increase in college attendance and completion.

Data from: John Bound and Sarah Turner, "Going to War and Going to College: Did the G.I. Bill Increase Educational Attainment for Returning Veterans?" *Journal of Labor Economics* 20 (October 2002): 784–815; and Keith W. Olson, *The G.I. Bill, the Veterans, and the Colleges* (Lexington: University Press of Kentucky, 1974).

Economists have begun to recognize that, beyond the effects of parenting, "peer effects" can also alter the psychic costs of attending school. If status with one's peers is enhanced by studying hard and getting good grades, the costs of studying are reduced—while the opposite occurs if status is reduced by academic achievement.[9]

In sum, there are several factors that cause the costs of college attendance to vary across individuals, and these factors help to explain why individuals facing the same general environment make different decisions about investing in human capital. We now turn to another set of forces that affect human capital decisions: the expected benefits associated with a human capital investment.

---

[9]Gordon C. Williams and David J. Zimmerman, "Peer Effects in Higher Education," in *College Choices: The Economics of Where to Go, When to Go, and How to Pay for It*, ed. Caroline M. Hoxby (Chicago: University of Chicago Press, 2004): 395–421; and David Austen-Smith and Roland G. Fryer Jr., "An Economic Analysis of 'Acting White,'" *Quarterly Journal of Economics* 120 (May 2005): 551–583.

Earnings Differentials   The fourth prediction of human capital theory is that the demand for education is positively related to the increases in *expected* lifetime earnings that a college education allows; however, the expected benefits for any individual are rather uncertain.[10] As a first approximation, however, it is reasonable to conjecture that the *average* returns received by recent college graduates have an important influence on students' decisions.

Dramatic changes in the average monetary returns to a college education over the past three decades are at least partially, if not largely, responsible for the changes in college enrollment rates noted earlier. It can be seen from the first and third columns of Table 9.1, for example, that the decline in male enrollment rates during the 1970s was correlated with a decline in the college/high school earnings differential, while the higher enrollment rates after 1980 were associated with larger earnings differentials.

The second and fourth columns of Table 9.1 document changes in enrollment rates and earnings differentials for women. Unlike enrollment rates for men, those for women rose throughout the four decades; however, it is notable that they rose most after 1980, when the college/high school earnings differential rose most sharply. Why did enrollment rates among women increase in the 1970s when the earnings differential fell? It is quite plausible that despite the reduced earnings differential, the expected returns to education for women actually rose because of increases in their intended labor force attachment and hours of work outside the home (both of which increase the period over which the earnings differential will be received).[11]

It is important to recognize that human capital investments, like other investments, entail uncertainty. While it is helpful for individuals to know the *average* earnings differentials between college and high school graduates, they must also assess their *own* probabilities of success in specific fields requiring a college degree. If, for example, the average returns to college are rising, but there is a growing spread between the earnings of the most successful college graduates and the least successful ones, individuals who believe they are likely to be in the

---

[10]For an historical analysis of earnings differentials and educational decisions, see Claudia Goldin and Lawrence F. Katz, *The Race between Education and Technology* (Cambridge, Mass.: Belknap Press, 2008). For a study that incorporates uncertainty into the projection of future earnings, see Joseph G. Altonji, "The Demand for and Return to Education When Education Outcomes Are Uncertain," *Journal of Labor Economics* 10 (January 1993): 48–83. For studies on the accuracy of students' knowledge about the salaries, see Julian R. Betts, "What Do Students Know about Wages? Evidence from a Survey of Undergraduates," and Jeff Dominitz and Charles F. Manski, "Eliciting Student Expectations of the Returns to Schooling," both in *Journal of Human Resources* 31 (Winter 1996): 1–56. For an article on locational variations in the returns to schooling, see Dan Black, Natalia Kolesnikova, and Lowell Taylor, "Earnings Functions When Wages and Prices Vary by Location," *Journal of Labor Economics* 27 (January 2009): 21–48.

[11]For evidence that women with "traditional" views of their economic roles receive lower rates of return on, and invest less in, human capital, see Francis Vella, "Gender Roles and Human Capital Investment: The Relationship between Traditional Attitudes and Female Labour Market Performance," *Economica* 61 (May 1994): 191–211. For an interesting analysis of historical trends in female college attendance, see Claudia Goldin, Lawrence Katz, and Ilyana Kuziemko, "The Homecoming of American College Women: The Reversal of the College Gender Gap," *Journal of Economic Perspectives* 20 (Fall 2006): 133–156.

Table 9.1

Changes in College Enrollments and the College/High School Earnings Differential, by Gender, 1970–2010

Year	College Enrollment Rates of New High School Graduates		Ratios of Mean Earnings of College to High School Graduates, Ages 25–34, Prior Year[a]	
	Male (%)	Female (%)	Male	Female
1970	55.2	48.5	1.38	1.42
1980	46.7	51.8	1.19	1.29
1990	58.0	62.2	1.48	1.59
2000	59.9	66.2	1.60	1.74
2010	62.8	74.0	1.59	1.66

[a]For year-round, full-time workers. Data for the first two years are for personal income, not earnings; however, in the years for which both income and earnings are available, the ratios are essentially equal.

Sources: U.S. Department of Education, *Digest of Education Statistics 2011* (June 2012), Table 209; U.S. Bureau of the Census, *Money Income of Families and Persons in the United States*, Current Population Reports P-60, no. 66 (Table 41), no. 129 (Table 53); U.S. Bureau of the Census, "Money Income in the United States: 1999," Detailed Person Income (P60 Package), Table PINC-04, at http://www.census .gov/hhes/www/cpstables/macro/032000/perinc/toc.htm; and U.S. Bureau of the Census, "Income, Poverty and Health Insurance in the United States: 2009," Person Income, Table PINC-04, at http:// www.census.gov/hhes/www/cpstables/032010/perinc/new04_000.htm.

latter group may be deterred from making an investment in college. Recent studies have pointed to the importance of friends, ethnic affiliation, and neighborhoods in the human capital decisions of individuals, even after controlling for the effects of parental income or education. While these peer effects can affect educational decisions by affecting costs, as discussed earlier, it is also likely that the presence of role models helps to reduce the uncertainty that inevitably surrounds estimates of future success in specific areas.[12]

Market Responses to Changes in College Attendance

Like other market prices, the returns to college attendance are determined by the forces of both employer demand and employee supply. If more high school students decide to attend college when presented with higher returns to such an investment, market forces are put into play that will tend to lower these returns in the future. Increased numbers of college graduates put downward pressure

---

[12]For papers on the issues discussed in this paragraph, see Kerwin Kofi Charles and Ming-Ching Luoh, "Gender Differences in Completed Schooling," *Review of Economics and Statistics* 85 (August 2003): 559–577; Ira N. Gang and Klaus F. Zimmermann, "Is Child Like Parent? Educational Attainment and Ethnic Origin," *Journal of Human Resources* 35 (Summer 2000): 550–569; and Eric Maurin and Sandra McNally, "Vive la Révolution! Long-Term Educational Returns of 1968 to the Angry Students," *Journal of Labor Economics* (January 2008): 1–33.

on the wages observed in labor markets for these graduates, other things equal, while a fall in the number of high school graduates will tend to raise wages in markets for less-educated workers.

Thus, adding to uncertainties about expected payoffs to an investment in college is the fact that current returns may be an unreliable estimate of future returns. A high return now might motivate an individual to opt for college, but it will also cause many *others* to do likewise. An influx of college graduates in four years could put downward pressure on returns at that time, which reminds us that all investments—even human capital ones—involve outlays now and uncertain returns in the future. (For an analysis of how the labor market might respond when workers behave as if the returns observed currently will persist into the future, see Appendix 9A.)

Education, Earnings, and Post-Schooling Investments in Human Capital

The preceding section used human capital theory to analyze the decision to undertake a formal educational program (college) on a full-time basis. We now turn to an analysis of workers' decisions to acquire training at work. The presence of on-the-job training is difficult for the economist to directly observe; much of it is informal and not publicly recorded. We can, however, use human capital theory and certain patterns in workers' lifetime earnings to draw inferences about their demand for this type of training.

Figures 9.3 and 9.4 graph the 2011 earnings of men and women of various ages with different levels of education. These figures reveal four notable characteristics:

1. Average earnings of full-time workers rise with the level of education.
2. The most rapid increase in earnings occurs early, thus giving a concave shape to the age/earnings profiles of both men and women.
3. Age/earnings profiles tend to fan out, so that education-related earnings differences later in workers' lives are greater than those early on.
4. The age/earnings profiles of men tend to be more concave and to fan out more than those for women.

Can human capital theory help explain the above empirical regularities?

Average Earnings and Educational Level

Our *investment* model of educational choice implies that earnings rise with the level of education, for if they did not, the incentives for students to invest in more education would disappear. It is thus not too surprising to see in Figures 9.3 and 9.4 that the average earnings of more-educated workers exceed those of less-educated workers.

Remember, however, that *earnings* are influenced by both wage rates and hours of work. Data on *wage rates* are probably most relevant when we look at the

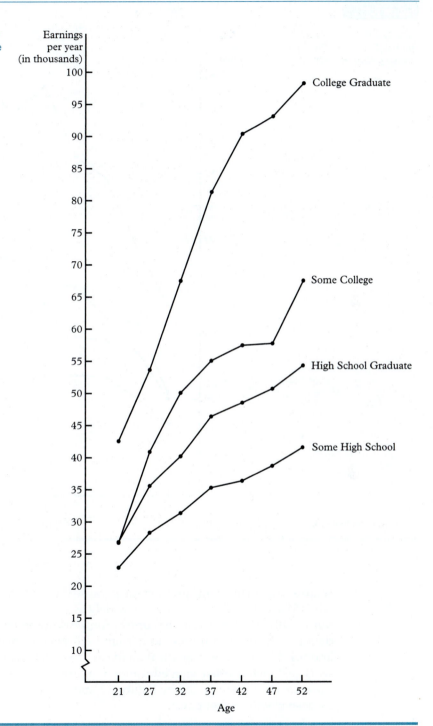

Figure 9.3

Money Earnings (Mean) for Full-Time, Year-Round Male Workers, 2011

Earnings per year (in thousands)

College Graduate

Some College

High School Graduate

Some High School

Age

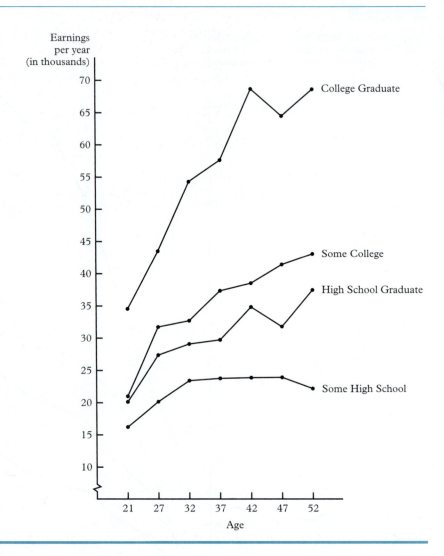

Figure 9.4

Money Earnings (Mean) for Full-Time, Year-Round Female Workers, 2011

Source: See footnote 13.

returns to an educational investment, because they indicate pay per unit of time at work. Wage data, however, are less widely available than earnings data. A crude, but readily available, way to control for working hours when using earnings data is to focus on full-time, year-round workers—which we do in Figures 9.3 and 9.4. More careful statistical analyses, however, which control for hours of work and factors other than education that can increase wage rates, come to the same conclusion suggested by Figure 9.3 and 9.4: namely, that more education is associated with higher pay.

On-the-Job Training and the Concavity of Age/Earnings Profiles

The age/earnings profiles in Figures 9.3 and 9.4 typically rise steeply early on, and then tend to flatten.[13] While in chapters 10 and 11 we will encounter other potential explanations for why earnings rise in this way with age, human capital theory explains the concavity of these profiles in terms of *on-the-job training*.[14]

Training Declines with Age   Training on the job can occur through learning by doing (skills improving with practice), through formal training programs at or away from the workplace, or by informally working under the tutelage of a more experienced worker. All forms entail reduced productivity among trainees during the learning process, and both formal and informal training also involve a commitment of time by those who serve as trainers or mentors. Training costs are either shared by workers and the employer, as with specific training, or are borne mostly by the employee (in the case of general training).

From the perspective of workers, training depresses wages during the learning period but allows them to rise with enhanced productivity afterward. Thus, workers who opt for jobs that require a training investment are willing to accept lower wages in the short run to get higher pay later on. As with other human capital investments, returns are generally larger when the post-investment period is longer, so we would expect workers' investments in on-the-job training to be greatest at younger ages and to fall gradually as they grow older.

Figure 9.5 graphically depicts the life cycle implications of human capital theory as it applies to on-the-job training. The individual depicted has completed full-time schooling and is able to earn E_s at age A_0. Without further training, if the knowledge and skills the worker possesses do not depreciate over time, earnings would remain at E_s over the life cycle. If the worker chooses to invest in on-the-job training, his or her future earnings potential can be enhanced, as shown by the (dashed) curve E_p in the figure. Investment in on-the-job training, however, has the near-term consequence that actual earnings are below potential; thus, in terms

---

[13]Data in these figures are from the U.S. Bureau of the Census Web site: http://www.census.gov/hhes/ www/cpstables/032012/perinc/pinc04_000.htm. These data match average earnings with age and education in a given year and do not follow individuals through time. For a paper using longitudinal data on *individuals*, see Richard W. Johnson and David Neumark, "Wage Declines and Older Men," *Review of Economics and Statistics* 78 (November 1996): 740–748; for a paper that follows *cohorts* of individuals through time, see David Card and Thomas Lemieux, "Can Falling Supply Explain the Rising Return to College for Younger Men? A Cohort-Based Approach," *Quarterly Journal of Economics* 116 (May 2001): 705–746.

[14]For discussions of the relative importance of the human capital explanation for rising age/earnings profiles, see Ann P. Bartel, "Training, Wage Growth, and Job Performance: Evidence from a Company Database," *Journal of Labor Economics* 13 (July 1995): 401–425; Charles Brown, "Empirical Evidence on Private Training," in *Research in Labor Economics*, vol. 11, eds. Lauri J. Bassi and David L. Crawford (Greenwich, Conn.: JAI Press, 1990): 97–114; and Jacob Mincer, "The Production of Human Capital and the Life Cycle of Earnings: Variations on a Theme," *Journal of Labor Economics* 15, no. 1, pt. 2 (January 1997): S26–S47.

Figure 9.5

Investment in On-the-Job Training over the Life Cycle

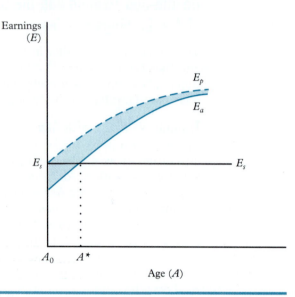

of Figure 9.5, actual earnings (E_a) lie below E_p as long as the worker is investing. In fact, the gap between E_p and E_a equals the worker's investment costs.

Figure 9.5 is drawn to reflect the theoretical implication, noted earlier, that human capital investments decline with age. With each succeeding year, actual earnings become closer to potential earnings; furthermore, because workers become less willing to invest in human capital as they age, the yearly *increases* in potential earnings become smaller and smaller. Thus, curve E_p takes on a concave shape, quickly rising above E_s but flattening later in the life cycle. Curve E_a (which is what we observe in Figures 9.3 and 9.4) takes on its concave shape for the same reasons.[15]

---

[15]For those who invest in on-the-job training, actual earnings start below E_s, approach it near age A^*, and continue to rise above it afterward. Age A^* is called the *overtaking age*, and it is the age at which workers with the same level of schooling have equivalent earnings regardless of whether they have invested in on-the-job training. The concept of an overtaking age has an interesting empirical implication.

We can observe educational levels workers possess, but we cannot observe workers' E_p or the time they have spent in on-the-job training. Thus, when we use statistical methods to analyze earnings differences across individuals, the correlation between earnings and education will be strongest at A^*, where $E_a = E_s$. Why? The correlation between schooling and earnings is weakened both before and after A^* by the presence of on-the-job training, which we cannot measure and for which we cannot therefore statistically control. Interestingly, we find that educational and earnings levels correlate most strongly at about 10 years after labor market entry. This finding offers support for the human capital explanation of age/earnings profiles based on job training. For the seminal work on estimating the effects of earnings on wages, see Jacob Mincer, *Schooling, Experience, and Earnings* (New York: Columbia University Press for National Bureau of Economic Research, 1974).

The Fanning Out of Age/Earnings Profiles

Earnings differences across workers with different educational backgrounds tend to become more pronounced as they age. This phenomenon is also consistent with what human capital theory would predict.

Investments in human capital tend to be more likely when the expected earnings differentials are greater, when the initial investment costs are lower, and when the investor has either a longer time to recoup the returns or a lower discount rate. The same can be said of people who have the ability to learn more quickly. The ability to learn rapidly shortens the training period, and fast learners probably also experience lower psychic costs (lower levels of frustration) during training.

Thus, people who have the ability to learn quickly are those most likely to seek out—and be presented by employers with—training opportunities. But who are these fast learners? They are most likely the people who, because of their abilities, were best able to reap benefits from formal schooling! Thus, human capital theory leads us to expect that workers who invested more in schooling will also invest more in post-schooling job training.[16]

The tendency of the better-educated workers to invest more in job training explains why their age/earnings profiles start low, rise quickly, and keep rising after the profiles of their less-educated counterparts have leveled off. Their earnings rise more quickly because they are investing more heavily in job training, and they rise for a longer time for the same reason. In other words, people with the ability to learn quickly select the ultimately high-paying jobs where much learning is required and thus put their abilities to greatest advantage.

Women and the Acquisition of Human Capital

A comparison of Figures 9.3 and 9.4 discloses immediately that the earnings of women who work full-time year-round are lower than those of men of equivalent age and education, and that women's earnings within each educational group rise less steeply with age. The purpose of this section is to analyze these differences in the context of human capital theory (a more complete analysis of male/female wage differentials is presented in chapter 12).

A major difference in the incentives of men and women to make human capital investments has historically been in the length of work life over which the costs of a human capital investment can be recouped. Chapters 6 and 7 clearly showed how rapidly working for pay has increased among women in recent decades, and this fact obviously should have made human capital investments more lucrative for women. Nevertheless, Table 9.2 shows it is still the case that, on

---

[16]For studies showing that on-the-job training is positively correlated with both educational level and ability, see Joseph G. Altonji and James R. Spletzer, "Worker Characteristics, Job Characteristics, and the Receipt of On-the-Job Training," *Industrial and Labor Relations Review* 45 (October 1991): 58–79; and Joseph Hight, "Younger Worker Participation in Post-School Education and Training," *Monthly Labor Review* 121 (June 1998): 14–21.

Table 9.2

Labor Force Participation Rates, Part-Time Employment Status, and Hours of Work in the United States, by Gender (2012)

	Women	Men
Labor force participation rate, age 16 and over	57.7%	70.2%
Percent of employed who worked full-time	68.0%	81.0%
Average weekly hours of full-time workers, by occupation:		
Management, business and financial	42.7	44.7
Professional specialty	40.9	42.3
Office/administrative support	39.9	40.3
Sales	41.0	43.2
Installation and repair	40.7	42.8

Sources: U.S. Bureau of Labor Statistics Web site: Labor Force Statistics from the Current Population survey: http://www.bls.gov/cps/cpsaat02.htm, Table 2; U.S. Bureau of Labor Statistics, *Labor Force Statistics from the Current Population Survey,* Table 23, at http://www.bls.gov/cps/cpsaat23.htm.

average, women are less likely than men to be in the labor force and, if employed, are less likely to work full-time. Furthermore, women employed full-time average fewer hours of work per week than men in each of the occupations shown.

To the extent that there is a shorter expected work life for women than for men, it is caused primarily by the role women have historically played in child-rearing and household production. This traditional role, while undergoing significant change, has caused many women to drop out of the labor market for a period of time in their childbearing years. Thus, female workers often have not had the continuity of experience that their male counterparts accumulate. If this historical experience causes younger women who are making important human capital decisions to expect a discontinuity in their own labor force participation, they might understandably avoid occupations or fields of study in which their skills depreciate during the period out of the labor market.[17] Moreover, historical experience could cause employers to avoid hiring women for jobs requiring much on-the-job training—a practice that itself will reduce the returns women

---

[17]For a discussion of the wage losses facing women who interrupt their labor force attachment at childbirth, see Shelly Lundberg and Elaina Rose, "Parenthood and the Earnings of Married Men and Women," *Labour Economics* 7 (November 2000): 689–710; and Jane Waldfogel, "Understanding the 'Family Gap' in Pay for Women with Children," *Journal of Economic Perspectives* 12 (Winter 1998): 137–156. Losses were also suffered by men who involuntarily withdrew from their careers by being drafted into military service during the Vietnam War; see Joshua D. Angrist, Stacy H. Chen, and Jae Song, "Long-term Consequences of Vietnam-Era Conscription: New Estimates Using Social Security Data," *American Economic Review: Papers and Proceedings* 101 (May 2011)): 334–338. A study comparing the wage effects of interruptions for both sexes is Christy Spivey, "Time Off at What Price? The Effects of Career Interruptions on Earnings," *Industrial and Labor Relations Review* 59 (October 2005): 119–140.

can expect from a human capital investment. Human capital theory, however, *also* predicts that recent changes in the labor force participation of women, especially married women of childbearing age, are causing dramatic changes in the acquisition of both job training and formal schooling by women. We turn now to a discussion of recent changes in these two areas.

Women and Job Training

Women appear to receive less on-the-job training than men, although the gap is probably narrowing. One survey of employer-provided training found that during a six-month period in 1995, women reported receiving 41.5 hours of both formal and informal training, while men received 47.6 hours; differences were mainly in the area of informal training.[18] To the extent that on-the-job training causes age/earnings profiles to be concave, an explanation for the flatter age/earnings profiles of women may be rooted in their lower levels of such training.

This human capital explanation for the flatter age/earnings profiles among women does not directly address whether the lower levels of job training emanate from the employer or the employee side of the market, but both possibilities are theoretically plausible. If employers expect women workers to have shorter work lives, they are less likely to provide training to them. Alternatively, if women themselves expect shorter work lives, they will be less inclined to seek out jobs requiring high levels of training. Finally, if women expect employers to bar them from occupations requiring a lot of training or experience, incentives to enter these occupations will be diminished.[19]

While human capital theory predicts that the traditional role of women in child-rearing will lead to reduced incentives for training investments, it also suggests that as this role changes, the incentives for women to acquire training will change. We should thus expect to observe a growing concavity in women's age/earnings profiles over the past decades, and Figure 9.6 indicates that this expectation is generally supported.

The darker lines in Figure 9.6 are the 2011 profiles for college and high school graduates that appeared in Figure 9.4. The lighter lines indicate the comparable profiles for 1977 (adjusted to 2011 dollars using the Consumer Price Index [CPI]). A visual comparison reveals that the earnings profiles for both high school and college graduates have become steeper for women in their twenties and thirties, especially among the college educated. This faster earnings growth among women at the early stages of their careers suggests that they may be receiving more on-the-job training than they did two decades ago.

Women and Formal Schooling

As Table 9.1 suggested, there have been dramatic changes in the level of formal education received by women in recent years. Their fields of study have also changed markedly. These changes undoubtedly

---

[18]H. Frazis, M. Gittleman, M. Horrigan, and M. Joyce, "Results from the 1995 Survey of Employer-Provided Training," *Monthly Labor Review* 121 (June 1998): 3–13.

[19]For an article on women's pay expectations and resulting outcomes, see Peter F. Orazem, James D. Werbel, and James C. McElroy, "Market Expectations, Job Search, and Gender Differences in Starting Pay," *Journal of Labor Research* 24 (Spring 2003): 307–321.

Figure 9.6

The Increased Concavity of Women's Age/Earnings Profiles

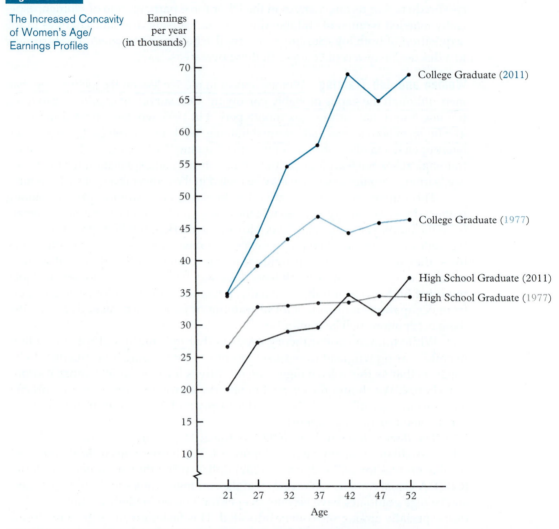

reflect the increased returns to human capital investments arising from women's increased attachment to the labor force and longer expected work lives. Table 9.3 outlines some of the magnitudes of these changes.

Women, who traditionally were less likely than men to graduate from college, now represent roughly 60% of both bachelor's and master's graduates. There have also been dramatic shifts in the fields in which women major, most notably in the areas of business (graduate and undergraduate), law, and medicine—fields in which women have gone from under 10 percent of all majors to 45 percent or more. While still underrepresented in computer science and engineering, women

Table 9.3

Percentages of Women among College and University Graduates, by Degree and Field of Study, 1971 and 2010

Percentage of Women among:	Bachelor's Degree		Master's Degree	
	1971	2010	1971	2010
Total	43.4%	57.2%	40.1%	60.3%
Business majors	9.1	49.0	3.9	45.6
Computer science majors	13.6	18.1	10.3	27.5
Education majors	74.5	79.5	56.2	77.3
Engineering majors	0.8	18.3	1.1	22.4
English majors	66.7	68.0	61.0	67.3
Health professionals	77.1	85.1	55.9	81.4
First professional degree[a]			6.3	49.7

[a]Degrees in this category are largely doctor's degrees in law, medicine, and dentistry.

Sources: U.S. National Center for Education Statistics, *Digest of Education Statistics 1993* (1993), Tables 235, 269, 271–273, 275, 278; *Digest of Education Statistics 20011* (2012), Tables 290, 311.

have posted gains in these areas as well.[20] What the data in Table 9.3 suggest is that women's expected labor force attachment has grown so fast that investing in bachelor's and master's degrees has become more attractive over the last four decades.

It is evident from Table 9.3 that, in the United States at least, women are now *more* likely than men to invest in a college degree. The growth in the percentage of women investing in a college degree can be clearly related to their lengthening attachment to the labor force (analyzed in chapter 6). Yet this attachment, on average, is still lower for women than men, and so attachment by itself cannot explain why women are so much more likely than men to attend college.

One potential explanation for why women invest more in schooling may have to do with gender differences in the earnings premium associated with college; it can also be seen from Table 9.1 that the earnings ratios of college to high school graduates are higher for women than men. Another potential explanation, however, is that the *psychic costs* of schooling are lower for women than men. It has been argued, for example, that the secondary-school performance of girls has exceeded that of boys for the last century, partly because they exhibit fewer behavioral problems in elementary and secondary schools, and partly because they spend more time than boys doing homework.[21]

---

[20]A study that measures gender changes in undergraduate majors differently, however, concludes that aside from business majors, changes since the 1970s have not been dramatic. See Sarah E. Turner and William G. Bowen, "Choice of Major: The Changing (Unchanging) Gender Gap," *Industrial and Labor Relations Review* 52 (January 1999): 289–313.

[21]Claudia Goldin, Lawrence F. Katz, and Ilyana Kuziemko, "The Homecoming of American College Women: The Reversal of the College Gender Gap," *Journal of Economic Perspectives* 20 (Fall 2006): 133–156.

Is Education a Good Investment?

The question of whether more education would be a good investment is one that concerns both individuals and government policymakers. Individuals ask, "Will I increase my monetary and psychic income enough to justify the costs of additional education?" Governments must decide if the expected social benefits of enhanced productivity outweigh the opportunity costs of investing more social resources in the educational sector. We pointed out earlier that these questions can be answered using either the *present-value* method (an illustration of which is in Example 9.4) or the *internal rate of return* method. The latter is primarily used in the sections that follow.

Is Education a Good Investment for Individuals?

Individuals about to make an investment in a college education are typically committing themselves to total monetary costs of at least $25,000 per year. Is there evidence that this investment pays off for the typical student? Several studies have tried to answer this question by calculating the internal rates of return to educational investments. While the methods and data used vary, these studies normally estimate benefits by calculating earnings differentials at each age from age/earnings profiles such as those in Figures 9.3 and 9.4. *Earnings* are usually used to measure benefits because higher wages and more stable jobs are both payoffs to more education. (While the estimated rates of return discussed later relate only to the monetary returns to education, we should note that many recent studies have found substantial non-monetary benefits—such as better health and more life satisfaction—to investments in more schooling.[22])

Estimating the monetary returns to an educational investment involves comparing the earnings of similar people who have different levels of education. Estimates using conventional data sets statistically analyze the earnings increases associated with increases in schooling, after controlling for the effects on earnings of *other* factors that can be measured, such as age, race, gender, health status, union status, and residential location. These studies, of which there have been hundreds, typically estimate rates of return that fall into the range of 5–12 percent.[23]

Ability Bias   One problem with these conventional estimates is that they may overstate the gain an individual could obtain by investing in education because they do not distinguish between the contribution that *ability* makes to higher earnings and

---

[22]Philip Oreopoulos and Kjell G. Salvanes, "Priceless: The Nonpecuniary Benefits of Schooling," *Journal of Economic Perspectives* 25 (Winter 2011): 159–184.

[23]See David Card, "Estimating the Return to Schooling: Progress on Some Persistent Econometric Problems," *Econometrica* 69 (September 2001): 1127–1160; and David Card, "The Causal Effect of Education on Earnings," in *Handbook of Labor Economics*, eds. Orley Ashenfelter and David Card (New York: Elsevier, 1999), 1802–1863, for comprehensive reviews. Graduating when the economy is in a recession might well lower the returns; for a discussion of this topic, see Philip Oreopoulos, Till von Wachter, and Andrew Heisz, "The Short- and Long-Term Career Effects of Graduating in a Recession," *American Economic Journal: Applied Economics* 4 (January 2012): 1–29.

EXAMPLE 9.4

Valuing a Human Asset: The Case of the Divorcing Doctor

State divorce laws typically provide for the assets acquired during marriage to be divided in some equitable fashion. Among the assets to be divided is often the value of human capital investments made by either spouse during marriage. How these acquired human capital values are estimated can be illustrated by the following example.

Dr. Doe married right after he had acquired a license to practice as a general practitioner. Instead of opening a general (family) practice, however, Dr. Doe undertook specialized training to become a surgeon. During his training (residency) period, the income of Dr. Doe and his wife was much lower than it would have been had he been working as a general practitioner. Thus, both spouses were investing, albeit to different degrees, in Dr. Doe's human capital.

Shortly after his residency was completed and he had acquired board certification as a general surgeon, Dr. Doe and his wife decided to divorce. She sued him for an equitable division of the asset value of his certification as a general surgeon. How can this asset value be estimated?

The asset value of Dr. Doe's certificate as a general surgeon is the present value of his estimated *increase in lifetime earnings* this certificate made possible. The most reasonable estimate of

his increase in yearly earnings is calculated by subtracting from what the typical general surgeon earns the average earnings of general practitioners (which is an estimate of what Dr. Doe could have earned in the absence of his training as a surgeon).

In 2012, the mean earnings of general surgeons were roughly $231,000 and those of general practitioners were $180,000. Thus, assuming Dr. Doe is an "average" doctor, obtaining his certificate as a surgeon increased his earnings capacity by $51,000 per year in 2012 dollars.[a] Assuming a remaining work life of 25 years and a real interest rate (which takes account of what inflation will do to the earnings differential) of 2 percent, the present value of the asset Dr. Doe acquired as the result of his surgical training comes to $994,000. (It would then be up to the court to divide this asset equitably between the two divorcing spouses.)

---

[a] Earnings data are from the U.S. Department of Labor, Bureau of Labor Statistics, "May 2012 National Occupational Employment and Wage Estimates, United States," Web site: http://www.bls.gov/oes/current/oes_nat.htm#29-0000. The formula used to calculate present value is the one given in footnote 2, where $X = \$51,000$, $r = 0.02$, and $n = 25$.

the contribution made by *schooling*.[24] The problem is that (a) people who are smarter, harder working, and more dynamic are likely to obtain more schooling, and (b) such people might be more productive, and hence earn higher-than-average wages, even if they did not complete more years of schooling than others. When measures of true ability are not observed or accounted for, the studies attribute *all* the earnings differentials associated with college to college itself and none to ability, even though *some* of the added earnings college graduates typically receive may have been received by an equally able high school graduate who did not attend college.

---

[24]An investment in education should also raise wages more than *overall* wealth—which (recalling chapters 6 and 7) should cause hours of work to rise. Thus, some of the increased earnings from more education could be associated with reduced leisure, which would constitute another source of upward bias. This point is made by C. M. Lindsay, "Measuring Human Capital Returns," *Journal of Political Economy* 79 (November/December 1971): 1195–1215.

Some studies have attempted to control for ability by using measures of intelligence quotient (IQ) or scores on aptitude tests, but there are continuing disputes over how much these tests reveal about innate abilities. One clever way to control for ability without relying on these tests is to analyze earnings differences among sets of identical twins (see the Empirical Study at the end of this chapter). Identical twins have the same genes, so they will have the same innate abilities, and one would think that measuring earnings differences that are associated with differences in schooling *within pairs of twins* would yield an unbiased estimate of the returns to education. The most recent studies of twins estimate rates of return that are not too different from the conventional estimates noted earlier; these studies, then, suggest that ability bias in the conventional estimates may not be very large.[25]

Returns for Whom?   As discussed earlier in this chapter, people who make educational investments are likely to differ from people who do not; for example, people who seek more schooling may have lower psychic costs of learning, or lower discount rates, than those who do not make the investment. Thus, the returns to schooling for those who *do* invest may be very different than the returns facing those who chose *not* to invest. For policies that attempt to encourage the non-investors to seek more schooling, what we really want to know is the rate of return they would experience if their choices about schooling were to change.

Economists have recently tried, therefore, to find contexts in which people have different levels of education, not because of choices they have made, but because of factors beyond their control. Compulsory schooling laws—laws that require children to start school at a certain age and remain in school until they reach the legal school-leaving age—have provided one such context. Comparing the years of education and earnings of high school dropouts, some of whom, by the accident of their birthday, will have been forced into more schooling than others, represents one approach that has been taken to estimate the returns facing those not currently investing in schooling. To date, there have not been enough studies of this type to arrive at a consensus estimate of these returns.[26]

---

[25]See Orley Ashenfelter and Cecilia Rouse, "Income, Schooling, and Ability: Evidence from a New Sample of Identical Twins," *Quarterly Journal of Economics* 113 (February 1998): 253–284; Andrew Leigh and Chris Ryan, "Estimating Returns to Education Using Different Natural Experiment Techniques," *Economics of Education Review* 27 (April 2008): 149–160; and Vikesh Amin, "Returns to Education: Evidence from UK Twins: Comment ," *American Economic Review* 101 (June 2011): 1629–1635.

[26]For a study that summarizes the issues and refers to similar studies, see Philip Oreopoulos, "Would More Compulsory Schooling Help Disadvantaged Youth? Evidence from Recent Changes to School-Leaving Laws," in *The Problems of Disadvantaged Youth: An Economic Perspective,* edited by Jonathan Gruber (Chicago and London: University of Chicago Press, 2009): 85–112. For a different approach to estimating the returns facing those who have *not* chosen to invest, see Pedro Carneiro, James J. Heckman, and Edward J. Vytlacil, "Estimating Marginal Returns to Education," *American Economic Review* 101 (October 2011): 2754–2781; and Andrew J. Hussey and Omari H. Swinton, "Estimating the *ex ante* Expected Returns To College," *American Economic Review; Papers and Proceedings* 101 (May 2011): 598–602.

Is Education a Good Social Investment?

The issue of education as a social investment has been of heightened interest in the United States in recent years, especially because of three related developments. First, product markets have become more global, increasing the elasticity of both product and labor demand. As a result, American workers are now facing more competition from workers in other countries. Second, the growing availability of high-technology capital has created new products and production systems that may require workers to have greater cognitive skills and to be more adaptable, efficient learners.[27] Third, American elementary and secondary school students have scored relatively poorly, as can be seen from data in Table 9.4, on achievement tests in mathematics and science.

The combination of these three developments has caused concern about the productivity of America's future workforce, relative to workers elsewhere, and has led to a series of questions about our educational system. Are we devoting enough resources to educating our current and future workforce? Should the resources we devote to education be reallocated in some way? Should we demand more of students in elementary and secondary schools?

The Social Cost   As can be seen from Table 9.4, the United States devotes relatively more resources to schooling than do some other developed countries—having spent over $12,000 per student in secondary schools in 2008. The relatively poor performance of American students on achievement tests, however, has led to questions about whether the United States is devoting too many or too few resources to education—or whether it is not using its educational resources wisely enough. These questions take on added urgency when we consider that if the forgone earnings of students are included, the United States

Table 9.4

International Comparisons of Schooling, 2008, 2009

Country	2008 Expenditures per Pupil, Secondary Level (U.S. $)	2009 Math Test Scores, 15-year-olds	2009 Science Test Scores, 15-year-olds
France	10,231	497	498
Germany	8,606	513	520
Japan	9,092	529	524
United Kingdom	9,487	492	514
United States	12,097	487	502

Source: U.S. National Center for Education Statistics, *Digest of Education Statistics, 2011,* Tables 416, 429 at the National Center for Education Statistics Web site: http://nces.ed.gov/pubs2012/2012001.pdf.

---

[27]For a discussion of cognitive skills and earnings, and a review of prior studies, see Eric A. Hanushek and Ludger Woessmann, "The Role of Cognitive Skills in Economic Development," *Journal of Economic Literature* 46 (September 2008): 607–668.

devotes *over a tenth of its gross domestic product* to education, from elementary schools to universities.[28] In beginning to answer these questions, we must try to understand how education and productivity are related.

The Social Benefit   The view that increased educational investments increase worker productivity is a natural outgrowth of the observation that such investments enhance the earnings of individuals who undertake them. If Individual A's productivity is increased because of more schooling, then *society's* stock of human capital has increased as a result. Some argue, however, that the additional education received by Individual A also creates benefits for Individual B, who must work with A. If more schooling causes A to communicate more clearly or solve problems more creatively, then B's productivity will also increase. In terms of concepts we introduced in chapter 1, education may create positive externalities so that the social benefits are *larger* than the private benefits.[29]

Others argue that the returns to society are *smaller* than the returns to individuals. They believe that the educational system is used by society as a screening device that sorts people by their (predetermined) ability. As discussed later, this alternative view, in its extreme form, sees the educational system as a means of *finding out* who is productive, not of enhancing worker productivity.

The Signaling Model   An employer seeking to hire workers is never completely sure of the actual productivity of any applicant, and in many cases, the employer may remain unsure long after an employee is hired. What an employer *can* observe are certain indicators that firms believe to be correlated with productivity: age, experience, education, and other personal characteristics. Some indicators, such as age, are immutable. Others, such as formal education, can be *acquired* by workers. Indicators that can be acquired by individuals can be called *signals*; our analysis here will focus on the signaling aspect of formal education.

Let us suppose that firms wanting to hire new employees for particular jobs know that there are two groups of applicants that exist in roughly equal proportions. One group has a productivity of 2, let us say, and the other has a productivity of 1. Furthermore, suppose that these productivity levels cannot be changed by education and that employers cannot readily distinguish which applicants are from which group. If they were unable to make such distinctions, firms would be forced

---

[28]About 7.5 percent of the gross domestic product in the United States has been devoted to the direct costs of formal schooling (elementary through university), but one study estimated that the forgone earnings of high school and college students add another 60 percent to these direct costs. See Theodore Schultz, *The Economic Value of Education* (New York: Columbia University Press, 1963).

[29]For an example of a study (with references to others) on the external effects of education, see Enrico Moretti, "Workers' Education, Spillovers, and Productivity: Evidence from Plant-Level Data," *American Economic Review* 94 (June 2004): 656–690; and Susana Iranzo and Giovanni Peri, "Schooling Externalities, Technology and Productivity: Theory and Evidence from U.S. States," National Bureau of Economic Research, Working Paper No. 12440 (August 2006).

to assume that all applicants are "average"; that is, they would have to assume that each had a productivity of 1.5 (and would offer them wages of up to 1.5).

While workers in this simple example would be receiving what they were worth on *average*, any firm that could devise a way to distinguish between the two groups (at little or no cost) could enhance its profits. When wages equal 1.5, workers with productivities equal to 1 are receiving more than they are worth. If these applicants could be discovered and either rejected or placed into lower-paying jobs, the firm could obviously increase its profits. It turns out that using educational attainment as a hiring standard can increase profits even if education does not enhance productivity. We can illustrate this with a simple example.

An Illustration of Signaling   To illustrate the use of educational signaling, suppose that employers come to believe that applicants with at least e^* years of education beyond high school are the ones with productivity 2 and that those with less than e^* are in the lower-productivity group. With this belief, workers with less than e^* years would be rejected for any job paying a wage above 1, while those with at least e^* would find that competition among employers drives their wages up to 2. This simple wage structure is illustrated in Figure 9.7.[30] If additional schooling does not enhance productivity, can requiring the signal of e^* really distinguish between the two groups of applicants? The answer is yes *if the costs to the worker of acquiring the added schooling are negatively related to his or her on-the-job productivity.*

Figure 9.7

The Benefits to Workers of Educational Signaling

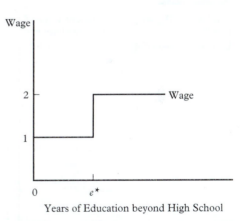

[30]This analysis is based on Michael Spence, "Job Market Signaling," *Quarterly Journal of Economics* 87 (August 1973): 205–221.

If workers with at least e^* years of education beyond high school can obtain a wage of 2, while those with less can earn a wage of only 1, all workers would want to acquire the signal of e^* if it were costless for them to do so. As we argued earlier, however, schooling costs are both large and different for different individuals. In particular, the psychic costs of education are probably inversely related to ability: those who learn easily can acquire the educational signal (of e^* in this case) more cheaply than others. If—and this is critical—those who have *lower* costs of acquiring education are *also* more productive on the job, then requiring educational signals can be useful for employers.

To understand the role of educational costs in signaling, refer to Figure 9.8, in which the reward structure from Figure 9.7 is expressed in terms of the present value of lifetime earnings (at a wage of 1, their discounted lifetime earnings sum to PVE_1, while at a wage of 2, they sum to PVE_2). Now assume that each year of education costs C for those with less productivity and $C/2$ for those with greater productivity.

Workers will choose the level of schooling at which the difference between their discounted lifetime earnings and their total educational costs is maximized. For those with yearly educational costs of C, the difference between lifetime earnings and total educational costs is maximized at zero years of education beyond high school. For these workers, the net benefit of an additional e^* years (distance BD) is less than the net benefit of zero additional years (distance $A0$). For them, the benefits of acquiring the signal of e^* years is not worth the added costs.

Figure 9.8

The Lifetime Benefits
and Costs of
Educational Signaling

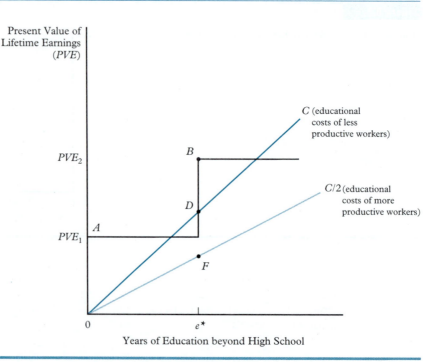

Years of Education beyond High School

For those whose costs are $C/2$, it can be seen that the net benefits of investing in e^* (distance BF) exceed the net benefits of other schooling choices. Therefore, only those with costs of $C/2$—the workers with productivities of 2—find it advantageous to acquire e^* years of schooling. In this example, then, schooling attainment signals productivity.

Some Cautions About Signaling   Our simple example demonstrated how education could have value even if it did not directly enhance worker productivity. It is necessary to stress, though, that for education to have signaling value in this case, on-the-job productivity and the costs of education must be *negatively* related. If the higher costs reflected along line C were associated with lower cognitive ability or a distaste for learning, then it is conceivable that these costs could be indicative of lower productivity. If, however, those with costs along C have higher costs only because of lower family wealth (and therefore smaller contributions from others toward their schooling costs), then they may be no less productive on the job than those along line $C/2$. In this latter case, signaling would fail, because it would only indicate those with low family wealth, not lower productivity.

Even when educational signaling is a useful way to predict future productivity, there is an *optimum* signal beyond which society would not find it desirable to go. Suppose, for example, that employers now requiring e^* years for entry into jobs paying a wage of 2 were to raise their hiring standards to e' years, as shown in Figure 9.9. Those with educational costs along

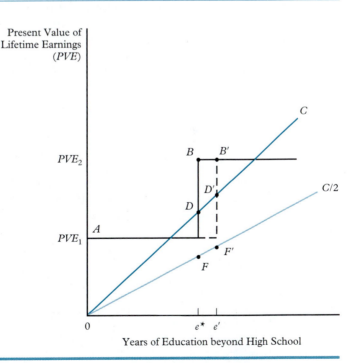

C would still find it in their best interests to remain at zero years of schooling beyond high school, and those with costs along *C*/2 would find it profitable to invest in the required signal of *e'* (because distance *B'F'* is greater than *A*0). Requiring more schooling of those who are selected for high-wage jobs, however, is more costly for those workers (and thus for society as a whole). While the new required signal would distinguish between the two groups of workers, it would do so at increased (and unnecessary) costs to individuals, which cannot be socially optimal.

It clearly can be beneficial for individuals to invest in educational signals, but if schooling *only* has signaling value, is it a worthy investment for society to make? If the only purpose of schools is to provide signals, why encourage investments in the expansion or qualitative upgrading of schooling? If 50 years ago being a high school graduate signaled above-average intelligence and work discipline, why incur the enormous costs of expanding college attendance only to find out that now these qualities are signaled by having a bachelor's degree? The issue is of even more importance in less-developed countries, where mistakes in allocating extremely scarce capital resources could be disastrous (see Example 9.5). Before attempting to decide if schooling has social value when all it produces are signals, let us first turn to the more basic question of whether we can figure out if schooling enhances, or merely signals, human capital.

Signaling or Human Capital?
Direct evidence on the role schooling plays in society is difficult to obtain. Advocates of the signaling viewpoint, for example, might point to the higher rates of return for college graduates than for college dropouts as evidence that schooling is a signaling device.[31] They argue that what is learned in school is proportional to the time spent there and that an added bonus (rate of return) just for a diploma is proof of the signaling hypothesis. Advocates of the view that schooling enhances human capital would counter that those who graduate after four years have learned more than four times what the freshman dropout has learned. They argue that dropouts are more likely to be poorer students—the ones who overestimated their returns on schooling and quit when they discovered their mistake. Thus, their relatively low rate of return is associated not with their dropping out but with their *reason* for dropping out.

To take another example, proponents of the human capital view could argue that the fact that earnings differentials between college and high school graduates grow with age supports their view. If schooling were just a signaling device, employers would rely on it *initially*, but as they accumulated direct information from experience

---

[31]Dropouts naturally have lower earnings than graduates, but because they have also invested less, it is not clear that their *rates of return* should be lower. For further discussion and evidence, see David A. Jaeger and Marianne E. Page, "Degrees Matter: New Evidence on Sheepskin Effects in the Returns to Education," *Review of Economics and Statistics* 78 (November 1996): 733–740. Thomas J. Kane and Cecilia Elena Rouse, "Comment on W. Norton Grubb: 'The Varied Economic Returns to Postsecondary Education: New Evidence from the Class of 1972,'" *Journal of Human Resources* 30 (Winter 1995): 205–221, calls into question the benefits of graduation independent of the number of *credits* taken.

EXAMPLE 9.5

The Socially Optimal Level of Educational Investment

In addition to asking whether schooling is a good social investment, we could also ask, "What is the socially optimal *level* of schooling?" The general principle guiding our answer to this question is that society should increase or reduce its educational investments until the marginal rate of return (to society) equals the marginal rate of return on other forms of capital investment (investment in physical capital, for example).

The rationale for this principle is that if society has some funds it wants to invest, it will desire to invest them in projects yielding the highest rates of return. If an investment in physical capital yields a 20 percent rate of return and the same funds invested in schooling yield (holding the riskiness of the investment constant) only a 10 percent return, society will clearly prefer to invest in physical capital. As long as the two rates of return differ, society could be made better off by reducing its investments in low-yield projects and increasing them in those with higher rates of return.

The text has discussed many of the difficulties and biases inherent in estimating rates of return to schooling. However, the general principle of equating the rates of social return on all forms of investments is still a useful one to consider. It suggests, for example, that capital-poor countries should invest in additional schooling only if the returns are very high—higher, in all probability, than the rates of return required for optimality in more-capital-rich countries.

Indeed, the rates of return to both secondary schooling and higher education appear to be generally higher in less-developed countries than in developed countries. One review estimated that the rate of return on secondary schooling investment was 10 percent for a developed country (on average), while for a less-developed country, it was 13 percent to 16 percent. Comparable rates of return on investments in higher education were 9.5 percent and 11 percent, respectively.

Data from: George Psacharopoulos and Harry Anthony Patrinos, "Returns to Investment in Education: A Further Update," World Bank Policy Research, working paper no. 2881, September 2002, Table 3.

with their employees, schooling would play a smaller role in determining earnings. Signaling advocates could counter that continued growth in earnings differentials only illustrates that educational attainment was a *successful* signaling device.[32]

School Quality   Given the difficulty of generating predictions of labor market outcomes that can directly distinguish the signaling from the human capital hypothesis, you may wonder if there are other ways to resolve the debate. A research strategy with some potential grows out of issues related to school quality.

---

[32]Attempts to distinguish between the two views include Joseph Altonji, "The Effects of High School Curriculum on Education and Labor Market Outcomes," *Journal of Human Resources* 30 (Summer 1995): 409–438; Andrew Weiss, "Human Capital vs. Signaling Explanations of Wages," *Journal of Economic Perspectives* 9 (Fall 1995): 133–154; Wim Groot and Hessel Oosterbeek, "Earnings Effects of Different Components of Schooling: Human Capital versus Screening," *Review of Economics and Statistics* 76 (May 1994): 317–321; Kelly Bedard, "Human Capital versus Signaling Models: University Access and High School Dropouts," *Journal of Political Economy* 109 (August 2001): 749–775; and Harley Frazis, "Human Capital, Signaling, and the Pattern of Returns to Education," *Oxford Economic Papers* 54 (April 2002): 298–320.

As mentioned earlier, concerns have been raised about the cognitive achievement of American students. If schooling primarily performs a signaling function, by helping to *discover* people's cognitive abilities, we would not necessarily look to the educational system to remedy the problem of low cognitive achievement. However, if schooling can enhance the kinds of skills that pay off in the labor market, then increased investment in the quality of the nation's schools could be warranted.

Proponents of the signaling and human capital views of education can agree that people of higher cognitive ability are likely to be more productive; where they disagree is whether better schools can enhance worker productivity by improving cognitive skills. Advocates of the signaling viewpoint cite a substantial literature suggesting it is difficult to demonstrate a relationship between schooling expenditures and student performance on *tests of cognitive skill*, although the evidence on this question is mixed.[33] Advocates of the human capital view, however, find support in studies of *earnings* and school quality. These studies generally indicate that students attending higher-quality schools (that is, ones with greater resources per student) have higher subsequent earnings, other things equal.[34]

Clearly, assessments of the social returns to schooling that examine the role of school quality have so far yielded somewhat ambiguous results. Better schools may enhance labor market earnings, but evidence that they enhance measured cognitive abilities is mixed. One possibility, of course, is that better schools enhance productivity by enhancing creative skills or better work habits—characteristics

---

[33]See, for example, Eric A. Hanushek, John F. Kain, Daniel M. O'Brien, and Steven G. Rivkin, "The Market for Teacher Quality," National Bureau of Economic Research, Working Paper No. 11154 (February 2005); Charles T. Clotfelter, Helen F. Ladd, and Jacob L. Vigdor, "How and Why Do Teacher Credentials Matter for Student Achievement?" National Bureau of Economic Research, Working Paper No. 12828 (January 2007); Thomas J. Kane, Jonah E. Rockoff, and Douglas Staigner, "What Does Certification Tell Us about Teacher Effectiveness? Evidence from New York City," National Bureau of Economic Research, Working Paper No. 12155 (July 2006); Eric A. Hanushek and Dennis D. Kimko, "Schooling, Labor Force Quality, and the Growth of Nations," *American Economic Review* 90 (December 2000): 1184–1208; and Alan B. Krueger and Diane M. Whitmore, "The Effect of Attending a Small Class in the Early Grades on College-Test Taking and Middle School Test Results: Evidence from Project STAR," *Economic Journal* 111 (January 2001): 1–28. It is also possible that the administrative and philosophical contributions of charter schools enhance cognitive skills; see Atila Abdulkadiroglu, Joshua D.Angrist, Susan M. Dynarski, Thomas J. Kane, and Parag A. Pathak, "Accountability and Flexibility in Public Schools: Evidence from Boston's Charters and Pilots," *Quarterly Journal of Economics* 126 (May 2011): 699–748.

[34]For citations to the literature analyzing links between school resources and student outcomes, see George A. Akerlof and Rachel E. Kranton, "Identity and Schooling: Some Lessons for the Economics of Education," *Journal of Economic Literature* 40 (December 2002): 1167–1201. This article attempts to identify sociological factors that might help resolve the disparate results obtained in economic analyses that relate schooling resources to educational results. For a more recent study, see Orley Ashenfelter, William J. Collins, and Albert Yoon, "Evaluating the Role of *Brown vs. Board of Education* in School Equalization, Desegregation, and the Income of African Americans," National Bureau of Economic Research, Working Paper No. 11394 (June 2005).

that may be valued in the labor market but not captured especially well by standardized tests of cognitive achievement. Another possibility, however, is that better schools give students better information about their own interests and abilities, thus helping them to make more successful career choices. Some important questions, then, remain unanswered.

Does the Debate Matter?   In the end, perhaps the debate between advocates of the signaling and human capital views of schooling is not terribly important. The fact is that schooling investments offer *individuals* monetary rates of return that are comparable to those received from other forms of investment. For individuals to recoup their human capital investment costs requires willingness on the part of employers to pay higher wages to people with more schooling; and for employers to be willing to do this, schools must be providing a service that they could not perform more cheaply themselves.

For example, we argued earlier that to profit from an investment of $100,000 in a college education, college graduates must be paid at least $3,652 more per year than they would have received otherwise. Naturally, this requires that they find employers who are willing to pay them the higher yearly wage. If college merely helps *reveal* who is more productive, employers who believe they could find this out for less than a yearly cost of $3,652 per worker would clearly have incentives to adopt their own methods of screening workers.

The fact that employers continue to emphasize (and pay for) educational requirements in the establishment of hiring standards suggests one of two things. Either more education *does* enhance worker productivity or it is a *less expensive* screening tool than any other that firms could use. In either case, the fact that employers are willing to pay a high price for an educated workforce seems to suggest that education produces social benefits.[35]

Is Public Sector Training a Good Social Investment?

Policymakers should also ask whether government job training programs can be justified based on their returns. During the past four decades, the federal government has funded a variety of these programs that primarily targeted disadvantaged men, women, and youth. Some programs have served trainees who applied voluntarily, and others have been mandatory programs for public assistance recipients (who stood to lose benefits if they did not enroll). Some of these programs have provided relatively inexpensive help in searching for work, while others have directly provided work experience or (in the case of the Job Corps) comprehensive services associated with living away from home. Over these decades, however, roughly half of those enrolled received classroom training at

[35]Kevin Lang, "Does the Human Capital/Educational Sorting Debate Matter for Development Policy?" *American Economic Review* 84 (March 1994): 353–358, comes to a similar conclusion through a more formal argument.

EMPIRICAL STUDY

ESTIMATING THE RETURNS TO EDUCATION USING A SAMPLE OF TWINS: COPING WITH THE PROBLEM OF UNOBSERVED DIFFERENCES IN ABILITY

Researchers doing empirical studies must always be aware of how their results are affected by the problem of *omitted variables*. It is rare that we have access to data on all relevant independent variables, and the regression techniques described in Appendix 1A contain an error term that explicitly assumes the variables we have do not fully explain all the variation in a given dependent variable. If an omitted variable is not correlated with any observed independent variable, there is no bias imparted to the estimates of how the independent variables affect the dependent variable.

However, if an omitted independent variable is correlated with a particular observed one, the estimated effect of the observed variable will be biased. The *omitted variables bias*, and one solution to it, can be illustrated by the problem of estimating the returns to schooling when researchers do not have data on innate learning ability (which is very difficult to observe).

The returns to education are conventionally estimated by using multivariate regression techniques to analyze, for a cross-section of workers, how much earnings are increased by an additional year of schooling—after controlling for other observed factors that influence earnings. However, if people with higher innate capacities for learning (higher *ability*) are the very ones who pursue more education, then estimates of the returns to schooling will also include any labor market rewards for *ability* unless researchers are able to measure innate learning ability. Put differently, if education and ability levels are positively correlated, but we do not observe data on innate ability, our estimates of the effects of schooling will be biased upward (we discussed this earlier as *ability bias*). Lacking a way to control for learning ability, then, makes it problematic to estimate how much more a typical person (with a given ability level) would earn if he or she invested in another year of schooling. Can we find a way to correct for ability bias, and if so, can we estimate how large that bias is?

A clever way to avoid the problems of ability bias is to use a sample of identical twins, because such twins have precisely the same genetic material and thus the same native abilities. With the same ability and family background, identical twins should have the same incentives for educational investments; however, random factors (marriage, divorce, career interests) can intervene and cause twins to have different schooling levels. By statistically analyzing, for several sets of twins, how the earnings differences between each twin in a pair are affected by differences in their years of schooling, we can estimate the returns to schooling in a way that is free of ability bias.

One careful study analyzed 340 pairs of identical twins who attended the annual Twinsburg Twins Festival in Twinsburg, Ohio, during the summers of 1991–1993. By looking at differences in earnings and education within each of the 340 pairs, the authors estimated that the returns to schooling were about 9 percent. In contrast, when they estimated the returns to schooling in the conventional way (not controlling for ability), the estimated rate of return was 10 percent. They thus conclude that failure to control for ability imparts only a small upward bias to the conventional estimates of the rate of return to schooling.

Source: Orley Ashenfelter and Cecilia Rouse, "Income, Schooling, and Ability: Evidence from a New Sample of Identical Twins," Quarterly Journal of Economics 113 (February 1998): 253–284.

vocational schools or community colleges, and another 15 percent received in-plant training. The per-student costs of these latter two types of programs have been in the range of $4,500 to $9,100 (in 2012 dollars).[36]

Evaluating these programs requires comparing their costs with an estimate of the present value of their benefits, which are measured by calculating the increase in wages made possible by the training program. Calculating the benefits involves estimating what trainees would have earned in the absence of training, and there are several thorny issues the researcher must successfully confront. Nevertheless, summaries of credible studies done to date have concluded that adult women are the one group among the disadvantaged that clearly benefits from these training programs; adult men and youth show no consistent earnings increases across studies. The average increase in earnings for women in training programs is roughly $1,980 per year (2012 dollars).[37] Were these increases large enough to justify program costs?

The programs had direct costs of $4,500 to $9,100 per trainee, but they also had opportunity costs in the form of forgone output. The typical trainee was in her program for 16 weeks, and while many of the trainees had been on welfare prior to training, the opportunity costs of their time surely were not zero. Recall from Chapter 7 that a person can be productive both at home and in the workplace. If we place an hourly value on trainee time equal to the minimum wage ($7.25 per hour in 2012), spending 16 weeks in training had opportunity costs

---

[36]Robert J. LaLonde, "The Promise of Public Sector–Sponsored Training Programs," *Journal of Economic Perspectives* 9 (Spring 1995): 149–168, gives a brief history of federally sponsored training programs and summarizes several issues relevant to evaluating their efficacy.

[37]David H. Greenberg, Charles Michalopoulos, and Philip K. Robins, "A Meta-Analysis of Government-Sponsored Training Programs," *Industrial and Labor Relations Review* 57 (October 2003): 31–53. Several studies find that the Job Corps training program for youth and young adults had a positive rate of return; see German Blanco, Carlos A. Flores, and Alfonso Flores-Lagunes, "The Effects of Job Corps Training on Wages of Adolescents and Young Adults," *American Economic Review: Papers and Proceedings* 103 (May 2013): 418–422.

of roughly $4,600; thus, the total costs of training were probably in the range of $9,100 to $13,700 per woman.

If benefits of $1,980 per year were received annually for 20 years after training, and if the appropriate discount rate is 2 percent, the present value of benefits comes to roughly $32,370. Benefits of this magnitude are clearly in excess of costs. Indeed, the present value of benefits for voluntary training would still be in excess of $11,400 (the approximate midpoint of the cost range) if the yearly earnings increases lasted for just 7 years.[38]

Review Questions

1. Women receive lower wages, on average, than men of equal age. What concepts of human capital help to explain this phenomenon? Explain. Why does the discrepancy between earnings for men and women grow with age?

2. "The vigorous pursuit by a society of tax policies that tend to equalize wages across skill groups will frustrate the goal of optimum resource allocation." Comment.

3. A few years ago, a prominent medical college inadvertently accepted more applicants than it could accommodate in its first-year class. Not wanting to arbitrarily delay the entrance date of the students admitted, it offered them one year of free tuition if they would delay their medical studies by one year. Discuss the factors entering into a student's assessment of whether he or she should take this offer.

4. Luigi, an 18-year-old man who finished secondary school, decides to look for a job rather than enroll in college. However, he is not sure whether he should work in the private sector (associated with both higher earnings prospects and risk of job loss) or in the public sector (lowers wages but safer jobs). For each scenario, plot Luigi's earnings prospects over the lifetime (similar to Figures 9.3 and 9.4), assuming that Luigi does not switch sectors. Add the present value of Luigi's utility derived (measured in $) to your figure(s). Which factors may determine Luigi's choice of occupational sector?

5. Why do those who argue that more education "signals" greater ability believe that the most able people will obtain the most education?

6. The advent of VoIP-services ("Voice over IP", e.g., Skype) allows cheap communication by voice or video over the internet. This development gave rise to new businesses: for instance, Indian math and science teachers started to provide private tutoring to children from developed English-speaking countries. Use human capital theory to discuss the effect on the propensity for studying math or science in India and developed English-speaking countries.

---

[38]Paul Lengermann, "How Long Do the Benefits of Training Last? Evidence of Long Term Effects Across Current and Previous Employers," *Research in Labor Economics* 18 (1999): 439–461, found that the gains from formal and company training last at least nine years. For an analysis of the returns to Job Corps training, see Peter Z. Schochet, John Burghardt, and Sheena McConnell, "Does Job Corps Work? Impact Findings from the National Job Corps Study," *American Economic Review* 98 (December 2008): 1864–1886. For reference to studies of vocational education, see Paul Ryan, "The School-to-Work Transition: A Cross-National Perspective," *Journal of Economic Literature* 29 (March 2001): 34–92.

7. In many countries, higher education is heavily subsidized by the government (that is, university students do not bear the full cost of their college education). While there may be good reasons for heavily subsidizing university education, there are also some dangers in it. Using human capital theory, explain what these dangers are.

8. Many crimes against property (burglary, for example) can be thought of as acts that have immediate gains but run the risk of long-run costs. If imprisoned, the criminal loses income from both criminal and noncriminal activities. Using the framework for occupational choice in the long run, analyze what kinds of people are most likely to engage in criminal activities. What can society do to reduce crime?

9. The human capital model (Equation 9.7) suggests that educational investments should be made if

$$\frac{B_1}{1 + r} + \frac{B_2}{(1 + r)^2} + \cdots + \frac{B_T}{(1 + r)^T} > C.$$

Why would you expect female labor supply to increase in response to better childcare provision? Explain in light of the human capital model.

10. The following statement was overheard at a party: "It is just not right that Joe, who never went to college, makes more than Ken, who has a master's degree. People with higher degrees deserve to earn more!" Use human capital theory to comment on this quotation.

Problems

1. Becky works in sales but is considering quitting work for two years to earn an MBA. Her current job pays $40,000 per year (after taxes), but she could earn $55,000 per year (after taxes) if she had a master's degree in business administration. Tuition is $10,000 per year, and the cost of an apartment near campus is equal to the $10,000 per year she is currently paying. Becky's discount rate is 6 percent per year. She just turned 48 and plans to retire when she turns 60, whether or not she gets her MBA. Based on this information, should she go to school to earn her MBA? Explain carefully.

2. (Appendix). Suppose that the supply curve for optometrists is given by $L_s = -6 + 0.6W$, while the demand curve is given by $L_D = 50 - W$, where W = annual earnings in thousands of dollars per year and L = thousands of optometrists.

   a. Find the equilibrium wage and employment levels.

   b. Now, suppose that the demand for optometrists increases and the new demand curve is $L'_D = 66 - W$. Assume that this market is subject to cobwebs because it takes about three years to produce people who specialize in optometry. While this adjustment is taking place, the short-run supply of optometrists is fixed. Calculate the wage and employment levels in each of the first three rounds, and find the new long-run equilibrium. Draw a graph to show these events.

3. Suppose you are offered $100 now or $125 in five years. Let the interest rate be 4 percent. Calculate the present value of

the $125 option. Which option should you take if your goal is to choose the option with the larger present value?

4. Recall Figure 9.3. Which regression model (see Appendix 1A) better fits the age-earnings profiles of male high school graduates?

Model 1: $earnings = \alpha_{HS} + \beta_{HS} age + \varepsilon$

Or

Model 2: $earnings = \alpha_{HS} + \beta_{HS} age + \gamma_{HS} age^2 + \varepsilon$

What sign do you expect for α, β, and γ? Finally, compare the coefficients α_{HS} with $\alpha_{college}$, β_{HS} and $\beta_{college}$, and γ_{HS} and $\gamma_{college}$ (for example, $\alpha_{college}$ denotes the intercept for college graduates).

5. Human capital theory identifies different determinants of wages. A famous study used data that contain information on a person's yearly wages *wage*, years of schooling *s*, labor market experience *exper*, and his or her *afqt* score. The *afqt* is a proxy for a person's ability, and the test is taken at around 17 years. Using regression techniques described in Appendix 1A, the study finds finds

$$\ln \widehat{wage} = \underset{(0.02)}{0.12}\, s - \underset{(0.03)}{0.10}\left(s \cdot \frac{exper}{10}\right)$$
$$- \underset{(0.05)}{0.04}\, afqt + \underset{(0.05)}{0.14}\left(afqt \cdot \frac{exper}{10}\right)$$

(standard errors in parentheses).

a. Compute a person's expected wage for $exper = 0$ and $exper = 10$.

b. What matters more in the long run, years of formal education s or a person's abilities as measured by *afqt*? Assume that employers can only observe s.

c. What is the reason for these findings?

Selected Readings

Becker, Gary. *Human Capital*. New York: National Bureau of Economic Research, 1975.

Borjas, George J. "Earnings Determination: A Survey of the Neoclassical Approach." In *Three Worlds of Labor Economics*, eds. Garth Mangum and Peter Philips. Armonk, N.Y.: M. E. Sharpe, 1988.

Card, David. "The Causal Effect of Education on Earnings." In *Handbook of Labor Economics*, eds. Orley Ashenfelter and David Card. New York: Elsevier, 1999.

Clotfelter, Charles T., Ronald G. Ehrenberg, Malcolm Getz, and John Siegfried. *Economic Challenges in Higher Education*. Chicago: University of Chicago Press, 1991.

Friendlander, Daniel, David H. Greenberg, and Philip K. Robins. "Evaluating Government Training Programs for the Economically Disadvantaged." *Journal of Economic Literature* 35 (December 1997): 1809–1855.

Goldin, Claudia, and Lawrence F. Katz. *The Race between Education and Technology*. Cambridge, Mass.: Belknap Press, 2008.

Krueger, Alan B., and Mikael Lindahl. "Education for Growth: Why and for Whom?" *Journal of Economic Literature* 39 (December 2001): 1101–1136.

Mincer, Jacob. *Schooling, Experience, and Earnings*. New York: National Bureau of Economic Research, 1974.

Schultz, Theodore. *The Economic Value of Education*. New York: Columbia University Press, 1963.

Spence, Michael. "Job Market Signaling." *Quarterly Journal of Economics* 87 (August 1973): 355–374.

A "Cobweb" Model of Labor Market Adjustment

The adjustment of college enrollments to changes in the returns to education is not always smooth or rapid, particularly in special fields, such as engineering and law, that are highly technical. The problem is that if engineering wages (say) were to go up suddenly in a given year, the supply of graduate engineers would not be affected until three or four years later (owing to the time it takes to learn the field). Likewise, if engineering wages were to fall, those students enrolled in an engineering curriculum would understandably be reluctant to immediately leave the field. They have already invested a lot of time and effort and may prefer to take their chances in engineering rather than devote more time and money to learning a new field.

The failure of supply to respond immediately to changed market conditions can cause *boom-and-bust cycles* in the market for highly technical workers. If educational planners in government or the private sector are unaware of these cycles, they may seek to stimulate or reduce enrollments at times when they should be doing exactly the opposite, as illustrated next.

An Example of "Cobweb" Adjustments

Suppose the market for engineers is in equilibrium, where the wage is W_0 and the number of engineers is N_0 (see Figure 9A.1). Let us now assume that the demand curve for engineers shifts from D_0 to D_1. Initially, this increase in the demand for engineers does *not* induce the supply of engineers to increase beyond N_0, because it takes a long time to become an engineer once one has decided to do so. Thus, while the increased demand for engineers causes more people to decide to enter the field, the number available for employment *at the moment* is N_0. These N_0 engineers,

The Labor Market for Engineers

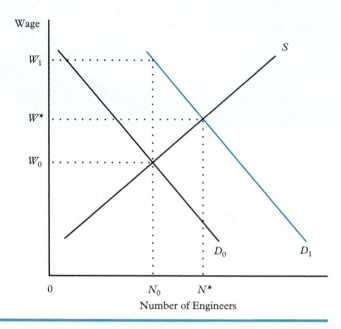

therefore, can *currently* obtain a wage of W_1 (in effect, there is a vertical supply curve, at N_0 for a few years until the supply of engineering graduates is increased).

The *current* engineering wage, W_1, is now above W^*, the new *long-run* equilibrium wage caused by the intersection of D_1 and S. The market, however, is unaware of W^*, observing only W_1. If people are myopic and assume W_1 is the new equilibrium wage, N_1 people will enter the engineering field (see Figure 9A.2). When these N_1 all graduate, there will be a *surplus* of engineers (remember that W_1 is *above* long-run equilibrium).

With the supply of engineers now temporarily fixed at N_1, the wage will fall to W_2. This fall will cause students and workers to shift *out* of engineering, but that effect will not be fully felt for a few years. In the meantime, note that W_2 is below long-run equilibrium (still at W^*). Thus, when supply *does* adjust, it will adjust too much—all the way to N_2. Now there will be another shortage of engineers, because after supply adjusts to N_2, demand exceeds supply at a wage rate of W_2. This causes wages to rise to W_3, and the cycle repeats itself. Over time, the swings become smaller and equilibrium is eventually reached. Because the adjustment path in Figure 9A.2 looks somewhat like a cobweb, the adjustment process described earlier is sometimes called a *cobweb model*.

Critical to cobweb models is the assumption that workers form myopic expectations about the future behavior of wages. In our example, they first assume that W_1 will prevail in the future and ignore the possibility that the occupational choice

Figure 9A.2

The Labor Market for Engineers:
A Cobweb Model

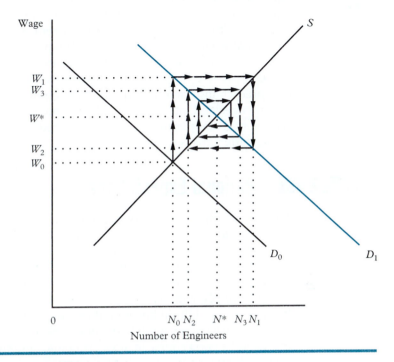

decisions of others will, in four years, drive the wage below W_1. Just how workers (and other economic actors, such as investors and taxpayers) form expectations about future wage (price) levels is very important to the understanding of many key issues affecting the labor market.[1]

Adaptive Expectations

The simplest and most naive way to predict future wage levels is to assume that what is observed today is what will be observed in the future; this naive assumption, as noted earlier, underlies the cobweb model. A more sophisticated way to form predictions about the future is with an *adaptive expectations* approach. Adaptive expectations are formed by setting future expected wages

---

[1]Also critical to cobweb models is that the demand curve be flatter than the supply curve; if it is not, the cobweb *explodes* when demand shifts and an equilibrium wage is never reached. An exploding cobweb model is an example from economics of the phenomenon of *chaos*. For a general introduction to this fascinating topic, see James Gleick, *Chaos* (New York: Penguin Books, 1987). For an article on chaos theory in the economic literature, see William J. Baumol and Jess Benhabib, "Chaos: Significance, Mechanism, and Economic Applications," *Journal of Economic Perspectives* 3 (Winter 1989): 77–106.

equal to a weighted average of current and past wages. While more weight may be given to current than past wages in forecasting future wage levels, changes in those levels prior to the current period are not ignored; thus, it is likely that wage expectations formed adaptively do not alternatively overshoot and undershoot the equilibrium wage *by as much as* those formed using the naive approach. If, however, adaptive expectations also lead workers to first overpredict and then underpredict the equilibrium wage, cobweb-like behavior of wages and labor supply will still be observed (although the fluctuations will be of a smaller magnitude if the predictions are closer to the mark than those made naively).

Rational Expectations

The most sophisticated way to predict future market outcomes is to use a full-blown model of the labor market. Those who believe in the *rational expectations* method of forming predictions about future wages assume that workers do have such a model in their heads, at least implicitly. Thus, they will realize that a marked increase in the earnings of engineers (say) is likely to be temporary, because supply will expand and eventually bring the returns to an investment in engineering skills in line with those for other occupations. Put differently, the rational expectations model assumes workers behave as if they have taken (and mastered!) a good course in labor economics and that they will not be fooled into overpredicting or underpredicting future wage levels.

Clearly, how people form expectations is an important empirical issue. In the case of engineers, lawyers, and dentists, periodic fluctuations in supply that characterize the cobweb model have been found, although the precise mix of naive and rational expectations is not clear.[2] Whether these fluctuations are the result of naive expectations or not, the lesson to be learned from cobweb models should not be lost on government policymakers. If the government chooses to take an active role in dealing with labor shortages and surpluses, it must be aware that because supply adjustments are slow in highly technical markets, wages in those markets tend to *over*-adjust. In other words, to the extent possible, governmental predictions and market interventions should be based on rational expectations. For example, at the initial stages of a shortage, when wages are rising toward W_1 (in our example), the government should be pointing out that W_1 is likely to be *above* the long-run equilibrium. If instead it attempts to meet the current shortage by *subsidizing* study in that field, it will be encouraging an even greater *surplus* later on. The moral of the story is that a complete knowledge of how markets adjust to changes in supply and demand is necessary before we can be sure that government intervention will do more good than harm.

---

[2]See Jaewoo Ryoo and Sherwin Rosen, "The Engineering Labor Market," *Journal of Political Economy* 112 (February 2004, supplement): S110–S140, for a recent analysis of both cobweb and rational-expectations models.

CHAPTER 10

Worker Mobility: Migration, Immigration, and Turnover

While the flow of workers across national borders is not a new phenomenon—after all, it was responsible for the settlement of Australia, Canada, and the United States—immigration over the last two or three decades has significantly raised the share of the foreign-born in Europe and North America. For example, the share of the foreign-born in the European population rose from 6.9 percent in 1990 to 9.5 percent in 2010; in Canada, the share of the foreign-born rose from 16.2 percent to 21.3 percent over this period, while in the United States it rose from 9.1 percent to 13.5 percent.[1] The dramatic increase in the presence of immigrants, who frequently speak a different language and are often from poorer countries, has stimulated some angry calls for stricter limits or tighter "border-security" measures—particularly in the United States, which shares a long border with a much poorer country (Mexico) and attracts many workers who have not been able to secure an official immigration visa. Proposals to impose stricter limits on immigration, including those to expel immigrants without work visas, are frequently justified with arguments that immigrants lower the wages of natives or otherwise impose a financial burden on the "host" country.

In this chapter, we will use economic theory to analyze the decision to emigrate and the labor-market effects of immigration. In the process,

---

[1]United Nations, "International Migrant Stock: The 2008 Revision Population Database: Country Profile," at http://esa.un.org/migration/.

we will examine how immigrants are likely to differ from others in personal characteristics (age and future-orientation), and what factors influence whether immigration raises the per-capita real income of the native-born in the host country. We begin the chapter, however, with an analysis of the causes and consequences of *worker mobility*—the larger category of which immigration is an important subset. Worker mobility plays a critical role in market economies. Because the purpose of any market is to promote voluntary exchange, society relies on the free movement of workers among employers to allocate labor in a way that achieves maximum satisfaction for both workers and consumers. The flow (either actual or threatened) of workers from lower-paying to higher-paying jobs, for example, is what forces firms that are paying below-equilibrium wages to increase their wage offers. The existence of compensating wage differentials, to take another example, also depends on the ability of informed workers to exercise choice among employment opportunities in the search for enhanced utility.

Mobility, however, is costly. Workers must take time to seek out information on other jobs, and for at least some workers, job search is most efficient if they quit their current job first (to look for work in a new geographic area, for example). Severing ties with the current employer means leaving friends and familiar surroundings, and it may mean giving up valuable employee benefits or the inside track on future promotions. Once a new job is found, workers may well face *monetary*, and will almost certainly face *psychic*, costs of moving to new surroundings—and in the case of immigration, the need to learn a new language and adapt to a new culture makes these costs particularly burdensome. In short, workers who move to new employers bear costs in the near term so that utility can be enhanced later on. Therefore, the human-capital model introduced in chapter 9 can be used to analyze mobility investments by workers.

The Determinants of Worker Mobility

The human-capital model views mobility as an investment in which costs are borne in some early period in order to obtain returns over a longer period of time. If the present value of the benefits associated with mobility exceeds the costs, both monetary and psychic, we assume that people will decide to change jobs or move, or both. If the discounted stream of benefits is not as large as the costs, then people will decide against such a change.

What determines the present value of the net benefits of mobility—that is, the benefits minus the costs—determines the mobility decision. These factors can be better identified by writing out the formula to use if we were to precisely calculate these net benefits:

$$\text{Present Value of Net Benefits} = \sum_{t=1}^{T} \frac{B_t}{(1 + r)^t} - C \qquad (10.1)$$

where

B_t = the increased utility in year t derived from changing jobs

T = the length of time (in years) one expects to work at the new job

r = the rate of discount

C = the utility lost in the move itself (direct and psychic costs)

Σ = a summation—in this case, the summation of the yearly discounted net benefits over a period running from year 1 to year T

Clearly, the present value of the net benefits of mobility will be larger the greater the utility derived from the new job, the less happy one is in the job of origin, the smaller the immediate costs associated with the change, and the longer one expects to be in the new job or live in the new area (that is, the greater T is). These observations lead to some clear-cut predictions about which groups in society will be most mobile and about the *patterns* of mobility we would expect to observe.

Geographic Mobility

Mobility of workers among countries, and among regions within a country, is an important fact of economic life. We have seen that the foreign-born comprise 10 percent to 20 percent of the population of Europe and North America. Moreover, migration within the United States is such that 1 of every 14 employees left their state of residence in the 5 years between 2005 and 2010.[2] Roughly one-third of those moving among states stay with their current employers, but taking into account those whose move is motivated by economic factors *and* who change employers, about half of all interstate moves are precipitated by a change in employment.[3] This emphasis on job change suggests that human-capital theory can help us understand which workers are most likely to undertake investments in geographic mobility and the directions in which mobility flows will take place.

The Direction of Migratory Flows

Human-capital theory predicts that migration will flow from areas of relatively poor earnings possibilities to places where opportunities are better. Studies of migratory flows support this prediction. In general, the results of such studies suggest that the *pull* of good opportunities in the areas of destination is stronger

---

[2]U.S. Census Bureau, "Geographical Mobility: 2005–2010: Detailed Tables," Table 3, at http://www.census.gov/hhes/migration/data/cps/cps2010-5yr.html.

[3]Ann P. Bartel, "The Migration Decision: What Role Does Job-Mobility Play?" *American Economic Review* 69 (December 1979): 775–786. See also Larry Schroeder, "Interrelatedness of Occupational and Geographical Labor Mobility," *Industrial and Labor Relations Review* 29 (April 1976): 405–411.

than the *push* of poor opportunities in the areas of origin. In other words, while people are more attracted to places where earnings are expected to be better, they do not necessarily come from areas where opportunities are poorest.

The most consistent finding in these detailed studies is that people are attracted to areas where the real earnings of full-time workers are highest. Studies find no consistent relationship, however, between unemployment and in-migration, perhaps because the number of people moving with a job already in hand is three times as large as the number moving *to look* for work. If one already has a job in a particular field, the area's unemployment rate is irrelevant.[4]

Most studies have found that contrary to what we might expect, the characteristics of the place of origin do not appear to have much net influence on migration. While those in the poorest places have the greatest *incentives* to move, the very poorest areas also tend to have people with lower levels of wealth, education, and skills—the very people who seem least *willing* (or able) to move. To understand this phenomenon, we must turn from the issue of *where* people go to a discussion of *who* is most likely to move. (In addition, there is the issue of *when* people move. See Example 10.1, which pulls together the issues of who, where, and when in analyzing one of the most momentous internal migrations in the history of the United States—the Great Migration of blacks from the South to the North in the first half of the twentieth century.)

Personal Characteristics of Movers

Migration is highly selective in the sense that it is not an activity in which all people are equally likely to be engaged. To be specific, mobility is much higher among the young and the better-educated, as human-capital theory would suggest.

Age   Age is one important factor in determining who migrates. Among Americans in their late twenties, 9 percent moved to another region within the United States, or to another country, between 2005 and 2010; for those in their late thirties and late forties, the corresponding percentages were 6 and 3 percent, respectively.[5]

There are two explanations for the fact that migration is an activity primarily for the young. First, the younger one is, the longer the period over which benefits from an investment can be obtained, and the larger the present value of these benefits.

---

[4]The level of *new hires* in an area appears to explain migration flows much better than the unemployment rate; see Gary Fields, "Place to Place Migration: Some New Evidence," *Review of Economics and Statistics* 61 (February 1979): 21–32. Robert H. Topel, "Local Labor Markets," *Journal of Political Economy* 94, no. 3, pt. 2 (June 1986): S111–S143, contains an analysis of how permanent and transitory shifts in an area's demand affect migration and wages.

[5]U.S. Census Bureau, "Geographical Mobility: 2005–2010: Detailed Tables," Table 1, at http://www .census.gov/hhes/migration/data/cps/cps2010-5yr.html. An analysis of internal migration in the United States, with a review of recent trends, see Raven Molloy, Christopher L. Smith, and Abigail Wozniak, "Internal Migration in the United States," *Journal of Economic Perspectives* 25 (Summer 2011): 173–196.

EXAMPLE 10.1

The Great Migration: Southern Blacks Move North

Our model predicts that workers will move whenever the present value of the net benefits of migration is positive. After the Civil War and emancipation, a huge wage gap opened up between the South and the North, with northern wages often twice as high as those in the South. Yet, black migration out of the South was very low—only 68,000 during the 1870s.

During World War I, however, the Great Migration began, and over half a million blacks moved out of the South in the 1910s. Black migration during the 1920s was almost twice this high, and it exceeded 1.5 million during the 1940s, so that by 1950, over 20 percent of southern-born blacks had left the region.

Why did this migration take so long to get going? One important factor was low education levels, which made obtaining information about outside opportunities very difficult. In 1880, more than 75 percent of African Americans over age 10 were illiterate, but this figure fell to about 20 percent by 1930. One study finds that in 1900, literate adult black males were three times more likely to have migrated than those who were illiterate. In 1940, blacks who had attended high school were twice as likely to have migrated than those with zero to four years of schooling. However, rising literacy alone cannot explain the sudden burst of migration.

The outbreak of World War I seems to have triggered the migration in two ways. First, it caused labor demand in northern industry to soar. Second, it brought the collapse of immigration inflows from abroad. Before World War I, growing northern industries had relied heavily on immigrants from Europe as a source of labor. With the immigration flood slowing to a trickle, employers began to hire black workers—even sending agents to recruit in the South. Job opportunities for blacks in the North finally opened up, and many blacks responded by moving.

A study using census data from 1870 to 1950 finds that, as expected, northern states in which wages were highest attracted more black migrants, as did those in which manufacturing growth was more rapid. Reduced European immigration seems to have spurred black migration, and it is estimated that if European immigration had been completely restricted at the turn of the century, the Great Migration would have started much sooner.

Data from: William J. Collins, "When the Tide Turned: Immigration and the Delay of the Great Black Migration," *Journal of Economic History* 57 (September 1997): 607–632; Robert A. Margo, *Race and Schooling in the South, 1880–1950* (Chicago: University of Chicago Press, 1990).

Second, a large part of the costs of migration is psychic—the losses associated with giving up friends, community ties, and the benefits of knowing one's way around. As we grow older, our ties to the community become stronger and the losses associated with leaving loom larger.

Education   Educational attainment is a second important predictor of who will move. For example, Americans with college degrees were twice as likely as those without to have moved out of their region between 2005 and 2010.[6]

---

[6]U.S. Census Bureau, "Geographical Mobility: 2005–2010: Detailed Tables," Table 1, at http://www.census.gov/hhes/migration/data/cps/cps2010-5yr.html.

One cost of migration is that of applying and interviewing for job offers. If one's occupation has a national (or international) labor market, as is the case for many college graduates, recruiters visit college campuses, and arrangements for interviews requiring fly-ins are commonplace—and often at the expense of the employer. However, if the relevant labor market for one's job is localized, the mechanisms for recruiting workers residing in distant areas are less likely to exist, and workers looking for a job far from home will find it relatively costly to interview.

The Role of Distance

Human-capital theory clearly predicts that as migration costs rise, the flow of migrants will fall. The costs of moving increase with distance, for two reasons. First, acquiring trustworthy *information* (often from friends or colleagues) on opportunities elsewhere is easier—especially for workers whose jobs are in "local" labor markets—when employment prospects are closer to home. Second, the time and money cost of a move and for trips back to see friends and relatives, and hence the *psychic* costs of the move, rise with distance. Indeed, we find that among those American workers who moved to a different labor market during 2005–2010, roughly 60% moved less than 500 miles—and most of those (35% of the total) moved less than 200 miles away from their original residence.[7]

Interestingly, lack of education appears to be a bigger deterrent to long-distance migration than does age (other influences held constant), a fact that can shed some light on whether information costs or psychic costs are the primary deterrent. As suggested by our arguments in the previous section, the age deterrent is closely related to psychic costs, while educational level and ease of access to information are closely linked. The apparently larger deterrent of educational level suggests that information costs may have more influence than psychic costs on the relation ship between migration and distance.[8]

The Earnings Distribution in Sending Countries and International Migration

To this point, our examples of factors that influence geographic mobility have related to domestic migration, but the influences of age, access to information, the potential gains in earnings, and distance are all relevant to international migration as well. Additionally, because immigrants are self-selected and the costs of immigration are so high, personal discount rates (or orientation toward the

---

[7]U.S. Census Bureau, "Geographical Mobility: 2005–2010: Detailed Tables," Table 24, at http://www.census.gov/hhes/migration/data/cps/cps2010-5yr.html.

[8]Aba Schwartz, "Interpreting the Effect of Distance on Migration," *Journal of Political Economy* 81 (September/October 1973): 1153–1167.

EXAMPLE 10.2

Migration and One's Time Horizon

Economic theory suggests that those with longer time horizons are more likely to make human-capital investments. Can we see evidence of this theoretical implication in the horizons of people who are most likely to migrate? A recent paper explores the possibility that people who give greater weight to the welfare of their children and grandchildren have a higher propensity to bear the considerable costs of immigration.

Before 1989, the Soviet Union made it difficult, although not impossible, for Jews to emigrate. Applying for emigration involved heavy fees; moreover, the applicant's property was often confiscated and his or her right to work was often suspended. However, after the collapse of the Soviet Union in 1989, these hassles were eliminated. The monetary benefits of migrating were approximately the same before and after 1989, but the costs fell considerably.

How did migrants from the earlier period—who were willing to bear the very high costs—differ from those who emigrated only when the costs were reduced? The study finds evidence that Jewish women who migrated to Israel during the earlier period brought with them larger families (on average, 0.4 to 0.8 more children) than otherwise similar migrants in the later period. This suggests that the benefits of migration to children may have been a decisive factor in the decision to migrate during the pre-1989 period.

Likewise, a survey of women aged 51 to 61 shows that grandmothers who have immigrated to the United States spend over 200 more hours per year with their grandchildren than American-born grandmothers. They are also more likely to report that they consider it important to leave an inheritance (rather than spending all their wealth on themselves).

Thus, there is evidence consistent with the theoretical implication that those who invest in immigration have longer time horizons (in the sense of putting greater weight on the welfare of their children and grandchildren) than those who do not.

Data from: Eli Berman and Zaur Rzakhanov, "Fertility, Migration and Altruism," National Bureau of Economic Research, working paper no. 7545 (February 2000).

future) are critical and likely to be very different for immigrants and nonmigrants. That is, as illustrated in Example 10.2, *immigrants—like others who make significant investments in human capital—are more likely to have lower-than-average personal discount rates.*

One aspect of the potential gains from migration that is uniquely important when analyzing international flows of labor is the distribution of earnings in the sending as compared with the receiving country. The relative distribution of earnings can help us predict which skill groups within a sending country are most likely to emigrate.[9]

Some countries have a more compressed (equal) earnings distribution than is found in the United States. In these countries, the average earnings differential between skilled and unskilled workers is smaller, implying that the returns

---

[9]The theory in this section is adapted from Andrew D. Roy, "Some Thoughts on the Distribution of Earnings," *Oxford Economic Papers* 3 (June 1951): 75–106; for a more thorough discussion of this issue, see George J. Borjas, *Friends or Strangers* (New York: Basic Books, 1990), especially chapters 1 and 7.

to human-capital investments are lower than in the United States. Skilled and professional workers from these countries (northern European countries are most notable in this regard) have the most to gain from emigration to the United States. Unskilled workers in countries with more equality of earnings are well paid compared with unskilled workers here and thus have less incentive to move. Immigrants to the United States from these countries, therefore, tend to be more skilled than the average worker who does not emigrate.

In countries with a less equal distribution of earnings than is found in the United States, skilled workers do relatively well, but there are large potential gains to the unskilled from emigrating to the United States. These unskilled workers may be blocked from making human-capital investments within their own countries (and thus from taking advantage of the high returns to such investments that are implied by the large earnings differentials). Instead, their human-capital investment may take the form of emigrating and seeking work in the United States. Less-developed countries tend to have relatively unequal earnings distributions, so it is to be expected that immigrants from these countries (and especially Mexico, which is closest) will be disproportionately unskilled.

The Returns to International and Domestic Migration

We have seen that migrants generally move to places that allow them greater earnings opportunities. How great these earnings increases are for individual migrants depends on the reasons and preparation for the move.

Internal Migration for Economic Reasons
The largest earnings increase from migration can be expected among those whose move is motivated by a better job offer and who have obtained this offer through a job-search process undertaken before quitting their prior jobs. A study of men and women in their twenties who were in this category found that for moves in the 1979–1985 period, earnings increased 14 percent to 18 percent more than earnings of nonmigrants. Even those who quit voluntarily and migrated for economic reasons *without* a prior job search earned 6 percent to 9 percent more than if they had stayed put.[10] The returns for women and men who migrated for economic reasons were very similar.

Family Migration
Most of us live in families, and if there is more than one employed person in a family, the decision to migrate is likely to have different earnings effects on the members. You will recall from chapter 7 that there is more than one plausible model for how those who live together actually make joint labor supply decisions, but with migration, a decision to move might well be made if the *family as a whole* experiences a net increase in total earnings. Total family earnings, of course, could be increased even if one partner's earnings were

---

[10]Kristen Keith and Abagail McWilliams, "The Returns to Mobility and Job Search by Gender," *Industrial and Labor Relations Review* 52 (April 1999): 460–477.

to fall as a result of the move, as long as the other partner experienced relatively large gains. Considering family migration decisions raises the issue of tied movers—those who agree to move for family reasons, not necessarily because the move improves their own earnings.

Among those in their twenties who migrated in the 1979–1985 period, quitting jobs and moving for *family* reasons caused earnings to decrease by an average of 10 percent to 15 percent—although searching for a new job before moving apparently held wage losses to zero.[11] Clearly, migrating as a tied mover can be costly to an individual. Women move more often than men for family reasons, but as more complete college or graduate school and enter careers, their willingness to move for family reasons may fall. The growing preference among college-educated couples for living in large urban areas, where both people have access to many alternative job opportunities without moving, reflects the costs of migrating as a tied mover.[12]

Returns to Immigration   Comparing the earnings of *international* immigrants with what they would have earned had they not emigrated is generally not feasible, owing to a lack of data on earnings in the home country—although a comparison of the wages received by Mexican immigrants in the United States with those paid to comparable workers in Mexico suggests that the gain from crossing the border was in the range of $9,000 to $16,000 per year in 2000 (a large percentage gain, given that the average per capita income in Mexico was $9,700 in that year).[13]

Most studies of the returns to immigration have focused on comparisons of immigrants' earnings with those of native-born workers in the host country. Figure 10.1 displays, for men who had immigrated to the United States decades ago, the path of their earnings relative to those of native-born Americans with similar amounts of labor market experience. While not reflecting the experience of recent immigrants, Figure 10.1 illustrates three generalizations about the relative earnings of immigrants over time. First, immigrants earn substantially less than their native-born counterparts when they first arrive in the United States. Second, each succeeding cohort of immigrants has done less well upon entry than its predecessor. Third, the *relative* earnings of immigrants rise over time, which means that their earnings rise faster than those of natives, especially in the first 10 years after immigration.

---

[11]Keith and McWilliams, "The Returns to Mobility and Job Search by Gender."

[12]Dora L. Costa and Matthew E. Kahn, "Power Couples: Changes in the Locational Choice of the College Educated, 1940–1990," *Quarterly Journal of Economics* 115 (November 2000): 1287–1315.

[13]The wage comparisons are expressed in 2000 dollars and represent U.S.-Mexico wage differences for workers of the same age and with the same education; see Gordon H. Hanson, "The Economic Consequences of the International Migration of Labor," *American Review of Economics* 1 (September 2009): 179–208. For a study that analyses the problems of estimating the monetary returns to those who immigrate, see Ran Abramitzky, Leah Boustan, and Katherine Eriksson, "Europe's Tired, Poor, Huddled Masses: Self-Selection and Economic Outcomes in the Age of Mass Migration," *American Economic Review* 102 (August 2012): 1832–1856.

Figure 10.1

Male Immigrant
Earnings Relative to
Those of the Native-
Born with Similar
Labor-Market
Experience, by
Immigrant Cohort

Source: Adapted from
Darren Lubotsky, "Chutes
or Ladders? A Longitudinal
Analysis of Immigrant
Earnings," working
paper no. 445, Industrial
Relations Section, Princeton
University, August 2000,
Figure 6.

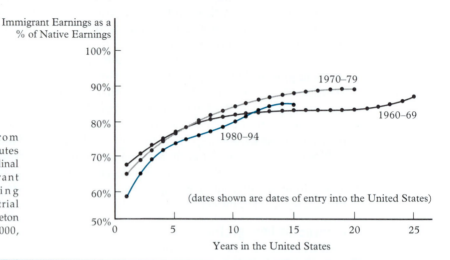

Immigrants' Initial Earnings
That immigrants initially earn substantially less than natives is hardly surprising. Even after controlling for the effects of education (the typical immigrant is less educated than the typical native), immigrants earn less owing to their difficulties with English, their unfamiliarity with American employment opportunities, and their lack of an American work history (and employers' consequent uncertainties about their productivity).

The fall in the initial earnings of successive immigrant groups relative to U.S. natives has been widely studied in recent years. It appears to reflect the fact that immigrants to the United States are coming increasingly from countries with relatively low levels of educational attainment, and they are therefore arriving in the United States with less and less human capital.[14]

Immigrants' Earnings Growth
Earnings of immigrants rise relatively quickly, which no doubt reflects their high rates of investment in human capital after arrival. After entry, immigrants typically invest in themselves by acquiring work experience and improved proficiency in English, and these investments raise the wages they can command. For example, one study found that English fluency raises immigrant earnings by an average of 17 percent in the United States, 12 percent in Canada, and 9 percent in Australia. Of course, not all immigrants have the same incentives to become proficient in English. Those who live in enclaves where business is conducted in their native tongue may have reduced

---

[14]George Borjas, "The Economics of Immigration," *Journal of Economic Literature* 32 (December 1994): 1667–1717; and George Borjas, *Heaven's Door: Immigration Policy and the American Economy* (Princeton, N.J.: Princeton University Press, 1999).

incentives to learn English, while those who are not able to return to their native countries have greater incentives to invest time and money in mastering English (political refugees are in the latter group; for an analysis, see the Empirical Study at the end of this chapter).[15]

Return Migration It is important to understand that the data underlying Figure 10.1 are from immigrants who remained working in the United States for at least 15 years after first entry. They are the ones for whom the investment in immigration was successful enough that they remained. Many of those for whom immigration does not yield the expected returns decide to return to their country of origin; indeed, about 20 percent of all moves are back to one's place of origin.[16] One study found that those who are most likely to return are the ones who were *closest to the margin* (expected the least net gains) when they first decided to come.[17] Return migration highlights another important fact: immigration, like other human-capital investments, entails risk—and not all such investments work out as hoped.

Policy Application: Restricting Immigration

Nowhere are the analytical tools of the economist more important than in the area of immigration policy. Immigration has both economic and cultural consequences, and there is some evidence that people's views on the desirability of immigration may be based largely on their attitudes toward cultural diversity.[18] However, the public debate about immigration is most often focused on claims about its economic consequences, so it is important to use economic theory to guide our analysis of these outcomes. After a brief outline of the history of U.S. immigration policy, this section will analyze in detail the economic effects of a phenomenon

---

[15]Barry R. Chiswick and Paul W. Miller, "The Endogeneity between Language and Earnings: International Analyses," *Journal of Labor Economics* 13 (April 1995): 246–288; Barry R. Chiswick and Paul W. Miller, "Language Skills and Earnings among Legalized Aliens," *Journal of Population Economics* 12 (February 1999): 63–91; Heather Antecol, Peter Kuhn, and Stephen J. Trejo, "Assimilation via Prices or Quantities? Sources of Immigrant Earnings Growth in Australia, Canada, and the United States," *Journal of Human Resources* 41 (Fall 2006): 821–840; and Eli Berman, Kevin Lang, and Erez Siniver, "Language-Skill Complementarity: Returns to Immigrant Language Acquisition," *Labour Economics* 10 (June 2003): 265–290.

[16]John Vanderkamp, "Migration Flows, Their Determinants and the Effects of Return Migration," *Journal of Political Economy* 79 (September/October 1971): 1012–1031; Fernando A. Ramos, "Outmigration and Return Migration of Puerto Ricans," in *Immigration and the Work Force*, eds. George J. Borjas and Richard B. Freeman (Chicago: University of Chicago Press, 1992); and Borjas, "The Economics of Immigration," 1691–1692.

[17]George J. Borjas and Bernt Bratsberg, "Who Leaves? The Outmigration of the Foreign-Born," *Review of Economics and Statistics* 78 (February 1996): 165–176.

[18]David Card, Christian Dustmann, and Ian Preston, "Immigration, Wages, And Compositional Amenities," *Journal of the European Economic Association,* 10 (February 2012): 78–119.

that is currently attracting much discussion in the United States: the immigration of workers whose immigration status is considered "unauthorized," because they do not have the documentation necessary to legally reside in the country.

U.S. Immigration History

The United States is a rich country whose wealth and high standard of living make it an attractive place for immigrants from nearly all parts of the world. For the first 140 years of its history as an independent country, the United States followed a policy of essentially unrestricted immigration (the only major immigration restrictions were placed on Asians and on convicts). The flow of immigrants was especially large after 1840, when U.S. industrialization and political and economic upheavals in Europe made immigration an attractive investment for millions. Officially recorded immigration peaked in the first decade of the twentieth century, when the *yearly* flow of immigrants was more than 1 percent of the population (see Table 10.1).

Restrictions   In 1921, Congress adopted the Quota Law, which set annual quotas on immigration on the basis of nationality. These quotas had the effect of reducing immigration from eastern and southern Europe. This act was followed by other laws in 1924 and 1929 that further restricted immigration from southeastern

Table 10.1

Officially Recorded Immigration: 1901 to 2012

Period	Number (in Thousands)	Annual Rate (per Thousand of U.S. Population)	Year	Number (in Thousands)	Annual Rate (per Thousand of U.S. Population)
1901–1910	8,795	10.4	2001	1,059	3.7
1911–1920	5,736	5.7	2002	1,059	3.7
1921–1930	4,107	3.5	2003	704	2.4
1931–1940	528	0.4	2004	958	3.3
1941–1950	1,035	0.7	2005	1,122	3.8
1951–1960	2,515	1.5	2006	1,266	4.2
1961–1970	3,322	1.7	2007	1,052	3.5
1971–1980	4,389	2.0	2008	1,107	3.6
1981–1990[a]	7,338	3.1	2009	1,131	3.7
1991–2000[a]	9,082	3.4	2010	1,043	3.4
			2011	1,062	3.4
			2012	1,031	3.3

[a]Includes illegal immigrants granted amnesty under the Immigration Reform and Control Act of 1986.

Source: U.S. Immigration and Naturalization Service, *Yearbook of Immigration Statistics: 2012*, Table 1, at http://www.dhs.gov/yearbook-immigration-statistics-2012-legal-permanent-residents.

Europe. These various revisions in immigration policy were motivated, in part, by widespread concern over the alleged adverse effect on native employment of the arrival of unskilled immigrants from eastern and southern Europe.

In 1965, the passage of the Immigration and Nationality Act abolished the quota system based on national origin that so heavily favored northern and western Europeans. Under this law, as amended in 1990, overall immigration is formally restricted, with most spots reserved for family-reunification purposes and relatively few (roughly 20 percent) reserved for immigrants with special skills who are admitted for employment purposes. Political refugees, who must meet certain criteria relating to persecution in their home countries, are admitted without numerical limit. The fact that immigration to the United States is a very worthwhile investment for many more people than can legally come, however, has created incentives for people to live in the country without official approval.

Unauthorized Immigration   Unauthorized immigration can be divided into two categories of roughly equal size: immigrants who enter legally but overstay or violate the provisions of their visas, and those who enter the country illegally. On an average day in 2011, roughly 150,000 people entered the United States under nonimmigrant visas, usually as students or visitors.[19] Once here, the foreigner can look for work, although working at a job under a student's or visitor's visa is not authorized. If the student or visitor is offered a job, he or she can apply for an "adjustment of status" to legally become a permanent resident, although the chances for approval as an employment-based immigrant are slim for the ordinary worker.

Many immigrants, however, enter the country without a visa. Immigrants from the Caribbean often enter through Puerto Rico, whose residents are U.S. citizens and thus are allowed free entry to the mainland. Others walk across the Mexican border. Still others are smuggled into the United States or use false documents to get through entry stations. Between 1995 and 2004, the *yearly increase* in the number of unauthorized immigrants residing in the United States was estimated to be close to 600,000, although with enhanced border security and fewer available jobs during the 2005–2010 period, yearly increases fell to about 300,000. It is thought that the total population of unauthorized immigrants peaked at roughly 12 million in 2007, but with the recession of 2008 and 2009, some of these immigrants left the country. By 2011, the population of unauthorized immigrants was estimated to be close to 11.5 million. Almost three-quarters of all unauthorized immigrants are from Mexico (59 percent) and Central America (14 percent).[20]

---

[19]Randall Monger, "Nonimmigrant Admissions to the United States: 2011," *Annual Flow Report*, U.S. Department of Homeland Security, Office of Immigration Statistics (Washington, D.C., July 2012), at http://www.dhs.gov/xlibrary/assets/statistics/publications/ni_fr_2011.pdf.

[20]Michael Hoefer, Nancy Rytina, and Bryan C. Baker, "Estimates of the Unauthorized Immigrant Population Residing in the United States: January 2011," U.S. Department of Homeland Security, Office of Immigration Statistics (Washington, D.C.: March 2012). Also see Gordon H. Hanson, "Illegal Migration from Mexico to the United States," *Journal of Economic Literature* 44 (December 2006): 869–924.

As of 2013, Americans were split over what to do about unauthorized immigration. There were calls for the enhancement of border security, especially along the Mexican border, accompanied by assertions that such immigration was harmful to Americans as a whole—by increasing the population of unskilled workers, reducing the wages of native-born workers, and putting greater demands on government spending than the unauthorized immigrants pay in taxes. On the other side, there were assertions that undocumented immigrants are fulfilling a useful economic function by performing tasks that Americans are increasingly less willing to do and that they should be given a path to achieve legal residency. Before we turn to an economic analysis of the effects of immigration on the receiving country, we will briefly describe the immigrants from Mexico, who are the focus of the current debate.

Immigrants from Mexico   Immigration to the United States from Mexico—both authorized and unauthorized—is large, for two reasons: the huge differential in income per capita between the two countries and the fact that they share a long border. In 2007, when almost 12 million Mexican immigrants were living in the United States, they constituted roughly one-third of the entire foreign-born population.[21] Of the 12 million, about half were undocumented.

Earlier, we reviewed theory suggesting that for a country with a *wider* distribution of earnings than is found in the United States, we would expect emigration to the United States to come largely from the lower end of its skill distribution. While the typical Mexican immigrant is less educated than the average American, because educational levels are generally lower in Mexico, the most recent immigrants from Mexico come from the *middle* of Mexico's skill distribution, not the bottom. For example, let us focus on Mexican men between the ages of 28 and 37. In Mexico, 23 percent of this group has between 10 and 15 years of schooling; however, among recent immigrants to the United States, 40 percent were in this educational group. In contrast, while in Mexico about two-thirds of this age group have less than 10 years of schooling, only about half of those who emigrate from Mexico have less than 10 years of education. Why is the *middle* of the Mexican educational distribution overrepresented in the immigrant group, not the lower level?

The cost of crossing the border is high, and it has become higher after the United States increased border surveillance in 2002 and beyond. Surveys done in areas of Mexico that are the source of much emigration to the United States suggest that between 80 and 95 percent of undocumented entrants use the services of a smuggler ("coyote"), whom they pay—in advance—to facilitate their crossing. The average fee charged by coyotes in 2004 was reported to be around $2,000 (in 2012 dollars)—a substantial fraction of the yearly per-capita income in Mexico.

---

[21]U.S. Census Bureau, "Race and Hispanic Origin of the Foreign-Born Population in the United States: 2007," American Community Survey Reports (Washington, D.C.: January 2010). Data in the remainder of this section are from Hanson, "Illegal Migration from Mexico to the United States."

Furthermore, the chances are probably around 50% that one will spend th
and still get caught (and returned to Mexico). While estimates sugges
investment can be recouped in 8–11 weeks of work, the fee represents a s
credit constraint that the poorest Mexicans probably cannot overcome.

The policies people advocate are based on their beliefs about the
consequences of immigration for employers, consumers, taxpayers, and workers
of various skill levels and ethnicities. Nearly everyone with an opinion on this
subject has an economic model implicitly or explicitly in mind when addressing these consequences; the purpose of the following sections is to make these
economic models explicit and to evaluate them.

Naive Views of Immigration

There are two opposing views of illegal immigration that can be considered
naive. One view is that every employed illegal immigrant deprives a citizen or
legal resident of a job. For example, a Department of Labor official told a House
committee studying immigration: "I think it is logical to conclude that if they are
actually employed, they are taking a job away from one of our American citizens."
According to this view, if x illegal immigrants are deported and others kept out,
the number of unemployed Americans would decline by x.

At the opposite end of the policy spectrum is the equally naive argument
that the illegals perform jobs no American citizen would do: "You couldn't
conduct a hotel in New York, you couldn't conduct a restaurant in New York . . .
if you didn't have rough laborers. We haven't got the rough laborers anymore. . . .
Where are we going to get the people to do that rough work?"[22]

Both arguments are simplistic because they ignore the slopes of the demand
and supply curves. Consider, for example, the labor market for the job of
"rough laborer"—any job most American citizens find distasteful. Without illegal immigrants, the restricted supply of Americans to this market would imply
a relatively high wage (W_1 in Figure 10.2). N_1 citizens would be employed. If
illegal immigrants entered the market, the supply curve would shift outward
and perhaps flatten (implying that immigrants were more responsive to wage
increases for rough laborers than citizens were). The influx of illegals would drive
the wage down to W_2, but employment would increase to N_2.

Are Americans unwilling to do the work of rough laborers? Clearly, at
the market wage of W_2, many more immigrants are willing to work at the job
than are U.S. citizens. Only N_3 citizens would want these jobs at this low wage,
while the remaining supply ($N_2 - N_3$) is made up entirely of immigrants. If there
were no immigrants, however, N_1 Americans would be employed at wage W_1
as rough laborers. Wages would be higher, as would the prices of the goods or
services produced with this labor, but the job would get done. The only shortage

---

[22]Both quotes in this section are from Elliott Abrams and Franklin S. Abrams, "Immigration Policy—
Who Gets In and Why?" *Public Interest* 38 (Winter 1975): 25–26.

Figure 10.2

Demand and Supply of Rough Laborers

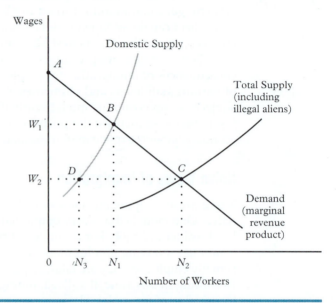

of American citizens is at the low wage of W_2; at W_1, there is no shortage (review chapter 2 for a discussion of labor shortages).

Would deporting those illegal immigrants working as rough laborers create the same number of jobs for U.S. citizens? The answer is clearly no. If the $N_2 - N_3$ immigrants working as laborers at wage W_2 were deported and all other illegal immigrants were kept from the market, the number of Americans employed as laborers would rise from N_3 to N_1 and their wages would rise from W_2 to W_1 (Figure 10.2). $N_2 - N_1$ jobs would be destroyed by the rising wage rate associated with deportation. Thus, while deportation would increase the employment and wage levels of Americans in the market for laborers, it would certainly not increase employment on a one-for-one basis.[23]

There is, however, one condition in which deportation *would* create jobs for American citizens on a one-for-one basis: when the federal minimum wage law creates a surplus of labor. Suppose, for example, that the supply of "native" laborers is represented by ABS_1 in Figure 10.3 and the total supply is represented by ABS_2. Because an artificially high wage has created a surplus, only N of the N' workers willing to work at the minimum wage can actually find employment. If some of them are illegal immigrants, deporting them—coupled with successful

---

[23]For a study suggesting that for every five Vietnamese manicurists who immigrated to California, a net of three new jobs were created, see Maya N. Federman, David E. Harrington, and Kathy J. Krynski, "Vietnamese Manicurists: Are Immigrants Displacing Natives or Finding New Nails to Polish?" *Industrial and Labor Relations Review* 59 (January 2006): 302–318.

Figure 10.3

Demand and Supply of Rough Laborers
with a Minimum Wage

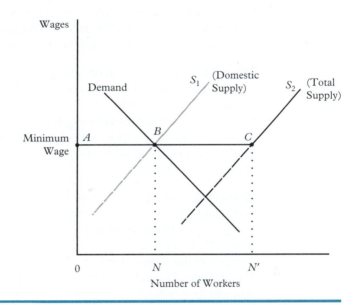

efforts to deny other immigrants access to these jobs—would create jobs for a comparable number of Americans. However, the demand curve would have to intersect the domestic supply curve (ABS_1) at or to the left of point B to prevent the wage level from rising (and thus destroying jobs) after deportation.

The analyses above ignore the possibility that if low-wage immigrant labor is prevented from coming to the jobs, employers may transfer the jobs to countries with abundant supplies of low-wage labor. Thus, it may well be the case that unskilled American workers are in competition with foreign unskilled workers anyway, whether those workers are employed in the United States or elsewhere. However, not all unskilled jobs can be moved abroad, because not all outputs can be imported (most unskilled services, for example, must be performed at the place of consumption); therefore, our analyses will continue to focus on situations in which the "export" of unskilled jobs is infeasible or very costly.

An Analysis of the Gainers and Losers

The claim that immigration is harmful to American workers is often based on a single-market analysis like that contained in Figure 10.2. It is argued that when immigration increases the supply of rough laborers, both the wages and the employment levels of American citizens working as laborers are reduced. The total wage bill paid to American laborers falls from $W_1 0 N_1 B$ in Figure 10.2 to $W_2 0 N_3 D$. Some American workers leave the market in response to the reduced wage, and those who stay earn less.

Even if the immigration of unskilled labor were to adversely affect domestic laborers, however, it would be a mistake to conclude that it is necessarily harmful to Americans as a *whole*. Let us look a bit more closely at the gains and losses we might expect to see from an influx of foreign laborers.

Consumers   Immigration of "cheap labor" clearly benefits consumers using the output of this labor. If wages are reduced and employment increases, the goods and services produced by this labor are increased in quantity and reduced in price. Indeed, a recent study suggests that the influx of low-skilled immigrants (who presumably provide household and childcare services) has made it easier for American college-educated women to pursue careers while simultaneously rearing children.[24]

Employers   Employers of rough labor (to continue our example) are obviously benefited, at least in the short run. In Figure 10.2, profits are increased from W_1AB to W_2AC. This rise in profitability will have two major effects. By raising the returns to capital, it will serve as a signal for investors to increase investments in plant and equipment. Increased profits will also induce more people to become employers. The increases in capital and the number of employers will eventually drive profits down to their normal level, but in the end, the country's stock of capital is increased and opportunities are created for some workers to become owners.

Employees in the "Rough Labor" Market   You will recall from chapters 3 and 4 that the demand curve for labor is affected by both the substitution and scale effects. A consideration of these two effects is critical to an understanding of how immigration affects native workers.

To begin our analysis of how immigration affects native workers, let us assume (as we implicitly did in drawing Figure 10.2) that immigrant and native laborers have exactly the same skills and are thus completely substitutable; put differently, we begin our analysis by assuming that low-skilled immigrants and low-skilled natives are in the same labor market. If supply to that market increases owing to immigration, the effects on wages and employment depend very much on the *elasticity* of the labor demand curve in that market. If, for example, the labor demand curve in Figure 10.2 were flatter (more elastic) than the one drawn, it is not difficult to see that the decline in laborers' wages would be smaller, and the increase in their employment would be larger, than the changes shown.

What would make for a more elastic labor demand curve? Our analyses in chapters 3 and 4 suggest that the labor demand curve is more elastic when both the substitution and scale effects are larger. That is, when wages of laborers start to fall owing to increased labor supply, the increase in labor demanded by

---

[24]Delia Furtado and Henrich Hock, "Low Skilled Immigration and Work-Fertility Tradeoffs Among High Skilled US Natives," *American Economic Review: Papers and Proceedings* 100 (May 2010): 224–228; and Patricia Cortes and Jose Tessada, "Low-Skilled Immigration and the Labor Supply of Highly Skilled Women," *American Economic Journal: Applied Economics* 3 (July 2011): 88–123.

employers will be larger if (a) the lower cost of production spurs a larger increase in consumer demand (the scale effect), and (b) there is greater use of laborers in producing any given level of output (the substitution effect). In the presence of an influx of immigrant laborers, then, larger scale and substitution effects will moderate the decline in native laborers' wages (and thus the extent to which they withdraw from work in that market).

Our analysis of the market for laborers has assumed so far that the influx of immigrants does not *shift* the demand curve for laborers (which was held fixed in Figure 10.2). Immigration, however, increases the population of consumers in the United States, thereby increasing the demand for mechanics, bus drivers, retail clerks, teachers, construction workers, truck drivers, and so forth. Some of this population increase may directly call for more rough laborers (such as roofers and meat packers), but the increased demand for other low-wage jobs (landscape workers, parking lot attendants, childcare workers) may arise because more natives are working, or working longer, outside the home.[25] If the labor demand curve in Figure 10.2 were to shift to the right, the downward effects on wages in the market for rough labor would be further moderated (if the shift in demand were large enough, wages for laborers might even rise).

Employees in Other Labor Markets   Let us now consider how the influx of rough laborers affects natives in *other* labor markets. For ease of exposition, we will call these other labor markets "skilled," although all we really mean by this term is that jobs in this market require characteristics (such as the ability to communicate clearly in English) that make the substitution of immigrants for natives difficult.[26]

For workers in skilled markets, a wage change in the market for rough labor will have scale and substitution effects that work in opposite directions. If wages for rough laborers fall, and if skilled and unskilled workers are substitutes in production, the substitution effect will tend to *reduce* the demand for skilled workers. The falling cost of unskilled labor, however, may also trigger a scale effect that *increases* the demand for skilled labor—and the size of this scale effect would be enhanced by the overall growth in population we noted earlier. Which effect will dominate?

Theoretical analysis cannot *prove* that the scale effect dominates and that the demand for skilled workers is therefore increased by the immigration of unskilled labor if the two grades of labor are substitutes in the production process; however, an increase in demand for skilled workers remains a distinct possibility. If the scale effect does dominate, the rightward shift in the demand for skilled workers will, as shown in Figure 10.4, tend to increase wages and employment in

---

[25]Delia Furtado and Henrich Hock, "Low Skilled Immigration and Work-Fertility Tradeoffs Among High Skilled US Natives"; and Patricia Cortes and Jose Tessada, "Low-Skilled Immigration and the Labor Supply of Highly Skilled Women."

[26]Giovanni Peri and Chad Sparber, "Task Specialization, Immigration, and Wages," *American Economic Journal: Applied Economics* 1 (July 2009): 135–169.

Figure 10.4

Market for "Skilled" Labor

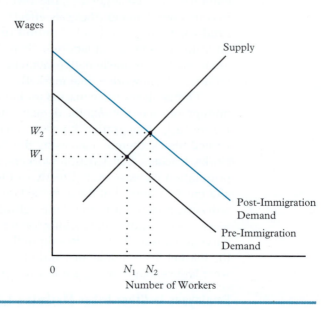

skilled markets. (Of course, any type of labor that is *complementary* with unskilled labor in the production process—supervisory workers, for example—can expect to gain from an influx of unskilled immigrants, because there would be no substitution effect.)

Empirical Estimates of the Effects on Natives

Because of the intense concern about the effects of illegal immigration on American workers, much of the empirical work has focused on the effects of an influx of low-skilled immigrants on those in the United States, especially in low-skilled sectors. Broadly speaking, there are two general approaches taken by these studies.

One approach is to look at how the proportion of unskilled immigrants in geographical areas affects the wages of natives, especially less-skilled workers, in those areas. In these studies, care must be taken to account for the likelihood that immigrants will go to cities with the best opportunities. Once account is taken of this likelihood, most studies taking this approach find that the influx of low-skilled immigrants in the last two decades has had rather small (or even negligible) effects on the wages of workers with a high school education or less.[27] A variant of this approach is summarized in Example 10.3.

---

[27]For reviews of the literature on this topic, see Hanson, "The Economic Consequences of the International Migration of Labor," and David Card, "Immigration and Inequality," *American Economic Review: Papers and Proceedings* 99 (May 2009): 1–21.

Some economists argue, however, that estimating the effects of immigration using cities as units of observation biases the estimated wage effects on natives toward zero. They argue that many low-skilled natives respond to an influx of immigrants (who compete with them for jobs) by leaving the city and that these studies thus fail to measure the ultimate effects on their wages. Whether natives respond to immigration in this way, and—if so—how quickly, is a factual issue that has not been settled.[28]

The possibility that area-based studies produce biased results because natives migrate in response to immigration has led to a second approach to estimating the effects of immigration on natives' wages—a methodology that analyzes, at the national level, how the wages in specific human-capital groups (defined by education and experience) are affected *over time* by changes in the immigrant composition of those groups. This approach requires making assumptions about (a) the degree of substitutability between immigrants and natives *within* human-capital groups and (b) the response of capital investments over time to changes in labor supplies. The results using this second approach are highly affected by these assumptions, and estimates of the effects on natives vary. Some find that immigration lowers the wages of natives with skills similar to those of the immigrants, while others find that the wages of both unskilled and skilled natives are increased—but the magnitudes of wage changes in both sets of studies tend to be small.[29] Researchers do agree, however, that the group of workers most likely to experience any negative wage effects from increased immigration are *prior* immigrants (who are the closest substitutes for new immigrants).[30]

It seems fair to say, then, that it is not entirely clear how immigration of less-skilled workers to the United States has affected the wages, on average, of native workers. There is general agreement among researchers that if there are negative effects on the wages of natives, they will be felt mostly in the market for the less-skilled (those with high school educations or less)—that is, among those with whom immigrants are most substitutable. *The larger question about immigration, however, is whether the losses of low-skilled native workers occur in the context of an overall gain to Americans as a whole. If so, as with the case of*

[28]Card, "Immigration and Inequality."

[29]Giovanni Peri, "Rethinking the Area Approach: Immigrants and the Labor Market in California," *Journal of International Economics* 84 (May 2011): 1–14; Gianmarco I. P. Ottaviano and Giovanni Peri, "Rethinking the Effect of Immigration on Wages," *Journal of the European Economic Association* 10 (February 2010): 152–197; George J. Borjas, Jeffrey Grogger, and Gordon H. Hanson, "Immigration and the Economic Status of African-American Men," *Economica* 77 (April 2010): 255–282; Abdurrahman Aydemir and George J. Borjas, "Attenuation Bias in Measuring the Wage Impact of Immigration," *Journal of Labor Economics* 29 (January 2011): 69–112; Gordon H. Hanson, "The Economic Consequences of the International Migration of Labor"; David Card, "Immigration and Inequality"; and Steven Raphael and Eugene Smolensky, "Immigration and Poverty in the United States," *American Economic Review: Papers and Proceedings* 99 (May 2009): 41–44.

[30]Hanson, "The Economic Consequences of the International Migration of Labor"; Ottaviano and Peri, "Rethinking the Effect of Immigration on Wages."

EXAMPLE 10.3

The Mariel Boatlift and Its Effects on Miami's Wage and Unemployment Rates

Between May and September of 1980, some 125,000 Cubans were allowed to emigrate to Miami from the port of Mariel in Cuba. These immigrants, half of whom permanently settled in Miami, increased Miami's overall labor force by 7 percent in under half a year. Because two-thirds of "the Mariels" had not completed high school, and because unskilled workers made up about 30 percent of Miami's workforce, it is likely that the number of *unskilled* workers in Miami increased by 16 percent or more during this short period! Such a marked and rapid increase in labor market size is highly unusual, but it provides an interesting "natural experiment" on the consequences of immigration for a host area.

If immigration has negative effects on wages in the receiving areas, we would expect to observe that the wages of Miami's unskilled workers fell relative to the wages of its skilled workers *and* relative to the wages of unskilled workers in otherwise comparable cities. Neither relative decline occurred; in fact, the wages of unskilled black workers in Miami actually rose relative to wages of unskilled blacks in four comparison cities (Atlanta, Los Angeles, Houston, and Tampa). Similarly, the unemployment rate among low-skilled blacks in Miami improved, on average, relative to that in other cities during the five years following the boatlift. Among Hispanic workers, there was an increase in Miami's unemployment rate relative to that in the other cities in 1981, but from 1982 to 1985, the Hispanic unemployment rate in Miami fell faster than in the comparison cities.

What accounts for the absence of adverse pressures on the wages and unemployment rates of unskilled workers in the Miami area? First, concurrent rightward shifts in the demand curve for labor probably tended to offset the rightward shifts in labor supply curves.

Second, it also appears that some residents left Miami in response to the influx of immigrants and that other potential migrants went elsewhere; the rate of Miami's population growth after 1980 slowed considerably relative to that of the rest of Florida, so that by 1986, its population was roughly equal to what it was projected to be by 1986 *before* the boatlift. For locational adjustments of residents and potential in-migrants to underlie the lack of wage and unemployment effects, these adjustments would have to have been very rapid. Their presence reinforces the theoretical prediction, made earlier in this chapter, that migration flows are sensitive to economic conditions in both sending and receiving areas.

Data from: David Card, "The Impact of the Mariel Boatlift on the Miami Labor Market," *Industrial and Labor Relations Review* 43 (January 1990): 245–257. For a recent study of mass migration to Israel, with references to similar studies for France and Portugal, see Sarit Cohen-Goldner and M. Daniele Paserman, "Mass Migration to Israel and Natives' Employment Transitions," *Industrial and Labor Relations Review* 59 (July 2006): 630–652.

technological change analyzed earlier (see the end of chapter 4), an important focus of immigration policy should be on shifting some of the overall gains from immigration to those who suffer economic losses because of it. We turn next to an analysis of the economic effects of immigration—especially unauthorized immigration—on society as a whole.

Do the Overall Gains from Immigration Exceed the Losses?

So far, we have used economic theory to analyze the likely effects of immigration on various groups of natives, including consumers, owners, and skilled and unskilled workers. Theory suggests that some of these groups should be clear-cut gainers; among these are owners, consumers, and workers who are complements in production with immigrants. Workers whose labor is highly substitutable in production with immigrant labor are the most likely losers from immigration, while the gains or losses for other groups of native workers are theoretically unpredictable, owing to potentially offsetting influences of the substitution and scale effects.

In this section, we use economic theory to analyze a slightly different question: "What does economic theory say about the *overall* effects of immigration—particularly unauthorized immigration—on the host country?" Put in the context of the *normative* criteria presented in chapter 1, this section asks, "If there are both gainers and losers from immigration among natives in the host country, is it likely that the gainers would be able to compensate the losers and still feel better off?" The answer to this question will be "yes" if immigration increases the aggregate disposable income of natives.

What Do Immigrants Add?   Immigrants, whether authorized or undocumented, are both consumers and producers, so whether their influx makes those already residing in the host country richer or poorer, in the aggregate, depends on how much the immigrants *add* to overall production as compared with how much they *consume*. Let us take a simple example of elderly immigrants allowed into the country to reunite with their adult children. If these immigrants do not work, and if they are dependent on their children or on American taxpayers for their consumption, then clearly the overall per capita disposable income among natives must fall. (This decline, of course, could well be offset by the increased utility of the reunited families, in which case it would be a price the host country might be willing to pay.)

If immigrants *work* after their arrival, our profit-maximizing models of employer behavior suggest that they will be paid no more than the value of their marginal revenue product. Thus, if they rely only on their own earnings to finance their consumption, immigrants who work do not reduce the per capita disposable income of natives in the host country. Moreover, if immigrant earnings are not equal to the *full* value of the output they add to the host country, then the total disposable income of natives will increase.[31]

---

[31]One study, for example, finds that an influx of immigrants from Country X to Country Y serves to increase the exports from Y to X; see Giovanni Peri and Francisco Requena, "The Trade Creation Effect of Immigrants: Evidence from the Remarkable Case of Spain," *Canadian Journal of Economics* 43 (August 2010): 1433–1459. Other studies have found that immigrants are disproportionately represented among American *inventors*; see William R. Kerr and William F. Lincoln, "The Supply Side of Innovation: H-1B Visa Reforms and U.S. Ethnic Invention," *Journal of Labor Economics* 28 (July 2010): 473–508; and Jennifer Hunt and Marjolaine Gauthier-Loiselle, "How Much Does Immigration Boost Innovation?" *American Economic Journal: Macroeconomics* 2 (April 2010): 31–56.

Immigrants, Taxes, and Public Subsidies   Most host countries (including the United States) have government programs that may distribute benefits to immigrants. If the taxes paid by immigrants are sufficient to cover the benefits they receive from such programs, then the presence of these immigrants does not threaten the per capita disposable income of natives. Indeed, some government programs, such as national defense, are true "public goods" (whose costs are not increased by immigration), and any taxes paid by immigrants help natives defray the expenses of these programs. However, if immigrants are relatively high users of government support services, and if the taxes they pay do not cover the value of their benefits, then it is possible that the "fiscal burden" of immigration could be large enough to reduce the aggregate income of natives.

Studies of the net fiscal effects of recent *authorized* immigration suggest that these effects—measured both immediately and over the lifetimes of the immigrants and their descendants—are apparently small. That is, authorized immigrants and their descendants typically pay about the same in taxes as they receive in government benefits; moreover, a recent study suggests that immigrants may even be *less* likely to put a burden on their host communities than the native-born.[32] But what can be said about the likely fiscal effects of unauthorized immigration?

Overall Effects of Unauthorized Immigration   Undocumented immigration has been the major focus in recent years of the immigration policy debate in the United States. It is widely asserted that these generally low-skilled workers are the beneficiaries of many government services, and that their undocumented status both allows them to escape taxation and is probably associated with a relatively high propensity to commit crimes. There are good reasons to doubt all three assertions; in fact, *unauthorized immigration may be more likely to increase native incomes than officially sanctioned immigration!*

First, undocumented immigrants come mainly to work.[33] Therefore, they clearly add to the production of domestic goods and services. Second, while unauthorized immigrants do receive emergency-room treatment and their children do get schooling, they are ineligible for most government programs (welfare, food stamps, Social Security, unemployment insurance) that transfer resources to low-income citizens. Moreover, as Example 10.4 discusses, poorly educated immigrants—most of whom will be undocumented—are *much* less likely to be incarcerated than similarly educated natives!

---

[32]Una Okonkwo Osili and Jia Xie, "Do Immigrants and Their Children Free Ride More Than Natives?" *American Economic Review: Papers and Proceedings* 99 (May 2009): 28–34.

[33]Attempted illegal immigration from Mexico is estimated to be extremely sensitive to changes in Mexico's real wage rate; see Gordon Hanson and Antonio Spilimbergo, "Illegal Immigration, Border Enforcement, and Relative Wages: Evidence from Apprehensions at the U.S.–Mexico Border," *American Economic Review* 89 (December 1999): 1337–1357.

EXAMPLE 10.4

Illegal Immigrants, Personal Discount Rates, and Crime

Immigrants to the United States, including those here illegally, are far less likely than the native-born to commit the kinds of violent or property crimes for which incarceration is the punishment. In 2000, for example, 3.4 percent of native-born Americans were institutionalized, with most of those in prison (the rest were in mental hospitals, drug treatment centers, or long-term-care facilities). In contrast, among immigrants, the rate of institutionalization was roughly *one-fifth* as high (at 0.7 percent). Among those with less than a high school education, a group in which crime rates are higher than average, the gap in the percentage institutionalized between the native-born and immigrants was even larger: 11 percent for the native-born, compared to 1 percent for immigrants.

While there could be several factors affecting the differential rates of incarceration, one reason for the difference may be rooted in a characteristic that human-capital theory implies that immigrants will possess: a lower-than-average personal discount rate. Immigrants, whether legal or illegal, are self-selected individuals who are willing to bear considerable costs to enter and adapt to a new country with the expectation of benefits that may lie well into the future. Among a group of people facing the same current costs and future benefits,

then, those most willing to leave their country of origin and emigrate to a new one are those with relatively low discount rates (that is, they are the most future-oriented).

People who commit crimes tend to be present-oriented; in economic terms, they have relatively high discount rates. For criminals, the perceived gains from their criminal act are in the present, while the costs—if caught—are in the future. With high discount rates, these future costs look relatively small compared to the current gains. Therefore, economic theory suggests that immigrants and criminals are likely to have very different orientations toward the future.

Within the general populace of any country, there will be a wide distribution of discount rates, and some of those who have high discount rates may turn to crime. However, immigrants are self-selected individuals who tend to have relatively low personal rates of discount, and therefore, it is not surprising that criminality among immigrants is so low.

For data on immigrants and incarceration, see Kristin F. Butcher and Anne Morrison Piehl, "Why Are Immigrants' Incarceration Rates So Low? Evidence on Selective Immigration, Deterrence, and Deportation," National Bureau of Economic Research, working paper no. 13229 (July 2007).

Third, despite their wish to hide from the government, unauthorized immigrants cannot avoid paying most taxes (especially payroll, sales, and property taxes); indeed, one study indicated that 75 percent of undocumented immigrants had income taxes withheld but that relatively few filed for a refund.[34] Additionally, since immigration reform legislation was passed in 1986, the typical way that undocumented immigrants qualify for jobs in the United States is to purchase a fake Social Security card. Employers then deduct payroll taxes and remit them to the government, and starting in the mid-1980s, the revenues that

---

[34]Gregory DeFreitas, *Inequality at Work: Hispanics in the U.S. Labor Force* (New York: Oxford University Press, 1991): 228. The same study showed minimal use of public services by illegal immigrants.

cannot be matched to a valid Social Security number (and therefore will not result in a future retirement payment) have risen dramatically—probably because of unauthorized immigration.[35]

Thus, we cannot rule out the possibility that despite governmental efforts to prohibit it, the "transaction" of unauthorized immigration is—to use the normative terminology of chapter 1—Pareto-improving. The immigrants themselves clearly gain (otherwise they would go back home), and the size of the gains experienced by Mexican immigrants relative to their incomes in Mexico suggest that these gains are large. Some natives clearly gain, while others may lose, but we have just seen that it is quite likely that the aggregate gain to natives is positive. Thus, economic theory suggests that with an overall gain to society, a critical part of the policy debate on unauthorized immigration should focus on programs or policies *that would tax the likely gainers in order to compensate those most likely to lose from such immigration*. We will return in chapter 16 to the issue of how best to compensate those who lose from policies that benefit society in general.

Employee Turnover

While this chapter has focused so far on the underlying causes and consequences of geographic mobility, it is important to remember that the mobility of employees among employers (also known as "turnover" or "separations") can take place *without* a change of residence. We noted in chapter 5 that employees generally find it costly to search for alternative job offers, and in this section, we use the principles of our human-capital model to highlight certain *patterns* in employee turnover.

Growing from our discussions in chapters 8 and 9, we would expect that individuals differ in their personal discount rates and in the psychic costs they attach to quitting one employer to find another. These differences imply that some workers are much more likely than others to move among employers, even if those in both groups face the same set of wage offers. Indeed, one study found that almost half of all turnover over a 3-year period involved the 13 percent of workers who had 3 or more separations during the period.[36] Despite individual idiosyncrasies, however, there are clearly *systematic* factors that influence the patterns of job mobility.

Wage Effects

Human-capital theory predicts that, *other things equal*, a given worker will have a greater probability of quitting a low-wage job than a higher-paying one. That is, workers employed at lower wages than they could obtain elsewhere are the

---

[35]See Office of the Inspector General, Social Security Administration. "Recent Efforts to Reduce the Size and Growth of the Social Security Administration's Earnings Suspense File," 16–18, May 2002; http://www.ssa.gov/oig/ADOBEPDF/A-03-01-30035.pdf.

[36]Patricia M. Anderson and Bruce D. Meyer, "The Extent and Consequences of Job Turnover," *Brookings Papers on Economic Activity: Microeconomics* (1994): 177–248.

most likely to quit. Indeed, a very strong and consistent finding in virtually all studies of worker quit behavior is that, holding worker characteristics constant, employees in industries with lower wages have higher quit rates. At the level of individual workers, research indicates that those who change employers have more to gain from a job change than those who stay and that, indeed, their wage growth after changing is faster than it would have been had they stayed.[37]

Effects of Employer Size

From Table 10.2, it can be seen that *quit rates tend to decline as firm size increases.* One explanation for this phenomenon is that large firms offer more possibilities for transfers and promotions. Another, however, builds on the fact that large firms generally pay higher wages.[38] This explanation asserts that large firms tend to have highly mechanized production processes, where the output of one work team is highly dependent on that of production groups preceding it in the production chain. Larger firms, it is argued, have greater needs for dependable and steady workers because employees who shirk their duties can impose great

Table 10.2

Monthly Quit Rates per 100 Workers by Firm Size, Selected Industries (1977–1981 Averages)

Industry	Number of Employees			
	<250	250–499	500–999	1,000 and Over
All manufacturing	3.28	3.12	2.40	1.50
Food and kindred products	3.46	4.11	3.95	2.28
Fabricated metal products	3.33	2.64	2.12	1.20
Electrical machinery	3.81	3.12	2.47	1.60
Transportation equipment	3.90	2.78	2.21	1.41

Source: Walter Oi, "The Durability of Worker-Firm Attachments," report to the U.S. Department of Labor, Office of the Assistant Secretary for Policy, Evaluation, and Research, March 25, 1983, Table 1.

---

[37]Donald O. Parsons, "Models of Labor Market Turnover: A Theoretical and Empirical Survey," in *Research in Labor Economics*, vol. 1, ed. Ronald Ehrenberg (Greenwich, Conn.: JAI Press, 1977): 185– 223; Michael G. Abbott and Charles M. Beach, "Wage Changes and Job Changes of Canadian Women: Evidence from the 1986–87 Labour Market Activity Survey," *Journal of Human Resources* 29 (Spring 1994): 429–460; Christopher J. Flinn, "Wages and Job Mobility of Young Workers," *Journal of Political Economy* 94, no. 3, pt. 2 (June 1986): S88–S110; and Monica Galizzi and Kevin Lang, "Relative Wages, Wage Growth, and Quit Behavior," *Journal of Labor Economics* 16 (April 1998): 367–391.

[38]Walter Oi, "The Fixed Employment Costs of Specialized Labor," in *The Measurement of Labor Cost*, ed. Jack E. Triplett (Chicago: University of Chicago Press, 1983).

costs on a highly interdependent production process. Large firms, then, establish "internal labor markets" for the reasons suggested in chapter 5; that is, they hire workers at entry-level jobs and carefully observe such hard-to-screen attributes as reliability, motivation, and attention to detail. Once having invested time and effort in selecting the best workers for its operation, a large firm finds it costly for such workers to quit. Thus, large firms pay high wages to reduce the probability of quitting because they have substantial firm-specific screening investments in their workers.[39]

Gender Differences

It has been widely observed that women workers have higher quit rates, and therefore shorter job tenures, than men. To a large degree, this higher quit rate probably reflects lower levels of firm-specific human-capital investments. We argued in chapter 9 that the interrupted careers of "traditional" women workers rendered many forms of human-capital investment less beneficial than would otherwise be the case, and lower levels of firm-specific training could account for lower wages, lower job tenures, and higher quit rates.[40] In fact, once the lower wages and shorter careers of women are controlled for, there appears to be no difference between the sexes in the propensity to quit a job, especially among those with more than a high school education.[41]

Cyclical Effects

Another implication of human-capital theory is that workers will have a higher probability of quitting when it is relatively easy for them to obtain a better job quickly. Thus, when labor markets are *tight* (jobs are more plentiful relative to job seekers), one would expect the quit rate to be higher than when labor markets are *loose* (few jobs are available and many workers are being laid off). This prediction is confirmed in studies of time-series data. Quit rates tend to rise when the labor market is tight and fall when it is loose. One measure of tightness is the unemployment rate; the negative relationship between the quit rate and unemployment can be readily seen in Figure 10.5.

---

[39]This argument is developed more fully and elegantly in Walter Oi, "Low Wages and Small Firms," in *Research in Labor Economics*, vol. 12, ed. Ronald Ehrenberg (Greenwich, Conn.: JAI Press, 1991).

[40]Jacob Mincer and Boyan Jovanovic, "Labor Mobility and Wages," in *Studies in Labor Markets*, ed. Sherwin Rosen (Chicago: University of Chicago Press, 1981).

[41]Anne Beeson Royalty, "Job-to-Job and Job-to-Nonemployment Turnover by Gender and Education Level," *Journal of Labor Economics* 16 (April 1998): 392–443; and Anders Frederiksen, "Explaining Individual Job Separations in a Segregated Labor Market," working paper no. 490, Industrial Relations Section, Princeton University, August 2004.

Figure 10.5

The Quit Rate and Labor Market Tightness

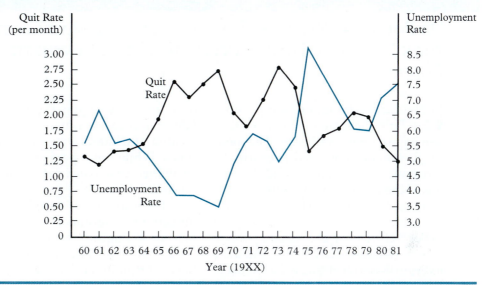

Employer Location

Economic theory predicts that when the costs of quitting a job are relatively low, mobility is more likely. Industries with high concentrations of employment in urban areas, where a worker's change of employer does not necessarily require investing in a change of residence, appear to have higher rates of turnover (holding wage rates and employee age constant) than industries concentrated in nonmetropolitan areas.[42]

Is More Mobility Better?

On the one hand, mobility is socially useful because it promotes both individual well-being and the quality of job matches. In chapter 8, we pointed out, for example, that mobility (or at least the *threat* of mobility) was essential to the creation of compensating wage differentials. Moreover, the greater the number of workers and employers in the market at any given time, the more flexibility an economy has in making job matches that best adapt to a changing environment. Indeed, when focusing on this aspect of job mobility, economists have

---

[42]Parsons, "Models of Labor Market Turnover"; and Farrell E. Bloch, "Labor Turnover in U.S. Manufacturing Industries," *Journal of Human Resources* 14 (Spring 1979): 236–246.

EMPIRICAL STUDY

Do Political Refugees Invest More in Human Capital than Economic Immigrants? The Use of Synthetic Cohorts

Individuals who immigrate presumably do so because they believe they will improve their well-being. For some, the decision is motivated primarily by economic considerations, and the timing of the move is both voluntary and planned; this group can be labeled "economic immigrants." Others may be forced to flee their country of origin for political reasons (often on short notice), and these individuals can often qualify for "refugee" status in the country of destination.

Because refugees have done less advance planning, we might expect that they earn less than comparably skilled economic immigrants immediately upon arrival in their new country. Unlike economic immigrants, however, who can return to their country of origin if the move does not work out, refugees cannot safely return. We might thus suppose that after arrival, refugees also have a greater incentive to invest in human capital (including the mastery of English) and in becoming citizens. Thus, we would expect that their earnings would rise faster than those of economic immigrants.

Ideally, in testing to see whether refugees invest more in human capital and have more rapid earnings growth than economic immigrants, we would like to have data that follow individual immigrants through time. Panel data are very expensive to collect, however, because individuals must be located and interviewed at multiple times. While not a perfect substitute, an alternative to panel data is the use of *synthetic cohorts*.

For example, one study sampled the earnings, educational level, and proficiency in English—as reported in the 1980 Census of Population—among the cohort of immigrants who came to the United States between 1975 and 1980. The study then sampled, again for those who immigrated in 1975–1980, data on the same variables from the 1990 Census. Because the workers in the 1980 sample are not necessarily the same as those in the 1990 sample (owing to randomized sampling and the possibility that some of those sampled in 1980 had died or had left the United States by 1990), we are not actually obtaining 1990 data on exactly the same group we observed in 1980; for this reason, the 1990 cohort can be called "synthetic" (an artificial representation of the earlier cohort).

If the sampling from both census years is random, and all departures from the sample between 1980 and 1990 were randomly determined, the results from this comparison should produce the same results, on average, as we would obtain if we were following the same individuals from 1980 to 1990. *The problem with this use of synthetic cohorts is that the economic immigrants who leave are likely to be those who were least successful here*; thus, the measured earnings gain for the group of economic immigrants from 1980 to 1990 will be biased upward (only those who are relatively successful stay on long enough to be counted in the 1990 data). If economic immigrants with the smallest earnings growth can leave, while refugees cannot, comparisons of the 1980–1990 earnings growth will be biased against finding evidence supportive of the hypothesis that refugees will exhibit *greater* earnings growth.

Despite the bias discussed earlier, the study found that while the earnings of refugees were 6 percent lower than those of economic immigrants in 1980, they were 20 percent greater by 1990. Moreover, refugees were more likely to be enrolled in school programs in 1980, a higher proportion of them achieved proficiency in English during the 1980s, and more had attained citizenship between 1980 and 1990. These data appear to be consistent with the hypothesis that refugees have greater incentives to invest in human capital than economic immigrants, presumably because they cannot return to their country of origin.

Source: Kalena E. Cortes, "Are Refugees Different from Economic Immigrants? Some Empirical Evidence on the Heterogeneity of Immigrant Groups in the United States," *Review of Economics and Statistics* 86 (May 2004): 465–480.

long worried whether economies have *enough* mobility. A case in point is the concern whether employers have created "job lock" by adopting pension plans and health insurance policies that are not portable if the employee leaves the firm.[43] As we saw in chapter 5, mobility costs introduce monopsonistic conditions into the labor market, which tend to lower wages relative to marginal revenue product.

On the other hand, however, lower mobility costs (and thus greater mobility) among workers also weaken the incentives of both employers and employees to invest in specific training or information particular to a job match. Failure to make these investments, it can be argued, reduces the productive potential of employees.

[43]See Stuart Dorsey, "Pension Portability and Labor Market Efficiency: A Survey of the Literature," *Industrial and Labor Relations Review* 48 (January 1995): 276–292; Kevin T. Stroupe, Eleanor D. Kinney, and Thomas J. Kniesner, "Chronic Illness and Health Insurance-Related Job Lock," *Journal of Policy Analysis and Management* 20 (Summer 2001): 525–544; Donna B. Gilleskie and Byron F. Lutz, "The Impact of Employer-Provided Health Insurance on Dynamic Employment Transitions," *Journal of Human Resources* 37 (Winter 2002): 129–162; and Mark C. Berger, Dan A. Black, and Frank A. Scott, "Is There Job Lock? Evidence from the Pre-HIPAA Era," *Southern Economic Journal* 70 (April 2004): 953–976.

Review Questions

1. The licensing of such occupations as nurses and doctors in the United States requires people in those occupations to pass a test administered by the state in which they seek to work. Saying that "every time a health-care worker moves, some bureaucrat tells him he can't work," a national newspaper argued that the United States could reduce health-care costs if it removed state-to-state licensing barriers.

   a. From the perspective of positive economics, what are the labor-market effects of having states, rather than the federal government, license professionals?

   b. Who would gain and who would lose from federalization of occupational licensing?

2. One way for the government to facilitate economic growth is for it to pay workers in depressed areas to move to regions where jobs are more plentiful. What would be the labor-market effects of such a policy?

3. A television program examining the issue of Mexican immigration stated that most economists believe immigration is a benefit to the United States.

   a. State the chain of reasoning underlying this view.

   b. From a normative perspective, is the key issue wage effects on native workers or subsidies of immigrants by the host country? Why?

4. Suppose the United States increases the penalties for illegal immigration to include long jail sentences for illegal *workers*. Analyze the effects of this increased penalty on the wages and employment levels of *all* affected groups of workers.

5. Other things equal, firms usually prefer their workers to have low quit rates. However, from a social perspective, quit rates can be too low. Why do businesses prefer low quit rates, and what are the social disadvantages of having such rates be "too low"?

6. The last three decades in the United States have been characterized by a very wide gap between the wages of those with more education and those with less. Suppose that workers eventually adjust to this gap by investing more in education, with the result that the wages of less-skilled workers rise faster than those of the more-skilled (so that the wage gap between the two falls). How would a decline in the wage gap between the skilled and the unskilled affect immigration to the United States?

7. It has been said, "The fact that quit rates in Japan are lower than in the United States suggests that Japanese workers are inherently more loyal to their employers than are American workers." Evaluate this assertion that where quit rates are lower, workers have stronger preferences for loyalty.

8. Two oil-rich Middle East countries compete with each other for the services of immigrants from India and Pakistan who perform menial jobs that local workers are unwilling to perform. Country A does not allow women to work, drive, or go out of the house without a chaperone. Country B has no such restrictions. Would you expect the wages that these two countries pay for otherwise comparable *male* immigrants to be roughly equal? Explain your answer.

9. If one were to build an economic model of crimes such as theft, it would contain the

same elements as the human-capital model of investments. The difference is that with theft, unlike with human-capital investments, the gains from the activity are *immediate* and the costs (if caught) are distributed across *future* years. With this distinction in mind, use the elements of human-capital theory to analyze whether immigrants are more or less likely than are citizens of similar income to commit the crime of theft.

10. A recent study by a noted economist has found evidence that a 10 percent increase in immigration within a given skill group reduces the wages of "natives" in that skill group by 3.5 percent. One social commentator has said, "These findings suggest only one conclusion: immigration is bad for American workers and therefore bad for American society." Using economic theory, comment on this quote.

Problems

1. Rose lives in a poor country where she earns $5,000 per year. She has the opportunity to move to a rich country as a temporary worker for 5 years. Doing the same work, she'll earn $35,000 per year in the rich country. The cost of moving is $2,000, and it would cost her $10,000 more per year to live in the rich country. Rose's discount rate is 10 percent. Rose decides not to move because she will be separated from her friends and family. Estimate the psychic costs of Rose's move.

2. Suppose that the demand for rough laborers is $L_D = 100 - 10W$, where $W =$ the wage in dollars per hour and $L =$ the number of workers. If immigration increases the number of rough laborers hired from 50 to 60, by how much will the short-run profits of employers in this market change?

3. Clare lives in France and earns $30,000 per year at her job. She is considering a job offer in the United States, which would give her a salary of $32,000 per year for the next 4 years, after which she will return to France and start her university education. Moving costs (to the United States and back) would be $6,000, living expenses are similar in both places, and her personal discount rate is 6 percent. If she moved to the United States for this 4-year experience, what is the present value of her net gain or loss?

Wage ($)	Demand	Domestic Supply	Supply
3	30	22	4
4	29	23	4
5	28	24	4
6	27	25	4
7	26	26	4
8	25	27	4
9	24	28	4
10	23	29	4

4. The following table summarizes the market for labor in an occupation. "Demand" is the number (in thousands) of employees firms would be interested in hiring at particular wages. "Domestic supply" is the number (in thousands) of native workers who are interested in working in the occupation at particular wages, and "immigrant supply" is the number (in thousands) of immigrants who are interested in working at particular wages.
   a. Graph the following curves for this labor market: demand for labor, domestic supply, and total supply of workers.

   b. What is the equilibrium wage rate before immigration? How many workers would be hired?

   c. What is the equilibrium wage rate after immigration? How many workers would be hired? How many domestic workers would be hired? How many immigrant workers would be hired?

   d. Comparing your answers in parts b and c, has immigration caused a change in the number of domestic workers hired? What was the change, if any? Why did the change, if any, occur?

5. The demand for labor in a domestic industry is $D = 36 - 2W$, where W = the wage rate and D = the number (in thousands) of employees whom the firms would be interested in hiring at particular wage rates. $S_{domestic} = 9 + W$, where

$S_{domestic}$ = the number (in thousands) of native workers who are interested in working in the industry at particular wages. $S_{total} = 10 + 2W$, where S_{total} is the *total* number (including immigrants) of workers who are interested in working in the industry at particular wages.

   a. Graph the following curves for this labor market: demand for labor, domestic supply, supply of immigrant workers, and total supply of workers.

   b. What is the equilibrium wage rate before immigration? How many workers would be hired?

   c. What is the equilibrium wage rate after immigration? How many workers would be hired? How many domestic workers would be hired? How many immigrant workers would be hired?

Selected Readings

Abowd, John M., and Richard B. Freeman, eds. *Immigration, Trade, and the Labor Market.* Chicago: University of Chicago Press, 1991.

Borjas, George. "The Economics of Immigration." *Journal of Economic Literature* 32 (December 1994): 1667–1717.

———. *Friends or Strangers.* New York: Basic Books, 1990.

———. *International Differences in the Labor Market Performance of Immigrants.* Kalamazoo, Mich.: W. E. Upjohn Institute for Employment Research, 1988.

Borjas, George J., ed. *Issues in the Economics of Immigration.* Chicago: University of Chicago Press, 2000.

Borjas, George J., and Richard B. Freeman, eds. *Immigrants and the Work Force.* Chicago: University of Chicago Press, 1992.

Chiswick, Barry. *Illegal Aliens: Their Employment and Employers.* Kalamazoo, Mich.: W. E. Upjohn Institute for Employment Research, 1988.

———. "Illegal Immigration and Immigration Control." *Journal of Economic Perspectives* 2 (Summer 1988): 101–115.

Hamermesh, Daniel S., and Frank D. Bean, eds. *Help or Hindrance? The Economic Implications of Immigration for African Americans.* New York: Russell Sage Foundation, 1998.

Hanson, Gordon H. "Illegal Migration from Mexico to the United States." *Journal of Economic Literature* 44 (December 2006): 869–924.

Parsons, Donald O. "Models of Labor Market Turnover: A Theoretical and Empirical Survey." In *Research in Labor Economics*, vol. 1, ed. Ronald Ehrenberg, 185–223. Greenwich, Conn.: JAI Press, 1977.

Smith, James P., and Barry Edmonston, eds. *The New Americans: Economic, Demographic, and Fiscal Effects of Immigration.* Washington, D.C.: National Academy Press, 1997.

CHAPTER 11

Pay and Productivity: Wage Determination within the Firm

In the simplest model of the demand for labor (presented in chapters 3 and 4), employers had few managerial decisions to make; they simply *found* the marginal productivity schedules and market wages of various kinds of labor and hired the profit-maximizing amount of each kind. In a model like this, there was no need for employers to design a compensation policy.

Most employers, however, appear to give considerable attention to their compensation policies, and some of the reasons have already been explored. For example, employers offering specific training (see chapter 5) have a zone into which the wage can feasibly fall, and they must balance the costs of raising the wages of their specifically trained workers against the savings generated from a higher probability of retaining these workers. Likewise, when the compensation package is expanded to include such items as employee benefits or job safety (see chapter 8), employers must decide on the mix of wages and other valued items in the compensation package. We have also seen (in chapter 5) that under certain conditions, employers will behave monopsonistically, in which case they set their wages rather than take them as given.

EXAMPLE 11.1

The Wide Range of Possible Productivities: The Case of the Factory That Could Not Cut Output

In 1987, a manufacturer of airguns ("BB guns") in New York State found that its sales were lagging behind production. Wanting to cut production by about 20 percent without engaging in widespread layoffs, the company decided to temporarily cut back from a 5-day to a 4-day workweek. To its amazement, the company found that despite this 20 percent reduction in working hours, production levels were not reduced—its workers produced as many airguns in 4 days as they previously had in 5!

Central to the problem of achieving its desired output reduction was that the company paid its workers on the basis of the number of items they produced. Faced with the prospect of a temporary cut in their earnings, its workers reduced time on breaks and increased their pace of work sufficiently to maintain their previous levels of output (and earnings). The company was therefore forced to institute artificial caps on employee production; when these individual output quotas had been met, the worker was not allowed to produce more.

The inability to cut output, despite cutting back on hours of work, suggests how wide the range of possible worker productivity can be in some operations. Clearly, then, careful attention by management to the motivation and morale of employees can have important consequences, both privately and socially.

This chapter will explore in more detail the complex relationship between compensation and productivity. Briefly put, employers must make managerial decisions rooted in the following practical realities:

1. Workers differ from each other in work habits that greatly affect productivity but are often difficult (costly) to observe before, and sometimes even after, hiring takes place.[1]
2. The productivity of a given worker with a given level of human capital can vary considerably over time or in different environments, depending on his or her level of motivation (see Example 11.1).
3. Worker productivity over a given period of time is a function of innate ability, the level of effort, and the environment (the weather, general business conditions, or the actions of other employees).
4. Being highly productive is usually not just a matter of slavishly following orders but rather of *taking the initiative* to help advance the employer's objectives.[2]

---

[1]The productivity of supervisors also varies considerably across individuals; see Edward Lazear, Kathryn Shaw, and Christopher Stanton, "The Value of Bosses," working paper no. 18317, National Bureau of Economic Research (Cambridge, Mass.: August 2012).

[2]For a stimulating article from which much of the ensuing discussion draws, see Herbert A. Simon, "Organizations and Markets," *Journal of Economic Perspectives* 5 (Spring 1991): 24–44. For more formal treatment of contracts and incentives, refer to James M. Malcomson, "Contracts, Hold-Up and Labor Markets," *Journal of Economic Literature* 35 (December 1997): 1916–1957, and Canice Prendergast, "The Provision of Incentives in Firms," *Journal of Economic Literature* 37 (March 1999): 7–63.

Employers, then, must choose management strategies and compensation policies to obtain the right (that is, profit-maximizing) kind of employees and offer them the optimum incentives for production. In doing so, they must weigh the costs of various policies against the benefits. The focus of this chapter is on the role of firms' compensation policies in optimizing worker productivity.

Motivating Workers: An Overview of the Fundamentals

Employers and workers each have their own objectives and concerns, and the incentives imbedded in the employment relationship are critical to aligning these separate interests. We first present an overview of the key features of this relationship before moving on in later sections to analyses of various compensation schemes that employers can adopt to induce high productivity among their workers.

The Employment Contract

The employment relationship can be thought of as a contract between the employer (the "principal") and the employee (the "agent"). The employee is hired to help advance the employer's objectives in return for receiving wages and other benefits. Often, there are understandings or implied promises that if employees work hard and perform well, they will be promoted to higher-paying jobs as their careers progress.

Formal Contracts The agreement by an employee to perform tasks for an employer in return for current and future pay can be thought of as a contract. A *formal* contract, such as one signed by a bank and a homeowner for the repayment of a loan, lays out quite explicitly all that each party promises to do and what will happen if either party fails to perform as promised. Once signed, a formal contract cannot be abrogated by either party without penalty. Disputes over performance can be referred to courts of law or other third parties for resolution.

Implicit Contracts Unlike formal contracts, most employment contracts are *incomplete* and *implicit*. They are usually incomplete in the sense that rarely are all the specific tasks that may be required of employees spelled out in advance. Doing so would limit the flexibility of employers in responding to changing conditions, and it would also require that employers and employees renegotiate their employment contract when each new situation arises—which would be costly to both parties.

Employment contracts are also implicit in the sense that they are normally a set of informal understandings that are too vague to be legally enforceable. For example, just what has an employee promised to do when she has agreed to "work hard," and how can it be proved she has failed to do so? Specifically, what has a firm promised to do when it has promised to "promote deserving employees as opportunities arise"? Furthermore, employees can almost always quit a job at will, and employers often have great latitude in firing employees; hence, the employment contract is one that can usually be abrogated by one party or the other without legal penalty.[3]

The severe limits on legal enforceability make it essential that implicit contracts be *self-enforcing*. We turn now to a discussion of the difficulties that must be surmounted in making employment contracts self-enforcing.

Coping with Information Asymmetries

It is often advantageous for one or both parties to cheat by reneging on their promises in one way or other. Opportunities for cheating are enhanced when information is *asymmetric*—that is, when one party knows more than the other about its intentions or performance under the contract. For example, suppose an insurance company promises a newly hired insurance adjuster that she will receive a big raise in four years if she "does a good job." The company may later try to refuse her the raise she deserves by falsely claiming her work was not good enough. Alternatively, the adjuster, who works out of the office and away from supervisory oversight most of the time, may have incentives to "take it easy" by doing cursory or overly generous estimates of client losses. How can these forms of cheating be avoided?

Of course, sanctions against cheating are embedded in the formal agreements made by employers and employees. Employers who break the provisions of agreements they have signed with their unions can be sued or legally subjected to a strike, for example, but this requires that cheating actually be *proved*. How can we reduce the chances of being cheated when contracts are informal and the threat of formal punishment is absent?

Discouraging Cheating: Signaling
One way to avoid being cheated is to transact with the "right kind" of person, and to do this, we must find a way to induce the other party to reveal—or *signal*—the truth about its actual characteristics or intentions. Suppose, for example, that an employer wants to hire employees who are willing to defer current gratification for long-term gain (that is, it wants employees who do not highly discount the future). Simply asking applicants if they are willing to delay gratification might not evoke honest answers. There are ways, however, an employer could cause applicants to signal their preferences indirectly.

---

[3]The doctrine of *employment-at-will*, under which employers (and employees) have the right to terminate an employment relationship at any time, has historically prevailed in the United States. Those not subject to this doctrine in the United States have included unionized workers with contract provisions governing discharges, tenured teachers, and workers under some civil service systems. A number of state courts also have adopted public policy and/or implicit contract exceptions to the doctrine. For a discussion of these issues, see Ronald Ehrenberg, "Workers' Rights: Rethinking Protective Labor Legislation," in *Rethinking Employment Policy*, eds. Lee Bawden and Felicity Skidmore (Washington, D.C.: Urban Institute Press, 1989). There is some evidence that making it less costly for employers to fire workers increases workers' effort; see Pedro S. Martins, "Dismissals for Cause: The Difference That Just Eight Paragraphs Can Make," *Journal of Labor Economics* 27 (April 2009): 257–279.

As pointed out in chapter 8, the employer could offer its applicants relatively low current wages and a large pension benefit upon retirement. Potential applicants with relatively high discount rates would find this pay package less attractive than applicants with low discount rates, and they would be discouraged from either applying for the job or accepting an offer if it were tendered.

Another way this firm could induce applicants to signal something about their true discount rate is to require a college degree or some other training investment as a hiring standard. As noted in chapter 9, people with high discount rates are less likely to make investments of any kind, so the firm's hiring standard should discourage those with high discount rates from seeking offers.

The essence of signaling, then, is the voluntary revelation of truth in *behavior*, not just statements. Many of the compensation policies discussed in the remainder of this chapter are at least partially aimed at eliciting truthful signals from job applicants or employees.[4]

Discouraging Cheating: Self-Enforcement

Even the "right kind" of people often have incentives to underperform on their promises. Economists have come to call this type of cheating *opportunistic behavior*, and it occurs not because people intend from the outset to be dishonest but because they generally try to advance their own interests by adjusting their behavior to unfolding opportunities. Thus, the challenge is to adopt compensation policies that more or less automatically induce both parties to adhere to their promises.[5]

The key to a self-enforcing agreement is that losses are imposed on the cheater that do not depend on proving a contract violation has occurred. In the labor market, the usual punishment for cheating on agreements is that the victim severs the employment relationship; consequently, self-enforcement requires that *both employer and employee derive more gains from honest continuation of the existing employment relationship than from severing it*. If workers are receiving more from the existing relationship than they expect to receive elsewhere, they will automatically lose if they shirk their duties and are fired. If employers profit more from keeping their existing workers than from investing in replacements, they will suffer by reneging on promises and having workers quit.

Creating a Surplus

Incentives for both parties to live up to an implicit agreement are strongest when workers are getting paid more than they could get in alternative employment yet less than the value of their marginal product to the firm. The gap between their marginal revenue product to the firm and their alternative

---

[4]For a formal model that uses educational attainment as a signal for innate ability (which is difficult for an employer to observe directly), refer back to chapter 9. For a thorough review of signaling theory, see John G. Riley, "Silver Signals: Twenty-Five Years of Screening and Signaling," *Journal of Economic Literature* 39 (June 2001): 432–478.

[5]See H. Lorne Carmichael, "Self-Enforcing Contracts, Shirking, and Life Cycle Incentives," *Journal of Economic Perspectives* 3 (Fall 1989): 65–84, for a more complete discussion of the importance of self-enforcement to implicit contracting.

wage represents a *surplus* that can be divided between employer and employee. This surplus must be *shared* if the implicit contract is to be self-enforcing, because if one party receives the entire surplus, the other party has nothing to lose by terminating the employment relationship. A graphic representation of the division of a surplus is given in Figure 11.1, where we see that attempts by one party to increase its share of the surplus will reduce the other party's losses from terminating the employment relationship.

Surpluses are usually associated with some earlier investment by the employer. In chapter 5, we saw that investments by the firm in specific training or in the hiring/evaluation process enabled workers' productivity and wages to exceed their alternatives. Firms can also create a surplus by investing in their *reputations*. For example, an employer that is well known for keeping its promises about future promotions or pay raises can attract workers of higher productivity at lower cost than can employers with poor reputations. (A firm with a poor reputation for performing on its promises must pay a compensating wage differential to attract workers of given quality away from employers with good reputations.) Because the good reputation increases productivity relative to the wage paid, a surplus is created that can be divided between the firm and its workers.

Figure 11.1

Two Alternative Divisions
of the Surplus

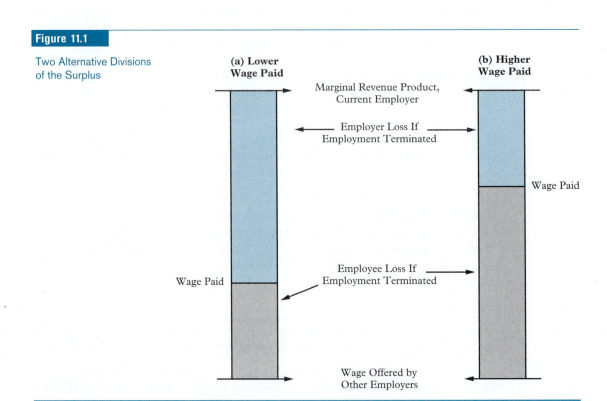

Motivating Workers

Beyond the issue of enforceability, employment contracts address the employer's need to motivate workers. Workers can be viewed as utility maximizers, and "putting forth their best efforts" may entail working hard when they are sick or distracted by personal problems, or it may involve a work pace that they find taxing. Employees can be assumed to do what they feel is in their own interests unless induced to do otherwise by the employer's system of rewards. How can we create rewards that give employees incentives to work toward the goals of their employers?

Pay for Performance   The most obvious way to motivate workers is to pay them based on their individual output. Linking pay to output creates the presumption of strong incentives for productivity, but there are two general problems that incentive pay schemes must confront.[6] One problem is that using output-based pay has both benefits and costs to an employer, and both are affected by the extent to which a worker's output is influenced by forces outside his or her control. Jane, for example, may be willing to put forth 10 percent more effort if she can be sure her output (and pay) will rise by 10 percent. If machine breakdowns are so common, however, that she can only count on a 5 percent increase, she may decide that the extra 10 percent of effort is not worth it. From the employer's perspective, then, output-based pay might provide only weak incentives if Jane's effort and the resulting output are not closely linked.

From Jane's perspective, a weak link between output and her own effort also puts her earnings at risk of variations that she cannot control—and she may be unwilling to take a job with such a pay scheme unless it pays a compensating wage differential. Thus, unless a worker's output and effort are very closely associated, output-based pay may have small benefits to the employer and yet come at added cost.[7]

The second general problem facing pay-for-performance plans is the need to pick an output measure that coincides with the employer's ultimate objective. Quantitative aspects of output (such as the number of complaints handled by a clerk in the customer service department) are easier to measure than the qualitative aspects of friendliness or helpfulness—and yet the qualitative aspects are critical to building a loyal customer base. Moreover, employees in modern plants are often asked to work in teams, and they thus produce several "outputs," including team planning, decision making, and problem solving. The quantity and quality of some of these outputs are difficult to measure. As we will see, imperfectly designed performance measures can backfire by inducing employees

---

[6]This section draws heavily on David E. Sappington, "Incentives in Principal–Agent Relationships," *Journal of Economic Perspectives* 5 (Spring 1991): 45–66, and George P. Baker, "Incentive Contracts and Performance Measurement," *Journal of Political Economy* 100 (June 1992): 598–614.

[7]For a more thorough discussion of this issue, see Canice Prendergast, "What Trade-off of Risk and Incentives?" *American Economic Review* 90 (May 2000): 421–425.

EXAMPLE 11.2

Calorie Consumption and the Type of Pay

We noted in the text that time-based pay raises the question of *moral hazard*; that is, because workers are paid regardless of their output, they may not put forth their best efforts. An interesting examination of this question comes from Bukidon in the Philippines, where it is common for workers to hold several different farming jobs during a year. In some of these jobs, they are paid by the hour, and in some, they are paid directly for their output. Therefore, we are able to observe how hard the same individual works under the two different types of pay system.

A clever study discovered clear-cut evidence that the workers put forth much less effort in these physically demanding jobs when paid by the hour rather than for their output. Measuring effort expended by both weight change and

calorie consumption, the study found that workers consumed *23 percent fewer calories* and *gained more weight per calorie consumed* when they were paid by the hour. Both facts suggest that less physical effort was put forth when workers were paid by the hour than when they were paid for their output.

_____

Data from: Andrew D. Foster and Mark R. Rosenzweig, "A Test for Moral Hazard in the Labor Market: Contractual Arrangements, Effort, and Health," *Review of Economics and Statistics* 76 (May 1994): 213–227. See Thomas Dohmen and Armin Falk, "Performance Pay and Multidimensional Sorting: Productivity, Preferences, and Gender," *American Economic Review* 101 (April 2011): 556–590, for additional evidence that workers paid for their performance work harder and experience greater levels of stress and exhaustion.

to allocate their effort toward what is being measured and away from other important aspects of their jobs.[8]

Time-Based Pay with Supervision   An alternative pay scheme is to compensate workers for the time they work. This reduces the risk of having Jane's pay—to continue our example—vary on a weekly basis, but guaranteeing her a wage without reference to her actual output creates a problem of *moral hazard*: why should she work hard if that effort is not rewarded? (See Example 11.2 for a comparison of actual work effort under output-based and time-based pay.) The danger that workers might only "put in their time" means that employers must closely monitor their behavior.

The problem with close supervision is that it is costly. Tasks in almost any workplace are divided so that the economies afforded by specialization are possible, and workers must continually adjust to changing situations within their areas of responsibility. Extremely close supervision would require supervisors to have the same information, at the same time, on the situations facing all their

_____

[8]An analysis of the two sets of incentive issues discussed in this section can be found in George Baker, "Distortion and Risk in Optimal Incentive Contracts," *Journal of Human Resources* 37 (Fall 2002): 728–751. For a study of the decline of piece-rate compensation in manufacturing, see Susan Helper, Morris M. Kleiner, and Yingchun Wang, "Analyzing Compensation Methods in Manufacturing: Piece Rates, Time Rates, or Gain Sharing?" working paper no. 16540, National Bureau of Economic Research (Cambridge, Mass.: November 2010).

subordinates, in which case they might as well make all the decisions themselves! In short, detailed supervision can destroy the advantages of specialization.

Motivating the Individual in a Group

If workers seek to maximize utility by increasing their *own* consumption of valued goods, then focusing on the link between each individual's pay and performance is sufficient in developing company policy. However, the concern for one's standing in a group is often a factor that also affects a worker's utility. The importance of the *group* in motivating *individuals* presents both problems and opportunities for the employer.

Issues of Fairness   People's concern about their treatment *relative to others* in their reference group means that issues of *status* and *fairness* pervade the employment relationship. A worker who obtains a 7 percent wage increase during a year in which both price and wage increases average 4 percent might be quite happy until he finds out that a colleague working in the same job for the same employer received a 10 percent increase (Example 11.3 offers an illustration). Workers who feel unfairly treated may quit, reduce their effort level, steal from the employer, or even sabotage output in order to "settle the score."[9] Unfortunately for employers, however, the fairness of identical policy decisions can often be perceived differently depending on their context.

For example, a sample of people was asked to consider the case of two small companies that were not growing as planned and therefore had a need to cut costs. Each paid workers $10 per hour, but Employer A paid that in salary and Employer B paid $9 in salary and $1 in the form of a bonus. Most respondents said it would be unfair for A to cut wages by 10 percent, but they thought it fair if B were to eliminate its bonus. Apparently, pay framed as "salary" connotes a greater entitlement than pay framed as "bonus."[10]

Consider a second example from the same survey. A majority of respondents thought it would be unfair for a successful house painter to cut wages from $9 to $7 if he discovered that reliable help could be hired for less. However, they felt that if he quit painting and went into landscaping (where wages were lower), paying a $7 wage would be justified. Clearly, the employer is included among

---

[9]For a recent review of the issue of fairness in pay, including effects of perceived fairness on productivity, see Ernst Fehr, Lorenz Goette, and Christian Zehnder, "A Behavioral Account of the Labor Market: The Role of Fairness Concerns," *Annual Review of Economics* 1 (September 2009): 355–384. That employee awards conveying status can be effective motivators is shown in Michael Kosfeld and Susanne Neckermann, "Getting More Work for Nothing? Symbolic Awards and Worker Performance," *American Economic Journal: Microeconomics* 3 (August 2011): 86–99.

[10]Daniel Kahneman, Jack L. Knetsch, and Richard Thaler, "Fairness as a Constraint on Profit-Seeking: Entitlements in the Market," *American Economic Review* 76 (September 1986): 728–741. Another study found that the prospect of *losing a bonus that had already been received* is a more powerful motivator than gaining a future bonus; see Roland G. Fryer, Jr., Steven Levitt, John List, and Sally Sadoff, "Enhancing the Efficacy of Teacher Incentives Through Loss Aversion," working paper no. 18237, National Bureau of Economic Research (Cambridge, Mass.: July 2012).

EXAMPLE 11.3

The Effects of Low Relative Pay on Worker Satisfaction

In March, 2008, a major newspaper in California posted a database containing the salaries of all California public employees, including all non-student workers at the University of California. Later that spring, four economists performed a study in which *some* faculty and staff members of the University of California system were sent an email informing them of this website and asking them only whether they were aware of this database. Later, the researchers sent an email to *all* University of California employees, asking them whether they knew about, and had used, the salary database; they were also asked about their level of job and pay satisfaction.

The study found that workers who went to the website and found their pay was *below the median*

pay for their department reported *lower levels of satisfaction* with their job than workers with similar pay who did not use the website (and presumably were less likely to know the salaries of their peers). Workers who discovered that their pay was above the median, however, were not more likely to report higher levels of job satisfaction. The results suggest, therefore, that workers are typically concerned about their pay *relative* to that of their peers but that that this concern is primarily about whether they are paid *less* than average.

Source: David Card, Alexandre Mas, Enrico Moretti, and Emmanual Saez, "Inequality at Work: The Effect of Peer Salaries on Job Satisfaction," *American Economic Review* 102 (October 2012): 2981–3003.

the reference groups used by workers in judging fairness, and the *context* of an employer's decision matters as much as its content!

Group Loyalty   Besides concern for their own levels of consumption and their relative treatment within the group, employees are also typically concerned with the status or well-being of the entire group. While there are always temptations to "free ride" in a group by taking it easy and enjoying the benefits of others' hard work, most people are willing to make at least some sacrifices for their team, school, work group, community, or country.[11] Because the essence of "doing a good job" so frequently means taking the initiative in many small ways to advance the organization's interests, employers with highly productive workers almost universally pay attention to policies that foster organizational loyalty. While many of the steps employers can take to nurture this loyalty go beyond the boundaries of economics, some compensation schemes we will analyze relate pay to *group* performance quite directly.

---

[11]One study found that workers were over 5 percent more productive during World War II and over 9 percent more productive in industries directly related to the war effort; see Mark Bils and Yongsung Chang, "Wages and the Allocation of Hours and Effort," National Bureau of Economic Research, working paper no. 7309, August 1999. For other considerations of altruistic behavior among workers, see Simon, "Organizations and Markets," 34–38; and Julio J. Rotemberg, "Human Relations in the Workplace," *Journal of Political Economy* 102 (August 1994): 684–717.

of pay in some apparel industries found that workers paid a piece rate earned about 14 percent more than workers paid by the hour. The study estimated that about one-third of this disparity was a compensating differential, with the remainder being related to the incentive and sorting effects.[13]

Employer Considerations

The willingness of employers to pay a premium to induce employees to accept piece rates depends on the costs and benefits to employers of incentive pay schemes. If workers are paid with piece rates or commissions, it is they who bear the consequences of low productivity, as noted earlier; thus, employers can afford to spend less time screening and supervising workers. If workers are paid on a *time* basis, the *employer* accepts the risk of variations in their productivity; when workers are exceptionally productive, profits increase, and when they are less productive, profits decline. Employers, however, may be less anxious about these variations than employees are. They typically have more assets and can thus weather the lean periods more comfortably than individual workers can. Employers also usually have several employees, and the chances are that not all will suffer the same swings in productivity at the same time (unless there is a morale problem in the firm). Thus, employers may not be as willing to pay for income certainty as workers are.

The other major employer consideration in deciding on the basis for pay concerns the incentives for employee effort. The considerations related to three major types of incentive plans in use are discussed here.

Pay for Output: Individual Incentives
From the employer's perspective, the big advantage of individually based output pay is that it induces employees to adopt a set of work goals that are directly related to output. Indeed, as with the increased output of incumbent workers at the automobile glass installer mentioned earlier, the estimated increases in an individual's productivity associated with switching from time-based pay to piece rates in the forestry industry have been in the range of 20 percent.[14] There are disadvantages, however.

First, the need to link output-based pay to some measure that can be objectively observed means that workers might be induced to allocate their efforts away from aspects of their performance that are not being measured. If they get paid only for the quantity of items they individually produce or sell, they

---

[13]Eric Seiler, "Piece Rate vs. Time Rate: The Effect of Incentives on Earnings," *Review of Economics and Statistics* 66 (August 1984): 363–376. For a later study that was able to control for unobserved differences among workers and firms, see Tuomas Pekkarinen and Chris Riddell, "Performance Pay and Earnings: Evidence from Personnel Records," *Industrial and Labor Relations Review* 61 (April 2008): 297–319.

[14]Bruce Shearer, "Piece Rates, Fixed Wages and Incentives: Evidence from a Field Experiment," *Review of Economic Studies* 71 (April 2004): 513–534. Increasing piece rates also increases effort; see M. Ryan Haley, "The Response of Worker Effort to Piece Rates: Evidence from the Midwest Logging Industry," *Journal of Human Resources* 38 (Fall 2003): 881–890.

may have minimal regard for quality, safety procedures, or the performance or professional development of others on their work team.[15] These problems can create a need for costly quality-control supervision unless workers can be induced to monitor quality themselves. Self-monitoring of quality is only easily induced when a particular item or service can be traced to the worker responsible. For example, the auto glass installer mentioned earlier requires workers who have installed a windshield improperly (which usually results in its breaking) to pay for the replacement glass and then to re-install it on their own time.

A second problem is that workers may be induced to work so quickly that machines and tools are damaged through lack of proper maintenance or use. While this problem is mitigated to the extent that production downtime can cause the worker's earnings to drop, it is of enough concern to employers that they frequently require piece-rate workers to provide their *own* machines or tools.

How can firms create pay schemes with the proper incentives when the overall value of individual output is difficult to measure? In the remainder of this section, we explore two options. One is payment based on some measure of *group* output, and the other bases pay at least partly on the *subjective* judgments of supervisors.

Pay for Output: Group Incentives   When individual output is difficult to monitor, when individual incentive plans are detrimental to output quality, or when output is generated by teams of interdependent workers, firms sometimes adopt group incentive pay schemes to more closely align the interests of employer and employee.[16] These plans may tie at least a portion of pay to some component of profits (group productivity, product quality, cost reductions) or they may directly link pay with the firm's overall profit level. In still other cases, workers might *own* the firm and split the profits among themselves.[17]

One drawback to group incentives is that groups are composed of individuals, and it is at the individual level that decisions about shirking are ultimately made. A person who works very hard to increase group output or the firm's profits winds up splitting the fruits of his or her labor with all the others,

---

[15]Robert Gibbons, "Incentives in Organizations," *Journal of Economic Perspectives* 12 (Fall 1998): 115–132, provides a summary of this issue, with extensive citations to the literature. For a discussion of "gaming" induced by piece rates (that is, engaging in behaviors that increase the *measure* upon which pay is based, while not actually increasing output), see Pascal Courty and Gerald Marschke, "An Empirical Investigation of Gaming Responses to Explicit Performance Incentives," *Journal of Labor Economics* 22 (January 2004): 23–56.

[16]Barton H. Hamilton, Jack A. Nickerson, and Hideo Owan, "Team Incentives and Worker Heterogeneity: An Empirical Analysis of the Impact of Teams on Productivity and Participation," *Journal of Political Economy* 111 (June 2003): 465–497; Susan Helper, Morris M. Kleiner, and Yingchun Wang, "Analyzing Compensation Methods in Manufacturing: Piece Rates, Time Rates, or Gain Sharing?"

[17]For a review of the literature on productivity in worker-owned or worker-managed firms, see James B. Rebitzer, "Radical Political Economy and the Economics of Labor Markets," *Journal of Economic Literature* 31 (September 1993): 1405–1409; and Michael A. Conte and Jan Svejnar, "The Performance Effects of Employee Ownership Plans," in *Paying for Productivity*, ed. Alan S. Blinder (Washington, D.C.: Brookings Institution, 1990), 142–181.

EXAMPLE 11.4

Poor Group Incentives Doom the Shakers

The Shakers were an unusual religious sect. They required strict celibacy and practiced communal ownership of property, with all members sharing the group's income equally—receiving the average product. They arrived in the United States in 1774 and numbered around 4,000 by 1850, but their membership dwindled thereafter. Their decline is generally attributed to their failure to reproduce and to their declining religious fervor, but economic historian John Murray argues that their group compensation plan was another important reason for their demise.

Those members with a higher-than-average marginal productivity would receive less than the value of their output—and usually less than they could make elsewhere. Thus, high-productivity members had an incentive to quit. Conversely, outsiders with a low marginal productivity had an incentive to join, receiving more than the value of their output and more than they could elsewhere.

Murray proxies marginal productivity by literacy. When the Shaker communes were established in Ohio and Kentucky, their members were full of religious zeal, which may have initially overcome the incentive problems.

These members had a literacy rate of almost 100 percent, far above that of the surrounding population. By the time of the Civil War, however, illiterates were joining the group in significant numbers, and the sect's literacy rates fell below the rates in the surrounding areas. Likewise, Murray finds that literate members were 30 to 40 percent more likely to quit the community (becoming "apostates") than were illiterate members.

Contemporaries began to question the sincerity of the new entrants: they were "bread and butter Shakers," intent on free-riding on their more productive brothers and sisters. Many had been unable or unwilling to provide for themselves in the world outside the commune. Eventually, the changing composition of the Shaker communities caused a crisis in the communes: the average product of the group fell, and the group was wracked by diminishing enthusiasm, internal stress, and declining membership.

Data from: John E. Murray, "Human Capital in Religious Communes: Literacy and Selection of Nineteenth Century Shakers," *Explorations in Economic History* 32 (April 1995): 217–235.

who may not have put out extra effort. Thus, *free-rider* opportunities give workers incentives to cheat on their fellow employees by shirking.[18] (Another downside of group incentives occurs when they attract the wrong sort of workers, and the good workers leave. One extreme case is discussed in Example 11.4.)

In very small groups, cheating may be easy to detect, and peer pressure can be effectively used to eliminate it. When the group of workers receiving incentive pay is large, however, employers may have to devote managerial resources to building organizational loyalties if shirking is to be discouraged. Interestingly,

---

[18]For a more in-depth analysis of this problem, see Haig R. Nalbantian, "Incentive Contracts in Perspective," in *Incentives, Cooperation, and Risk Sharing*, ed. Haig R. Nalbantian (Totowa, N.J.: Rowman & Littlefield, 1987); and Eugene Kandel and Edward Lazear, "Peer Pressure and Partnerships," *Journal of Political Economy* 100 (August 1992): 801–817. For an analysis of peer pressure as a way of overcoming the "free rider" problem, see Alexandre Mas and Enrico Moretti, "Peers at Work," *American Economic Review* 99 (March 2009): 112–145.

despite free-rider problems, studies have found that there is a positive correlation between compensation tied to group outcomes and the productivity of workers in those groups.[19]

Group Incentives and Executive Pay

Compensation for top executives provides an interesting example of the potential and the problems of basing pay on group results. Executives run a company but do not own it, and like other employees, they want to advance their own interests.[20] How can companies align the interests of these key players with those of the owners (shareholders)?

Because firms are trying to maximize profits, we might consider basing executive pay on the firm's profits. But over what time period should profits be measured? Basing this year's pay on current-year profits might create the same adverse incentives discussed earlier with piece rates. A focus on current-year profits could induce executives to pursue only short-run strategies (or accounting tricks), which run counter to the firm's long-run interests, in the hopes they can "take the money and run" to another corporation before the long-run consequences of their decisions are fully observed.

One might think that the strongest way to align the interests of corporate executives and company owners may be to pay them with company stock or the options to buy it. This seemingly rewards top executives for efforts that increase shareholder wealth and punishes them for actions they initiate that reduce it. Paying high-ranking corporate decision-makers with company stock, however, has three drawbacks. First, a company's stock price is affected by more than company performance; it is also influenced by overall investor "bullishness." Moreover, even to the extent a stock's price reflects the company profitability, that profitability—as in the case of an oil company benefiting from a rise in the price of oil—may have nothing to do with the quality of decisions or the effort of a company's management team. Thus, executives paid with stock are rewarded for luck as well as effort—a fact that may reduce the efforts they devote to advancing the interests of their firms.

Second, beyond reducing incentives, economy-wide fluctuations in stock prices also cause executives' pay to vary because of things beyond their control, which may force firms to pay them a compensating differential for the added riskiness of their pay. Third, the incentives stocks provide are related mainly to the *long-term* perspective they induce corporate executives to take when making decisions that affect a company's strength; once an executive sells his or her stock in the company, these

---

[19]Brent Boning, Casey Ichniowski, and Kathryn Shaw, "Opportunity Counts: Teams and the Effectiveness of Production Incentives," *Journal of Labor Economics* 25 (October 2007): 613–650; Douglas Kruse, Joseph Blasi, and Richard Freeman, "Does Linking Worker Pay to Firm Performance Help the Best Firms Do Even Better?" working paper no. 17745, National Bureau of Economic Research (Cambridge, Mass.: January 2012).

[20]As noted in chapter 3's discussion of the demand for labor under monopoly, executives can buy some peace and quiet on the job by forgoing profit maximization when possible. For an example, see Marianne Bertrand and Sendhil Mullainathan, "Is There Discretion in Wage Setting? A Test Using Takeover Legislation," *RAND Journal of Economics* 30 (Autumn 1999): 535–554.

incentives are lost. Thus, policy-makers interested in executive pay have frequently proposed limits on the ability of executives to sell their company's stock.[21]

In practice, the compensation of chief executive officers (CEOs) in the United States has become increasingly responsive to shareholder value. In 1984, 17 percent of CEO pay was in the form of stock or stock options, while around 2000 the comparable figure was close to 30 percent.[22] (The remainder of CEO pay was in the form of salary, benefits, and bonuses based on current-year profits.) Companies in industries with higher volatility in sales—and thus for whom pay based on profits or share values exposes CEO incomes to greater variations beyond their control—rely more on salary payments, and less on company performance, to attract top executives.[23]

It appears that, on balance, paying CEOs with stock or stock options does work. Generally speaking, those firms with executive compensation plans more heavily weighted toward stock or stock options have tended to enjoy greater increases in corporate wealth. There is some evidence, however, that tying pay to stock market values might make CEOs excessively worried about fluctuations in their own income, causing them to shy away from risky projects even when the projects appear profitable.[24]

Recent scandals involving CEOs have raised another concern about aligning their incentives with those of stockholders. The issue is whether CEOs use their close relationship with members of their board of directors (many of whom have been with the company a long time) to negotiate compensation packages that are excessive. More precisely, do they use their "insider" relationship with those who set their pay to receive compensation that is greater than what is consistent with maximizing shareholder value? While researchers differ in their answers to this question, most agree that collusion between CEOs and directors is a potential problem and that greater use of "outside" directors or the presence of well-informed stockholders (institutional investors, say) may be a critical ingredient in aligning incentives.[25]

Pay for Time, with Merit Increases   Given employee risk aversion and the problem of devising appropriate measurable outcomes for individual- and group-incentive plans, most employers opt for some form of time-based pay.

[21]See, for example, Gene Sperling, "Opening Statement before the U.S. House of Representatives Committee on Financial Services," June 11, 2009, at http://www.treas.gov/press/releases/tg166.htm.

[22]John M. Abowd and David S. Kaplan, "Executive Compensation: Six Questions That Need Answering," *Journal of Economic Perspectives* 13 (Fall 1999): 145–168. For other reviews of issues with CEO pay, see Marianne Bertrand, "CEOs," *Annual Review of Economics* 1 (September 2009): 121–150; and Carola Frydman and Raven E. Saks, "Executive Compensation: A New View from a Long-Term Perspective, 1936–2005," *Review of Financial Studies* 23 (May 2010): 2099–2138.

[23]Brian J. Hall and Jeffrey B. Liebman, "Are CEOs Really Paid Like Bureaucrats?" *Quarterly Journal of Economics* 113 (August 1998): 653–691.

[24]Abowd and Kaplan, "Executive Compensation," 158–159.

[25]Bertrand, "CEO"; Kevin J. Murphy and Tatiana Sandino, "Executive Pay and 'Independent' Compensation Consultants," *Journal of Accounting and Economics* 49 (April 2010): 247–262.

While satisfying employees' desires for pay stability, time pay creates an incentive problem because compensation and output are not directly linked. Employers often try to cope with this problem through the use of *merit-pay* plans, which award larger pay increases to workers whose supervisors rate them as the better performers.

On the one hand, basing pay on supervisory ratings has the potential to create superior incentives for workers, because these ratings can take account of the more subjective aspects of performance (friendliness, being a team player) that may be critical to the welfare of the employer.[26] On the other hand, merit-based pay still faces two incentive problems similar to those with output-based pay.

If supervisors are told to base their ratings on worker contributions toward *actual* output, merit pay runs up against the (by now familiar) problem that individual effort and output may not correlate well, owing to forces beyond the control of workers. For this reason, supervisors are often asked to rate their subordinates *relative* to each other, on the theory that all face the same external forces of snowstorms, machine breakdowns, and so forth.

The problem of relative rankings for merit-pay purposes is that the *effort* induced among employees may not be consistent with the employer's interests. For example, one way to enhance one's *relative* status is to sabotage the work of others. Finding pages torn out of library books on reserve shortly before major examinations is not unknown at colleges or universities, where grading is often based on relative performance. Somewhat less sinister than sabotage, but equally inconsistent with employer interests, is noncooperation; one study has shown that the stronger the rewards based on relative performance, the less likely employees are to share their equipment and tools with fellow workers.[27]

Because relative performance ratings usually have a subjective component, another kind of counterproductive effort may take place: *politicking*.[28] Workers may spend valuable work time "marketing" their services or otherwise ingratiating themselves with their supervisors. Thus, efforts are directed away from productivity itself to generate what is, at best, the *appearance* of productivity.[29]

---

[26]For a study indicating that subjective evaluations can enhance performance, see Eric S. Taylor and John H. Tyler, "The Effect of Evaluation on Teacher Performance," *American Economic Review* 102 (December 2012): 3628–3651.

[27]Robert Drago and Gerald T. Garvey, "Incentives for Helping on the Job: Theory and Evidence," *Journal of Labor Economics* 16 (January 1998): 1–25.

[28]Paul Milgrom, "Employment Contracts, Influence Activities, and Efficient Organization Design," *Journal of Political Economy* 96 (February 1988): 42–60; and Canice Prendergast, "A Theory of 'Yes Men,'" *American Economic Review* 83 (September 1993): 757–770. For a theoretical analysis incorporating the important element of trust between workers and supervisors, see George Baker, Robert Gibbons, and Kevin J. Murphy, "Subjective Performance Measures in Optimal Incentive Contracts," *Quarterly Journal of Economics* 109 (November 1994): 1125–1156.

[29]While we discuss individually the tools that can be used to motivate workers—incentive pay, supervision, stock ownership, or profit-sharing, for example—they should all be seen as part of a firm's system for motivating its workers. For example, see Casey Ichniowski and Kathryn Shaw, "Beyond Incentive Pay: Insiders' Estimates of the Value of Complementary Human Resource Management Practices," *Journal of Economic Perspectives* 17 (Winter 2003): 155–180.

Productivity and the Level of Pay

Given difficulties created for both employers and employees by pay-for-performance plans (including merit pay), employers are often driven to search for other monetary incentives that can be used to motivate their workers. In this section, we discuss motivational issues related to the *level* of pay.

Why Higher Pay Might Increase Worker Productivity

Paying higher wages is thought to increase worker productivity for several reasons. One involves the *type* of worker the firm can attract; the others are related to the productivity that can be elicited from *given* workers.

Attracting Better Workers
Higher wages can attract better employees by enlarging the firm's applicant pool. A larger pool means that the firm can be more selective, skimming the cream off the top to employ only the most experienced, dependable, or highly motivated applicants.[30]

Building Employee Commitment
The reasons higher wages are thought to generate greater productivity from given workers all relate to the commitment to the firm they build. The higher the wages are relative to what workers could receive elsewhere, the less likely it is that the workers will quit; knowing this, employers are more likely to offer training and more likely to demand longer hours and a faster pace of work from their workers. Employees, on their part, realize that even though supervision may not be detailed enough to detect shirking with certainty, if they are caught cheating on their promises to work hard and are fired as a result, the loss of a job paying above-market wages is costly both now and over their remaining work life.

Perceptions of Equity
A related reason higher wages might generate more productivity from given employees arises from their concern about being treated fairly. Workers who believe they are being treated fairly are likely to put forth effort, while those who think their treatment is unfair may "get even" by withholding effort or even engaging in sabotage.[31]

One comparison workers make in judging their treatment is the extent to which they see the employer as profiting from their services. It is often considered unfair if a highly profitable employer is ungenerous in sharing its good fortune with its workers, even if the wages it pays already are relatively high. Likewise, workers who are asked to sacrifice leisure and put forth extraordinary effort on

---

[30]Stephen G. Bronars and Melissa Famulari, "Wage, Tenure, and Wage Growth Variation within and across Establishments," *Journal of Labor Economics* 15 (April 1997): 285–317.

[31]This assertion is based on what psychologists call equity theory. For works by economists that employ this theory, see George A. Akerlof and Janet Yellen, "The Fair Wage–Effort Hypothesis and Unemployment," *Quarterly Journal of Economics* 105 (May 1990): 255–283; and Robert M. Solow, *The Labor Market as a Social Institution* (Cambridge, Mass.: Basil Blackwell, 1990).

EXAMPLE 11.5

Did Henry Ford Pay Efficiency Wages?

The 1908–1914 period saw the introduction of "scientific management" and assembly-line production processes at the Ford Motor Company. The change in production methods led to a change in the occupational composition of Ford's workforce, and by 1914, most of its workers were relatively unskilled and foreign-born. Although these changes proved extremely profitable, worker dissatisfaction was high. In 1913, turnover rates reached 370 percent (370 workers had to be hired each year to keep every 100 positions filled), which was high even by the standards of the Detroit automobile industry at the time. Similarly, absenteeism typically averaged 10 percent a day. However, while Henry Ford was obviously having difficulty retaining and eliciting effort from workers, he had little difficulty finding replacements: there were always long lines of applicants at the factory gates. Hence, Ford's daily wage in 1913 of about $2.50 was at least at the competitive level.

In January 1914, Ford instituted a $5-a-day wage; this doubling of pay was granted only to workers who had been employed at the company for at least six months. At roughly the same time, residency in the Detroit area for at least six months was made a hiring standard for new job applicants. Since the company was limiting the potential applicant flow and was apparently not screening job applicants any more carefully after the pay increase, it appears the motivation for this extraordinary increase in wages was not to increase the quality of new hires.

It is clear, however, that the increase *did* affect the behavior of existing employees. Between March 1913 and March 1914, the quit rate of Ford employees fell by 87 percent and discharges fell by 90 percent. Similarly, the absentee rate was reduced by a factor of 75 percent during the October 1913 to October 1914 period. Morale and productivity increased, and the company continued to be profitable.

There is some evidence that at least initially, however, Ford's productivity gains were less than the wage increase. Historians have pointed to the noneconomic factors that influenced Ford's decision, including his paternalistic desire to teach his workers good living habits. (For workers to receive these increases, investigators from Ford first had to certify that they did not pursue lifestyles that included behavior like excessive gambling or drinking.) While the wage increase thus probably did not lead to a wage level that maximized the company's profits (a smaller increase probably would have done that), the policy did have a substantial positive effect on worker turnover, effort, morale, and productivity.

Data from: Daniel Raff and Lawrence Summers, "Did Henry Ford Pay Efficiency Wages?" *Journal of Labor Economics* 5 (October 1987): S57–S86.

the job are likely to expect the firm to make an extraordinary financial sacrifice (that is, the offer of high pay) to them in return.[32]

Employees also judge the fairness of their pay by comparing it with what they could obtain elsewhere. Raising compensation above the level that workers can earn elsewhere, of course, has both benefits and costs to the employer, as we discuss in the following section.

---

[32]For a study indicating a link between profits and wages, see Andrew K. G. Hildreth and Andrew J. Oswald, "Rent-Sharing and Wages: Evidence from Company and Establishment Panels," *Journal of Labor Economics* 15 (April 1997): 318–337.

Efficiency Wages

While initial increases in pay may well serve to increase productivity and therefore the profits of the firm, after a point, the costs to the employer of further increases will exceed the benefits. The above-market pay level at which the marginal revenues to the employer from a further pay increase equal the marginal costs is the level that will maximize profits; this has become known as the *efficiency wage* (see Example 11.5).[33]

The payment of efficiency wages has a wide set of implications that, in recent years, have begun to be explored by economists. For example, the persistence of unemployment is thought by some to result from the widespread payment of above-market wages (see chapter 14).[34] Furthermore, persistently different wage rates paid to qualitatively similar workers in different industries are the hypothesized result of efficiency-wage considerations.[35]

For our purposes here, however, the most important implications of efficiency wages relate to their effects on productivity, and two types of empirical studies are of interest. One set of studies *infers* the effects of efficiency wages on productivity from the types of firms that pay these wages. That is, if some firms raise wages above the market level for profit-maximizing purposes, we ought to observe that those who do are the ones that (a) stand to gain the most from enhancing worker reliability (perhaps because they have a lot invested in expensive equipment), or (b) find it most difficult to properly motivate their workers through output-based pay or supervision.[36] The other kind of study

---

[33]It should be clear that the efficiency wage refers to all forms of compensation, not just cash wages. Lawrence Katz, "Efficiency Wage Theories: A Partial Evaluation," in *NBER Macroeconomics Annual, 1986*, ed. Stanley Fischer (Cambridge, Mass.: MIT Press, 1986); Joseph E. Stiglitz, "The Causes and Consequences of the Dependence of Quality on Price," *Journal of Economic Literature* 25 (March 1987): 1–48; and Kevin M. Murphy and Robert H. Topel, "Efficiency Wages Reconsidered: Theory and Evidence," in *Advances in Theory and Measurement of Unemployment*, eds. Yoram Weiss and Gideon Fishelson (London: Macmillan, 1990), offer detailed analyses of efficiency-wage theories.

[34]Janet Yellen, "Efficiency Wage Models of Unemployment," *American Economic Review* 74 (May 1984): 200–208; and Andrew Weiss, *Efficiency Wages: Models of Unemployment, Layoffs, and Wage Dispersion* (Princeton, N.J.: Princeton University Press, 1990).

[35]Richard Thaler, "Anomalies: Interindustry Wage Differentials," *Journal of Economic Perspectives* 3 (Spring 1989): 181–193; Surendra Gera and Gilles Grenier, "Interindustry Wage Differentials and Efficiency Wages: Some Canadian Evidence," *Canadian Journal of Economics* 27 (February 1994): 81–100; and Paul Chen and Per-Anders Edin, "Efficiency Wages and Industry Wage Differentials: A Comparison Across Methods of Pay," *Review of Economics and Statistics* 84 (November 2002): 617–631.

[36]Alan B. Krueger, "Ownership, Agency and Wages: An Examination of Franchising in the Fast Food Industry," *Quarterly Journal of Economics* 106 (February 1991): 75–101; Erica L. Groshen and Alan B. Krueger, "The Structure of Supervision and Pay in Hospitals," *Industrial and Labor Relations Review* 43 (February 1990): 134S–146S; Carl M. Campbell III, "Do Firms Pay Efficiency Wages? Evidence with Data at the Firm Level," *Journal of Labor Economics* 11 (July 1993): 442–470; Bradley T. Ewing and James E. Payne, "The Trade-Off Between Supervision and Wages: Evidence of Efficiency Wages from the NLSY," *Southern Economic Journal* 66 (October 1999): 424–432; and Bjorn Bartling, Ernst Fehr, and Klaus M. Schmidt, "Screening, Competition, and Job Design: Economic Origins of Good Jobs," *American Economic Review* 102 (April 2012): 834–864.

directly relates the effects of efficiency wages to measures of productivity, rates of disciplinary dismissals, or changes in the employer's product market share.[37] The studies so far are limited in number, but they are generally supportive of efficiency-wage theory.

Note that the payment of wages above what workers could earn elsewhere makes sense only because workers expect to have long-term employment relationships with firms. If workers switched jobs every period, they would face no incentive to reduce shirking when a firm paid above-market wages, because firing someone who is going to quit anyway is not an effective penalty; as a result, firms would have no incentive to pursue an efficiency-wage policy. Thus, efficiency wages are likely to arise only in situations where structured internal labor markets exist. The existence of internal labor markets, however, raises *other* possibilities for using pay to motivate workers, and it is to these possibilities that we now turn.

Productivity and the Sequencing of Pay

Employers with internal labor markets have options for motivating workers that grow out of their employees' expected *careers* with the organization. Applicants to and employees of employers with internal labor markets are concerned with the present value of *career* compensation. This "lifetime" perspective increases employers' options for developing compensation policies, because both the pay levels at each step in one's career and the swiftness of promotion to given steps can be varied by the firm while still living within the constraint of having to offer an attractive present value of career compensation. In this section, we analyze several possibilities for sequencing pay over workers' careers that are thought to provide incentives for greater productivity.

Underpayment Followed by Overpayment

It may be beneficial to both employer and employee to arrange workers' pay over time so that employees are "underpaid" early in their careers and "overpaid" later on.[38] This sequencing of pay, it can be argued, will increase worker productivity and enable firms to pay *higher* present values of compensation than otherwise, for reasons related both to worker sorting and to work incentives. An understanding of these reasons takes us back to the problem of avoiding cheating on an implicit contract in the presence of asymmetric information.

---

[37]Peter Cappelli and Keith Chauvin, "An Interplant Test of the Efficiency Wage Hypothesis," *Quarterly Journal of Economics* 106 (August 1991): 769–787; and Jozef Konings and Patrick P. Walsh, "Evidence of Efficiency Wage Payments in U.K. Firm Level Panel Data," *Economic Journal* 104 (May 1994): 542–555.

[38]Our discussion here draws on Edward Lazear, "Why Is There Mandatory Retirement?" *Journal of Political Economy* 87 (December 1979): 1261–1284. For a review of issues raised in this and succeeding sections, see H. Lorne Carmichael, "Self-Enforcing Contracts, Shirking, and Life Cycle Incentives." Also see Steffen Huck, Andrew J. Seltzer, and Brian Wallace, "Deferred Compensation in Multiperiod Labor Contracts: An Experimental Test of Lazear's Model," *American Economic Review* 101 (April 2011): 819–843.

Worker Sorting   Pay plans that delay at least a part of employees' compensation to a time later in their careers have an important signaling component. They will appeal most (and perhaps only) to those workers who intend to stay with the employer a long time and work hard enough to avoid being fired before collecting their delayed pay. In the absence of being able to predict which workers intend to stick around and work diligently, an employer might find an underpay-now, overpay-later compensation plan attractive because of the type of workers likely to sort themselves into their applicant pool.[39]

Work Incentives   A company that pays poorly to begin with but well later on increases the incentives of its employees to work industriously. Once in the job, an employee has incentives to work diligently in order to qualify for the later overpayment. The employer need not devote as many resources to supervision each year as would otherwise be the case, because the firm has several years in which to identify shirkers and withhold from them the delayed reward. Because all employees work harder than they otherwise would, compensation within the firm tends to be higher also.

Constraints   One feasible compensation-sequencing scheme would pay workers *less* than their marginal product early in their careers and *more* than their marginal product later on. This scheme, however, must satisfy two constraints. First, the present value of the earnings streams offered to employees must be at least equal to alternative streams offered to workers in the labor market; if not, the firm cannot attract the workers it wants.

Second, the scheme must also satisfy the equilibrium conditions that the firm maximizes profits and does not earn supernormal profits. If profits are not maximized, the firm's existence is threatened; if firms make supernormal profits, new firms will be induced to enter the market. Thus, in neither case would equilibrium exist.

These two conditions will be met if hiring is done until the present value of one's career-long marginal revenue product equals the present value of one's career earnings stream. (This career-long condition is the multiyear analogue of the single-year profit-maximization conditions discussed in chapter 3.) Thus, for firms choosing the "underpayment-now, overpayment-later" compensation scheme to be competitive in both the labor and product markets, the present value of the yearly amounts by which marginal revenue product (*MRP*) *exceeds* compensation early on must equal the present value of the later amounts by which *MRP falls short* of pay.

[39]The lower turnover rate among workers who have been promised larger pensions upon retirement is apparently mostly the result of self-selection, not the threat of lost pension wealth; see Steven G. Allen, Robert L. Clark, and Ann A. McDermed, "Pensions, Bonding, and Lifetime Jobs," *Journal of Human Resources* 28 (Summer 1993): 463–481.

Graphical Analysis   The above compensation plan is diagrammed in Figure 11.2. We assume that *MRP* rises over a worker's career but that in the first t^* years of employment, compensation remains below *MRP*. At some point in the worker's career with the firm—year t^* in the diagram—compensation begins to exceed *MRP*. From t^* until retirement in year r is the period during which diligent employees are rewarded by receiving compensation in excess of what they could receive elsewhere (namely, their *MRP*). For the firm to be competitive in both the labor and the product markets, the *present value* of area A in the diagram must equal the *present value* of area B. (Area B is larger than area A in Figure 11.2 because sums received further in the future are subjected to heavier discounting when present values are calculated.)

Risks   To be sure, there are risks to both parties in making this kind of agreement. On the one hand, employees agreeing to this compensation scheme take a chance that they may be fired without cause or that their employer may go bankrupt before they have collected their reward in the years beyond t^*. It is easy to see that employers will have some incentives to renege, since older workers are being paid a wage that exceeds their immediate value (at the margin) to the firm.

On the other hand, employers who do not wish to fire older people face the risk that these "overpaid" employees will stay on the job longer than is necessary to collect their reward—that is, stay on longer than time r in Figure 11.2. Knowing that their current wage is greater than the wage they can get elsewhere, since it reflects payment for more than current output, older employees will have incentives to keep working longer than is profitable for the firm.

Figure 11.2

A Compensation-Sequencing
Scheme to Increase Worker
Motivation

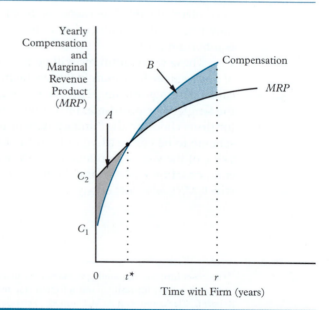

Employee Safeguards   Some safeguards for employees can be built into the employment contract when this type of pay sequencing is utilized. Employers can guarantee seniority rights for older workers, under which workers with the shortest durations of employment with the firm are laid off first if the firm cuts back its workforce. Without these seniority rights, firms might be tempted to lay off older workers, whose wages are greater than *MRP*, and keep the younger ones, who are paid less than *MRP* at this point in their careers.

Employees can also be protected later in their careers by obtaining part of their overpayment in the form of vested pension rights. Once vested (within five years of service, under federal law), employees covered by pension plans have rights to a benefit upon retirement even if they are separated from their employer before retirement age.

Ultimately, however, the best protection older workers have may be the employer's need to recruit *younger* workers. If a certain employer gains a reputation for firing older workers despite an implicit agreement not to do so, that employer will have trouble recruiting new employees. However, if the company is in permanent decline, if it faces an unusually adverse market, or if information on its employment policies is not easily available, incentives to renege on its promises could be very strong.

Employer Safeguards   Before 1978, many employers had mandatory retirement ages for their employees so that they could enforce retirement at point r, for example. However, amendments to the Age Discrimination in Employment Act in 1978 and 1986 precluded mandatory retirement for most workers. Age-discrimination legislation also makes it very difficult for employers to reduce the wages of workers who stay past point r. Thus, employers with underpay–overpay plans are now faced with greater difficulties in getting employees to retire.

One action employers with these plans have taken is to offer large inducements for workers to retire at a certain age. For example, a study of pension plans in 190 of the largest companies in the United States (employing about one-quarter of all workers) found that it is common for the present value of pension benefits, summed over the expected lifetime of the retirees, to decline as retirement is postponed. This study discovered that for workers with typical earnings and years of service, the present value of pension benefits was over 25 percent greater if retirement occurred five years before, rather than at, normal retirement age.[40]

Who Adopts Delayed Compensation?   One implication of the underpayment–overpayment compensation scheme is that it is more likely to exist for jobs in which close supervision of workers is not feasible. Indeed, a study that separated jobs into those that were conducive to close supervision and those

---

[40]Edward Lazear, "Pensions as Severance Pay," in *Financial Aspects of the United States Pension System*, eds. Zvi Bodie and John Shoven (Chicago: University of Chicago Press, 1983).

that were not found that jobs in the latter category were more likely to have relatively high wages for older workers and (in the past, at least) mandatory retirement rules.[41]

Promotion Tournaments

Another form of worker motivation within the context of internal labor markets might best be called a *promotion tournament*. Tournaments have three central features: who will win is uncertain, the winner is selected based on *relative* performance (that is, performance compared with that of the other "contestants"), and the rewards are concentrated in the hands of the winner so that there is a big difference between winning and losing. Not all promotions within firms satisfy this definition of a tournament, largely because the rewards are relatively small and the winners are easy to predict. For example, one study found that promotions were typically associated with increased wage growth of 2 percent to 3 percent, and those who received their first promotion most quickly tended to be promoted most quickly later on as well.[42]

Promotions to very senior leadership positions, however, often take place through a process that fits the description of a tournament.[43] The fortunate vice presidents who are promoted above their rivals to CEO in America's largest corporations, for example, can expect to receive an addition to lifetime income that is in excess of $4 million.[44] The magnitude of this payoff suggests it is a prize offered at the end of a tournament; after all, if one vice president were actually that much more productive than all the others, he or she would have been promoted (or the others fired) long ago! What determines a tournament's strength of incentives, and what are the problems that promotion tournaments must address?

Incentives for Effort   In any tournament, athletic or otherwise, the contestants must decide how much effort to devote to winning. In tennis, for example, a player must decide how much to risk injury by diving or straining for a ball that is difficult to reach. In the corporate world, parents need to consider whether working another week of nights at the office (on a project, say) is worth sacrificing the time with their children. We can hypothesize that contestants will decide to expend the extra effort if the marginal benefits they expect to gain exceed the added risk, inconvenience, or disutility.

---

[41]Robert Hutchens, "A Test of Lazear's Theory of Delayed Payment Contracts," *Journal of Labor Economics* 5, no. 4, pt. 2 (October 1987): S153–S170. For a consideration of how age-discrimination laws affect delayed-payment pay plans, see David Neumark and Wendy A. Stock, "Age Discrimination Laws and Labor Market Efficiency," *Journal of Political Economy* 107 (October 1999): 1081–1125.

[42]George Baker and Bengt Holmstrom, "Internal Labor Markets: Too Many Theories, Too Few Facts," *American Economic Review* 85 (May 1995): 255–259.

[43]Michael L. Bognanno, "Corporate Tournaments," *Journal of Labor Economics* 19 (April 2001): 290–315. The growth of tournaments in a variety of economic sectors, and the social disadvantages of huge gains tied to what may be small relative differences in productivity, are accessibly analyzed in Robert H. Frank and Philip J. Cook, *The Winner-Take-All Society* (New York: Free Press, 1995).

[44]Bognanno, "Corporate Tournaments," 299 (adjusted for inflation).

The marginal benefit that the extra effort produces is a function of two things: the *increased probability of winning* and the value (including prestige) of the *winner's prize*. The extent to which one's chances of winning are improved depends on the now familiar issue of how closely effort is linked to output. If winning is largely a matter of luck, for example, spending extra effort may have little effect on the outcome.[45]

The value of the winner's prize, of course, depends on the disparity between what the winner and losers receive. Tournaments designed to elicit effort that entails great personal sacrifice or that have so many contestants that extra effort improves one's chances only to a small degree require a large prize to create incentives.

Tournaments also enhance output because of their sorting value. People who have confidence in their own abilities and a willingness to sacrifice now for a shot at the prize are much more likely to enter a tournament than others. Thus, employees self-select into (or out of) promotion tournaments, and by so doing, they signal things about themselves that employers might otherwise find difficult to judge.[46] (See Example 11.6 for a discussion of the selection issue in law firms.)

Problems While there may be self-selection benefits to a firm that adopts promotion tournaments, there are also self-selection problems. Promotion tournaments tend to attract "entrants" who are overconfident about their abilities and may harm the interests of their employer by making too many risky decisions—and they tend to discourage entry by those who are averse to risk or who do not work well in a highly competitive environment. There is growing evidence, for example, that women are less attracted to tournaments than equally productive men and that their performance may be less enhanced by the competition tournaments induce.[47]

Another problem with tournaments is that, as with merit pay based on relative performance, contestants may allocate effort away from increasing their own output and toward reducing the output of their rivals. Indeed, where sabotage is possible, promotion tournaments can actually reduce an organization's total output.[48]

Organizations running promotion tournaments also have to be concerned about how to treat the losers. A large disparity in earnings produces large

---

[45]For a paper that analyzes the criteria firms set for winning a tournament in the context of (a) stimulating effort among executives while (b) discouraging them from undertaking programs that place the firm at excessive risk, see Hans K. Hvide, "Tournament Rewards and Risk Taking," *Journal of Labor Economics* 20 (October 2002): 877–898.

[46]For a paper that attempts to separate the "sorting" effects of tournaments from the incentive effects on individual performance, see Bentley Coffey and M. T. Maloney, "The Thrill of Victory: Measuring the Incentive to Win," *Journal of Labor Economics* 28 (January 2010): 87–112.

[47]Rachel Croson and Uri Gneezy, "Gender Differences in Preferences," *Journal of Economic Literature* 47 (June 2009): 448–474; Victor Lavy, "Gender Differences in Market Competitiveness in a Real Workplace: Evidence from Performance-Based Pay Tournaments Among Teachers," *Economic Journal* 123 (June 2013): 540–573.

[48]Jeffrey Carpenter, Peter Hans Matthews, and John Schirm, "Tournaments and Office Politics: Evidence from a Real Effort Experiment," *American Economic Review* 100 (March 2010): 504–517.

EXAMPLE 11.6

The "Rat Race" in Law Firms

Within law firms, partners—who share with each other in the firm's profits—need to be very careful about selecting which associates (lawyers who are not partners) to promote into their ranks. In particular, they will want to promote only those associates who are the most capable and most hard-working—that is, those who will contribute more than their share to profits. They thus tend to rely on "billable hours" as an indicator of an associate's productivity.

All applicants out of law school will claim to be hard workers, of course, and even those who have strong preferences for relatively short (or even "normal") hours can pretend to be "long-hours workers" for a time after hire. Employers therefore need to elicit a signal from their applicants or employees about their *long-run* work orientation, and one way to do this is to announce to all applicants that very long hours are expected for a very long time. These expectations obviously must be reasonable enough that the firms can generate applicants, but in terms of our signaling discussion in chapter 9, the announced work requirements

must be demanding enough to discourage pretenders from applying.

Discouraging pretenders, however, may simultaneously require hours of work that are in excess of what even what those who choose to work for the firm would prefer!

For example, one study of two large law firms in the northeastern United States found that over half of their associates worked more than 50 hours a week—and 70 percent normally worked at least half a day on the weekends. The study also found evidence that, if offered a 5 percent wage increase, fully 65 percent of associates would prefer to cut their hours by 5 percent rather than keeping their hours constant and having their incomes rise. Among those whose *spouses had full-time jobs*—and who therefore had to share household duties—those wanting to work fewer hours exceeded 75 percent.

Source: Renée M. Landers, James B. Rebitzer, and Lowell J. Taylor, "Rat Race Redux: Adverse Selection in the Determination of Work Hours in Law Firms," *American Economic Review* 86 (June 1996): 329–348.

incentives during tournament play, but it also means that the losers do relatively badly. If a firm is perceived as treating losers callously, it will have problems attracting contestants in the first place (after all, most contestants lose). Thus, the firm has to specify a disparity that is large enough to provide incentives but small enough to provide contestants!

Promotion-related incentive plans face additional problems, however, when employees find it feasible to seek careers outside their current organization and are able to send at least some signals of their productivity to other potential employers. We turn now to an analysis of situations in which the career concerns of employees might orient their efforts toward seeking employment elsewhere.

Career Concerns and Productivity

Employees often define themselves more as members of a profession or field than as members of a particular organization. As such, they may be as motivated to impress *other* employers (in the hopes of receiving future offers) as they are their own. What are the implications of these "career concerns"?

The Distortion of Effort   Other employers can observe objective measures of performance more easily than subjective measures ("quality," for example). As a result, employees with career concerns have an incentive to allocate their efforts toward measurable areas of performance and deemphasize areas that other employers cannot observe. As discussed earlier, executives looking for opportunities elsewhere have incentives to pursue strategies that yield short-run profits (which are highly visible) even if doing so harms the long-term interests of their current employer.[49]

Piece Rates and Effort   While job possibilities with other employers can distort workers' allocations of their effort, they can also solve yet another problem with piece-rate pay. In a world in which products and technologies are constantly changing, piece rates must be continually reset. In establishing a piece rate, the employer makes a guess about how long it takes to complete the task and calibrates the piece rate so that the average hourly earnings of its workers are attractive enough to recruit and retain a workforce.

Management, however, can never know for sure just how long it takes to complete a task, given a reasonably high level of effort by production workers. Moreover, as noted earlier, workers have incentives to "go slow" in trial runs so that management will overestimate the time it takes to complete the task and set a relatively high piece rate. If workers know that the estimated time for task completion is too high, they may deliberately work slowly out of fear that the firm will later reduce the piece rate if it finds out the truth.

Employees who are mobile across firms, however, will be less concerned about their *current* employer's future actions. They are more likely to decide to work at top speed so that other employers are sufficiently impressed to hire them in the future. Where workers' pay is at least partially based on a piece rate, then, career concerns can be helpful in eliciting maximum effort from one's employees.

The Sequencing of Effort   For employees who are concerned about future promotions, whether with their current employer or elsewhere, there are usually two general incentives for high productivity: one's current pay and the chances of future promotion. When career (that is, promotion) concerns are strong, employers may not need much in the way of current pay-for-performance incentives to motivate their employees. As career concerns weaken, firms may need to adopt more current incentives to maintain worker effort.[50]

---

[49]When workers' current employers can observe their true productive characteristics better than outsiders can, outsiders (that is, other employers) wanting to make "talent raids" may reasonably infer who are the most valuable employees from observing who is promoted. Thus, promotion itself sends information to other employers, which may help the employee who is promoted but harm his or her current employer. Several papers have addressed this issue, among which are Dan Bernhardt, "Strategic Promotion and Compensation," *Review of Economic Studies* 62 (April 1995): 315–339; and Derek Laing, "Involuntary Layoffs in a Model with Asymmetric Information Concerning Worker Ability," *Review of Economic Studies* 61 (April 1994): 375–392.

[50]Robert Gibbons and Kevin J. Murphy, "Optimal Incentive Contracts in the Presence of Career Concerns: Theory and Evidence," *Journal of Political Economy* 100 (June 1992): 468–505.

Workers are more likely to be motivated by career concerns and less by pay for current performance when they are inexperienced. Paying them for current performance runs into the problem that output is a function of ability, effort, and luck—and when workers are young, their abilities are unknown to themselves and their employers. Relating pay to the performance of inexperienced workers may not increase their incentives much because, with ability unknown, the connection between effort and output is unclear. The incentive to work hard is strong for those with career concerns, however, because they realize that employers are observing them to estimate their abilities and their willingness to put forth effort.

Moreover, the inability of employers (especially outside employers) to closely monitor workers' efforts can, in the presence of career concerns, lead to *more* effort. Employees realize that future promotions depend in part on employers' beliefs about their *ability*. Because some of their efforts can be hidden, inexperienced workers have incentives to put in extra, hidden effort in an attempt to mislead employers about their ability. For example, an employee expected to work 50 hours a week may put in an extra 20 hours at home to boost performance in an attempt to raise employers' perceptions of his or her ability.

As one's career progresses, however, ability becomes known with more certainty and the career-based incentives for extraordinary effort decline. Fortunately, as noted earlier, the case for performance-based current pay also becomes stronger. Indeed, one study found that older CEOs were paid more on the basis of current performance than were younger CEOs.[51]

Applications of the Theory: Explaining Two Puzzles

The conceptual issues outlined in this chapter can help to shed light on two compensation questions that puzzle labor economists: why pay increases with seniority and why larger employers pay higher wages. In both cases, multiple theoretical or data-related reasons can be called upon to explain the empirical phenomenon; some of these were presented in this chapter and some were introduced earlier. This section briefly summarizes these reasons and, where relevant, reviews the results of empirical studies to evaluate which ones seem most relevant.

Why Do Earnings Increase with Job Tenure?

Earnings rise with age and general labor market experience, as we saw in chapter 9; however, *within* age groups, wages additionally rise as *tenure* with one's employer increases. Why does the length of time with one's employer matter? There are three sets of explanations for why wage increases should be associated with job tenure, holding age (or general labor market experience) constant.[52]

---

[51]Gibbons and Murphy, "Optimal Incentive Contracts in the Presence of Career Concerns."

[52]A review of this puzzle and the early empirical work on it can be found in Robert Hutchens, "Seniority, Wages, and Productivity: A Turbulent Decade," *Journal of Economic Perspectives* 3 (Fall 1989): 49–64.

The simplest assumption is that workers are paid wages equal to their *MRP* at all times—see panel (a) in Figure 11.3—so that wages and productivity rise together as length of time with an employer increases. Clearly, if general training, which is useful to a number of potential employers, is taking place, wages will rise with *age*—but our question is why they *additionally* rise as tenure with an employer rises. A reason explored in chapter 5 is related to the *matches* between the job and the worker. With many potential employers for any given worker, and with the costs entailed in any job search, it is very unlikely that all workers will quickly find the job that puts their skills to the highest-value (and therefore best-paying) use. Some will get lucky early on, of course, and the lucky ones will tend to stay with their employers and cease further searching. Those who are not so lucky will continue searching for better jobs (and pay) and will therefore have shorter job tenures. Thus, it can be argued that longer tenure and higher wages both reflect the same phenomenon: better (more productive) matches between the job and the worker.

The second explanation asserts that *firm-specific* investments are jointly undertaken by workers and their employers (see chapter 5). The joint investment creates a surplus that is *shared* by the worker and the firm; therefore, workers generally receive wage increases that are *less* than the increase in their productivity. As illustrated in panel (b) of Figure 11.3, with firm-specific investments, wages are below—and rise more slowly than—marginal revenue productivity.

Finally, this chapter has offered yet a third explanation for rising wage profiles: they may be part of a delayed-compensation incentive system designed to attract and motivate workers who have long-term attachments to their employers. Under this third explanation, which is depicted in panel

---

Figure 11.3

Alternative Explanations for the Effect of Job Tenure on Wages

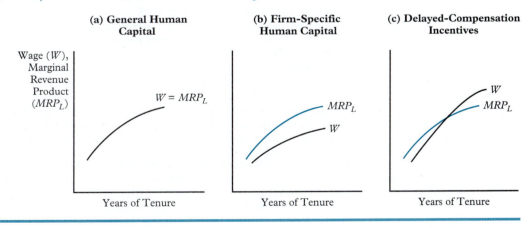

(c), wages rise *faster* than marginal revenue productivity and ultimately rise above it.[53]

Economists have been interested in devising empirical analyses that distinguish among these competing theories, but directly measuring *productivity* is not generally feasible.[54] Therefore, most studies have identified workers for whom theory suggests that one or another of the earlier explanations is very likely (or unlikely) and then compares their wage profiles with those of other workers. Support for an explanation can be inferred if the relative wage profiles display their predicted patterns. For example, delayed-compensation plans are unnecessary if the output of a worker is easily monitored or if the worker is self-employed or paid a piece rate. If we can find evidence that wages for these workers rise *more slowly than average*, it would lend support for the existence of delayed-payment schemes.[55] Likewise, if tenure profiles are steepest during periods when workers are most likely to be receiving training, support for the human-capital explanations could be inferred.[56] To date, the best of the explanations for rising tenure profiles has by no means been discovered—and, of course, it may be that each correctly provides a *partial* explanation for the increase of earnings with job tenure.

Why Do Large Firms Pay More?

Roughly 20 percent of all American private sector employees work in firms with fewer than 20 workers, while about 45% work in firms with more than 500. Workers in the latter group, however, are much better paid than workers in the former group with the same education and experience. It is also apparent that, especially for supervisory workers, wages rise faster with experience in larger firms.[57]

---

[53]A variant of this third explanation is that employers offer rising wage profiles because employees *prefer* them. It is argued in Robert H. Frank and Robert M. Hutchens, "Wages, Seniority, and the Demand for Rising Consumption Profiles," *Journal of Economic Behavior and Organization* 21 (August 1993): 251–276, that employees' utility is in part a function of their wage *increases* (not only their wage level). Therefore, to be competitive in the labor market, employers are induced to offer them wage profiles that start lower and rise faster than they otherwise would.

[54]For a study that did have productivity data, see Judith K. Hellerstein and David Neumark, "Are Earnings Profiles Steeper Than Productivity Profiles? Evidence from Israeli Firm-Level Data," *Journal of Human Resources* 30 (Winter 1995): 89–112.

[55]Edward P. Lazear and Robert L. Moore, "Incentives, Productivity, and Labor Contracts," *Quarterly Journal of Economics* 99 (May 1984): 275–296; and Robert Hutchens, "A Test of Lazear's Theory of Delayed Payment Contracts."

[56]James N. Brown, "Why Do Wages Increase with Tenure?" *American Economic Review* 79 (December 1989): 971–991. For somewhat similar studies, see Sheldon E. Haber and Robert S. Goldfarb, "Does Salaried Status Affect Human Capital Accumulation?" *Industrial and Labor Relations Review* 48 (January 1995): 322–337; David Neumark and Paul Taubman, "Why Do Wage Profiles Slope Upward? Tests of the General Human Capital Model," *Journal of Labor Economics* 13 (October 1995): 736–761; and Erling Barth, "Firm-Specific Seniority and Wages," *Journal of Labor Economics* 15, no. 3, pt. 1 (July 1997): 495–506.

[57]For a recent study that refers to the literature on this topic, see Jeremy T. Fox, "Firm-Size Wage Gaps, Job Responsibility, and Hierarchical Matching," *Journal of Labor Economics* 27 (January 2009): 83–126.

The explanations that have been offered for why larger firms pay higher wages are rooted in claims that they *need better workers* and/or that they have better *opportunities* to make their workers more productive.[58] One potential explanation, for example, is that there are economies of scale in job training; larger firms are therefore more likely to offer it and, of course, have greater need to attract workers willing to undertake it.[59]

A second possible explanation is that large firms more often use highly interdependent production processes, which require that workers be exceptionally dependable and disciplined (one shirking worker can reduce the output of an entire team). Workers in a highly interdependent production environment are more regimented and have less ability to act independently, and their higher wages can be seen as a compensating wage differential for the unattractiveness of a job requiring rigid discipline.

A third hypothesis is that larger firms find job vacancies more costly. They tend to be more capital-intensive and, as noted earlier, have more interdependent production processes. Therefore, an unfilled job or an unexpected quit could more severely disrupt production in larger firms and, by idling much of its labor and capital, impose huge costs on the firm. In an effort to reduce quits and ensure that vacancies can be filled quickly, larger firms thus decide to pay higher wages—even when the work environment is not unattractive and efficiency wages are otherwise unnecessary (because other work incentives exist).[60]

A fourth hypothesis argues that workers in larger firms are more productive because larger firms have more options for allocating workers to various tasks and machines efficiently. They have enough capital, labor, and customers, so the argument goes, that their workers experience less idleness and the most productive workers can be paired with the newest and most productive machines.[61]

The remaining hypotheses are rooted in concepts discussed in this chapter. One is that large firms make available to workers many steps in a career ladder so that long-term attachments between worker and employer are more attractive than in smaller firms. As has been noted in this chapter, employers whose workers

[58]For studies that try to distinguish between the two factors, see Rudolf Winter-Ebmer and Josef Zweimuller, "Firm-Size Differentials in Switzerland: Evidence from Job Changers," *American Economic Review* 89 (May 1999): 89–93; and John M. Abowd and Francis Kramarz, "Inter-Industry and Firm-Size Wage Differentials: New Evidence from Linked Employer-Employee Data," Cornell University, School of Industrial and Labor Relations Institute for Labor Market Policies, July 2000.

[59]Kevin T. Reilly, "Human Capital and Information: The Employer Size-Wage Effect," *Journal of Human Resources* 30 (Winter 1995): 1–18; and Dan A. Black, Brett J. Noel, and Zheng Wang, "On-the-Job Training, Establishment Size, and Firm Size: Evidence for Economies of Scale in the Production of Human Capital," *Southern Economic Journal* 66 (July 1999): 82–100.

[60]For some evidence along the lines of this argument, see James B. Rebitzer and Lowell J. Taylor, "Efficiency Wages and Employment Rents: The Employer Size-Wage Effect in the Job Market for Lawyers," *Journal of Labor Economics* 13 (October 1995): 678–708.

[61]Todd L. Idson and Walter Y. Oi, "Workers Are More Productive in Large Firms," *American Economic Review* 89 (May 1999): 104–107.

EMPIRICAL STUDY

ARE WORKERS WILLING TO PAY FOR FAIRNESS? USING LABORATORY EXPERIMENTS TO STUDY ECONOMIC BEHAVIOR

When discussing the problems of motivating individuals in a group, we noted that opinion surveys of both workers and human-resource managers suggest that perceptions of *fairness* will affect the productivity of employees. Can we obtain independent evidence on whether workers derive utility just from their *own* earnings and the consumption such earnings permit, or whether their *earnings relative to those of others* also affect their utility? Putting the question differently, do workers care only about their absolute level of earnings, or does their concern for fairness cause them also to care about how their earnings level compares with that of others?

If fairness is something workers value, economic theory predicts that they should be willing to pay a price to obtain it. Finding natural experiments that test this prediction is difficult, so some economists have turned to laboratory experiments as a way to gain insights into what motivates people.

Consider the following game conducted with 112 economics and business students at the University of Wisconsin, Madison. The students were anonymously paired (they never found out with whom they were paired). One was designated the "proposer" and the other the "responder." The objective of the game was to divide up to $12. The proposer indicated how each dollar was to be divided, and the responder then chose how many dollars (zero to 12) were to be divided.

If the proposer indicated, for example, that he or she would keep 75 percent of all dollars divided, the responder could walk away with at most $3—by proposing to split the whole $12. In this case, the proposer would receive $9. If responders cared only about their own gains and not about rewards to others, they would not choose to shrink the pool. However, if responders cared so much about their relative payoffs that they were willing to give up some gains to retaliate against what they considered unfair treatment by the proposer, they could do so by shrinking the pool. For example, if a responder thought the 75/25 split was unfair, he or she might shrink the pool to $8, in which case the responder would walk away with $2 and the proposer would receive only $6. In this case, we would observe responders giving up $1 for the utility gained by inflicting $3 of loss on the proposer.

The results of the above laboratory experiment indicated that about half of the responders accepted whatever split was proposed and did not choose to shrink the pool. That is, roughly half were concerned only about their own, absolute payments.

Among the roughly half who were concerned enough about fairness to pay something to retaliate, how much were they willing to pay? The average proposal was for the responder to receive about 40 cents of each dollar split, and with proposals of a 60/40 split, those who were willing to retaliate shrunk the pool by about $3. With a pool now shrunk by $3, these responders indicated that they were willing to give up $1.20 (0.4 × $3) to inflict a loss of $1.80 (0.6 × $3) on the proposer.

While we might question whether the players chosen for the game and the amounts of money at risk accurately portray preferences of real workers in real jobs, laboratory experiments such as this one do offer a major advantage

over opinion surveys. The players are not merely responding hypothetically to questions; rather, they are engaging in *actual behavior that has a consequential (monetary) outcome*. In recent years, laboratory experiments have become an accepted tool for gaining insight into economic behavior when it is difficult or infeasible to generate behavioral data from real markets.

Source: James Andreoni, Marco Castillo, and Ragan Petrie, "What Do Bargainers' Preferences Look Like? Experiments with a Convex Ultimatum Game," *American Economic Review* 93 (June 2003): 672–685. Also see Morris Altman, "The Nobel Prize in Behavioral and Experimental Economics: A Contextual and Critical Appraisal of the Contributions of Daniel Kahneman and Vernon Smith," *Journal of Political Economy* 16 (January 2004): 3–41.

are seeking long-term attachments have more options for using pay to motivate productivity. Efficiency wages are a more effective motivator when there is an expected long-term attachment, because workers' losses from being terminated rise with both their wage level *and* the length of their future expected tenure. Deferred-compensation schemes and promotion tournaments obviously can be used *only* in the context of long-term attachment.

While large firms have more opportunities for adopting efficiency wages, deferred-compensation plans, or promotion tournaments, they may also have a greater need to adopt one or more of these schemes. Owing to sheer size, it is argued, they find it more difficult to monitor their employees and thus must turn to other methods to encourage high levels of effort. One study concluded that the firm-size effect is more related to the presence of efficiency wages than to compensating wage differentials for a demanding work environment.[62]

[62]David Fairris and Lee J. Alston, "Wages and the Intensity of Labor Effort: Efficiency Wages Versus Compensating Payments," *Southern Economic Journal* 61 (July 1994): 149–160. An extensive review of papers on both the "monitoring" and the "compensating differentials" explanations can be found in Rebitzer, "Radical Political Economy and the Economics of Labor Markets," 1417–1419.

Review Questions

1. Explain the underlying principle and the necessary conditions for implicit contracts in the labor market to be self-enforcing.

2. The earnings of piece-rate workers usually exceed those of hourly paid workers performing the same tasks. Theory suggests three reasons why. What are they?

3. Suppose that as employment shifts out of manufacturing to the service sector, a higher proportion of workers are employed in small firms. What effect would this growth of employment in small firms have on the types of compensation schemes used to stimulate productivity?

4. Tournaments induce higher effort levels at low career stages by offering very good earnings prospects to winners. Theory suggests that a worker's effort is positively related to both the probability of winning and (the value of) the winner's prize. Discuss how tournament theory can explain the positive relationship between firm size and CEO compensation.

5. "The way to get power over workers is to underpay them." Comment.

6. Briefly summarize the main characteristics of the following compensation schemes: piece rates, efficiency wages, merit pay, tournaments, group compensation, and deferred compensation. Draw a table with five columns: (i) "Change from time-base pay to ... name of scheme," (ii) "Observability of worker output," (iii) "Expected changes in worker behavior that are in line with the employer's objectives," (iv) "Expected detrimental changes in worker behavior,"

and (v) "Expected change in the pool of applicants."

7. In recent years, many plants have closed, forcing thousands of workers out of their jobs and into new ones. Studies of wage loss suffered by these displaced workers find that *among groups of workers with exactly the same skills and types of training*, workers who had been with the firm for many years and were in the 55–64 age range had greater wage losses than those in the 25–34 age range. How might a compensation scheme designed to enhance worker motivation lead to this result?

8. Suppose that, in commenting on Japan's system of offering some workers lifetime jobs, an analyst claims that Japanese employers are paying their senior workers more than they are worth. Is this comment consistent with economic theory? Explain.

9. A recent magazine article argued that there has been a shift in CEO pay away from stock options, which are often not closely related to a CEO's performance, and toward bonuses that are more discretionary in nature. Use economic theory to analyze the dual claim that stock options are not closely related to CEO performance and that moving away from them and toward discretionary bonuses will strengthen incentives for CEOs to perform well.

   Use economic theory to analyze the dual claim that stock options are tenuously related to CEO performance and that moving away from them and toward bonuses will strengthen incentives for CEOs to perform well.

Problems

1. Suppose that the market wage is $5 per hour, but Charlie will work harder if his employer pays him a higher wage. The relationship between Charlie's wage and MRP_L is given in the following table. What is the efficient wage for Charlie?

Wage ($/hour)	MRP_L ($/hour)
4	6.00
5	8.00
6	9.50
7	10.25
8	11.00
9	11.50
10	12.00
11	12.25
12	12.50
13	12.75

2. Hans works at a company that pays a piece rate, i.e., he is free to choose q, his output level.
   a. Hans's utility $U(q)$ from producing q units is $U(q) = earnings(q) - effort(q)$. Complete the third column of the following table:

	Earnings(q)	Effort(q)	U(q)
0	0	0.0	
1	2	0.5	
2	4	2.0	
3	6	4.5	
4	8	8.0	
5	10	12.5	
...	...	...	

How many units will Hans produce?

   b. Hans's effort function is $effort(q) = \frac{1}{2}q^2$. Plot this function and discuss the key idea behind it.
   c. Suppose that the employer knew Hans's effort function $effort(q) = \frac{1}{2}q^2$. Given that the employer can sell the product for $4 per unit, which of the following two earnings functions should he implement, $earnings(q) = 2q$ or $earnings(q) = 3q$?

3. a. The MRP of labor is given by the following equation: $MRP_0 = 20 - L$, where L = number of workers. If the market wage is $5 per hour, how many workers will the employer want to hire?
   b. The employer now finds that employees will work harder if they are paid a higher wage. If the wage rate paid to the workers is at least $6 per hour, the higher productivity of labor is represented by the new marginal product of labor curve: $MRP_1 = 22 - L$. How many workers would the employer want to hire at $6 per hour?
   c. Use economic theory to explain the change in employment levels associated with paying $6 instead of $5.

4. Jane works on a time-base pay. Every day, she spends $h = 8$ hours on two types of duties. The more time she spends on the first (second) duty, the higher the quantity (quality) of the product. Let $V = q \cdot x$ denote the market value of Jane's daily output: q reflects the quantity and x reflects the quality. Assume $q = 3 + \frac{hq}{2}$ and $x = 1 + h_x$ with $h_q + h_x = 8$.
   a. Jane's employment contract requires her to "do her best." Consequently, Jane decides to spend 4 hours on each

task; i.e., $h_q = h_x = 4$. What is the market value of her daily output?

b. The company cannot afford close supervision of Jane's work; that is, it does not know Jane's time allocation. Would you recommend the company to base Jane's compensation solely on output?

Selected Readings

Akerlof, George A., and Janet L. Yellen, eds. *Efficiency Wage Models of the Labor Market*. New York: Cambridge University Press, 1986.

Bertrand, Marianne. "CEOs." *Annual Review of Economics* 1 (September 2009): 121–150.

Carmichael, H. Lorne. "Self-Enforcing Contracts, Shirking, and Life Cycle Incentives." *Journal of Economic Perspectives* 3 (Fall 1989): 65–84.

Frank, Robert H., and Philip J. Cook. *The Winner-Take-All Society*. New York: Free Press, 1995.

Gibbons, Robert. "Incentives in Organizations." *Journal of Economic Perspectives* 12 (Fall 1998): 115–132.

Hallock, Kevin F. *Pay: Why People Earn What They Earn and What You Can Do Now to Make More*. New York: Cambridge University Press, 2012.

Lazear, Edward P., and Kathryn L. Shaw. "Personnel Economics: The Economist's View of Human Resources." *Journal of Economic Perspectives* 21 (Fall 2007): 91–114.

Sappington, David E. "Incentives in Principal–Agent Relationships." *Journal of Economic Perspectives* 5 (Spring 1991): 45–66.

Simon, Herbert A. "Organizations and Markets." *Journal of Economic Perspectives* 5 (Spring 1991): 24–44.

CHAPTER 12

Gender, Race, and Ethnicity in the Labor Market

The American labor force has gone through a period of remarkable demographic change in recent decades. Some forces for change have been rooted in the different expectations of women regarding the balance between household and market work. Other forces for change have arisen from immigration, both legal and illegal, and from different birthrates among racial/ethnic groups. The result has been a pronounced and continuing change in the mix of groups in the labor force.

Table 12.1 contains both changes occurring from 1990 to 2010 and projections that are foreseeable by the year 2020. White workers, who were about 78 percent of the labor force in 1990, constituted less than 68 percent by 2010, and their share is projected to fall to around 62 percent by 2020. The share of women in the labor force is steadily rising, as are the shares of African and Asian Americans, while the share of Hispanics is rising quickly—from 8.5 percent in 1990 to almost 15 percent in 2010.

With the exception of Asian Americans, the groups in the labor force that are growing as a fraction of the labor force are those whose members earn substantially less, on average, than white males for full-time work. A glance at Figure 12.1 suggests that as of 2011, none of the non-Asian groups with rapid growth rates averaged more than 70 percent of white male earnings for full-time work. In contrast, Asian-American men had average earnings for full-time work that were virtually equal to the average for white men.

Table 12.1

Shares of the Civilian Labor Force for Major Demographic Groups: 1990, 2000, 2010, 2020

	Year			
	1990	**2000**	**2010**	**2020 (Projected)**
White (non-Hispanic)	77.7%	72.0%	67.5%	62.3%
Women (all races)	45.2%	46.5%	46.7%	47.0%
Blacks (both genders)	10.9%	11.5%	11.6%	12.0%
Asian	3.7%	4.4%	4.7%	5.7%
Hispanics (all races, both genders)	8.5%	11.7%	14.8%	18.6%

[a]Includes Alaskan Natives and Pacific Islanders.

Source: Mitra Toossi, "Labor Force Projections to 2020: A More Slowly Growing Workforce," *Monthly Labor Review* 135 (January 2012): 43–64, Table 1.

The growing numerical significance of demographic groups whose members are relatively poorly paid has heightened interest in understanding the sources of earnings differences across groups. The purpose of this chapter is to analyze such differences, with special attention to the topic of discrimination.

Measured and Unmeasured Sources of Earnings Differences

This section focuses on explaining the earnings differentials for three of the larger (and partially overlapping) groups whose members have been targeted by government policy as potential victims of employment discrimination:

Figure 12.1

Mean Earnings as a Percentage of White Male Earnings, Various Demographic Groups, Full-Time Workers over 24 Years Old, 2011

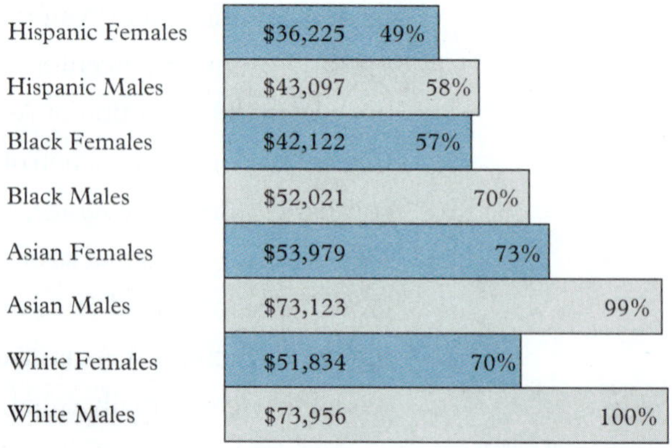

Source: Data in this figure are from U.S. Bureau of the Census, "2012 Current Population Survey, Annual Social and Economic Supplement, Person Income," at http://www.census.gov/hhes/www/cpstables/032012/perinc/pinc03_000.htm.

Group	Earnings	Percentage
Hispanic Females	$36,225	49%
Hispanic Males	$43,097	58%
Black Females	$42,122	57%
Black Males	$52,021	70%
Asian Females	$53,979	73%
Asian Males	$73,123	99%
White Females	$51,834	70%
White Males	$73,956	100%

women, blacks, and Hispanics. The focus is on these groups because data and studies are more readily available for them than for groups defined by such characteristics as physical limitation or sexual preference.[1] We analyze *earnings* rather than total *compensation* (which would be preferable) for the practical reason that data on the value of employee benefits are not generally available by demographic group.[2]

In looking at earnings across demographic groups, we will be comparing the earnings of people who (as in Figure 12.1) *worked full-time, year-round*. Earnings differences among workers employed full-time during the entire year are driven mainly (but not entirely) by differences in *wage rates*, and it is explaining differences in wage rates that is the main focus of this chapter. However, by comparing only the pay of full-time workers, we overlook the large effects on *hours* of work caused by both part-time work and unemployment during the year—differences that we will need to take account of as well when analyzing the topic of discrimination.

Earnings Differences by Gender

Combining all races and ethnic groups, women over the age of 24 who worked full-time earned an average of 62 percent of what males earned in the year 2011. This percentage was slightly higher than the 58 percent observed in 1970 and 1980.[3] Understanding the sources of this difference is critical to a determination of what policies, if any, might be needed to address the gap in pay.[4]

Age and Education   The first step in analyzing earnings differentials is to think of potential *sources* of difference, many of which can be measured. We know from chapter 9 that two important and measurable factors that influence earnings are education and age (which is correlated with potential labor market experience). While the most recent cohorts of women have levels of schooling at least equal to those of men, the same cannot be said of older cohorts. Moreover, we also

---

[1]For papers on these two topics, see Thomas DeLeire, "Changes in Wage Discrimination Against People with Disabilities: 1984–93," *Journal of Human Resources* 36 (Winter 2001): 144–158; and Christopher S. Carpenter, "Self-Reported Sexual Orientation and Earnings: Evidence from California," *Industrial and Labor Relations Review* 58 (January 2005): 258–273.

[2]For discussions of this issue in the context of gender pay gaps, see Aaron Lowen and Paul Sicilian, "'Family-Friendly' Fringe Benefits and the Gender Wage Gap," *Journal of Labor Research* 30 (2009): 101–119; and Eric Solberg and Teresa Laughlin, "The Gender Pay Gap, Fringe Benefits, and Occupational Crowding," *Industrial and Labor Relations Review* 48 (1995): 692–708.

[3]Data can be found at U.S. Bureau of the Census, "2012 Current Population Survey, Annual Social and Economic Supplement, Person Income," at http://www.census.gov/hhes/www/cpstables/032012/perinc/pinc03_000.htm.

[4]As noted, the pay differences presented and analyzed in this chapter relate to wages and earnings, not to measures of total compensation (which would include employee benefits). There is some indication that women are less likely than comparable men to have pension, health insurance, or disability benefits; see Janet Currie, "Gender Gaps in Benefits Coverage," in *The Human Resource Management Handbook*, eds. David Lewin, Daniel Mitchell, and Mahmood Zaidi (Greenwich, Conn.: JAI Press, 1997), chapter 23.

know that the age/earnings profiles for women are flatter than the ones for men. Therefore, we would expect that controlling for age and education would account for at least some of the female/male differences in earnings.

The data in Table 12.2, which categorizes women and men by age and education, suggest that, as expected, female/male earnings ratios tend to fall with age. Even for the youngest cohort of women in the table, however, these ratios are so low (0.80 is the highest) that we must look elsewhere for a complete explanation of the female/male earnings difference.

Occupation   A measurable factor that could help explain female/male earnings ratios is occupation. As can be seen in Table 12.3, women tend to be overrepresented in low-paying occupations and underrepresented in high-paying ones; thus, at least some of the difference between the average pay of women and men is the result of different occupational distributions. Moreover, Table 12.3 also suggests that even in the *same* occupations, women earn less than men. Since the higher-paying occupations selected for inclusion in Table 12.3 generally require specialized college or postgraduate education, it can be reasonably assumed that women and men entering them share a "career" orientation—yet even for these occupations in 2012, the female/male earnings ratios are substantially below 1.0 in three of the four occupations listed.

Hours and Experience   Within occupations, earnings are affected by one's *weekly hours* of work and one's *years of experience*. We saw in chapter 9 that women average fewer hours of market work per week than do men in the same occupation. Putting aside the effects of part-time employment by focusing on those working full-time, Table 9.2 indicated that women in given occupations average 1 percent to 5 percent fewer hours per week than do men. Because salaried workers presumably receive a compensating wage differential for longer hours of work, some of the earnings differentials in Table 12.3 could be associated with fewer hours of work among women.

Table 12.2

Female Earnings as a Percentage of Male Earnings, by Age and Education, Full-Time Workers, 2011

Age	High School Graduate (%)	Bachelor's Degree (%)	Master's Degree (%)
25–34	75	80	69
35–44	67	74	76
45–54	66	70	61
55–64	70	72	68

Source: Data in this table are from U.S. Bureau of the Census, "2012 Current Population Survey, Annual Social and Economic Supplement, Person Income," at http://www.census.gov/hhes/www/cpstables/032012/perinc/pinc03_000.htm.

Table 12.3

Female/Male Earnings Ratios and Percentages of Female Jobholders, Full-Time Wage and Salary Workers, by Selected High- and Low-Paying Occupations, 2012

	Percentage Female in Occupation	Female-to-Male Earnings Ratio
High-Paying[a]		
Chief executives	26	0.76
Computer systems managers	26	0.88
Lawyers	33	0.80
Pharmacists	52	1.00
Low-Paying[a]		
Cashiers	70	0.92
Cooks	33	0.90
Food preparation	56	0.88
Dining room/cafeteria attendants	49	0.98

[a]"High-paying" occupations are those in which women earned more than $1,500 per week in 2012; "low-paying" ones are those in which men earned less than $410 per week. Occupations in which so few of either gender were employed that earnings data were not published are omitted.

Source: U.S. Bureau of Labor Statistics, *2013 Employment and Earnings Online,* Annual Average Household Survey Data (January 2013), Table 39 at http://www.bls.gov/opub/ee/2013/cps /annavg39_2012.pdf.

Analyses suggest that within occupations, women typically have less (and sometimes, interrupted) work experience and are less likely to be promoted.[5] One study of those who graduated with a Master of Business Administration (MBA) degree from the same highly ranked business school, for example, found that women earned about the same as men immediately after graduation, but after 15 years, they earned 40 percent less. Some of this difference at 15 years was associated with fewer current hours of work, but most was associated with less accumulated experience (women in the sample had fewer total months of experience and more months of *part-time* work than did their male counterparts). Given the primary role women have typically played in child-rearing, the authors attributed much of this "experience gap" to child care.[6] Indeed, another study

[5]Edward P. Lazear and Sherwin Rosen, "Male-Female Wage Differentials in Job Ladders," *Journal of Labor Economics* 8 (January 1990): S106–S123; Erica L. Groshen, "The Structure of the Female/Male Wage Differential: Is It Who You Are, What You Do, or Where You Work?" *Journal of Human Resources* 26 (Summer 1991): 457–472; and Stephen J. Spurr and Glenn J. Sueyoshi, "Turnover and Promotion of Lawyers: An Inquiry into Gender Differences," *Journal of Human Resources* 29 (Summer 1994): 813–842.

[6]Marianne Bertrand, Claudia Goldin, and Lawrence F. Katz, "Dynamics of the Gender Gap for Young Professionals in the Financial and Corporate Sectors," *American Economic Journal: Applied Economics* 2 (July 2010): 228–255.

reports that in 1991, among all women working at age 30, those who were mothers earned 23 percent less than 30-year-old men, while those who were not mothers earned 10 percent less.[7]

Unexplained Differences   Clearly, controlling for occupation, education, age, experience, and hours of work probably goes a long way toward explaining earnings differentials by gender, and other measurable variables added to this list could explain some of the rest. It is possible, however, that some differences would remain unexplained even if all measurable factors were included in our analysis. If so, there are two possible interpretations. One is that these remaining differences are the result of characteristics affecting productivity that might differ by gender but *cannot be observed* by the researcher (for example, the relative priorities individual men and women assign to market and household activities, if the two conflict). Alternatively, the unexplained differential could be interpreted as resulting from *discriminatory treatment* in the labor market. (See Example 12.1 for an illustration of discriminatory behavior against women in symphony orchestras.)

Defining Discrimination   Labor market discrimination is said to exist if individual workers who have *identical productive characteristics* are treated differently because of the demographic groups to which they belong. Put differently, the average wage differentials we observe between demographic groups result from (a) differences in the productive characteristics with which the groups enter the labor market (often called *pre-market differences*) and (b) differences in the way the groups are treated by actors *within* the labor market. Differential treatment within the labor market is what we refer to as *labor market discrimination*.

Gender discrimination in the labor market is alleged to take two prominent forms. First, employers are sometimes suspected of paying women less than men with the same experience and working under the same conditions in the same occupations; this is labeled *wage discrimination*. Second, women with the same education and productive potential are seen as shunted into lower-paying occupations or levels of responsibility by employers who reserve the higher-paying jobs for men. This latter form of discrimination has been called *occupational discrimination*.

Wage Discrimination   Basic to the concept of labor market discrimination is that workers' wages are a function of both their *productive characteristics* (their human capital, the size of the firm for which they work, and so on) and the *price* each

---

[7]Jane Waldfogel, "Understanding the 'Family Gap' in Pay for Women with Children," *Journal of Economic Perspectives* 12 (Winter 1998): 137–156. For more recent papers on this topic, see Nabanita Datta Gupta and Nina Smith, "Children and Career Interruptions: The Family Gap in Denmark," *Economica* 69 (November 2002): 609–629; and Christy Spivey, "Time Off at What Price? The Effects of Career Interruptions on Earnings," *Industrial and Labor Relations Review* 59 (October 2005): 119–140. See Andrea Ichino and Enrico Moretti, "Biological Gender Differences, Absenteeism, and the Earnings Gap," *American Economic Journal: Applied Economics* 1 (January 2009): 183–218, for research indicating that absenteeism related to the menstrual cycle may account for some of the wage disadvantage experienced by women.

EXAMPLE 12.1

Bias in the Selection of Musicians by Symphony Orchestras

Symphony orchestras contain about 100 musicians who must audition in front of a selection committee consisting of the conductor and some orchestra members. Prior to 1970, nearly all orchestras had auditions in which the identity of each candidate was known by the committee. This process favored males—particularly those who were students of a select group of teachers—with the result that only 10 percent of newly hired orchestra members were women. By the 1990s, some 35 percent of new hires were women. What can account for this change?

While it is likely true that the relative pool of female musicians rose during this period, another significant change occurred. Throughout the 1970s and 1980s, most orchestras adopted a selection process that concealed behind a screen those auditioning from the selection committee so that the identity and sex of the candidates could not be discovered. The fact that orchestras adopted these "blind" procedures at different times allows us to estimate the separate effects of these procedures, and one careful study found that about one-third of the 25 percentage-point increase in the hiring of women could be traced to blind auditioning. Put differently, the findings suggest that if the sex of a candidate were known to selection committees, the percentage of women hired would be lower by about 8 percentage points (27 percent instead of 35 percent).

Source: Claudia Goldin and Cecilia Rouse, "Orchestrating Impartiality: The Impact of 'Blind' Auditions on Female Musicians," *American Economic Review* 90 (September 2000): 715–741.

characteristic commands in the labor market. Thus, economic theory suggests that the wages of women and men might differ because of differences in their levels of job experience, for example, or they might differ because men and women are compensated differently for each added year of experience. *Wage discrimination is said to be present when the prices paid by employers for given productive characteristics are systematically different for different demographic groups.* In other words, if men and women (or minorities and nonminorities) with equal productive characteristics are paid unequally, even in the same occupations, then wage discrimination exists.

Occupational Discrimination   Critical to a worker's human capital are the occupational preparation and skills acquired through schooling, job training, or experience. Women and men have very different occupational distributions, but proving occupational *segregation* is a lot easier than proving occupational *discrimination*.

Occupational segregation can be said to exist when the distribution of occupations within one demographic group is very different from the distribution in another. With respect to gender, occupational segregation is reflected in there being female-dominated occupations and male-dominated ones.

If occupational choices are directly limited or if they are influenced by lower payoffs to given human capital characteristics, then occupational segregation certainly reflects labor market discrimination. If, however, these choices reflect different preferences or different household responsibilities (particularly related to child care), then two arguments can be made. One is that there is no particular problem, that occupational preferences—including those toward household work—form naturally from one's life experiences and should be respected in a market economy. The other view is that these preferences are the result of *premarket* discrimination—differential treatment by parents, schools, and society at large that points girls toward lower-paying (including household) pursuits long before they reach adulthood and enter the labor market.

We now turn to issues of measuring occupational segregation and wage discrimination. In both cases, we discuss the available measures and then briefly discuss the extent to which they can be said to accurately reflect discriminatory treatment.

Measurement: Occupational Segregation   As seen in Table 12.3, women and men are not equally represented in the various occupations. While dramatic changes have occurred in recent decades, women are still underrepresented in higher-paying jobs and overrepresented in the lower-paying ones. Various measures are used to summarize the inequality of gender representation across detailed occupational categories, all of which are based on comparing the existing distribution of men and women in occupations with the distribution that would exist if assignment to occupations were random with respect to gender.[8]

One measure is the *index of dissimilarity*. Assuming workers of one gender remain in their jobs, this index indicates the percentage of the other gender that would have to change occupations for the two genders to have equal occupational distributions. If all occupations were completely segregated, the index would equal 100, while if men and women were equally distributed across occupations, it would equal zero. Analyses of gender-related employment patterns in some 500 narrowly defined occupations suggest that the index of dissimiliarity has declined from 64.5 in 1970, to 58.4 in 1980, to 54.1 in 1990, to 52.0 in 2000 and to 51.0 in 2009.[9]

Despite a decline in occupational segregation, studies generally find that its effects on women's wages are substantial. It is typically estimated that if American women with given educational attainment and experience levels were in the same occupations and industries as their male counterparts, their wages would rise by as much as 3 percent to 10 percent.[10]

---

[8]Dale Boisso, Kathy Hayes, Joseph Hirschberg, and Jacques Silber, "Occupational Segregation in the Multidimensional Case: Decomposition and Tests of Significance," *Journal of Econometrics* 61 (March 1994): 161–171; and Martin Watts, "Divergent Trends in Gender Segregation by Occupation in the United States: 1970–92," *Journal of Post-Keynesian Economics* 17 (Spring 1995): 357–379.

[9]Francine D. Blau, Peter Brummund and Albert Yung-Hsu Liu, "Trends in Occupational Segregation by Gender 1970-2009: Adjusting for the Impact of Changes in the Occupational Coding System," working paper no. 17993, National Bureau of Economic Research (Cambridge, Mass.: April 2012).

[10]Francine D. Blau, Marianne A. Ferber, and Anne E. Winkler, *The Economics of Women, Men, and Work*, 6th ed. (Boston: Prentice Hall, 2010), 196; Marjorie L. Baldwin, Richard J. Butler, and William G. Johnson, "A Hierarchical Theory of Occupational Segregation and Wage Discrimination," *Economic Inquiry* 39 (January 2001): 94–110; June O'Neill, "The Gender Gap in Wages circa 2000," *American Economic Review* 93 (May 2003): 309–314; and Michael Ransom and Ronald L. Oaxaca, "Intrafirm Mobility and Sex Differences in Pay," *Industrial and Labor Relations Review* 58 (January 2005): 219–237.

As noted previously, however, not all gender segregation is the result of labor market discrimination; at least some may be the result of either preferences formed before labor market entry or choices made later, perhaps in the context of family decision making (refer back to Example 8.2). For example, there is a growing literature pointing to the possibility that women are more averse to risk, and that they tend to avoid occupations in which pay is negotiable or related to performance – either absolute or relative to other workers.[11] As yet, no measure has been devised to estimate that portion of occupational segregation that can be attributed to unequal treatment by employers.

The decline in observable occupational segregation, and our inability to measure the role of preferences in that segregation, should not imply that discrimination is no longer an issue. Even within narrowly defined occupations, men and women are often segregated across employers. For example, it is common for restaurants to employ only waiters or only waitresses but not both. Furthermore, waitresses earn only 87 percent of what waiters earn, and a hiring audit of Philadelphia restaurants suggests that discrimination might play a role. In 1994, two matched pairs of men and women (with equivalent résumés) applied for jobs in 65 restaurants, and it was found that the high-priced restaurants, where earnings are higher, were much less likely to interview and extend an offer to the female applicant.[12]

Measurement: Wage Discrimination   We pointed out earlier that average earnings can differ between women and men either because of pre-market differences in average levels of productive characteristics or because of differences in what women and men are paid for possessing each characteristic. Ideally, wage discrimination could be identified and measured in the following four-step process.[13]

---

[11]See Rachel Croson and Uri Gneezy, "Gender Differences in Preferences," *Journal of Economic Literature* 47 (June 2009): 448–474; Victor Lavy, "Gender Differences in Market Competitiveness in a Real Workplace: Evidence from Performance-Based Pay Tournaments Among Teachers," *Economic Journal* 123 (June 2013): 540–573; Andreas Leibbrandt and John List, "Do Women Avoid Salary Negotiations? Evidence from a Large Scale Natural Field Experiment," working paper no. 18511, National Bureau of Economic Research (Cambridge, Mass.: November 2012); and Alan Manning and Farzad Saidi, "Understanding the Gender Pay Gap: What's Competition Got to Do with It," *Industrial and Labor Relations Review* 63 (July 2010): 681–698.

[12]Kimberly Bayard, Judith Hellerstein, David Neumark, and Kenneth Troske, "New Evidence on Sex Segregation and Sex Differences in Wages from Matched Employee-Employer Data," *Journal of Labor Economics* 21 (October 2003): 887–922; David Neumark, "Sex Discrimination in Restaurant Hiring: An Audit Study," *Quarterly Journal of Economics* 111 (August 1996): 915–941. Intrafirm promotion differences between men and women can also account for some job segregation; see Michael Ransom and Ronald L. Oaxaca, "Intrafirm Mobility and Sex Differences in Pay," *Industrial and Labor Relations Review* 58 (January 2005): 219–237, and Francine Blau and Jed DeVaro, "New Evidence on Gender Differences in Promotion Rates: An Empirical Analysis of a Sample of New Hires," *Industrial Relations* 46 (July 2007): 511–550.

[13]This procedure was first described in Ronald Oaxaca, "Male-Female Wage Differentials in Urban Labor Markets," *International Economic Review* 14 (October 1973): 693–709. For refinements, see Ronald L. Oaxaca and Michael R. Ransom, "On Discrimination and the Decomposition of Wage Differentials," *Journal of Econometrics* 61 (March 1994): 5–21; and Moon-Kak Kim and Solomon W. Polachek, "Panel Estimates of Male-Female Earnings Functions," *Journal of Human Resources* 29 (Spring 1994): 406–428.

1. We would collect data, for men and women separately, on *all* human capital and other characteristics that are theoretically relevant to the determination of earnings. Based on discussions in earlier chapters, the characteristics of age, education and training, experience, tenure with current employer, hours of work, firm size, region, intensity of work effort, industry, and the job's duties, location, and working conditions come readily to mind.

2. We would then estimate (statistically) how each of these characteristics contributes to the earnings of women. That is, we would use statistical techniques to estimate the payoffs to women associated with each characteristic. (The basic statistical technique used is called *regression analysis,* and it allows us to estimate how changes in a productive characteristic affect earnings, holding other productive characteristics constant. A computer must be used to make these estimates when, as in the case at hand, there are *several* relevant productive characteristics to be jointly analyzed. However, the general idea behind this technique is graphically illustrated in Appendix 12A by using the simple example of estimating how wages are affected by changes in a single composite measure of job *"difficulty."*)

3. Having measured levels of the productive characteristics typically possessed by men and women (step 1) and having estimated how changes in each productive characteristic affect the earnings of women (step 2), we would next estimate how much women *would* earn if their productive characteristics were exactly the same as those of men. This would be done by applying the payoffs *women* receive for each productive characteristic to the average level of those characteristics possessed by *men*.

4. Finally, we would compare the *hypothetical* average earnings level calculated for women (in step 3) with the *actual* average earnings of men. This latter comparison would yield an estimate of wage discrimination, because it reflects the effects of the different prices for productive characteristics paid to men and women. (In the absence of discrimination, women and men who have identical productive characteristics should have identical earnings.)

Can We Infer Wage Discrimination?   There are two problems with this "ideal" measure of wage discrimination. First, as explained earlier, isolating the effects of labor market discrimination requires us to separately categorize the effects of pre-market *differences in productive characteristics* on overall wage differentials. The residual part of the wage gap that cannot be explained by different levels of productive characteristics—and instead is categorized as different *payoffs* to these characteristics—is what can be ascribed to labor market discrimination. Pre-market differences are the result of choices (primarily about investments in human capital and occupation) that individuals make, and these choices often vary across demographic groups. *A question that is difficult to answer is the extent to which these pre-market choices are themselves affected by discrimination in the labor market.*

Occupational choice is a case in point. For example, when making choices about occupational preparation are women able to freely exercise their occupational preferences, or do they avoid occupations for which they believe their entry will be made very difficult by discrimination in the labor market? On the one hand, if we assume women are able to freely choose their occupations, then gender-related occupational differences reflect preferences, and *occupation* becomes one of the pre-market variables for which we would want to control when trying to isolate the effects of labor market discrimination. On the other hand, if women's occupational choices are constrained by discriminatory behavior in the labor market, then we would not want to include occupation among the pre-market control variables—because the effects of occupational choice on the gender wage differential reflect labor market discrimination, not the exercise of pre-market preferences.[14]

Thus, the first problem with our procedure for measuring wage discrimination is that because the labor market payoffs to productive characteristics can affect pre-market choices about them, the distinction between these two categories is not clear-cut. If we include among the pre-market controls a variable whose level is affected by labor market discrimination, we may *understate* the effects of such discrimination (by putting these effects in the "pre-market" category).

The second problem is that frequently we do not have data on *all* the pre-market variables that affect wages, and in this case, the above procedure may *overstate* the extent of labor market discrimination. For example, because of greater household responsibilities, women may be more likely than men to seek work close to home, may be less available for work outside normal business hours, or may more often be the parent "on call" if a child becomes ill at school. These choices reduce the earnings of women, and variables reflecting such choices should be included in the list of pre-market variables used in step 2—but because we lack data on them, their effects show up (in step 4) as reduced payoffs to the female human capital variables we do observe. Thus, if we believe that the omitted pre-market variables are ones that reduce women's wages, *we cannot conclude that all the unexplained residual is caused by labor market discrimination* (because some of the residual will be derived from the effects on women's wages of the omitted characteristics).

Analyzing Wage Differences   These measurement problems notwithstanding, it is interesting to follow the four-step procedure outlined earlier and see what the earnings gap between women and men would be if observed productive characteristics were equalized. A study using 1998 data estimated that while women in the sample earned about 80 percent as much as men, if their productive characteristics (including occupation) had been equalized, they would have earned about 91 percent as much.[15]

---

[14]One attempt to measure the effects of current labor market discrimination on subsequent human capital accumulation is reported in David Neumark and Michele McLennan, "Sex Discrimination and Women's Labor Market Outcomes," *Journal of Human Resources* 30 (Fall 1995): 713–740.

[15]Blau, Ferber, and Winkler, *The Economics of Men, Women, and Work*, 196.

A similar analysis of data for the year 2000, but which focused just on 35- to 43-year-olds, found that women's earnings would have risen from 78 percent of men's to between 91 and 98 percent if they had the same human capital characteristics, worked for the same types of employers, and had the same occupational distribution as men.[16] Differences in labor market experience explained the largest part of the observed gender gap in earnings, while differences in the occupational distribution contributed roughly 3 percentage points to the original 22 percent gap. Thus, labor market discrimination could account for as much as 2 to 9 percentage points of the gap if occupational choice is assumed to reflect preferences, or from roughly 5 to 12 points if occupational choices for women are assumed to be constrained.

The observed productive characteristic that contributes most to the wage gap between women and men in the same occupation is labor market *experience*. Women typically have less work experience than men of comparable age, education, and occupation; furthermore, an extra year of total experience also appears to have a *lower payoff* to women. Economists have increasingly recognized the need to go beyond measuring total years of experience to analyze the effects on wages of the *frequency* and *timing* of periods when women (and men) are out of the labor force.[17] There is also evidence that it is experience as a *full-time* worker that is crucial for both men and women.[18] Thus, in the absence of data on the frequency and timing of nonwork spells (data not normally available to the researcher), at least some of the lower payoff to work experience for women may be the result of an unmeasured productive characteristic.

Earnings Differences between Black and White Americans

We saw in Figure 12.1 that black males who worked full-time in 2011 earned just 70 percent as much as white males; black females earned just 57 percent as much. The black/white earnings gap for men narrowed in the 1970s,

---

[16]O'Neill, "The Gender Gap in Wages circa 2000." The estimated range of effects (from 91 percent to 98 percent) is produced by slightly different estimating procedures.

[17]Julie L. Hotchkiss and M. Melinda Pitts, "At What Level of Labor-Market Intermittency Are Women Penalized?" *American Economic Review* 93 (May 2003): 233–237; and Spivey, "Time Off at What Price? The Effects of Career Interruptions on Earnings." For a related article on informal training, see Catherine J. Weinberger and Peter J. Kuhn, "Changing Levels or Changing Slopes? The Narrowing of the U.S. Gender Earnings Gap, 1959–1999," *Industrial and Labor Relations Review* 63 (April 2010): 384–406.

[18]A study by Francine D. Blau and Lawrence M. Kahn, "Swimming Upstream: Trends in the Gender Wage Differential in the 1980s," *Journal of Labor Economics* 15, no. 1, pt. 1 (January 1997): 1–42, finds that women's returns to *full-time* experience were lower than men's in 1979 but similar by 1988. For a study with similar implications, see Audra J. Bowlus, "A Search Interpretation of Male-Female Wage Differentials," *Journal of Labor Economics* 15 (October 1997): 625–657. T. D. Stanley and Stephen B. Jarrell, "Gender Wage Discrimination Bias? A Meta-Regression Analysis," *Journal of Human Resources* 32 (Fall 1998): 947–973, summarizes and references several studies of gender wage discrimination. More recently, see Catherine J. Weinberger and Peter J. Kuhn, "Changing Levels or Changing Slopes? The Narrowing of the Gender Earnings Gap 1959–1999," *Industrial and Labor Relations Review* 63 (April 2010): 384–406.

became somewhat larger in the 1980s, narrowed again in the 1990s, and has stayed relatively constant since 2000.[19]

The earnings of full-time workers, however, do not tell the whole story of the economic disparities between black and white Americans. There is no major difference in the fraction of adult male employees in the two groups who usually work part-time, and there is a *lower* percentage of employed black women (13.5 percent in 2012) than white women (20.7 percent) who report that they usually work part-time.[20] There are significant disparities, however, in the *employment-to-population ratios* (the ratios of employed adults to the entire population of adults in a particular demographic group who are not in the military or institutionalized). It can be seen in the first two columns of Table 12.4 that, as compared with the white population, a lower percentage of the black population is employed. The differences are particularly striking for males. We begin our analysis of black/white disparities by first considering these differences in the employment ratios.

Differences in Employment Ratios   The employment ratio for a given demographic group is completely determined by the percentage of the group seeking employment (the labor-force participation rate) and the percentage of those seeking employment who find it. Because the latter is equal to 100 percent minus the group's unemployment rate, the employment ratio can be expressed as a function of two widely published rates: the group's labor-force participation rate and its unemployment rate.

Table 12.4 contains data on labor-force participation rates and unemployment rates by race and gender. Looking first at labor force participation, we see that black women have had *higher* labor force participation rates than white women over the 1970 to 2012 period. Among men, however, the picture is much different. Black men have had consistently lower participation rates than white men, and while both groups of men experienced reductions in labor-force participation rates from 1970 to 2012, the reductions were greater for blacks.

The declining labor-force participation rates of men are not just the result of earlier labor force withdrawal among older men or more postsecondary schooling by the young (although as we saw in chapter 6, both phenomena have played a role). The participation rates even of men aged 35 to 44 have dropped for both blacks and whites, with these reductions being more or less confined

---

[19]Kevin Lang and Jee-Yeon K. Lehman, "Racial Discrimination in the Labor Market: Theory and Empirics," *Journal of Economic Literature* 50 (December 2012): 959–1006. For analyses of these earnings gaps, see Chinhui Juhn, "Labor Market Dropouts and Trends in the Wages of Black and White Men," *Industrial and Labor Relations Review* 56 (July 2003): 643–662; and Derek Neal, "The Measured Black-White Wage Gap among Women Is Too Small," *Journal of Political Economy* 112, no. 1, pt. 2 (February 2004): S1–S28.

[20]U.S. Bureau of Labor Statistics, *Employment and Earnings Online*, Annual Average Household Data, Characteristics of the Employed, Table 22, at http://www.bls.gov/opub/ee/2013/cps/annavg22_2012.pdf.

Table 12.4

Employment Ratios, Labor-Force Participation Rates, and Unemployment Rates, by Race and Gender,[a] 1970–2012

	Employment Ratio		Labor-Force Participation Rate		Unemployment Rate	
			Men			
Year	Blacks (%)	Whites (%)	Blacks (%)	Whites (%)	Blacks (%)	Whites (%)
1970	71.9	77.8	77.6	81.0	7.3	4.0
1980	62.5	74.0	72.1	78.8	13.3	6.1
1990	61.8	73.2	70.1	76.9	11.8	4.8
2000	63.4	72.9	69.0	75.4	8.1	3.4
2012	54.1	65.8	63.6	71.0	15.0	7.4
			Women			
1970	44.9	40.3	49.5	42.6	9.3	5.4
1980	46.6	48.1	53.6	51.4	13.1	6.5
1990	51.5	54.8	57.8	57.5	10.8	4.6
2000	58.7	57.7	63.2	59.8	7.2	3.6
2012	52.2	53.3	59.8	57.4	12.8	7.0

[a]For 1970 and 1980, data on blacks include other racial minorities. Data in all years are for persons aged 16 or older.

Sources: U.S. Bureau of Labor Statistics, *Employment and Earnings* 17 (January 1971), Table A-1; 28 (January 1981), Table A-3; 38 (January 1991), Table 3; 48 (January 2001); *Employment and Earnings Online*, Annual Average Household Data, Employment Status, Table 3, at http://www.bls.gov /opub/ee/2013/cps/annavg3_2012.pdf

to those with a high school education or less. The wages of poorly educated workers—especially men—have fallen in recent years, and many of these men apparently have become "discouraged workers" and have dropped out of the labor force. It appears that at least some of the larger declines in labor force participation among black males are a consequence of their lower average levels of education.[21]

Table 12.4 also suggests that the higher unemployment rates of blacks are a cause of their lower employment-to-population ratios. For both men and women, the unemployment rate among blacks is approximately twice that among whites.

---

[21]See Amitabh Chandra, "Labor-Market Dropouts and the Racial Wage Gap: 1940–1990," *American Economic Review* 90 (May 2000): 333–338; and John Bound and Richard B. Freeman, "What Went Wrong? The Erosion of Relative Earnings and Employment of Young Black Men in the 1980s," *Quarterly Journal of Economics* 107 (February 1992): 202–232; and Kevin Lang and Jee-Yeon K. Lehman, "Racial Discrimination in the Labor Market: Theory and Empirics."

This pattern is *not* just a function of differences in education, age, experience or region of residence; the black unemployment rate has been roughly double the rate for whites in *every* group.[22]

The relative constancy of the black/white *ratio* of unemployment rates suggests that this ratio is not affected much by the business cycle. It would be erroneous to conclude from this constancy, however, that recessions have equal proportionate effects on black and white employment; in fact, the constant ratio means that black workers suffer *disproportionately* in a recession.

Suppose, for example, that the white unemployment rate were 5 percent and the black unemployment rate were 10 percent; these rates imply, of course, that 95 percent of the white labor force and 90 percent of the black labor force are employed. Suppose now that a recession occurs and that the white and black unemployment rates rise to 8 and 16 percent, respectively. Among whites, the employment rate falls from 95 percent to 92 percent, which implies that a bit over 3 percent of whites who had jobs lost them (3/95 = 0.032). Among blacks, however, the employment rate falls from 90 percent to 84 percent, indicating that almost 7 percent of employed blacks lost their jobs (6/90 = 0.067). The greater sensitivity of black employment to aggregate economic activity has led many observers to conclude that blacks are the last hired and first fired.

Occupational Segregation and Wage Discrimination   Among black workers who are employed, analyses similar to those for women can be made to measure the extent of occupational segregation and the degree to which measurable productive characteristics explain the black/white gap in earnings. Occupational segregation appears to be less prevalent by race than by gender. Recent studies that calculated indices of occupational dissimilarity by both race and gender found that the indices comparing black and white occupational distributions had values roughly *half* the size of indices comparing male/female occupational distributions. While racial occupational dissimilarities are smaller and have fallen faster over time than gender-related ones, economists continue to study what role, if any, discrimination plays in generating occupational differences by race.[23]

Turning to the issue of *wage discrimination*, researchers have attempted to determine, using the statistical method outlined earlier in this chapter for explaining gender pay gaps, what factors are most responsible for the large gap that exists between the wages of blacks and whites. Some of the premarket variables that must be taken into account in explaining black/white differences in wages are readily observed in most data sets: education, experience, age, hours of work, region, occupation, industry, and firm size. While these

---

[22]For an analysis of the growth in the unemployment ratio, see Robert W. Fairlie and William A. Sundstrom, "The Emergence, Persistence, and Recent Widening of the Racial Unemployment Gap," *Industrial and Labor Relations Review* 52 (January 1999): 252–270.

[23]Andrew M. Gill, "Incorporating the Cause of Occupational Differences in Studies of Racial Wage Differentials," *Journal of Human Resources* 29 (Winter 1994): 20–41. For a study of racial segregation across firms, see Judith Hellerstein and David Neumark, "Workplace Segregation in the United States: Race, Ethnicity, and Skill," *Review of Economics and Statistics* 90 (August 2008): 459–477.

variables explain some of the black/white pay gap, they are not a complete list of premarket differences that can, and should, be used.

One premarket (or human-capital) characteristic that plays a key role in explaining black/white wage differentials is cognitive achievement, as measured by scores on the Armed Forces Qualification Test (AFQT). Black Americans have lower AFQT scores, on average, which is associated with poorer-quality schooling and/or the influences of poverty on home and neighborhood characteristics.[24] A recent study controlling for observable human capital characteristics—including levels of education and AFQT scores, along with some measures of school quality and family background—found that *two-thirds* of the pay gap between black and white men could be explained by these observable variables.[25] This finding suggests, however, that a gap of around 11 percent could *not* be explained. Can this unexplained gap be interpreted as labor-market evidence of discrimination?

As with the issue of occupational choice when analyzing gender pay gaps, there are questions about whether the premarket educational and occupational choices of black Americans are themselves affected by anticipated labor market discrimination. Perhaps, it can be argued, blacks choose different levels of education than whites *because of their expectation of discrimination in the labor market.* If the choice of educational level, for example, is *reflective* of labor-market discrimination, then it should not be included in the list of *premarket* variables used to estimate what wages of blacks would be in the absence of discrimination. There is currently a lively debate among economists about whether including educational attainment among the list of premarket variables increases or reduces the pay gap that can be attributed to discrimination.[26] While we cannot be sure that the existence and size of the unexplained pay gap between black and white men

---

[24]For example, see David Card and Jesse Rothstein, "Racial Segregation and the Black-White Test Score Gap," *Journal of Public Economics* 91 (December 2007): 2158–2184; and Rucker C. Johnson, "Long-Run Impacts of School Desegregation and School Quality on Adult Attainments," working paper no. 16664, National Bureau of Economic Research (Cambridge, Mass.: January 2011). Other studies that examine this test-score gap include Roland G. Fryer, Jr. and Steven D. Levitt, "The Black-White Test Score Gap through Third Grade," and Alan Krueger, Jesse Rothstein, and Sarah Turner, "Race, Income, and College in 25 Years: Evaluating Justice O'Connor's Conjecture," both in *American Law and Economics Review* 8 (Summer 2006): 249–311. Also see Derek Neal, "Why Has Black-White Skill Convergence Stopped?" National Bureau of Economic Research, working paper no. 11090 (January 2005).

[25]Kevin Lang and Michael Manove, "Education and Labor Market Discrimination," *American Economic Review* 101 (June 2011): 1467–1496. The controls for school inputs (such as teacher qualification and class size) and family background are attempts to control for the quality of schooling and the non-cognitive characteristics that are associated with success in school; for a discussion of the latter set of characteristics, see Pedro Carneiro, James J. Heckman, and Dimitriy V. Masterov, "Labor Market Discrimination and Racial Differences in Premarket Factors," *Journal of Law and Economics* 48 (April 2005): 1–39.

[26]For a discussion of this issue, see Pedro Carneiro, James J. Heckman, and Dimitriy V. Masterov, "Labor Market Discrimination and Racial Differences in Premarket Factors"; Kevin Lang and Michael Manove, "Education and Labor Market Discrimination"; Kevin Lang and Jee-Yeon K. Lehman, "Racial Discrimination in the Labor Market: Theory and Empirics"; and Lisa Barrow and Cecilia Elena Rouse, "Do Returns to Schooling Differ by Race and Ethnicity?" *American Economic Review* 95 (May 2005): 83–87.

is evidence of labor market discrimination, there are indications from other kinds of studies that discrimination in the labor market does exist. For example, there is direct evidence—from hiring audits and government complaints, as well as from studies like the one summarized in Example 12.2 that labor market discrimination

---

EXAMPLE 12.2

Race Discrimination May "Strike" When Few Are Looking: The Case of Umpires in Major League Baseball

Racial discrimination in the workplace can lower wages among disfavored groups in three ways: (a) fewer workers in these groups may be hired; (b) if hired, workers in these groups may be assigned to lower-paying jobs; or, (3) if hired into the same jobs, workers in the disfavored groups may receive lower performance ratings from their supervisors. Much of the research by economists on labor-market discrimination has focused on hiring and occupational distributions, because these outcomes are objectively observable by researchers. Supervisory ratings are more difficult to judge, because in most workplace settings, employee performance is not objectively measured by those outside the particular workplace. A wealth of performance data, however, is observable from the world of sports, and one clever study found evidence consistent with race discrimination in Major League Baseball—by umpires (supervisors) against pitchers (employees).

If umpires have more positive feelings toward pitchers of their own race, we would expect that they would be more likely to call pitches close to the strike zone as "strikes" (a favorable call) rather than "balls" if the pitcher is of their same race. Conversely, umpires with racial preferences would be more likely to call a close pitch a "ball" if the pitcher is of a different race. Since umpires are themselves being monitored and judged by their supervisors (and baseball fans), however, economists would expect that any racial bias in judging pitches would be most prominent when the monitoring of umpires is least effective or least likely.

In the years 2004 to 2008, Major League Baseball installed pitch monitoring cameras in about one-third of its ballparks. This photographic system allowed umpires to be monitored, and in a study of over 3.5 million pitches thrown in the 2004–2008 period, the researchers found that in ballparks with these cameras, the race of umpires and pitchers had no role in judging how a pitch was called. In parks without these monitoring cameras, however, racial preferences among umpires was evident; that is, when the umpire and pitcher were of *different* races, pitches that were "close" to the strike zone were *less* likely to be called a "strike." Racial discrimination in pitch calling was even more evident when crowds were small and the game situations were not critical—that is, when fewer people were watching or likely to be paying close attention.

Fortunately, the magnitude of discrimination, while statistically observable, was found to be small. On average, a pitch that is not swung at by the batter is called a strike 31.9 percent of the time. In situations where umpires are not closely monitored (that is, in poorly attended games in parks without the monitoring cameras, and in situations that are not likely to be critical to the outcome of the game), the likelihood of a pitch being called a strike falls to 31 percent if the umpire and pitcher are of different races.

Source: Christopher A. Parsons, Johan Sulaman, Michael C. Yates, and Daniel S. Hamermesh, "Strike Three: Discrimination, Incentives, and Evaluation," *American Economic Review* 101 (June 2011): 1410–1435. Similar behaviors were found in a study of professional basketball referees; see Joseph Price and Justice Wolfers, "Racial Discrimination Among NBA Referees," *Quarterly Journal of Economics* 125 (November 2010): 1859–1887.

persists, although it is difficult to generalize about its overall effect on wages.[27] Moreover, as long as black unemployment rates are twice those of whites, blacks will continue to fall short of whites, on average, in terms of job experience and the tenure-related benefits of on-the-job training.[28]

Earnings Differences by Ethnicity

Increased immigration has sparked a renewed interest in the relative earnings of various ancestral groups in the United States, most especially because the earnings differences are so pronounced. Table 12.5 contains earnings data from a study of men using data from the 1990 *Census of Population*. The first column displays full-time earnings of men from selected ancestral groups relative to the U.S. average, and from it, we can note the relatively high earnings of men whose ancestry was Russian, Italian, or Japanese. Conversely, men whose ancestry is Native American, Mexican, or Puerto Rican had especially low earnings.

Drawing upon our discussion of earnings differences across gender and race, we must ask to what extent these differences resulted from different levels of productive (or pre-market) characteristics. Educational attainment, for example, across ethnic groups is widely divergent. Men of Japanese, Chinese, and Russian ancestry had average levels of college attainment roughly twice the national average of 1.6 years in 1990, while men from Puerto Rican and Mexican backgrounds had average levels that were under half the national average. The second column in Table 12.5 presents estimates of what earnings in each group would have been if observed productive characteristics, including education and fluency in English, were equalized across all groups. The results suggest that if observed productive characteristics were equalized, men of Japanese or Russian ancestry

[27]Marianne Bertrand and Sendhil Mullainathan, "Are Emily and Greg More Employable Than Lakisha and Jamal? A Field Experiment on Labor Market Discrimination," *American Economic Review* 94 (September 2004): 991–1013; and Michael A. Stoll, Steven Raphael, and Harry Holzer, "Black Job Applicants and the Hiring Officer's Race," *Industrial and Labor Relations Review* 57 (January 2004): 267–287. For an article suggesting that the discrimination may be implicit rather than intentional, see Marianne Bertrand, Dolly Chugh, and Sendhil Mullainathan, "Implicit Discrimination," *American Economic Review* 95 (May 2005): 94–98.

[28]Edwin A. Sexton and Reed Neil Olsen, "The Returns to On-the-Job Training: Are They the Same for Blacks and Whites?" *Southern Economic Journal* 61 (October 1994): 328–342. A recent study on the probability of employment suggests that black women with darker skin tone – a group that historically had lower probabilities of employment, given their human capital characteristics – no longer have employment probabilities lower than white women or blacks with lighter skin tone; the employment probabilities for black men, however, showed no such improvements; see Randall Akee and Mutlu Yuksel, "The Decreasing Effect of Skin Tone on Women's Full-Time Employment," *Industrial and labor Relations Review* 65 (April 2012): 398–426.

Table 12.5

Male Earnings Differences, by Ancestry, 1990

Ancestral Group	Earnings as a Percentage of U.S. Average	Estimated Earnings as a Percentage of U.S. Average If Productive Characteristics of Group Were Average
U.S. total	100	100
Mexican	71	95
Puerto Rican	87	98
Cuban	90	102
Chinese	99	95
Japanese	133	115
Native American	85	95
English	113	102
Italian	121	109
Russian	157	118

Source: William Darity Jr., David Guilkey, and William Winfrey, "Ethnicity, Race and Earnings," *Economics Letters* 47 (1995): 401–408.

would have earned 15 percent to 18 percent more than average, while those of Mexican, Chinese, or Native American ancestry would have earned roughly 5 percent less.[29]

Because of social concern about labor market discrimination, it is natural to focus on groups whose earnings appear to be low, given their productive characteristics. In recent years, however, there has also been interest in the diversity of earnings across white ethnic groups, for which discrimination is of less concern. Of particular interest is whether there are unmeasured qualitative differences in education or background across ethnic groups. Indeed, recent studies have found evidence that there are important intergenerational transfers of "ethnic human capital," some of which is manifest in divergent rates of return to education.[30]

Research interest in ancestral groups that are suspected victims of labor market discrimination have centered on "Hispanics," a categorization including people from such diverse backgrounds as Mexican, Puerto Rican, Cuban, and

---

[29]An analysis of wage differences in rural America estimates that equalizing the productive characteristics of Native Americans would result in their earning 3 to 7 percent less than rural whites. See Jean Kimmel, "Rural Wages and Returns to Education: Differences between Whites, Blacks, and American Indians," *Economics of Education Review* 16 (February 1997): 81–96. Similar findings come from a study of native groups in Canada; see Peter George and Peter Kuhn, "The Size and Structure of Native–White Wage Differentials in Canada," *Canadian Journal of Economics* 27 (February 1994): 20–42.

[30]George J. Borjas, "Ethnic Capital and Intergenerational Mobility," *Quarterly Journal of Economics* 107 (February 1992): 123–150; and Barry R. Chiswick, "The Skills and Economic Status of American Jewry: Trends over the Last Half-Century," *Journal of Labor Economics* 11, no. 1, pt. 1 (January 1993): 229–242.

Central and South American. While these groups share a common linguistic heritage, one can infer from Table 12.5 that they have somewhat different earnings and human capital levels.

The influx of Spanish-speaking immigrants into the United States has resulted in the growth of a group of workers characterized by its youth, low levels of education, inexperience in the American labor market, and relatively low levels of proficiency in English. Motivated in part by concerns about discrimination, recent research on earnings differences between Hispanics and non-Hispanic whites has focused on the effects of English-language proficiency on earnings. Language proficiency is not measured in the data sets normally used to analyze earnings, yet it clearly affects productivity in just about any job; hence, if measures of it are omitted from the analysis, we cannot conclude anything about the presence or absence of discrimination against immigrant groups.

The handful of studies (including the one underlying the data in Table 12.5) that have had access to data on language proficiency estimate that equalizing all productive characteristics, including language proficiency, would bring the earnings of Hispanics up to equality with, or within 3 percent to 7 percent of, the earnings of non-Hispanic whites. One study, however, found that the effects on earnings of either unmeasured productive characteristics are far larger for black Hispanics than for non-black Hispanics.[31]

Theories of Market Discrimination

We cannot rule out the presence of discrimination against women and minorities in the labor market. Before designing policies to end discrimination, however, we must understand the *sources* and *mechanisms* causing it. The goal of this section is to lay out and evaluate the different theories of discrimination proposed by economists.

Three general sources of labor market discrimination have been hypothesized, and each source suggests an associated model of how discrimination is implemented and what its consequences are. The first source of discrimination is *personal prejudice,* wherein employers, fellow employees, or customers dislike associating with workers of a given race or sex.[32] The second general source is statistical *prejudgment,* whereby employers project onto individuals certain perceived group characteristics. Finally, there are models based on the presence of *noncompetitive* forces in the labor market. While all the models generate useful, suggestive insights, we will see that none has been convincingly established as superior.

---

[31]Hoyt Bleakley and Aimee Chin, "Language Skills and Earnings: Evidence from Childhood Immigrants," *Review of Economics and Statistics* 86 (May 2004): 481–496; Pedro Carneiro, James J. Heckman, and Dimitriy V. Masterov, "Labor Market Discrimination and Racial Differences in Premarket Factors"; and Joni Hersch, "Profiling the New Immigrant Worker: The Effects of Skin Color and Height," *Journal of Labor Economics* 26 (April 2008): 345–386.

[32]The models of personal prejudice are based on Gary S. Becker, *The Economics of Discrimination,* 2nd ed. (Chicago: University of Chicago Press, 1971).

Personal-Prejudice Models: Employer Discrimination

The models based on personal prejudice assume that employers, customers, or employees have prejudicial tastes; that is, they have preferences for not associating with members of certain demographic groups. Suppose first that white male *employers* are prejudiced against women and minorities but (for simplicity's sake) that customers and fellow employees are not. Furthermore, assume for the purposes of this model that the women and minorities in question have the same productive characteristics as white males. (This assumption directs our focus to labor market discrimination by putting aside pre-market differences.)

If employers have a decided preference for hiring white males in high-paying jobs despite the availability of equally qualified women and minorities, they will act as *if* the latter were less productive than the former. By virtue of our assumption that the women and minorities involved are equally productive in every way, the devaluing of their productivity by employers is purely subjective and is a manifestation of personal prejudice. The more prejudiced an employer is, the more actual productivity will be discounted.

Suppose that MRP stands for the actual marginal revenue productivity of all workers in a particular labor market and d represents the extent to which this productivity is subjectively devalued for minorities and women. In this case, market equilibrium for white males is reached when their wage (W_M) equals MRP:

$$MRP = W_M \tag{12.1}$$

For the women and minorities, however, equilibrium is achieved only when their wage (W_F) equals their *subjective* value to firms:

$$MRP - d = W_F \tag{12.2}$$

or

$$MRP = W_F + d \tag{12.2a}$$

Since the actual marginal revenue productivities are equal by assumption, equations (12.1) and (12.2a) are equal to each other, and we can easily see that W_F must be less than W_M:

$$W_M = W_F + d \tag{12.3}$$

or

$$W_F = W_M - d \tag{12.3a}$$

What this says algebraically has a very simple economic logic: if the actual productivity of women and minorities is devalued by employers, workers in these groups must offer their services at lower wages than white males to compete for jobs.

Profits under Employer Discrimination

This model of employer discrimination has two major implications, as illustrated by Figure 12.2, which is a graphic representation of equation (12.2a). The first concerns profits. A discriminatory employer faced with a market wage rate of W_F for women and minorities will hire N_0, for at that point $MRP = W_F + d$. *Profit-maximizing* employers, however, will hire N_1; that is, they will hire until $MRP = W_F$. The effects on profits can be readily seen in Figure 12.2 if we remember that the area under the MRP curve represents total revenues of the firm. Subtracting the area representing the wage bill of the discriminatory employer ($0EFN_0$) yields profits for these employers equal to the area $AEFB$. Profits for a profit-maximizing (nondiscriminatory) employer, however, are AEG. These latter employers hire women and minorities to the point where their marginal product equals their wage, while the discriminators end their hiring short of that point. Discriminators thus give up profits in order to indulge their prejudices.

Pay gaps Under Employer Discrimination

The second implication of our employer discrimination model concerns the size of the gap between W_M and W_F. The determinants of this gap can be best understood by moving to an analysis of

---

Figure 12.2

Equilibrium Employment of Women or Minorities in Firms That Discriminate

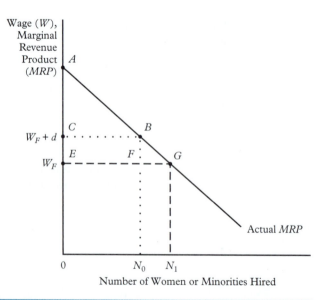

the *market* demand curve for women or minorities. In Figure 12.3, the market's demand for women or minorities is expressed in terms of their wage rate *relative* to the wage for white males. The figure assumes that there are a number of nondiscriminatory employers who will hire up to N_a women or minorities at a relative wage of unity (that is, at $W_F = W_M$). For those employers with discriminatory preferences, W_F must fall below W_M to induce them to hire women or minorities. These employers are assumed to differ in their preferences, with some willing to hire women or minorities at small wage differentials and others requiring larger ones. Thus, the market's relative demand curve is assumed to bend downward at point A, reflecting the fact that to employ more than N_a of women or minorities would require a fall in W_F relative to W_M.

If the supply of women or minorities is relatively small (supply curve S_1 in Figure 12.3), then such workers will all be hired by nondiscriminatory employers and there will be no wage differential. If the number of women or minorities seeking jobs is relatively large (see supply curve S_2), then some discriminatory employers will have to be induced to hire women or minorities, driving W_F down below W_M. In Figure 12.3, combining supply curve S_2 with the demand curve drives the relative wage down to 0.75.

Besides changes in the labor supply curves of women or minorities, there are two other factors that can cause the market differential between W_F and W_M to change. First, given the supply curve, if the number of nondiscriminators were to increase, as shown in Figure 12.4, the wage differential would decrease. The increase in the nondiscriminators shows up graphically in the figure as an extension of the horizontal segment of the demand curve to A', and the relative wage is driven up (to 0.85 in the figure). Behaviorally, the influx of nondiscriminators absorbs more of

---

Figure 12.3

Market Demand for Women or Minorities
as a Function of Relative Wages

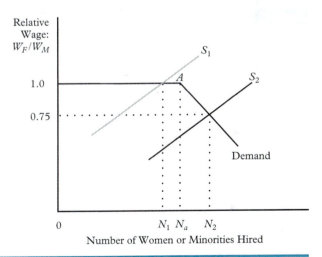

Figure 12.4

Effects on Relative Wages of an Increased
Number of Nondiscriminatory Employers

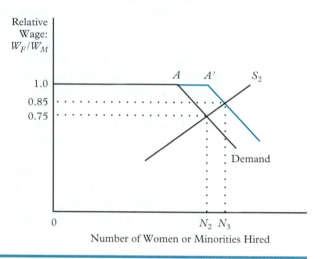

Number of Women or Minorities Hired

the supply than before, leaving fewer minorities or women who must find employment with discriminatory employers. Moreover, the few who must still find work with discriminatory employers are able to bypass the worst discriminators and can go to work for those with smaller preferences for discrimination.

Second, the same rise in W_F relative to W_M could occur if the number of prejudiced employers stayed the same but their discriminatory preferences were reduced. Such reduction would show up graphically as a flattening of the downward-sloping part of the market's relative demand curve, shown in Figure 12.5. The changes

Figure 12.5

Effects on Relative Wages of a Decline in
the Discriminatory Preferences of Employers

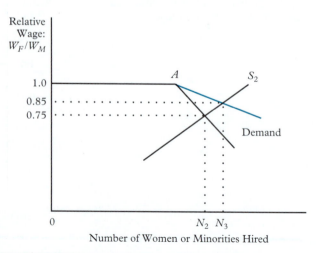

Number of Women or Minorities Hired

hypothesized in this figure cause W_F to rise relative to W_M, because the induce-ment required by each discriminatory employer to hire women or minorities is now smaller.

There are three empirical predictions about race-related wage gaps that arise from our discussion of Figures 12.3, 12.4, and 12.5. First, holding human capital constant, race-related pay gaps will be greater when the black population in a region is greater (see Figure 12.3). Second, pay gaps will be larger, other things equal, when the prejudice of the white employers who hire blacks is greater (see Figures 12.4 and 12.5). Third, pay gaps will be unaffected by the level of preju-dice of the most prejudiced employers (the ones who do not hire blacks). A recent study—using attitudes about interracial marriages and voting for a black presi-dential candidate—finds support for all three predictions.[33]

Which Employers Can Afford to Discriminate?   The employer discrimination model implies that discriminators maximize *utility* (satisfying their prejudicial preferences) instead of *profits*. This practice should immediately raise the question of how they survive. Since profit-maximizing (nondiscriminatory) firms would normally make more money from a given set of assets than would discriminators, we should observe nondiscriminatory firms buying out others and gradually tak-ing over the market.[34] In short, if competitive forces were at work in the product market, firms that discriminate would be punished and discrimination could not persist unless their owners were willing to accept below-market rates of return.

Theory suggests, then, that employer discrimination is most likely to persist when owners or managers do not have to maximize profits in order to stay in business. The opportunity to indulge in discriminatory preferences is especially strong among monopolies that face government regulation, because the costs of this wasteful practice make profits look smaller to regulatory bodies.

Studies of both the banking and trucking industries provide evidence consistent with the greater presence of race and gender discrimination among regulated monopolies. Both industries were historically regulated in ways that limited competition, both were deregulated in recent decades, and in both cases, race and gender wage differentials were considerably narrowed by greater productmarket competition.[35]

---

[33]Kerwin Kofi Charles and Jonathan Guryan, "Prejudice and Wages: An Empirical Assessment of Becker's *The Economics of Discrimination*," *Journal of Political Economy* 116 (October 2008): 773–809.

[34]There is evidence from a recent study, for example, that when a company is taken over by new own-ership, discrimination faced by women in both promotions and wages falls; see Frederik Heyman, Helena Svaleryd and Jonas Vlachos, "Competition, Takeovers, and Gender Discrimination," *ILR Review* 66 (April 2013): 409–432.

[35]Sandra E. Black and Philip E. Strahan, "The Division of Spoils: Rent-Sharing and Discrimination in a Regulated Industry," *American Economic Review* 91 (September 2001): 814–831; and James Peoples Jr. and Wayne K. Talley, "Black-White Earnings Differentials: Privatization versus Deregulation," *American Economic Review* 91 (May 2001): 164–168. For a related study, see Judith K. Hellerstein, David Neumark, and Kenneth R. Troske, "Market Forces and Sex Discrimination," *Journal of Human Resources* 37 (Spring 2002): 353–380.

Personal-Prejudice Models: Customer Discrimination

A second personal-prejudice model stresses *customer* prejudice as a source of discrimination. Customers may prefer to be served by white males in some situations and by minorities or women in others. If their preferences for white males extend to jobs requiring major responsibility, such as physician or airline pilot, then occupational segregation that works to the disadvantage of women and minorities will occur. If women or minorities are to find employment in these jobs, they must either accept lower wages or be more qualified than the average white male, because their marginal revenue productivity to their employers is reduced by customers' prejudices.

One of the implications of customer discrimination is that it will lead to segregation in the occupations with high customer contact. Firms that cater to discriminatory customers will hire only the preferred group of workers, pay higher wages, and charge higher prices than firms that employ workers from disfavored groups and that serve nondiscriminatory customers. To continue their discriminatory ways, then, customers must be willing to pay the added costs.

Empirical studies have found evidence consistent with customer discrimination. For example, the racial composition of a firm's customers is reflected in the racial composition of its employees, especially in jobs with high customer contact. Similarly, a study of television viewership for professional basketball games in the United States found that ratings rose, other things equal, when there was greater participation by white players. Because a team's revenues are affected by its television viewership, the latter finding implies that customer discrimination causes white players to have higher marginal revenue product—and higher pay—than black players with comparable skills.[36]

Personal-Prejudice Models: Employee Discrimination

A third source of discrimination based on personal prejudice might be found on the supply side of the market, where white male workers may avoid situations in which they will have to interact with minorities or women in ways they consider distasteful. For example, they may resist taking orders from a woman or sharing responsibility with a minority member.

If white male workers, for example, have discriminatory preferences, they will tend to quit or avoid employers who hire and promote on a nondiscriminatory basis. Employers who wish to employ workers in a nondiscriminatory fashion, therefore, would have to pay white males a wage premium (a compensating wage differential) to keep them.

If employers were nondiscriminatory, however, why would they pay a premium to keep white males when they could hire equally qualified and less

[36]Harry J. Holzer and Keith R. Ihlanfeldt, "Customer Discrimination and Employment Outcomes for Minority Workers," *Quarterly Journal of Economics* 113 (August 1998): 835–867; Neumark, "Sex Discrimination in Restaurant Hiring"; Mark T. Kanazawa and Jonas P. Funk, "Racial Discrimination in Professional Basketball: Evidence from Nielsen Ratings," *Economic Inquiry* 39 (October 2001): 599–608.

expensive women or minorities? One answer is that white males constitute a large fraction of the labor force, so it is difficult to imagine producing without them. Moreover, the pressure for women and minorities to be employed outside of "traditional" occupations is relatively recent, so white males hired under one set of implicit promises relating to future promotion possibilities now must adjust to a new set of competitors for positions within the firm. Firms realize that changing their practices involves reneging on past promises, so they may seek to accommodate the preferences for discrimination among their workers. Put differently, employee discrimination may be costly to employers but so is getting rid of it.

One way to accommodate employee discrimination is to hire on a segregated basis. While it is usually not economically feasible to completely segregate a plant, it *is* possible to segregate workers by job title. Thus, both the employee and the customer models of discrimination can help to explain the finding of one study that employers usually hire only women or only men into any single job title— even if *other* employers hire members of the opposite sex into that job title.[37]

The most direct test for the presence of employee discrimination comes from a study that found young white males earned more in *racially integrated* workplaces than if they worked in segregated environments. Furthermore, some studies suggest that the lack of women in top executive jobs may be related to distaste among men for working under female bosses—although this distaste may be diminishing over time.[38] (Example 12.3 provides an interesting historical example of employee discrimination.)

Statistical Discrimination

We discussed in chapter 5 the need for employers to acquire information on their job applicants in one way or another, all of which entail some cost. Obviously, the firm will evaluate the *personal* characteristics of its applicants, but in seeking to guess their potential productivity, it may also utilize information on the average characteristics of the groups to which they belong. If group characteristics are factored into the hiring decision, *statistical discrimination* can result (at least in the short run) even in the absence of personal prejudice.[39]

Statistical discrimination can be viewed as a part of the *screening problem* that arises when observable personal characteristics that are correlated with productivity are not perfect predictors. By way of example, suppose two grades

---

[37]Groshen, "The Structure of the Female/Male Wage Differential."

[38]James F. Ragan Jr. and Carol Horton Tremblay, "Testing for Employee Discrimination by Race and Sex," *Journal of Human Resources* 23 (Winter 1988): 123–137; Baldwin, Butler, and Johnson, "A Hierarchical Theory of Occupational Segregation and Wage Discrimination"; Marianne Bertrand and Kevin F. Hallock, "The Gender Gap in Top Corporate Jobs," *Industrial and Labor Relations Review* 55 (October 2001): 3–21; Jonathan S. Leonard and David I. Levine, "The Effect of Diversity on Turnover: A Large Case Study," *Industrial and Labor Relations Review* 59 (July 2006): 547–572.

[39]For an extensive analysis of statistical discrimination, with references to the literature on this topic, see Kevin Lang and Jee-Yeon K. Lehman, "Racial Discrimination in the Labor Market: Theory and Empirics."

EXAMPLE 12.3

Fear and Lathing in the Michigan Furniture Industry

In the late nineteenth century, America attracted several hundreds of thousands of immigrants every year. Ethnicity was very important, as people divided along ethnic lines into separate neighborhoods, churches, trade unions, and social clubs. This flood of immigrants encouraged a growing tide of nativism during the late 1800s. The most recognizable face of this nativism was hostility by the American-born toward Catholics and the new immigrant groups from southern and eastern Europe. In addition, many of the newcomers distrusted and disliked one another, carrying over animosities from the old country.

How did these ethnic sensibilities play out in the labor market? Data from the Michigan furniture industry in 1889 allow us a remarkable view, as they include the wages of workers and measures of their human capital, plus information on the ethnicity of coworkers and supervisors.

During this period, the supervisors or foremen had tremendous latitude in hiring and setting the wages of those who worked under them. If *employers* were the source of discrimination, then we would expect a worker to earn more when supervisors were from the same ethnic group and less when they were not. If fellow *employees* were the source of discrimination, we would

expect a compensating wage differential to arise, with workers receiving higher pay to offset the disamenity of working with members of other ethnic groups and lower pay when working only with members of their own ethnic group.

Both of these indications of discrimination occurred in the Michigan furniture industry, but employee-based discrimination appears to have been much more important. Working with foremen from one's own ethnic group was associated with earning wages about 2 percent higher.

However, the ethnicity of coworkers had a fairly large effect: workers who were the only member of their ethnic group in the workplace earned about 11 percent *more* than those whose ethnic group made up about one-quarter of the labor force. Those working in a factory where over 90 percent of coworkers were from their own ethnic group earned about 9 percent *less*. Thus, a worker could pay a big price for avoiding—and could reap big rewards from working with— workers from the other ethnic groups.

Data from: David Buffum and Robert Whaples, "Fear and Lathing in the Michigan Furniture Industry: Employee-Based Discrimination a Century Ago," *Economic Inquiry* 33 (April 1995): 234–252.

of workers apply for a secretarial job: those who can type 70 words per minute (wpm) over the long haul and those who can type 40 wpm. These actual productivities are unknown to the employer, however. What the employer can observe are the results of a 5-minute keyboarding test whose results reflect skill but also are affected by test-taking abilities and luck.

Figure 12.6 shows the test-score distributions for both groups of workers. Those who can actually type 70 wpm score 70 on average, but half score less. Likewise, half of the other group score better than 40 on the test. If an applicant scores 55, say, the employer does not know if the applicant is a good (70 wpm) or a bad (40 wpm) keyboarder. If those scoring 55 are automatically rejected, the firm will be rejecting some good workers, and if it accepts those scoring 55, some bad workers will be hired.

Figure 12.6

The Screening Problem

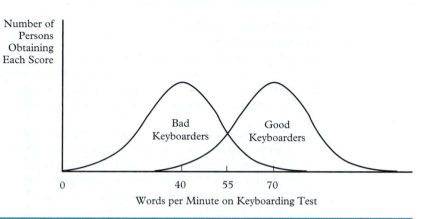

Number of Persons Obtaining Each Score

Bad Keyboarders

Good Keyboarders

0   40   55   70

Words per Minute on Keyboarding Test

Suppose the employer, in an effort to avoid the above dilemma, does some research and finds out that applicants from a particular training school are specifically coached to perform well on 5-minute keyboarding tests. Thus, applicants who can actually type X wpm over a normal day will tend to score *higher* than X wpm on a 5-minute test. Recognizing that students from this school will have average test scores above their long-run productivity, the firm might decide to reject all applicants from this school who score 55 or below (on the grounds that, for most, the test score overestimates their ability).

The general lesson of this example is that firms can legitimately use both *individual* data (test scores, educational attainment, experience) and *group* data in making hiring decisions when the former are not perfect predictors of productivity. However, this use of group data can give rise to market discrimination because people with the same *measured productive characteristics* (test scores, education, etc.) will be treated differently depending on *group* affiliation. The use by employers of race and sex in evaluating job applicants could lead them to prefer white males over other groups.[40] While it is obvious that this preference could be rooted in prejudice, it is also possible that it is based on nonmalicious grounds (for example, the fact that women work fewer hours on average than men). However, if statistical discrimination does not derive from prejudice, then employers will show evidence of "learning" (relying less on group affiliation) as more accurate information on individuals becomes available.[41]

---

[40]For an example of preferences for the native-born (who may speak English better than immigrants), see Philip Oreopoulos, "Why Do Skilled Immigrants Struggle in the Labor Market? A Field Experiment with Thirteen Thousand Resumes," *American Economic Journal* 3 (November 2011): 148–171.

[41]For recent papers on this topic, see Joshua C. Pinkston, "A Test of Screening Discrimination with Employer Learning," *Industrial and Labor Relations Review* 59 (January 2006): 267–284; and Fabian Lange, "The Speed of Employer Learning," *Journal of Labor Economics* 25 (January 2007): 1–35.

Noncompetitive Models of Discrimination

The discriminatory models discussed so far have traced out the wage and employment implications of personal prejudices or informational problems for labor markets in which firms were assumed to be wage-takers. The rather diverse models to which we now turn are all based on the assumption that individual firms have some degree of influence over the wages they pay, either through *collusion* or through some source of *monopsonistic* power.

Crowding   The existence and extent of occupational segregation, especially by gender, have caused some to argue that it is the result of a deliberate *crowding* policy intended to lower wages in certain occupations. Graphically, the "crowding hypothesis" is very simple and can be easily seen in Figure 12.7. Panel (a) illustrates a market in which supply is small relative to demand, and the wage (W_H) is thus relatively high. Panel (b) depicts a market in which crowding causes supply to be large relative to demand, resulting in a wage (W_L) that is comparatively low.

While the effects of crowding are easily seen, the phenomenon of crowding itself is less easily explained. If men and women were equally productive in a given job or set of jobs, for example, one would think that the lower wages of women caused by their being artificially crowded into certain jobs would make it attractive for firms now employing only men to replace them with less-expensive women workers; this profit-maximizing behavior should eventually eliminate any wage differential. The failure of crowding, or occupational segregation, to disappear suggests the presence of noncompeting groups (and therefore barriers to employee mobility), but we are still left with trying to explain why such groups exist in the first place. Over the past 70 years, various possible explanations have been put forth: the establishment of some jobs as "male" and others as "female" through social custom, differences in aptitude that are either innate or acquired,

---

Figure 12.7

Labor Market
Crowding

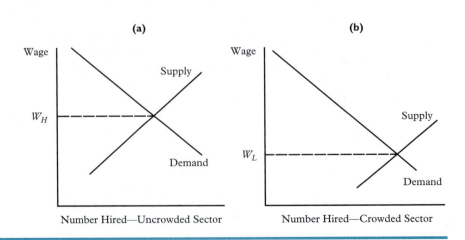

and different supply curves of men and women to monopsonistic employers (discussed later). None of these explanations is complete in the sense of getting at the ultimate source of discrimination, but it is undeniable that the more female dominated an occupation is, the lower its wages are, even after controlling for the human capital of the workers in it.[42]

Dual Labor Markets

A variant of the crowding hypothesis with more recent origins is the view that the labor market is divided into two noncompeting sectors: a *primary* and a *secondary* sector. Jobs in the primary sector offer relatively high wages, stable employment, good working conditions, and opportunities for advancement. Secondary-sector jobs, however, tend to be low-wage, unstable, dead-end jobs with poor working conditions; the returns to education and experience are thought to be close to zero in this sector. Workers (primarily minorities and women) relegated to the secondary sector are tagged as unstable, undesirable workers and are thought to have little hope of acquiring primary-sector jobs.

The dual labor market description of discrimination does not really explain why noncompeting sectors arose or why women and minorities were confined to the secondary sector. Some view the dual labor market as arising out of employer collusion (see the section Collusive Behavior), and others see it as rooted in the factors that lead to internal labor markets and efficiency wages. Whatever the cause, there is evidence that two distinct sectors of the labor market exist— one in which education and experience are associated with higher wages and one in which they are not.[43]

Evidence in support of the dual labor market hypothesis offers an explanation of why discrimination can persist. It also calls into question the levels of competition and mobility that exist, and it suggests that the initial existence of noncompeting race/sex groups will be self-perpetuating. In short, the dual labor market hypothesis is consistent with any of the models of discrimination analyzed above; what it does suggest is that if any of these theories *are* applicable, we cannot count on natural market forces to eliminate the discrimination that results.

Search-Related Monopsony

The crowding and dual labor market explanations for discrimination are grounded in the assumption that workers are "assigned" to occupational groups from which mobility to other groups is severely restricted; how or why assignments are made is not entirely clear. A third model of restricted mobility is built around the presence of job search costs for employees.[44] This model combines a monopsonistic model of firm behavior (discussed in chapter 5) with the phenomenon of prejudice.

---

[42]See Blau, Ferber, and Winkler, *The Economics of Women, Men and Work,* p. 203. An excellent history of crowding theories is provided in Janice F. Madden, *The Economics of Sex Discrimination* (Lexington, Mass.: Lexington Books, 1973), 30–36.

[43]For a review of the literature on this topic, see James Rebitzer, "Radical Political Economy and the Economics of Labor Markets," *Journal of Economic Literature* 31 (September 1993): 1417.

[44]For a more rigorous discussion of this model, see Dan A. Black, "Discrimination in an Equilibrium Search Model," *Journal of Labor Economics* 13 (April 1995): 309–334.

Suppose that some, but not all, employers refuse to hire minorities or women owing to their own prejudices, those of their customers, or those of their employees. Suppose further that, in contrast, no employers rule out the hiring of white males. Minorities and women looking for jobs do not readily know who will refuse them out of hand, so they have to search longer and harder than do white men to generate the same number of job offers. As we saw in chapter 5, employee job search costs cause firms' labor supply curves to slope upward, and the monopsonistic outcomes that follow become more pronounced when these search costs are greater.[45]

Figure 12.8 graphically illustrates the implications of a situation in which two groups of workers have the same productivity (that is, they both have a marginal revenue product of labor equal to MRP_L^*), but one group has higher search costs than the other. Panel (a) depicts the supply and the marginal revenue product of labor curves for the group (white males, presumably) with relatively low search costs.

Figure 12.8

Search-Related Monopsony and Wage Discrimination

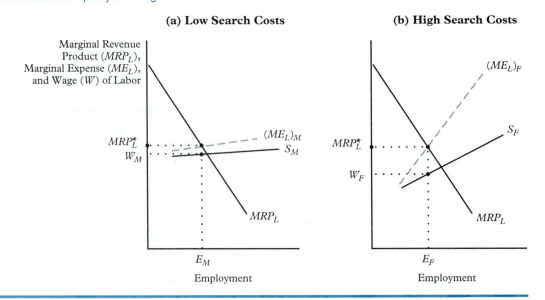

[45]Support for this theoretical implication can be found in Michael R. Ransom and Ronald L. Oaxaca, "New Market Power Models and Sex Differences in Pay," *Journal of Labor Economics* 28 (April 2010): 267–289; Boris Hirsch, Thorsten Schank, and Claus Schnabel, "Differences in Labor Supply to Monopsonistic Firms and the Gender Pay Gap: An Empirical Analysis Using Linked Employer-Employee Data from Germany," *Journal of Labor Economics* 28 (April 2010): 291–330; and Torberg Falch, "Teacher Mobility Responses to Wage Changes: Evidence from a Quasi-Natural Experiment," *American Economic Review: Papers and Proceedings* 101 (May 2011): 460–465.

The labor supply curve of this group to their employers (S_M) is relatively flat, which also means that the associated *marginal* expense of labor curve ($ME_L)_M$ is relatively flat. Profit-maximizing employers will hire E_M workers from this group and pay them a wage of W_M, which is only slightly below MRP_L^*.

Panel (b) illustrates the relevant curves for a group (minorities or women) with higher search costs created by the existence of prejudice. These workers are assumed to have exactly the same marginal revenue product of labor, but their higher search costs imply a more steeply sloped labor supply curve (S_F), a more steeply sloped marginal expense of labor curve ($ME_L)_F$, and a greater divergence between marginal revenue product and the wage rate. E_F workers in this group are hired, and they are paid a wage of W_F. Comparing panels (a) and (b), it is readily seen that despite having the same marginal productivity, workers with higher search costs are paid lower wages (that is, $W_F < W_M$). At a practical level, if members of both groups are hired by a given firm, those with higher search costs may be placed into lower job titles.

Our discussion of search-related monopsony invites two comments. First, we introduced the monopsony model in chapter 5 as a potential explanation for the small and uncertain responses of employment to *mandated* wage increases under minimum wage laws. The monopsony model has also been invoked to explain the lack of employment declines associated with mandated wage increases for women under the United Kingdom's Equal Pay Act of 1970.[46]

Second, if prejudice increases the job search costs for women and minorities so that members of these groups are less likely to search for alternative offers of employment, their job matches will be of lower quality than the job matches for white men. Individual women and minority-group members, then, would be less likely to find the employers who can best utilize their talents. Thus, even within narrowly defined occupational groups, minorities and women would tend to be less productive and receive less pay than white men, owing to poorer-quality matches.

Collusive Behavior   Some theories are grounded in an assumption that employers collude with each other to subjugate minorities or women, thus creating a situation in which monopsonistic wages can be forced on the subjugated group. One of the more explicit collusive theories of discrimination argues that prejudice and the conflicts it creates are inherent in a capitalist society because they serve the interests of owners.[47] Workers divided by race or gender are harder to organize and, if they *are* unionized, are less cohesive in their demands. Hence, it is argued that owners of capital gain, while *all* workers—but particularly minorities and women—lose from discrimination.

---

[46]Alan Manning, "The Equal Pay Act as an Experiment to Test Theories of the Labour Market," *Economica* 63 (May 1996): 191–212.

[47]Michael Reich, "The Economics of Racism," in *Problems in Political Economy: An Urban Perspective*, ed. David M. Gordon (Lexington, Mass.: D. C. Heath, 1971): 107–113.

If discrimination is created or at least perpetuated by capitalists, however, how do we account for its existence in pre-capitalist or socialist societies? Furthermore, it may be true that if all white employers conspire to keep women and minorities in low-wage, low-status jobs, they can all reap monopoly profits. However, if employers A through Y adhere to the agreement, employer Z will always have incentives to *break* the agreement. Z can hire women or minorities cheaply because of the agreement among *other* employers not to hire them, and Z can enhance profits by hiring these otherwise equally productive workers to fill jobs that A through Y are staffing with high-priced white males. Since every other employer has the same incentives as Z, the conspiracy will tend to break down unless cheaters can be disciplined in some way. The collusive-behavior model does not tell us how the conspiracy is maintained and coordinated among the millions of U.S. employers.

A Final Word on the Theories of Discrimination

It would appear that all models of discrimination agree on one thing: any persistence of labor market discrimination is the result of forces that are either noncompetitive or very slow to adjust to competitive forces. While no one model yet can be demonstrated to be superior to the others in explaining the facts, the various theories and the facts they seek to explain suggest that government intervention might be useful in eliminating the noncompetitive (or sluggish) influences. In analyzing these governmental programs, it will be helpful to keep in mind that discriminatory pressures can come from a variety of sources and that discrimination is not necessarily profitable for those who engage in it.

Federal Programs to End Discrimination

Broadly speaking, the government has taken two somewhat conflicting approaches to combat the causes or effects of discrimination. One approach is to mandate *nondiscrimination*, which implies that race, ethnicity, or sex should play no role in hiring, promoting, or compensating workers. The other approach can be characterized as *affirmative action*, in which employers are required to be conscious of race, ethnicity, and gender in their personnel decisions and take steps to ensure that "protected" groups are not underrepresented.

Equal Pay Act of 1963

Before the 1960s, sex discrimination was officially sanctioned by laws that limited women's total weekly hours of work and prohibited them from working at night, lifting heavy objects, and working during pregnancy. Not all states placed all these restrictions on women, but the effect of these laws was to limit the access of women to many jobs. These laws were overturned by the Equal Pay Act of 1963, which also outlawed separate pay scales for men and women using similar skills and performing work under the same conditions.

The act was seriously deficient as an antidiscrimination tool, however, because it said nothing about equal opportunity in hiring and promotions. This flaw can be easily understood by a quick review of our theories of discrimination. If there is prejudice against women from whatever source, employers will treat female employees as less productive or more costly to hire than equally productive males. The market response is for female wages to fall below male wages, because, otherwise, women cannot hope to be able to successfully compete with men in obtaining jobs. The Equal Pay Act took a step toward the elimination of wage differentials, but in so doing, it tended to suppress a market mechanism that helped women obtain greater access to jobs.[48] The act failed to acknowledge that if labor market discrimination is to be eliminated, legislation must require *both* equal pay and equal opportunities in hiring and promotions for people of comparable productivity.

Title VII of the Civil Rights Act

Some defects in the Equal Pay Act of 1963 were corrected the next year. Title VII of the Civil Rights Act of 1964 made it unlawful for any employer "to refuse to hire or to discharge any individual, or otherwise to discriminate against any individual with respect to his compensation, terms, condition, or privileges of employment, because of such individual's race, color, religion, sex or national origin." Title VII applies to all employers in interstate commerce with at least 15 employees and is enforced by the Equal Employment Opportunity Commission (EEOC), which has the authority to mediate complaints, encourage lawsuits by private parties or the U.S. attorney general, or bring suits itself against employers. To enhance the force of the law, the courts permitted individual plaintiffs to expand their suits into *class actions* in which the potential discriminatory impact of an organization's employment practices on an entire group of workers is assessed.

Over the years, the federal courts have fashioned two standards of discrimination that may be applied when discriminatory employment practices are alleged—*disparate treatment* and *disparate impact*. Disparate treatment occurs under Title VII if individuals are treated differently because of their race, sex, color, religion, or national origin and if it can be shown that there was an intent to discriminate. The difficulty raised by this standard is that policies that appear to be neutral in the sense that they ignore race, gender, etc., may nevertheless perpetuate the effects of past discrimination. For example, word-of-mouth recruiting (a seemingly neutral policy) in a plant with a largely white workforce would be suspect under Title VII even if the selection of new employees from among the applicants was done on a nondiscriminatory basis.

The concern with addressing the present effects of past discrimination led to the *disparate impact standard*. Under this approach, it is the result, not the

---

[48]For evidence that state equal-pay laws reduced the relative employment of women, see David Neumark and Wendy A. Stock, "The Labor Market Effects of Sex and Race Discrimination Laws," *Economic Inquiry* 44 (July 2006): 385–419.

motivation, that matters. Policies that appear to be neutral but lead to different effects by race, gender, etc., are prohibited under Title VII unless they can be related to job performance.[49] As a result, plaintiffs, employers, and the courts have become interested in how closely the race or gender composition of those selected for employment, promotion, training, or termination accords with the race or gender composition of the pool of workers available for selection.

Enforcing Title VII using the disparate impact standard has raised several issues regarding hiring, promotion, and pay decisions. One is defining who should be considered in a firm's potential hiring pool; for example, should prospective applicants residing quite far from the workplace be given the same weight as those who live in nearby neighborhoods? Another is statistical: what constitutes convincing (significant) evidence of underrepresentation? Two other issues relate to how employers award seniority to workers and how to judge "equal pay" when occupations are segregated.

Seniority   Many firms use seniority as a consideration in allocating promotion opportunities. Moreover, employees are frequently laid off in order of reverse seniority, the least-senior first, in a recession. Seniority can be calculated either as tenure within the *plant* or as time served within a *department* of the plant; in both cases, such systems have worked against minorities and women who have been hired or promoted to nontraditional jobs as a result of Title VII or some other antidiscrimination program. The most egregious cases occurred under departmental seniority systems when, during a business downturn, women or minorities who had recently been promoted to new departments were laid off ahead of those who had less plant seniority! The argument that the effects of seniority systems lock in past discrimination led to much litigation, but departmental seniority systems are still permitted,[50] and laying off more-senior white employees instead of recently hired minorities to preserve racial balance has been ruled unconstitutional.[51]

Comparable Worth: In Theory   Many contend that achieving "equal pay for equal work" would be a rather hollow victory, since occupations are so segregated by gender that men and women rarely do "equal work." As a result, some have come to support the goal of equal pay for jobs of "comparable worth." Proponents of comparable worth can point to the fact that the "male" occupation of maintaining *machines* (general maintenance mechanic) pays $15 per hour, for example, while the "female" job of maintaining *children* (child-care worker) pays $8.50. Why, they might ask, should those who take care of human beings be paid less than those who take care of machines?

---

[49]*Griggs v. Duke Power Company* 401 U.S. 424 (1971).

[50]*International Brotherhood of Teamsters* v. *United States* 431 U.S. 324, 14 FEP 1514 (1977).

[51]*Franks v. Bowman Transportation* 424 U.S. 747, 12 FEP Cases 549 (1976); *Fire Fighters Local* 1784 v. Stotts, U.S. S. Ct. no. 82–206, June 12, 1984; and *Wygant* v. *Jackson Board of Education*, U.S. S. Ct. no. 84–1340, May 19, 1986.

When asked why mechanics are paid more than child-care workers, economists answer in terms of market forces: for some reason, the supply of mechanics must be smaller relative to the demand for them than the supply of child-care workers. Perhaps this reason has to do with working conditions, or perhaps it is more difficult to learn and keep abreast of the skills required of a mechanic, or perhaps occupational crowding increases the supply of child-care workers. Whatever the reason, it is argued, wages are the price of labor—and prices play such a critical *practical* role in the allocation of resources that they are best left unregulated.

Thus, in fighting discrimination, most economists would advise modifying the demand or supply behaviors that *cause* unequal outcomes rather than treating the *symptoms* by regulating wages. If the wages of child-care workers were to be raised above their market-clearing level, to take the case at hand, a surplus would be created in that labor market. Above-market wages would mean fewer jobs and more unemployed applicants—hardly the outcome envisioned by those wanting to end discrimination. (A lengthy analysis of these unintended side effects is given in Example 12.4, in the context of equalizing the pay of university professors across the various disciplines.)

Comparable Worth: In Practice   Comparable-worth policies have generally relied on job-rating schemes often used by employers with internal labor markets to determine or justify pay differentials associated with various job titles or promotion steps. The process involves assigning points to each job according to the knowledge and problem-solving abilities required, its level of accountability, the physical conditions of work, and perhaps other characteristics. Jobs with equal point values would receive equal pay and, of course, jobs assigned higher point values would receive higher pay (Appendix 12A provides an example). The process by which points are awarded to each job is obviously critical, and both sides of the comparable-worth issue see it as a problem. Opponents claim that job ratings can be used to unjustifiably raise the pay in targeted jobs above market levels, while proponents argue that the job ratings now used within firms unfairly lower the value of women's jobs.[52]

The relatively few cases in which comparable-worth policies have been used to address unequal pay in the United Kingdom and the United States, for example, have required equalization only *within the boundaries of a single employer.* In contrast to the United Kingdom, however, where cases involving both public and private employers have come before the tribunals specially created to hear comparable-worth complaints,[53] the major push for comparable worth in the United States has come in the state and local government sector.

To date, the estimated effects of implementing comparable worth in the United States, Canada, and the United Kingdom have been neither as positive

---

[52]See Donald J. Treiman and Heidi L. Hartmann, eds., *Women, Work and Wages: Equal Pay for Jobs of Equal Value* (Washington, D.C.: National Academy Press, 1981); and Steven E. Rhoads, *Incomparable Worth* (Cambridge: Cambridge University Press, 1993): 160–165.

[53]Rhoads, *Incomparable Worth*, 148–160.

EXAMPLE 12.4

Comparable Worth and the University

Some of the difficulties involved with the concept of *comparable worth* can be illustrated by an example in which gender does not even enter. Consider the labor market for university professors in the fields of computer science and English, and suppose that initially, the demand and supply curves for both are given by D_{0C} and S_{0C} and D_{0E} and S_{0E}, respectively. As the figure indicates, in this circumstance, the same wage (W_0) will prevail in both markets, and N_{0C} computer science professors and N_{0E} English professors will be hired. Suppose also that in some objective sense, the quality of the two groups of professors is equal.

Presumably this is a situation that advocates of comparable worth would applaud. Both types of professors require the same amount of training, represented by a Ph.D., and both are required to engage in the same activities: teaching and research. Unless we are willing to assign different values to the teaching and research produced in different academic fields, we must conclude that the jobs are truly comparable. Hence, if the two groups are equal in quality, equal wages would be justified according to the concept of comparable worth.

Suppose now, however, that the demand for computer science professors rises to D_{1C} as a result of the increasing number of students who want to take computer science courses. Suppose at the same time the demand for English professors falls to D_{1E} because fewer students want to take elective courses in English. At the old equilibrium wage rate, there is now an excess demand for computer science professors of $N_{1C} - N_{0C}$ and an excess supply of English professors of $N_{0E} - N_{1E}$.

How can universities respond? One possibility is to let the market work; the wage of computer science professors will rise to W_{1C} and that of English professors will fall to W_{1E}. Employment of the former will rise to N_{2C}, while employment of the latter will become N_{2E}.

Another possibility is to keep the wages of the two groups of professors equal at the old wage rate of W_0. Universities could respond to the excess demand for computer scientists and the excess supply of English professors by lowering hiring standards for the former and raising them for the latter. Since the average quality of English professors would then exceed the average quality of computer scientists, the wage paid per "quality-unit" would now be higher for the computer scientists. Hence, true comparable worth—equal pay for *equal-quality* workers performing comparable jobs—would not be achieved. Moreover, employment and course offerings in this situation would not change to meet changing student demands.

Alternatively, some advocates of comparable worth might argue that universities should respond by raising the wages of *all* professors to W_{1C}. While this would eliminate the shortage of computer science professors, it would exacerbate the excess supply of English professors, raising

as its proponents had hoped nor as dire as its critics had portended. The effects on male/female wage differentials appear small, as do any negative effects on female employment.[54]

[54]Peter E. Orazem, J. Peter Mattila, and Sherry K. Welkum, "Comparable Worth and Factor Point Pay Analysis in State Government," *Industrial Relations* 31 (Winter 1992): 195–215; Mark R. Killingsworth, *The Economics of Comparable Worth* (Kalamazoo, Mich.: W. E. Upjohn Institute for Employment Research, 1990); Shulamit Kahn, "Economic Implications of Public Sector Comparable Worth: The Case of San Jose, California," *Industrial Relations* 31 (Spring 1992): 270–291; Ronald G. Ehrenberg and Robert S. Smith, "Comparable Worth Wage Adjustments and Female Employment in the State and Local Sector," *Journal of Labor Economics* 5 (January 1987): 43–62; and Manning, "The Equal Pay Act as an Experiment to Test Theories of the Labour Market."

EXAMPLE 12.4

Comparable Worth and the University (*Continued*)

it to $N_{4E} - N_{3E}$. Universities would respond by reducing the employment of English professors to N_{3E} (and reducing course offerings). Moreover, the excess supply again would permit universities to raise hiring standards for English professors, so again average quality would rise. As a result, once more the wage per quality-unit of English professors would be less than that of computer science professors, and again true comparable worth would not be achieved.

The message we can take away from this example is that it is difficult to "trick the market." In the face of changing relative demand conditions, either wage differentials for the two types of professors must be allowed to arise or quality differentials will arise. In neither case, however, can comparable worth be achieved. Put another way, the value of a job cannot be determined independently of market conditions.

The Market for Computer Science and English Professors

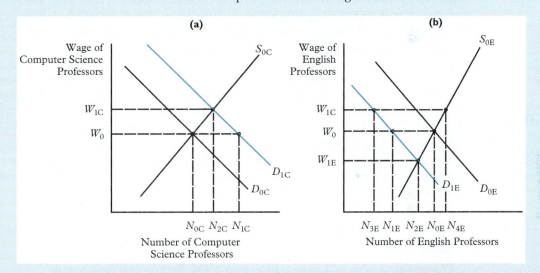

The Federal Contract Compliance Program

In 1965, the U.S. Office of Federal Contract Compliance Programs (OFCCP) was established to monitor the hiring and promotion practices of federal contractors (firms supplying goods or services to the federal government). OFCCP requires contractors above a certain size to analyze the extent of their underutilization of women and minorities and to propose a plan to remedy any such underutilization. Such a plan is called an *affirmative action plan.* Contractors submitting unacceptable plans or failing to meet their goals are threatened with cancellation of their contracts and their eligibility for future contracts, although these drastic steps are rarely taken.

Affirmative action planning is intended to commit firms to a schedule for rapidly overcoming unequal career opportunities afforded to women and minorities. Such planning affects both *hiring* and *promotion* practices, and like requirements under the disparate impact standard, the contract compliance program requires covered employers to take race, ethnicity, and gender into account when developing personnel policies.

Those who favor affirmative action point out that even if nondiscrimination in personnel actions were to be scrupulously followed, it still would not be an expeditious way to overcome the adverse effects of past discrimination. For example, consider the data in Table 12.6 for a hypothetical firm that has just agreed to follow a policy of nondiscrimination in hiring. Black workers represent 12 percent of the firm's hiring pool, but right now, they are only 6.25 percent of the firm's 1,600-person workforce. The firm is not growing, so the only hiring opportunities come when workers quit, which they do at a rate of 20 percent each year. Because of these limited hiring opportunities, and because 20 percent of black workers hired subsequently leave each year, the table illustrates that nondiscrimination in hiring would not achieve proportionate representation even in 10 years (and progress would be slower with a lower quit rate).

Besides the argument that affirmative action represents *reverse* discrimination (against white males), the potential effects of the contract compliance program have been questioned on two other grounds. First, if underrepresented groups are to be given preference in hiring, will firms be required to hire less-qualified workers? Second, because the program covers only federal contractors, will qualified minorities and women just be shifted from the noncovered to the covered sector, with no overall gain in employment? These questions lead us to a review of the effects that antidiscrimination programs have had in the United States.

Table 12.6

Change in the Racial Composition of a 1,600-Person Job Group with Nondiscriminatory Hiring from a Pool That Is 12 Percent Black (20 Percent Yearly Turnover Rate)

	Year						
	0	1	2	3	4	5	10
Number of blacks							
Loss		20	24	26	29	31	36
New hires		38	38	38	38	38	38
Net gain		18	14	12	11	7	2
Cumulative level	100	118	132	144	155	162	181
Percent black	6.25	7.37	8.25	9.00	9.69	10.12	11.31

Effectiveness of Federal Antidiscrimination Programs

A comprehensive review of federal affirmative action programs concluded that they have redistributed employment opportunities among federal contractors (who generally pay more than noncontractors) toward blacks and women, although the extent of this redistribution does not seem to have been very large. It also appears that with respect to women, there is no evidence that affirmative action was associated with lower levels of human capital or job performance. Weaker labor market credentials were found among minorities hired, but there is scant evidence that job performance levels were lower.[55] Can we conclude that the improvements for minorities and women in this one sector have translated to improvements overall?[56] This question has been most extensively addressed with respect to African Americans.

The ratio of black to white incomes has risen since 1960, and it is natural to ask, is this rise a result of government efforts or were other forces working to accomplish this result? Three other forces are commonly cited. First, an improvement in the *educational attainment* of black workers relative to that of whites during this period is thought to have played an important role in raising the ratio of black to white earnings; in fact, one study estimated that increased educational attainment accounts for 20 percent to 25 percent of the post-1960 gain in the earnings ratio.[57] Second, there is evidence that the *quality* of schooling improved more after 1960 for blacks than for whites, and one study has estimated that from 15 percent to 20 percent of the increased earnings ratio can be attributed to enhanced school quality.[58] Finally, it has been argued that because the relatively large reduction in labor-force participation rates among blacks was centered in the least-educated group of workers, the average earnings of those who remained employed were thereby increased, giving

[55]Harry Holzer and David Neumark, "Assessing Affirmative Action," *Journal of Economic Literature* 38 (September 2000): 483–568; and Harry Holzer and David Neumark, "Affirmative Action: What Do We Know?" *Journal of Policy Analysis and Management* 25 (Spring 2006): 463–490. For a study of an apparently successful program aimed at improving opportunities for black workers among defense contractors during World War II, see William J. Collins, "Race, Roosevelt, and Wartime Production: Fair Employment in World War II Labor Markets," *American Economic Review* 91 (March 2001): 272–286; and for one that analyzes the effects of ending of an affirmative action program, see Caitlin Knowles Myers, "A Cure for Discrimination? Affirmative Action and the Case of California's Proposition 209," *Industrial and Labor Relations Review* 60 (April 2007): 379–396. Court-ordered affirmative action may have stronger effects; see Justin McCrary, "The Effect of Court-Ordered Hiring Quotas on the Composition and Quality of Police," *American Economic Review* 97 (March 2007): 318–353.

[56]For a comprehensive review of the contributions to economic development of programs to empower women in developing countries, see Ester Duflo, "Women Empowerment and Economic Development," *Journal of Economic Literature* 50 (December 2012): 1051–1079.

[57]James P. Smith and Finis R. Welch, "Black Economic Progress after Myrdal," *Journal of Economic Literature* 27 (June 1989): 519–564.

[58]David Card and Alan B. Krueger, "School Quality and Black-White Relative Earnings: A Direct Assessment," *Quarterly Journal of Economics* 107 (February 1992): 151–200. For a study of how school desegregation affected the wages of blacks in the South, see Orley Ashenfelter, William J. Collins, and Albert Yoon, "Evaluating the Role of *Brown vs. Board of Education* in School Equalization, Desegregation, and the Income of African Americans," *American Law and Economics Review* 8 (Summer 2006): 213–248.

EMPIRICAL STUDY

CAN WE CATCH DISCRIMINATORS IN THE ACT?
THE USE OF FIELD EXPERIMENTS IN IDENTIFYING
LABOR MARKET DISCRIMINATION

As we saw earlier in this chapter, the statistical methods economists employ to measure labor market discrimination against, say, African Americans, essentially break the observed black/white wage differential into two parts: the part that can be explained by differences in *measurable* productive characteristics and the residual associated with the payoffs to those characteristics. While some may assert that the residual reflects discrimination, others will point to this residual as attributable (in whole or in part) to productive characteristics that could not be measured. In the legal terms introduced toward the end of this chapter, statistical analyses are useful in identifying *disparate impact*, but they are not usually conclusive in this regard. Furthermore, they fall short of proving *disparate treatment* because they focus on results, not on the behaviors that produced them. Can we find ways to actually catch discriminators in the act?

One method used to observe discrimination is to conduct an *audit*—or field experiment—in which employers (if the focus is on the labor market) with advertised job openings are approached by auditors of different races posing as applicants. Each "applicant" is paired with an auditor of a different race, and both are given fictional work histories and educational backgrounds that are carefully constructed to be equivalent in terms of job qualifications. Discrimination can be inferred if auditors who are black, say, are systematically treated worse than whites.

Constructing convincing audits is challenging, because if the auditors know the purpose of the study, they may behave during interviews in ways that induce employers to respond in the way they believe the researchers expect. Sending auditors to interview for jobs is also very time-consuming and expensive, so large samples are usually not feasible. It is also challenging to match auditors in terms of size and appearance and train them to present themselves in the same way at interviews.

One recent study, however, circumvented these problems with audits by sending some 5,000 résumés to firms in Boston and Chicago that advertised a total of 1,300 job openings. The researchers then analyzed how likely each résumé was to elicit a callback. The résumés were paired to achieve equivalence, and the names assigned were used to suggest race: Lakisha Washington and Jamal Jones, for example, were among the names used as indicators of African-American applicants, while names such as Emily Walsh and Greg Baker were used to suggest that the applicant was white. If the résumés with African-American–sounding names elicited significantly fewer invitations for the applicant to come in for an interview, we could conclude that race discrimination occurred.

The findings were remarkable. Job applicants with white-sounding names needed to send 10 résumés to receive one callback, while those whose names sounded African American needed to send 15 résumés to receive one callback. This 50 percent gap was statistically significant, and it grew larger as the quality of résumés rose (that is, in jobs with greater skill demands, the racial differential was even larger). If these fictitious résumés indicated the applicants lived in a wealthier or more-educated neighborhood, callback probabilities increased for both blacks and whites, but the size of the racial differential remained constant. While newspaper ads represent only one hiring channel, and the audit ended at the callback stage

(rather than going through to job offers), this study demonstrates that racial discrimination persists in the labor market to this day.

Source: Marianne Bertrand and Sendhil Mullainathan, "Are Emily and Greg More Employable than Lakisha and Jamal? A Field Experiment on Labor Market Discrimination," *American Economic Review* 94 (September 2004): 991–1013. For a subsequent analysis of the apparent causes and economic effects of distinctively African-American names, see Roland G. Fryer, Jr. and Steven D. Levitt, "The Causes and Consequences of Distinctively Black Names," *Quarterly Journal of Economics* 119 (August 2004): 767–805. For a study of Asian, African, and Slavic immigrants to Sweden who changed their names to hide their ethnicity, see Mahmood Arai and Peter Skogman Thoursie, "Renouncing Personal Names: An Empirical Examination of Surname Change and Earnings," *Journal of Labor Economics* 27 (January 2009): 127–147. A study from Canada is contained in Philip Oreopoulos, "Why Do Skilled Immigrants Struggle in the Labor Market? A Field Experiment with Thirteen Thousand Resumes," *American Economic Journal* 3 (November 2011): 148–171.

the *appearance* of overall improvement. Roughly 10 percent to 20 percent of the improved earnings ratio has been attributed to this last factor.[59]

Taking the upper estimates of the three sources of earnings increases cited earlier, at least a third of the improvement in the black/white earnings ratio for men remains to be explained. Is it possible that federal efforts to reduce discrimination in the labor market were responsible? One review of the literature and the evidence on this issue concluded that, overall, federal efforts were successful in raising earnings levels of African Americans.[60]

---

[59]John J. Donohue III and James Heckman, "Continuous versus Episodic Change: The Impact of Civil Rights Policy on the Economic Status of Blacks," *Journal of Economic Literature* 29 (December 1991): 1603–1643.

[60]Donohue and Heckman, "Continuous versus Episodic Change." For a thumbnail sketch of this comprehensive review, see James Heckman, "Accounting for the Economic Progress of Black Americans," in *New Approaches to Economic and Social Analyses of Discrimination*, eds. Richard R. Cornwall and Phanindra V. Wunnava (New York: Praeger, 1991): 331–337. A paper by Kenneth Y. Chay, "The Impact of Federal Civil Rights Policy on Black Economic Progress: Evidence from the Equal Employment Opportunity Act of 1972," *Industrial and Labor Relations Review* 51 (July 1998): 608–632, supports the view that federal efforts helped to reduce the black/white pay gap.

One important fact about black economic progress is that there was a discontinuous jump in the black/white earnings ratio between 1960 and 1975. This sudden improvement coincided with the onset of federal antidiscrimination programs, and it cannot be explained by the rather continuous increases taking place in such other factors as schooling quality or attainment. A second important fact is that the greatest gains in the black/white earnings ratio during the 1960–1975 period were in the South, where segregation was most blatant and where federal antidiscrimination efforts were greatest.

The conclusion that federal antidiscrimination efforts were at least partially successful in raising the relative earnings of blacks must be acknowledged as somewhat surprising, because studies of individual programs (such as the contract compliance program) have estimated rather meager results. The paradox of overall improvement resulting from programs that appear to have been individually weak may be resolved by noting that each program was part of a comprehensive set of programs—largely aimed at the South—to dismantle all forms of racial segregation, register blacks to vote, and provide legal remedies for victims of discrimination. In the words of one analyst:

> There is evidence that southern employers were eager to employ blacks if they were given the proper excuse. This produced a strong leverage effect for the new laws. . . . An entire pattern of racial exclusion was challenged. This helps to explain how an apparent straw (the Equal Employment Opportunity Commission and the Office of Federal Contract Compliance) could have broken the back of southern employment discrimination. They were only the tip of a federal iceberg launched against the South.[61]

While optimism about the effects of federal antidiscrimination programs in the 1960s and 1970s is warranted, it is not clear that such programs were successful after 1980, when the market for less-educated workers turned poor. It might be possible to argue that the earnings of blacks after 1980 would have been even *lower* were it not for federal efforts, but the evidence so far is that once the most blatant forms of discrimination were attacked, the effects of federal efforts have weakened.[62]

---

[61]Heckman, "Accounting for the Economic Progress of Black Americans," 336.

[62]Donohue and Heckman, "Continuous versus Episodic Change," 1640. Harry J. Holzer, "Why Do Small Establishments Hire Fewer Blacks Than Large Ones?" *Journal of Human Resources* 32 (Fall 1998): 896–914, documents that small firms lag behind larger ones in the hiring of blacks. While the source of this lag is unknown, the lag does indicate a sector in which further gains might be possible.

Review Questions

1. Chinese and Japanese Americans have average earnings that are equal to, or above, those of white Americans. Does this fact imply that they are not victims of labor market discrimination?

2. "In recent years, the wage gap between skilled and unskilled workers in the United States has grown. This growth means that measured labor market discrimination against unskilled Mexican immigrants is also growing." Comment on whether the second part of this statement is implied by the first part.

3. An Associated Press article quoted a report saying that male high school teachers were paid more than female high school teachers. Assuming this is true, what information would you require before judging this to be evidence of wage discrimination?

4. Will government-mandated requirements to hire qualified minorities (at nondiscriminatory wages) in the same proportions they are found in the relevant labor force reduce the profits of firms that formerly engaged in employer discrimination? Fully explain your answer.

5. Suppose that the United States were to adopt, on a permanent basis, a wage subsidy to be paid to employers who hire black, disadvantaged workers (those with relatively little education and few marketable skills). Analyze the potential effectiveness of this subsidy in overcoming (a) labor market discrimination against blacks and (b) pre-market differences between blacks and whites in the long run.

6. You are involved in an investigation of charges that a large university in a small town is discriminating against female employees. You find that the salaries for professors in the nearly all-female School of Social Work are 20 percent below average salaries paid to those of comparable rank elsewhere in the university. Is this university exhibiting behavior associated with *employer* discrimination? Explain.

7. Suppose a city pays its building inspectors (all male) $16 an hour and its public health nurses (all female) $10 an hour. Suppose that the city council passes a comparable-worth law that in effect requires the wages of public health nurses to be equal to the wages of building inspectors. Evaluate the assertion that this comparable-worth policy would primarily benefit high-quality nurses and low-quality building inspectors.

8. In the 1920s, South Africa passed laws that effectively prohibited black Africans from working in jobs that required high degrees of skill; skilled jobs were reserved for whites. Analyze the consequences of this law for black and white South African workers.

9. Assume that women live longer than men, on the average. Suppose an employer hires men and women, pays them the same wage for the same job, and contributes an equal amount per person toward a pension. However, the promised monthly pension after retirement is smaller for women than for men because the pension funds for them have to last longer. According to a decision by the Supreme Court, the above employer would be guilty of discrimination because of the unequal monthly pension benefits after retirement.

   a. Comment on the Court's implicit definition of discrimination. Is it consistent with the definition normally used by economists? Why or why not?

   b. Analyze the economic effects of this decision on men and women.

Problems

1. Calculate the Index of Dissimilarity for males and females, given the information below.

Occupation	Males	Females
A	40	20
B	40	25
C	20	25
Total	100	70

2. Suppose that $MRP_L = 20 - 0.5L$ for left-handed workers, where $L =$ the number of left-handed workers and MRP_L is measured in dollars per hour. The going wage for left-handed workers is $10 per hour, but employer A discriminates against these workers and has a discrimination coefficient, D, of $2 per hour. Graph the MRP_L curve and show how many left-handed workers employer A hires. How much profit has employer A lost by discriminating?

3. Suppose that (similar to Figure 12.3 in the text) the market demand for female workers depends on the relative wage of females to males, W_F/W_M, in the following manner: $W_F/W_M = 1.1 - 0.0001N_F$ if the number of female workers is less than 1,000, where N_F is the number of female workers hired in the market; $W_F/W_M = 1$ if the number of female workers is between 1,001 and 5,000; and $W_F/W_M = 1.5 - 0.0001N_F$ if the number of female workers is above 5,000. Graph this demand curve, and calculate the relative wage of female workers when the number hired is 200, 2,000, and 7,000. When does discrimination harm female workers in this market?

4. (Appendix). In the market for delivery truck drivers, $L_S = -45 + 5W$ and $L_D = 180 - 10W$, where $L =$ number

   of workers and $W =$ wage in dollars per hour. In the market for librarians, $L_S = -15 + 5W$ and $L_D = 190 - 10W$. Find the equilibrium wage and employment level in each occupation, and explain what will happen if a comparable-worth law mandates that the librarians' wage be increased to equal the delivery truck drivers' wage. Use a graph.

5. (Appendix) The following table gives the Hay Point (HP) total for five female jobs and the corresponding monthly salary (S).

Hay Point	Average Salary of Females ($)
200	1200
310	1300
425	1500
500	1580
550	1635

   A least squares regression applied to data for the *male* occupations yielded the following relationship: $S_i = 1200 + 0.90 \, HP_i$. Using the "male" equation, estimate the earnings that the females would have earned based on the HP level of the occupation. Analyze whether discrimination appears to exist. Is there a pattern by skill level?

6. Suppose the hourly marginal revenue product of all workers in a particular labor market is $MRP_L = 20 - L$, where $L =$ the number of workers. The hourly wage rate for women in this market is $W = \$5.75$. What is the gap between MRP_L and wage in this labor market if $L = 12$? Is this gap a reliable measure of discrimination against women in this market?

7. Suppose the marginal revenue product of all workers in a particular labor market is $MRP_L = 20 - L$, where $L =$ the number of workers. Suppose women are receiving

$8 per hour and 10 women are hired. How many workers would a nondiscriminatory employer hire? How much profit is the employer willing to forgo by hiring these 10 female workers?

8. Suppose a researcher estimated the relationship between salary, gender, and age among a group consisting of male and female workers but ignored the fact that, on average, male workers have more work experience than females. The estimated regression of salary on gender and age is

$$S_i = 21354.83 + 239.45\,G_i + 93.17\,A_i$$
$$(15252.9) \quad (95.6) \quad (29.58)$$

where S_i = salary of a worker, $G_i = 1$ if the worker is male and 0 if the worker is female, and A_i = the employee's age. Standard errors of the coefficients are in parentheses.

When experience was included in the regression, the estimated regression is

$$S_i = 21177.75 + 226.27\,G_i + 89.73\,A_i + 443.41\,X_i$$
$$(16111.3) \quad (186.8) \quad (34.64) \quad (47.7)$$

where X_i = the years of work experience of the worker. Comparing the two estimated regressions, does there appear to be salary discrimination by gender? Discuss the implications of omitting the experience variable in the first regression.

Selected Readings

Aigner, Dennis J., and Glen G. Cain. "Statistical Theories of Discrimination in Labor Markets." *Industrial and Labor Relations Review* 30 (January 1977): 175–187.

Altonji, Joseph G., and Rebecca M. Blank. "Race and Gender in the Labor Market." In *Handbook of Labor Economics*, eds. Orley Ashenfelter and David Card. New York: Elsevier, 1999.

Becker, Gary. *The Economics of Discrimination.* 2nd ed. Chicago: University of Chicago Press, 1971.

Blau, Francine D., Marianne A. Ferber, and Anne E. Winkler. *The Economics of Women, Men, and Work.* 5th ed. Upper Saddle River, N.J.: Prentice-Hall, 2006.

Blau, Francine D., and Lawrence M. Kahn. "Gender Differences in Pay." *Journal of Economic Perspectives* 14 (Fall 2000): 75–99.

Cain, Glen G. "The Challenge of Segmented Labor Market Theories to Orthodox Theory: A Survey." *Journal of Economic Literature* 14 (December 1976): 1215–1257.

Cornwall, Richard R., and Phanindra V. Wunnava, eds. *New Approaches to Economic* and Social Analyses of Discrimination. New York: Praeger, 1991.

Donohue, John H., III, and James Heckman. "Continuous versus Episodic Change: The Impact of Civil Rights Policy on the Economic Status of Blacks." *Journal of Economic Literature* 24 (December 1991): 1603–1643.

Goldin, Claudia. *Understanding the Gender Gap: An Economic History of American Women.* New York: Oxford University Press, 1990.

Holzer, Harry, and David Neumark. "Assessing Affirmative Action." *Journal of Economic Literature* 38 (September 2000): 483–568.

Killingsworth, Mark R. *The Economics of Comparable Worth.* Kalamazoo, Mich.: W. E. Upjohn Institute for Employment Research, 1990.

Lang, Kevin, and Jee-Yeon K. Lehman. "Racial Discrimination in the Labor Market: Theory and Empirics." *Journal of Economic Literature* 50 (December 2012): 959–1006.

Smith, James P., and Finis R. Welch. "Black Economic Progress after Myrdal." *Journal of Economic Literature* 27 (June 1989): 519–564.

Estimating Comparable-Worth Earnings Gaps: An Application of Regression Analysis

Although many economists have difficulty with the notion that the worth of a job can be established independently of market factors, formal job evaluation methods have existed for a long time. The state of Minnesota is one of the few states that began to implement comparable-worth pay adjustments for their employees based on such an evaluation method. How might we use data from job evaluations to estimate whether discriminatory wage differentials exist?[1]

Minnesota, in conjunction with Hay Associates, a prominent national compensation consulting company, began an evaluation of state government jobs in 1979. Initially evaluated were 188 positions in which at least 10 workers were employed and which could be classified as either *male* (at least 70 percent male incumbents) or *female* (at least 70 percent female incumbents) positions. Each position was evaluated by trained job evaluators and awarded a specified number of "Hay Points" for each of four job characteristics or factors: required know-how, problem-solving, accountability, and working conditions. The scores for each factor were then added to obtain a total Hay Point (HP), or job evaluation, score for each job. These scores varied across the 188 job titles from below 100 to over 800 points.

Given these job evaluation scores, the next step is to ask what the relationship is between the salary (S_i) each male job pays and its total HP_i score. Each dot in Figure 12A.1 represents a male job, and this figure plots the monthly salary for each job against its total HP score. On average, it is clear that jobs with higher scores receive higher pay.

---

[1]For a more complete discussion of the Minnesota job evaluation and comparable-worth study, see *Pay Equity and Public Employment* (St. Paul, Minn.: Council on the Economic Status of Women, March 1982).

Figure 12A.1

Estimated Male Comparable-Worth Salary Equation

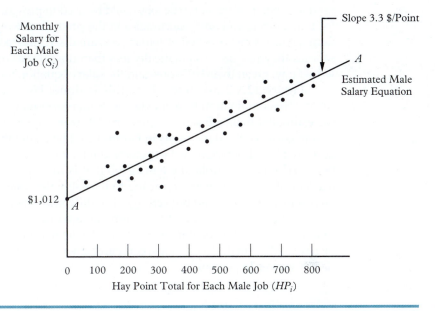

Although these points obviously do not all lie on a single straight line, it is natural to ask what straight line fits the data best. An infinite number of lines can be drawn through these points, and some precise criterion must be used to decide which line fits best. As discussed in Appendix 1A, the procedure typically used by statisticians and economists is to choose that line for which the sum (across data points) of the squared vertical distances between the line and the individual data points is minimized. The line estimated from the data using this method—the *method of least squares*—has a number of desirable statistical properties.[2]

Application of this method to data for the male occupations contained in the Minnesota data yielded the estimated line:[3]

$$S_i = 1012 + 3.3\ HP_i \qquad\qquad (12A.1)$$

So, for example, if male job i were rated at 200 *HPs*, we would predict that the monthly salary associated with job i would be $1,012 + (3.3)(200), or $1,672. This estimated male salary equation is drawn in Figure 12A.1 as line AA.

Now, if the value of a job could be determined solely by reference to its job evaluation score, one would expect that in the absence of wage discrimination against women, male and female jobs rated equal in terms of total HP scores would

---

[2]See Appendix 1A.

[3]These estimates are obtained in Ronald Ehrenberg and Robert Smith, "Comparable Worth in the Public Sector," in *Public Sector Payrolls,* ed. David Wise (Chicago: University of Chicago Press, 1987).

pay equal salaries (at least on average). Put another way, the same salary equation used to predict salaries of male jobs could be used to provide predictions of salaries for female jobs, and any inaccuracies in the prediction would be completely random. Hence, a test of whether female jobs are discriminated against is to see if the salaries they pay are systematically less than the salaries one would predict they would pay, given their *HP* scores and the salary equation for male jobs.

Figure 12A.2 illustrates how this is done. Here, each dot represents a salary/*HP* combination for a female job. Superimposed on this scatter of points is the estimated male job salary equation, *AA*, from Figure 12A.1. The fact that the vast majority of the data points in Figure 12A.2 lie below the male salary line suggests that female jobs tend to be underpaid relative to male jobs with the same number of *HP*s. For example, the female job that is rated at 300 *HP*s (point *a*) is paid a salary of S_{300}^F. However, according to the estimated male salary line, if that job were a male job, it would be paid S_{300}^M. The difference in percentage terms between S_{300}^M and S_{300}^F is an estimate of the comparable-worth earnings gap—the extent of underpayment—for the female job. Indeed, calculations suggest that the average (across all the female occupations) comparable-worth earnings gap in the Minnesota data was over 16 percent.[4]

Figure 12A.2

Using the Estimated Male Comparable-Worth Salary Equation to Estimate the Extent of Underpayment in Female Jobs

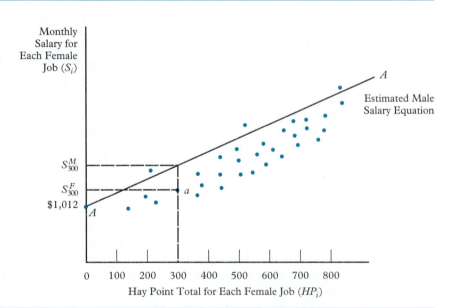

[4]See Ehrenberg and Smith, "Comparable Worth in the Public Sector." Analogous estimates for four other states are presented there and in Elaine Sorensen, "Implementing Comparable Worth: A Survey of Recent Job Evaluation Studies," *American Economic Review* 76 (May 1986): 364–367.

This brief presentation has glossed over a number of complications that must be addressed before such estimates can be considered estimates of wage discrimination against female jobs.[5] These include issues relating to the reliability and/or potential sex bias in the evaluation methods, whether salaries and *HP* scores may be related in a nonlinear fashion, whether the *composition* of any given total *HP* score (across the four sets of job characteristics) affects salaries, and whether variables other than the job evaluation scores can legitimately affect salaries. Nonetheless, it should give the reader a sense of how comparable-worth wage gap estimates are computed.

---

[5]For a more complete discussion of these issues and empirical studies relating to comparable worth, see Ehrenberg and Smith, "Comparable Worth in the Public Sector"; M. Anne Hill and Mark R. Killingsworth, eds., *Comparable Worth: Analyses and Evidence* (Ithaca, N.Y.: ILR Press, 1989); Robert T. Michael, Heidi L. Hartmann, and Brigid O'Farrell, eds., *Pay Equity: Empirical Inquiries* (Washington, D.C.: National Academy Press, 1989); and Killingsworth, *The Economics of Comparable Worth*.

CHAPTER 13

Unions and the Labor Market

O ur analysis of the workings of labor markets has, for the most part, omitted any mention of the role of labor unions and collective bargaining. Because many people have strong and conflicting opinions about the role of unions in our society, it is often difficult to remain objective when discussing them. Some people view labor unions as forms of monopolies that, while benefiting their own members, impose substantial costs on other members of society. In contrast, others view unions as the major means by which working persons have improved their economic status and as important forces behind much social legislation.

The purpose of this chapter is to analyze the goals, major activities, and overall effects of unions in the context of economic theory. We begin with some general descriptive material on unions internationally, with a more comprehensive description of unions in the United States, and then move to a fundamental theoretical question: what are the economic forces on the demand side of the market that constrain unions in their desire to improve the welfare of their members? With these constraints in mind, we devote the last half of the chapter to analyzing the primary activities of the collective bargaining process and to discussing empirical evidence on how unions affect wages, employment, labor productivity, and profits.

Union Structure and Membership

Labor unions are organizations of workers whose primary objectives are to improve the pecuniary and nonpecuniary conditions of employment among their members. Unions can be classified into two types: an *industrial* union represents most or all of the workers in an industry or firm regardless of their occupations, and a *craft* union represents workers in a single occupational group. Examples of industrial unions are the unions representing automobile workers, bituminous coal miners, and rubber workers; craft unions include those representing the various building trades, printers, and dockworkers.

Unions bargain with employers over various aspects of the employment contract, including pay and employee benefits; conditions of work; policies regarding hiring, overtime, job assignment, promotion, and layoff; and the means by which grievances between workers and management are to be resolved. Bargaining can occur at different levels.

At one end of the spectrum, bargaining can be highly *centralized*, with representatives of entire industries sitting at the bargaining table to decide on contracts that bind multiple employers. At the *decentralized* end of the spectrum, bargaining can take place between a union and a single company—or even between the workers and management at a single plant within a company. In the middle are multiemployer agreements reached at the local level between a union and several employers; an example of such agreements would be the ones typically signed between construction craft unions (plumbers, say) and the construction contractors that operate in a given metropolitan area.

As large collective organizations, unions also represent a *political* force in democratic countries. Often, unions will use the political process in the attempt to gain benefits they could not as easily win through collective bargaining. In some countries (Great Britain, for example), unions have their own political party. In others, such as the United States, unions are not affiliated with any single political party; rather, they act as lobbyists for various bills and policies at the federal, state, and local levels of government.

International Comparisons of Unionism

Table 13.1 displays two measures of unionization in several countries. One measure is the percentage of workers who are members of unions, and the other is the percentage of workers in each country whose conditions of employment are covered by a collective bargaining agreement. Three characteristics of this table stand out. First, the United States and Japan are notable in the relatively small percentages of their workers—less than 20 percent—who are currently covered by collectively bargained agreements. Collective bargaining in these countries and Canada takes place at the level of firms and plants, and provisions of the resulting agreements rarely extend beyond the membership of the unions that signed them.

Table 13.1

Union Membership and Bargaining Coverage, Selected Countries, 1990, 2009–2010

Country	Union Membership as a Percentage of Workers		Percentage of Workers Covered by a Collective Bargaining Agreement	
	1990	2010*	1990	2009**
Austria	46.9	28.1	98.0	99.0
France	9.9	7.6	92.0	90.0
Sweden	80.0	68.4	89.0	91.0
Australia	39.6	18.0	80.0	40.0
Italy	38.8	35.1	83.0	80.0
Netherlands	24.3	19.4	82.0	82.3
Germany	31.2	18.6	72.0	62.0
Switzerland	22.7	17.8	48.0	48.0
United Kingdom	38.2	26.5	54.0	32.7
Canada	34.0	27.5	38.0	31.6
Japan	25.4	18.4	23.0	16.0
United States	15.5	11.4	18.3	13.6

*Data for the Netherlands and Switzerland are for 2009.

**Data for Austria and Australia are for 2007; data for France, Sweden, Netherlands and Switzerland are for 2008.

Source: Organisation for Economic Co-operation and Development, http://www.oecd-ilibrary.org/employment/oecd-employment-outlook-2012/trade-union-density-and-collective-bargaining-coverage-1990-and-latest-year_empl_outlook-2012-graph50-en

Second, in Australia and most European countries, collective bargaining coverage is extended to a very high fraction of workers who are not members of unions. In Austria, for example, collective bargaining is highly centralized, in that agreements are national in their scope, and in most of continental Europe, the parties at the bargaining table represent entire sectors of the economy. Clearly, the historical and legal contexts within which unions operate in each country are critical to an understanding of the differing levels of membership and labor-market influence.[1]

Third, the data in Table 13.1 indicate large declines in union membership in every country listed over the two decades from 1990 to 2010. The declines in membership, however, tend to be larger than the declines in the percentage of workers *covered* by a collective bargaining agreement—with roughly half of the countries shown having virtually the same coverage percentages in 2009 as in 1990.

---

[1] Richard B. Freeman, "Labor Market Institutions Around the World," working paper no. 13242, National Bureau of Economic Research (Cambridge, Mass.: July 2007); Harry Katz, "The Decentralization of Collective Bargaining: A Literature Review and Comparative Analysis," *Industrial and Labor Relations Review* 47 (October 1993): 3–22; and Richard B. Freeman, "American Exceptionalism in the Labor Market: Union–Nonunion Differentials in the United States and Other Countries," in *Labor Economics and Industrial Relations: Markets and Institutions*, eds. Clark Kerr and Paul D. Staudohar (Cambridge, Mass.: Harvard University Press, 1994): 272–299.

Clearly, then, there are country-specific differences in the legal and institutional contexts within which unions operate.

Much of the empirical work on unions has been done in the United States, where bargaining is decentralized and, as we have seen, the majority of workers are nonunion. While the study of unions in one country does not easily generalize to others, given the different legal and historical environments, this empirical work may be of growing interest elsewhere, owing to what may be a trend toward a greater decentralization of bargaining in most developed economies during the last decade or two.[2] No matter how well (or poorly) studies of U.S. unions generalize, however, their results must still be understood within the context of American institutions. We therefore turn to a brief history of the legal structure within which American unions have operated.

The Legal Structure of Unions in the United States

Public attitudes and federal legislation have not always been favorably disposed toward labor unions and the collective bargaining process in the United States. For example, during the early part of the twentieth century, employers were often able to claim that unions acted like monopolies in the labor market and hence were illegal under existing antitrust laws. Such employers were often able to get court orders or injunctions that prohibited union activity and aided them in stopping union organization drives. Given this environment, it is not surprising that the fraction of the labor force who were union members stood at less than 7 percent in 1930. Since that date, however, legislation has changed the environment in which American unions operate.

National Labor Relations Act
The National Labor Relations Act (NLRA) of 1935 required employers to bargain with unions that represented the majority of their employees and made it illegal for employers to interfere with their employees' right to organize collectively.[3] The National Labor Relations Board (NLRB) was established by the NLRA and given power both to conduct *certification elections* to see which union, if any, employees wanted to represent them and to investigate claims that employers were either violating election rules or refusing to bargain with elected unions. In the event violations were found, the NLRB was given further power to order violators to "cease and desist."

---

[2]Katz, "The Decentralization of Collective Bargaining." Michael Wallerstein, Miriam Golden, and Peter Lange, "Unions, Employers' Associations, and Wage-Setting Institutions in Northern and Central Europe, 1950–1992," *Industrial and Labor Relations Review* 50 (April 1997): 379–401, present evidence for Austria, Germany, Belgium, the Netherlands, and Scandinavia, suggesting that a general process of decentralization has not occurred in those countries. For a more recent study of the effects of decentralized bargaining in Spain, see David Card and Sara De La Rica, "Firm-Level Contracting and the Structure of Wages in Spain," *Industrial and Labor Relations Review* 59 (July 2006): 573–592.

[3]Actually the NLRA was much less pro-labor than our brief discussion indicates; the NLRA also gave the NLRB power to investigate employers' claims that their employees, or unions, were violating provisions of the act.

Taft-Hartley Act   After World War II, the pendulum shifted decidedly in an antiunion direction. The Labor-Management Relations Act of 1947 (better known as the Taft-Hartley Act) restricted some aspects of union activity and permitted workers to vote in elections that could decertify a union from representing them in collective bargaining. Perhaps its most famous provision is Section 14B, which permits individual states to pass *right-to-work laws*. These laws prohibit the "union shop" requirement, often written into collective bargaining agreements, that a person become a union member as a condition of employment. Twenty-four states, located primarily in the South, Southwest, and Plains areas, have passed such laws—the most recent of which are in Indiana and Michigan (2012).

Landrum-Griffin Act   In 1959, Congress passed the Labor-Management Reporting and Disclosure Act (the Landrum-Griffin Act). This law, which was designed to protect the rights of union members in relation to their leaders, contained provisions that increased union democracy. As argued later, such provisions may well have had the side effect of increasing the level of strike activity in the economy.

Government Unions   The laws that have been discussed to this point relate only to the private sector, where unionism in the United States first flourished. Indeed, prior to the 1960s, public sector workers were prohibited from organizing. In 1962, however, President Kennedy signed Executive Order 10988, which gave federal workers the right to organize and bargain over working conditions but not wages.[4] The influence of federal unions on wages, then, operates primarily through the political pressure they can exert on the president to recommend, or on Congress to approve, pay increases.

Beginning with Wisconsin in 1959, a number of states have extended to employees of state and local governments (including teachers) the rights to organize and collectively bargain. Generally speaking, public sector unions are barred from going on strike, so laws permitting their right to bargain were accompanied by provisions for some form of binding arbitration (through which neutral parties would ultimately decide on disputes that could not be voluntarily resolved).[5] Ironically, in 2011, Wisconsin adopted a controversial law that limited the bargaining of public-sector unions and governmental employers—except in the case of public safety workers—to base wages (not to other forms of pay, such as benefits or performance pay).[6] As of 2013, the role and power of public sector

----

[4]There were some major exceptions—namely, postal workers and employees of federal government authorities, such as the Tennessee Valley Authority. In each of these cases, the prices of the products or services produced (mail delivery, hydroelectric power) can be raised to cover the cost of the contract settlement. In other federal agencies, salaries are paid out of general revenues.

[5]See Richard B. Freeman, "Unionism Comes to the Public Sector," *Journal of Economic Literature* 24 (March 1986): 41–86, for a more complete discussion of the evolution of legislation governing bargaining in the public sector.

[6]State of Wisconsin, "Summary of Provisions of 2011 Act 10," at http://legis.wisconsin.gov/lfb/publications/budget/2011-13-Budget/documents/act32/act%2010.pdf.

unions are being increasingly challenged—across several countries—by politicians and taxpayer groups interested in controlling government spending.[7]

Union Membership   Union membership as a fraction of all American workers peaked in the years following World War II at about one-third. Since then, the percentage of all workers who are union members has dropped continuously, except among government workers. Figure 13.1 graphs the trends in union membership starting in 1973, when the membership percentages in the private and public sectors (and hence, overall) were about 24 percent. As of 2012, membership among private sector workers has fallen to 6.6 percent, membership among government workers has risen to 35.9 percent, and the overall rate of membership now stands at 11.2 percent.

Figure 13.1

Union Membership as a Percentage of All Workers, by Sector, United States, 1973–2012

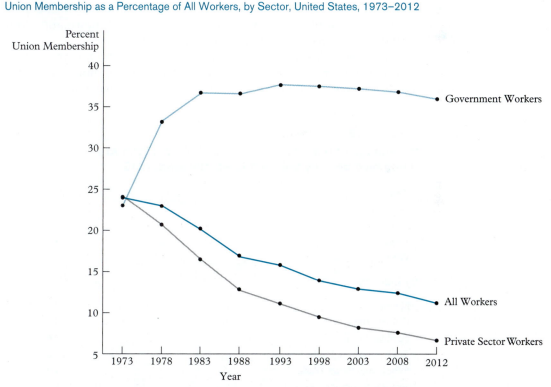

Source: Barry T. Hirsch and David A. Macpherson, *Union Membership and Earnings Data Book* (Arlington, Va.: Bureau of National Affairs, 2013), Table 1.

---

[7]David Lewin, Jeffrey Keefe, and Thomas A. Kochan, "The New Great Debate about Unionism and Collective Bargaining in U.S. State and Local Governments," *ILR Review* 65 (October 2012): 749–778.

Unionized workers in the United States are members of "local" unions, organized at the level of the plant, the employer, or (especially for construction unions) the metropolitan area. We have noted that in the United States, bargaining is relatively decentralized, so it is local unions that bear the brunt of negotiations. These locals, however, are usually members of larger "national" or "international" (usually meaning they include Canadian workers) unions, which provide help and advice to the locals with their organization drives and, later, their negotiations. If bargaining is being done at the industry level or with one firm at the national level, it is representatives of the national or international union who sit at the bargaining table.

In turn, most of the nationals and internationals (and therefore some three-quarters of all union members) are affiliated with the AFL-CIO, which stands for the American Federation of Labor and Congress of Industrial Organizations. The AFL-CIO is not a union but rather an association of unions organized both nationally and at the state level. Its main functions are to provide a unified political voice for its diverse member unions, to recommend and coordinate membership initiatives among its affiliates, and to provide research and information to its members. It does not directly negotiate with employers.

Table 13.2 provides another way of looking at union membership in the United States. From this table, we can see that men are more likely to be unionized than women and that African American workers have higher rates of

Table 13.2

Percentage of U.S. Wage and Salary Workers Who Are Union Members, by Selected Characteristics, 2012

Men	12.0
Women	10.5
African American	13.4
Hispanic	9.8
White	11.1
By Industry	
Mining	7.2
Construction	13.2
Manufacturing	9.6
Transportation, Public Utilities	20.6
Wholesale, Retail Trade	4.7
Finance, Insurance	1.2
Public Sector	35.9

Source: Barry T. Hirsch and David A. Macpherson, *Union Membership and Earnings Data Book* (Arlington, Va.: Bureau of National Affairs, 2013), Table 3a; and U.S. Bureau of Labor Statistics Web site, http://www.bls.gov/news.release/union2.t03.htm.

unionization than other groups. By sector, the highest rates of unionization are clearly among government workers; in the private sector, only in construction and transportation/public utilities are membership rates above 10 percent.

What Do Unions Want?   The founder of the American Federation of Labor, Samuel Gompers, was once asked what unions wanted. His answer was quite simple: "More." Hardly anyone who has studied union behavior believes unions' objectives are quite that simple, but it is self-evident that unions want to advance the welfare of their members in one way or another.

Some objectives of unions are *procedural*, in that unions give workers some "voice" in the way employers manage the workplace—especially in the handling of various human-resource issues, such as job assignment, the allocation of overtime, the handling of worker discipline and grievances, the composition of employee-benefit packages, and the establishment of joint labor-management safety committees and work teams. Procedural objectives are not always costly to the employer, who (especially with modern management techniques) may want a mechanism through which employee participation in management decisions can be achieved. Other procedural objectives, however, put limits on managerial prerogatives that, while difficult to quantify, are often seen by employers as costly.[8] We will close this chapter with a fuller discussion of the "voice" mechanism that unions can provide.

Wanting "more," however, is usually associated with the union goal of increasing the *compensation* levels of its members. The most visible element of compensation is the wage rate, but bargaining in the United States also occurs over such employee benefits as pensions, health insurance, and vacations. (In many other developed countries, these benefits are mandated by the government and therefore are not subject to collective bargaining.) The attempts to achieve "more," of course, take place in the context of *constraints*. We now turn to an analysis of these constraints.

Constraints on the Achievement of Union Objectives

Employers are on the other side of the bargaining table, and they must make agreements that permit them to operate successfully both with their workers *and* within their product markets. Increased compensation for their workers will give them incentives to *substitute* capital for labor, and to the extent that their costs of production rise, there will also be pressures to reduce the *scale* of operations. In short, unions must ultimately reckon with the downward-sloping demand curve for labor (for an example from professional sports, see Example 13.1). As a result, both the position and the elasticity of this curve become fundamental market constraints on the ability of unions to accomplish their objectives.

---

[8]For a useful summary of the "voice" model of unions, see John T. Addison and Clive R. Belfield, "Union Voice," *Journal of Labor Research* 25 (Fall 2004): 563–596.

A Downward Sloping Demand Curve for Football Players?

Do unions behave as if the labor demand curve slopes down? Put differently, do unions appear to recognize that higher wages can limit employment opportunities for their members? Some evidence that they do comes from the National Football League (NFL).

The collective bargaining agreement signed in 2011 by the union and ownership of the NFL contained clauses that, among other things, specified (a) *minimum salaries* for NFL players that rise with a player's years of service in the league, and (b) a limit on the *total* salaries that each team can pay to its players (a team *salary cap*). Provision (a) is essentially a minimum-wage provision, where the minimum rises as the player ages, and it is intended to put a "floor" under the salaries of "bench" players who are not the stars that teams bid against each other to attract. Provision (b) is intended to foster competitiveness in the league by limiting the ability of a team to stockpile star (expensive) players.

Apparently, however, the players' union was concerned that the service-related minimum wages would give teams incentives to replace older, more experienced bench players with younger (lower-paid) ones. The 2011 agreement, therefore, contains a "Minimum Salary Benefit," specifying that when a player with over 4 years of experience is paid at the minimum for his service time, only the *minimum salary for a 2-year player* gets counted against the team's salary cap. For example, in 2013, a player with 5 years of experience must be paid \$715,000 per year, but only \$555,000 (the minimum salary for a player with 2 years of service) is charged against the team's salary cap. In essence, then, while an older bench player must be paid the minimum salary for his service level, his team is allowed to go above its salary cap to do so. Teams thus have at least some incentive to retain the services of their more experienced (and hence more expensive) bench players rather than replacing them with younger players.

_____

Source: This provision of the NFL's collective bargaining agreement was brought to our attention by our colleague, Lawrence Kahn. For more details, see NFL-NFL Players' Association, "Collective Bargaining Agreement," August 4, 2011.

To see this, ignore employee benefits and working conditions for the moment and consider Figure 13.2, which shows two demand curves, D_e^0 and D_i^0, which intersect at an initial wage W_0 and employment level E_0. Suppose a union seeks to raise the wage rate of its members to W_1. To do so would cause employment to fall to E_e^1 if the union faced the relatively elastic demand curve D_e^0 or to E_i^1 if it faced the relatively inelastic demand curve D_i^0. Other things equal, the more elastic the demand curve for labor is, the greater will be the reduction in employment associated with any given increase in wages.

Suppose now that the demand curve D_i^0 shifts out to D_i^1 while the negotiations are under way, owing perhaps to growing demand for the final product. If the union succeeds in raising its members' wages to W_1, there will be no absolute decrease in employment in this case. Rather, the union will have only slowed the rate of growth of employment to E_i^2 instead of E_i^3. More generally, other things

Figure 13.2

Effects of Demand Growth and the
Wage Elasticity of Demand on the
Market Constraints Faced by Unions

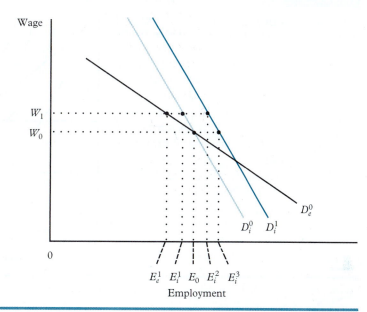

equal, the more rapidly the labor demand curve is shifting out (in), the smaller (larger) will be the reduction *in employment* or the reduction *in the rate of growth of employment* associated with any given increase in wages. Hence, unions' ability to raise their members' wages will be strongest in rapidly growing industries with inelastic labor demand curves. Conversely, unions will be weakest in industries in which the wage elasticity of demand is highly elastic and in which the demand curve for labor is shifting in.

We now turn to two alternative models of how unions and employers behave in their agreements about wages and benefits, given the market constraints they face. Each of the models analyzes the interaction of—and trade-offs between—wages and employment.

The Monopoly-Union Model

The simplest model of the union–employer relationship has been called one of *monopoly unionism*, whereby the union sets the price of labor and the employer responds by adjusting employment to maximize profits, given the new wage rate with which it is confronted. This model is formally illustrated by Figure 13.3, which shows the labor demand curve, D, facing workers as a simple function of the wage rate (for simplicity, we abstract from other elements in the compensation package).

Figure 13.3

Union Maximizes Utility Subject
to the Constraint of the Labor
Demand Curve

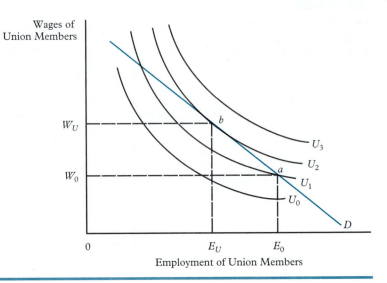

In Figure 13.3, we assume that the union values both the wages and
the employment levels of its members and that it can aggregate its members'
preferences so that we can meaningfully speak of a union utility function that
depends on these two variables. This utility function is summarized by the
family of indifference curves U_0, U_1, U_2, U_3. Each curve represents a locus of
employment/wage combinations about which the union is indifferent. The indifference curves are negatively sloped, because to maintain a given utility level, the
union must be compensated for a decline in one variable (employment or wages)
by an increase in the other. They exhibit the property of diminishing marginal
rates of substitution (they are convex to the origin) because we assume the loss of
employment that unions are willing to tolerate in return for a given wage increase
grows smaller as employment falls. Finally, higher indifference curves represent
higher levels of union utility.

Suppose that in the absence of a union, market forces would cause the wage
to be W_0 and employment to be E_0 (point a in Figure 13.3). How does collective
bargaining affect this solution? One possibility is that the union and the employer
will agree on a higher wage rate and then, given the wage rate, the employer will
determine the number of union members to employ. Given a bargained wage rate,
the employer will maximize profits and determine employment from its labor
demand curve. Since the union presumably knows this, its goal is to choose the
wage that maximizes its utility subject to the constraint that the resultant wage/
employment combination will lie on the demand curve.

In terms of Figure 13.3, the union will seek to move to point b, where indifference curve U_2 is just tangent to the labor demand curve. At this point, wages would be W_U and employment E_U. Given the constraint posed by the labor demand curve, point b represents the highest level of utility the union can attain.

The Efficient-Contracts Model

An interesting feature of the simple monopoly-union model is that it is not *efficient*. Instead of having unions set the wage and then having employers determine employment, both parties could be better off if they agreed to jointly determine wages and employment. Put succinctly in terms of Figure 13.3, there is a whole set of wage/employment combinations that at least one of the parties would prefer and that would leave the other no worse off; these combinations have been called *efficient contracts*. (While the term *efficient* recalls our discussion of *Pareto efficiency* in chapter 1, it is being used more narrowly here. Pareto efficiency refers to *social* welfare, and a transaction is said to be Pareto-improving if *society* is made better off—that is, if some gain and no one else loses. *Efficiency* in the current context denotes only that the welfare of the two parties can be improved; it does not imply that society, as a whole, gains. Indeed, we will see in the next section that, in general, these efficient contracts lead to a socially wasteful use of labor.)

The Formal Model   To begin our analysis, we must recall from chapter 3 that the labor demand curve is defined by the employer's choosing an employment level that maximizes profits at each wage rate. In Figure 13.3, for example, if we start at point a on the demand curve with the wage at W_0 and employment at E_0, profits would fall if the employer were to either expand or contract employment. Thus, if employment were to be changed from E_0, a lower wage rate would have to be paid to keep profits from falling. The larger the deviation of employment from E_0, the lower wages would have to be to keep profits constant.

We can formalize this by reintroducing the concept of *isoprofit curves*, first discussed in chapter 8. Here, an isoprofit curve is a locus of wage/employment combinations along which an employer's profits are unchanged. Figure 13.4 shows three isoprofit curves for the employer whose labor demand curve is D. As discussed earlier, each curve reaches a maximum at its intersection with the demand curve; as we move along a given isoprofit curve in either direction away from the demand curve, wages must fall to keep profits constant. A higher isoprofit curve represents a lower level of employer profits because the wage associated with each level of employment is greater along the higher curve. So, for example, the employer would prefer any point on I_0, which includes the original wage/employment combination (point a), to any point on I_2, which includes the monopoly-union wage/employment solution (point b).

Figure 13.4

Employer Isoprofit
Curves

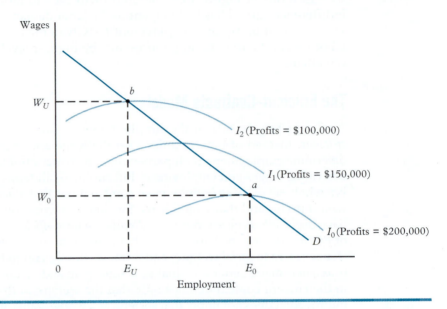

Figure 13.5 superimposes the family of employer isoprofit curves from Figure 13.4 onto the family of union indifference curves from Figure 13.3 and illustrates why the monopoly-union solution, point b, is not an *efficient contract*. Suppose that rather than locating at point b, the parties negotiated a contract that called for them to locate at point d, where the wage rate (W_d) would be lower but employment of union members (E_d) would be higher. At point d, the union would be better off, since it would now be on a higher indifference curve, U_3, while the firm would be no worse off, since it would still be on isoprofit curve I_2.

Similarly, suppose that rather than negotiating a contract to wind up at b, the parties agreed to a contract that called for them to locate at point e, with a wage rate of W_e and an employment level of E_e. Compared with the monopoly-union solution (point b), the union is equally well off, since it remains on indifference curve U_2, but now the firm is better off because it has been able to reach isoprofit curve I_1. Because I_1 lies below I_2, it represents a higher level of profits.

In fact, there is a whole set of contracts that both parties will find at least as good as point b; these are represented by the shaded area in Figure 13.5. Among this set, the ones that are efficient contracts—contracts in which no party can be made better off without hurting the other—are the ones in which employer isoprofit curves are just tangent to union indifference curves, such as at points d and e. Indeed, there is a whole locus of such points, and they are represented in the figure by the curve ed. Each point on ed represents a tangency of a union indifference curve and an employer isoprofit curve; these are points at which the employer and the union are equally willing to substitute wages for employment at the margin (so that no more mutually beneficial trades of wages for employment are possible).

Figure 13.5

The Contract Curve—The Locus
of Efficient Contracts

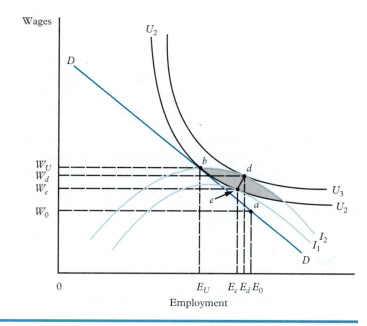

All of the points on *ed*, which is often called the *contract curve* (or locus of efficient contracts), will leave both parties at least as well off as at point b and at least one party better off. However, the parties are not indifferent to where along *ed* the settlement is reached. Obviously, the union would prefer to be close to *d* and the employer close to *e*. Where on the contract curve a settlement actually occurs in this model depends upon the bargaining power of the parties.[9]

The Contract Curve   Two points need to be made about the contract curve. First, as shown in Figure 13.5, it lies off and to the right of the firm's labor demand curve. This implies that the firm is using more labor at any given wage rate than it would if it had unilateral control over employment, and it implies that the collective bargaining agreement will contain clauses that create (more precisely, ratify the use of) excess labor in the plant. For example, there may be clauses pertaining to minimum crew sizes or to rigid rules governing which workers must do specific tasks; some agreements may even have no-layoff clauses for certain workers. While the employer may be better off with these clauses, because it can induce the union to agree to a lower wage, its failure to minimize costs is socially wasteful (society could increase its aggregate output if labor were reallocated and used more productively).

---

[9]For an attempt to model how bargaining power affects the nature of contract settlements, see Jan Svejnar, "Bargaining Power, Fear of Disagreement, and Wage Settlements: Theory and Empirical Evidence from U.S. Industry," *Econometrica* 54 (September 1986): 1055–1078.

Second, it is not necessary that the slope of the contract curve be up and to the right, as shown in Figure 13.5. Depending on the shapes of the union's indifference curves and the firm's isoprofit curves, the contract curve could slope up and to the left or even be *vertical*.

An interesting special case involving a vertical contract curve is created when the curve is *vertical at the original (preunion) level of employment*. In this case, the firm agrees to maintain employment at the level that *maximizes profits*, given the *market* wage rate. The union and firm in effect bargain over how these profits are split; every dollar gained by the union is a dollar lost by the employer, and there are no changes in output or employment. If the union succeeds in raising wages above their original (market) level, however, it is reasonable to ask how the firm could afford to pay higher wages, maintain its original employment level, and still operate successfully in the product market. The answer must be that it is in a *noncompetitive* product market and is therefore receiving profits in excess of those required for it to remain in business; a reduction in these excess profits might make management unhappy, but it does not cause the employer to change its behavior.[10] Further implications of a vertical contract curve are discussed in the final section of this chapter, in which the social gains or losses of unionization are considered.

Are Contracts Really Efficient?   How realistic is the efficient-contracts model as a description of the wage-determination process in unionized workplaces in the United States? The most obvious way to answer this question would be to look at the language of collective bargaining agreements to see if there is evidence of joint agreement on employment levels. Many contracts covering public school teachers specify maximum class sizes or minimum teacher/student ratios, and a few private sector contracts include no-layoff provisions for certain core workers, but the world is too uncertain for an employer to explicitly guarantee a certain *level* of employment.

Contracts, however, often contain language that perpetuates the use of excess labor. Many require that duties cannot be performed "out of job title," so a custodian, for example, could not paint a scuffed wall (a painter would be required) or an off-stage actress could not perform any of the duties of a lighting technician. These rigidities in job assignment are clearly designed to protect jobs even though the level of employment is not explicitly determined in the contract.

There are also *indirect* tests of the efficient-contracts model. This model and the monopoly-union model yield different implications about how wages and employment will vary in response to changes in variables that affect either the demand for labor or union preferences. A number of studies have analyzed these implications, and it is fair to say that at the moment, there is evidence that both supports and goes against the efficient-contracts model.[11]

---

[10]Brian E. Becker, "Union Rents as a Source of Takeover Gains among Target Shareholders," *Industrial and Labor Relations Review* 49 (October 1995): 3–19. An empirical test for a vertical contract curve can be found in John M. Abowd, "The Effect of Wage Bargains on the Stock Market Value of the Firm," *American Economic Review* 79 (September 1989): 774–800.

[11]Nicholas Lawson, "Is Collective Bargaining Pareto Efficient? A Survey of the Literature," *Journal of Labor Research* 32 (September 2011): 282–304.

The Activities and Tools of Collective Bargaining

Having analyzed the general constraints facing unions as they seek to accomplish their goals, we now turn to an economic analysis of several activities that affect their power. We begin with a simple model of union *membership* and use it to help understand the decline in membership faced by U.S. unions in recent decades. Next, we briefly discuss the ways in which unions use the *political* process in an attempt to alter the market constraints they face. Finally we analyze the ultimate threats—of calling a *strike* or having an unresolved dispute decided by third-party *arbitration*—that unions can carefully use in the collective bargaining process.

Union Membership: An Analysis of Demand and Supply

A simple model of the demand for and supply of union activity can be used to explain the forces that influence union membership.[12] On the demand side, employees' desire to be union members will be a function of the *price* of union membership; this price includes initiation fees, monthly dues, the value of the time an individual is expected to spend on union activities, and so on. Other things equal, the higher the price, the lower the fraction of employees that will want to be union members, as represented by the demand curve D_0 in Figure 13.6.

Figure 13.6

The Demand for and Supply of Unionization

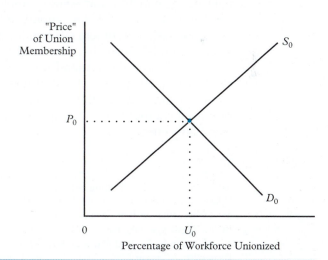

<hr />

[12]This model is based on the approach found in Orley Ashenfelter and John Pencavel, "American Trade Union Growth, 1900–1960," *Quarterly Journal of Economics* 83 (August 1969): 434–448; and John Pencavel, "The Demand for Union Services: An Exercise," *Industrial and Labor Relations Review* 24 (January 1971): 180–191.

It is costly to represent workers in collective bargaining negotiations and to supervise the administration of union contracts. Therefore, it is reasonable to conclude that, other things equal, the willingness of unions to supply their services is an upward-sloping function of the price of union membership, as represented by the supply curve S_0 in Figure 13.6. The intersection of these demand and supply curves yields an equilibrium percentage of the workforce that is unionized (U_0) and an equilibrium price of union services (P_0).

What are the forces that determine the *positions* of the demand and supply curves? Anything that causes either the demand curve or the supply curve to shift to the right will increase the level of unionization in the economy, other things equal. Conversely, if either of these curves shifts to the left, other things equal, the level of unionization will fall. Identifying the factors that shift these curves would enable us to explain *changes* in the level of unionization in the economy over time.

On the demand side, it is likely that individuals' demand for union membership is positively related to their perceptions of the *net benefits* from being union members. For example, the larger the wage gain they think unions will win for them, the further to the right the demand curve will be. Another factor is *tastes*; if individuals' tastes for union membership increase, perhaps because of changes in social attitudes, the demand curve will also shift to the right.

On the supply side, anything that changes the *costs* of union-organizing activities will affect the supply curve. Introduction of labor legislation that makes it easier for unions to win representation elections will shift the supply curve to the right. Changes in the composition of employment that make it more difficult to organize the workforce will shift the curve to the left and reduce the level of unionization.[13]

The decline in unionization rates that has taken place in the United States since the mid-1950s is hypothesized to be at least partially explained by five factors related to the demand for, or supply of, union services: demographic changes in the labor force, a shifting industrial mix, a heavier mix of employment in states in which the environment is not particularly favorable for unions, increased competitive pressures, and increased employer resistance to union-organizing efforts.[14]

[13]Rebecca S. Demsetz, "Voting Behavior in Union Representation Elections: The Influence of Skill Homogeneity and Skill Group Size," *Industrial and Labor Relations Review* 47 (October 1993): 99–113, finds that plants with more homogeneously skilled workers are more supportive of unions, other things equal.

[14]For a discussion of the factors underlying the rise and fall of unionization rates in the United States, see the essays by Edward P. Lazear, Richard B. Freeman, and Melvin W. Reder in *Journal of Economic Perspectives* 2 (Spring 1988): 59–110. For quantitative estimates of the extent to which the factors discussed in this section are responsible for the decline in unionization, see Henry Farber, "The Decline of Unionization in the United States: What Can Be Learned from Recent Experience?" *Journal of Labor Economics* 8, no. 1, pt. 2 (January 1990): S75–S105; Henry Farber and Alan Krueger, "Union Membership in the United States: The Decline Continues," in *Employee Representation: Alternatives and Future Decisions*, eds. Bruce Kaufman and Morris Kleiner (Madison, Wis.: Industrial Relations Research Association, 1993).

Demographic Changes   The fraction of the labor force that is female has increased substantially (see chapter 6), and women have historically tended not to join unions. The benefits from union membership are a function of individuals' expected tenure with firms; seniority provisions, job security provisions, and retirement benefits are not worth much to individuals who expect to be employed at a firm for only a short while. *In the past*, women tended to have shorter expected job tenure than men and to have more intermittent labor force participation. Given the *growing* labor force attachment of women, however, demographic changes are an unlikely explanation for the decline in union membership.[15]

Changing Industrial Mix   A second possible factor in the decline of union membership is the shift in the industrial composition of employment, first discussed in chapter 2. The fraction of workers in government, the most heavily unionized sector in the United States, has held more or less constant since the mid-1970s, while there has been a substantial decline in the employment shares of the most heavily unionized industries in the *private* sector (see Table 13.2): manufacturing, mining, construction, transportation, and public utilities. Employment has increased most notably in wholesale and retail trade; in finance, insurance, and real estate; and in the service industries—all of which are the least-unionized sectors of the economy.

Why do the latter industries tend not to be unionized? These industries tend to be highly competitive, with high price elasticities of product demand and therefore high wage elasticities of labor demand, which limit unions' abilities to increase wages without suffering substantial employment declines. For this reason, the net benefits individuals perceive from union membership may be lower in these industries, and an increase in their importance in the economy would shift the demand for union services to the left in Figure 13.6, thereby reducing the percentage of the workforce that is unionized.

These industries also tend to be populated by small establishments. The demand for unionization is thought to be lower for employees who work in small firms, because they often feel less alienated from their supervisors. Similarly, since it is more costly to try to organize 1,000 workers spread over 100 firms than it is to organize 1,000 workers at one plant, it is often thought that the supply of union services would shift left as the share of employment going to small firms increased. Both of these factors tend to suggest (in terms of Figure 13.6) that unionization will decline as the share of employment in small establishments increases, providing another reason the shift in industrial distribution of employment may have affected the extent of unionization.

---

[15]Farber and Krueger, "Union Membership in the United States: The Decline Continues," argue that demographic changes have played almost no role in the decline.

Regional Shifts in Employment   A third factor that may have contributed to the decline in union strength is the movement in population and employment that has occurred since 1955 from the industrial Northeast and Midwest to the South and West. As noted earlier, the South and Southwest are heavily represented among the 24 states that have right-to-work laws. Such laws raise the costs of expanding union membership, because individuals who accept employment with a firm cannot be compelled to become union members as a condition of employment. In terms of Figure 13.6, these laws shift the supply curve of union services to the left, thereby reducing the level of unionization. Between 1955 and 2010, the proportion of employees working in right-to-work states increased from 24 to 44 percent. This shifting geographic distribution of the workforce, coupled with the existence of these laws, undoubtedly tended to depress union membership.

It is not at all obvious, however, that the decline in unionization occasioned by the move to the South and West can be attributed to right-to-work laws per se. The extent of unionization in right-to-work states tended to be lower than that in other states even before the passage of the laws. These laws may only reflect attitudes toward unions that already exist in these communities.[16]

Competitive Pressures   A fourth factor is increased foreign competition in manufacturing and the deregulation of the airline, trucking, and telephone industries (see Example 13.2). In these industries, which tend to be highly unionized, increased product-market competition has served to reduce the power of unions to raise wages; that is, more product-market competition increases the price elasticity of product demand and hence (as we saw in chapter 4) increases the elasticity of labor demand. To the extent that union members' wages did not fall substantially in the face of increased product-market competition, unionized employment within these industries could have been expected to fall. Indeed, the share of unionized employment in these previously heavily unionized industries has fallen substantially in the past two decades as competition from both foreign firms and new, nonunion employers in the deregulated industries has increased.[17]

By making labor demand curves more elastic, increased competitive pressures reduce the benefits to workers of collective action, hence shifting the demand curve for union membership to the left. Moreover, increased product-market

---

[16]For a recent study that cites earlier literature on the effects of right-to-work laws, see Steven E. Abraham and Paula B. Voos, "Right-to-Work Laws: New Evidence from the Stock Market," *Southern Economic Journal* 67 (October 2000): 345–362.

[17]Evidence that the effects of foreign competition are felt primarily in union members' employment levels, not in their wages, is found in John Abowd and Thomas Lemieux, "The Effects of International Trade on Union Wages and Employment: Evidence from the U.S. and Canada," *in Immigration, Trade, and the Labor Market*, eds. John Abowd and Richard Freeman (Chicago: University of Chicago Press, 1991). Also see Matthew J. Slaughter, "Globalization and Declining Unionization in the United States," *Industrial Relations* 46 (April 2007): 329–346.

EXAMPLE 13.2

The Effects of Deregulation on Trucking and Airlines

Before the late 1970s, the heavily unionized trucking and airline industries were regulated by the U.S. government, which restricted the entry of potential competitors and granted existing carriers a degree of monopoly power. From 1978 to 1980, however, these restrictions were largely removed. The resulting increase in product-market competition increased the price elasticity of product demand and, of course, the wage elasticity of labor demand in those industries—thus reducing the power of unions to raise wages.

These changes reduced the desirability of being unionized, and indeed, both industries experienced sharp declines in unionized employment. In the airline industry, for example, the employment of union mechanics had fallen 15 percent to 20 percent by 1983. In trucking, the rate of unionization throughout the industry fell from 88 percent to 65 percent by 1990.

Data from: David Card, "The Impact of Deregulation on the Employment and Wages of Airline Mechanics," *Industrial and Labor Relations Review* 39 (July 1986): 527–538; and Michael H. Belzer, *Sweatshops on Wheels: Winners and Losers in Trucking Deregulation* (New York: Oxford University Press, 2000).

competition may well call forth *employer* responses that affect workers' demand for unions. For example, if firms find that foreign competition has intensified, they may seek to relocate in areas where workers are less likely to unionize; similarly, they may seek to employ workers in demographic groups whose demands for union membership are relatively low. Increased competition may also cause employers to resist union-organizing efforts more vigorously, which could well increase the costs of such efforts and shift the supply curve of union services to the left.

Employer Resistance   U.S. employers can, and often do, play an active role in opposing union-organizing campaigns, using both legal and illegal means. For example, under the NLRA, it is legal for employers to present arguments to employees detailing why they think it is in the workers' best interests to vote against a union and for employers to hire consultants to advise them how to best conduct a campaign to prevent a union from winning an election. However, it is illegal for an employer to threaten to withhold planned wage increases if the union wins the election or for a firm to discriminate against employees involved in the organizing effort. If a union believes an employer is involved in illegal activities during a campaign, it can file an unfair labor practices charge with the NLRB that, if sustained, can lead the NLRB to issue a formal complaint.

Table 13.3 chronicles, from 1970 to 2010, the number of union representation elections, the percent won by the union, and the number of unfair labor practice complaints filed by the NLRB against employers. While not all unfair practices occur during representation elections, the ratio of such complaints to the number of elections held gives us at least some idea of the intensity of employer resistance.

Table 13.3

Union Representation Elections and Unfair Labor Practice Complaints Issued by NLRB, 1970–2010

	Representation Elections		NLRB Complaints against Employers	
Year	Number	Percent Won by Union	Number	Ratio: Complaints to Elections
1970	8,074	55.2	1,474	0.183
1975	8,577	48.2	2,335	0.272
1980	8,198	45.7	5,164	0.630
1985	4,614	42.4	2,840	0.616
1990	4,210	46.7	3,182	0.756
1993	3,586	47.6	3,576	0.997
1996	3,277	44.8	2,919	0.891
1999	3,585	50.5	2,036	0.568
2003	2,937	53.8	1,767	0.601
2005	2,649	56.8	1,160	0.438
2010	1,823	62.3	1,166	0.640

Source: *Annual Report of the National Labor Relations Board*, Appendix Tables 3A, 13 (various years).

This ratio rose steeply in the 1970s and 1980s, peaked in 1993 (at a ratio over five times greater than it had been two decades earlier), and in the last decade has more or less returned to the levels experienced in the 1980s.

Why did employers offer increased resistance to unions after 1975? Some argue that employers were more disposed, on purely ideological grounds, to maintain union-free workplaces. Others suggest, however, that the change in employer behavior was the result of an increase in the costs that employers expected to face if the unions won. During the 1970s and early 1980s, wages of unionized workers grew more rapidly than the wages of nonunion workers just as competition from foreign producers increased sharply. Thus, the perceived economic benefits to nonunion employers of keeping their workplaces nonunion increased. This factor, it is argued, encouraged them to increasingly and aggressively combat union election campaigns, through both legal and illegal means.[18]

Union Actions to Alter the Labor Demand Curve

Many actions that unions take are direct attempts to relax the market constraints they face: either to *increase the demand* for union labor or to *reduce the wage elasticity of demand* for their members' services. Many of these attempts have *not* occurred through the collective bargaining process per se. Rather, they have occurred

---

[18]William T. Dickens, "The Effect of Company Campaigns on Certification Elections: Law and Reality Once Again," *Industrial and Labor Relations Review* 36 (July 1983): 560–575; Robert Flanagan, *Labor Relations and the Litigation Explosion* (Washington, D.C.: Brookings Institution, 1987); and Farber, "The Decline in Unionization in the United States."

through union support for legislation that at least indirectly achieved union goals and through direct public relations campaigns to increase the demand for products produced by union members.

Shifting Product Demand

To increase the demand for the final product—and hence shift the labor demand curve for union workers to the right—unions have lobbied for import quotas, which restrict the quantities of foreign-made goods that can be imported into the United States, and for *domestic content* legislation, which requires goods from abroad to have a certain percentage of American-made components. Unions have also lobbied strongly against legislation, such as the North American Free Trade Agreement, that reduces tariffs on imported goods. Some unions have sought to directly influence people's tastes for the products they produce, urging consumers to "Buy American" or "Look for the union label."

Restricting Substitution: Legislation

An implication of our earlier discussion of labor demand elasticity (chapter 4) is that the demand for union labor is likely to become less elastic, other things equal, when it becomes more difficult or expensive to replace union labor with alternative factors of production. Unions have therefore often sought, by means of legislation, to pursue strategies that increase the costs of other inputs that are potential substitutes for union members. Construction unions, for example, have often persuaded states to require that nonunion contractors working on public projects pay the "prevailing wage" (usually the union wage in that area); furthermore, labor unions have been among the primary supporters of higher minimum wages.[19] While such support may be motivated by a concern for the welfare of low-wage workers, increases in the mandated wage also raise the relative costs to employers of hiring nonunion workers, thereby both increasing the costs of the products they produce and reducing employers' incentives to substitute them for higher-paid union workers.

Restricting Substitution: Bargaining

Union attempts to restrict the substitution of other inputs for union labor also can occur through the collective bargaining process. In the past, some unions, notably those in the airline, railroad, and printing industries, sought and won guarantees of minimum crew sizes (for example, at least three pilots were required to fly certain jet aircrafts). Such *staffing requirements* prevented employers from substituting capital for labor.[20] Other

---

[19]See Daniel P. Kessler and Lawrence F. Katz, "Prevailing Wage Laws and Construction Labor Markets," *Industrial and Labor Relations Review* 54 (January 2001): 259–274. For evidence that union support for minimum wage legislation is often transformed into pro-minimum wage votes by members of Congress, see James Cox and Ronald Oaxaca, "The Determinants of Minimum Wage Levels and Coverage in State Minimum Wage Laws," in *The Economics of Legal Minimum Wages*, ed. Simon Rottenberg (Washington, D.C.: American Enterprise Institute for Public Policy Research, 1981).

[20]In cases in which these requirements call for the employment of workers whose functions are redundant—for example, fire-stokers in diesel-operated railroad engines—*featherbedding* is said to take place. For an economic analysis of this phenomenon, see George Johnson, "Work Rules, Featherbedding and Pareto Optimal Union Management Bargaining," *Journal of Labor Economics* 8, no. 1, pt. 2 (January 1990): S237–S259.

unions have won contract provisions that prohibit employers from *subcontracting* for some or all of the services they provide. For example, a union representing a company's janitorial employees may win a contract provision preventing the firm from hiring external firms to provide it with janitorial services. Such provisions may limit the substitution of nonunion for union workers.

Craft unions often negotiate specific contract provisions that restrict the functions that members of each individual craft can perform, thereby limiting the substitution of one type of union labor for another. They also limit the substitution of unskilled union labor for skilled union labor by establishing rules about the maximum number of *apprentice* workers that can be employed relative to the experienced *journeymen* workers. Apprenticeship rules also limit the supply of skilled workers to a craft, which is another way to limit substitution for current union members.

Bargaining and the Threat of Strikes

How do unions persuade employers to agree to changes that reduce the wage elasticity of demand or shift the demand curve for union labor to the right? Given the elasticity and position of demand curves, how are unions able to bargain for, and win, real wage increases when in most cases an increase in the price of an input reduces a firm's profits?

In some cases, a union and an employer may agree to a settlement in which real wages are increased in return for the union agreeing to certain work-rule changes that will result in increased productivity. If such an agreement is explicit and is tied to the resulting change in productivity, the process is often referred to as *productivity bargaining*. More typically, however, unions are able to win management concessions at the bargaining table because of the unions' ability to impose costs on management. These costs typically take the form of work slowdowns and strikes. A *strike* is an attempt to deny the firm the labor services of all union members.

Strikes, for all the publicity generated when they occur, are relatively rare—and becoming ever rarer—in the United States. In 1970, for example, there were 381 work stoppages in the United States involving 1,000 or more workers, and these strikes caused a loss of about one-fourth of 1 percent of all work hours in the economy. By way of contrast, in 1997 and 2007 (years of comparable economic activity, as measured by the unemployment rate), there were 29 and 21 such strikes, respectively—and the time lost was less than one-hundredth of 1 percent.[21] Despite their infrequency, the *threat* of a strike hangs over virtually every bargaining situation in the private sector, and therefore, models of the bargaining process and its outcomes must address this threat.

---

[21]U.S. Department of Labor, Bureau of Labor Statistics, "Major Work Stoppages in 2009," *Economic News Release* USDL-10-0170 (February 10, 2010), Table 1.

A Simple Model of Strikes and Bargaining   The first, and also simplest, model of strikes in the bargaining process was developed by Sir John Hicks.[22] Suppose that management and labor are bargaining over only one issue: the size of the wage increase to be granted. How would the percentage increase that the union demands and the increase that the employer is willing to grant vary with the expected duration of a strike? Hicks analyzed this question with a diagram like the one shown in Figure 13.7, in which W is the percentage wage increase over which labor and management are bargaining.

On the employer side, the firm's highest pre-strike wage offer is assumed to be W_f. If that offer is rejected and a strike ensues, the employer may be able to service its customers for a relatively short period of time through accumulated inventories or the use of nonstriking employees (including managers) in production jobs. As a strike progresses, however, the costs of lost business or dissatisfied customers mount; indeed, recent papers suggest that productivity and product quality—whether measured by tread separations in tire plants or patient mortality rates in hospitals—can suffer quite markedly during periods of labor strife.[23] Faced with these losses, the employer can be expected to increase its wage offer

---

Figure 13.7

Hicks's Bargaining Model and Expected Strike Length

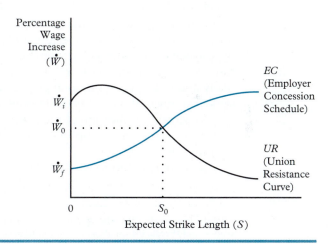

---

[22]John R. Hicks, *The Theory of Wages*, 2nd ed. (New York: St. Martin's Press, 1966): 136–157.

[23]Alan B. Krueger and Alexandre Mas, "Strikes, Scabs and Tread Separations: Labor Strife and the Production of Defective Bridgestone/Firestone Tires," *Journal of Political Economy* 112 (April 2004): 253–289; Morris M. Kleiner, Jonathan S. Leonard, and Adam M. Pilarski, "How Industrial Relations Affects Plant Performance: The Case of Commercial Aircraft Manufacturing," *Industrial and Labor Relations Review* 55 (January 2002): 195–218; Alexandre Mas, "Labor Unrest and the Quality of Production: Evidence from the Construction Equipment Resale Market," *Review of Economic Studies* 75 (January 2008): 229–258; Jonathan Gruber and Samuel A. Kleiner, "Do Strikes Kill? Evidence from New York State," *American Economic Journal: Economic Policy* 4 (February 2012): 127–157.

in an effort to end the strike. The expected willingness of employers to increase their wage offers as a strike lengthens is depicted by the upward-sloping *employer concession schedule, EC,* in Figure 13.7.

The union is assumed initially willing to accept some wage increase (W_i) without a strike, but after a strike begins, worker attitudes may harden, and the union may actually increase its wage demands early on. After some point in the strike, however, the loss of income workers are suffering begins to color their attitudes, and the union will begin to reduce its wage demands. This reduction is indicated by the *union resistance curve, UR,* in Figure 13.7, which eventually becomes downward-sloping.

As the strike proceeds, we expect the union's demands to decrease and the employer's offer to increase, until at strike duration S_0, the two will coincide. At this point, a settlement is reached on a wage increase of W_0 and the strike is expected to end. This simple model has several implications.

Implications of the Model   First, holding the *EC* schedule constant, anything that shifts the *UR* schedule upward (that is, increases union resistance to management) will both lengthen the expected strike duration and raise the wage increase that can be expected. This heightened resistance may be manifest in either a higher "no-strike" wage demand (an increase in $\dot{W}_i$) or a flatter slope to the *UR* curve, which would indicate that the union is less willing to modify its wage demands as the strike proceeds.[24] Union resistance can be expected to increase, for example, if the unemployment rate is so low that strikers can easily obtain temporary jobs or if strikers are able to collect some form of unemployment benefits (either from the government or from the union). Indeed, we do find that strikes are both more likely and of longer duration in periods of relative prosperity; the availability to strikers of unemployment benefits similarly affects strike activity.[25]

A second implication of the simple Hicks model is that anything strengthening the resistance of employers will lower the *EC* curve, thereby lengthening expected strike duration and reducing the expected wage settlement. Thus, firms will be more likely to resist—and less likely to raise their wage offers very much

---

[24]For evidence on the hypothesized downward slope to the *UR* curve, see Sheena McConnell, "Strikes, Wages, and Private Information," *American Economic Review* 79 (September 1989): 801–815; and David Card, "Strikes and Wages: A Test of an Asymmetric Information Model," *Quarterly Journal of Economics* 105 (August 1990): 625–659.

[25]Orley Ashenfelter and George Johnson, "Bargaining Theory, Trade Unions, and Industrial Strike Activity," *American Economic Review* 59 (March 1969): 35–49; Susan B. Vroman, "A Longitudinal Analysis of Strike Activity in U.S. Manufacturing: 1957–1984," *American Economic Review* 79 (September 1989): 816–826; Peter C. Cramton and Joseph S. Tracy, "The Determinants of U.S. Labor Disputes," *Journal of Labor Economics* 12 (April 1994): 180–209; and Robert Hutchens, David Lipsky, and Robert Stern, "Unemployment Insurance and Strikes," *Journal of Labor Research* 13 (Fall 1992): 337–354. For similar evidence on strikes and the business cycle in Canada and Great Britain, see Alan Harrison and Mark Stewart, "Is Strike Behavior Cyclical?" *Journal of Labor Economics* 12 (October 1994): 524–553; and A. P. Dickerson, "The Cyclicality of British Strike Frequency," *Oxford Bulletin of Economics and Statistics* 56 (August 1994): 285–303.

Permanent Replacement of Strikers

The collective bargaining laws of most nations permit a company whose workforce is on strike to hire *temporary* replacement workers to keep the business operating. The United States is one of the few nations that permit firms to hire *permanent* replacement workers. That is, workers on strike in the United States are at risk of permanently losing their jobs.

Although the right of companies to hire permanent replacements dates back to a 1938 Supreme Court decision, only since the early 1980s are large companies doing so or seriously threatening to do so. In 1981, for example, the Reagan administration "broke" the air traffic controllers' union by permanently replacing striking controllers. Subsequently, a number of large companies, including Eastern Airlines and Greyhound, permanently replaced striking workers. One study estimated that the increased threat of using permanent replacements reduced strikes in the 1980s by about 8 percent.

Why did large companies begin using permanent replacement workers in the 1980s when they had typically failed to do so during the previous four decades? Some attributed it to increasingly antiunion attitudes on the part of the federal government, a declining number of high-wage union jobs, and high unemployment—which led many workers to apply for permanent replacement positions, even at the risk of being ostracized as "scabs" by fellow workers. Still others attributed it to the pressures of international competition, which increased employers' needs to cut costs.

Does the increased use of permanent replacements, which reduced union bargaining power, portend the end of unions in the United States? The answer is probably no. While employers may derive benefits from the use of permanent replacements, they also face costs. The costs are particularly high when new employees must be carefully screened and training needs to be extensive. There is also likely to be friction between replacements and any union workers brought back after the strike, and the commitment of workers to the employer may suffer in the long run.

Source: Peter Cramton and Joseph Tracy, "The Use of Replacement Workers in Union Contract Negotiations: The U.S. Experience, 1980–1989," *Journal of Labor Economics* 16 (October 1998): 667–701.

as the strike progresses—if they are less profitable, face an elastic product demand curve, can stockpile product inventories in advance of a strike, or can easily hire replacement workers (see Example 13.3).[26]

A final implication is that strikes appear to be unnecessarily wasteful. Had the expected settlement of $\dot{W}_0$ been reached *without* a strike, or with a *shorter* strike, both sides would have been spared some losses. When strikes are likely to be very costly to both parties, the two might agree in advance to certain *bargaining protocols* that will help avert future strikes. For example, the parties might agree to start bargaining well in advance of a contract's expiration date, to limit the number of contract

---

[26]Melvin W. Reder and George R. Neumann, "Conflict and Contract: The Case of Strikes," *Journal of Political Economy* 88 (October 1980): 867–886; John F. Schnell and Cynthia L. Gramm, "The Empirical Relations between Employers' Striker Replacement Strategies and Strike Duration," *Industrial and Labor Relations Review* 47 (January 1994): 189–206; and Peter Cramton, Morley Gunderson, and Joseph Tracy, "The Effect of Collective Bargaining Legislation on Strikes and Wages," *Review of Economics and Statistics* 81 (August 1999): 475–487.

items they will discuss, or to submit the dispute to binding arbitration if they fail to reach agreement on their own. Indeed, there is some evidence that strikes are less frequent, and shorter, when the *joint costs* of any strike are likely to be greater.[27]

If strikes are costly, and if they can be averted in advance, why do they occur at all? Some argue that to enhance their bargaining positions and retain the credibility of the *threat* of a strike, unions have to periodically use the strike weapon; that is, a strike may be designed to *influence future* negotiations. Strikes also may be useful devices by which the internal solidarity of a union can be enhanced against the common adversary—the employer. More fundamentally, however, strikes are thought to occur because the information that both sides have about each other's goals and intentions to resist may be imperfect.

Strikes and Asymmetric Information   Most recent economic models of strike activity in the United States are based on the assumption of information asymmetry. Workers may want to share in the firm's profits, for example, but they will doubt management's willingness to be completely truthful about current and expected profit levels. The reason is not difficult to understand: management knows more about the firm's profitability than does labor, and if it can convince workers that the enterprise is not very profitable, the union can be expected to moderate its wage demands.

Knowing management's informational advantages and its incentives to understate profitability, the union may try to elicit a signal from management about the true level of profits. A strike would be one such signal. If the firm is lying, and profits are greater than stated, the firm may be unwilling to put up a fight (management may figure that since giving in is financially feasible, it is better off avoiding the costs of a strike). If, however, the firm is telling the truth about its low level of profits, giving in may not be feasible; taking a strike, then, sends a signal that the firm believes labor's demands are far enough above what it can feasibly pay that they must be strongly resisted.

An implication of the asymmetric-information model of strike activity is that greater uncertainty about an employer's willingness and ability to pay for wage increases should raise both the probability that a strike will occur and the duration of the strike. It does appear that the more variable a firm's profitability is over time, other things equal, the greater this uncertainty will be and the greater will be the expected incidence and duration of strike activity.[28] If the parties realize this, however, they may avert a strike by establishing a reputation for revealing their true positions rather quickly.

---

[27]Barry Sopher, "Bargaining and the Joint-Cost Theory of Strikes: An Experimental Study," *Journal of Labor Economics* 8, no. 1, pt. 1 (January 1990): 48–74.

[28]Joseph Tracy, "An Empirical Test of an Asymmetric Information Model of Strikes," *Journal of Labor Economics* 5 (April 1987): 149–173; and "An Investigation into the Determinants of U.S. Strike Activity," *American Economic Review* 76 (June 1986): 423–436. For other evidence supporting the asymmetric information model, see Peter Kuhn and Wulong Gu, "Learning in Sequential Wage Negotiations: Theory and Evidence," *Journal of Labor Economics* 17 (January 1999): 109–140.

Union Leaders and the Union Members   One barrier to elimination of the misunderstandings caused by asymmetric information is that there are really *three* major parties to a negotiation, not just two. On the employee side of the negotiations are two groups: union *leaders* and the *rank-and-file* union members, who rely on their leaders for information.[29] The rank and file may understandably suspect their leaders of withholding information from them so that their negotiations are less stressful; put differently the rank and file may suspect their leaders will sell them out. Conversely the leadership may be unsure just how strongly their members feel about certain demands being made of management. Thus, there are also information asymmetries (and hence possibilities for misunderstandings) within the *employee* side of the negotiating table.

Union leaders have much better information than rank-and-file union members about the employer's true financial position. If the offered settlement is smaller than the membership wants, union leaders face two options.

On the one hand, they can return to their members, try to convince them of the employer's true financial picture, and recommend that management's offer be accepted. The danger is that the members may vote down the recommendation, accuse the leaders of selling out to management, and ultimately vote them out of office.

On the other hand, union leaders can return to their members and recommend that the members go out on strike. This recommendation will allow them to appear to be strong, militant leaders, even though the leaders themselves know that the strike will probably not lead to a larger settlement. After a strike of some duration, however, in accordance with the notion of the union resistance curve in Figure 13.7, union members will begin to moderate their wage demands, and ultimately, a settlement for which the union leaders will receive credit will be reached.

Because the latter strategy is the one that is more likely to maintain the union's strength *and* keep the leaders in office, it is the strategy leaders may opt for even though it is clearly not in their members' best interests in the short run (the members have to bear the costs of the strike). Interestingly, strike activity rose markedly right after passage of the Landrum-Griffin Act in 1959, possibly because this act increased union democracy—thereby giving the wishes of the rank and file greater weight in the bargaining process.[30]

Bargaining in the Public Sector: The Threat of Arbitration

Although some states have granted to selected public sector employees the right to strike in one form or another, most have continued historic prohibitions against strikes by state and local government workers. When strikes are forbidden,

---

[29]The model described here was put forth by Ashenfelter and Johnson, "Bargaining Theory, Trade Unions, and Industrial Strike Activity."

[30]Ashenfelter and Johnson, "Bargaining Theory, Trade Unions, and Industrial Strike Activity."

however, laws often provide for third parties to enter the dispute-resolution process if bargaining between the parties comes to an impasse. The first step in this process is typically some form of *mediation*, in which a neutral third party attempts to facilitate a settlement by listening to each party separately, making suggestions on how each might modify its position to have more appeal to the other, and doing anything else possible to bring the parties to a voluntary settlement.

If a mediator is unable to bring the parties to a settlement, the dispute-resolution process sometimes calls for the next step to *be fact-finding*, in which a neutral party, after listening to both sides and gathering information, writes a report that proposes a settlement. The report is not binding for either party, but it may be considered by each to be a forecast of the settlement that binding arbitration would impose if the impasse were to continue.

If noncoercive methods fail to bring a voluntary settlement, *arbitration* becomes the final step of the dispute-resolution process. A single arbitrator may hear the case, or the case may be heard by a panel, usually consisting of one representative from labor, one from management, and one "neutral." Whether the parties *choose* to go to arbitration to settle their dispute, or whether by law they *must* go to arbitration, once the arbitration report is issued, the parties are bound by its contents. Arbitration associated with the bargaining process is called *interest arbitration* (to distinguish it from the *grievance-arbitration* process so widely used in resolving contract-administration disputes during the life of a contract).

Forms of Arbitration   Interest arbitration can take two forms. With *conventional arbitration*, the arbitrators are free to decide on any wage settlement of their choosing. They listen to both sides make their case and then render their own decision. Some have suspected that under this conventional procedure, arbitrators tend to split the difference between the two parties, thereby encouraging the parties to take extreme positions (in the hope of dragging the arbitrator toward their true goal).

Some jurisdictions have chosen to adopt *final-offer arbitration*, in which the arbitrator is constrained to choose the final, pre-arbitration offer either of the union or of management; no other option is possible for the arbitrator. Final-offer arbitration, it was theorized, would induce the parties to make more reasonable final offers to each other, because by so doing, they would increase the chances of their offer being the one accepted by the arbitrator.

The Contract Zone   No matter what form arbitration may take, going to arbitration is a risk for both parties because neither knows how the arbitrator will decide. A party wins the gamble only if the arbitrator reaches a more favorable wage decision than it could get through voluntary agreement. Thus, in deciding whether to continue bargaining—or, instead, take a rigid position and let the dispute go to arbitration—a party needs to develop expectations of various possible arbitrator decisions. By calculating the likelihood of each possible outcome *and* the utility associated with it, the party can develop a set of voluntary agreements it would prefer over taking its chances with arbitration. If the preferred decision sets of the two parties happen to overlap, there is a *contract zone* of possible voluntary agreements that *both* parties will prefer to the gamble of arbitration. If there is no overlap, the parties cannot agree voluntarily and the dispute will definitely go to arbitration.

A party's preferences for negotiation over gambling on arbitration are increased by greater aversion to risk and greater uncertainty about how the arbitrator might decide. If the parties become increasingly averse to losing, or if they become increasingly unable to predict what arguments or facts an arbitrator will find persuasive, then the set of negotiated outcomes they prefer to the arbitration gamble will widen. (Appendix 13A presents a more formal model underlying this conclusion.)

While logic dictates that a bargaining situation with *no* contract zone will produce no voluntary agreement, it is not obvious that a wider contract zone will make reaching a voluntary agreement more likely.[31] A wider contract zone opens up more feasible outcomes to the two parties, so one might think that the chances of voluntary agreement are enhanced, but it also gives the parties more to argue about. To take an extreme example, if there were only one wage increase that both parties preferred to arbitration, then perhaps agreement would be reached more quickly and with more certainty than if there were several possible outcomes to be thoroughly debated.

Persuading the Arbitrator   Although going to arbitration is clearly risky, the parties are not helpless in their abilities to influence the arbitrator's decision. If they are going to final-offer arbitration, they can improve their chances of winning by developing a final, pre-arbitration offer that the arbitrator is likely to regard as reasonable. The influence they exert in final-offer arbitration, then, amounts to guessing what the arbitrator thinks the outcome should be and then crafting an offer that approaches it. (Obviously, the union will approach it from *above* and management will approach it from *below*, as each tries to drag the arbitrator in its direction.)

If the parties are going to conventional arbitration, it is less certain how their offers can influence the arbitrator's decision. Some people might reason that the arbitrator will decide on a wage increase that lies between those of the two parties or, in the extreme, simply split the difference. If so, the parties might then be tempted to make final offers that are far from where they eventually expect to end up.

It might be more reasonable to believe, however, that arbitrators initially have their own views of a proper settlement, which can then be modified by listening to the arguments and positions of each party. Their own beliefs of what constitutes a reasonable outcome are not easily changed, and if a party's position (offer) is far from the outcome they consider appropriate, little weight will be given to it.[32] This latter view of how arbitrators behave implies that the parties

---

[31]Vincent Crawford, "Arbitration and Conflict Resolution in Labor-Management Bargaining," *American Economic Review* 71 (May 1981): 205–210.

[32]For experimental evidence in support of this view of arbitrator behavior, see Henry S. Farber and Max H. Bazerman, "The General Basis of Arbitrator Behavior: An Empirical Analysis of Conventional and Final-Offer Arbitration," *Econometrica* 54 (July 1986): 819–844.

can gain influence only by making offers that are close to what they think the arbitrator will decide. If both parties make the same (correct) guess about the arbitrator's preferred outcome, their final offers will bracket the arbitrator's decision. To outsiders it will look as though the arbitrator followed a simple, split-the-difference rule, but what really happened was that the parties strategically placed their offers around the arbitrator's expected position.[33]

Effects of Arbitration   If arbitrators have their own strongly held views on the appropriate outcome in a particular case, and if the parties position their offers around what they expect to be the arbitrator's preferred outcome, then whatever form of arbitration is used, the behavior of the parties and the arbitrator should be more or less the same. Indeed, one study of police officers' contracts in a state where either form could be used found the wage outcomes chosen by the arbitrators were very similar in each.[34] But how do arbitrated settlements compare with negotiated ones?

It is not surprising that negotiated wage settlements are comparable with arbitrated settlements in states requiring that disputed settlements go to arbitration, because all negotiations in those states take place under the threat of arbitration. What is somewhat surprising, however, is that another study of police contracts found wages in states requiring arbitration of disputed settlements are more or less the same as those in states *without* that requirement.[35] Thus, it may well be that the effects of arbitration on wage levels are actually quite small.[36]

The Effects of Unions

Economists have long been interested in the effects of unions on wages, and recently, attention has also been given to their effects on total compensation (including employee benefits), employment levels, hours of work, productivity, and profits. In this section, we review the theory and the evidence on these effects.

---

[33]Henry S. Farber, "Splitting-the-Difference in Interest Arbitration," *Industrial and Labor Relations Review* 35 (October 1981): 70–77.

[34]Orley Ashenfelter and David Bloom, "Models of Arbitrator Behavior: Theory and Evidence," *American Economic Review* 74 (March 1984): 111–124.

[35]Orley Ashenfelter and Dean Hyslop, "Measuring the Effect of Arbitration on Wage Levels: The Case of Police Officers," *Industrial and Labor Relations Review* 54 (January 2001): 316–328.

[36]One study found that if only one side of a dispute hires a lawyer to present its case to the arbitrator, the side hiring the lawyer obtains a better outcome; however, if *both* sides hire lawyers, neither side benefits—despite the added costs to each of hiring lawyers; see Orley Ashenfelter and Gordon B. Dahl, "Bargaining and the Role of Expert Agents: An Empirical Study of Final-Offer Arbitration," *Review of Economics and Statistics* 94 (February 2012): 116–132.

The Theory of Union Wage Effects

Suppose we had data on the wage rates paid to two groups of workers identical in every respect except that one group was unionized and the other was not. Let W_u denote the wage paid to union members and W_n the wage paid to nonunion workers. If the difference between the two could be attributed solely to the presence of unions, then the *relative wage advantage* (R) that unions would have achieved for their members would be given, in percentage terms, by

$$R = (W_u - W_n)/W_n \qquad (13.1)$$

This relative wage advantage does *not* represent the absolute amount, in percentage terms, by which unions would have increased the wages of their members, because unions both directly and indirectly affect *nonunion* wage rates also. Moreover, we cannot say for sure whether estimates of R will overstate or understate the absolute effect of unions on their members' real wage levels. To illustrate the difficulties in interpreting union–nonunion wage differentials, we begin with the simple model of the labor market depicted in Figure 13.8.

Figure 13.8 represents two sectors of the labor market, both of which hire similar workers. Panel (a) is the union sector and panel (b) is the nonunion sector. Suppose *initially* that both sectors are nonunion and that mobility between them is costless. Workers will therefore move between the two sectors until wages are equal in both. With demand curves D_u and D_n, workers will move between sectors until the supply curves are S_u^0 and S_n^0, respectively. The common equilibrium wage will be W_0, and employment will be E_u^0 and E_n^0, respectively, in the two sectors.

Figure 13.8

Spillover Effects of
Unions on Wages and
Employment

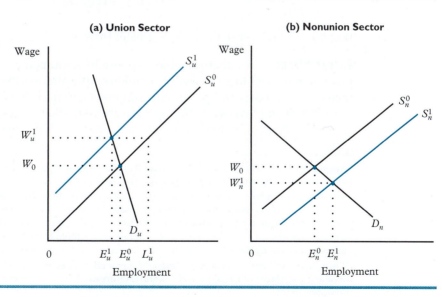

Once one sector becomes unionized, and its wage rises to W_u^1, what happens to wages in the other sector depends on the responses of employees who are not employed in the union sector. In the following sections, we discuss four possible reactions.[37]

Spillover Effects   If the union succeeds in raising wages in the union sector to W_u^1, this increase will cause employment to decline to E_u^1 workers, resulting in $L_u^1 - E_u^1$ unemployed workers in that sector. If all the unemployed workers *spill over* into the nonunion sector, the supply curves in the two sectors will shift to S_u^1 and S_n^1, respectively. Unemployment will be eliminated in the union sector; in the nonunion sector, however, an excess supply of labor will exist at the old market-clearing wage, W_0. As a result, downward pressure will be exerted on the wage rate in the nonunion sector until the labor market in that sector clears at a *lower* wage (W_n^1) and a higher employment level (E_n^1).

In the context of this model, the union has succeeded in raising the wages of its members who kept their jobs. However, it has done so by shifting some of its members to lower-wage jobs in the nonunion sector and, because of this spillover effect, by actually lowering the wage rate paid to individuals initially employed in the nonunion sector. As a result, the observed union *relative wage* advantage (R_1), computed as

$$R_1 = (W_u^1 - W_n^1)/W_n^1 \qquad (13.2)$$

will tend to be greater than the true *absolute* effect of the union on its members' real wage. This true absolute effect (A), stated in percentage terms, is defined as

$$A = (W_u^1 - W_0)/W_0 \qquad (13.3)$$

Because W_n^1 is lower than W_0, R_1 is greater than A.

Threat Effects   Another possible response by nonunion employees is to want a union to represent them as well. Nonunion employers, fearing that a union would increase labor costs and place limits on managerial prerogatives, might seek to buy off their employees by offering them above-market wages.[38] Because there are costs to workers (as noted earlier) of union membership, some wage less than W_u^1

---

[37]Much of the discussion in this section is based on the pioneering work of H. G. Lewis, *Unionism and Relative Wages in the United States* (Chicago: University of Chicago Press, 1963). In Figure 13.8, our analysis employs a two-sector model with labor supply curves to each sector. Remember that a labor supply curve to one sector is drawn holding the wages in other sectors ("alternative wages") constant; whenever the wage in one sector changes, the labor supply curve to the other sector may shift. We *sometimes* ignore this complexity to keep our exposition as simple as possible and to highlight the various behaviors that might occur in either sector in response to unionization.

[38]For a theoretical and empirical treatment of threat effects, see Henry S. Farber, "Nonunion Wage Rates and the Threat of Unionization," National Bureau of Economic Research, working paper no. 9705 (May 2003).

but higher than W_0 would presumably be sufficient to assure employers that the majority of their employees would not vote for a union (assuming that the employees are happy with their nonwage conditions of employment).

The implications of such *threat effects*—nonunion wage increases resulting from the threat of union entry—are traced in Figure 13.9. The increase in wage in the union sector, and resulting decline in employment there, is again assumed to cause the supply of workers to the nonunion sector to shift to S_n^1. In response to the threat of union entry, however, nonunion employers are assumed to *increase* their employees' wages to W_n^*, which lies between W_0 and W_u^1. This wage increase causes nonunion employment to decline to E_n^*; at the higher wage, nonunion employers demand fewer workers. Moreover, since the nonunion wage is now not free to be bid down, an excess supply of labor, $L_n^* - E_n^*$, exists, resulting in unemployment. Finally, because the nonunion wage is now higher than the original wage, the observed union relative wage advantage

$$R_2 = (W_u^1 - W_n^*)/W_n^* \qquad (13.4)$$

is smaller than the absolute effect of unions on their members' real wages.

Wait Unemployment   Do workers who lose (or do not have) a union job necessarily leave the union sector and take jobs in the nonunion sector? Even with reduced employment in the union sector, job vacancies occur as a result of retirements, deaths, and voluntary turnover. Some of those who do not have union jobs will find it attractive to search for work in the union sector, and their search might be more effective if they are not simultaneously employed elsewhere. Workers who reject

---

Figure 13.9

Threat Effects of Unions on Wages and Employment in Nonunion Sector

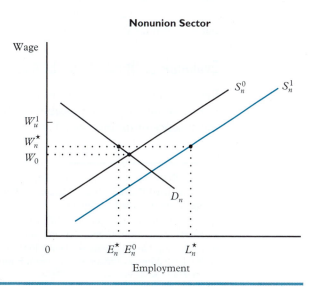

Nonunion Sector

lower-paying nonunion jobs so they can search for higher-paying union ones create the phenomenon of *wait unemployment* (they are waiting for union jobs to open up).[39]

The main behavior behind the wait-unemployment response is that workers will move from one sector to another if the latter offers higher *expected* wages. Expected wages in a sector are equal to the sector's wage rate multiplied by the probability of obtaining a job in that sector. Thus, even if one were always able to find a job in the nonunion sector, rejecting employment there might be beneficial if there were a reasonable chance (even if it were less than 100 percent) of obtaining a higher-paying union job. The importance of the resultant wait unemployment for our current discussion is that not everyone who loses a job in the union sector will spill over into the nonunion sector; in fact, it is even theoretically possible that some workers originally in the nonunion sector would quit their jobs to take a chance on finding work in the union sector.

The presence of wait unemployment in the union sector will reduce the spillover of workers to the nonunion sector, thus moderating downward pressure on nonunion wages. Moreover, if enough nonunion workers decide to search for union jobs, the labor supply curve to the nonunion sector could even shift to the left. In this case, unionization in one sector could cause wages in the nonunion sector to rise, just as with the threat effect (in fact, a "threat" here is being carried out: workers are leaving the nonunion employers to search for union jobs).

Shifts in Labor Demand   Finally, recall that we discussed earlier the activities unions undertake to alter the demand for their members' labor services. In some cases, these activities involve attempts to shift the product demand curve facing unionized firms (and hence their labor demand curve) to the right. If unions were successful in their efforts to increase product demand in the unionized sector, perhaps at the expense of the nonunion sector, the rightward shift in the union-sector labor demand curve—and the associated leftward shift in the labor demand curve in the nonunion sector—would again serve to lower wages in the nonunion sector below what they were originally.[40]

Evidence of Union Wage Effects

Because the presence of unions can influence both the union and the nonunion wage rate, it is not possible to observe the wage that would have existed in the absence of unions (W_0). Hence, estimates of a union's effects on the absolute

---

[39]See Jacob Mincer, "Unemployment Effects of Minimum Wages," *Journal of Political Economy* 84, no. 4, pt. 2 (August 1976): S87–S104. Although Mincer discusses minimum wage effects, union-imposed wages can be analyzed analogously.

[40]Our discussion of these four responses has assumed a partial equilibrium model. Once one considers a general equilibrium framework and allows capital to move between sectors, even more possibilities may exist. On this point, see Harry Johnson and Peter Mieszkowski, "The Effects of Unionization on the Distribution of Income: A General Equilibrium Approach," *Quarterly Journal of Economics* 84 (November 1969): 539–561.

level (*A*) of its members' real wages—see equation (13.3)—cannot be obtained. Care must be taken not to mistake the relative wage effects we can observe (equations 13.2 and 13.4) for the absolute effects.

Economists have expended considerable effort to estimate the extent to which unions have raised the wages of their members relative to the wages of comparable nonunion workers in the private sector. These studies have tended to use data on large samples of individuals and sought to estimate how much more union members get paid than nonunion workers, after controlling for any differences between the two groups in other factors that might be expected to influence wages. Most of the work has been done on the United States, where levels of unionization are so modest that it is relatively easy to find comparable nonunion workers.

Because the studies of union–nonunion wage differences have used various data sets and statistical methodologies, there is no single estimate of the gap upon which all researchers agree. Enough work has been done on the topic, however, for certain patterns to emerge.

1. The union relative wage advantage in the United States appears to fall into the range of *10 percent to 20 percent*;[41] that is, our best estimate is that American union workers receive wages that are some 10 percent to 20 percent higher than those of comparable nonunion workers.[42]
2. The *private sector* union wage advantage in the United States is larger than that in the *public* sector. For example, one study that used the same data and the same statistical methodology for both sectors estimated that the private sector wage gap was in the 18 percent to 20 percent range from 2000 to 2012, while in the public sector over the same period, it was in the 8 percent to 12 percent range.[43]
3. The union relative wage advantage in the United States is larger than it is in most other countries for which comparable estimates are available. For example, one study found the following union–nonunion wage gaps during the late 1990s: United States, 18 percent; Australia, 12 percent;

[41]For surveys of these estimates, see David G. Blanchflower and Alex Bryson, "What Effect Do Unions Have on Wages Now and Would Freeman and Medoff be Surprised?" *Journal of Labor Research* 25 (Summer 2004): 383–414; Richard Freeman and James Medoff, *What Do Unions Do?* (New York: Basic Books, 1984); H. Gregg Lewis, *Union Relative Wage Effects: A Survey* (Chicago: University of Chicago Press, 1986); Barry T. Hirsch and John T. Addison, *The Economic Analysis of Unions: New Approaches and Evidence* (Boston: Allen and Unwin, 1986); and Pencavel, *Labor Markets under Trade Unionism*. For articles with citations to earlier studies, see Steven Raphael, "Estimating the Union Earnings Effect Using a Sample of Displaced Workers," *Industrial and Labor Relations Review* 53 (April 2000): 503–521;; Barry T. Hirsch, "Reconsidering Union Wage Effects: Surveying New Evidence on an Old Topic," *Journal of Labor Research* 25 (Spring 2004): 233–266; and Ozkan Eren, "Does Membership Pay Off for Covered Workers? A Distributional Analysis of the Free Rider Problem," *Industrial and Labor Relations Review* 62 (April 2009): 367–380.

[42]For a study that differs in methodology from prior research and finds that the wages of newly unionized workers are not increased, see John DiNardo and David S. Lee, "Impacts of New Unionization on Private Sector Employees: 1984–2001," *Quarterly Journal of Economics* 116 (November 2004): 1383–1441.

[43]Barry T. Hirsch and David A. Macpherson, *Union Membership and Earnings Data Book: Compilations from the Current Population Survey* (Washington, D.C.: Bureau of National Affairs, 2013): Table 2a.

United Kingdom, 10 percent; Canada, 8 percent; Germany, 4 percent; and France, 3 percent.[44]

4. Unions everywhere tend to reduce the dispersion of earnings among workers, especially men. They raise the wages of less-skilled workers relative to higher-skilled workers within the union sector, thereby reducing the payoff to human-capital investments. They standardize wages within and across firms in the same industry, and they reduce the earnings gaps between production and office workers.[45] They also reduce the wage gap between white and black workers in the United States.[46]

5. The union relative wage advantage in the United States, at least in recent decades, has tended to grow larger during recessionary periods.[47] While evidence prior to the 1980s is mixed, the wage changes of union members have been less sensitive to business conditions than the wages of nonunion workers in recent years.

6. Although the findings do not yet fit a pattern, researchers have attempted to discover whether greater levels of unionization tend to increase or decrease wages in the *nonunion* sector. These studies have tried to see whether the spillover or the threat effect dominates among nonunion employers. The evidence so far is ambiguous. One study found, for example, that threat effects dominated within *cities* (that is, in more highly unionized cities, the wages of nonunion workers were higher). It also found, however, that the spillover effect dominated within *industries* (in more highly unionized industries, nonunion wages tended to be lower). These contradictory results mirror those of earlier studies.[48]

Evidence of Union Total Compensation Effects

Estimates of the extent to which the wages of union workers exceed the wages of otherwise comparable nonunion workers may prove misleading for two reasons. First, such estimates ignore the fact that wages are only part of the compensation

---

[44]David Blanchflower and Alex Bryson, "Changes over Time in Union Relative Wage Effects in the U.K. and the U.S. Revisited," National Bureau of Economic Research, working paper no. 9395 (December 2002).

[45]Richard B. Freeman, "Labor Market Institutions Around the World," working paper no. 13242, National Bureau of Economic Research (Cambridge, Mass.: 2007); Lawrence M. Kahn, "Wage Inequality, Collective Bargaining and Relative Employment 1985–94: Evidence from 15 OECD Countries," *Review of Economics and Statistics* 82 (November 2000): 564–579; and David Card, Thomas Lemieux, and W. Craig Riddell, "Unions and Wage Inequality," *Journal of Labor Research* 25 (Fall 2004): 519–562.

[46]James Peoples Jr., "Monopolistic Market Structure, Unionization, and Racial Wage Differentials," *Review of Economics and Statistics* 76 (February 1994): 207–211; and Richard Freeman and James Medoff, *What Do Unions Do?* chapter 5.

[47]Darren Grant, "A Comparison of the Cyclical Behavior of Union and Nonunion Wages in the United States," *Journal of Human Resources* 36 (Winter 2001): 31–57; David Blanchflower and Alex Bryson, "What Effect Do Unions Have on Wages Now and Would Freeman and Medoff be Surprised?"

[48]See David Neumark and Michael L. Wachter, "Union Effects on Nonunion Wages: Evidence from Panel Data on Industries and Cities," *Industrial and Labor Relations Review* 49 (October 1995): 20–38.

package. It has often been argued that *employee benefits*, such as paid holidays, vacation pay, sick leave, and retirement benefits, will be higher in firms that are unionized than in nonunion firms. The argument states that because tastes for the various benefits differ across individuals and because there is no easy way to communicate the preferences of the average employee to the employer in a non-union firm, nonunion firms tend to pay a higher fraction of total compensation in the form of money wages. Empirical evidence tends to support this contention; employee benefits and the share of compensation that goes to benefits do appear to be higher in union than in nonunion firms. Furthermore, studies also suggest that unionization increases the probability that workers apply for employer-financed government benefits for which they are eligible.[49] Ignoring benefits may therefore *understate* the true union–nonunion total compensation differential.

Second, ignoring *conditions of employment* may cause one to *overstate* the effect of unions on their members' overall welfare levels compared with those of nonunion workers. For example, studies have shown that for blue-collar work-ers, unionized firms tend to have more-structured work settings, more-hazardous jobs, less-flexible hours of work, faster work paces, lower worker job satisfaction, and less employee control over the assignment of overtime hours than do non-union firms.[50] This situation may arise because production settings that call for more interdependence among workers and the need for rigid work requirements by employers also give rise to unions. While unions often strive to affect these working conditions, they do not always succeed. Part of the estimated union–nonunion earnings differential thus may be a premium paid to union workers to compensate them for these unfavorable working conditions. One study estimates that two-fifths of the estimated union–nonunion earnings differential reflects such compensation, suggesting that the observed earnings differential may overstate the true differential in overall levels of worker well-being.[51]

The Effects of Unions on Employment

If unions raise the wages and employee benefits of their members, and if they impose constraints on managerial prerogatives, economic theory suggests their presence will have a negative effect on employment. In recent years, several

---

[49]Barry T. Hirsch, David A. Macpherson, and J. Michael Dumond, "Workers' Compensation Recipiency in Union and Nonunion Workplaces," *Industrial and Labor Relations Review* 50 (January 1997): 213–236; John W. Budd and Brian P. McCall, "The Effects of Unions on the Receipt of Unemployment Insurance Benefits," *Industrial and Labor Relations Review* 51 (April 1997): 478–492; Thomas C. Buchmuller, John DiNardo, and Robert G. Valletta, "Union Effects on Health Insurance Provision and Coverage in the United States," *Industrial and Labor Relations Review* 55 (July 2002): 610–627; and John W. Budd, "Non-Wage Forms of Compensation," *Journal of Labor Research* 25 (Fall 2004): 587–622.

[50]Greg Duncan and Frank Stafford, "Do Union Members Receive Compensating Wage Differentials?" *American Economic Review* 70 (June 1980): 355–371; Keith A. Bender and Peter J. Sloane, "Job Satisfaction, Trade Unions, and Exit-Voice Revisited," *Industrial and Labor Relations Review* 51 (January 1998): 222–240; and John S. Heywood, W. S. Siebert, and Xiangdong Wei, "Worker Sorting and Job Satisfaction: The Case of Union and Government Jobs," *Industrial and Labor Relations Review* 55 (July 2002): 595–609.

[51]Duncan and Stafford, "Do Union Members Receive Compensating Wage Differentials?"

studies have investigated this theoretical prediction, and the results suggest that unions do reduce employment growth. A study of plants in California during the late 1970s, for example, estimated that employment grew some 2 to 4 percentage points more slowly per year in union than in nonunion firms; in fact, the growth rates were so different that about 60 percent of the decline in California's unionization rate was attributed to slower employment growth in union jobs.[52] Other studies have found similar employment effects for the United States as a whole as well as for Australia, Canada, and the United Kingdom.[53] Finally, even when employment is not much changed in the face of unionization, the total yearly hours of work might still fall.[54]

The Effects of Unions on Productivity and Profits

There are two views on how unions affect labor productivity (output per worker). One is that unions *increase* worker productivity, given the firm's level of capital, by providing a "voice" mechanism through which workers' suggestions and preferences can be communicated to management.[55] With a direct means for expressing their ideas or concerns, workers may have enhanced motivation levels and be less likely to quit. With lower quit rates, firms have more incentives to invest in training, which should also raise worker productivity.

The other view on how unions affect worker productivity stresses the limits they place on managerial prerogatives, especially with respect to using cost-minimizing levels of the labor input. We argued earlier that if unions care about the employment as well as the wages of their members, they will put pressure on management to agree to staffing requirements, restrictions on

---

[52]Jonathan S. Leonard, "Unions and Employment Growth," *Industrial Relations* 31 (Winter 1992): 80–94.

[53]Timothy Dunne and David A. Macpherson, "Unionism and Gross Employment Flows," *Southern Economic Journal* 60 (January 1994): 727–738; Stephen G. Bronars, Donald R. Deere, and Joseph Tracy, "The Effects of Unions on Firm Behavior: An Empirical Analysis Using Firm-Level Data," *Industrial Relations* 33 (October 1994): 426–451; Robert G. Valletta, "Union Effects on Municipal Employment and Wages: A Longitudinal Approach," *Journal of Labor Economics* 11 (July 1993): 545–574; Richard J. Long, "The Impact of Unionization on Employment Growth of Canadian Companies," *Industrial and Labor Relations Review* 46 (July 1993): 691–703; David G. Blanchflower, Neil Millward, and Andrew J. Oswald, "Unions and Employment Behaviour," *Economic Journal* 101 (July 1991): 815–834; Giuseppe Bertola, Francine D. Blau, and Lawrence M. Kahn, "Labor Market Institutions and Demographic Employment Patterns," *Journal of Population Economics* 20 (October 2007): 833–867; and Michelle Brown and John S. Heywood, "Investigating the Cause of Death: Industrial Relations and Plant Closures in Australia," *Industrial and Labor Relations Review* 59 (July 2006): 593–612.

[54]William M. Boal and John Pencavel, "The Effects of Labor Unions on Employment, Wages, and Days of Operation: Coal Mining in West Virginia," *Quarterly Journal of Economics* 109 (February 1994): 267–298.

[55]For a more complete statement of this argument, see Freeman and Medoff, *What Do Unions Do?* Note that there is another, more mechanical way in which unions can raise worker productivity. We have seen that unions raise wages, and theory suggests that the response by profit-maximizing employers will be to reduce employment and substitute capital for labor. Thus, as firms move up and to the left along their marginal product of labor curves, the marginal product of labor rises in response to the wage increase.

work out of job title, cumbersome methods through which the disciplining of nonproductive workers must take place, and other policies that increase labor costs per unit of output.

Empirical analyses of union productivity effects have yielded conflicting results. The effects of unions on workers' output apparently depend very much on the quality of the relationship between labor and management in each particular collective bargaining setting. In fact, one study found that unionized firms with human-resource practices that combined joint labor-management decision-making with output-based pay had higher productivity than similar nonunion firms; unionized firms without such practices had lower productivity than comparable nonunion employers.[56]

When unions raise wages but do not raise worker productivity, then we might expect them to reduce firms' profits. Some studies directly analyze unionization and profit levels, holding other things constant; these rather consistently estimate that profits in unionized firms are lower, both in the United States and in the United Kingdom.[57] Another way of studying unions' effects on profits, however, is to make use of evidence that the stock market reflects changes in a firm's profitability. For example, a recent study found that when a firm's workers become unionized, the price of the firm's stock typically falls about 10 percent over the next year and one-half.[58]

Normative Analyses of Unions

We have seen throughout this text that economic theory can be used in both its *positive* and its *normative* modes. The analyses of union effects in this section so far have been of a positive nature, in that we have summarized both theory and evidence on how unions affect various labor market outcomes. We now turn to a normative question that often underlies discussions of unions and the government policies that affect them: do unions enhance or reduce social welfare? As one might expect, opinions differ.

---

[56]Sandra Black and Lisa Lynch, "How to Compete: The Impact of Workplace Practices and Information Technology on Productivity," *Review of Economics and Statistics* 83 (August 2001): 434–445. Also see David G. Blanchflower and Richard B. Freeman, "Unionism in the U.S. and Other OECD Countries," *Industrial Relations* 31 (Winter 1992): 56–79; and Michael Ash and Jean Ann Seago, "The Effect of Registered Nurses' Unions on Heart-Attack Mortality," *Industrial and Labor Relations Review* 57 (April 2004): 422–442.

[57]Bronars, Deere, and Tracy, "The Effects of Unions on Firm Behavior"; Blanchflower and Freeman, "Unionism in the U.S. and Other OECD Countries"; Barry T. Hirsch, "Unionization and Economic Performance: Evidence on Productivity, Profits, Investment, and Growth," in *Unions and Right-to-Work Laws*, ed. Fazil Mihlar (Vancouver: Fraser Institute, 1997), 35–70; Richard B. Freeman and Morris M. Kleiner, "Do Unions Make Enterprises Insolvent?" *Industrial and Labor Relations Review* 52 (July 1999): 510–527; and Elisabetta Magnani and David Prentice, "Did Lower Unionization in the United States Result in More Flexible Industries?" *Industrial and Labor Relations Review* 63 (July 2010): 662–680.

[58]David S. Lee and Alexandre Mas, "Long-Run Impacts of Unions on Firms: New Evidence from Financial Markets: 1961–1999," *Quarterly Journal of Economics* 127 (February 2012): 333–378.

Potential Reductions in Social Welfare   We saw in chapter 1 that the role of any market, including the labor market, is to facilitate mutually beneficial transactions by providing a mechanism for voluntary exchange. The ultimate goal of this exchange is to arrive at an allocation of goods and services that generates as much utility as possible, given a society's resources, for the individuals in that society. If a market has facilitated *all* such transactions, then it can be said to have arrived at a point of Pareto efficiency. A requirement for the existence of Pareto efficiency is that all productive resources, including labor, be used in a way that generates maximum utility for society (this includes the utility of the workers as well as that of the consumers who purchase the goods or services they produce).

Arguments that unions reduce social welfare generally stem from the proposition that they represent the interests of only their members, not of others.[59] One argument points to the production lost (the labor resources wasted) when workers go on strike. A second argument is similar: when labor and management agree to restrictive work rules (as noted in our discussion of the efficient-contracts model), the use of excess workers in the production process creates wastage—and therefore social loss—in the use of labor. A third argument is more subtle, however.

Simple reasoning suggests that for Pareto efficiency to be achieved, resources that have the same *potential* productivity must have the same *actual* productivity. Consider, for example, a group of workers who are equally skilled, experienced, and motivated. If some of these workers are in jobs that produce $15 worth of goods or services per hour, while others in the group are in jobs that produce only $10, the value of society's output could be enhanced by the voluntary movement of members from the latter subset of jobs into the higher-productivity jobs. Reducing the number of workers in the $10 jobs would serve to raise the marginal productivity of those who remain in those jobs, while increasing the number of workers in the $15 jobs would put downward pressure on the wage (and marginal productivity) in that sector. As long as the marginal productivities of workers in the skill group continue to differ, however, the value of society's output could be increased still further by having members of the lower-paid subset move into the higher-paying jobs. Only when the marginal productivities are equal, and all Pareto-improving moves by workers have been completed, can it be said that Pareto efficiency is achieved.

The third argument that unions reduce social welfare, then, rests on two propositions. The first is that unions create wage (and therefore productivity) differentials among equivalent workers by raising wages in the union sector above those in the nonunion sector. The second proposition is that the higher and inflexible union wage reduces employment in the high-paid sector and prevents workers in lower-paying jobs from moving into the higher-productivity sector, with the result that society's output is lower than it would be otherwise. Some economists have attempted to estimate these losses, and their estimates have generally been small—in the range of 0.2 percent to 0.4 percent of national output.[60]

---

[59]Assar Lindbeck and Dennis J. Snower, "Insiders versus Outsiders," *Journal of Economic Perspectives* 15 (Winter 2001): 165–188.

[60]Freeman and Medoff, *What Do Unions Do?* 57.

Potential Increases in Social Welfare   Arguments that unions reduce social welfare lose some of their force if, in the absence of unions, labor or product markets are not as competitive as assumed by standard economic theory. Suppose, for example, that the cost of mobility is so great that workers do not freely move to preferable jobs. Compensating wage differentials may fail to correctly guide the allocation of workers across jobs that have varying levels of unpleasant (or pleasant) characteristics. If so, too many workers may end up in dangerous or otherwise unpleasant jobs, which they would gladly leave (even for a lower-paying one) if they had the chance.

With respect to working conditions, there are two general means by which employer behavior can be influenced. The mechanism relied upon by the market, with its individual transactions, is one of *exit and entry*. If a worker is unhappy with certain conditions of employment, he or she is free to leave; if enough workers do so, the employer will be forced to alter the offending condition or else increase wages enough to induce the workers it has to remain. An alternative to the exit mechanism is the mechanism of *voice*: workers can vocalize their concerns and hope that the employer will respond.

The voicing of requests by *individuals* is potentially very costly. First, many workplace conditions (such as lighting, scheduling, safety precautions) are examples of "public goods" within the plant. All workers are benefited by any improvements, whether or not they contributed to the campaign to secure them. Therefore, the possibility of free riders inhibits individuals (acting alone) from bearing the costs of a campaign to change workplace conditions. Second, because the employer may respond to complaints by firing "troublemakers," an individual worker who uses the voice mechanism without some form of job protection must be prepared to suffer the costs of exit.

Those who hold the view that unions improve social welfare argue that in the face of high mobility costs, unions offer workers the mechanism of *collective* voice in the establishment of their working conditions. They solve the free-rider problem and relieve their members of the risks and burdens associated with individual voice. Furthermore, collective bargaining agreements almost always establish a grievance procedure through which certain employee complaints can be formally addressed by a neutral third party. In short, unions provide mechanisms of collective voice that substitute for an expensive-to-use exit mechanism in the determination of the workplace conditions that affect workers' utility. They therefore promote Pareto-improving transactions that otherwise would not have been induced because of the high costs of employee mobility.

Other arguments that unions enhance (or at least do not reduce) social welfare also rest on market conditions that call into question key assumptions underlying the standard economic model of employer behavior. For example, one possibility (mentioned earlier in this chapter) is that unionized employers have substantial monopoly power in their product markets, which yields them excess profits. If the efficient-contracts model of bargaining holds, and if the associated contract curve is vertical, then employment remains equal to its preunionization level, and the union and the employer end up simply splitting the employer's excess profits. Income is transferred from owners to workers, but because total output is unaffected, there would be no social losses associated with higher union wages.

EMPIRICAL STUDY

WHAT IS THE GAP BETWEEN UNION AND NONUNION PAY? THE IMPORTANCE OF REPLICATION IN PRODUCING CREDIBLE ESTIMATES

The question of whether unions raise the wages of their members relative to the wages of nonunion workers has been of enduring interest to labor economists ever since the 1940s. There have been hundreds of studies on this topic, using a variety of data sources and statistical techniques, and these studies (at least those up through the early 1980s) were scrutinized and compared by H. Gregg Lewis, whom many regard as the father of modern labor economics. Lewis produced two books, some 20 years apart, on the subject of union–nonunion wage differentials—and his painstaking concern with methodological details of the research projects he synthesized serves as a standard to be emulated among empirically oriented social scientists.

Lewis spent most of his career at the University of Chicago, where he was a significant advisor to almost 90 doctoral students and a teacher to many more—many of whom went on to become leaders in the field of labor economics. Lewis published very few books or articles, however, because his insistence on checking and cross-checking data, replicating results of prior studies, looking for biases in estimating equations, and reconciling results with prior estimates ruled out quick publication. His first book on union–nonunion wage differentials, published in 1963, was an exhaustive survey of 20 earlier studies on the subject. This survey involved detailed checks for transcription or arithmetic errors in the data analyzed, the replication of estimates to make sure that the results were accurately reported, and his *reestimation* of results when he believed the original estimates were faulty or when newer data had been made available. The result of this work was his conclusion that in 1957–1958, union wages exceeded nonunion wages by 10 percent to 15 percent, assuming other factors affecting wages were held constant.

Lewis published his second book on the topic in 1986. This book analyzed the findings of some 200 studies that had been done in the preceding two decades, during which the advent of the computer and large data sets allowed more sophisticated analyses of union–nonunion wage differentials in various industries and regions and among different demographic groups. These studies used regression analysis to determine whether those in unions received higher wages, holding other productive characteristics constant. Lewis was concerned about biases in the estimates of the union differential if union membership is not randomly determined (the issue of *selection bias* or *unobserved heterogeneity*), if important variables were either omitted (the *omitted variables* problem) from the estimating equation or mismeasured (the *errors in variables* problem), and if certain groups of people were excluded from the samples. He devoted whole chapters to investigations and estimates of these biases.

In analyzing the estimates of *overall* union pay differentials within the United States, Lewis sought in his second book to reconcile the different estimates of some 117 studies. He adjusted each estimate for the biases his analyses found that were introduced by such factors as nonrandom data sampling; the omission of nonmanufacturing workers, minorities, or young employees from the sample; the failure to control for industry or occupation in the regression equation; and the omission of employee benefits from the pay variable. His painstaking analyses resulted in the conclusion that, on average, union workers received roughly 15 percent higher pay than otherwise equivalent nonunion workers in the 1967–1979 period. While this result was remarkably consistent with his earlier conclusions, Lewis was careful to point out that he regarded his 15 percent estimate as an upper-bound approximation of the true wage differential.

One prominent labor economist characterized the legacy of H. Gregg Lewis in this way: "Lewis influenced the way a generation of labor economists did empirical work. He was a conscience against the quick and dirty and shoddy.... [His books] never lose sight that the goal of social science is to measure purported effects of economic institutions or changes in markets nor of the limitations nonexperimental data place on meeting the goal."[a]

---

[a]Richard Freeman, "H. G. Lewis and the Study of Union Wage Effects," *Journal of Labor Economics* 12 (January 1994): 144, 147.

Sources: H. G. Lewis, *Unionism and Relative Wages in the United States: An Empirical Inquiry* (Chicago: University of Chicago Press, 1963); and H. Gregg Lewis, *Union Relative Wage Effects: A Survey* (Chicago: University of Chicago Press, 1986).

Another argument is that employers are not as knowledgeable about how to maximize profits as standard economic theory assumes. Because management finds it costly to search for better (or less costly) ways to produce, so the argument goes, we cannot be sure that it will always use labor in the most productive ways possible. (Clearly, this argument rests on the implicit assumption that entry into the product market is difficult enough that inefficient producers are not necessarily punished by competitive forces.) When unions organize and raise the wages of their members, firms may be shocked into the search for better ways to produce. Moreover, by establishing formal channels of communication between workers and management, unionization at least *potentially* provides a mechanism through which employers and employees can more effectively communicate about workplace processes.[61]

---

[61]For a fuller development of this argument, see Freeman and Medoff, *What Do Unions Do?*; Barry T. Hirsch, "What Do Unions Do for Economic Performance?" *Journal of Labor Research* 25 (Summer 2004): 415–455; and John T. Addison and Clive R. Belfield, "Union Voice."

Review Questions

1. Suppose that a proposal for tax reductions associated with the purchase of capital equipment is up for debate. Suppose, too, that union leaders are called upon to comment on the proposal from the perspective of how it will affect the welfare of their members as workers (not consumers). Will they all agree on the effects of the proposal? Explain your answer.

2. Some collective bargaining agreements contain "union standards" clauses that prohibit the employer from farming out work normally done in the plant to other firms that pay less than the union wage.
   a. What is the union's rationale for seeking a union standards clause?
   b. Under what conditions will a union standards clause most likely be sought by a labor union?

3. The Jones Act mandates that at least 50 percent of all U.S. government-financed cargo must be transported in U.S.-owned ships and that any U.S. ship leaving a U.S. port must have at least 90 percent of its crew composed of U.S. citizens. What would you expect the impact of this act to be on the demand for labor in the shipping industry and the ability of unions to push up the wages of U.S. seafarers?

4. It has been observed that unions in the capital-intensive steel industry were able to negotiate higher-than-average wage increases during the very period in which steel output in the United States was declining. Using economic theory, how can this pattern be explained?

5. In Germany, temporary layoffs and dismissals on short notice are often illegal. A dismissal is illegal if it is "socially unjustified," and it is considered "socially unjustified" if the worker could be employed in a different position or establishment of the firm, even one requiring retraining. Workers illegally dismissed may sue their employers. What are the likely consequences of this German law for the ability of German unions to raise wages?

6. American unions often try to win public support for boycotting goods made in less-developed countries by workers who work very long hours at low pay in unhealthy conditions.
   a. If successful, will these efforts unambiguously help the targeted foreign workers receive better pay? Explain fully.
   b. Will these efforts unambiguously help the union's American workers? Explain fully.

7. Suppose that a union argues that unionized workers are generally more productive than nonunion workers, and therefore that employers should take a much more positive approach to unionism and collective bargaining. Use economic theory to analyze why union workers are likely to be more productive (in terms of output per worker), and to analyze whether greater labor productivity enhances the profitability of firms.

8. A certain country has very centralized collective bargaining, under which wage bargains are applied nationally. This country is thinking about adopting a bargaining structure that is more decentralized so that wage bargains will be made at the individual plant or firm level. How would you expect decentralization to affect wages and employment? Explain your answer.

Problems

1. For a local tire factory, the employer concession curve is $W = 2 + 0.5S$ and the union resistance curve is $W = 11 + 0.5S0.1S^2$, where W = percentage increase in wages and S = expected length of strike in days. Using Hicks' simple model, calculate the percentage of wage increase and expected strike length when the union bargains for a wage increase.

2. The city-cleaning workers guild faces an own wage elasticity of demand for labor equal to −0.3. The gardening workers association faces an own wage elasticity of −3.3. If the leaders of both unions bargain for a 15% increase but have no power to set the employment levels directly, which union will favor the wage increase and which one will not?

3. The unionized baby caregivers in a town earn $8 per hour whereas the nonunionized baby caregivers earn $6 per hour. The equilibrium wage in the unionized sector is $5. Calculate the relative wage advantage and the absolute effect of the union on its members' wages. Comment on the relation between them.

4. The following table gives the demand for labor in two firms.

Wage Rate ($)	Firm 1	Firm 2
8	22	24
10	20	20
12	18	16

The current wage rate in both firms is $10. A union would like to organize them and bargain for a wage increase of $12. Which firm is more likely to be unionized?

5. The following table gives the demand for labor at a chocolate factory. The factory is unionized, and the union is negotiating to raise the wage rate for its members from $7 per hour to $8 per hour. At the same time, more people are realizing how delicious the chocolate products produced at the factory are, resulting in an increase in the demand for the chocolate. The labor demand after the increase in the demand for the company's product is shown in column 3.

Wage Rate ($)	Labor Demand (Original)	Labor Demand (New)
3	38	42
4	35	39
5	32	36
6	29	33
7	26	30
8	23	27
9	20	24
10	17	21

A company official announces, "This wage increase will cost jobs in this factory!" In response, a union leader asserts, "What the company official said is incorrect; not a single union member will lose his or her job if the wage goes to $8." Who is correct? Justify your answer.

6. There are two sectors of the construction industry that currently pay their employees the market-clearing wage. The demand for labor in each sector is $MRP_L = 12 - L$, where L = the number (in thousands) of workers. The supply of labor in each sector is $L = W - 2$, where W = the wage rate (dollars per hour).

   A union organizes in one of the sectors, and it restricts supply to that sector by insisting that only those in the union are hired by firms in that sector (and it is difficult to get into the union). When the employees in this sector unionize, the supply of labor in that sector changes to $L = W - 4$.

   a. What is the wage rate in both sectors before unionization? How many employees will be hired in each sector?
   b. What is the wage rate in the unionized sector? How many employees will be hired in the unionized sector?
   c. If the unemployed workers in the newly unionized sector spill over into the nonunion sector, what will be the wage rate in the nonunion sector? How many employees will be hired in that sector?
   d. What is the union relative wage advantage? What is the true absolute effect?

7. Suppose the employees in the nonunionized sector in Problem #6 want a union to represent them as well. In an attempt to discourage a union from forming in this sector, the employers in that sector offer a wage rate of $7.50. How many nonunion workers will be hired? What is the union relative wage advantage?

Selected Readings

Atherton, Wallace. *Theory of Union Bargaining Goals*. Princeton, N.J.: Princeton University Press, 1973.

Bennett, James, and Bruce E. Kaufman, eds. *What Do Unions Do: A Twenty-Year Perspective*. New Brunswick, N.J.: Transaction, 2007.

Freeman, Richard B., and James L. Medoff. *What Do Unions Do?* New York: Basic Books, 1984.

Hirsch, Barry T., and John T. Addison. *The Economic Analysis of Unions: New Approaches and Evidence*. Boston: Allen and Unwin, 1986.

Kerr, Clark, and Paul D. Staudohar, eds. *Labor Economics and Industrial Relations: Markets and Institutions*. Cambridge, Mass.: Harvard University Press, 1994.

Lewis, H. Gregg. *Union Relative Wage Effects: A Survey*. Chicago: University of Chicago Press, 1986.

Pencavel, John. *Labor Markets under Trade Unionism*. Cambridge, Mass.: Basil Black-well, 1991.

Arbitration and the Bargaining Contract Zone

W hat incentive do the parties to collective bargaining negotiations have to settle their negotiations on their own rather than go to arbitration and have an outside party impose a settlement? The answer may well be that the uncertainty about an arbitrator's likely decision imposes costs on both parties that give them an incentive to come to an agreement on their own. This appendix provides a simple model that illustrates this proposition; it highlights the roles of both *uncertainty* about an arbitrator's likely decision and the parties' *attitudes toward risk* in determining whether a negotiation will wind up in arbitration.[1]

Consider a simple two-party bargaining problem in which the parties, A and B, are negotiating over how to split a "pie" of fixed size. Each party's utility function depends only on the share of the pie that it receives. Figure 13A.1 plots the utility function for party A. When A's share of the pie is zero, A's utility (U_A) is assumed to be zero, and as A's share (S_A) increases, A's utility increases. Crucially, this utility function is also assumed to exhibit the property of *diminishing marginal utility*; equal increments in S_A lead to progressively smaller increments in U_A. As we shall show later, this is equivalent to assuming that the party is *risk averse*, which means that the party would prefer the certainty of having a given share of the pie to an uncertain outcome that, on average, would yield the same share.[2]

---

[1]The discussion here is a simplified version of some of the material found in Henry S. Farber and Harry C. Katz, "Interest Arbitration, Outcomes, and the Incentive to Bargain," *Industrial and Labor Relations Review* 33 (October 1979): 55–63.

[2]Refer to Appendix 8A, especially footnote 4, for an introduction to this use of cardinal utility functions.

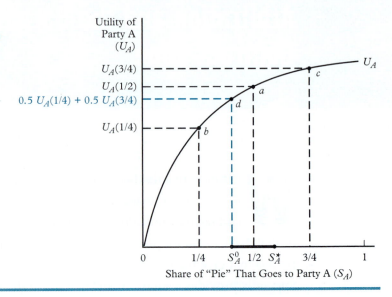

Figure 13A.1

Utility Function for a Risk-Averse Party: Uncertainty about Arbitrator's Decision Leads to a Contract Zone

Now, suppose party A believes that, on average, the arbitrator would award it one-half of the pie if the negotiations went to arbitration. If it knew with certainty that the arbitrator would do this, party A's utility from going to arbitration would be $U_A(1/2)$, at point a in Figure 13A.1. Suppose, however, that party A is uncertain about the arbitrator's decision and instead believes the arbitrator will assign it one-quarter of the pie with probability one-half, or three-quarters of the pie also with probability one-half. Utility in these two states is given by $U_A(1/4)$, point b, and $U_A(3/4)$, point c, respectively. Although, on average, party A expects to be awarded one-half of the pie, its average or *expected* utility in this case is $0.5U_A(1/4) + 0.5U_A(3/4)$, which, as Figure 13A.1 indicates (see point d), is less than $U_A(1/2)$. This reflects the fact that party A is risk averse, preferring a certain outcome (point a) to an uncertain outcome (point d) that yields the same expected share.

Note that if party A were awarded the share S_A^0 with certainty, it would receive the same utility level it receives under the uncertain situation, where it expects, with equal probability, the arbitrator to award it either one-quarter or three-quarters of the pie. Indeed, it would prefer any *certain* share above S_A^0 to bearing the cost of the uncertainty associated with having to face the arbitrator's decision. The set of contracts it potentially would voluntarily agree to, then, is the set S_A, such that

$$S_A^0 \le S_A \le 1; S_A^0 < 1/2 \qquad (13A.1)$$

Suppose party B is similarly risk averse and has identical expectations about what the arbitrator's decision will look like. It should be obvious, using the same logic as earlier, that the set of contracts, *SB*, that party B would potentially voluntarily agree to is given by a similar expression:

$$S_B^0 \leq S_B \leq 1; S_B^0 < 1/2 \qquad (13A.2)$$

Now, any share that party B voluntarily agrees to receive implies that what B is willing to give party A is 1 minus that share. Since the *minimum* share B would agree to receive, S_B^0, is less than one-half, it follows that the *maximum* share B would voluntarily agree to give A in negotiations, S_A^* (which equals $1 - S_B^0$), is greater than one-half. Party B would potentially be willing to voluntarily agree to any settlement that gives party A a share of less than S_A^*.

Referring to Figure 13A.1, observe that party A would be willing to voluntarily agree to contracts that offer it at least *SA*, while party B would be willing to agree to contracts that give party A S_A^* or less. Hence, the set of contracts that *both* parties would find preferable to going to arbitration (and thus *potentially* would voluntarily agree to) is given by all the shares for A (S_A) that lie between these two extremes:

$$S_A^0 \leq S_A \leq S_A^* \qquad (13A.3)$$

This set of potential voluntary solutions to the bargaining problem is indicated by the bold-line segment on the horizontal axis of Figure 13A.1 and is called the *contract zone*. As long as both parties are risk averse and are uncertain what the arbitrator will do, a contract zone will exist.

The extent of the parties' *uncertainty* about the arbitrator's decision and the extent of their *risk aversion* are important determinants of the size of the contract zone. To see this, first suppose that party A continues to expect that, on average, the arbitrator will assign it one-half of the pie but now believes that this will occur by receiving shares of one-eighth and seven-eighths with equal probability. Figure 13A.2 indicates its utility in each of these states (points *e* and *f*) and shows that while its expected share is still one-half, the greater uncertainty—or "spread" of possible outcomes—has led to a reduction in its expected utility (compare points *d* and *g*). Indeed, party A would now be as happy to receive the share S_A^1 with certainty as it would to face the risks associated with going to arbitration. Since S_A^1 is less than S_A, the size of the contract zone has increased. Hence, increased uncertainty about the arbitrator's decision leads to a larger contract zone.

Next, consider Figure 13A.3, where we have drawn a utility function for a *risk-neutral* party. A risk-neutral party has a linear utility function because its utility depends only on its expected share, not the uncertainty associated with the outcome. So, for example, in Figure 13A.3, party A gets the same utility from having a share of one-half with certainty as it does from facing an arbitrated outcome in which there is equal probability that the arbitrator will award it either a share of one-quarter or a share of three-quarters. As a result, faced with

Figure 13A.2

Increased Uncertainty about
Arbitrator's Decision Increases
Size of the Contract Zone

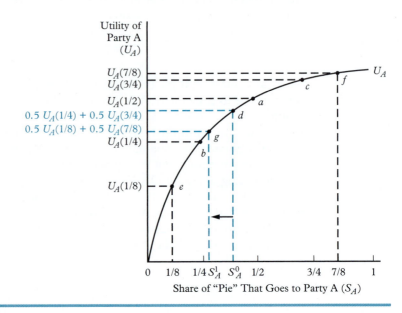

Figure 13A.3

Utility Function for a Risk-Neutral
Party: Contract Zone Is
Reduced to a Single Point

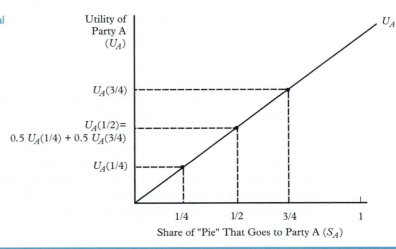

the possibility of going to arbitration, there is no share less than one-half that party A would voluntarily agree to settle for prior to arbitration. If party B had similar expectations about the arbitrator's behavior and was similarly risk neutral, it would also refuse to settle for any share of less than one-half, which on average is what it expects to win from the arbitrator. Hence, the contract zone would reduce to one point—the point where both parties receive a share of one-half. The only voluntary agreement the parties will reach is what they expect to receive on average if they go to arbitration. (This illustrates how the arbitration process itself may influence the nature of negotiated settlements.)

More generally, one can show that as a party's risk aversion increases (the utility function becomes more curved), the size of the contract zone will increase. Hence, increases in either the parties' risk aversion or their uncertainty about the arbitrator's decision will increase the size of the contract zone.

Larger contract zones mean that there are more potential settlements that *both* parties would prefer to an arbitrated settlement, and some people have argued that this increased menu of choices increases the probability that the parties would settle on their own prior to going to arbitration.[3] An immediate implication of this argument is that if one believes it is preferable for the parties to settle on their own, the arbitration system should be structured so that the arbitrator's behavior does *not* become completely predictable. As we discussed in the text, however, others argue that a *smaller* contract zone implies the parties have less to argue about and that, therefore, *smaller* zones lead to more rapid voluntary settlements.

---

[3]Farber and Katz, "Interest Arbitration, Outcomes, and the Incentive to Bargain."

CHAPTER 14

Unemployment

With the dramatic rise in unemployment after 2007 has come a renewed interest in understanding both the measurement and—more importantly—the causes of unemployment. As noted in chapter 2, the population can be divided into those people who are in the labor force (*L*) and those who are not (*N*). The labor force consists of those people who are employed (*E*) and those who are unemployed but would like to be employed (*U*). The concept of unemployment is somewhat ambiguous, since, in theory, virtually anyone would be willing to be employed in return for a generous enough compensation package. Economists tend to resolve this dilemma by defining unemployment in terms of an individual's willingness to be employed at some prevailing market wage. Government statistics take a more pragmatic approach, defining the unemployed as those who are on temporary layoff waiting to be recalled by their previous employer, or those without a job who have actively searched for work in the previous month (of course, "actively" is not precisely defined).

Given these definitions, the unemployment rate (**u**) is measured as the ratio of the number of the unemployed to the number in the labor force:

$$\mathbf{u} = \frac{U}{L} \tag{14.1}$$

Much attention is focused on how the national unemployment rate varies over time and how unemployment rates vary across geographic areas and age/race/gender/ethnic groups.

It is important, however, to understand the limitations of unemployment rate data. They *do* reflect the proportion of a group that, at a point in time, actively want to work but are not employed. For a number of reasons, however, they *do not* necessarily provide an accurate reflection of the economic hardship that members of a group are suffering. First, individuals who are not actively searching for work, including those who searched unsuccessfully and then gave up, are not counted among the unemployed (see chapter 7). Second, unemployment statistics tell us nothing about the earnings levels of those who are employed, including whether these exceed the poverty level. Third, in most years, a substantial fraction of the unemployed come from families in which other earners are present— for example, many of the unemployed are teenagers—and the unemployed often are not the primary source of their family's support. Fourth, a substantial fraction of the unemployed receive some income support while they are unemployed, in the form of either government unemployment compensation payments or private supplementary unemployment benefits.

Finally, while unemployment rate data give us information on the fraction of the *labor force* that is not working, they tell us little about the fraction of the *population* that is *employed*. Table 14.1 contains U.S. data on the aggregate unemployment rate, the labor force participation rate, and the *employment rate*—the last being defined as employment divided by the adult population—for 2000 and 2012, as well as for two pairs of earlier years over which roughly equal changes in the unemployment rate were experienced. From 1948 to 1958, for example, the unemployment rate rose from 3.8 percent to 6.8 percent and the employment rate fell from 56.6 percent to 55.4 percent. In contrast, from 1968 to 1991, the unemployment rate rose by a similar magnitude, but the employment rate *rose* substantially! The reason for the opposite correlations between the unemployment and the employment rates for these two

Table 14.1

Civilian Labor Force Participation, Employment, and Unemployment Rates in the United States (in Percentages)

Year	Labor Force Unemployment Rate (U/L)	Participation Rate (L/POP)	Employment Rate (E/POP)
1948	3.8	58.8	56.6
1958	6.8	59.5	55.4
1968	3.6	59.6	57.5
1991	6.8	66.2	61.7
2000	4.0	67.1	64.4
2012	8.1	63.7	58.6

U = the number of people unemployed

L = the number of people in the labor force

E = the number of people employed

POP = the total population over age 16

Sources: U.S. Department of Labor, *2013 Employment and Earnings Online*, Household Survey Data (February 2013), Table 1, at http://www.bls.gov/opub/ee/2013/cps/annavg1_2012.pdf.

periods is that in the earlier period, labor force participation grew only slowly, while in the latter period, it was growing very rapidly. In contrast, the very high unemployment rate in 2012 was accompanied by declines in *both* the employment rate and the labor force participation rate (the latter decline is evidence of the "discouraged-worker" effect discussed in chapter 7).

Nonetheless, the unemployment rate remains a useful indicator of labor market conditions. This chapter will be concerned with the causes of unemployment and with how various government policies affect, in an either intended or unintended manner, the level of unemployment.

■ A Stock-Flow Model of the Labor Market

We begin with a simple conceptual model of a labor market that emphasizes the importance of considering the *flows* between labor market states (for example, the *movement* of people from employed to unemployed status) as well as the *number* of people in each labor market state (for example, the *number* of the unemployed). Knowledge of the determinants of these flows is crucial to any understanding of the causes of unemployment.

Data on the number of Americans who are employed, unemployed, and not in the labor force are provided each month from the national Current Population Survey (CPS). As Figure 14.1 indicates, in May 2013 there were 144.8 million employed, 12.2 million unemployed, and 88.6 million over the age of 16 who were not in the labor force. The impression we get when tracing these data over short periods of time is that of relative stability; for example, it is highly unusual for the unemployment rate to change by more than a few tenths of a percentage point from one month to the next (it was 7.3% on May 1, 2013 and 7.8% on June 1).

Figure 14.1

Labor Market Stocks and Flows: May to June, 2013

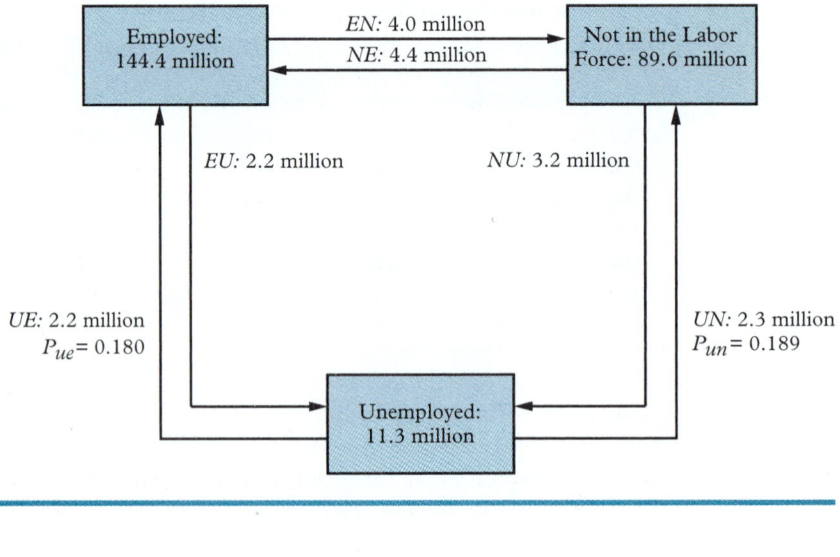

Source: U.S. Bureau of Labor Statistics, "Labor Force Statistics from the Current Population Survey: Labor Force Status Flows by Sex," at http://www.bls.gov/web/empsit/cps_flows_recent.htm.

- Employed: 144.4 million
- Not in the Labor Force: 89.6 million
- Unemployed: 11.3 million
- *EN:* 4.0 million
- *NE:* 4.4 million
- *EU:* 2.2 million
- *NU:* 3.2 million
- *UE:* 2.2 million, $P_{ue} = 0.180$
- *UN:* 2.3 million, $P_{un} = 0.189$

Taking month-to-month snapshots of the number of people who are employed, unemployed, or out of the labor market misses a considerable amount of movement into and out of these categories *during* the month. Figure 14.1 contains data on the flows of workers among the various categories during the month of May 2013. During this month, approximately 2.2 million of the unemployed found employment (the flow denoted by *UE* in Figure 14.1) and 2.3 million of the unemployed dropped out of the labor force (the flow denoted by *UN*). These numbers represent the proportions 0.180 (P_{ue}) and 0.189 (P_{un}) of the stock of unemployed, respectively; thus, we can conclude that about one-third of the individuals who were unemployed at the beginning of May left unemployment by month's end. These individuals were replaced in the pool of unemployed by flows of individuals into unemployment from the stocks of employed individuals (2.2 million, the flow *EU*) and those not in the labor force (3.2 million, the flow *NU*).[1] The flow *EU* consists of individuals who voluntarily left or involuntarily lost their last job, while the flow *NU* consists of people entering the labor force. The fact that the flows into unemployment (5.4 million) were greater than the flows out of unemployment (4.5 million) means that during this period, unemployment was rising.

Sources of Unemployment

When we think of the unemployed, the image of an individual laid off from his or her previous job often springs to mind. However, the view that such individuals constitute all the unemployed is incorrect. Table 14.2 provides some data that bear on this point for years between 1970 and 2012, during which the unemployment rate varied considerably. In the typical year, roughly half of the unemployed were job losers—although the fraction of job losers was highest in the years of very high unemployment (reaching almost two-thirds in 2009).

In each year except 2009, more than one-third of the unemployed came from out-of-labor-force status—that is, they were individuals who were either entering the labor force for the first time (*new entrants*) or individuals who had some previous employment experience and were reentering the labor force after a period of time out of the labor force (*reentrants*). Some of these reentrants, of course, will be job losers who dropped out of the labor force for a time. Finally, although the vast majority of individuals who quit their jobs obtain new jobs prior to quitting and never pass through unemployment status, in most years, 10 percent to 15 percent of the unemployed were voluntary job leavers.

Among those who lose their jobs, the duration and the consequences of unemployment depend on whether the layoff is temporary or permanent. Of the

---

[1]From the perspective of actual measurement, those who are classified as "unemployed" are distinguished from those considered "out of the labor force" only by self-reported information on job search. Thus, the empirical distinction between the two categories, as well as errors in recording movements between them, have attracted the attention of researchers. For an analysis of the former issue, see Füsun Gönsül, "New Evidence on Whether Unemployment and Out of the Labor Force Are Distinct States," *Journal of Human Resources* 27 (Spring 1992): 329–361. On the latter topic, see Paul Flaim and Carma Hogue, "Measuring Labor Force Flows: A Special Conference Examines the Problems," *Monthly Labor Review* (July 1985): 7–15.

Table 14.2

Sources of Unemployment, United States, Various Years

Year	Unemployment Rate	Percent of Unemployed Who Were:			
		Job Losers	Job Leavers	Reentrants	New Entrants
1970	4.9	44.3	13.4	30.0	12.3
1974	5.6	43.5	14.9	28.4	13.2
1978	6.1	41.6	14.1	30.0	14.3
1982	9.7	58.7	7.9	22.3	11.1
1986	6.9	48.9	12.3	26.2	12.5
1990	5.5	48.3	14.8	27.4	9.5
1994	6.1	47.7	9.4	34.8	7.6
1998	4.5	45.5	11.8	34.3	8.4
2002	5.8	55.0	10.3	28.3	6.4
2006	4.6	47.4	11.8	32.0	8.8
2009	9.3	64.2	6.2	22.3	7.3
2012	8.1	55.0	7.7	26.7	10.5

Sources: U.S. Department of Labor, *1982 Employment and Training Report of the President* (Washington, D.C.: U.S. Government Printing Office, 1982), Table A-36; U.S. Department of Labor, *Monthly Labor Review*, various issues.

0.6 percent of American workers who were laid off in the average month during the 1990s, a bit less than half were laid off temporarily and returned relatively quickly to their jobs (usually within three to six weeks). Those who were permanently discharged—whether for cause or because of plant closure or "downsizing"— were unemployed for over twice as long. Furthermore, when they returned to work, it was typically at a much lower pay level.[2] Unfortunately, layoffs are now less likely to be temporary than in earlier decades, reflecting the permanent adjustments required by a business environment that is increasingly competitive.

Rates of Flow Affect Unemployment Levels

Although ultimately public concern focuses on the *level* of unemployment, to understand the determinants of this level, we must analyze the *flows* of individuals between the various labor market states. A group's unemployment rate might be high because its members have difficulty finding jobs once unemployed, because they have difficulty (for voluntary or involuntary reasons) remaining

[2]See Hoyt Bleakley, Ann E. Ferris, and Jeffrey C. Fuhrer, "New Data on Worker Flows During Business Cycles," *New England Economic Review* (July–August 1999): 49–76. For more on the subject of job loss, see Kenneth A. Couch and Dana W. Placzek, "Earnings Losses of Displaced Workers Revisited," *American Economic Review* 100 (March 2010): 572–589; and Kevin Hallock, "Job Loss and the Fraying of the Implicit Employment Contract," *Journal of Economic Perspectives* 23 (Fall 2009): 69–93.

employed once a job is found, or because they frequently enter and leave the labor force. The appropriate policy prescription to reduce the unemployment rate will depend on which one of these labor market flows is responsible for the high rate.

Somewhat more formally, we can show that if labor markets are roughly in balance, with the flows into and out of unemployment equal, the unemployment rate (**u**) for a group depends on the various labor market flows in the following manner:

$$\mathbf{u} = F(\overset{+}{P_{en}}, \overset{-}{P_{ne}}, \overset{-}{P_{un}}, \overset{+}{P_{nu}}, \overset{+}{P_{eu}}, \overset{-}{P_{ue}}) \qquad (14.2)$$

In this equation, F means "a function of" and

$P_{en} =$ the fraction of employed who leave the labor force
$P_{ne} =$ the fraction of those not in the labor force who enter the labor force and find employment
$P_{un} =$ the fraction of unemployed who leave the labor force
$P_{nu} =$ the fraction of those not in the labor force who enter the labor force and become unemployed
$P_{eu} =$ the fraction of employed who become unemployed
$P_{ue} =$ the fraction of unemployed who become employed

So, for example, if there were initially 100 employed individuals in a group and 15 of them became unemployed during a period, P_{eu} would equal 0.15.

A plus sign over a variable in equation (14.2) means that an increase in that variable will increase the unemployment rate, while a minus sign means that an increase in the variable will decrease the unemployment rate. The equation thus asserts that, other things equal, increases in the proportions of individuals who voluntarily or involuntarily leave their jobs and become unemployed (P_{eu}) or leave the labor force (P_{en}) will increase a group's unemployment rate, as will an increase in the proportion of the group that enters the labor force without first having a job lined up (P_{nu}). Similarly, the greater the proportion of individuals who leave unemployment status, either to become employed (P_{ue}) or to leave the labor force (P_{un}), the lower a group's unemployment rate. Finally, the greater the proportion of individuals who enter the labor force and immediately find jobs (P_{ne}), the lower a group's unemployment rate.[3]

Equation (14.2) and Figure 14.1 make clear that social concern over any given level of unemployment should focus on both the *incidence* of unemployment (or the fraction of people in a group who become unemployed) and the *duration* of spells of unemployment. Society is probably more concerned if small groups of

---

[3]The specific functional form for equation (14.2) is found in Stephen T. Marston, "Employment Instability and High Unemployment Rates," *Brookings Papers on Economic Activity* 1976: 1, 169–203. An intuitive understanding of why each of the results summarized in equation (14.2) holds can be obtained from the definition of the unemployment rate in equation (14.1). A movement from one labor market state to another may affect the numerator or the denominator or both. For example, an increase in P_{en} does not affect the number of unemployed individuals directly, but it does reduce the size of the labor force. According to equation (14.1), this reduction leads to an increase in the unemployment rate.

individuals are unemployed for long periods of time than if many individuals rapidly pass through unemployment status.

Table 14.3 documents some remarkable differences in both the incidence and duration of unemployment across years and across selected European and North American countries. The more notable examples are as follows:

a. In most countries (Denmark and Norway are exceptions), the unemployment rate and long-term unemployment moved in the same direction from 2005 to 2011;

b. Canada had a higher unemployment rate than Germany in 2011, but the unemployed in Canada typically found jobs much more quickly (only 13.5 percent of the Canadian unemployed had been out of work for over a year, compared to roughly 50 percent in Germany);

c. The Netherlands and Norway had similar levels of unemployment in both 2005 and 2011, but in Norway long-term unemployment is much less common.

d. Finally, both Denmark and the United States experienced sizeable increases in their unemployment rates between 2005 and 2011, but in Denmark the percentage of those out of work for over a year dipped slightly, while it almost tripled in the United States over the period.

Clearly, then, there are important differences across countries in labor-market conditions, institutions, or policies that underlie these unemployment outcomes.

While this textbook cannot offer detailed analyses of all the differences across countries shown in Table 14.3, the various theories of unemployment

Table 14.3

Unemployment and Long-Term Unemployment, Selected European and North American Countries, 2005 and 2011

	Unemployment Overall Rate		Percent of Unemployed Out of Work > One Year	
	2005	2011	2005	2011
Belgium	8.4%	7.2%	51.6%	48.3%
Canada	6.8	7.4	9.6	13.5
Denmark	4.8	7.6	25.9	24.4
France	9.5	9.7	42.5	41.4
Germany	9.5	5.9	54.0	48.0
Ireland	4.3	14.5	34.3	59.4
Netherlands	4.8	4.4	40.1	33.6
Norway	4.6	3.3	9.4	11.6
United Kingdom	4.7	8.0	22.4	33.4
United States	5.1	9.0	11.8	31.3

Source: OECD, *Employment Outlook* (Paris: OECD, 2006), Tables A and G; and OECD, *Employment Outlook* (Paris: OECD, 2012), Tables A and H.

■ Demand-Deficient (Cyclical) Unemployment

Frictional unemployment arises because labor markets are dynamic and information flows are imperfect; structural unemployment arises because of long-lasting imbalances in demand and supply. *Demand-deficient unemployment* is associated with fluctuations in business activity (the "business cycle"), and it occurs when a decline in aggregate demand in the output market causes the *aggregate demand for labor* to decline in the face of downward inflexibility in real wages. The most recent example of such a decline took place during the "Great Recession" of 2007 to 2009, during which time the unemployment rate in the United States rose from 4.4 percent in the spring of 2007 to 10 percent in the fall of 2009.[23]

Returning to our simple demand and supply model of Figure 14.2, suppose that a temporary decline in aggregate demand leads to a shift in the labor demand curve to D_1. If real wages are inflexible downward, employment will fall to E_1, and $E_0 - E_1$ additional workers will become unemployed. This employment decline occurs when firms temporarily lay off workers (increasing P_{eu}) and reduce the rate at which they replace those who quit or retire (decreasing P_{ne} and P_{ue}); that is, flows into unemployment increase while flows into employment decline.

Unemployment, however, is not the inevitable outcome of reduced aggregate demand. Employers, for example, could reduce the wages they pay to their workers. If the latter response occurred, employment would move to E_2 and real wages to W_2 in Figure 14.2. Although employment would be lower than its initial level, E_0, there would be no measured demand-deficient unemployment, because $E_0 - E_2$ workers would have dropped out of the labor force in response to this lower wage. While this textbook cannot discuss the macroeconomic forces that cause (or ameliorate) reductions in aggregate demand, we will analyze two features of the U.S. labor market thought to *contribute* to demand-deficient unemployment: (1) institutional and profit-maximizing reasons for rigid money wages, and (2) the way in which the U.S. unemployment compensation program is financed.

Downward Wage Rigidity

Stock and commodity prices fluctuate with demand and supply, and product market retailers have sales or offer discounts when demand is down, but do the wage rates paid to individual workers fall when the demand for labor shifts to the left? If such decreases are not very likely, what might be the reasons?

Wages, of course, can be measured in both nominal and real terms. *Nominal* wages (the money wages quoted to workers) may be relatively rigid, yet the *real* wage (the nominal wage divided by an index of prices) can fall if prices are rising. It will come as no great surprise that the real wages received by individual workers quite commonly fall; all that needs to happen for real wages to fall is for the increase in nominal wages to be less than the increase in prices. One study that followed individuals in the United States from 1970 to 1991 found that when the

---

[23]Edward Lazear and James Spletzer, "The United States Labor Market: Status Quo or a New Normal?" working paper no. 18386, National Bureau of Economic Research (Cambridge, Mass.: September 2012).

unemployment rate went up by one percentage point, the average real hourly earnings among workers who did not change employers went down by about 0.5 percent. Hourly earnings reductions were greatest among those paid by piece rates or commissions, or whose compensation packages included bonuses; those paid by salary were least likely to experience such reductions.[24]

Despite evidence of at least modest downward flexibility of real wages, it is also important to see how common cuts in workers' nominal wages are. If real wages fall only when prices rise, they may not be able to fall fast enough to prevent an increase in unemployment during business downturns. One study of workers who did not change employers found that nominal wages fell from one year to the next in 18 percent of the cases between the years 1976 and 1988; similar estimates come from a study using different employee-provided data, although this latter study extended into the early 1990s, when some 18 percent to 20 percent of hourly paid workers experienced nominal-wage cuts.[25] These studies suggest that nominal wages are not completely rigid in a downward direction, although compensation in the form of bonuses or other forms of contingent pay (such as profit sharing) appears to be more flexible than time-based pay.[26] However, the studies also conclude that nominal wages are resistant to cuts, and as a result, employment adjustments during periods of downturn are larger and more common than they would be with complete nominal-wage flexibility.

Explanations for why employment levels are more likely to be reduced than nominal wages during business downturns must confront two questions: why do firms find it more profitable to reduce employment than wages, and why are workers who face unemployment not more willing to take wage cuts to save their jobs? The hypotheses concerning wage rigidity that have come to the forefront recently address both questions.

---

[24]Thomas Lemieux, W. Bentley MacLeod, and Daniel Parent, "Contract Form, Wage Flexibility, and Employment," *American Economic Review: Papers and Proceedings* 102 (May 2012): 526–531; Paul J. Devereux, "The Cyclicality of Real Wages within Employer–Employee Matches," *Industrial and Labor Relations Review* 54 (July 2001): 835–850. For a study of real wage flexibility in Britain, see Paul J. Devereux and Robert A. Hart, "Real Wage Flexibility of Job Stayers, Within-Company Job Movers, and Between-Company Job Movers," *Industrial and Labor Relations Review* 60 (October 2006): 105–119.

[25]Shulamit Kahn, "Evidence of Nominal Wage Stickiness from Microdata," *American Economic Review* 87 (December 1997): 993–1008; and David Card and Dean Hyslop, "Does Inflation Grease the Wheels of the Labor Market?" in *Reducing Inflation: Motivation and Strategy*, eds. Christina D. Romer and David H. Romer (Cambridge, Mass.: National Bureau of Economic Research, 1997): 71–121. Also see Christopher Hanes and John A. James, "Wage Adjustment Under Low Inflation: Evidence from U.S. History," *American Economic Review* 93 (September 2003): 1414–1424; and Louis N. Christofides and Thanasis Stengos, "Wage Rigidity in Canadian Collective Bargaining Agreements," *Industrial and Labor Relations Review* 56 (April 2003): 429–448. For an international study of wage rigidity among workers who do not change employers, using data from both employees and employers, see William T. Dickens, Lorenz Goette, Erica L. Groshen, Steinar Holden, Julian Messina, Mark E. Schweitzer, Jarkko Turunen, and Melanie E. Ward, "How Wages Change: Micro Evidence from the International Wage Flexibility Project," *Journal of Economic Perspectives* 21 (Spring 2007): 195–214.

[26]Thomas Lemieux, W. Bentley MacLeod, and Daniel Parent, "Contract Form, Wage Flexibility, and Employment"; and Harry J. Holzer and Edward B. Montgomery, "Asymmetries and Rigidities in Wage Adjustments by Firms," *Review of Economics and Statistics* 75 (August 1993): 397–408.

Wage Rigidity and Unions   According to one explanation for rigid money wages, employers are not free to unilaterally cut nominal wages because of the presence of unions. This cannot be a complete explanation for the United States, because less than 14 percent of American workers are covered by union agreements (see chapter 13), and unions could, in any case, agree to temporary wage cuts to save jobs instead of subjecting their members to layoffs. Why they fail to make such arrangements is instructive.

A temporary wage reduction would reduce the earnings of all workers, while layoffs would affect, in most cases, only those workers most recently hired. Because these workers represent a minority of the union's membership in most instances, because union leaders are elected by majority rule, and because these leaders are most likely drawn from the ranks of the more experienced workers (who are often immune from layoff), unions tend to favor a policy of layoffs rather than one that reduces wages for all members.[27] A variant of this explanation is the *insider-outsider hypothesis*, which sees union members as *insiders* who have little or no concern for nonmembers or former members now on layoff (*outsiders*); these insiders gain from keeping their numbers small and may choose to negotiate wages that effectively prevent the recall or employment of outsiders.[28]

Wage Rigidity and Specific Human Capital   Layoffs do occur in *nonunion* firms, although perhaps less frequently than in unionized ones, so wage rigidity cannot be completely attributed to unionization. One possible explanation lies with employer investments in workers. In the presence of firm-specific human capital investments, for example, employers have incentives both to minimize voluntary turnover and to maximize their employees' work effort and productivity. Across-the-board temporary wage reductions would increase all employees' propensities to quit and could lead to reduced work effort on their part. In contrast, layoffs affect only the least-experienced workers—the workers in whom the firm has invested the smallest amount of resources. It is likely, then, that the firm will find the layoff strategy a more profitable alternative.[29]

---

[27]See James Medoff, "Layoffs and Alternatives under Trade Unions in United States Manufacturing," *American Economic Review* 69 (June 1979): 380–395, for evidence. This hypothesis suggests that unions are much more likely to bargain for wage reductions when projected layoffs exceed 50 percent of the union's membership. For evidence that this occurred in the early 1980s, see Robert J. Flanagan, "Wage Concessions and Long-Term Union Flexibility," *Brookings Papers on Economic Activity*, 1984–1: 183–216.

[28]Assar Lindbeck and Dennis J. Snower, "Insiders versus Outsiders," *Journal of Economic Perspectives* 15 (Winter 2001): 165–188.

[29]See Truman F. Bewley, *Why Wages Don't Fall during a Recession* (Cambridge, Mass.: Harvard University Press, 1999); and Weiss, *Efficiency Wages: Models of Unemployment, Layoffs and Wage Dispersion*. Wendy L. Rayack, "Fixed and Flexible Wages: Evidence from Panel Data," *Industrial and Labor Relations Review* 44 (January 1991): 288–298, presents empirical evidence that the sensitivity of wages to unemployment is confined largely to workers with short job tenure; however, somewhat different results were obtained by Mark Bils, Yongsung Chang, and Sun-Bin Kim, "Comparative Advantage in Cyclical Unemployment," National Bureau of Economic Research, working paper no. 13231 (July 2007). For a study finding, for recent years, that rising layoffs are less important than slower rates of hire in causing unemployment during recessions, see Robert E. Hall, "Employment Efficiency and Sticky Wages: Evidence from Flows in the Labor Market," *Review of Economics and Statistics* 87 (August 2005): 397–407.

Wage Rigidity and Asymmetric Information   Employers with internal labor markets frequently promise, at least implicitly, a certain path of earnings to employees over their careers. As we saw in chapter 11, firms may pay relatively low salaries to new employees with the promise (expectation) that if they work diligently, these employees will be paid relatively high wages toward the end of their careers. The firm's promises are, of necessity, conditional on how well it is performing, but the firm has more accurate information on the true state of its demand than do its workers. If a firm asks its employees to take a wage cut in periods of low demand, employees may believe that the employer is falsely stating that demand is low, and their productivity could be reduced by a loss of trust or a decline in morale. If, instead, a firm temporarily lays off some of its workers, it loses the output these workers would have produced, and workers may therefore accept such an action as a signal that the firm is indeed in trouble (that is, wages exceed current marginal productivity). Put another way, the *asymmetry of information* between employers and employees may make layoffs the preferred policy.[30]

Wage Rigidity and Risk Aversion   Firms with internal labor markets, and therefore long employer–employee job attachments, may be encouraged by the risk aversion of older employees to engage in seniority-based layoffs (last hired, first laid off) rather than wage cuts for all its workers. That is, the desire to have a constant income stream, rather than a fluctuating one with the same average value over time, is something for which older, more-experienced workers may be willing to pay.[31] Thus, if the risks of income fluctuation are confined to one's initial years of employment, the firm may be able to pay its experienced workers wages lower than would otherwise be required. Of course, during the initial period, workers will be subject to potential earnings variability and may demand higher wages then to compensate them for these risks. However, if the fraction of the workforce subject to layoffs is small, on average, employers' costs could be reduced by seniority-based layoffs.

Wage Rigidity: Worker Status and Social Norms   The explanations given earlier pertain mainly to firms with internal labor markets, which can be roughly thought of as large employers. If these firms have rigid wages and lay off workers during a business downturn, why don't workers who are laid off take jobs with smaller employers? These smaller firms pay lower wages and have few of the reasons cited earlier to avoid reducing them further when aggregate demand falls; hence, increased employment in these jobs would lower the average nominal

---

[30]See, for example, Sanford Grossman, Oliver Hart, and Eric Maskin, "Unemployment with Observable Aggregate Shocks," *Journal of Political Economy* 91 (December 1983): 907–928; Sanford Grossman and Oliver Hart, "Implicit Contracts, Moral Hazard and Unemployment," *American Economic Review* 71 (May 1981): 301–307; Costas Azariadis, "Employment with Asymmetric Information," *Quarterly Journal of Economics* 98 (Supplement, 1983): 157–172; and Daiji Kawaguchi and Fumio Ohtake, "Testing the Morale Theory of Nominal Wage Rigidity," *Industrial and Labor Relations Review* 61 (October 2007): 59–74.

[31]This line of reasoning follows that in Costas Azariadis, "Implicit Contracts and Underemployment Equilibria," *Journal of Political Economy* 83 (December 1975): 1183–1202; and Martin Baily, "Wages and Employment under Uncertain Demand," *Review of Economic Studies* 41 (January 1974): 37–50.

wage paid in the economy and help reduce unemployment. Some theorists believe that the failure of unemployed workers to flock to low-wage jobs derives from their sense of status (their relative standing in society).

It is possible, for example, that individuals prefer unemployment in a "good" job to employment in an inferior one, at least for a period longer than the typical recession.[32] A sense of *status*, then, may prevent a reduction in wages and the expansion of low-wage jobs during recessionary periods. It is also possible, however, that considerations of social status may operate in a different way: prevailing market wages may be accepted as *social norms*, which inhibit the unemployed from trying to find work by appearing to undercut the wages of the employed.[33]

Financing U.S. Unemployment Compensation

The incentives for employers to engage in temporary layoffs are also affected by a key characteristic of the U.S. UI system: *its methods of financing benefits.* As we will see, the way in which the government raises the funds to pay for UI benefits has a rather large effect on cyclical layoffs.

The UI Payroll Tax   The benefits paid out by the UI system are financed by a payroll tax. Unlike the Social Security payroll tax, in almost all states the UI tax is paid solely by employers.[34] The UI tax payment (T) that an employer must make for each employee is given by

$$T = tW \quad \text{if} \quad W \le W_B \qquad (14.3a)$$

and

$$T = tW_B \quad \text{if} \quad W > W_B \qquad (14.3b)$$

where t is the employer's UI tax rate, W is an employee's earnings during the calendar year, and W_B is the *taxable wage base* (the level of earnings after which no UI tax payments are required). In 2010, the taxable wage base ranged from $7,000 to $14,000 in about two-thirds of the states; thus, depending on the state, employers had to pay UI taxes on just the first $7,000 to $14,000 of each employee's earnings. The other one-third of the states had taxable wage bases that were higher.

The employer's UI tax rate is determined by general economic conditions in the state, the industry the employer is operating in, and the employer's *layoff experience.* The last term is defined differently in different states; the underlying

---

[32]See Alan S. Blinder, "The Challenge of High Unemployment," *American Economic Review* 78 (May 1988): 1–15.

[33]See Robert M. Solow, *The Labor Market as an Institution* (Cambridge, Mass.: Basil Blackwell, 1990), chapter 2.

[34]Recall from our discussion in chapter 3 that this fact tells us nothing about who really bears the burden of the tax.

notion is that since the UI system is an insurance system, employers who lay off workers frequently and make heavy demands on the system's resources should be assigned a higher UI tax rate. This practice is referred to as *experience rating*.

Imperfect Experience Rating   Experience rating is typically *imperfect* in the sense that the marginal cost to an employer of laying off an additional worker (in terms of a higher UI tax rate) is often less than the added UI benefits the system must pay out to that worker. Imperfect experience rating is illustrated in Figure 14.7, which plots the relationship between an employer's UI tax rate and that firm's layoff experience. (We shall interpret *layoff experience* to mean the probability that employees in the firm will be on layoff. Clearly, this probability depends both on the frequency with which the firm lays off workers and the average duration of time until they are recalled to their positions.)

Each state has a minimum UI tax rate, and below this rate (t_{min} in Figure 14.7), the firm's UI tax rate cannot fall. After a firm's layoff experience reaches some critical value (l_{min}), the firm's UI tax rate rises with increased layoff experience over some range.[35] In each state, there is also a ceiling on the UI tax rate (t_{max}); after this tax rate is reached, additional layoffs will not alter the firm's tax rate. The system is *imperfectly* experience-rated because for firms below l_{min} or above l_{max}, variations in their layoff rate have no effect on their UI tax rate.[36] Furthermore, over

---

Figure 14.7

Imperfectly Experience-Rated
Unemployment Insurance Tax Rates

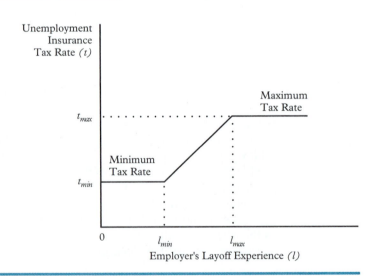

---

[35]In actuality, the UI tax rate changes discretely (as a step function) over the range l_{min} to l_{max}, not continuously as drawn in Figure 14.7. For expository convenience, we ignore this complication.

[36]Such a system of UI financing leads to inter-industry subsidies, in which industries with virtually no layoffs still must pay the minimum tax, and these industries subsidize industries (such as construction) that have very high layoffs but pay only the maximum rate.

the range in which the tax rate is increasing with layoff experience, the increase is not large enough in most states to make the employer's marginal cost of a layoff (in terms of the increased UI taxes the firm must pay) equal to the marginal UI benefits the laid-off employees receive.

Does the UI Tax Encourage Layoffs?   The key characteristic of the UI system that influences the desirability of temporary layoffs is the *imperfect experience rating* of the UI payroll tax. To understand the influence of this characteristic, suppose first that the UI system were constructed in such a way that its tax rates were perfectly experience-rated. A firm laying off a worker would have to pay added UI taxes equal to the full UI benefit (50 percent of normal earnings) received by the worker, so it saves just half of the worker's wages by the layoff. Now, suppose instead that the UI tax rate employers must pay is totally independent of their layoff experience (no experience rating). In this case, a firm saves a laid-off worker's *entire* wages because its UI taxes do not rise as a result of the layoff. Thus, compared with a UI system with perfect experience rating, it is easy to see that a system with incomplete experience rating will tend to enhance the attractiveness of layoffs to employers.

Empirical analyses of the effect of imperfect experience rating on employer behavior suggest that it is substantial. These studies have estimated that unemployment would fall by 10 percent to 33 percent if UI taxes in the United States were perfectly experience-rated (so that employers laying off workers would have to pay the full cost of the added UI benefits).[37]

Seasonal Unemployment

Seasonal unemployment is similar to demand-deficient unemployment, in that it is induced by fluctuations in the demand for labor. Here, however, the fluctuations can be regularly anticipated and follow a systematic pattern over the course of a year. For example, the demand for agricultural employees declines after the planting season and remains low until the harvest season. Similarly, the demand for production workers falls in certain industries during the season of the year when plants are retooling to handle annual model changes.

The issue remains: why do employers respond to seasonal patterns of demand by laying off workers rather than reducing wage rates or hours of work? All the reasons cited for the existence of cyclical unemployment and temporary layoffs for cyclical reasons also pertain here. Indeed, one study has shown that the expansion (in the early 1970s) of the UI system that led to the coverage of most agricultural employees was associated with a substantial increase in seasonal

---

[37]Patricia M. Anderson and Bruce D. Meyer, "The Effects of the Unemployment Insurance Payroll Tax on Wages, Employment, Claims, and Denials," *Journal of Public Economics* 78 (October 2000): 81–106; and Robert H. Topel, "Financing Unemployment Insurance: History, Incentives, and Reform," in *Unemployment Insurance: The Second Half-Century*, eds. W. Lee Hansen and James F. Byers (Madison: University of Wisconsin Press, 1990): 108–135.

EXAMPLE 14.2

Unemployment Insurance and Seasonal Unemployment: A Historical Perspective

The current American UI system was established during the Great Depression of the 1930s. At that time, labor economist John Commons urged that legislation include a penalty on firms with higher unemployment rates. He believed that employers had enough leeway to reduce seasonal and other layoffs substantially, and he thus championed a system that included incentives to avoid higher layoffs. Others were unconvinced that employers had much discretion over unemployment. But ultimately, the Commons plan was adopted in most states. It was rarely adopted outside the United States, however.

Evidence on seasonal unemployment seems to support Commons's contentions: over time, as the economy has diversified, seasonal unemployment has fallen, but it has fallen much more rapidly where employers are penalized for layoffs. One study found that within the United States, seasonal

fluctuations in employment have fallen most in states where UI experience rating is highest.

Even more striking is the comparison between the United States and Canada, which established an UI system without *any* experience rating. Seasonality in the Canadian construction industry (an industry notorious for its seasonality) fell by half between 1929 and the 1947–1963 period, as construction practices improved and changed. However, in American states along the Canadian border, seasonality dropped by an even greater two-thirds!

Source: Katherine Baicker, Claudia Goldin, and Lawrence F. Katz, "A Distinctive System: Origins and Impact of U.S. Unemployment Compensation," in *The Defining Moment: The Great Depression and the American Economy in the Twentieth Century*, eds. Michael D. Bordo, Claudia Goldin, and Eugene N. White (Chicago: University of Chicago Press, 1998): 259.

unemployment in agriculture. Studies of seasonal layoffs in nonagricultural industries also suggest that imperfect experience rating of the UI tax significantly increases seasonal unemployment.[38] (See Example 14.2 for a longer-term perspective on UI and seasonal unemployment.)

We may question why workers would accept jobs in industries in which they knew in advance they would be unemployed for a portion of the year. For some workers, the existence of UI benefits along with the knowledge that they will be rehired as a matter of course at the end of the slack-demand season may allow them to treat such periods as paid vacations.[39] However, since UI benefits typically replace less than half of an unemployed worker's previous gross earnings and even smaller fractions for high-wage workers (see Figure 14.4), most

---

[38]Barry Chiswick, "The Effect of Unemployment Compensation on a Seasonal Industry: Agriculture," *Journal of Political Economy* 84 (June 1976): 591–602; Patricia M. Anderson, "Linear Adjustment Costs and Seasonal Labor Demand: Evidence from Retail Trade Firms," *Quarterly Journal of Economics* 108 (November 1993): 1015–1042; and David Card and Phillip B. Levine, "Unemployment Insurance Taxes and the Cyclical and Seasonal Properties of Unemployment," *Journal of Public Economics* 53 (January 1994): 1–29.

[39]The incidence of part-year work is much higher in the Canadian province of New Brunswick than it is across the border in Maine, where unemployment benefits are much less generous; see Peter Kuhn and Chris Riddell, "The Long-Term Effects of a Generous Income Support Program: Unemployment Insurance in New Brunswick and Maine, 1940–1991."

workers will not find such a situation desirable. To attract workers to seasonal industries, firms will have to pay workers higher wages to compensate them for being periodically unemployed. One recent study, for example, found that agricultural workers in seasonal jobs earned about 10 percent more per hour than they would have earned in permanent farm jobs.[40]

The existence of wage differentials that compensate workers in high-unemployment industries for the risk of unemployment makes it difficult to evaluate whether this type of unemployment is voluntary or involuntary in nature. On the one hand, workers have voluntarily agreed to be employed in industries that offer higher wages *and* higher probabilities of unemployment. On the other hand, once on the job, employees usually prefer to remain employed rather than becoming unemployed. Such unemployment may be considered either voluntary or involuntary, then, depending on one's perspective.

When Do We Have Full Employment?

Governments constantly worry about the unemployment rate, because it is seen as a handy barometer of an economy's health. An unemployment rate that is deemed to be too high is seen as a national concern, because it implies that many people are unable to support themselves and that many of the country's workers are not contributing to national output. Often, governments will take steps to stimulate the demand for labor in one way or another when they believe unemployment to be excessive.

Governments also worry about unemployment being too low. An unusually low rate of unemployment is thought by many to reflect a situation in which there is excess demand in the labor market. If labor demand exceeds supply, wages will tend to rise, it is argued, and wage increases will lead to price inflation. In addition, excessively low unemployment rates may increase shirking among workers and reduce the pool of available talent on which new or expanding employers can draw.

Defining the Natural Rate of Unemployment

If both too much and too little unemployment are undesirable, how much is just right? Put differently, what unemployment rate represents full employment? The *full-employment* (or *natural*) rate of unemployment is difficult to define precisely, and there are several alternative concepts from which to choose. One defines the natural rate of unemployment as that rate at which wage and price inflation are either stable or at acceptable levels. Another defines full employment as the rate of unemployment at which job vacancies equal the number of unemployed workers, and yet

---

[40]Enrico Moretti, "Do Wages Compensate for Risk of Unemployment? Parametric and Semiparametric Evidence from Seasonal Jobs," *Journal of Risk and Uncertainty* 20 (January 2000): 45–66. Also see Susan Averett, Howard Bodenhorn, and Justas Staisiunas, "Unemployment Risk and Compensating Differentials in Late-Nineteenth Century New Jersey Manufacturing," *Economic Inquiry* 43 (October 2005): 734–749.

another defines it as the level of unemployment at which any increases in aggregate demand will cause no further reductions in unemployment. A variant of the latter defines the natural rate as the unemployment rate at which all unemployment is voluntary (frictional and perhaps seasonal). A final definition of the natural rate is that rate at which the level of unemployment is unchanging and both the flows into unemployment and the duration of unemployment are normal.[41]

All the various earlier definitions try to define in a specific way a more general concept of full employment as the rate that prevails in "normal" times. If we assume that frictional and seasonal unemployment exist even in labor markets characterized by equilibrium (i.e., markets having neither excess demand nor excess supply), it is clear that the natural rate of unemployment is affected by such factors as voluntary turnover rates among employed workers, movements in and out of the labor force, and the length of time it takes for the unemployed to find acceptable jobs. These factors vary widely across demographic groups, so the natural rate during any period is strongly influenced by the demographic composition of the labor force.

Unemployment and Demographic Characteristics

Table 14.4 presents data on actual unemployment rates for various age/race/gender/ethnic groups in 2005, a year in which the overall unemployment was a moderate 5.1 percent. The patterns indicated in Table 14.4 for 2005 are similar to the patterns for other recent years: high unemployment rates for teens and young adults of each race/gender group relative to older adults in these groups; black unemployment rates at least double white unemployment rates for most age/gender groups, with Hispanic-American unemployment rates tending to lie in between; and female unemployment rates roughly equal to, or lower than, male unemployment rates for each group except Hispanics and those of prime age. The high unemployment rates of black teenagers, which ranged between 7 percent and 45 percent in 2005, have been of particular concern to policymakers.

Over recent decades, the demographic composition of the labor force has changed dramatically with the growth in labor force participation rates of females and substantial changes in the relative size of the teenage, black, and Hispanic populations. Between 1975 and 2005, the proportion of the labor force that was female grew from 40 percent to 46 percent. The growth in the Hispanic labor force was over three times faster than average over this time span, and the Hispanic share in the labor force grew from 4 percent to 13 percent. In contrast, the teenage share of the labor force dropped from over 9 percent in 1975 to roughly 5 percent by 2005.[42]

---

[41]James Tobin, "Inflation and Unemployment," *American Economic Review* 62 (March 1972): 1–18; and John Haltiwanger, "The Natural Rate of Unemployment," In *The New Palgrave*, eds. J. Eatwell, M. Milgate, and P. Newman (New York: Stockton Press, 1987): 610–612.

[42]See U.S. Department of Labor, *Employment and Earnings* 53 (January 2006), Tables 1–4, and earlier years' issues. For an analysis of the racial gap in unemployment rates, see Robert W. Fairlie and William A. Sundstrom, "The Emergence, Persistence, and Recent Widening of the Racial Unemployment Gap," *Industrial and Labor Relations Review* 52 (January 1999): 252–270.

Table 14.4

Unemployment Rates in 2005 by Demographic Group

Age	White Male	White Female	Black Male	Black Female	Hispanic Male	Hispanic Female	All
16–17	18.9	14.0	45.1	37.3	23.4	23.8	
18–19	14.3	11.1	31.5	26.6	17.5	14.0	
20–24	7.9	6.4	20.5	16.3	8.2	9.2	
25–54	3.5	3.8	7.8	7.8	4.1	5.9	
55–64	3.0	3.0	5.9	5.3	4.0	5.0	
Total	4.4	4.4	10.5	9.5	5.4	6.9	5.1

"Hispanic" refers to those of Hispanic origin; depending on their race, these individuals are also included in both the white and black population group totals.

Source: U.S. Department of Labor, *Employment and Earnings* 53 (January 2006), Tables 3 and 4.

The overall unemployment rate reflects both the tightness of the labor market and the composition of the labor force. If demographic groups with relatively high unemployment rates grow as a fraction of the labor force, then the overall unemployment rate accompanying any given level of labor market tightness will rise; similarly, the unemployment rate will tend to fall, other things equal, if the labor force share of groups with relatively high unemployment rates falls. Since 1975, changes in the composition of the labor force have had effects that tend to be offsetting. The percent of the labor force that is African American has been stable (at about 11.5 percent), and the rising share of women has had a neutral effect, given that their unemployment rates are about the same as those of men. However, the rising share of Hispanics has tended to increase the overall unemployment rate, while the falling share of teenagers has served to reduce the unemployment rate.

What Is the Natural Rate?

Economists' estimates of the natural rate have varied over time, going from something like 5.4 percent in the 1960s, to about 7 percent in the 1970s, to 6 or 6.5 percent in the 1980s, to around 5 or 6 percent in the last decade.[43] We must wonder, though, how useful estimates of the natural rate are for policy purposes if they keep changing; indeed, Milton Friedman, a Nobel-prize winner

---

[43]Mary C. Daly, Bart Hobijn, Aysegul Sahin, and Robert Valletta, "A Search and Matching Approach to Labor Markets: Did the Natural Rate of Unemployment Rise?" *Journal of Economic Perspectives* 26 (Summer 2012): 3–26; George A. Akerlof, William T. Dickens, and George L. Perry, "Near-Rational Wage and Price Setting and the Long-Run Phillips Curve," *Brookings Papers on Economic Activity*, 2000–1: 1–44; and Laurence Ball and N. Gregory Mankiw, "The NAIRU in Theory and Practice," *Journal of Economic Perspectives* 16 (Fall 2002): 115–136.

EMPIRICAL STUDY

DO REEMPLOYMENT BONUSES REDUCE UNEMPLOYMENT? THE RESULTS OF SOCIAL EXPERIMENTS

In earlier chapters, we have emphasized that empirical research in the social sciences requires analyzing the behavior of a *treatment* group against that of a *comparison* (or *control*) group. Ideally, researchers would create controlled experiments in which otherwise identical subjects are randomly assigned to the two groups and a carefully crafted treatment is applied to one but not the other.

The predictions growing out of economic theory, however, typically apply to outcomes generated by the behavior of those *at the margin* within large groups of people, and they are most credibly tested under conditions where the behaviors observed have *real-world consequences*. Thus, controlled experiments are usually infeasible in economics because of the required sample size and expense involved. Such experiments are also morally objectionable in a wide variety of cases; it is inconceivable, for example, that we could test the theory of compensating differentials by deliberately exposing the treatment group to high risk. Outside of unusual cases (see the empirical studies summarized in chapters 11 and 12), economists must normally look for *natural experiments* caused by economic conditions or government policies that happen to affect similar workers differently.

One set of controlled social experiments that did take place was designed to see if unemployment rates could be reduced by awarding cash bonuses to unemployed workers who found new jobs "quickly." The hope was that by offering these reemployment bonuses, the duration of unemployment—and therefore the unemployment rate—could be reduced.

Four states conducted such experiments in the mid- to late-1980s, and each assigned UI recipients to the treatment and control groups randomly—by using the last two digits of their Social Security numbers. While details differed, recipients in the treatment group who took jobs in under 11 to 13 weeks—and who held them for at least four months—received cash bonuses averaging around $500 in most cases but ranging as high as $1,600 in one state. The bonuses were not offered to members of the control group.

The analyses of these experiments estimated that those in the treatment group took jobs about one-half week faster, on average, than those in the control group. Put differently, the bonuses appeared to reduce the duration of unemployment by an average of about 3 percent, and most of the estimated effects in the four states were statistically significant. The experiments also found that in the states that offered bonuses of differing sizes, larger bonuses did *not* produce estimated declines in duration that were statistically significant.

Can the modest estimated effects of these experiments be generalized to an environment in which all workers on UI would be given a reemployment bonus if they found a job quickly? The experiments were adopted on a temporary basis, and the UI recipients in the experiment neither expected them nor could be sure of being in the treatment group; therefore, whether they applied for UI was unaffected by the presence of a bonus. However, if the bonuses were to become a permanent part of the UI system and available to all UI recipients, the benefits paid to those with short spells of unemployment would be enhanced, and this might cause more people to engage in behaviors that make them eligible for UI benefits.

We cannot be very certain, then, that reemployment bonuses would reduce the unemployment rate, because even if they reduced the duration of unemployment, they might also increase the number who qualify for the UI program. This problem illustrates an unfortunate drawback of social experiments: of necessity, they are temporary, and the behavioral responses they generate are often not completely transferable to those we might observe if a program were permanently adopted.

Source: Bruce D. Meyer, "Lessons from the U.S. Unemployment Insurance Experiments," *Journal of Economic Literature* 33 (March 1995): 91–131.

in economics and a leader in the development of the natural-rate concept, disavowed any attempts at forecasting it. He said, "I don't know what the natural rate is . . . and neither does anyone else."[44]

Certainly, some level of unemployment is unavoidably associated with the frictions in a dynamic labor market fraught with imperfect information. Moreover, as we have seen, the parameters of the UI system encourage unemployment associated with job search and with both cyclical and seasonal layoff. Nonetheless, when unemployment rises above its full-employment or natural level, resources are being wasted. Some 40 years ago, economist Arthur Okun pointed out that every one-percentage-point decline in the aggregate unemployment rate was associated with a three-percentage-point increase in the output the United States produces. More recent estimates suggest that the relationship is now more in the range of a two-percentage-point increase in output.[45] Even this last number, however, suggests the great costs a society pays for excessively high rates of unemployment.

---

[44]Amanda Bennett, "Business and Academia Clash over a Concept: 'Natural' Jobless Rate," *Wall Street Journal*, January 24, 1995, A8.

[45]Arthur Okun, "Potential GNP: Its Measurement and Significance," reprinted in *The Political Economy of Prosperity*, ed. Arthur Okun (Washington, D.C.: Brookings Institution, 1970); and Clifford L. F. Attfield and Brian Silverstone, "Okun's Coefficient: A Comment," *Review of Economics and Statistics* 79 (May 1997): 326–329.

Review Questions

1. A presidential hopeful is campaigning to raise unemployment compensation benefits and lower the unemployment rate. Comment on the compatibility of these goals.

2. Marie lost her job in January, 2013. She was looking for a job during the first 4 weeks of her unemployment, but has stopped now and feels that it is better to look after her own child rather than hire a babysitter. Is Marie to be counted as unemployed? Comment on her status and job search.

3. Recent empirical evidence suggests that unemployed workers' reservation wages decline as their spells of unemployment lengthen. That is, the longer they have been unemployed, the lower their reservation wages become. Explain why this might be true.

4. Is the following assertion true, false, or uncertain? "Increasing the level of UI benefits will prolong the average length of spells of unemployment. Hence, a policy of raising UI benefit levels is not socially desirable." Explain your answer.

5. In recent years, the federal government has introduced and then expanded a requirement that UI beneficiaries pay income tax on their unemployment benefits. Explain what effect you would expect this taxation of UI benefits to have on the unemployment rate.

6. "With the growth of free trade, Mexican employers have sought to reduce union control over internal labor markets, and they have eliminated promotion by seniority, rules against subcontracting, and restrictions on the use of temporary workers—all in the name of greater flexibility." Would you expect greater employer flexibility in hiring and assigning workers to increase or decrease unemployment in Mexico? Explain.

7. The "employment-at-will" doctrine is one that allows employers to discharge workers for any reason whatsoever. This doctrine has generally prevailed in the United States except where modified by union agreements or by laws preventing discrimination. Recent policies have begun to erode the employment-at-will doctrine by moving closer to the notion that one's job becomes a property right that the worker cannot be deprived of unless there is a compelling reason. If employers lose the right to discharge workers without "cause," what effects will this have on the unemployment rate?

8. One student of the labor market effects of free trade argues that the government should offer "wage insurance" to workers who lose a job because of free trade. Under this proposal, the government would replace a substantial portion of lost earnings if, upon reemployment, eligible workers find that their new job pays less than the one they lost. This wage insurance would be available for up to two years after the initial date of job loss. Would this wage insurance program reduce unemployment? Explain.

Problems

1. Suppose that at the beginning of the month, the number employed, E, equals 120 million; the number not in the labor force, N, equals 70 million; and the number unemployed, U, equals 10 million. During the course of the month, the flows indicated in the following table occurred.

EU	1.8 million
EN	3.0 million
UE	2.2 million
UN	1.7 million
NE	4.5 million
NU	1.3 million

Assuming that the population has not grown, calculate the unemployment and labor force participation rates at the beginning and end of the month.

2. In a particular economy, at the initial equilibrium the labor supply is $L_S = 25{,}000 + 200W$ and labor demand is $L_D = 37{,}000 - 400W$, where L is the number of work hours and W is the prevailing wage rate in thousand dollars. If labor demand is forced to shift downward to $L_D = 31{,}000 - 400W$ due to structural forces in the economy but the wages are inflexible, calculate the number of unemployed in the economy, and work out the unemployment rate.

3. a. For weekly wages of $100, $200, and $1000, calculate the replacement rate provided the benefit function is $B = 0.4W + 100$.

   b. For the same unemployment function, if $B_{min} = \$100$ and $B_{max} = \$400$,

calculate the minimum wage and the maximum wage and draw the graph showing the relation between weekly unemployment benefits as a function of previous earnings.

4. The demographics of a country are as given in the following table:

Details	2010	2011
Population	100	110
Employed	67	75
Unemployed	3	3.5
Discouraged Workers	1	2

   a. Calculate the labor force participation rate for the given years and compare them.

   b. Calculate the unemployment rate (including the discouraged workers) for the year 2011.

5. Suppose that the UI system is structured so that the minimum tax rate is 1.5 percent, the maximum tax rate is 6.2 percent, and the tax rate in between is calculated according to the following formula: $t = .1 + 2.4l$, where $t =$ the employer's UI tax rate and $l =$ the employer's layoff experience. Layoff experience is the probability that employees in the firm will be on layoff, expressed as a percentage of the firm's workforce, and generally lies in the range of less than 1 percent to 5 percent. Graph this tax rate formula, and calculate the firm's critical value of layoff

experience (l_{min}) and ceiling value of layoff experience (l_{max}).

6. On July 24, 2007, the federal minimum wage was increased from $5.15 per hour to $5.85 per hour. Consider the effect of this increase on an unemployed job seeker. Using a job-search model, what is the effect on the probability of finding an acceptable job in any given period? How does this increase affect the expected duration of unemployment and the expected wage (once employed)?

Selected Readings

Atkinson, Anthony, and John Micklewright. "Unemployment Compensation and Labor Market Transitions: A Critical Review." *Journal of Economic Literature* 29 (December 1991): 1679–1727.

Blanchflower, David G., and Andrew J. Oswald. *The Wage Curve.* Cambridge, Mass.: MIT Press, 1994.

Blank, Rebecca M., ed. *Social Protection versus Economic Flexibility: Is There a Trade-off?* Chicago: University of Chicago Press, 1994.

Freeman, Richard, and Harry Holzer, eds. *The Black Youth Unemployment Crisis.* Chicago: University of Chicago Press, 1986.

Lang, Kevin, and Jonathan Leonard, eds. *Unemployment and the Structure of Labor Markets.* New York: Basil Blackwell, 1987.

Meyer, Bruce D. "Lessons from the U.S. Unemployment Insurance Experiments." *Journal of Economic Literature* 33 (March 1995): 91–131.

Reducing Unemployment: Current Issues and Policy Options. Kansas City, Mo.: Federal Reserve Bank of Kansas City, 1994.

CHAPTER 15

Inequality in Earnings

Workers as individuals, and society as a whole, are concerned with both the *level* and the *dispersion* of income in the economy. The level of income obviously determines the consumption of goods and services that individuals find it possible to enjoy. Concerns about the distribution of income stem from the importance that we, as individuals, place on our relative standing in society and the importance that our society, as a collective, places on equity.

For purposes of assessing issues of poverty and relative consumption opportunities, the distribution of *family incomes* is of interest. An examination of family incomes, however, involves an analysis of unearned as well as earned income; thus, it must incorporate discussions of inheritance, investment returns, welfare transfers, and tax policies. It must also deal with family size and how families are defined, formed, and dissolved. Many of these topics are beyond the scope of a labor economics text.

Consistent with our examination of the labor market, the focus of this chapter is on the distribution of *earnings*. While clearly only part of overall income, earnings are a reflection of marginal productivity; the investment in (and returns to) education, training, and migration activities; and the access to opportunities. This chapter begins with a discussion of how to conceptualize and measure the equality or inequality of earnings. We then describe how the earnings distribution in the United States has changed since 1980 using published data readily accessible to the student. Finally, we analyze the basic forces that economists believe underlie these changes in earnings inequality.

Measuring Inequality

To understand certain basic concepts related to the distribution of earnings,[1] it is helpful to think in graphic terms. Consider a simple plotting of the number of people receiving each given level of earnings. If everyone had the same earnings, say $20,000 per year, there would be no dispersion. The graph of the earnings distribution would look like Figure 15.1.

If there were disparities in the earnings people received, these disparities could be relatively large or relatively small. If the average level of earnings were $20,000 and virtually all people received earnings very close to the average, the *dispersion* of earnings would be small. If the average were $20,000, but some made much more and some much less, the dispersion of earnings would be large. Figure 15.2 illustrates two hypothetical earnings distributions. While both distributions are centered on the same average level ($20,000), distribution A exhibits

---

Figure 15.1

Earnings Distribution with Perfect Equality

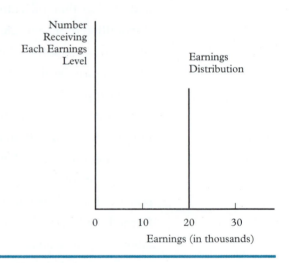

---

[1]Ideally, the focus would be on total compensation so that the analyses would include employee benefits. As a practical matter, however, data on the *value* of employee benefits are not widely available in a form that permits an examination of their *distribution* either over time or across individuals. For a study that analyzes the dispersion in total compensation, see Brooks Pierce, "Compensation Inequality," *Quarterly Journal of Economics* 116 (November 2001): 1493–1525. It is also important to keep in mind that earnings reflect both wages and hours worked; for a study suggesting that recent increases in leisure hours may have contributed to the rise in earnings inequality, see Mark Aguiar and Erik Hurst, "Measuring Trends in Leisure: The Allocation of Time Over Five Decades," *Quarterly Journal of Economics* 122 (August 2007): 969–1006.

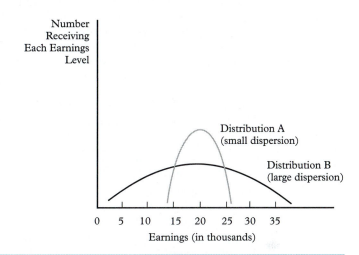

Figure 15.2

Distributions of Earnings
with Different Degrees of Dispersion

smaller dispersion than distribution B. Earnings in B are more widely dispersed and thus exhibit *a greater degree of inequality.*[2]

Graphs can help illustrate the concepts of dispersion, but they are a clumsy tool for *measuring* inequality. Various quantitative indicators of earnings inequality can be devised, and they all vary in ease of computation, ease of comprehension, and how accurately they represent the socially relevant dimensions of inequality.

The most obvious measure of inequality is the *variance* of the distribution. Variance is a common measure of dispersion calculated as follows:

$$\text{Variance} = \frac{\sum_i (E_i - \overline{E})^2}{n} \tag{15.1}$$

where E_i represents the earnings of person i in the population, n represents the number of people in the population, $\overline{E}$ is the mean level of earnings in the population, and Σ indicates that we are summing over all persons in the population. One problem with using the variance, however, is that it tends to rise as earnings grow larger. For example, if all earnings in the population were to double, so that the

---

[2]A summary of various inequality measures can be found in Frank Levy and Richard J. Murnane, "U.S. Earnings Levels and Earnings Inequality: A Review of Recent Trends and Proposed Explanations," *Journal of Economic Literature* 30 (September 1991): 1333–1381. It is also interesting to inquire whether the distribution of earnings is *symmetric* or not. If a distribution is symmetric, as in Figure 15.2, then as many people earn $X less than average as earn $X more than average. If not, we say it is *skewed*, meaning that one part of the distribution is bunched together and the other part is relatively dispersed. For example, many less-developed countries do not have a sizable middle class. Such countries have a huge number of very poor families and a tiny minority of very wealthy families (the distribution of income is highly skewed to the right).

ratio of each person's earnings to the mean (or to the earnings of anyone else for that matter) remained constant, the variance would quadruple. Variance is thus a better measure of the absolute than of the *relative* dispersion of earnings.

An alternative to the variance is the *coefficient of variation:* the square root of the variance (called the *standard deviation*) divided by the mean. If all earnings were to double, the coefficient of variation, unlike the variance, would remain unchanged. Because we must have access to the underlying data on each individual's earnings to calculate the coefficient of variation, however, it is impractical to construct it from published data. Unless the coefficient of variation is itself *published*, or unless the researcher has access to the *entire* data set, other more readily constructed measures must be found.

The most widely used measures of earnings inequality start with ranking the population by earnings level and by establishing into which percentile a given level of earnings falls. For example, in 2011, men between the ages of 25 and 64 with earnings of $42,492 were at the *median* (50th percentile), meaning that half of all men earned less and half earned more. Men with earnings of $21,361 were at the 20th percentile of the earnings distribution (20 percent earned less; 80 percent earned more), while those with earnings of $80,561 were at the 80th percentile.

Having determined the earnings levels associated with each percentile, we can either compare the earnings *levels* associated with given percentiles or compare the *share* of total earnings received by each. Comparing shares of total *income* received by the top and bottom fifth (or "quintiles") of households in the population is a widely used measure of *income* inequality. Using this measure, we find, for example, that in 2010, households in the top fifth of the income distribution received 50.2 percent of all income, while those in the bottom fifth received 3.3 percent.[3]

Unfortunately, information on *shares* received by each segment of the distribution is not as readily available for individual *earnings* as it is for family income. Comparing the earnings *level* associated with each percentile is readily feasible, however. A commonly used measure of this sort is the ratio of earnings at, say, the 80th percentile to earnings at the 20th. Ratios such as this are intended to indicate how far apart the two ends of the earnings distribution are, and as a measure of dispersion, they are easily understood and readily computed.

How useful is it to know that in 2011, for example, men at the 80th percentile of the earnings distribution earned 3.77 times more than men at the 20th? In truth, the ratio in a given year is not very enlightening unless it is *compared* with something. One natural comparison is with ratios for prior years. An increase in these ratios over time, for example, would indicate that the earnings distribution was becoming stretched, so that the distance between the two ends was growing and earnings were becoming more unequally distributed.

---

[3]U.S. Bureau of the Census, "Selected Measures of Household Income Dispersion: 1967 to 2010" Table A-3 (2013), at http://www.census.gov/hhes/www/income/data/historical/inequality/IE-1.pdf.). A more sophisticated measure would take into account the shares of income received by each of the five quintiles, and a way to quantify the deviation from strict equality (when the income share of each quintile is 20 percent) is discussed in Appendix 15A. For a review of studies of income at the very top of income distributions across countries and across time, see Anthony B. Atkinson, Thomas Piketty, and Emmanuel Saez, "Top Incomes in the Long Run of History," *Journal of Economic Literature* 49 (March 2011): 3–71.

As a rough measure of increasing distance between the two ends of the earnings distribution, the ratio of earnings at the 80th and 20th percentiles is satisfactory; however, this simple ratio is by no means a complete description of inequality. Its focus on earnings at two arbitrarily chosen points in the distribution ignores what happens on either side of the chosen percentiles. For example, if earnings at the 10th percentile fell and those at the 20th percentile rose, while all other earnings remained constant, the above ratio would decline even though the very lowest end of the distribution had moved down. Likewise, if earnings at the 20th and 80th percentiles were to remain the same, but earnings in between were to become much more similar, this step toward greater overall earnings equality would not be captured by the simple 80:20 ratio. In the next section, we will examine trends in ratios at other points in the earnings distribution (the 90:10 ratio, for example) to more closely examine distributional changes in the last three decades.

These drawbacks notwithstanding, we present in the next section descriptive data on changes in earnings inequality based on comparisons of earnings levels at the 80th and 20th percentiles of the distribution. While crude, these measures indicate that earnings became more unequal after 1980.

Earnings Inequality Since 1980: Some Descriptive Data

Table 15.1 displays changes in earnings inequality from 1980 to 2011 for men and women between the ages of 25 and 64 using the 80:20 ratio discussed earlier. Among men, earnings at the 80th percentile were constant (in 2011 dollars) from 1980 to 1990, but earnings at the 20th percentile fell during that period. The result was a big jump in the 80:20 ratio, from 3.08 to 3.52. From 1990 to 2005, earnings at both percentiles rose modestly, and the 80:20 ratio was more or less stable. Unemployment associated with the Great Recession that started in 2008 reduced earnings at both percentiles, but the reductions were greater at the lower end and the 80:20 ratio rose from 3.41 in 2005 to 3.77 in 2011.[4] While earnings at the 20th percentile for women are so low that they are likely to be

---

[4]Recall from the discussion of Table 2.2 that the Consumer Price Index, which we use in Table 15.1 to adjust all earnings figures to 2011 dollars, may overstate inflation by about one percentage point per year. If that is the case, then the real earnings of men at the 80th percentile grew by 21 percent (not the 5 percent shown in Table 15.1) from 1980 to 2005, for example, while those at the 20th percentile grew by 9 percent (instead of falling by 5 percent). For a paper concluding that use of the Consumer Price Index may overstate the extent of poverty, see Bruce D. Meyer and James X. Sullivan, "Winning the War: Poverty from the Great Society to the Great Recession," working paper no. 18718, National Bureau of Economic Research (Cambridge, Mass.: January 2013). The major point made in Table 15.1, however, is that the 80:20 ratio has grown for men over this period, and it is important to realize that the *ratios* in any given year are not affected by assumptions about overall inflation (because the same inflationary adjustments are made to both the numerator and the denominator of the ratio). One study, however, found that college graduates have experienced larger increases in the cost of living, so that growth in their *real* earnings has not been as large as the growth in their nominal earnings; see Enrico Moretti, "Real Wage Inequality," *American Economic Journal: Applied Economics* 5 (January 2013): 65–103.

Table 15.1

The Dispersion of Earnings by Gender, Ages 25–64, 1980–2011 (Expressed in 2011 Dollars)

	Earnings at		
	80th Percentile (a)	20th Percentile (b)	Ratio: (a) ÷ (b)
Men			
1980	77,759	25,284	3.08
1990	77,798	22,123	3.52
2005	81,737	23,939	3.41
2011	80,561	21,361	3.77
Women			
1980	41,500	11,208	3.70
1990	47,032	10,236	4.60
2005	55,310	14,028	3.94
2011	55,610	14,110	3.94

Sources: U.S. Bureau of the Census, *Money Incomes of Households, Families, and Persons in the United States*, Series P-60: no. 132 (1980), Table 54; no. 174 (1990), Table 29; and U.S. Bureau of the Census, http://pubdb3.census.gov/macro/032006/perinc/new03_000.htm (2005); http://www.census.gov/hhes/www/cpstables/032012/perinc/pinc03_000.htm (2011).

received by those working part-time (in 2005, for example, roughly 32 percent of women worked part-time), the overall changes in inequality are similar to those for men. Inequality rose during the 1980s, driven by earnings increases at the 80th percentile and earnings decreases at the 20th percentile. After 1990, inequality decreased as earnings at the 20th percentile rose relatively rapidly; both the pre-recession increase in pay at this percentile and the overall decrease in inequality were larger for women than for men (the recession also appears not to have increased earnings inequality among women).

As discussed earlier, the 80:20 ratio does not tell the complete story about the growth in inequality. Specifically, the two points in the earnings distribution are arbitrarily chosen, and the ratio of earnings at these points does not capture what is happening both between these two percentiles and beyond them (that is, in the middle of the distribution and at either end). Table 15.2 provides a more detailed look at changes in earnings inequality from 1980 to 2011 by focusing on two aspects of change in inequality.

First, we want to know whether the changes in the upper end of the earnings distribution and the changes in the lower end are roughly similar; in other words, are *both* halves of the earnings distribution becoming more stretched? One way to obtain some insight into this question is to calculate the 80:50 and 50:20 ratios; both ratios indicate how earnings at the upper end (80th percentile) and lower end (20th percentile) are changing over time compared to the median (50th percentile). Inspecting the first three rows for both men and women in Table 15.2, it is clear

Table 15.2

Earnings Ratios at Various Percentiles of the Earnings Distribution, 1980, 1990, 2005, 2011

Ratio of Earnings at Given Percentiles	1980	1990	2005	2011
Men				
80:20 (see Table 15.1)	3.08	3.52	3.41	3.77
80:50	1.53	1.74	1.77	1.90
50:20	2.01	2.03	1.93	1.99
Women				
80:20 (see Table 15.1)	3.70	4.60	3.94	3.94
80:50	1.66	1.79	1.78	1.79
50:20	2.24	2.57	2.22	2.20
Men				
90:10	4.68	7.31	7.97	8.94*
90:50	1.87	2.14	2.49	2.59*
50:10	2.50	3.41	3.20	3.45
Women				
90:10	9.12	13.88	9.74	9.89
90:50	2.07	2.27	2.34	2.43
50:10	4.41	6.12	4.16	4.07

*Because published earnings at the 90th percentile fell into an "open" range ("$100,000 and above"), earnings at this percentile had to be estimated.

Sources: U.S. Bureau of the Census, *Money Incomes of Households, Families, and Persons in the United States,* Series P-60: no. 132 (1980), Table 54; no. 174 (1990), Table 29; and U.S. Bureau of the Census, http://pubdb3.census.gov/macro/032006/perinc/new03_000.htm (2005); http://www.census.gov/hhes/www/cpstables/032012/perinc/pinc03_000.htm (2011)

that inequality in both halves grew during the 1980s, but that between 1990 and 2005, inequality in the upper half remained more or less constant while it *became smaller* in the lower half. As the recession took hold after 2008, earnings inequality among men once again grew in both halves of the earnings distribution (among women, however, inequality was more or less stable in both halves between 2005 and 2011).

Second, we might ask what was happening to earnings in each *tail* of the earnings distribution over this period. The 90:10 ratio represents a measure of inequality that focuses on the top and bottom 10 percent of the earnings distribution, and it can therefore shed light on changes beyond the 80:20 boundaries. Table 15.2 also contains (in the shaded rows) the 90:10 earnings ratio and its two components (90:50 and 50:10).

For the period from 1980 to 1990, the 90:10 ratios (and their upper and lower components) tell the same story for men and women as did the 80:20 ratios; that is, earnings inequality clearly grew among both men and women during the

1980s, and it grew in both halves of the earnings distribution. However, while increases in the 90:50 and 80:50 ratios are roughly comparable, the 50:10 ratios increase much more markedly than the 50:20 ratios over the 1980s—indicating that the drop in relative earnings at the very bottom of the earnings distribution was especially pronounced.

After 1990, the 90:10 ratio fell for women but—unlike the 80:20 ratio—continued to rise for men. In the lower half of the distribution, the 50:10 ratios (like the 50:20 ratios) for both men and women were lower in 2005 than in 1990, indicating that earnings in the lower half of the earnings distribution became more equal during that period. By 2011, however, the Great Recession had brought the 50:10 ratio for men back to its level in 1990.

In the upper half of the earnings distribution, the 90:50 ratios for both men and women rose more after 1990 than did the 80:50 ratios. Clearly, then, both men and women at the very highest levels of earnings continued to experience increases (relative to the median) after 1990—increases that were not shared by those only slightly below them in the distribution.

To summarize, the tables reviewed earlier suggest the following major changes in earnings inequality since 1980:

a. There was an unambiguous increase in inequality during the 1980s, with earnings in both the upper and lower halves of the earnings distribution becoming more dispersed.

b. During the 1980s, there was an especially pronounced fall in relative earnings at the very bottom of the distribution (lowest 10th percentile), indicating downward pressures on the earnings of the lowest-skilled workers.

c. From 1990–2005, earnings became less dispersed in the lower half of the earnings distribution, as earnings at the bottom increased relative to the median; however, joblessness associated with the Great Recession reduced pay at the lower end of the earnings distribution, causing increases in the 50:20 and 50:10 ratios among men.

d. Since 1990, earnings at the 90th percentile for both women and men have pulled farther away from the median than have earnings at the 80th percentile—which is indicative of continued increases in relative earnings at the very top of the earnings distribution.

(See Example 15.1 for an overall comparison of the level of earnings inequality across selected developed countries.)

Generally speaking, changes in the distribution of earnings since 1980 have occurred along two dimensions. One is the increased returns to investments in higher education, which have raised the relative earnings of those at the top of the distribution (those with higher levels of human capital). The other dimension is the growth in earnings disparities *within* human-capital groups, which stretches out the earnings at both the higher and lower ends of the distribution. In the next two sections, we will discuss changes in these two dimensions.

EXAMPLE 15.1

Differences in Earnings Inequality across Developed Countries

The United States stands out from other developed countries in its much higher *level* of earnings inequality. Below are the 90:10 ratios for several developed countries in 2005 (the earnings distributions these ratios characterize are different than those presented in this text, because they are for full-time workers and combine both men and women):

Country	90:10 Ratios in 2005
Australia	3.12
Canada	3.74
France	3.10
Japan	3.13
Netherlands	3.12
Norway	2.91
Sweden	2.33
United States	4.88

One reason for greater inequality in the United States may lie in the greater *dispersion of skills* among American workers. Countries that have workers among whom skills are vastly different will naturally have earnings disparities that reflect those differences. One study proposed that a way to measure skill level is to examine scores in "quantitative literacy" on the International Adult Literacy Survey. This study found that scores on this test varied most among workers in the United States, and least (among the countries listed earlier) in the Scandinavian countries, Germany, and the Netherlands—with Canada and Australia in the middle. The study found that the statistical correlation between the dispersion in test scores and the dispersion in earnings was very strong. This finding illustrates one significant outcome of the relatively poor performance of American high school students on achievement tests, which was noted in chapter 9.

Sources: Organisation for Economic Co-operation and Development, *OECD Employment Outlook* 2007 (Paris: June 19, 2007), Table H; and Stephen Nickell, "Is the U.S. Labor Market Really that Exceptional: A Review of Richard Freeman's *America Works: The Exceptional U.S. Labor Market*," *Journal of Economic Literature* 46 (June 2008): 384–395.

The Increased Returns to Higher Education

To illustrate the rising returns to higher education, let us focus first on male workers between the ages of 35 and 44 who are working full-time. As can be seen in the upper panel of Table 15.3, the real earnings of men in this age group with a college or graduate school education are higher than they were in 1980—particularly among those with graduate degrees—while those with a high school education or less have experienced decreases in real earnings. The earnings advantages of acquiring a bachelor's degree or a graduate degree (as seen by the earnings ratios) are higher in recent years than in 1980, but the earnings advantages of obtaining a high school degree (as opposed to dropping out) did not change much over this period.

The rising returns to investing in a bachelor's degree or a graduate degree are also observed for women, although the underlying changes within each level of education are different. The earnings of women with high school degrees actually rose in the 1980s, both absolutely and relative to those of dropouts, but

Table 15.3

Mean Earnings and the Returns to Education among Full-Time, Year-Round Workers between the Ages of 35 and 44 (Expressed in 2011 Dollars)

	Earnings				Earnings Ratios		
	Dropout ($)	H.S. Grad ($)	Bachelor's ($)	Grad School[a] ($)	H.S./ Drop	Bachelor's/ H.S.	Grad/ Bachelor's
Men							
1980	40,083	55,926	78,807	90,026	1.40	1.41	1.14
1990	35,269	49,801	81,567	100,738	1.41	1.64	1.24
2005	33,698	48,520	92,609	127,044	1.44	1.91	1.37
2011	32,467	47,607	85,947	115,075	1.47	1.81	1.34
Women							
1980	24,800	32,056	43,671	51,029	1.29	1.36	1.17
1990	24,699	34,220	54,430	64,700	1.39	1.59	1.19
2005	23,314	33,743	62,558	81,805	1.45	1.85	1.31
2011	22,469	32,701	63,362	81,035	1.46	1.94	1.28

[a]The data for 2005 and 2011 are a weighted average of earnings for those with various levels of graduate degrees; data for 1980 and 1990 are for those who completed more than four years of college.

Sources: U.S. Bureau of the Census, *Money Income of Households, Families, and Persons in the United States,* Series P-60: no. 132 (1980), Table 52; no. 174 (1990), Table 30; and U.S. Bureau of the Census Web site: http://pubdb3.census.gov/macro/032006/perinc/new03_190.htm and http://pubdb3.census.gov/macro/032006/perinc/new03_316.htm (2005); http://www.census.gov/hhes/www/cpstables/032012/perinc/pinc03_000.htm (2011).

because the earnings for those with bachelor's and graduate degrees rose even more, the increased returns to higher education parallel those for men. Increases for women in the earnings advantages of obtaining a bachelor's or graduate degree are similar to those for men, except for the period 2005–2011, when the advantages associated with a bachelor's degree continued to grow for women.

(It is important to recall from chapter 9 that rising returns to higher education should call forth an increase in university students and an eventual shift in the supply curve of the college-educated to the right. Rightward supply-curve shifts will tend to moderate the wages commanded by the college-educated, so the fact that the earnings advantages they experienced after 1980 increased suggests that the rightward shifts in supply were smaller than the rightward shifts in demand. As seen in Example 15.2, important changes in office technology, which increased the demand for better-educated workers, were introduced in the early 1900s, but during that period, the supply response was such that the returns to education actually fell!)

Growth of Earnings Dispersion within Human-Capital Groups

While one factor in the growing diversity of earnings is the enlarged gap between the average pay of more-educated and less-educated workers, another possible dimension of growing inequality is that earnings *within* narrowly defined

EXAMPLE 15.2

Changes in the Premium to Education at the Beginning of the Twentieth Century

While the premium to education has recently risen and is currently relatively high, the premium appears to have been even higher at the beginning of the twentieth century. However, the premium did not stay high for too long because, despite increasing demand for educated workers, the *supply* increased at an even more rapid clip. In 1914, office workers, whose positions generally required a high school diploma, earned considerably more than less-educated manual workers. Female office workers earned 107 percent more than female production workers, while male office workers earned 70 percent more than male production workers. This premium fell rapidly during World War I and the early 1920s, so that by 1923, the high school premium was only 41 percent for females and merely 10 percent for males. These rates drifted just a little higher during the remainder of the 1920s and 1930s.

What makes these dramatically falling premiums for a high school degree so surprising is that changes in the economy were increasing the relative demand for these workers. New office machines (such as improved typewriters, adding machines, address machines, dictaphones, and mimeo machines) lowered the cost of information technology and increased the demand for a complementary factor of production: high school-educated office workers. In the two decades after 1910, office employment's share of total employment in the United States rose by 47 percent.

Counteracting this demand shift, however, was an even more substantial shift in the supply of high school graduates, as high schools opened up to the masses throughout much of the country. Between 1910 and 1920, for example, high school enrollment rates climbed from 25 percent to 43 percent in New England and from 29 percent to 60 percent in the Pacific region. The internal combustion engine, paved roads, and consolidated school districts brought secondary education to rural areas for the first time during the 1920s. Within cities, schools moved away from offering only college preparatory courses and attracted more students. From 1910 to 1930, the share of the labor force made up of high school graduates increased by almost 130 percent.

Thus, relative growth in the demand for more-educated workers was similar in the early and late decades of the twentieth century, but changes in the premiums for education diverged. As emphasized throughout this text, supply *and* demand are important in understanding wages!

Data from: Claudia Goldin and Lawrence F. Katz, "The Decline of Non-Competing Groups: Changes in the Premium to Education, 1890–1940," National Bureau of Economic Research, working paper no. 5202, August 1995.

human-capital groups has become more diverse. To understand how within-group inequality affects *overall* measures of inequality, suppose that those at the top of the earnings distribution are older workers with college educations, while those at the bottom are younger workers who dropped out of high school. If earnings *within* each group become more diverse, some in the top earning group will become even better-paid, while some in the least-skilled group would have even lower wages; the end result would be an increase in the *overall* 80:20 or 90:10 ratio.

To get a sense of trends in earnings differences within human-capital groups, Table 15.4 divides men into six such groups, defined by age and education. The table displays the earnings ratios of those at the 80th percentile to those at

Table 15.4

Ratio of Earnings at the 80th to 20th Percentiles for Males, by Age and Education, 1980–2005

	1980	1990	2005
Male Bachelor's Graduates			
Ages 25–34	2.27	2.49	2.88
35–44	2.47	2.52	2.78
45–54	2.62	2.93	3.00
Male High School Graduates			
Ages 25–34	2.47	2.78	2.80
35–44	2.48	2.85	2.65
45–54	2.45	2.75	2.73

Source: U.S. Bureau of the Census, *Money Incomes of Households, Families, and Persons in the United States*, Series P-60: no. 132 (1980), Table 51; no. 174 (1990), Table 29; and U.S. Bureau of the Census, http://pubdb3.census.gov/macro/032006/perinc/new03_163.htm, http://pubdb3.census.gov/macro/032006/perinc/new03_181.htm, http://pubdb3.census.gov/macro/032006/perinc/new03_199.htm (2005).

the 20th percentile inside of each human-capital group from 1980 to 2005.[5] Among college graduates, earnings disparities grew throughout the three decades in each age group. Earnings disparities also grew among high school graduates in the 1980s, but afterward, they tended to stabilize or even shrink. Thus, it is likely that the growth in earnings disparities *within* human-capital groups played at least some role in generating overall earnings inequality during the 1980s and afterward.[6]

The Underlying Causes of Growing Inequality

The major phenomenon we must explain is the widening gap between the wages of highly educated and less-educated workers, and our basic economic model suggests three possible causes. First, the *supply* of less-educated workers might have risen faster than the supply of college graduates, driving down the relative wages

[5]The focus is on men, because women at the 20th percentile are typically part-time workers. The year 2005 is used as the end point of our comparison, rather than a more recent year, because recessionary conditions (after 2008) have a short-term effect on earnings inequality – because of unemployment – that is distinct from the long-term trends we are attempting to analyze here.

[6]For analyses of within-group dispersion of earnings, see Thomas Lemieux, "Postsecondary Education and Increasing Wage Inequality," *American Economic Review* 96 (May 2006): 195–199; Thomas Lemieux, "Increasing Residual Wage Inequality: Composition Effects, Noisy Data, or Rising Demand for Skill?" *American Economic Review* 96 (June 2006): 461–498; and Anders Akerman, Elhanan Helpman, Oleg Itskhoki, Marc-Andreas Muendler, and Stephen J. Redding, "Sources of Wage Inequality," *American Economic Review: Papers and Proceedings* (May 2013): 214–219. For a study finding that much of the increased dispersion at the top of the earnings distribution is related to the increased use of pay-for-performance pay systems, see Thomas Lemieux, W. Bentley MacLeod, and Daniel Parent, "Performance Pay and Wage Inequality," *Quarterly Journal of Economics* 124 (February 2009): 1–49.

of less-skilled workers. Second, the demand for more-educated workers might have increased relative to the demand for less-educated workers. Finally, changes in *institutional* forces, such as the minimum wage or the decline in unions, might have reduced the relative wages of less-educated workers. We discuss these possibilities here.

Changes in Supply

In reality, shifts in supply and demand curves, and even changes in the influence of institutions, occur both simultaneously and continually. Sophisticated statistical studies can often sort through the possible influences underlying a change and estimate the separate contributions of each. For the most part, however, the details of these studies are beyond the scope of this text; instead, our focus will be on identifying the *dominant* forces behind the growth of wage inequality in recent years.

For the market-clearing wage rate of a particular group of workers to be reduced primarily by a shift in supply, that shift must be rightward and therefore accompanied by an increase in employment (see panel "a" of Figure 15.3 for a graphic illustration). Conversely, if a leftward shift in the supply curve is the dominant cause of a wage increase, this wage increase will be accompanied by a decrease in the market-clearing level of employment (see panel "b" of Figure 15.3). Other things equal, the larger these shifts are, the larger will be the effects on the equilibrium wage.

The major phenomenon we are trying to explain is the increasing gap between the wages of highly educated and less-educated workers. If *supply* shifts are primarily responsible, we should observe that the employment of less-educated

---

Figure 15.3

Changes in Supply as the Dominant Cause of Wage Changes

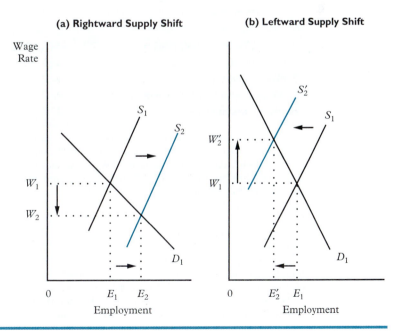

workers *increased* relative to the employment of the college-educated workforce. Table 15.5 contains data indicating that supply shifts could *not* have been the primary cause. Comparing the employment shares of those whose relative earnings rose after 1980 (rows A to D) to the employment shares of those whose earnings fell (rows E to H), it is clear that earnings and employment increases were *positively* correlated. The groups that experienced increases in their relative earnings also experienced more rapid employment growth, and the groups whose earnings fell also experienced falling shares of employment. Thus, shifts in supply cannot be the dominant explanation for the growing returns to education.[7]

To say that shifts in supply were not the *dominant* influence underlying the increased returns to education is not to say, of course, that they had no effect at all. We saw in chapter 10 that immigration to the United States rose during the period and that it was especially heavy among unskilled, less-educated workers—the very groups whose relative earnings fell most during that period. While the very presence of low-skilled immigrants can increase overall earnings inequality, estimates differ on whether immigration has had much effect on earnings inequality

Table 15.5

Employment Shares (within Gender) of Educational Groups, Workers 25 and Older: 1980, 1990, 2005, 2011

Groups Whose Relative Earnings Rose	1980	1990	2005	2011
A. Men with graduate degree (%)	9.1	10.5	11.6	12.8
B. Men with bachelor's degree (%)	11.4	14.0	20.5	22.4
C. Women with graduate degree (%)	5.7	8.2	11.1	13.7
D. Women with bachelor's degree (%)	10.3	13.9	21.8	24.1
Groups Whose Relative Earnings Fell				
E. Men with high school degree (%)	38.2	38.1	30.8	29.2
F. Male dropouts (%)	22.7	16.3	11.6	9.8
G. Women with high school degree (%)	46.4	42.1	28.6	25.4
H. Female dropouts (%)	17.8	12.2	7.8	6.8

Sources: U.S. Bureau of the Census, *Money Income of Households, Families, and Individuals in the United States,* Series P-60: no. 132 (1980), Table 52; no. 174 (1990), Table 30; and U.S. Bureau of the Census, http://pubdb3.census.gov/macro/032006/perinc/new03_127.htm, http://pubdb3.census.gov/macro/032006/perinc/new03_253.htm (2005), and http://www.census.gov/hhes/www/cpstables/032012/perinc/pinc03_000.htm (2011).

---

[7]The generally small role played by *supply* shifts in generating wage inequality is also found in more sophisticated studies: Lawrence F. Katz and Kevin M. Murphy, "Changes in Relative Wages, 1963–1987: Supply and Demand Factors," *Quarterly Journal of Economics* 107 (February 1992): 35–78; John Bound and George Johnson, "Changes in the Structure of Wages in the 1980s: An Evaluation of Alternative Explanations," *American Economic Review* 82 (June 1992): 371–392; and John Bound and George Johnson, "What Are the Causes of Rising Wage Inequality in the United States?" *Federal Reserve Bank of New York Economic Policy Review* 1 (January 1995): 9–17.

among *natives*.[8] Because of immigration, however, the percentage of less-skilled workers in the labor force fell less than it would otherwise have fallen, and therefore the supply-related upward pressures on unskilled wages were probably smaller.

Changes in Demand: Technological Change

The fact that human-capital groups whose earnings were experiencing faster growth also experienced relative gains in employment suggests that shifts in labor *demand* curves were a prominent factor raising inequality since 1980. Rightward shifts in the labor demand curve will, other things equal, result in both increased wages and increased employment, while leftward shifts will reduce both wages and employment. Thus, the data in Table 15.5 are consistent with a rightward shift in the demand for workers with a university education and a leftward shift in the demand for workers with a high school education or less.

Economists generally agree that one phenomenon underlying these shifts in labor demand is "skill-biased technological change"—technological change that increased the productivity of highly skilled workers and reduced the need for low-skilled workers. During the 1980s, firms in virtually every industry adopted production and office systems that relied on the computerization of many functions. "High-tech" investments—in robots, automated measuring devices, data-management systems, word-processing, and communications networks, for example—far outstripped conventional forms of mechanization, such as larger or faster machines. The percentage of workers using computers in their jobs rose from 25 percent in 1984, to 37 percent in 1989, to 47 percent in 1993.[9] There are good reasons to suspect that, generally speaking, the computerization of many processes increased the demand for highly skilled workers and reduced the demand for others.

As noted in chapter 4, technological change is equivalent to a decrease in the price of capital, and the effects on the demand for labor depend on the relative size of scale and substitution effects. If a category of labor is a complement in production with the capital whose price has been reduced, or if it is a substitute in production but a *gross* complement, then technological change will increase the demand for that category. If the category of labor is a gross substitute with

---

[8]See George J. Borjas, Richard B. Freeman, and Lawrence F. Katz, "On the Labor Market Effects of Immigration and Trade," in *Immigration and the Work Force*, eds. George J. Borjas and Richard B. Freeman (Chicago: University of Chicago Press, 1992): 213–244. For studies that did not find that immigration of the unskilled influenced inequality much, see James J. Heckman, Lance Lochner, and Christopher Taber, "Explaining Rising Wage Inequality: Explorations with a Dynamic General Equilibrium Model of Labor Earnings and Heterogeneous Agents," *Review of Economic Dynamics* 1 (January 1998): 1–58, and David Card, "Immigration and Inequality," *American Economic Review* 99 (May 2009): 1–21.

[9]See Daron Acemoglu, "Technical Change, Inequality, and the Labor Market," *Journal of Economic Literature* 40 (March 2002): 7–72; and David H. Autor, Lawrence F. Katz, and Alan B. Krueger, "Computing Inequality: Have Computers Changed the Labor Market?" *Quarterly Journal of Economics* 113 (November 1998): 1169–1213.

capital, however, then technological change will reduce its demand. We know from chapter 4 that, at least in recent decades, capital and skilled labor tend to be gross complements, while capital and less-skilled labor are more likely to be gross substitutes. If these generalizations apply to high-tech capital, then the falling price of such capital, and its consequent spread, would have shifted the demand curve for skilled workers to the right and the demand curve for less-skilled workers to the left.

It appears that the industries with the largest increases in high-tech capital were those with the highest proportions of college-educated workers, and that computer usage in 1993 was far higher among the college-educated (at 70 percent) than among high school graduates (35 percent). Furthermore, those who used computers apparently had increased productivity, as it is estimated that they received 20 percent higher wages than they otherwise would have received—a differential that grew between 1984 and 1993.[10]

Finally, the rapidity and scope of workplace technological change associated with the introduction of computerized processes required workers to acquire new skills (even ones current students think of as elementary, such as learning to type or how to use various computer programs). We saw in chapter 9 that the costs of learning a new skill are not the same for everyone; those who learn most quickly tend to have the lowest psychic costs of learning. The abrupt need to learn new skills, combined with differential learning costs across workers, generated two sources of greater inequality.

First, as suggested by economic theory, those with lower learning costs are likely to invest more in education, so it would not be surprising to find that workers with more schooling were the ones who adapted more quickly to the new, high-tech environment. Second, even *within* human-capital groups, the psychic costs of learning cause some workers to be more resistant to change than others. During a period of rapid change, as some adapt more quickly and completely than others, it is quite likely that earnings disparities within human-capital groups will grow.

The view that the falling price and greater use of high-tech capital increased the demand for skilled workers across the board seems *generally* consistent with the changing inequality in the 1980s. Earnings rose for the highly skilled and fell for the less-skilled, and they became more dispersed within both the high- and low-skilled human-capital groups (and more dispersed within both the upper and lower halves of the earnings distribution). However, if the introduction of high-tech capital raised the demand for skill at every level, how do we account for the fact that the earnings advantage of staying in high school stayed more or less constant, at least for men? Furthermore, if rapid technological change—which continued after 1990—increased the demand for skills across the board, how do we account for *reduced* inequality in the lower half of the earnings distribution (and within less-educated, human-capital groups) after 1990?

---

[10]Autor, Katz, and Krueger, "Computing Inequality: Have Computers Changed the Labor Market?"

Recent work by economists suggests that the high-tech revolution might have had effects on the demand for labor that were more complex than simply increasing the demand for skilled workers.[11] Instead, it may be that computerized technologies were readily substituted for labor in processes that were *routine* in nature: feeding machines, making accounting calculations, typing correspondence, inspecting manufactured products for defects, processing customer orders, and so forth. Computers, however, cannot replace the abstract and interpersonal skills used by the highly educated—nor can they replace the nonroutine manual skills used in many very low-skilled jobs (parking lot attendants, landscaping workers, hospital aides, and restaurant servers). Thus, it is possible that computerization had a polarizing effect on job growth, reducing the demand for many factory and clerical workers, whose earnings were in the middle of the distribution, and increasing the demand for both the highly educated and (through the scale effect) those in nonroutine manual jobs—many of whom are among the lowest paid.

Some support for the hypothesis that technological change has had a polarizing effect on employment can be seen in Table 15.6, which contains changes in the share of total employment in four occupational groups: managers, professionals, office and administrative support workers, and service workers (those in health-care support, protective services, food preparation, and custodial or personal-care jobs).[12] Consistent with the polarization hypothesis, from 1983 to 2012, the share of

Table 15.6

Changes in the Share of Employment for Four Major Occupational Groups, 1983–2012

Occupational Group (2012 Weekly Earnings)	Share in Total Employment		
	1983 (%)	1990 (%)	2012 (%)
Managers ($1,171)	10.7	12.6	15.9
Professionals ($1,053)	12.7	13.4	22.0
Office and Administrative Support ($643)	16.3	15.8	12.4
Service ($485)	13.7	13.4	17.9

Sources: U.S. Bureau of Labor Statistics, *Employment and Earnings:* 31 (January 1984), Table 20 (1983); 38 (January 1991), Table 22 (1990); *Employment and Earnings Online,* (January 2013), Tables 10, 39 (2012) at http://www.bls.gov/opub/ee/2013/cps/annavg10_2012.pdf, and http://www.bls.gov/opub/ee/2013/cps/annavg39_2012.pdf

[11]Maarten Goos and Alan Manning, "Lousy and Lovely Jobs: The Rising Polarization of Work in Britain," *Review of Economics and Statistics* 89 (February 2007): 118–133; and David H. Autor and David Dorn, "The Growth of Low Skill Service Jobs and the Polarization of the U.S. Labor Market," *American Economic Review* 103 (August 2013): 1553–1597.

[12]These four groups were selected because their definitions were essentially unchanged from 1983 to the present. Other groupings were changed over that period, making comparisons using published data infeasible.

workers who are managers or professionals rose, the share of workers in office and administrative support jobs declined, and the share of service workers increased. Thus, it is possible that increased demand for jobs at the lower end of the earnings distribution—especially after 1990 and before the Great Recession—played a role in reducing inequality in the lower half of the earnings distribution.[13]

Changes in Demand: Earnings Instability

As argued earlier, technological change appears to have played a critical role in changing the market wages for workers of various skill levels since 1980. However, the technological developments just described, coupled with growing competition within product markets through deregulation and the globalization of production (see chapter 16), also may have led to a growth in the *instability* of earnings for individual workers. In periods of rapid change, some firms grow while others die, and some workers work overtime while others are laid off. Any growth in the instability of earnings—the year-to-year fluctuations in earnings of individual workers—could also have contributed to the growth of earnings inequality that we have documented.

To see how earnings instability can affect measured earnings inequality, let us focus on the lower fifth of the earnings distribution. Assume, initially, that each worker in this lowest quintile had earnings that did not vary from year to year. Then suppose that technological or product-market changes cause the earnings of these workers to fluctuate; in some years, half (say) of these workers are unlucky and experience unemployment that *reduces* their earnings, while the other half are lucky enough to experience temporary earnings *increases* through overtime work or profit-sharing bonuses. The *average* pay among this lower fifth of the earnings distribution might not change, but the earnings at the 10th percentile would fall (reflecting the experience of the unlucky workers) while earnings at the 20th percentile would rise. If earnings instability in the upper quintile of the distribution did not change, the 80:20 ratio would shrink but the 90:10 ratio would grow.

A recent study has found evidence that the degree of earnings instability is higher now than in 1980, particularly in the lower end of the earnings distribution. Most of this increase occurred from 1980 to 1990, and degree of instability since then has been maintained but has not trended upward.[14]

---

[13]This argument is made in David H. Autor, Lawrence F. Katz, and Melissa S. Kearney, "Trends in U.S. Wage Inequality: Revising the Revisionists," *Review of Economics and Statistics* 90 (May 2008): 300–323; and Lemieux, "Increasing Residual Wage Inequality." One study found that job polarization is especially pronounced in recessions; see Nir Jaimovich and Henry Siu, "The Trend Is the Cycle: Job Polarization and Jobless Recoveries," working paper no. 18334, National Bureau of Economic Research (Cambridge, Mass.: August 2012).

[14]For a more detailed analysis of this potential explanation for growing inequality, see Peter Gottschalk and Robert Moffitt, "The Rising Instability of U.S. Earnings," *Journal of Economic Perspectives* 23 (Fall 2009): 3–24. The "earnings instability" explanation for increased inequality might also explain the rise in inequality among men from 2005 to 2011—because during the recession that began in 2008, men in the lower part of the earnings distribution were especially prone to layoff.

Changes in Institutional Forces

In addition to the market forces of demand and supply, two other causes of growing earnings inequality have been considered by economists: the decline of unions
and the fact that the minimum wage was held constant over much of the period
since 1980, while wages in general rose. Because unionized workers tended to
have earnings in the middle of the distribution, the decline in unions could have
served to increase the 80:50 or 90:50 ratios, while a falling real minimum wage
could have reduced wages at the very bottom of the earning distribution—which,
other things equal, would increase the 50:20 or 50:10 ratios.

There are two *a priori* reasons to doubt that the decline of labor unions
has been a significant causal factor of the increased returns to education after
1980. First, as noted in chapter 13, the declining share of unionized workers in
the United States is a phenomenon that started in the 1950s and has continued
unabated throughout each decade—even in the 1970s, when the returns to education *fell* (see chapter 9). Second, women are less highly unionized than men
(see chapter 13), and the fall in their rates of unionization has been considerably
smaller, yet increases in the returns to education were as large among women as
among men, or larger, after 1980.

Studies that have estimated the effects of declining unionization on wage
inequality generally conclude that it explains perhaps 20 percent of the growth
in inequality for men (but not women) in the 1980s but played no important role
after 1990.[15] These carefully produced findings are consistent with the summary
observations, made earlier, that growth in the 80:50 ratio, which was sizable in
the 1980s, stopped after 1990—and that increases in the 90:50 ratio after 1990 were
thus a function only of rising relative earnings at the very top of the distribution
(which unionization does not affect).

Another institutional factor that has been considered as a possible explanation for the rising returns to education is the declining real level of the minimum
wage, especially during the 1980s. In 1981, the minimum wage was set at $3.35 per
hour, which was 45 percent of the average wage for nonsupervisory workers in
manufacturing. The nominal minimum wage was held constant throughout the
rest of the 1980s, and with increases in wages generally, the legal minimum had
fallen to about one-third of the average wage by the time it was again increased
in the early 1990s. This decline in the real minimum wage appears to explain
the sharp fall in relative earnings at the very bottom of the earnings distribution

---

[15]David Card, "The Effect of Unions on Wage Inequality in the U.S. Labor Market," *Industrial and Labor Relations Review* 54 (January 2001): 296–315; Nicole M. Fortin and Thomas Lemieux, "Institutional Changes and Rising Wage Inequality: Is There a Linkage?" *Journal of Economic Perspectives* 11 (Spring 1997): 75–96; and David Card, Thomas Lemieux, and W. Craig Riddell, "Unions and Wage Inequality," *Journal of Labor Research* 25 (Fall 2004): 519–562.

EMPIRICAL STUDY

DO PARENTS' EARNINGS DETERMINE THE EARNINGS OF THEIR CHILDREN? THE USE OF INTERGENERATIONAL DATA IN STUDYING ECONOMIC MOBILITY

While our analysis of earnings inequality has focused on the distribution of earnings at a point in time, another important aspect of inequality is the opportunity for children—especially in households at the bottom of the earnings distribution—to improve on the economic status of their parents. Put differently, a country with growing earnings inequality is likely to be more concerned about this trend if children appear to inherit the earnings inequality of their parents; the country might be less concerned if access to education and job opportunities are such that they offer significant chances for upward mobility.

Studying intergenerational mobility requires a data set with the unusual property that it contains earnings data on both parents and their adult children. When such data can be found, the heart of the statistical analysis is to measure the elasticity of the children's earnings with respect to the earnings of their parents. That is, if the parents' earnings were to rise by 10 percent, by what percentage do we expect their children's earnings to rise? An elasticity of unity implies a very rigid earnings distribution across generations, in that earnings differences across one generation are completely inherited by the next. An elasticity of zero would mean that there

is no correlation between the earnings of parents and children and that earnings status is not passed from one generation to another.

The above elasticities can be estimated using regression analysis, in which the dependent variable is the earnings of the child and the independent variables include earnings of the parent. Of course, earnings of both parent and child will vary year by year, owing to such transitory factors as unemployment, illness, family problems, and overall economic activity. Thus, we would like our measure of parental earnings to reflect their *permanent*—or long-run average—earnings level. If the data are such that only one or two years of parental earnings are available to researchers, the regression procedure will yield estimated elasticities that are biased toward zero by the *errors in variables* problem (discussed in the empirical study of chapter 8). This is a serious problem for studying intergenerational mobility, because an elasticity of zero implies substantial intergenerational mobility, and it may lead us to conclude that a society permits substantial upward mobility when in fact it does not.

Estimates of the elasticity of American sons' earnings with respect to those of their fathers offer a good example of this statistical problem. When just one year of the fathers' incomes is used, the estimated elasticity is in the range of 0.25 to 0.35. When a 5-year average of fathers' earnings is used, the estimated elasticity rises to roughly 0.40—and when the data permit a 16-year average to be used, the estimated elasticity is 0.60.

Thus, as data sets have been improved to permit more years of observations on the earnings of fathers, estimated elasticities have risen and economists have become more pessimistic about the extent

of upward mobility in the United States. The most recent estimates imply that if the earnings gap between high- and low-earning men were currently 200 percent, the gap between the earnings of their sons 25 or 30 years from now would be about 120 percent if other factors affecting earnings were held constant.

Sources: Gary Solon, "Intergenerational Income Mobility in the United States," *American Economic Review* 82 (June 1992): 393–408; and Bhashkar Mazumder, "Analyzing Income Mobility over Generations," *Chicago Fed Letter,* issue 181 (Federal Reserve Bank of Chicago, September 2002): 1–4.

during the 1980s.[16] However, the increasing equality in the lower half of the earnings distribution and the relative wage growth in the very upper tail suggest that declines in the real minimum wage—which were once again marked after 1997— did not play much of a role after 1990.

Review Questions

1. Analyze how increasing the investment tax credit given to firms that make expenditures on new capital affects the dispersion of earnings. (For a review of relevant concepts, see chapter 4.)
2. Laws affecting employment have a huge impact on earnings, contractual power, and eventually, inequality in society. List some of them and explain the adverse effects they

can cause. (For a review of relevant concepts, refer to Chapters 12 and 15.)
3. One of organized labor's primary objectives is legislation forbidding employers to replace workers who are on strike. If such legislation passes, what will be its effects on earnings inequality? (For a review of relevant concepts, see chapter 13.)

[16]David S. Lee, "Wage Inequality in the United States During the 1980s: Rising Dispersion or Falling Minimum Wage? *Quarterly Journal of Economics* 114 (August 1999): 977–1023; John DiNardo, Nicole M. Fortin, and Thomas Lemieux, "Labor Market Institutions and the Distribution of Wages, 1973–1992: A Semiparametric Approach," *Econometrica* (September 1996): 1001–1044; and Autor, Katz, and Kearney, "Trends in Wage Inequality: Revising the Revisionists." For a study of how labor market institutions in their entirety affect wage inequality across countries, see Winfried Koeniger, Marco Leonardi, and Luca Nunziata, "Labor Market Institutions and Wage Inequality," *Industrial and Labor Relations Review* 60 (April 2007): 340–356.

4. How can tax breaks on MNEs and international companies negatively affect domestic workers? Explain with an example. (For a review of relevant concepts, refer to Chapters 4 and 16.)

5. "The labor supply responses to programs designed to help equalize *incomes* can either narrow or widen the dispersion of *earnings*." Comment on this statement in the context of an increase in the subsidy paid under a "negative income tax" program to those who do not work. Assume that this program creates an effective wage that is greater than zero but less than the market wage, and assume that this effective wage is unchanged by the increased subsidy to those who do not work. (For a review of relevant concepts, see chapter 6.)

6. Illustrate the relevance and the importance of education subsidies on workers. (For a review of relevant concepts, refer to Chapter 15.)

7. Suppose a country's government is concerned about growing inequality of incomes and wants to undertake a program that will increase the total earnings of the unskilled. It is considering two alternative changes to its current payroll tax, which is levied on employers as a percentage of the first $100,000 of employee earnings:

   a. Extending employer payroll taxes to all earnings over $100,000 per year and increasing the cost of capital by eliminating certain tax deductions related to plant and equipment.

   b. Reducing to zero employer payroll taxes on the first $30,000 of earnings but continuing the payroll tax on all employee earnings between $30,000 and $100,000 (there would be no taxes on earnings above $100,000).

   Analyze proposal a and proposal b separately (one, but not both, will be adopted). Which is more likely to accomplish the aim of increasing the earnings of the unskilled? Why?

8. One economist has observed that by age 20, the cognitive and noncognitive skills of people are set in such a way that those who are not good at learning new skills or concepts cannot be helped much by education or training programs. Assuming this observation is true, use economic theory to analyze its implications for the issue of earnings inequality in the world today.

Problems

1. (Appendix) Ten college seniors have accepted job offers for the year after they graduate. Their starting salaries are given here. Organize the data into quintiles and then, using these data, draw the Lorenz curve for this group. Finally, calculate the relevant Gini coefficient.

Becky	$42,000
Billy	$20,000
Charlie	$31,000
Kasia	$24,000
Nina	$34,000
Raul	$37,000
Rose	$29,000
Thomas	$35,000
Willis	$60,000
Yukiko	$32,000

2. Suppose that the wage distribution for a small town is given here.

Sector	Number of Workers	Wage ($)
A	50	10 per hour
B	25	5 per hour
C	25	5 per hour

Assume a minimum wage law is passed that doesn't affect the market in high-wage sector A but boosts wages to $7 per hour in sector B, the covered sector, while reducing employment to 20. Displaced workers in sector B move into the uncovered sector, C, where wages fall to $4.50 per hour as employment grows to 30. Has wage inequality risen or fallen? Explain.

3. The following table gives the average wage rate for the indicated percentiles of the wage distribution for customer service representatives in New York City.

Percentile	1990	2005
10th	$9.13	$10.51
50th	$11.23	$12.15
90th	$13.98	$14.78

a. Calculate the earnings ratios at various percentiles of the earnings distribution for both years.

b. Describe the changes in wage inequality in this local labor market.

4. Calculate the coefficient of variation for the workers listed in Problem 1.

5. (Appendix) The following table gives data on the shares of household income by quintile in the United States in 2005. Draw the Lorenz curve, and calculate the Gini coefficient.

Quintile	Percent Share of Income
Lowest	3.4
Second	8.6
Third	14.6
Fourth	23.0
Highest	50.4

Selected Readings

Author, David H., Lawrence F. Katz, and Melissa S. Kearney. "Trends in U.S. Wage Inequality: Revising the Revisionists." *Review of Economics and Statistics* 90 (May 2008): 300–323.

Bound, John, and George Johnson. "Changes in the Structure of Wages in the 1980s: An Evaluation of Alternative Explanations." *American Economic Review* 82 (June 1992): 371–392.

Burtless, Gary, ed. *A Future of Lousy Jobs? The Changing Structure of U.S. Wages.* Washington, D.C.: Brookings Institution, 1990.

Freeman, Richard B., and Lawrence F. Katz, eds. *Differences and Changes in Wage Structures.* Chicago: University of Chicago Press, 1995.

Gordon, Robert J., and Gordon Ian Dew-Becker. "Controversies About the Rise of American Inequality: A Survey." Cambridge, Mass.: National Bureau of Economic Research, working paper no. 13982 (April 2008).

Levy, Frank, and Richard J. Murnane. "U.S. Earnings Levels and Earnings Inequality: A Review of Recent Trends and Proposed Explanations." *Journal of Economic Literature* 30 (September 1992): 1333–1381.

Lorenz Curves and Gini Coefficients

The most commonly used measures of distributional inequality involve grouping the distribution into deciles or quintiles and comparing the earnings (or income) received by each. As we did in the body of this chapter, we can compare the earnings levels at points high in the distribution (the 80th percentile, say) with points at the low end (the 20th percentile, for example). A richer and more fully descriptive measure, however, employs data on the *share* of total earnings or income received by those in each group.

Suppose that each household in the population has the same income. In this case of perfect equality, each fifth of the population receives a fifth of the total income. In graphic terms, this equality can be shown by the straight line *AB* in Figure 15A.1, which plots the cumulative share of income (vertical axis) received by each quintile and the ones below it (horizontal axis). Thus, the first quintile (with a 0.2 share, or 20 percent of all households) would receive a 0.2 share (20 percent) of total income, the first and second quintiles (four-tenths of the population) would receive four-tenths of total income, and so forth.

If the distribution of income is not perfectly equal, then the curve connecting the cumulative percentages of income received by the cumulated quintiles—the *Lorenz curve*—is convex and lies below the line of perfect equality. For example, in 2002, the lowest fifth of U.S. households received 3.5 percent of total income, the second fifth received 8.8 percent, the third fifth 14.8 percent, the next fifth 23.3 percent, and the highest fifth 49.7 percent. Plotting the cumulative data in Figure 15A.1 yields Lorenz curve *ACDEFB*. This curve displays the convexity we would expect from the clearly unequal distribution of household income in the United States.

Lorenz Curves for 1980
and 2002 Distributions of
Income in the United
States

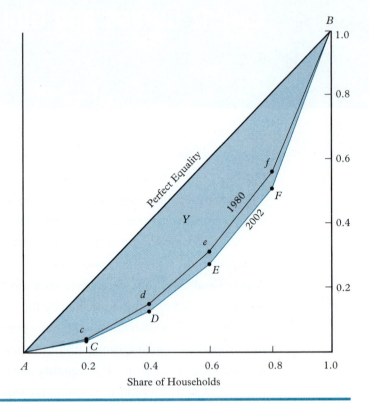

Comparing the equality of two different income distributions results in
unambiguous conclusions if one Lorenz curve lies completely inside the other
(closer to the line of perfect equality). If, for example, we were interested in comparing the American income distributions of 1980 and 2002, we could observe
that plotting the 1980 data results in a Lorenz curve, *AcdefB* in Figure 15A.1, that
lies everywhere closer to the line of perfect equality than the one for 2002.

If two Lorenz curves cross, however, conclusions about which one represents greater equality are not possible. Comparing curves *A* and *B* in Figure 15A.2,
for example, we can see that the distribution represented by *A* has a lower proportion of total income received by the poorest quintile than does the distribution
represented by curve *B*; however, the cumulative share of income received by the
lowest two quintiles (taken together) is equal for *A* and *B*, and the cumulative
proportions received by the bottom three and bottom four quintiles are higher for
A than for *B*.

Another measure of inequality, which seems at first glance to yield unambiguous answers when various distributions are compared, is the *Gini coefficient*: the
ratio of the area between the Lorenz curve and the line of perfect equality (for 2002,
the shaded area labeled *Y* in Figure 15A.1) to the total area under the line of perfect
equality. Obviously, with perfect equality, the Gini coefficient would equal zero.

Figure 15A.2

Lorenz Curves That
Cross

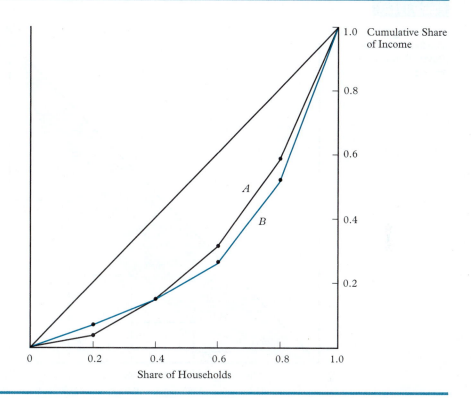

One way to calculate the Gini coefficient is to split the area under the Lorenz curve into a series of triangles and rectangles, as shown in Figure 15A.3 (which repeats the Lorenz curve for 2002 shown in Figure 15A.1). Each triangle has a base equal to 0.2—the horizontal distance for each of the five quintiles—and a height equal to the percentage of income received by that quintile (the cumulative percentage less the percentages received by lower quintiles). Because the base of each triangle is the same and their heights sum to unity, the *sum* of the areas of each triangle is always equal to $0.5 \times 0.2 \times 1.0 = 0.1$ (one-half base times height).

The rectangles in Figure 15A.3 all have one side equal to 0.2 and another equal to the cumulated percentages of total income received by the previous quintiles. Rectangle $Q_1CC'Q_2$, for example, has an area of $0.2 \times 0.035 = 0.007$, while $Q_2DD'Q_3$ has an area of $0.2 \times 0.123 = 0.0246$. Analogously, $Q_3EE'Q_4$ has an area of 0.0542 and $Q_4FF'Q_5$ an area of 0.1008; together, all four rectangles in Figure 15A.3 have an area that sums to 0.1866.

The area under the Lorenz curve in Figure 15A.3 is thus $0.1866 + 0.1 = 0.2866$. Given that the total area under the line of perfect equality is $0.5 \times 1 \times 1 = 0.5$, the Gini coefficient for 2002 is calculated as follows:

$$\text{Gini coefficient (1992)} = \frac{0.5 - 0.2866}{0.5} = 0.4268 \qquad (15A.1)$$

Calculating the Gini
Coefficient for the
2002 Distribution of
Household Income

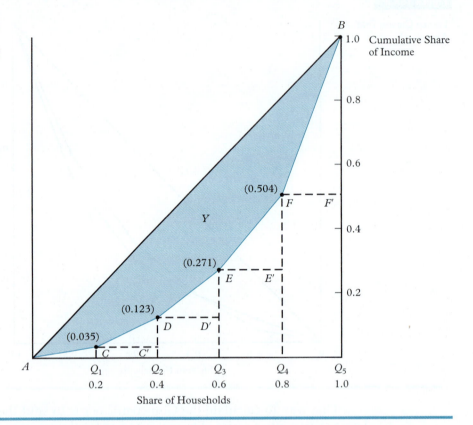

For comparison purposes, the Gini coefficient for the income distribution in 1980 can be calculated as 0.3768—which, because it lies closer to zero than the Gini coefficient for 2002, is evidence of greater equality in 1980.

Unfortunately, the Gini coefficient will become smaller when the rich give up some of their income to the middle class as well as when they give up income in favor of the poor. Thus, the Gini coefficient may yield a "definitive" answer about comparative equality when none is warranted. As we saw in the case of Figure 15A.2, in which the Lorenz curves being compared cross, judging the relative equality of two distributions is not always susceptible of an unambiguous answer.

To this point in the appendix, we have analyzed the Lorenz curve and Gini coefficient in terms of *household income* for the simple reason that published data permit these calculations. The underlying data on the *shares* of individual *earnings* are not published, but the Gini coefficients associated with earnings distributions were published on a comparable basis from 1967 to 1992. The Gini coefficients for the *earnings* distributions of both men and women who worked full-time year-round were relatively stagnant in the 1970s but rose roughly 15 percent in the 1980s.[1]

[1]U.S. Bureau of the Census, *The Changing Shape of the Nation's Income Distribution, 1947–1998*, P-60: no. 204 (June 2000): 2–3.

CHAPTER 16

The Labor-Market Effects of International Trade and Production Sharing

Countries have traditionally protected many of their industries from competition with foreign firms by imposing taxes ("tariffs") or quotas on their imports. In recent years, the restrictions on imports have been eased in many places, usually by mutual agreement with one or more trading partners. Furthermore, recent developments in telecommunications have created the ability to communicate virtually instantaneously across the entire world, which has greatly expanded the possibilities for producing goods and services in locations that are remote from the customer. As a result of these changes, the increased movement of goods, services, financial resources, and information flows across international borders has been significant.

In the United States, for example, imports of goods and services from foreign countries constituted less than 10 percent of all purchases in 1985, but by 2012, roughly 17 percent of American purchases were of goods or services produced elsewhere. Likewise, in 1985, about 7 percent of goods and services produced in the United States were sold to those in other countries, and in 2012, 14 percent of American output was sold abroad.[1] It is also increasingly unclear just what "American" output is; for example, the laptop computers sold by an American company may be designed in the United States, use a microprocessor made in Costa Rica or Malaysia,

---

[1]U.S. President, *Economic Report of the President* (Washington, D.C.: Government Printing Office, 2013), Table B-1.

589

have a keyboard manufactured in Korea, be assembled in Taiwan, and be supported by a telephone help-line staffed by technicians in India! This geographic dispersion of the various steps in the production process has been called "production sharing."

The increased movement of components, services, and final goods across international borders has led to concerns that highly paid American workers now face increased competition from a huge number of lower-paid foreigners, that production sharing means their work is being outsourced (or "offshored") to other countries, and that their jobs are thereby being destroyed and their wages reduced. The implication of these assertions is typically that American workers— or at least a large segment of them—are being made worse off by a more integrated world economy.

This chapter will use economic concepts developed earlier in the text to analyze the labor-market effects of increased trade, in both products and factors of production, with other countries. As with chapter 15, our goal is to provide an analysis of a much-discussed topic in a way that uses and reviews concepts developed throughout the book—and our analysis will utilize both positive and normative concepts. We start with an examination of just why trade among individuals or firms, whether within a country or between countries, takes place.

Why Does Trade Take Place?

We emphasized in chapter 1 that the function of a market is to facilitate mutually beneficial transactions. These transactions will be socially beneficial (Pareto-improving) if some gain and no one loses—a state that can be reached if those who gain are willing to compensate anyone who loses. Because transactions across international borders—just as those within a country—take place among individuals or firms, we must understand the motivations of these decision-makers.

Trade between Individuals and the Principle of Comparative Advantage

Every individual household, as we saw in chapter 7, faces a variety of make-or-buy decisions on almost a daily basis. We must decide what daily tasks to do ourselves and which we want to outsource to (buy from) others. Do we assemble food and make a meal ourselves or do we buy it from a restaurant? Do we spend two days painting our living room or do we hire a painter? Do we change the oil in our car, prepare our own income tax forms, mow our lawn, and/or care for an aging parent—or do we pay others to perform these chores?

Make-or-buy decisions are made by weighing the opportunity costs of doing tasks ourselves against the costs of buying the goods or services from others. If we decide to specialize in one activity and buy the rest from others, we are engaging in *trade*; that is, we are selling the work in which we specialize and using the money obtained to buy other goods or services from outsiders.

Performing all the household activities listed above by ourselves would entail two types of costs. First, we are not specialists in all these tasks, so if we did them all ourselves, we might end up with inferior outcomes. Second, if we did them ourselves, we would give up the opportunity to spend our time in other ways, which may be either more productive or more pleasant. For example, does a lawyer who can earn $400 per day really want to spend two days painting her living room when she can hire a painter for $120 per day?

To better understand the factors influencing these make-or-buy decisions, let us take a simple example. Suppose that Doris is the lawyer mentioned above and that she lives across the street from Daryl, who is self-employed doing shoe-repair work. Doris can earn $400 per day, and she is currently in need of three new suits to wear. Both Doris and Daryl can sew, although at different speeds, and Doris is trying to decide whether she should make the suits or buy them from Daryl.

If Doris took time from her work as a lawyer and sewed full-time, she could make the three suits in a week. Thus, she will calculate that her three suits would cost $2,000 (plus the cost of materials), because she would forgo five days of work as a lawyer at $400 per day. Clearly, unless she really loves to sew, she would be happy to buy her suits from Daryl if he charged her less than $2,000 for his labor.

Daryl is less talented. He can earn only $120 per day, and while he can sew competently, it would take him *two* weeks of full-time sewing to produce three suits of the quality Doris wants. If he decides to sew, he will give up two weeks of work—or $1,200 (10 days of work at $120 per day). Note, however, that his opportunity cost of making suits is much less than Doris's opportunity cost of $2,000.

If Daryl agreed to make the three suits and charge $1,500 (say) for his labor, both would be better off. Daryl would earn $300 more than he normally would by repairing shoes, and Doris would save $500 compared to sewing the suits herself. Not only are both individuals better off, *society's* output is enhanced if Doris specializes in legal work and buys her suits from Daryl! When Daryl makes the suits, society loses his alternative output, which is valued at $1,200. If Doris were to make the suits, society would lose $2,000 of legal services. Thus, it is less costly from a social perspective if Daryl makes the suits.

The inquisitive reader will see an interesting puzzle in this example. Daryl is much less productive in everything than is Doris—he can earn less in his alternative activities and he sews more slowly—yet, he ends up with demand for his services as a tailor! Why? The first step in make-or-buy decisions is for each party to perform an *internal* comparison: individuals must consider their *own* opportunity costs of producing the good or service in question. Put differently, because those trying to decide whether to make or buy some good cannot do two things at once, they must first calculate the value of the activity they would have to give up if they were to make that good.

In the earlier example, Daryl would calculate that the labor cost of his making the three suits is $1,200, while Doris calculates that her cost is $2,000. Once they make their internal calculations, they are in a position to negotiate with each other to see if there is a mutually beneficial trade that both can agree to. Even though Doris can make suits faster than Daryl, her opportunity costs are higher because she is so much more productive at her alternative activity (legal services) than he is at his (shoe repair). Economists would thus conclude that Daryl has the *comparative advantage* in making suits. That is, his opportunity cost (his value of lost production) in making suits is less than hers—and because their opportunity costs differ, there is room for a mutually beneficial trade to take place.

This principle of comparative advantage underlies all decisions about trading with others. Generally speaking, individuals have a strong incentive to *specialize* in the production of goods or services in which they have a comparative advantage and buy from others the goods or services they would find more expensive to produce themselves.

The Incentives for Trade across Different Countries

If trade among individuals within a city, state, or country can benefit both the individuals and society at large, can transactions among individuals or firms across international borders have similar benefits? Economists generally agree that international trade has the *potential* for enlarging the output of the countries engaging in it, although there is much debate about whether that potential is realized in practice. To understand the debate, we must first ask ourselves why economic theory considers trade between two countries to be potentially beneficial to both. Whereas our analysis in the prior section was conducted at the level of individuals, the analysis in this section is at the aggregate (country) level.

Production Possibilities without Trade   Let us assume that in the past, trade between two countries was severely limited either by the imposition of tariffs on imported goods or by technological restrictions, such as the difficulties in transporting goods or communicating vital information about transactions across international borders. The effect of these restrictions was that each country had to satisfy its consumer demands only with goods or services it made domestically.

To keep the analysis simple, suppose we look at countries A and B, each of which can produce two goods—food and clothing—with the resources it has available. Because the resources of A and B are fixed at any time, increasing the output of food in each country requires giving up clothing; likewise, producing more clothing requires giving up food. Countries A and B have different productive resources, and the various combinations of food and clothing that each country can produce with its resources can be plotted on a graph; the result is called the *production possibilities curve* (which we introduced toward the end of chapter 4 when discussing the effects of technological change).

The straight black lines in Figures 16.1 and 16.2—XY in Figure 16.1 and $X'Y'$ in Figure 16.2—are the production possibilities curves that we assume for A and B, respectively. We also assume (again for the sake of simplicity) that the opportunity costs of production in each country do not change as the mix of food and clothing changes, so the production possibilities "curves" are depicted as straight lines in the two figures.

Inspecting Figure 16.1, note that if Country A devoted all its resources to the production of food, it could produce 200 million units of food and no clothing (it would be at point Y). If all of Country A's productive resources were devoted to

Figure 16.1

Production Possibilities for Country A

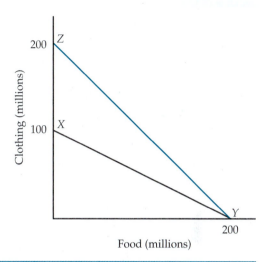

making clothing, we assume that 100 million units of clothing and no food could be produced (point *X*). Absent trade with Country B, Country A would most likely choose to produce a *mix* of both outputs, thus ending up at a point along the production possibilities curve between *X* and *Y*. The exact point it chooses would depend on its preferences.

Turning to Figure 16.2 and Country B, we assume that if it devoted all its resources to making food, it could produce 200 million units of food and no clothing (point *Y′*), and if it instead devoted all its resources to the production of clothing, 400 million units of clothing and no food could be produced (point *X′*). You will note that we have assumed the production possibilities curves in the two countries are different; this difference could be rooted in the natural, human, or technological resources available to each country.

Comparative Advantage   Can we infer comparative advantage from these production possibilities curves? As noted earlier, identifying comparative advantage starts with calculating the *domestic* (internal) opportunity costs of production, so let us analyze the opportunity costs of producing food in each country. If Country A had been producing only clothing, but it decided to produce only food, it would gain 200 million units of food at an opportunity cost of giving up 100 million units of clothing. Thus, in Country A, an additional unit of food can be gained by giving up a half-unit of clothing. In Country B, 200 million units of food could be produced only by giving up 400 million units of clothing; thus, in Country B, an additional unit of food requires giving up 2 units of clothing. Clearly, the opportunity cost of producing food is lower in Country A than in Country B—because in Country A, less clothing needs to be given up to obtain an extra unit of food. Therefore, as between the two countries in our example, Country A has the comparative advantage in producing food.

Figure 16.2

Production Possibilities for Country B

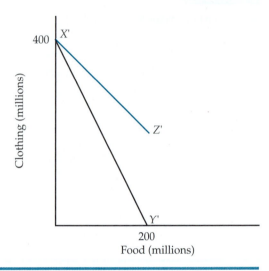

Which country has the comparative advantage in producing clothing? In Country A, obtaining 100 million units of clothing requires giving up 200 million units of food, so producing an additional unit of clothing means two fewer units of food. In Country B, the 400 million units of clothing would require forgoing 200 million units of food, so each unit of clothing costs one-half unit of food. Country B has the comparative advantage in clothing production.

Is it coincidence that Country A has a comparative advantage in one good, while Country B has it in the other? No. Because Country A has resources that produce food very efficiently, if it had to produce its own clothing—rather than being able to specialize in the production of food—it would be giving up a lot of food as a result! Country B is not as efficient in food production, so producing clothing there has lower opportunity costs. Country B has a comparative advantage in producing clothing precisely because it is not as efficient as Country A in producing food! Thus, the comparative advantage of Country A in producing food implies it has a comparative *disadvantage* in producing clothing.

Production Possibilities with Trade   Analogous to our example with Doris and Daryl earlier, the differences in the internal costs of producing food and clothing create a situation in which each country would be better off by specializing in making the good in which it has a comparative advantage and trading for the other good. To understand this, let us assume that, with trade, Country B makes only clothing, Country A only produces food, and firms in both Country A and Country B agree to trade with each other on the basis of one unit of clothing for one unit of food. We will first focus on the effects in Country A.

We noted that, before trade, each unit of clothing in Country A could be obtained only by giving up two units of food. With trade, people in Country A can obtain a unit of clothing at a cost of only one unit of food. At the extreme, if Country A were willing to trade away all its food, it could now obtain 200 million units of clothing (see point Z in Figure 16.1). In graphic terms, the production possibilities curve for Country A has shifted out, from the black line (XY) in Figure 16.1 to the blue line (ZY). Clearly, trade with Country B has made it possible for people in Country A to consume more of *both* clothing and food.

At this point, we must stop to explain that for Country A, the movement from XY to ZY in Figure 16.1 is identical to the shift that took place in Figure 4.6 (see p. 144). In Figure 4.6, we started—by assumption—with the same production possibilities curve (XY) and illustrated the shift that would take place if *technological change* doubled productivity in the clothing industry. In Figure 16.1, exactly the same shift occurs as a result of trade. In fact, from the viewpoint of Country A, *trade can be thought of as creating a new technology* for making its clothing. Because its clothing is now made in Country B, the clothing worn in Country A is indeed being produced using a new technology!

In Country B, an analogous outward shift in the production possibilities curve will occur. Before trade was possible, to consume an extra unit of food required giving up two units of clothing (along production possibilities curve X'Y' in Figure 16.2). With trade, people in Country B can obtain a unit of food by giving up only one unit of clothing (see the blue line, X'Z'). This change in the cost of food is equivalent to an invention that doubles Country B's productivity in the food industry. In Country B prior to trade, it took the resources needed to produce 400 million units of clothing to internally produce 200 million units of food; with trade, Country B can obtain 200 million units of food at half its internal opportunity cost.

Reallocating Resources   For the potential gains from trade to be realized in both Country A and Country B, however, resources must flow from one sector to another *within* each country—from clothing production to the food sector in Country A and from food to clothing production in Country B. These sectoral changes are costly and often painful for those workers and owners who are displaced. If the shift of productive resources from one sector to the other is impeded for some reason, increased trade could cause long-term unemployment—and the gains from trade would be reduced or eliminated completely. Thus, the normative judgment that trade can enhance national output rests in part on the assumption that any unemployment associated with these sectoral shifts is short term—and does not become long term, or "structural" (as defined in chapter 14). Normative analysis—as we saw in chapter 1 and again when we discussed technological change in chapter 4—also implies that society should take steps to compensate those on whom the costs of expanded trade fall; we will return to this topic at the end of the chapter.

Despite the very real costs of moving capital and labor across sectors when trade is expanded, the promise of ultimate gains from specialization and trade illustrated in Figures 16.1 and 16.2 has provided a powerful argument among economists for encouraging international trade. Theory suggests that Doris and Daryl—and the society in which they live—will be better off for having traded with each other.

(Similarly, few would doubt that the citizens of New York will be better off, individually and in the aggregate, if they can trade freely with those in New Jersey and Florida.) The principle of comparative advantage, which drives make-or-buy decisions by individuals, also underlies transactions across international borders. Theory suggests, then, that the people in both countries can gain, on the whole, if they are able to conclude mutually beneficial trades with those in the other country.

Unfortunately, it is difficult to gather convincing empirical evidence on whether an increase in international trade causes an increase in the overall output of a country. Many studies, for example, have tried to test whether countries that are more open to trade have faster growth rates, other things equal; however, the research problems with which the studies must contend have cast doubt on their findings.[2] There are various measures of "openness" to trade, and the results of studies appear sensitive to which ones are used. Furthermore, even if it could be shown that more openness and faster growth are positively correlated, researchers must find a way to make sure their studies deal successfully with the possibility that more growth could lead to more openness—that is, that the causality, instead of running from more openness to greater growth, could run in the opposite direction! Finally, more openness to trade is just one of many factors within a country that could affect its growth rate, so researchers must have a way to successfully account for all the other factors that are relevant to growth.[3] To date, the most careful empirical studies suggest that the effects of expanded trade are positive but probably relatively small.[4] (For an interesting natural experiment on how the sudden openness to trade can affect economic growth, see Example 16.1.)

Effects of Trade on the Demand for Labor

We have seen that, in theory, the effects of expanded international trade on a country's production possibilities curve are similar to the effects of technological change, because both trade and technological change open up new opportunities for acquiring goods and services. As we will see later, the effects of expanded trade on the demand for labor are also similar to those of technological change; thus, our analysis of how increased trade affects the demand for labor will parallel our analysis in chapter 4 of how technological change affects employment and wages.

---

[2]A nice summary of studies that try to measure the overall gains to countries from trade can be found in Richard Freeman, "Trade Wars: The Exaggerated Impact of Trade in Economic Debate," National Bureau of Economic Research, working paper no. 10000 (September 2003).

[3]For studies that cite and evaluate earlier literature, see Timothy J. Kehoe and Kim J. Ruhl, "Why Have Economic Reforms in Mexico Not Generated Growth?" *Journal of Economic Literature* 48 (December 2010): 1005–1027; David Greenaway, Wyn Morgan, and Peter Wright, "Trade Liberalisation and Growth in Developing Countries," *Journal of Economic Development* 67 (February 2002): 229–244; and L. Alan Winters, Neil McCulloch, and Andrew McKay, "Trade Liberalization and Poverty: The Evidence So Far," *Journal of Economic Literature* 42 (March 2004): 72–115.

[4]For a theoretical analysis that comes to this conclusion, see Costas Arkolakis, Arnaud Costinot, and Andrés Rodríguez-Clare, "New Trade Models, Same Old Gains?" *American Economic Review* 102 (February 2012): 94–130.

EXAMPLE 16.1

The Growth Effects of the Openness to Trade: Japan's Sudden Move to Openness in 1859

Most empirical studies of how greater openness to trade affects economic growth estimate what happens when the barriers to trade *change*, and such changes are—in reality—relatively small. It is rare to actually observe countries like A and B in our textbook example, moving from complete self-sufficiency (which economists call "autarky") to completely free trade. One such example, however, can be found in nineteenth-century Japan, which, after 200 years of self-imposed autarky, opened itself to trade with the rest of the world in 1859.

In 1639, Japan's Tokugawa rulers, responding to what it saw as threats posed by Portuguese attempts to Christianize Japanese citizens, prohibited all Japanese from traveling to foreign countries and severely restricted imports. The Dutch and Chinese were the only countries allowed to trade with Japan, and the trade permitted was tiny. The Dutch were limited to one ship a year, which could be unloaded only on a small island in the harbor of Nagasaki; by the 1820s, the Chinese were allowed only three or four small ships per year. British victories over China in the Opium Wars of the early 1840s opened Chinese markets, and Japan's military weakness at the time kept it from opposing the demands from Western countries to open its markets to foreign trade after 1859.

Japan thus offers an excellent "natural experiment" on how trade affects a country's economic growth. It suddenly switched from nearly complete autarky in the early 1850s to virtually free trade by 1870, and the price changes for the goods it imported and exported were large. Moreover, Japan's adoption of free trade was not done for economic reasons but because of outside political and military pressure; thus, it cannot be argued that greater Japanese openness was caused by economic growth or the lack thereof (that is, the causation in this case runs from openness to growth, not the reverse). Finally, during this period, Japan did not experience much technological change, so there were not major factors other than trade that would have affected economic growth.

A recent study that compares the prices and quantities of goods facing Japanese consumers in the early 1850s with those of the early 1870s finds that the gains from trade were positive but surprisingly small. It estimates that had Japan adopted free trade in the early 1850s (instead of later), its per-capita income would have been higher by no more than 8 percent or 9 percent.

Source: Daniel M. Bernhofen and John C. Brown, "An Empirical Assessment of the Comparative Advantage Gains from Trade: Evidence from Japan," *American Economic Review* 95 (March 2005): 208–225.

We begin with a reminder that the demand for a given type of labor is derived from (a) conditions in the product market and (b) the prices and productivities of other factors of production. Because trade affects both product demand and the availability of other factors of production, we must consider each source of change.

Product Demand Shifts

Because trade involves *exchange*, a country's move toward greater international trade generally means that both its imports and exports will increase. When its exports increase, the demand for workers involved in the production of those exports will shift to the right, owing to the expanded scale of production, and both employment opportunities and wages in export industries will tend to increase.

Furthermore, if the expansion of trade makes a country richer, the increase in the overall demand for goods and services, including those made domestically, will tend to cause a rightward shift (a scale effect) in demand for the workers who produce these goods or services. Thus, as people become wealthier, they may want, for example, larger houses, a nicer personal appearance, and better education for their children—and these changes would increase the demand for carpenters, cosmetologists, and teachers.

The increase in imports associated with increased trade, however, will tend to directly or indirectly *reduce* the demand for some domestically produced goods or services. Less-expensive clothing made in Asia, for example, might be so attractive to American consumers that domestic clothing producers would be forced to reduce their production of clothing—and, consequently, their demand for American clothing workers. Similarly, if the United States cannot grow bananas, the increased importation of that fruit might cause the demand for domestically produced apples to fall, and the demand for workers involved in the growing and distribution of American apples would shift to the left.

The shifts in product demand associated with increased international trade thus also create shifts in labor demand. Workers for whom the labor demand curve shifts to the right will experience expanded employment opportunities and perhaps higher wages, with the mix between these two labor market outcomes being dependent on the shape of the labor supply curves to the relevant occupations or industries. That is, when the labor supply curve is relatively elastic (flat), the rightward shift in the demand for labor will expand employment without much increase in the wage; when the market labor supply curve is less elastic, the wage increase will be greater and the increase in employment will be smaller.

Those workers for whom trade causes the labor demand curve to shift *left*, however, may not share in the overall potential benefits of increased trade—even if expanded trade lowers consumer prices. They are forced to change jobs, which could entail a period of unemployment while they search for new work. The costs of change could also involve wage loss or require a significant investment in learning new skills. The mix of reduced employment and wage loss associated with the leftward shift in labor demand also depends on the shape of the market labor supply curve. The more costly it is for the workers facing a leftward shift in demand to learn new skills, the less elastic will be the labor supply curves to their occupations, and the larger will be the decline in their wages.

While a leftward shift in the labor demand curve will put downward pressure on both employment and *nominal* wage levels, it is possible that greater trade may also bring about a fall in the prices of at least some consumer goods or services. Thus, the fall in workers' *real* wages may not be as large as the fall in their nominal wages.[5]

[5]See Laurence Ball, "Has Globalization Changed Inflation?" National Bureau of Economic Research, working paper no. 12687 (November 2006), for an analysis of the effects of expanded trade on inflation.

Shifts in the Supply of Alternative Factors of Production

In recent years, many American (and other rich-country) firms have relocated all or parts of their production to poorer areas of the world—most notably, Asia and Latin America.[6] This production sharing has effectively brought a huge number of lower-paid foreigners into direct competition for jobs with higher-paid Americans. In terms of the production process, the access to lower-paid workers in other parts of the world has reduced the cost of an alternative source of labor for American firms (which, if they could not tap this source before, could be thought of as formerly facing an infinitely high cost of employing foreign labor). What are the effects on American labor when lower-wage labor becomes available in other countries?

You will recall from chapter 4 that when the cost of an alternative factor of production falls, there is a *cross-wage effect* on the demand for labor; that is, the overall effect on the demand for a given kind of labor is the summation of the *substitution and scale effects*, which work in opposite directions. We will begin our analysis with a review of the substitution effect.

The Substitution Effect   The incentive to substitute foreign labor for American labor does not derive from a simple comparison of wage levels in both places; rather, what matters to employers is the *ratio of wages to marginal productivity* in both countries. These ratios, as you will recall from chapter 3 (equation 3.8c), indicate the cost of producing an extra unit of output using each source of labor. Thus, in considering whether to substitute one country's labor for another's, firms will consider the wage level *and* the marginal productivity of workers in each country. Only if the ratio of wages to marginal productivity is lower for foreign workers will firms consider substituting foreign workers for Americans.

To analyze the *size* of a potential substitution effect, we must review the two Hicks–Marshall laws of derived demand (see chapter 4) that bear most directly on substitution. One law suggests that the size of the substitution effect depends in part on the supply response of *American* workers. If Americans quickly leave for new occupations when the substitution of foreign workers begins—that is, if the labor supply curve to their current occupation is relatively flat—then the wages of Americans who remain in the current occupation will not fall very much, and substitution will not be mitigated. If, however, the supply curve is relatively steep, so that American wages in the occupation fall to a greater extent, that fall would tend to reduce the incentives of firms to continue their substitution. (In the latter case, of course, American jobs are saved only through wage reductions.) Thus, the substitution effect will be greater if the *supply of Americans to the relevant occupations is more elastic*.

The other Hicks–Marshall law strongly related to the substitution effect is the *ease with which foreigners can be substituted for Americans*. Many American workers

---

[6]Clearly, firms in high-wage countries have recently found it more profitable to utilize cheaper labor in poorer countries. The reasons for this increased use of foreign labor may be related to improvements in telecommunications technologies, better transportation systems both within and among countries, the miniaturization of components that comprise final output, and/or a reduction in political barriers to relocation.

are in jobs that manufacture goods, which can be transported across borders. Thus, production jobs in the manufacturing sector—which are often filled by workers with relatively little education—are at comparatively high risk of being sent to lower-wage countries. While we will see later that the costs of expanded trade appear to have fallen mostly on the less-skilled, even some highly skilled workers (such as those in the area of finance) have found that they are at risk of competition with comparably educated, but lower-paid, workers in poorer countries.

Other (perhaps most) jobs simply cannot be performed in a remote location: the tasks of barbers, landscapers, surgeons, and physical therapists—to take just a few examples—cannot be sent offshore because they require face-to-face contact with customers. The language barrier is another deterrent to substitution, as are transportation and long-distance communications costs, training needs, the necessity for employers to acquire a working knowledge of local laws and practices regarding the workplace, and real or perceived cultural differences in work habits, attitudes toward managerial authority, and openness to change. The greater the barriers to substitution, the smaller the substitution effect.

The Scale Effect   Recalling our discussion of cross-wage elasticity of demand in chapter 4 reminds us that there will also be a *scale effect* associated with the substitution of foreign for American labor. If lower-cost labor in poorer countries is substituted for American labor in a particular industry, the resulting fall in production costs will tend to be accompanied by a fall in product price and an associated increase in product demand. Thus, while the substitution effect of offshoring will push toward reducing the demand for American labor, the scale effect associated with lower costs will tend to increase it—so it is not theoretically clear that the overall number of jobs in the directly affected sectors will fall. For example, if clothing is stitched together at a much lower cost overseas, the resulting fall in clothing prices could induce American consumers to buy more of it. The increased consumption of clothing will increase the demand for American workers who are *complements in production* with the overseas production workers, and the demand for clothing buyers, designers, packers, truckers, retail clerks, and their supervisors will tend to rise.

The *size* of the scale effect that accompanies the use of lower-wage labor depends principally on two factors discussed in chapter 4. One is the *elasticity of demand for the final product* in the industry that is cutting its labor costs. To the extent that consumers are more sensitive to price reductions, the increase in the demand for the good or service being produced will be greater.

The other factor affecting the size of the scale effect is the *share of labor (in this case, foreign labor) in total cost*. If the foreign workers' wages constitute a larger part of production costs, the resulting effect on production costs and product price will be greater, and the larger will be the associated scale effect.

Changes in the Elasticity of Demand for Labor   Besides causing the labor demand curve for industries or occupations to shift to the right or left, reducing the barriers to international transactions will tend to *increase the elasticity of demand for labor*, for two major reasons. First, a greater ability to substitute foreign for domestic workers will increase the strength of the substitution effect, other things equal. Second, as foreign-made goods and services are allowed to compete with those produced domestically, the elasticity of *product* demand will tend to increase. Workers facing more elastic labor demand curves will experience greater employment losses if their wages are raised by some nonmarket force, such as the minimum wage or a collective bargaining agreement. Indeed, as we speculated in chapter 13, greater openness to international transactions may well have played a role, along with several other factors, in reducing the power of unions in the United States in recent decades.

The Net Effect on Labor Demand

We have seen that, in theory, increased trade in goods or services (including production sharing) with foreign countries will benefit some workers but displace others. Those Americans, for example, most likely to *lose* from trade are in jobs (often, less-skilled ones) that foreign workers can readily perform; in sectors, such as manufacturing, that shrink domestically once trade is expanded; or in industries for which lower costs do not significantly increase product demand. Workers who are displaced will suffer greater losses if it is difficult or costly for them to switch occupations or industries. Those workers most likely to *gain* are in sectors that have a comparative advantage in production (and thus expand with increased trade) or are in jobs that are complementary with production workers overseas.

Estimates of Employment Effects
There have been hundreds of studies attempting to estimate the effects of increased trade or the offshoring of employment in affected sectors. Isolating the effects of trade on employment levels is inherently difficult, however, for two broad reasons. On the one hand, changes in trade occur in the context of continual change in several other forces that affect labor supply and demand. Technological change, for example, has displaced the same group of workers most threatened by trade or offshoring,[7] and responses to both trade and technological change take place amidst changes in immigration, personal incomes, and consumer preferences. On the other hand, studies often try to focus on the employment effects in sectors thought to be especially hurt by a change in trade barriers, such as those manufacturing industries facing competition from imports, occupational groups (unskilled factory workers, for example) whose jobs are at risk of going overseas, or areas of the country more affected than others by trade. While these studies are useful in trying to assess the number of workers on whom the costs of trade might fall, they do not measure the *total* effect of trade on employment—because they typically find it difficult to account for employment gains that might be created by trade in other industries, occupations or regions.

---

[7]See Ann Harrison and Margaret McMillan, "Offshoring Jobs? Multinationals and U.S. Manufacturing Employment," *Review of Economics and Statistics* 93 (August 2011): 857–875; and David H. Autor, David Dorn, and Gordon H. Hanson, "Untangling Trade and Technology: Evidence from Local Labor Markets," working paper no. 18938, National Bureau of Economic Research (Cambridge, Mass.: April 2013).

Barriers to trade among the United States, Canada, and Mexico have fallen in the last two decades, and there have been many studies estimating the number of workers displaced by greater trade among these countries. For example, one study estimated that when the Canada–United States Free Trade Agreement— implemented in 1989—reduced Canadian tariffs on imports from the United States, Canadian employment fell by 12 percent in the industries whose tariffs fell the most (these were the industries most affected by an increase in imports from the United States).[8] While this study suggests that a very large fraction of Canadian workers in the affected sectors lost their jobs when trade was expanded, its author pointed to the fact that the *overall employment rate* in Canada was the same in 2002 as it was in 1988—and he speculated that those who were displaced thus moved to new jobs relatively rapidly.

Estimates of the job losses in the United States from the offshoring of jobs to foreign countries suggest that the percentage losses have been considerably smaller. One study has estimated that as of 2002, some 300,000 American workers could expect to lose their jobs each year—or about 25,000 per month—owing to offshoring.[9] Is this number large or small? To gain some perspective on this level of job loss, from May 2001 through April 2002, there were roughly 1.6 million American workers *per month* who lost their jobs (another 2.9 million voluntarily quit their jobs each month).[10] If the estimates of the number of jobs lost to offshoring are correct, these jobs represent only about 1.5 percent of all jobs lost in a month. Other estimates of the American workers displaced by increased trade more generally (not just offshoring) have tended to be correspondingly small,[11] although the large and rapid growth of imports from China may have increased job displacements in recent years.[12] As suggested in Example 16.2, however, the *potential* displacement of American workers by offshoring may be far larger than has occurred to date.

However large or small the number of workers displaced by expanded international trade is, economic theory suggests that in the long run, *total employment* in a country is no more affected by its openness to international trade than it is

---

[8]Daniel Trefler, "The Long and Short of the Canada–U.S. Free Trade Agreement," *American Economic Review* 94 (September 2004): 870–895.

[9]See Jagdish Bhagwati, Arvind Panagariya, and T. N. Srinivasan, "The Muddles over Outsourcing," *Journal of Economic Perspectives* 18 (Fall 2004): 93–114.

[10]U.S. Bureau of Labor Statistics, "New Monthly Data Series on Job Openings and Labor Turnover Announced by BLS," News Release USDL 02-412, July 30, 2002. The number of monthly layoffs published by the Bureau of Labor Statistics may be significantly understated, which would imply that offshored jobs are even a smaller percent of overall monthly job loss; see Steven J. Davis, R. Jason Faberman, John C. Haltiwanger, and Ian Rucker, "Adjusted Estimates of Worker Flows and Job Openings in JOLTS," National Bureau of Economic Research, working paper no. 14137 (June 2008).

[11]For example, see Ann Harrison and Margaret McMillan, "Offshoring Jobs? Multinationals and U.S. Manufacturing Employment"; Mary E. Burfisher, Sherman Robinson, and Karen Thierfelder, "The Impact of NAFTA on the United States," *Journal of Economic Perspectives* 15 (Winter 2001): 125–144; Bhagwati, Panagariya, and Srinivasan, "The Muddles over Outsourcing"; and Freeman, "Trade Wars: The Exaggerated Impact of Trade in Economic Debate."

[12]David H. Autor, David Dorn, and Gordon H. Hanson, "The China Syndrome: Local Labor Market Effects of Import Competition in the United States," *American Economic Review* (forthcoming).

EXAMPLE 16.2

Could a Quarter of American Jobs Be Offshored? Might Your Future Job Be among Them?

The estimates of American workers displaced because their jobs have been sent abroad are based on levels or patterns of offshoring that have occurred to date. One prominent economist, however, believes that the number of American jobs that are *potentially* at risk of offshoring is in the neighborhood of 30 to 40 million—roughly one-quarter of those currently employed! He arrives at this rough estimate by identifying occupations whose services must be performed face to face and those involved in making goods or performing services that can be done in remote locations.

For example, he believes that most of the 14 million American workers in manufacturing—who make goods that can be transported around the world—could well be in competition with the 1.5 billion workers in China, India, or other relatively poor countries that are fast becoming part of the global economy. He also believes that many jobs in computer programming and financial services can be performed in locations distant from the customer or client. In contrast, most jobs in repair, maintenance, education, health care, leisure, and retailing services must be done face to face.

No one can say, of course, just how many jobs will *actually* be offshored, because there are still large costs of transacting with those in other countries. However, the exercise of trying to assess what sorts of services can be performed remotely suggests that students, in planning their careers, could improve their future job security by preparing themselves for jobs that must be performed in person!

Source: Alan S. Blinder, "Offshoring: The Next Industrial Revolution?" *Foreign Affairs* 85 (March/April 2006): 113–128. For a similar article that focuses on service jobs, see Roger J. Moncarz, Michael G. Wolf, and Benjamin Wright, "Service-Providing Occupations, Offshoring, and the Labor Market," *Monthly Labor Review* 131 (December 2008): 71–86.

by technological change (see chapter 4). What affects total employment is how well the labor market works to equate supply and demand. If displaced workers can find new jobs with relative ease, and if wages are flexible enough that labor markets equilibrate supply and demand, spells of unemployment for those who lose their jobs could be relatively short. We saw earlier that, although 12 percent of Canadian workers in certain sectors lost their jobs after tariffs on Canadian imports were reduced, the overall percentage of Canadians who were employed a decade later was unchanged. Likewise, we pointed out in chapter 4 that the employment rate in the United States actually rose between 1979 and 2006—a period of time over which both technological change *and* increases in international trade were particularly large.

Even if total employment rates are potentially maintained in the long run when international trade expands, those who are displaced from their jobs will bear the costs of qualifying for and finding new jobs. Recent work suggests that these costs of adjustment are high and that full adjustment may take years.[13] Many affected workers experience a significant fall in earnings owing

---

[13]Erhan Artuc, Shubham Chaudhuri, and John McLaren, "Trade Shocks and Labor Adjustment: A Structural Empirical Approach," *American Economic Review* 100 (June 2010): 1008–1045.

to joblessness and falling wages, and withdrawals from the labor force and the receipt of income support payments (from the disability and retirement programs, for example) increase.[14] Adjustment costs are larger for workers with lower levels of education.[15]

Estimates of Wage Effects   Studies that estimate the *wage* effects of trade run into the same problems that confront researchers concerned with estimating its employment effects: trade is but one of many factors that affect the demand for labor and the level of wages in a country. One recent study tried to account for these other factors by comparing wage changes across regions that were differentially affected by manufacturing imports, and it found no changes in the manufacturing wage from increased trade, but it did find that wages in the nonmanufacturing sector fell.[16] As manufacturing jobs decline and displaced workers seek jobs in nonmanufacturing industries, then, the workers who must change jobs may experience reduced wages.

Most studies of wage effects from increased trade have concentrated on *relative* wages—the differences in wages received by skilled and unskilled workers within a country of interest. Some estimates of the effects of trade on relative wages in the United States suggest that these effects are small when compared to the contributions of other forces (primarily technological change), accounting for less than 10 percent of the fall in wages of high school dropouts relative to the wages of high school graduates.[17] Others, however, estimate that increased trade and the offshoring of jobs have had a significant effect on raising the relative wages of skilled workers (however, this same study concluded that trade did not

---

[14]David H. Autor, David Dorn, and Gordon H. Hanson, "The China Syndrome: Local Labor Market Effects of Import Competition in the United States."

[15]David H. Autor, David Dorn, Gordon H. Hanson, and Jae Song, "Trade Adjustment: Worker Level Evidence," working paper no. 19226, National Bureau of Economic Research (Cambridge, Mass.: July 2013).

[16]David H. Autor, David Dorn, and Gordon H. Hanson, "The China Syndrome: Local Labor Market Effects of Import Competition in the United States."

[17]The study estimates that trade accounts for even less of the fall in the wages of high school graduates relative to college graduates; see George J. Borjas, Richard B. Freeman, and Lawrence F. Katz, "How Much Do Immigration and Trade Affect Labor Market Outcomes?" *Brookings Papers on Economic Activity* (1997: 1): 1–67. Similar conclusions are made by Robert Z. Lawrence, *Blue-Collar Blues: Is Trade to Blame for Rising US Income Inequality?* (Washington, D.C.: Peterson Institute for International Economics, 2008), and Jonathan Haskel, Robert Z. Lawrence, Edward E. Leamer, and Matthew J. Slaughter, "Globalization and U.S. Wages: Modifying Classic Theory to Explain Recent Facts," *Journal of Economic Perspectives* 26 (Spring 2012): 119–140. However, greater competition from foreign firms does appear to increase the extent to which pay-for-performance compensation plans are utilized (and thus could contribute to growing inequality *within* human-capital groups); see Vicente Cuñat and Maria Guadalupe, "Globalization and the Provision of Incentives Inside the Firm: The Effect of Foreign Competition," *Journal of Labor Economics* 27 (April 2009): 179–212, and Anders Akerman, Elhanan Helpman, Oleg Itskhoki, Marc-Andreas Muendler, and Stephen Redding, "Sources of Wage Inequality," *American Economic Review: Papers and Proceedings* 103 (May 2013): 214–219.

reduce the real earnings of less-skilled American workers).[18] A study of wages in Hong Kong, which began to outsource production jobs to mainland China when the latter dropped its barriers in the 1980s, also found that trade and outsourcing played an important role in increasing the wage differences between skilled and unskilled workers.[19]

The wage effects of trade and production sharing on poorer countries—the recipients of outsourced jobs—have also been studied, and the results are surprising: these countries have *also* experienced increased differences between the wages of skilled and unskilled workers that can be traced to increased trade and outsourcing! Apparently, the jobs offshored from richer countries, while often low-skilled by rich-country standards, are comparatively high-skilled within poorer countries; thus, production sharing may increase the demand for relatively skilled workers in both rich and poor countries alike.

Moreover, labor mobility appears to be restricted in many poorer countries, so the reallocation of employment from declining to growing sectors is sluggish. Put differently, occupation- or industry-specific labor supply curves in these countries may be relatively inelastic, so the changes in labor demand accompanying increased trade and outsourcing occur mainly in wages rates, not employment levels.[20] These wage adjustments put further downward pressure on the wages of low-skilled workers in poor countries.

Will Wages Converge across Countries?

One of the concerns that many people have about reducing the barriers to international transactions is that it puts workers (especially the less-skilled) in the United States and other high-wage countries in direct competition with many millions of much lower-paid workers in Asia, Latin America, and Africa. They worry that this competition will drive wages in richer countries down to the level faced by workers in poorer countries. The purpose of this section is to analyze the forces affecting wage convergence across countries.

In the process of minimizing the cost of producing their optimal level of output, firms will compare the cost of producing an extra unit of output using American labor, say, with the cost of producing the added unit using Chinese,

---

[18]Robert C. Feenstra and Gordon H. Hanson, "The Impact of Outsourcing and High-Technology Capital on Wages: Estimates for the U.S., 1979–1990," *Quarterly Journal of Economics* 114 (August 1999): 907–940; and Robert C. Feenstra and Gordon H. Hanson, "Global Production Sharing and Rising Inequality: A Survey of Trade and Wages," National Bureau of Economic Research, working paper no. 8372 (July 2001).

[19]Chang-Tai Hsieh and Keong T. Woo, "The Impact of Outsourcing to China on Hong Kong's Labor Market," *American Economic Review* 95 (December 2005): 1673–1687.

[20]Pinelopi Koujianou Goldberg and Nina Pavcnik, "Distributional Effects of Globalization in Developing Countries," *Journal of Economic Literature* 45 (March 2007): 39–82. The effects on wages of capital inflows to developing countries is analyzed in Peter Blair Henry and Diego Sasson, "Capital Market Integration and Wages," National Bureau of Economic Research, working paper no. 15204 (July 2009).

Indian, or Mexican labor; as we saw earlier, these costs are represented by the ratio of wages to the marginal productivity of workers in each country. When this ratio is lower in one country than another, firms will want to consider moving production to the lower-cost country, and the incentives to consider shifting production from higher- to lower-cost locations will persist until the ratios are equalized across countries. Thus, if firms are free to move production from country to country, the profit-maximization process would produce a result consistent with the *law of one price*: namely, the equalization within narrowly defined occupations of wage-to-marginal-productivity ratios across countries.

In applying the law of one price to international transactions, it is important to note that it is the *ratios* of wage to marginal productivity that would equalize if production could be readily relocated, not the wage itself. Wages would equalize only if marginal productivities equalized; thus, cross-country differences in educational levels, work practices, managerial and organizational skills, and the technology used in the production process could all affect the degree to which wage levels are equalized.

To say, however, that differences in the wage-to-marginal-productivity ratio across countries lead firms to *consider* shifting production to the lowest-cost location does not imply that firms will *actually* do so. The costs of moving and trading across national borders are very high, with one estimate suggesting that these costs add almost 75 percent to the cost of the typical product.[21] While the costs imposed by tariffs have fallen over time in most countries, there are significant costs of communicating in other languages, transporting goods (especially from poorer countries), dealing in foreign currencies, acquiring information on local laws and regulations, and enforcing contracts internationally. The costs associated with international transactions reduce the incentives for firms to relocate to lower-cost areas, and they thus impede the convergence of wage-to-marginal-productivity ratios predicted by the law of one price (we saw earlier, in chapter 5, other examples in which mobility costs impede the convergence of wages across firms within labor markets).

Tendencies toward convergence will also be concentrated among jobs whose output can be produced in locations remote from the end user, because these are the jobs that can be moved from place to place if the cost barriers are small relative to the savings. As discussed in Example 16.2, manufacturing workers and those in services that can be performed using telecommunications are most in competition with similar workers in other countries. Perhaps 75 percent of American workers, however, are in jobs that cannot be moved overseas; they perform health, transportation, maintenance, repair, leisure, educational, or merchandising services that must be performed at the point of sale. These latter workers are not in direct competition with similar workers in other countries.

---

[21]James E. Anderson and Eric van Wincoop, "Trade Costs," *Journal of Economic Literature* 42 (September 2004): 691–751.

To the extent the demand for workers in the face-to-face services grows, then, workers displaced by foreign competition will have opportunities—if they can qualify—for jobs that are not subject to foreign competition (we saw in chapter 2 that over the last decades, employment in the United States has shifted out of manufacturing and into services, which as a group are more difficult than goods to produce remotely). Additionally, earlier in this chapter, we saw that expanded trade means that there will be growing export sectors, even in high-wage economies, because international transactions are driven by comparative advantage—that is, by the *internal opportunity costs* of producing goods or services. Thus, the availability of jobs that either are not in competition with foreigners or are in sectors that have an international comparative advantage will serve to limit the fall in wages owing to competition from workers in low-wage countries. Indeed, one study of increased trade between the United States and Mexico found no evidence of wage convergence.[22]

While the creation of jobs in expanding sectors can offer a "brake" on the fall of wages for workers displaced by trade, it is critical that these displaced workers be able to find, qualify for, and move to the newly created jobs with relative ease. Furthermore, normative theory requires that those who lose from expanded trade be compensated for their losses by those who gain. We thus close this chapter with an analysis of the kinds of policies that can minimize the costs of trade-related displacement and spread the benefits of expanded international transactions more widely.

Policy Issues

Our theoretical analysis of the effects on workers of expanded international trade and production sharing leads to two broad conclusions. First, removing the barriers to transactions across an international border can enhance aggregate consumption in both countries—through greater specialization and the exploitation of comparative advantage. Second, the movement of resources within each country that is needed to adjust to greater specialization imposes costs on workers whose jobs are displaced; thus, while a society may gain in the aggregate, many within that society are likely to lose when trade and production sharing are expanded. We have seen that, to date, it is generally the less-skilled within a country that seem most at risk of losing from expanded trade.

In chapter 1, and when discussing the effects of technological change in chapter 4, we must emphasize that we can only conclude that society as a whole is

---

[22]Gordon H. Hanson, "What Has Happened to Wages in Mexico Since NAFTA?" National Bureau of Economic Research, working paper no. 9563 (March 2003). The concern that competition from low-paid workers in poor countries will encourage a "race to the bottom" in terms of wages and working conditions has led some to propose the worldwide adoption of a uniform set of labor standards; for an economic analysis of these proposals, see Drusilla K. Brown, "Labor Standards: Where Do They Belong on the International Trade Agenda?" *Journal of Economic Perspectives* 15 (Summer 2001): 89–112.

better off with some policy change if (a) everyone gains from it, (b) some gain and no one else loses, or (c) some gain and some lose, but the gainers fully compensate the losers—which converts condition (c) into condition (b). Because enhanced trade—just as is the case with technological change—does displace some workers in a society, normative considerations require that those who gain from reducing the barriers to international transactions compensate those who lose from this policy change. We can use the theory developed earlier in this text to analyze the forms such compensation might usefully take.

Subsidizing Human-Capital Investments

Much of the losses suffered by those who are displaced arise from their having to change jobs and possibly face a cut in wages. Because having to search for a new job takes time, workers who lose their jobs will probably experience a spell of unemployment as they conduct their search (see chapter 14). Furthermore, displaced workers may have to invest in training to qualify for another job (chapter 9)[23], and they may also have to invest in moving to a new city or state to secure employment (chapter 10). In short, those who are displaced by expanded trade or offshoring are forced to make new human-capital investments.

Government programs that subsidize these human-capital investments, if paid for by those who gain from the expansion of international transactions,[24] can serve two important purposes. First, they can help to compensate workers who are displaced as a result of policy change by reducing the financial burden of the investments they need to make. Second, by helping the displaced qualify for and find new jobs, they can minimize unemployment and speed the process of real-locating resources to more efficient uses—thus helping society as a whole realize the consumption gains from expanded trade.

In the United States, the Trade Adjustment Assistance program, as amended in 2002, is an example of a program that is designed to subsidize human-capital investments by workers who have been displaced by trade or production sharing. To be eligible for benefits, groups of three or more workers (or a union or company official acting on their behalf) must apply and be able to demonstrate that layoffs of a certain magnitude have occurred in their firm because of increased imports or offshoring.[25] Once certified for eligibility, displaced workers

---

[23]For evidence that workers do make human-capital investments after being displaced, see Daniel C. Hickman and William W. Olney, "Globalization and Investment in Human Capital," *ILR Review* 64 (July 2011): 652–670.

[24]Because the gains from trade appear to be concentrated among the more skilled, some economists point out that governments should raise revenues by increasing the progressivity of their tax systems, which would increase taxes paid by those with relatively high incomes; see, for example, Joseph E. Stiglitz, *Making Globalization Work* (New York: W. W. Norton and Company, 2006): 100.

[25]The program requires that in the 12 months preceding the date of the application for benefits, at least three workers in work groups of fewer than 50, or at least 5 percent of the workforce in groups of 50 or more, have been laid off (or threatened with layoff) owing to offshoring or imports.

can receive up to 104 weeks of training or remedial education, during which they receive unemployment benefits (and partially subsidized health insurance); in addition to training investments, eligible workers can receive up to $1,250 as a reimbursement for job search costs and another $1,250 to help subsidize relocation costs. To date, however, the number of workers declared eligible for this program has been relatively small.[26]

Recognizing that those who lose from expanded trade are required to make an *investment* to adjust to their displacement suggests that we review the factors influencing human-capital investment decisions, which were analyzed in chapters 5, 9, and 10. Those workers who are most likely (other things equal) to benefit from investing in mobility and training, or to find an employer willing to share these investment costs with them, are those who are young enough to have a relatively long expected period over which the benefits of investment can be "collected." The net benefits from training will also be greater for workers who learn easily or who do not find the psychic costs of learning to be very large. Finally, the net benefits of any investment are larger for those who have relatively low discount rates—that is, for those who are not too present-oriented.

Given that using resources in any *particular* way precludes their use in *other* ways, society will want to make sure that it only invests in human-capital subsidies when the social benefits exceed the social costs. Consideration of the factors affecting human-capital decisions suggests some of the conditions under which the costs might exceed the benefits. For older (or even middle-aged) workers, the present value of the future benefits from an investment may be so limited that they fall short of the costs. Costs could also exceed the benefits for workers who are present-oriented or who find learning new skills difficult—and many of the less-skilled workers displaced by trade may have avoided earlier human-capital investments for these very reasons. Thus, training subsidies may not represent a wise use of resources for many displaced workers. (Indeed, based on evaluations of more widely targeted government-sponsored training programs, both in the United States—see chapter 9—and Europe,[27] the net benefits of government training appear to be, at best, rather modest.)

Income Support Programs

One response to the problem that some training or relocation investments may not be worth making is for the government to offer extended unemployment benefits for displaced workers or provide funds so that older workers affected by displacement can retire early. While more generous unemployment and pension benefits

---

[26]For a more detailed description of the program and its antecedents, see Katherine Baicker and M. Marit Rehavi, "Policy Watch: Trade Adjustment Assistance," *Journal of Economic Perspectives* 18 (Spring 2004): 239–255; and U.S. Department of Labor website at http://www.dol.gov.

[27]Jochen Kluve et al., *Active Labor Market Policies in Europe: Performance and Perspectives* (Berlin: Springer, 2007).

would help to compensate those displaced by expanded trade, the provision of these benefits—as we saw in chapters 6, 7, and 14—encourages nonemployment. A reduction in the workforce, of course, tends to reduce the output gains associated with greater trade.

An alternative form of income support, which encourages employment, is to directly subsidize targeted individuals who work. The Earned Income Tax Credit Program, analyzed in chapter 6, is an example of such a program—although it does not specifically target workers displaced by trade. A program that does target those displaced by trade is "wage insurance," under which displaced workers whose new jobs pay less than the one from which they were displaced receive a payment from the government that makes up at least part of the difference. For example, the United States has a program, for certain older workers who are eligible for the Trade Adjustment Assistance program, that pays them half of their annual earnings losses—for a period of two years—if they take a new job within 26 weeks of layoff and earn less than $50,000 per year.[28] While relatively new, this program is clearly aimed at encouraging rapid reemployment, even if it means lower wages, among displaced workers in whom training investments may not be worthwhile.

Subsidized Employment

Another response to the problem that not all training will create net social benefits is for government to subsidize the employers of displaced workers for whom training costs are relatively high or the expected benefits are relatively low.[29] One way to do this is to offer employers payroll subsidies if they hire, for example, older or lower-skilled workers who have been displaced by trade or offshoring. We saw in chapter 3 that employer payroll subsidies will tend to increase employment and wages among the targeted workers, with the mix of these two outcomes depending on the shape of the market labor supply curves for the targeted workers. The research described in the empirical study at the end of this chapter suggests that private employment subsidies are more effective than training in speeding the reemployment of workers.

Another form of subsidized employment is for the government to become the "employer of last resort," directly employing targeted workers to perform public works projects for a period of time. These programs appear to be relatively ineffective in helping workers acquire unsubsidized jobs later on (see the empirical study for this chapter).

---

[28]Workers must be over age 50 and have limited skills. Furthermore, their new job must be full-time, and the subsidy is capped at $10,000 over the two-year period. See Baicker and Rehavi, "Policy Watch: Trade Adjustment Assistance," for additional details. For a monograph on wage insurance, see Robert J. LaLonde, "The Case for Wage Insurance," Council on Foreign Relations, Council Special Report no. 30 (September 2007).

[29]These subsidies are suggested by Adrian Wood, *North-South Trade, Employment, and Inequality: Changing Fortunes in a Skill-Driven World* (Oxford: Clarendon Press, 1994).

How Narrowly Should We Target Compensation?

Our analysis has shown that the displacement effects of greater trade and production sharing are similar to those of technological change, and in practice, it is very difficult to identify which of the two forces actually caused the displacement of a given individual. Indeed, we have pointed out that there are myriad other forces that also serve to shift the demand for, and supply of, workers in a dynamic economy: changes in incomes, preferences, and demographic characteristics, to highlight a few. Therefore, while a drop in the barriers to international transactions will tend to increase the number of workers whose jobs will be displaced, this displacement occurs in the larger context of labor market changes that are constantly occurring for other reasons.

Because the compensation principle suggested by normative economics applies to *all* transactions in which some in society are forced to bear losses for the good of the collective, and because expanded international transactions are but one (and perhaps a relatively small) force causing worker displacement, it is difficult to justify a set of compensation programs targeted *only* on trade-related displacement. In fact, the resources and time needed to verify that it was international trade or production sharing that caused the displacement of a particular set of workers could very well be one reason why the benefits of the American Trade Adjustment Assistance program are received by so few workers.[30] Many European countries, in contrast, offer a range of "Active Labor Market Policies" under which workers displaced—for whatever reasons—are the intended beneficiaries of training and employment subsidies. While these European policies are not universally successful, they do represent attempts to smooth transitions to a wide set of economic forces.[31]

We must also recognize that the costs of greater trade and production sharing do not fall exclusively on those who are displaced. When the forces for change in an economy are increased, whether by technological advances, greater openness to international transactions, or some other factor, workers other than those who are actually displaced face greater uncertainty about their futures. They may also experience wider swings in their earnings over time.

For example, we argued earlier that falling barriers to international transactions tend to create a more elastic labor demand curve in an affected labor market. To see how a change in the elasticity of labor demand can affect employment and wages, consider the relatively inelastic (D_0) and the relatively elastic (D_1) demand curves in Figure 16.3. Suppose, given the supply curve shown, the initial equilibrium for both curves is at wage W^* and employment E^*. Now, suppose that product prices fall, shifting both demand curves down by an equal vertical distance (ab). The new wage and employment equilibria

---

[30]See Baicker and Rehavi, "Policy Watch: Trade Adjustment Assistance."

[31]See Kluve et al., *Active Labor Market Policies in Europe.*

EMPIRICAL STUDY

EVALUATING EUROPEAN ACTIVE LABOR MARKET POLICIES: THE USE OF META-ANALYSIS

In discussing how societies might help those workers adversely affected by expanded trade, we saw that many European countries have adopted one or more "Active Labor Market Policies"—training programs, private sector employment subsidies, or direct government employment, for example—to help displaced workers qualify for and find new jobs. In the last decade, dozens of statistical studies of programs in 15 European countries have evaluated the success of given policies in either reducing workers' durations of unemployment or increasing their probability of reemployment. Each program, however, has a unique context and its own set of characteristics. Furthermore, in the empirical studies presented earlier in this text, we have seen that the methodological problems confronting researchers in any study can be coped with in different ways and using different assumptions. Thus, while no single evaluative study is likely to be definitive, it is natural to ask whether—taking various studies together—we can develop some generalizations that would be useful in crafting national policies.

The number of Active Labor Market Policies in Europe and the variety of institutional contexts in which they take place actually prove quite useful in coming to some conclusions about their effectiveness, because each program can be considered as a separate experiment. If the results from these many experiments can be compared in a meaningful way, we should be able to find out which programmatic characteristics are likely to help workers transition to new employers most successfully. "Meta-analysis" offers a statistical methodology for summarizing and analyzing the results of different studies.

A recently published meta-analysis of 137 evaluative studies categorized their research outcomes as indicating either a success or a failure in speeding the transition of displaced workers to new jobs. An "outcome" variable was then created and given the value of 1 if the program analyzed by a study was considered successful—and a value of zero if not. With the outcome of programs as the variable to be explained (the dependent variable), the meta-analysis also captured data on four categories of independent (explanatory) variables: the type of Active Labor Market Policy and its level of funding; the country's unemployment and economic growth rates; the decade during which the outcome was measured; and various laws in the country regarding how "protected" workers are from being fired.

Essentially, the meta-analysis consisted of regressing the dichotomous outcome variable against the independent variables above.[a] The analysis found that, holding variables in the other categories constant, those Active Labor Market Policies using employment subsidies and providing help with—and incentives for—job searches were more effective than training programs in helping workers transition to new jobs. Programs to employ the displaced on public works projects were less successful than training in helping workers to obtain jobs in the long run. All types of Active Labor Market Policy programs, the analysis found, tended to be *less* successful in reducing the duration of unemployment in countries that strongly protect workers from being fired (recall from chapter 5 that increasing employers' costs of firing workers also increases their costs of hiring them).

---

[a]Using a dichotomous variable, which varies only between 0 and 1, as the dependent variable in a regression analysis presents a serious statistical issue, which was addressed in this study by using a widely known methodology called "probit analysis."

Source: Jochen Kluve, et. al., *Active Labor Market Policies in Europe: Performance and Perspectives* (Berlin: Springer, 2007): 172–185.

Figure 16.3

Comparing the Outcomes of Equal Vertical Shifts of Inelastic and Elastic Labor Demand Curves

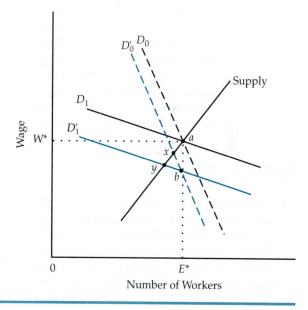

would be at point x with the inelastic demand curve and at point y with the elastic curve; the employment and wage losses created by this fall in product price are thus greater when the demand curve is more elastic. Thus, if labor demand curves are—because of increased international competition—becoming more elastic over time, any price fluctuations in the product market will be associated with larger swings in employment and wage outcomes in the labor market. The actual extent to which labor demand curves are made more elastic by greater openness, however, is still unclear.[32]

While technology and trade, in theory, can enhance consumption levels in a society, we must remember that individuals are trying to maximize their *utility*, not their income. Greater worry about a more uncertain future, therefore, is an additional cost of expanding international transactions, and if those who see gains from trade are to persuade others to go along with reducing the barriers to international transactions, they may have to agree to a larger "safety net" of compensation policies. Indeed, one study found that countries that are more open to international transactions also have larger governments, presumably because government spending plays a role in risk reduction.[33]

Summary

We have seen that reducing the barriers to international transactions has reinforced the labor-market effects brought on by other forces, such as technological change, in raising the relative demand for skilled workers. As the returns to educational investments have risen, and as workers are put at greater risk of having to adjust to changes in labor demand over their careers, the case for governments to extend and improve *schooling* has been strengthened. Workers with higher levels of cognitive skill will be able to qualify for a wider variety of jobs, and they will also be able to learn new skills with greater ease (and thus lower cost). *Providing youth greater access to a high-quality education is perhaps the single most important program a government can undertake to help its workers cope with the changes in labor demand associated with an expansion in international transactions.*[34]

Review Questions

1. In explaining and illustrating the principle of comparative advantage, this chapter compared the production possibilities for two countries, A and B, with and without being able to trade with each other. The student will notice that, although the potential total output in Country B was larger than in Country A (compare Figures 16.1 and 16.2), the discussion did not specify the population in each country. Would it matter to the analysis of comparative advantage whether

---

[32]For citations to the literature on this topic, see Goldberg and Pavcnik, "Distributional Effects of Globalization in Developing Countries."

[33]Dani Rodrik, "Why Do More Open Economies Have Bigger Governments?" *Journal of Political Economy* 106 (October 1998): 997–1032.

[34]See Stiglitz, *Making Globalization Work*, especially chapter 2, for a thorough analysis of what is required of governments to bring about (and more widely distribute) the gains societies can achieve from greater openness to international transactions. For an essentially complementary view, also see Dennis J. Snower, Alessio J. G. Brown, and Christian Merkl, "Globalization and the Welfare State: A Review of Hans-Werner Sinn's *Can Germany Be Saved?*" *Journal of Economic Literature* 47 (March 2009): 136–158.

Country B's population was (a) equal in size to that of Country A or (b) 10 times as large as that of Country A (therefore making Country B much poorer on a per-capita basis than A)? Explain.

2. Illustrate with examples why education has such a substantial impact on the job market and eventually on income distribution, and which kind of action governments are often led to adopt.

3. Suppose the many American firms making home burglar alarm systems decide (independently) to shift the *production* of their alarms to Asia or Latin America, where they can be made at a much lower cost. Using economic theory, analyze the effects on American employment levels in the burglar alarm industry. What factors make these effects larger or smaller?

4. One of the criticisms of free trade is the claim that it destroys domestic jobs by putting workers out of the market. This is due to the fact that imported goods are often cheaper than domestically produced ones. Analyze the claim and offer your views, using a case-study to support them.

5. Television commentator B makes the following statement: "Tearing down tariff and other protections for American producers from competition with low-wage countries can only reduce the number of jobs in the United States." Comment using economic theory.

6. Globalization has often attracted a lot of criticism, not just from emerging countries, but also from advanced economies like the United States and EU members. Discuss this, taking this chapter's content and real case-studies into consideration.

7. Television commentator D makes the following statement: "The fact that greater trade increases overall national income tells us all we need to know: greater trade is good for our society." Comment using economic theory.

Problems

1. Country M can produce 50 million bicycles or 60 million refrigerators per year. Country N can produce 75 million bicycles or 50 million refrigerators per year. The production possibilities curve for each country is linear.
   a. What is the opportunity cost of bicycles in each country? What is the opportunity cost of refrigerators in each?
   b. Which country has a comparative advantage in producing bicycles? Why?
   c. Should these two countries trade? If not, why not? If so, which country would produce bicycles and which country would produce refrigerators?

2. Country C can produce 200 tons of wheat or 50 million automobiles per year. Country D can produce 500 tons of wheat or 125 million automobiles per year. The production possibilities curve for each country is linear.
   a. What is the opportunity cost of wheat in each country? What is the opportunity cost of automobiles in each?
   b. Which country has a comparative advantage in producing wheat? Why?
   c. Should these two countries trade? If not, why not? If so, which country should produce wheat and which country should produce automobiles?

3. Suppose the marginal productivity of customer service representatives in a rich country is $MP_L = 17 - .6L$, where L = the number (in thousands) of workers. The marginal productivity of customer service representatives in a poorer country is $MP_L = 11 - .8L$. Currently, there are 10,000 workers in the rich country who are employed as customer service representatives at a wage rate of $20 per hour. In the poor country, there are 5,000 workers who are employed as customer service representatives at a wage rate of $10 per hour. A firm in the rich country is thinking about transferring 1,000 customer service jobs from the rich country to the poor one. Do you think it should do so? Why or why not?

Selected Readings

Anderson, James E., and Eric van Wincoop. "Trade Costs." *Journal of Economic Literature* 42 (September 2004): 691–751.

Freeman, Richard. "Trade Wars: The Exaggerated Impact of Trade in Economic Debate." National Bureau of Economic Research, working paper no. 10000 (September 2003).

Goldberg, Pinelopi Koujianou, and Nina Pavcnik. "Distributional Effects of Globalization in Developing Countries." *Journal of Economic Literature* 45 (March 2007): 39–82.

Lawrence, Robert Z. *Blue-Collar Blues: Is Trade to Blame for Rising US Income Inequality?* Washington, D.C.: Peterson Institute for International Economics, 2008.

Stiglitz, Joseph. *Making Globalization Work.* New York: W. W. Norton and Company, 2006.

Answers to Odd-Numbered Review Questions and Problems

Chapter 1

Review Questions

1. The basic value premise underlying normative analysis is that if a given transaction is beneficial to the parties agreeing to it and hurts no one else, then accomplishing that transaction is said to be "good." This criterion implies, of course, that anyone harmed by a transaction must be compensated for that harm (a condition tantamount to saying that all parties to a transaction must voluntarily agree to it). The labor market will reach a point of optimality when all mutually beneficial transactions have been accomplished. If there are mutually beneficial transactions remaining unconsummated, the labor market will not be at a point of optimality.

   One condition preventing the accomplishment of a mutually beneficial transaction would be ignorance. A party to a transaction may voluntarily agree to it because he or she is uninformed about some adverse effect of that transaction. Likewise, a party to a potential transaction may fail to enter into the transaction because he or she is uninformed about a benefit of the transaction. Informed individuals may fail to consummate a transaction, however, because of underlying transaction barriers. These may arise because of government prohibitions against certain kinds of transactions, imperfections in the market's ability to bring buyers and sellers together, or the nonexistence of a market where one could potentially exist.

3. Both scenarios are identical from the view of normative economics if all compelled workers had been willing to work for w anyway. Note that this result does not imply that the same workers are hired in either scenario; it only states that both sides (the demand and supply sides of labor) perform mutually beneficial transactions.

5. a. This behavior is entirely consistent with the model of job quitting described in the text. Workers are assumed by economic theory to be attempting to maximize utility (happiness). If all other aspects of two jobs are similar, this theory predicts that workers will prefer a higher-paying job to a lower-paying job. However, two jobs frequently differ in many important respects, including the work environment, personalities of managers, and the stresses placed on employees. Thus, one way to interpret this woman's

behavior is that she was willing to give up 50 cents an hour to be able to work in an environment freer of stress.

b. There is no way to prove that her behavior was grounded in "rationality." Economists define rationality as the ability to make considered decisions that are expected (at the time the decision is made) to advance one's self-interest. We cannot tell from any one individual act whether the person involved is being rational or not. Certainly, as described earlier, this woman's decision to quit could be interpreted as a move calculated to increase her utility (or level of happiness). However, it could also be that she became uncontrollably angry and made her decision without any thought of the consequences.

c. Economic theory does not predict that everyone will act alike. Since economic agents are assumed to maximize utility, and since each person can be assumed to have a unique set of preferences, it is entirely consistent with economic theory that some workers would respond to a given set of incentives and that others would not. Thus, it could not be correctly concluded from the situation described that economic theory applied to one group of workers but not to another. It might well be that the other workers were less bothered by stress and that they were not willing to give up 50 cents an hour to avoid this stress.

7. The prohibitions of child labor laws would seem to violate the principle of mutual benefit by outlawing certain transactions that might be voluntarily entered into. However, there are at least two conditions under which such prohibitions would be consistent with the principles of normative economics. First, the children entering into an employment transaction may be uninformed of the dangers or the consequences of their decision to work in a particular environment. By their very nature, children are inexperienced, and society frequently adopts legislation to protect them from their own ignorance.

Second, society may adopt child labor legislation to protect children from their parents. A child forced by a parent to work in a dangerous or unhealthy environment has not voluntarily agreed to the employment transaction. Thus, a law prohibiting such a child from engaging in certain employment would not be violating the principle of mutual benefit when parental compulsion was present.

9. Positive economics asserts that people respond positively to benefits and negatively to costs. Therefore, the reform may motivate some unemployed workers to stay unemployed for more than six months. If the government's budget is fixed over time, an increase in the average length of unemployment will induce adjustments in governmental spending. For instance, the government may reduce educational spending. In that case, some people are adversely affected by the reform (e.g., students).

Problems

1. (Appendix) Plotting the data shows that age and wage rise together. The appropriate linear model would be $W_i = a_0 + a_1 A_i + e_i$, where W_i is the wage of the ith person, A_i is the age of the ith person, a_0 and a_1 are the parameters of the line, and e_i is the random error term for the ith person. Notice that wage must be the dependent variable and age the explanatory variable, not the other way around.

3. Yes, the *t statistic* (the coefficient divided by the standard error) equals .3/.1, or 3. When the *t statistic* exceeds 2, one can be fairly confident that the true value of the coefficient is not 0.

5. The *t statistic* equals the coefficient divided by the standard error. For the coefficient on age, the *t statistic* is .25/.10, or 2.5. For the coefficient on full time status, the *t statistic* is .75/.20, or 3.75. Thus, both estimated coefficients are statistically significant, implying that the hypothesis that the true value of the coefficient equals zero can be rejected.

Chapter 2

Review Questions

1. As shown in the figure, the outflow of construction workers shifted the labor supply curve relevant to Egypt's construction sector to the *left* (from S_1 to S_2), while the demand curve for the services of construction workers shifted to the *right* (D_1 to D_2). Because both shifts, by themselves, tended to increase the

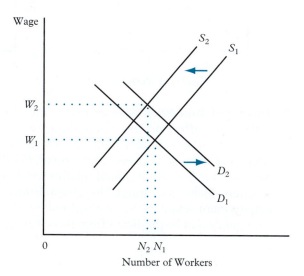

equilibrium wage rate from W_1 to W_2, we would clearly expect wages in the Egyptian construction sector to have risen faster than average. However, the two shifts by themselves had opposite effects on employment, so the expected net change in employment is theoretically ambiguous.

3. Many engineers are employed in research and development tasks. Therefore, if a major demander of research and development were to reduce its demand, the demand curve for engineers would shift left, causing their wages and employment to fall.

5. If the wages for arc welders are above the equilibrium wage, the company is paying more for its arc welders than it needs to and, as a result, is hiring fewer than it could. Thus, the definition of overpayment that makes the most sense in this case is one in which the wage rate is above the equilibrium wage.

   A ready indicator of an above-equilibrium wage rate is a long queue of applicants whenever a position in a company becomes available. Another indicator is an abnormally low quit rate as workers (in this case arc welders) who are lucky enough to obtain the above-equilibrium wage cling tenaciously to their jobs.

7.

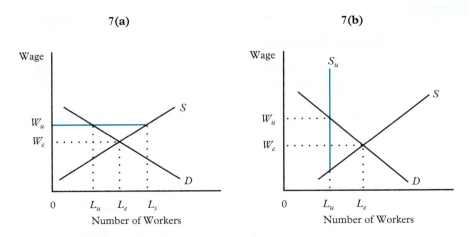

9. This regulation essentially increases the cost of capital and will have an ambiguous effect on the demand curve for labor. On the one hand, the increased cost of capital will increase the cost of production and cause a scale effect that tends to depress employment. On the other hand, this regulation will increase the cost of capital relative to labor and could stimulate the substitution of labor for capital. Thus, the substitution effect will work to increase employment while the scale effect will work to decrease it. Which effect is stronger cannot be predicted from theory alone.

11. a. Economic growth tends to shift the labor demand curve to the right (more workers are demanded at each wage rate).
    b. Greater job growth accompanied by slower positive wage changes will result if the labor supply curve in Canada is flatter (has a smaller positive slope) than the labor supply curve in the United States.

Problems

1. Unemployment rate = (Unemployed/Labor force) × 100 = 5.11%
   Labor force participation rate = (L/population) × 100 = 50.8%
3. The quickest places to find the relevant data are probably at http://www.bls .gov/ces/, "Tables from Employment and Earnings" (Table B-11), and http://www.bls.gov, Consumer Price Index. If average hourly earnings are rising faster than the Consumer Price Index (CPI), then real wages have been rising. In addition, we should consider the impact of mismeasurement in the CPI. If the CPI overstates inflation (as discussed in the text), then real wages have risen more rapidly than the official statistics suggest. The Bureau of Labor Statistics Web site contains links to recent research on changes in the construction of the CPI that are intended to remove some of the historical bias.
5. Real hourly minimum wage in 1990 = nominal wage in 1990/CPI in 1990
   $$= (\$3.80/130.7) \times 100$$
   $$= \$2.91$$

   Real hourly minimum wage in 2006 = nominal wage in 2006/CPI in 2006
   $$= (\$5.15/201.6) \times 100$$
   $$= \$2.55$$

   The federal minimum wage decreased in real dollars from 1990 to 2006.
7. If cashiers are being paid $8.00 per hour, they are being paid more than the market equilibrium wage for their job. At $8.00 per hour, employers will hire 110 cashiers, but 175 workers are available for work as a cashier. There are 65 workers who would like a job as a cashier at a wage of $8.00 per hour but cannot get such a job. Because a labor surplus exists for jobs that are overpaid, a wage above equilibrium has two implications. First, employers are paying more than necessary to produce their output; they could cut wages and still find enough qualified workers for their job openings. In fact, if they did cut wages, they could expand output and make their product cheaper and more accessible to consumers. Second, more workers want jobs than can find them. If wages were reduced a bit, more of these disappointed workers could find work.

Chapter 3

Review Questions

1. Profit maximization requires that firms hire labor until marginal revenue productivity equals the market wage. If wages are low, a profit maximizer will hire labor in abundant quantity, driving the marginal revenue productivity down to the low level of the wage. This statement, then, seems to imply that firms are not maximizing profits.

3. The potential employment effects of OSHA standards differ with the type of approach taken. If the standards apply to capital (machinery), they will increase the cost of capital equipment. This increase in cost has a scale effect, which will reduce the quantity demanded of all inputs (including labor). On the other hand, it also provides employers with an incentive to substitute labor (which is now relatively cheaper) for capital in producing any given desired level of output. This substitution will moderate the decline in employment.

   In contrast, requiring employers to furnish personal protective devices to employees increases the cost of labor. In this case, employers have an incentive to substitute now relatively cheaper capital for labor when producing any given level of output (as above, the increased cost of production causes a scale effect that also tends to reduce employment).

   Other things equal, then, the employment reduction induced by safety standards will be greater if the personal protective device method is used. However, to fully answer the question requires information on the costs of meeting the standards using the two methods. For example, if the "capital" approach increases capital costs by 50 percent while the "personal protective" approach increases labor costs by only 1 percent, the scale effect in the first method will probably be large enough that greater employment loss will be associated with the first method.

5. The wage and employment effects in both service industries and manufacturing industries must be considered. In the service sector, the wage tax on employers can be analyzed in much the same way that payroll taxes are analyzed in the text. That is, a tax on wages, collected from the employer, will cause the demand curve to shift leftward if the curve is drawn with respect to the wage that employees take home. At any given hourly wage that employees take home, the cost to the employer has risen by the amount of the tax. An increase in cost associated with any employee wage dampens the employer's appetite for labor and causes the demand curve to shift down and to the left.

   The effects on employment and wages depend on the shape of the labor supply curve. If the labor supply curve is upward-sloping, both employment and the wage employees take home will fall. If the supply curve is vertical, employment will not fall, but wages will fall by the full amount of the tax. If the supply curve is horizontal, the wage rate will not fall, but employment will.

  The reduced employment and/or wages in the service sector should cause the supply of labor to the manufacturing sector to shift to the right (as people formerly employed in the service sector seek employment elsewhere). This shift in the supply curve should cause employment in manufacturing to increase even if the demand curve there remains stationary. If the demand curve does remain stationary, the employment increase would be accompanied by a decrease in manufacturing wages. However, the demand for labor in manufacturing may also shift to the right as consumers substitute away from the now more expensive services and buy the now relatively cheaper manufactured goods. If this demand shift occurs, the increase in employment would be accompanied by either a wage increase or a smaller wage reduction than would occur if the demand curve for labor in manufacturing were to remain stationary.

7. The imposition of financial penalties on employers who are discovered to have hired illegal immigrants essentially raises the cost of hiring them. The employers now must pay whatever the prevailing wage of the immigrants is, and they also face the possibility of a fine if they are discovered to have illegally employed workers. This penalty can be viewed as increasing the cost of hiring illegal workers so that this cost now exceeds the wage. This effect can be seen as a leftward shift of the demand curve for illegal immigrants, thus reducing their employment and wages.

  The effects on the demand for skilled "natives" depend on whether skilled and unskilled labor are gross substitutes or gross complements. Raising the cost of unskilled labor produces a scale effect that tends to increase the cost of production and reduce skilled employment. If skilled and unskilled labor are complements in production, the demand for skilled labor will clearly shift to the left as a result of the government's policy. However, if they are substitutes in production, the increased costs of unskilled labor would stimulate the substitution of skilled for unskilled labor. In this case, the demand for skilled labor could shift either right (if the substitution effect dominated the scale effect) or left (if the scale effect dominated).

9. Wage subsidies shift the demand for labor curve (in terms of employee wages) to the right. The effect on employment depends on the slope of the labor supply curve, which affects how much of the increased demand is translated into wage increases. The increases in employment will be greater when the supply curve is flatter and the associated wage increase received by workers is smaller.

Problems

1. The marginal product (as measured by these test scores) is 0.
3. See the figure below. Since the supply curve is vertical, the workers will bear the entire tax. The wage will fall by $1 per hour, from $4 to $3.

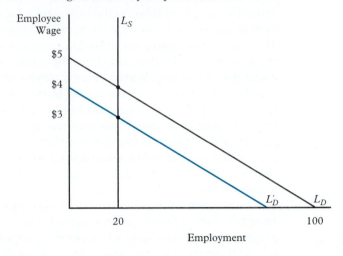

5. Applying the rule $W/MP_L = K/MP_K$, the profit maximizing labor–capital ratio is 10:1.

7. a. Pick K and L so that $(MP_L/MP_K = W/C$ or $(25K/25L) = 8/8 = 1$.
   b. Since the cost-minimizing capital-labor ratio is 1, the firm should use equal amounts of capital and labor. To produce 10,000 pairs of earrings, the calculation is as follows:

   $$Q = 25K \times L$$
   $$10{,}000 = 25K \times L$$
   $$400 = K \times L$$

   Since $K = L$, $400 = K \times K$. 20 units of both K and L must be used, and at $8 per unit the cost comes to $320.
   c. Costs are minimized when $MP_L/MP_K = W/C$. MP_L equals 25K, and MP_K equals 25L, so their ratio equals K/L. For costs to be minimized, K/L must now equal 8/6, meaning that the capital-labor ratio rises from 1 to 1.33. Once capital becomes cheaper, capital is substituted for labor.

Chapter 4

Review Questions

1. The overall conditions making for a smaller employment loss among teenagers are (a) a small substitution effect and (b) a small scale effect. The substitution effect is relatively small when it is difficult to substitute capital or adult workers for teenagers or when those substitutes rise in price when the demand for them grows. A small scale effect is associated with having the labor cost of teenagers be a small part of overall cost and with the industry's product demand curve being relatively inelastic.

3. The tax credit for capital purchases effectively lowers the cost of capital, so the question thus becomes, under what conditions will a reduced price of capital increase employment the most? Employment will be most beneficially affected if a particular industry has a large scale effect and a small substitution effect associated with the tax credit. The scale effect will be largest when the share of capital is relatively large (so that the reduced price of capital results in a relatively large reduction in product price) and when the product demand elasticity facing the industry is relatively large (the product price decline causes a large increase in product demand). The substitution effect will be nonexistent if labor and capital are complements in production; it will be relatively small when they are substitutes in production but capital is not easily substituted for labor or when the supply of labor is inelastic (so that if the demand for labor goes down as capital is substituted for it, wages will also go down—which will blunt the substitution effect).

5. Both options increase the costs of firms not already providing employees with acceptable health coverage. Since noncoverage is a characteristic mostly of small firms, all options would increase costs of small firms relative to costs in large firms. This would create a scale effect, tending to reduce employment in small firms relative to that in large ones. The magnitude of this scale effect will be greater the more elastic product demand is and (usually) the greater labor's share is in total cost.

   Option A has, in addition to the scale effect, a substitution effect that tends to decrease the number of workers a firm hires. This substitution effect will be larger the more easily capital can be substituted for labor and the more elastic the supply of capital is.

   Option B is a tax on a firm's revenues, so it would have just a scale effect on the demand for labor, not a substitution effect. It would increase total costs and cause downward pressures on employment and wages, but it does not raise the ratio of labor costs to capital costs. Thus, its effects on wages and employment would be smaller than under option A.

7. a. An increased tariff on steel imports will tend to make domestic product demand, and therefore the demand for domestic labor, more inelastic.

   b. A law forbidding workers from being laid off for economic reasons will discourage the substitution of capital for labor and therefore tend to make the own-wage elasticity of demand for labor more inelastic.

   c. A boom in the machinery industry will shift the product demand curve in the steel industry to the right, thereby shifting the labor demand curve to the right. The effects of this shift on the own-wage elasticity of demand for labor cannot be predicted (except that a parallel shift to the right of a straight-line demand curve will reduce the elasticity at each wage rate).

   d. Because capital and labor are most substitutable in the long run, when new production processes can be installed, a decision to delay the adoption of new technologies reduces the substitutability of capital for labor and makes the labor demand curve more inelastic.

   e. An increase in wages will move the firm along its labor demand curve and does not change the shape of that curve. However, if the demand curve happens to be a straight line, movement up and to the left along the demand curve will tend to increase elasticity in the range in which firms are operating.

   f. A tax placed on each ton of steel output will tend to shift the labor demand curve to the left but will not necessarily change its elasticity. However, if the demand curve happened to be a straight line, this leftward shift would tend to increase the elasticity of demand for labor at each wage rate.

Problems

1. At wage $= \$100$, $L_D = 2000 - (5 \times 100) = 1500$

    At wage $= \$200$, $L_D = 2000 - (5 \times 200) = 1000$

    % change in wage $= (100 - 200)/((200 + 100)/2) = 0.667 \times 100 = 66.7\%$

    % change in labor demand $= (1500 - 1000)/((1500 + 1000)/2) = 40\%$

    Own wage elasticity $\eta = 1.667$

    The absolute value is greater than one. Thus, the demand curve at this point is elastic.

3. a. See the following figure. The higher wage will cause a movement along the demand curve, and L_D will fall from -20 ($300 - 20 \times 4$) to 200 ($300 - 20 \times 5$).

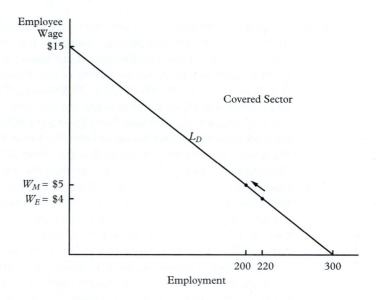

b. The initial equilibrium wage in the uncovered sector is $4 per hour and $L = 220$. Then, the labor supply curve shifts over by 20 to $L_{S'} = -80 + 80W$. The new equilibrium is $W = \$3.80$ per hour and $L = 224$.

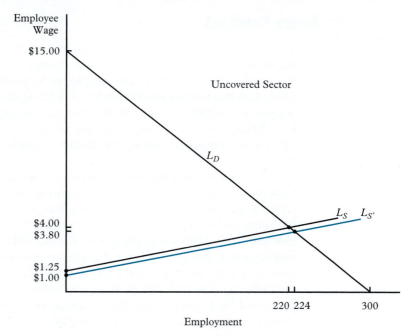

5. a. The elasticity of demand is defined as the percentage change in employment divided by the percentage change in the wage. Using the starting values for employment and wages as our bases, the percentage change in employment of Union A's members when the wage rises from $4 to $5 (a 25% increase) is (10,000–20,000)/20,000—or a 50% decrease in employment. Thus, the elasticity of demand for A's members is −50%/25% = −2. For Union B, a wage decrease from $6 to $5 (a 16% decrease) is associated with an increase in employment from 30,000 to 33,000—a 10% increase. The elasticity of demand facing B is therefore 10%/−16% = −0.625. The demand curve facing A is more elastic than the one facing B.

    b. One cannot say which union will be more successful in increasing its members' total earnings. This depends upon a number of factors, including the bargaining power of the two unions and the firms with which they deal. It is true, however, that the union with the more elastic demand curve will suffer a larger percentage employment loss for any given percentage increase in wages, and this is likely to reduce its incentive to push for large wage gains. Thus, the union facing the less elastic demand curve is likely to be more successful in raising its members' wages.

7. The cross-wage elasticity = (−)8/(−)15 = (+) 0.53; since it is positive the coffee-making machines and coffee brewers are gross substitutes.

Chapter 5

Review Questions

1. The labor supply curve to a firm depicts how the number of workers willing to work for that firm responds to changes in the firm's offered wage. If workers can move from one employer to another without costs of any kind, then small changes in the wage will bring about large changes in labor supply (as workers seek out the highest-paying employer in their labor market). Thus, if mobility costs are truly zero, the wage a firm offers cannot differ from the market wage, and its labor supply curve is horizontal at the market wage.

    If workers find it costly to move among employers, then they will only move if the wage gains from the move are large enough to offset the costs of the move—and some wage changes will be too small to induce mobility. *Furthermore, some workers are likely to find moving more costly—or less beneficial—than others* (they find it more difficult to generate offers of employment, are less open to change, are more emotionally tied to their current workplaces, or have a shorter time horizon over which to collect the benefits). The differences among workers in the incentives for mobility produced by a given wage change mean that some workers will want to change employers and some will stay put.

Because not everyone in a labor market is lured to a firm that raises its wage, and because not all employees of a firm that reduces its wage will quit, the labor supply curve to the firm is not horizontal. Rather, it is upward-sloping. The positive slope indicates that the larger the wage increase is, the greater will be the number of workers attracted to the firm. Conversely, the larger the reduction in wages is, the greater will be the likelihood that an employer will lose its current workers to other firms.

3. One reason firms are slow to hire in expansions is that they are slow to lay off workers during a recession. Workers in whom the firm has made an investment are paid less than the value of their marginal product so the firm can recoup investment costs, and this difference offers employment protection when productivity falls in a recession (because investment costs are sunk and the firm will continue to employ a worker in the short run as long as marginal revenue productivity exceeds the wage). As productivity rises during expansion, firms will not hire workers (which involves an investment) until the gap between marginal revenue productivity and wages is again large enough so that the firm can recoup investment costs.

5. Low-wage jobs typically involve less training than high-wage jobs, and if the training in high-wage jobs is at least partly paid for by employers, the cost of training will induce employers to substitute longer hours of work for hiring more workers. Thus, it is consistent with economic theory for employers to require longer hours of work for workers with more skills.

7. This change would convert a quasi-fixed labor cost to a variable one, inducing employers to substitute added workers for weekly hours (especially overtime hours) of work. Because this new financing scheme increases the cost of higher-paid workers relative to lower-paid ones, it also induces firms to substitute unskilled for skilled workers. (Both these effects emphasize labor–labor substitution; scale effects are minimal if total premiums are held constant.)

9. Hiring and training investments by employers (and employees) are more attractive, other things equal, when the period over which returns can be received is longer. A cap on weekly hours of work limits this period, and it therefore serves to reduce incentives for such skill formation. Furthermore, while intended to increase employment by "spreading the work," the cap increases labor costs by constraining how employers allocate their resources, creating a scale effect that tends to reduce employment.

Problems

1. a. $E = 5W$, so $W = 0.2E$. Thus, the wage must rise by 20 cents for every one-person increase in desired number of employees.

   b. Total labor costs (C) are $E \cdot W$, so $C = E(0.2E) = 0.2E^2$.

   c. The marginal expense of labor (ME_L) is found by taking the derivative of C with respect to E: $dC/dE = 0.4E$. Note that while wages must rise by

20 cents for every additional employee desired, the marginal expense of labor rises by 40 cents (refer back to footnote 7 in the text).

3. Given the lack of mobility costs for employees, the firm cannot recoup its costs of providing general training. Thus, the worker must pay for the training:

$$W = MRP_L - \text{cost of training} = \$3,000 - \$1,000 = \$2,000.$$

5. a. The total labor cost is equal to the offered wage $\times$ supply of labor. The marginal expense of labor is equal to Δ(total labor cost)$/\Delta$(supply of labor). (See the following table.)

Offered Wage ($)	Supply of Labor (Number of Hours)	Total Labor Cost ($)	ME_L
4	18	72	—
5	19	95	23
6	20	120	25
7	21	147	27
8	22	176	29

b.

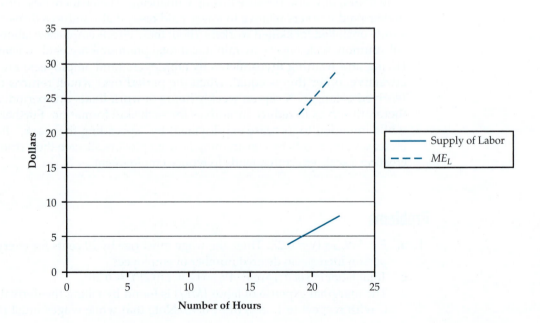

7. a.

Offered Wage ($)	Supply of Labor (Number of Hours)	Total Labor Cost ($)	ME_L
4	19	76	—
5	20	100	24
6	21	126	26
7	22	154	28
8	23	184	30

b.

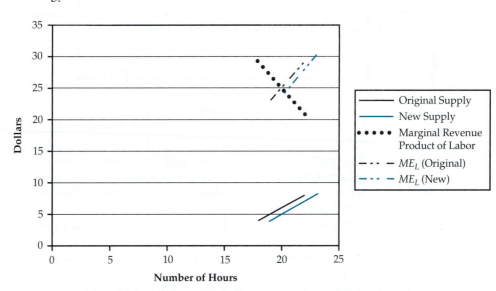

c. The supply curve of labor and the marginal expense of labor curve both shifted to the right.

d. There will be an increase in employment to between 20 and 21 hours of labor, and the firm will offer a wage between $5 and $6.

9. a.

Quantity of Labor (Hours)	Offered Wage ($)	Total Hourly Labor Cost	ME_L	MRP_L
5	6	30	—	—
6	8	48	18	50
7	10	70	22	38
8	12	96	26	26
9	14	126	30	14
10	16	160	34	2
11	18	198	38	1

b.

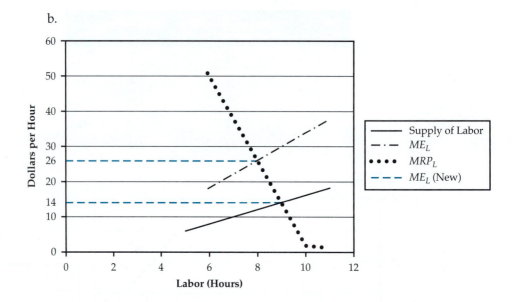

c. The profit-maximizing firm will determine the quantity of hours by equating ME_L with MRP_L and offer a wage as indicated by the supply of labor curve. At Toasty Tasties, 8 hours of labor will be employed at a wage of $12 per hour.

d. If the mandated wage is $14 per hour, there will be an increase in the number of hours employed to 9 hours.

e. If the mandated wage is $26 per hour, there will be 8 hours of labor employed.

f. If the mandated wage is above $26 per hour, there will be fewer than 8 hours of labor employed.

Chapter 6

Review Questions

1. False. An inferior good is defined as one that people consume less of as their incomes rise (if the price of the good remains constant). A labor supply curve is drawn with respect to a person's wage rate. Thus, for a labor supply curve to be backward-bending, the supply curve must be positively sloped in some range and then become negatively sloped in another. A typical way of illustrating a backward-bending supply curve is shown below.

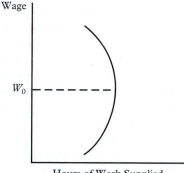

Hours of Work Supplied

Along the positively sloped section of this backward-bending supply curve, the substitution effect of a wage increase dominates the income effect, and as wages rise, the person increases his or her labor supply. However, after the wage reaches W_0 in the figure, further increases in the wage are accompanied by a reduction in labor supply. In this negatively sloped portion of the supply curve, the income effect dominates the substitution effect.

We have assumed that the income effect is negative and that, therefore, leisure is a normal good. Had we assumed leisure to be an inferior good, the increases in wealth brought about by increased wages would have worked *with* the underlying substitution effect and caused the labor supply curve to be unambiguously positively sloped.

3. The graphs for each option are shown below, with the new constraints shown as dashed lines. By mandating that 5 percent of each hour be worked for free, option A reduces lawyers' wages, creating income and substitution effects that work in opposite directions on their desired labor supply.

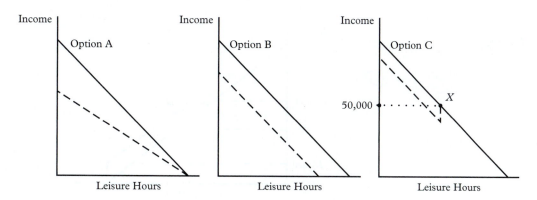

Option B essentially reduces the time lawyers have available for leisure and paid work, which shifts the budget constraint to the left in a parallel manner (keeping the wage rate constant). This creates an income effect that increases their incentives to work for pay.

Option C leaves unchanged the budget constraint of lawyers who work relatively few hours, but for those who work enough to earn over $50,000, there is an income effect that tends to increase work incentives. For some whose incomes were only slightly above $50,000, however, the $5,000 tax may drive them to reduce hours of work, thereby reducing their earnings to $50,000 and avoiding the tax. These lawyers find their utilities are maximized at point X in the graph of option C's budget constraint.

5. Absenteeism is one dimension of labor supply, so the proposals must be analyzed using labor supply theory. Both proposals increase worker income, because employees now have paid sick days; this increase in income will tend to increase absenteeism through the income effect. The first proposal also raises the *hourly wage*, however, because any unused sick leave can be converted to cash in direct proportion to the unused days. Thus, this first proposal will tend to have a substitution effect accompanying the income effect, so the overall expected change in absenteeism is ambiguous.

The second proposal raises the cost of the *first* sick day because, if absent, the worker loses the entire promised insurance policy. Thus, there is a huge substitution effect offsetting the income effect for the first day of absence. However, once sick leave is used at all, *further* days of absence cause no further loss of pay; thus, after the first day, there is no substitution effect to offset the income effect, and this will tend to increase the incentives for absenteeism.

7. In the following figure, the straight line *AB* represents the person's market constraint (that is, the constraint in a world with no subsidies). *ACDEB* is the constraint that would apply if the housing subsidy proposal became effective.

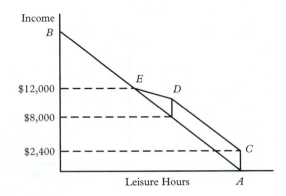

The effects on labor supply depend on which segment of *ACDEB* the person finds relevant. There are four possible cases. First, if the indifference curves are very steeply pitched (reflecting a strong desire to consume leisure), the housing subsidy proposal will not affect work incentives. The person strongly desiring leisure would continue to not work (would be at point *C*) but would receive the housing subsidy of $2,400. The second case occurs when the person has a tangency along segment *CD*. Along this segment, the person's effective wage rate is the same as the market wage, so there is a pure income effect tending to reduce work incentives.

If the person has a tangency point along segment *DE*, there are likewise reduced incentives to work because the income effect caused by the northeast shifting out of the budget constraint is accompanied by a reduction in the effective wage rate. Finally, those with tangency points along *EB* will not qualify for the housing subsidy program and therefore will not alter their labor supply behavior. (An exception to this case occurs when a person with a tangency point near point *E* before the initiation of the housing subsidy program now has a tangency point along segment *DE* and, of course, works less than before.)

9. The old constraint is *ABC* below, and the new one is *BADEC*.

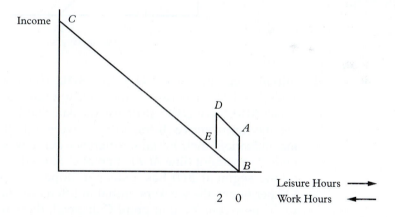

The work-incentive effects of the new constraint depend on worker preferences. For those with relatively strong preferences for leisure, who may not have been in the labor force before, there is an increased incentive to join the labor force and work part-time. For workers with very weak preferences for leisure (who had a tangency along the upper part of *EC* before), there will be no effect. However, for workers whose earlier tangency was along the lower middle part of *EC*, the new constraint may create incentives to cut the hours of work and maximize utility at point *D*.

Problems

1. a. See the following figure, where the initial budget constraint is given by *ACE*. After the new law is passed, the budget constraint bends upward after 8 hours of work. Thus, the new wage rate and overtime constraint is given by *ABCD*, which intersects the old constraint at point *C*—the original combination of income and working hours (10 hours of work in this example).

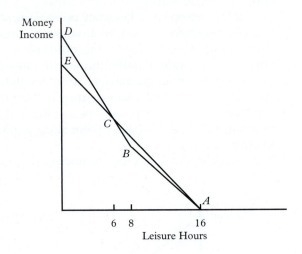

b. Initially, earnings were $11 × 10 = $110. The new earnings formula is $8W + 2 × 1.5W$, where W = the hourly wage. Pick W so that this total equals $110. Since $11W = $110, we calculate that $W = $10 per hour.

c. See the figure above. If the workers were initially at a point of utility maximization, their initial indifference curve was tangent to the initial budget constraint (line *ACE*) at point *C*. Since the new budget constraint (along segment *BD*) has a steeper slope ($15 per hour rather than $11 per hour), the workers' initial indifference curve cannot be tangent to the new constraint at point *C*. Instead, there will be a new point of tangency along segment *CD*, and hours of work must increase—tangency points along *CD* lie to the left of point *C*. (Income in the vicinity of point *C* is effectively being held constant, and the substitution effect always pulls in the direction of less leisure whenever the wage rate has risen.)

3. a. Δ hours worked per year = Δ hours worked per week × weeks worked per year = $(-10)(50) = -500$
Income Effect = $(\Delta H / \Delta Y) \mid W(\text{constant}) = -500/50000 = -1/100$
Interpretation: For every $100 increase in nonlabor income, you work 1 hour less each year.

    b. The substitution effect is zero. The lottery win enhances wealth (income) independent of the hours of work. Thus, income is increased without a change in the compensation received from an hour of work.

5.

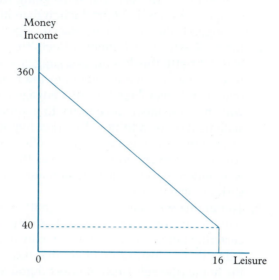

7. At point b, leisure hours = 6, therefore he works for 10 hours.
At point a, the earnings = $8 \times 8 = \$64$. At point b the earnings = $10 \times 10 = \$100$. The increase in earnings = $100 - 64 = \$36$.

      The substitution effect is stronger because this increase in wage rate made him reduce the leisure hours.

Chapter 7

Review Questions

1. a. $6,000 - 5,600 = 400$.
    b. The labor force participation rate drops from 60 percent to 56 percent, a reduction of 4 percentage points.
    c. One implication of hidden unemployment is that the unemployment rate may not fully reflect the degree of joblessness. That is, some people who want to work but do not have work are not counted as unemployed because they place such a low probability on obtaining employment that they stop looking for work. While this observation may suggest that hidden unemployment should be included in the published unemployment figures, to do so would call into question the theoretical

underpinnings of our measure of unemployment. Economic theory suggests that unemployment exists if there are more people willing to work at the going wage than there are people employed at that wage. If economic conditions are such that at the going wage some decide that time is better spent in household production than in seeking market work, our theory suggests that they have in fact dropped out of the labor force.

3. Jimmy Carter's statement reflects the "additional-worker hypothesis." Stated briefly this hypothesis suggests that as the economy moves into a recession and some members of the labor force are thrown out of work, other family members currently engaged in household production or leisure will enter the labor force to try to maintain family income. While Carter's statement of the additional-worker hypothesis is an apt description of that hypothesis, his statement fails to reflect the fact that studies show the "discouraged worker" effect dominates the added-worker effect (that is, as the economy moves into a recession and workers are laid off, the labor force shrinks, on balance).

5. To parents who must care for small children, this subsidy of day care is tantamount to an increase in the wage rate. For those parents who are currently out of the labor force, the increased wage will be accompanied by a dominant substitution effect that induces more of them to work outside the home (the substitution effect dominates in *participation* decisions). For those who are currently working outside the home, this increase in the take-home wage will cause both an income and a substitution effect, the net result of which is not theoretically predictable. If the substitution effect is dominant, then the change in policy would increase the hours of work. If the income effect is dominant, then this increase in the take-home wage rate might cause a reduction in work hours.

7. For workers close to retirement age, this change in government policy creates a significant decrease in postretirement income. The basic postretirement pension has been cut in half, so these workers experience a substantial income effect that would drive them in the direction of more work (delayed retirement).

   For very young workers, the reduction in pension benefits facing them in their retirement years is offset by a reduction in payroll taxes (which, of course, acts as an increase in their take-home wage rate). Thus, if we assume that these workers will pay for their retirement benefits through the payroll taxes they pay over their careers, this change in Social Security might leave their lifetime wealth unaffected. If so, the cut in payroll taxes would increase their wages without causing an increase in lifetime wealth, which would create a "pure" substitution effect inducing more labor supply (and possibly later retirement).

9. $C(\$)$

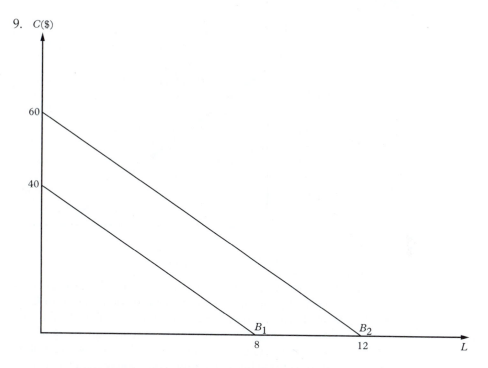

a. & b. The key point is that $H\downarrow$ is equivalent to a northeast-shift of the budget line. Put differently, a decrease in H frees up additional time that can be spent either on paid work or leisure.

11. a. The constraint for Company X is ABC in the following diagram, while the constraint for Company Y is AD; both assume maximum work hours per year are 4,000.

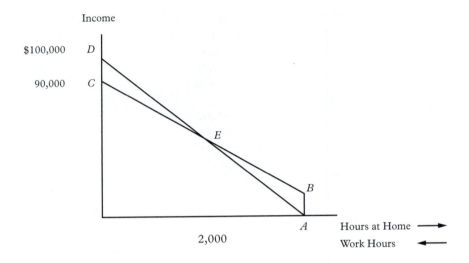

b. A woman preferring to work more than 2,000 hours for Company X would have a tangency along segment *EC* if she worked for Company X. If she is now offered a job at $25 per hour at Company Y, she would *prefer the offer from Y*, because her tangency would end up along segment *ED*. Segment *ED* has a higher slope than segment *EC*, so the effect of the new offer from Y is to increase her wage rate. Thus, the income effect of the wage increase will push her toward fewer work hours, while the substitution effect of the wage increase will push her toward more work hours; the overall effect on her hours of work is therefore uncertain.

Problems

1. a. Unemployment rate (official) = (# unemployed/# in labor force) $\times$ 100
        For June 2006: unemployment rate = (7,341/152,557) $\times$ 100 = 4.81 percent
        For June 2007: unemployment rate = (7,295/154,252) $\times$ 100 = 4.73 percent
        The officially defined unemployment rate fell by 0.08 percentage points.
    b. Unemployment rate (unofficial) = (# unemployed + # discouraged)/(# in labor force + # discouraged) $\times$ 100
        For June 2006: Unemployment rate (w/discouraged workers) = (7,341 + 481)/(152,557 + 481) $\times$ 100 = (7,822/153,038) $\times$ 100 = 5.11 percent
        For June 2007: Unemployment rate (w/discouraged workers) = (7,295 + 401)/(154,252 + 401) $\times$ 100 = (7,696/154,653) $\times$ 100 = 4.98 percent
        The unofficially defined unemployment rate fell by 0.13 percentage points.
    c. If job opportunities are expanding, the officially defined unemployment rate will tend to fall, but the number of discouraged individuals will also tend to decrease. Since these people no longer feel as discouraged, they will enter the labor force and search for a job as unemployed workers, thus moderating the decrease in the officially defined unemployment rate.

3. a.

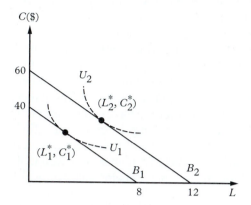

     The microwave oven raises Sally's household productivity, which frees up additional time for both leisure and paid work. In the leisure-consumption diagram, a reduction in H leads to a parallel shift of the budget line (i.e., there are no substitution effects). As consumption goods and leisure are normal goods, demand for both goods will increase because of the income effect.

b.

Model:	Household Time-Consumption	(Extended) Leisure-Consumption
Household productivity ↑:	Indifference curves become flatter.	Slope of indifference curves does not change. Instead, $H\downarrow$.
Consequence:	Hours in paid work ↑.	Hours in paid work ↑.

     In both models, the key result is the same: labor supply increases if purchased goods can be substituted more easily for household time.

Chapter 8

Review Questions

1. To fix ideas, suppose that a university graduate can either work for a company or start a PhD in the humanities (and stay in academia thereafter). The graduate's decision could be determined by the following comparison of job characteristics:

	Research	Company
Salary	low	medium to high
Job security	low	medium to high
following own interests/intrinsic motives	high	low to medium

For most people, the benefits of doing research in the humanities are outweighed by the opportunity costs.

3. A society unwilling to use force or trickery to fill jobs that are dangerous, say, must essentially bribe workers into voluntarily choosing these jobs. To induce workers to choose a dangerous job over a safer one requires that the former be made more attractive than the latter in other dimensions, and one way is to have elevated compensation levels. These increased levels of compensation are what in this chapter we have called compensating wage differentials.

    These compensating wage differentials will arise if workers are well-informed and can select from an adequate number of job choices. If workers are without *choice*, then society essentially forces them to take what is offered through the threat of being jailed or of not being able to obtain a means of livelihood.

    If, instead of lacking choice, workers lack information about working conditions in the jobs from which they have to choose, then society is in effect using trickery to allocate labor. That is, if workers are ignorant of true working conditions and remain ignorant of these conditions for a long period after they have taken a job, they have not made their choice with full information. They have been tricked into making the choice they have made.

5. False. Whether government policy is required in a particular labor market depends on how well that market is functioning. If the outcomes of the market take into account worker preferences (with full information and choice), then the labor market decisions will lead to utility maximization among workers. In this case, efforts by government to impose a level of safety greater than the market outcome could lead to a reduction in worker welfare (as argued in the text).

    If the market fails to take full account of worker preferences, owing to either lack of information or lack of choice, then the private decision-makers do not weigh all the costs and benefits of greater safety. There is a very good chance that the market outcome will not be socially optimal, and an appropriate setting of governmental standards could improve the utility of workers.

    Of course, if society does not trust workers' preferences or seeks to change those preferences, it would not want to rely on the market even if it were functioning perfectly, because the market would reflect worker preferences.

7. Compensating wage differentials arise only under three conditions: (i) workers are utility maximizers (which is the case here), (ii) workers are informed, i.e., they (roughly) know all relevant job characteristics (this is also the case), (iii) workers can choose from a range of job offers (worker mobility).

    The theory of compensating wage differentials therefore suggests that, unfortunately, workers in underpaid risky jobs in the garment industry simply lack better job alternatives. If a poor worker can only choose between subsistence agriculture and an "informal" job in the garment industry, the latter might indeed maximize his or her utility.

9. From the perspective of positive economics, banning Sunday work drives down the profits of employers, which will have a scale effect on employment,

and drives up the cost of labor relative to capital (machines are not banned from running on Sunday). Overall, firms will tend to hire less labor.

Furthermore, in the absence of government prohibitions, most workers presumably preferred to celebrate a Sabbath, and in Germany, Sunday was most likely the typical choice. With most workers preferring Sunday off, employers who wanted to remain open had to hire from a small pool of workers who did not celebrate Sunday as a Sabbath. If this pool was small relative to the demand for Sunday workers, employers had to pay a compensating wage differential to lure workers into offering their services on Sundays. The workers most easily lured were those who cared least about having Sunday off. These workers will lose their premium pay (unless exempt from the law).

Normatively, this law prevents some voluntary transactions. It makes society worse off by preventing workers who are willing to work on Sundays (for a price) from transacting with employers who want Sunday workers, and it thus discourages some mutually beneficial transactions.

Problems

1. See the following figure. A's wage at 3 meters is $10 + .5 \times 3 = \$11.50$ per hour. At 5 meters, B's wage is $10 + .5 \times 5 = \$12.50$ per hour. A's indifference curve must be tangent to the offer curve at 3 meters—B's must be tangent at 5 meters. Because both indifference curves are tangent to a straight line, both

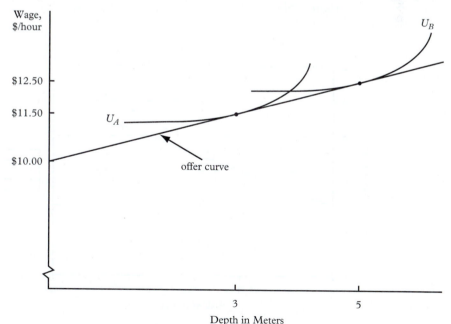

must have the same slope at their points of tangency; therefore, both workers are willing to pay (or receive) 50 cents per hour for reduced (added) depth of 1 meter. Worker A, who chooses to work at 3 meters, has a steeper indifference curve (a greater willingness to pay for reduced depth) at each level of depth; that is why worker A chooses to work at a shallower depth.

3. (Appendix) He will be fully compensated when his expected utility is the same on the two jobs.

Utility from the first job is $\sqrt{Y} = \sqrt{40{,}000} = 200$.

Utility from the second job is $U = .5 \times \sqrt{Y_{bad}} + .5 \times \sqrt{Y_{good}} = .5 \times \sqrt{22{,}500} + .5 \times \sqrt{Y_{good}}$. This equals the utility of the first job when $\sqrt{Y_{good}} = 62{,}500$ ($.5 \times 150 + .5 \times \sqrt{Y_{good}} = 200$). If he earns \$22,500 half the time and \$62,500 half the time, his expected earnings are \$42,500. Thus, his expected extra pay for the layoff risk is \$2,500 per year.

5. a. Sheldon is willing to trade 1 percent risk of injury for \$3 per hour. Shelby is willing to trade 1 percent risk of injury for \$2 per hour. Since Sheldon requires a larger wage increase to compensate him for a 1 percent increase in risk of injury, he has a stronger aversion to risk of injury.

   b. An isoprofit curve that is concave (from below) exhibits diminishing marginal returns to safety expenditures. Where the curve is steeply sloped, wages will have to be reduced by a lot if the firm is to reduce risk and still maintain its profits; this trade-off between wage and risk is more similar to Sheldon's willingness to trade wage and risk. Thus, an individual with a stronger aversion to risk is more likely to attain a match farther to the left along a concave isoprofit curve. Shelby's tangency point will be to the right of Sheldon's.

7. a.

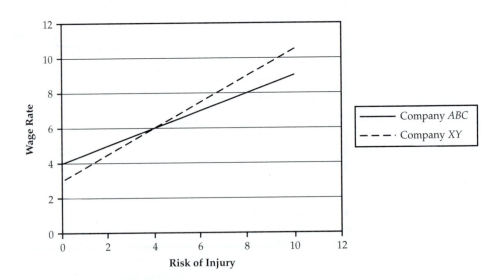

A linear isoprofit curve is a graphic representation of the assumption of constant marginal returns to safety expenditures. In this situation, the trade-off between risk of injury and wages does not vary.

b. $W_{ABC} = 4 + .5R$
    $W_{XY} = 3 + .75R$
    Solving for R: $4 + .5R = 3 + .75R$
$$1 = .25R$$
$$4 = R$$
    Now solve for W: $W = 4 + .5(4) = 4 + 2 = \$6$
    At a risk level of 4, both firms will offer a wage rate of $6.00 per hour.

c.   At risk levels lower than 4, workers would prefer to work at Company ABC, which is offering higher wage rates for those risk levels. At risk levels higher than 4, workers would prefer to work at Company XY, which is offering higher wage rates for those risk levels.

Chapter 9

Review Questions

1. Understanding why women receive lower wages than men of comparable age requires an analysis of many possible causes, including discrimination. This answer will explore the insights provided by human capital theory.

Women have traditionally exhibited interrupted labor market careers, which shortens the time over which human capital investments can be recouped. Even recently, when educational attainment levels between relatively young men and women have equalized, women graduates are still bunched in occupations for which an interrupted working life is least damaging. Lower human capital investments and occupational bunching are undoubtedly associated with lower wages.

The fact that female age/earnings profiles are relatively flat, while men have age/earnings profiles that are more upward-sloping and concave, can also be explained by human capital analysis. If men acquire more on-the-job training in their early years than women do, their wages will be relatively depressed by these investments (this will cause wages of men and women at younger ages to be more equal than they would otherwise be). In their later years, those who have made human capital investments will be recouping them, and this will cause the wages of men and women to become less equal.

3. Delaying reduces tuition costs, but it also delays the benefits of a medical education (generally measured as the difference between what doctors earn and what can be earned without a medical degree). This difference in benefits will be greatest for those with the smallest alternative (pre-medical-school) earnings. Furthermore, it reduces by one the number of years that the investment's payoff

can be recouped. Thus, those expecting the greatest payoff to an investment in medical education, and those who are older and therefore have fewer years over which to recoup its returns, will be least likely to take this offer.

5. One cost of educational investment is related to the time students need to devote to studying in order to ensure success. People who can learn quickly are going to have lower costs of obtaining an education. If one assumes that learning ability and ability in general (including productive capacity in a job) are correlated, then the implication of human capital theory is that the most-able people, other things being equal, will obtain the most education.

7. Government subsidies will, of course, lower the costs to individuals of obtaining an education (of making a human capital investment). Reduced university costs will, from an individual perspective, raise the individual rate of return to making an investment in education. This will induce more people to attend college than would have attended otherwise. Students who would, in the absence of a college subsidy, have required a postcollege earnings differential (as compared with that of a high school graduate) of $6,000 per year (say) may now be induced to attend college if the earnings differential is only $3,000 per year. From a social perspective, however, the increase in productivity of $3,000 per year may be insufficient to pay back society for its investments in college students.

9. Childcare allows mothers to work more hours, which has a positive impact on B_T; for example, depreciation of human capital$\downarrow$ and on-the-job training$\uparrow$. Childcare may further reduce the number of career interruptions. Additionally, childcare provision during the study or training period is equivalent to a decrease in C.

Problems

1. She needs to compare the present value of the costs and benefits from getting the MBA. Costs equal forgone income at ages 48 and 49, plus tuition. The cost of an apartment is not included, because she will need to live somewhere whether she's working or in school. Benefits equal the $15,000 in extra wages that she'll get at ages 50 through 59. Present value of costs = $50,000 + $50,000/(1.06) = $97,170. Present value of benefits = $15,000/(1.06)^2 + $15,000/(1.06)^3 + \ldots + 15,000/(1.06)^{10} + 15,000/(1.06)^{11} = 104,152$.

Thus, Becky enrolls in the MBA program, because the present value of the net benefits of doing so is $6,982.

3. $PV = B_5/(1 + r)^5$
$= \$125/(1 + .04)^5$
$= \$125/(1.04)^5$
$= \$125/(1.217)$
$= \$102.71$

You should opt for $125 in five years, since the present value is worth more than $100 now.

5. a. For *exper* = 0, we have
$$\text{In}\,\widehat{wage} = 0.12s - 0.04sfqt$$
$$\approx 0.12s.$$

For *exper* = 10, the prediction dramatically changes:
$$\text{In}\,\widehat{wage} = 0.12s - 0.10s + 0.14sfqt - 0.04afqt$$
$$\approx 0.10afqt.$$

   b. For graduates, i.e., persons with *exper* = 0, schooling clearly dominates over ability (in terms of relevance) because In $\widehat{wage}$ = 0.12s for persons with *exper* = 0. Over time, however, schooling basically becomes irrelevant: if, for instance, *exper* = 10, In $\widehat{wage}$ ≈ 0.10*afqt*

   c. As *afqt* is unknown to employers, they may initially base their wage offer on observable characteristics like formal education *s*. Over time, however, employers observe a worker's true ability (as proxied by *afqt*), leading to adjustments in the worker's wage. (Additionally, formal schooling *s* may become less relevant due to depreciation.)

Chapter 10 _____

Review Questions

1. a. State licensing increases the costs of interstate mobility among licensed professionals, thus tending to reduce the overall supply to these occupations and to drive up their wages. In addition, the flows from low-to high-earnings areas are inhibited, which slows the geographic equalization of wages among these professionals.

   b. The gainers from federalization would be licensed professionals who are in low-earnings areas, because their labor market mobility is enhanced. (One could also argue that clients in high-earnings areas similarly gain from the enhanced mobility of the professionals from whom they purchase services.) The losers are already licensed professionals in high-earnings areas who face increased competition now because of enhanced mobility.

3. a. Immigrant workers create goods or perform services that have value to the rest of society. Thus, whether their presence enriches native-born Americans (in the aggregate) depends on the total value of these services, net of what they are paid. If immigrants receive no more than their marginal revenue product, the native-born cannot lose and in fact will reap inframarginal gains. If immigrants are subsidized by the native-born, so that they are net consumers of goods and services, then the native-born could be worse off in the aggregate.

   b. There are two critical issues from a normative perspective. The first is whether immigrants are subsidized, on balance, by the native-born (as noted earlier). If they are not, then there is a second issue: are there mechanisms whereby the native-born gainers from immigration can compensate the losers? Many economists argue that compensation of losers must take place for a potentially Pareto-improving policy to be socially defensible, so identifying whose wages are reduced and by how much is a critical social issue.

5. One factor inducing quit rates to be low is that the cost of job changing may be high (pension losses, seniority losses, and difficulties finding information about other jobs are examples of factors that can increase the cost of quitting). If there are cost barriers to mobility, then employees are more likely to tolerate adverse conditions within the firm without resorting to leaving.

Firms are also more likely to provide their employees with firm-specific training if quit rates are low. Thus, if firms need to train their employees in firm-specific skills, they clearly prefer a low quit rate.

Finally, firms prefer low quit rates because hiring costs are kept to a minimum. Every time a worker quits, a replacement must be hired, and to the extent that finding and hiring a replacement is costly, firms want to avoid incurring these costs.

From a social perspective, the disadvantage of having a low quit rate is related to the failure of the market to adjust quickly to shortages and surpluses. Changing relative demands for labor require constant flux in the employment distribution, and factors that inhibit change will also inhibit adaptation to new conditions.

Furthermore, high costs of quitting will be associated not only with lower quit rates but also with larger wage differentials across firms or regions for the same grade of labor. Since firms hire labor until marginal productivity equals the wage they must pay, these large wage differentials will also be accompanied by large differentials in marginal productivities within the same skill group. As implied by our discussion of job-matching, if marginal productivities differ widely among workers with the same skills, national output could be increased by reallocating labor so that marginal productivities of the low-paid workers are enhanced.

7. It is possible that Japanese workers, say, do have stronger preferences for loyalty (meaning that they are more willing to pass up monetary gains from mobility for the sake of "consuming" loyalty to their current employers). It is also true that quit rates are affected by incentives as well as preferences, and incentives for lower quit rates can be altered by employer policies. Thus, quit rates do not by themselves allow us to measure differentials in inherent employee loyalties.

Lower quit rates in Japan, however, could result from poorer information flows about jobs in other areas, greater costs of changing jobs (employee benefits may be strongly linked to seniority within the firm so that when workers quit, they lose benefits that are not immediately replaced by their new employer), smaller wage differentials among employers, or other employer policies adopted because of a greater reliance on firm-specific human capital investments by Japanese employers.

9. Criminals presumably weigh the benefits of their crimes against the expected future costs (which can be thought of as the discounted present value of the expected loss of income and freedom if jailed). These costs will be smaller— and crime more attractive, other things equal—the *higher* one's discount rate

is. Thus, criminals tend to have higher-than-average discount rates. In contrast, because the act of immigration entails very high initial costs and returns that flow only over future years, we can infer that those who decide to immigrate tend to have *lower*-than-average personal discount rates. Thus, theory would lead us to expect that immigrants will have lower-than-average crime rates.

Problems

1. The present value of net benefits from the move is given by equation (10.1) in the text. Assuming that the benefits of the two identical jobs are summarized by the real wage, the present value of the gains from moving are $20,000 + $20,000/1.1 + $20,000/1.1^2 + $20,000/1.1^3 + $20,000/1.1^4 = $83,397$.

    Because she doesn't move, we know that the costs of moving outweigh the benefits. The direct cost of the move is only $2,000, so the psychic costs must be greater than $81,397.

3. Clare should compare the present value of her choices.

$$PV_{US} = $32,000/(1 + .06) + $32,000/(1 + .06)^2 + $32,000/(1 + .06)^3 + $32,000$$
$$/(1 + .06)^4 - $6,000$$
$$= $30,189 + $28,480 + $26,868 + $25,347 - $6,000$$
$$= $104,884$$
$$PV_{France} = $30,000/(1 + .06) + $30,000/(1 + .06)^2 + $30,000/(1 + .06)^3$$
$$+ $30,000/(1 + .06)^4$$
$$= $28,302 + $26,700 + $25,189 + $23,762$$
$$= $103,953$$

Clare should take the job offer in the United States. She would be financially ahead by $931.

5. a. Draw curves from the following table:

Wage ($)	Demand	Domestic Supply	Total Supply	Immigrants
3	30	12	16	4
4	28	13	18	5
5	26	14	20	6
6	24	15	22	7
7	22	16	24	8
8	20	17	26	9
9	18	18	28	10
10	16	19	30	11

Note: The number of immigrants in column 5 is calculated by subtracting the domestic supply of labor from the total supply of labor at particular wage rates.

b.
$$D = S_{\text{domestic}}$$
$$36 - 2W = W + 9$$
$$27 = 3W$$
$$9 = W$$
$$36 - 2(9) = 18{,}000 \text{ domestic workers}$$

Before immigration, the equilibrium wage is $9.00 per hour, and 18,000 domestic workers will be hired.

c.
$$D = S_{\text{total}}$$
$$36 - 2W = 10 + 2W$$
$$26 = 4W$$
$$\$6.50 = W$$
$$S_{\text{total}} = 2(6.50) + 10 = 13 + 10 = 23 \text{ thousand total employed}$$
$$S_{\text{domestic}} = 9 + W = 9 + 6.50 = 15.5 \text{ thousand domestic workers employed}$$
$$S_{\text{immigrants}} = S_{\text{total}} - S_{\text{domestic}} = 23 - 15.5 = 7.5 \text{ thousand immigrants}$$

After immigration, the equilibrium wage is $6.50 per hour. Twenty-three thousand workers will be hired, of which there are 15,500 domestic workers and 7,500 immigrant workers.

Chapter 11

Review Questions

1. With an implicit labor-market contract, which is not legally enforceable, the punishment for cheating is that the other party terminates the employment relationship. Therefore, the principle underlying self-enforcement is that both parties must lose if the relationship is terminated. For both parties to lose, workers must be paid above what they could get elsewhere but below what they are worth to the employer. The latter conditions imply the existence of a surplus (a gap between marginal revenue product and alternative wages) that is divided between employer and employee.

3. Compensation schemes, such as efficiency wages, deferred payments, and tournaments, are made feasible by an expected long-term attachment between worker and firm. If small firms do not offer long enough job ladders to provide for career-long employment, long-term attachments will become less prevalent and the above three schemes less feasible. The growth of small firms, then, may mean more reliance on individual or group output-based pay schemes (or on closer supervision).

5. If management already has power over workers because workers' ability to go to other jobs is severely limited by unemployment or monopsony, then low wages may result. However, paying low wages is definitely not the way to *acquire* power if management currently lacks it. Underpaid workers have no incentives to tolerate demanding requirements from management, because their current job is not better (and may be worse) than one they could find elsewhere. However, if workers are paid more by one firm than they

could get elsewhere, they will tolerate heavy demands from their supervisors before deciding to quit. One way to acquire power over workers, therefore, is to overpay, not underpay, them.

7. The compensation scheme that pays workers less than they are worth initially, and more than they are worth later on, could result in this outcome. Older workers end up getting pay that is high relative to their productivity, and when they have to find another employer, their pay drops substantially. Younger workers, who are lower-paid under this scheme to begin with, do not experience such a drop in wages.

9. For strong performance incentives, the performance measure upon which pay is based (stock prices) must be strongly affected by CEO *effort*. The problem with using stock options as a performance measure is that they are affected by *overall* market conditions (both in the stock market and in the product market) as well as by CEO efforts to enhance the company's performance relative to its competitors. A bonus, if awarded based on the CEO's success in boosting the firm's *relative* performance, is superior in terms of incentives.

Problems

1. Charlie's employer will pay him $6 per hour. Increasing his wage from $5 to $6 per hour induces enough extra output to cause revenue to climb from $8 to $9.50—that is, a raise of $1 per hour yields $1.50 per hour in extra output, so the employer benefits from increasing his wage from $5 to $6. Increasing his wage beyond $6 per hour won't benefit his employer. An increase from $6 to $7 induces an increase in output from $9.50 to $10.25—only 75 cents per hour, not enough to pay for a $1 per hour increase in his wage.

3. a. The employer will hire such that the wage = *MRP*. If the wage rate is $5 per hour, the employer will want to hire 15 workers.
   b. If the wage rate is $6 per hour, with the new marginal product of labor, the employer will want to hire 16 workers.
   c. At a higher wage rate, the employer will want to hire more workers because the marginal productivity of labor increased with the higher ("efficiency") wage rate.

Chapter 12

Review Questions

1. Labor market discrimination is said to exist when workers who are productively equivalent are systematically paid different wages based on their race or ethnicity (or some other demographic characteristic unrelated to productivity). Because simple averages of earnings do not control for these characteristics, we cannot tell from them if labor market discrimination exists (Chinese and Japanese Americans, for example, may have average productive characteristics that greatly exceed those of white Americans).

3. Wage discrimination in the labor market is present when workers with the same productive characteristics are systematically paid differently because of the demographic group to which they belong. The critical issue in judging discrimination in this case is whether male and female high school teachers have the same productive characteristics.

   One area of information we would want to obtain concerns the human capital characteristics: do male and female teachers have the same levels of education and experience, and do they teach in comparable fields? A second area of information concerns working conditions. Are male teachers working longer hours (coaching sports or sponsoring clubs) or working in geographical areas that are associated with compensating wage differentials?

5. a. A wage subsidy paid to employers who hire disadvantaged black workers will shift the demand curve for such workers (stated in terms of the employee wage) to the right. This shift can cause employment to increase, the wage rate paid to black disadvantaged workers to increase, or both. The mix of wage and employment changes will depend on the shape of the supply curve of these workers. The changes in wages and employment induced by the subsidy will tend to overcome the adverse effect on unskilled blacks of labor market discrimination.

   b. Increasing the wages and employment opportunities of unskilled black workers will reduce incentives of these workers to invest in the training required to become skilled. Thus, one consequence of a wage subsidy just for unskilled black workers is that the subsidy may induce more to remain unskilled than would otherwise have been the case.

7. When nursing wages are raised above market-clearing levels, a surplus of nursing applicants will arise. The high wages, of course, will attract not only a large number of applicants but also a large number of very high-quality applicants; the fact that applicants are so plentiful allows the city to select only the best. Therefore, comparable worth may reduce the number of nursing jobs available, but it will also tend to increase the employment of high-quality nurses.

   Since the wages of nurses are tied to those of building inspectors, the city will be very reluctant to raise the wages of building inspectors even if there are shortages. Rather than raising wages as a recruiting device for building inspectors, the city may be tempted to lower its hiring standards and to employ building inspectors it would previously have rejected. Thus, employment opportunities for low-quality building inspectors may be enhanced by the comparable worth law.

9. a. Wage discrimination exists when compensation levels paid to one demographic group are lower than those paid to another demographic group that is exactly comparable in terms of productive characteristics. Using this definition, there would be no discrimination because both men and women would receive equal yearly compensation while working. This equal yearly compensation would, in fact, result in a pension fund for each man and woman that would have exactly the same present value at retirement age. However, because women live longer than men, this retirement

fund would be paid out over a longer period of time and thus would be paid out to retired women in smaller yearly amounts. The Supreme Court decision would require employers to put aside more pension funds for women, and it thus requires that working women have greater yearly compensation (while working) than comparable men.

b. The decision essentially mandates greater labor costs for women than for men of comparable productive characteristics, and by raising the firm's costs of hiring women, it could give firms incentives to substitute male for female workers (or capital for female workers).

Problems

1. Assuming that workers of one gender remain in their jobs, the index of dissimilarity indicates the percentage of the other group that would have to change occupations for the two genders to have equal occupational distributions. Assume that the males stay in the same jobs and then find the number of females in each job that would give them the same percentage distribution as males.

Occupation	Actual Female Distribution	If Female % = Male %	No. Needing to Change
A	20	40% = 28	28 − 20 = 8
B	25	40% = 28	28 − 25 = 3
C	25	20% = 14	14 − 25 = −11

As this table shows, 11 females need to change jobs—these 11 leave occupation C and move into occupations A and B. Eleven females equal 15.7 percent of the total, which is the index of dissimilarity.

3. See the following figure.

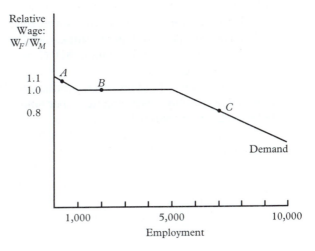

$W_F/W_M = 1.08$ when 200 women are hired at point A.
$W_F/W_M = 1$ when 2,000 women are hired at point B.
$W_F/W_M = 0.8$ when 7,000 women are hired at point C.

Discrimination only hinders female workers in this market if there are more than 5,000 hired. In fact, discrimination goes in favor of female workers when there are fewer than 1,000 hired.

5. The third column in the following table gives the estimated salary for each job based on the number of Hay Points according the estimated regression for males. The fourth column gives the percentage difference between the female salary and the male salary, relative to the male salary.

Hay Point	Salary ($)	Estimated Salary ($)	C-W Gap
200	1,200	1,380	180
310	1,300	1,479	179
425	1,500	1,582.5	82.5
500	1,580	1,650	70
550	1,635	1,695	60

Women, on average, are paid less than men with comparable Hay Point levels. As we see in the fourth column, the comparable worth gap appears to diminish with skill level.

7. The following graph shows the marginal product of labor. If the wage rate is $8 per hour, in the absence of discrimination, the employer would want to hire 12 workers. The profits to the employer would be equal to the area under the MRP_L (demand curve) above the (blue) horizontal wage line. If 12 workers are hired, this triangular area ABC is calculated as $.5(20 - 8)(12) = \$72$.

If the employer discriminates and only hires 10 female workers, the profits can be calculated as the trapezoidal area $ABDF$, which is the sum of the triangle AGF and the rectangle $BDFG$, as follows: Area $= .5(20 - 10)(10) + (2)(10) = 50 + 20 = \$70$.

Thus, if the employer discriminates and hires only 10 females, the discriminating employer is giving up $2 per hour in profits, which is the difference between the two areas (CDF).

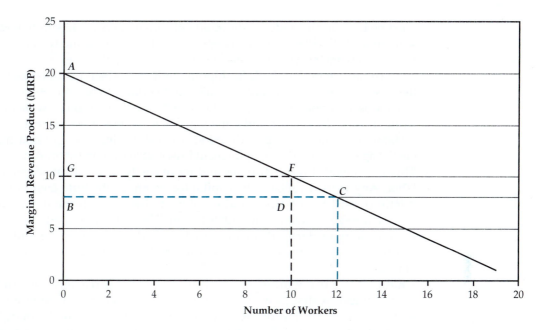

Chapter 13

Review Questions

1. Since a reduction in the price of capital equipment will stimulate the purchase of capital equipment, a union should be concerned whether its members are gross complements or gross substitutes with capital. In the former case, the proposed policy (reducing the price of capital) would cause the demand for union members to rise, while in the latter, their demand would fall. Other things equal, the more rapidly the demand for labor is shifting out, the smaller will be the reduction in employment associated with any union-induced wage gain (assuming the collective bargaining agreement lies on the labor demand curve). Hence, unions representing groups that are gross complements (substitutes) with capital would benefit (lose) from the policy change.

   Evidence cited in the text suggests that capital and skilled labor may be gross complements, but capital and unskilled labor are gross substitutes. This suggests that union leaders representing the latter type of workers will be opposed to the legislation, while union leaders representing the former may favor it.

3. The provisions of the Jones Act affect the demand for labor in the U.S. shipping industry in at least two ways. First, the provision that 50 percent of all U.S. government cargo must be transported in U.S.-owned ships makes the price elasticity of demand for U.S. shipping in the output market less elastic. Second, the restriction that at least 90 percent of the crews of U.S. ships

must be U.S. citizens reduces the ability of ship owners to substitute foreign seamen for U.S. citizens. Both changes cause the wage elasticity of demand for U.S. crew members to be less elastic than it would otherwise be.

To the extent that the U.S. shipping industry is heavily unionized and there is little competition between union and nonunion crew members (a reasonable assumption), the wage elasticity of demand for union crew members would become less elastic under the Jones Act. As stressed in the text, inelastic labor demand curves permit unions to push for increases in their members' wages without large employment losses, at least in the short run.

5. This law makes it more difficult and more costly to substitute capital for labor. Any worker replaced by capital (or another substitute factor of production) must be retrained and employed elsewhere in the firm, which clearly raises the cost of this substitution. Thus, this law tends to reduce the elasticity of demand for union labor, and it increases the ability of unions to raise wages without reducing their members' employment very much.

7. Unions may raise worker productivity for several reasons. One of the more obvious is that as wages are increased, firms cut back employment and substitute capital for labor. Both actions tend to raise the marginal productivity of labor. To survive in a competitive market, profit-maximizing firms must raise the marginal productivity of labor whenever wages increase.

Another reason unions raise productivity is that the high wages unionized employers offer attract a large pool of applicants, and employers are able to select the best applicants. Moreover, the reduction in turnover that we observe in unionized plants increases firms' incentives to provide specific training to their workers, and the seniority system that unions typically implement encourages older workers to help train younger workers (they can do so without fear that the younger workers will compete for their jobs when fully trained).

Because many of these sources of increased productivity are responses by firms to higher wages, they tend to mitigate the effects of unionization on costs. Some nonunion firms deliberately pay high wages to attract and retain able employees, and they often pursue this strategy even without the implicit threat of becoming unionized. However, the fact that firms generally pay the union wage only after their employees become organized suggests that they believe unions raise labor costs to a greater extent than they raise worker productivity.

What the quotation in question 7 overlooks is that increases in productivity must be measured against increases in costs. If unions enhance productivity to a greater extent than they increase costs of production, then clearly, employers should take a much less antagonistic approach to unions. If, however, enhancements in labor productivity are smaller than increases in labor costs, employer profitability will decline under unionization.

Problems

1. Equating the employer concession curve and the union resistance curve,

$$2 + 0.5S = 11 + 0.5S0.1S^2$$
$$S^2 = 9/0.1; S = 9.486 \text{ days}$$
$$W = 2 + 0.5S = 2 + 0.5(9.486) = 6.75\%$$

3. Relative wage advantage $= (8 - 5)/5 = 60\%$
   True absolute effect $= (8 - 6)/6 = 33\%$

   Because the nonunionized wage is lower than the equilibrium wage, the relative wage advantage of the unionized workers is greater than their true absolute effect.

5. The demand curves for the factory are graphed in the following figure.

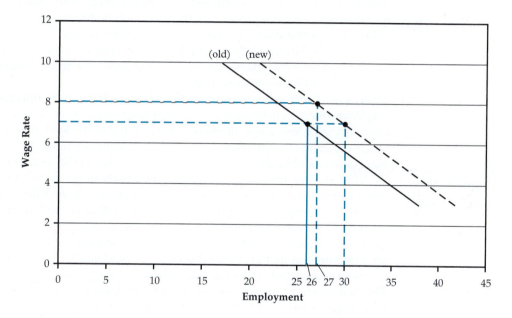

Both the company official and the union leader are correct. Currently at $7 per hour, the employers would like to hire 26 employees. If the union were successful with the wage negotiations, along with the growing demand, the firm would want to hire 27 employees. So the union leader is correct. But, if the union were not successful in its attempt to raise wages, the firm would want to hire 30 employees. So the company official is also correct. The effect of a successful wage negotiation in the presence of growing demand is to reduce the rate of growth of employment.

7. At a wage rate of $7.50, there will be 4,500 workers employed. The union relative wage advantage is $R = (8 - 7.5)/7.5 = .067$.

Chapter 14

Review Questions

1. The two policy goals are not compatible in the short run. An increase in unemployment compensation benefits reduces the costs to unemployed workers of additional job search; this will lead them to extend their duration of unemployment and search for better-paying jobs. In the short run, increasing unemployment compensation benefits will increase the unemployment rate.

   In the long run, however, the two policy goals may be compatible. If the prolonged durations of job search lead to better matches of workers and jobs, the chances that workers will become unemployed in the future will diminish. That is, the better matches will reduce both the probability that workers will quit their jobs and the probability that they will be fired. This reduced probability of entering unemployment will reduce the unemployment rate in the long run. Whether the reduction in the unemployment rate due to the smaller incidence of unemployment outweighs the increase due to the longer spells of unemployment is an open question.

3. When a worker first becomes unemployed, he or she may be optimistic about employment opportunities and set a high reservation wage. However, if over time only very low wage offers are received, the individual may realize that the distribution of wage offers is lower than initially assumed. This revision of expectations would also cause a downward revision of the reservation wage.

   In fact, even if workers' initial perceptions about the distribution of wage offers were correct, this distribution might systematically shift down over time. For example, employers might use the length of time an individual had been unemployed as a signal of the individual's relatively low productivity and might moderate wage offers accordingly. A systematically declining wage-offer distribution that arises for this reason would similarly cause reservation wages to decline as durations of unemployment lengthened.

5. This policy should have two effects on the unemployment rate. First, by reducing the value of benefits to unemployed workers, it should reduce the duration of their spells of unemployment. In other words, by taxing unemployment insurance benefits, the government is in effect reducing those benefits, and the reduction in benefits increases the marginal costs of remaining unemployed for an additional period of time. Thus, workers will tend to be less choosy about job offers they accept and should be induced to reduce the amount of time they spend searching for additional job offers. However, by reducing job search, the taxation of UI benefits may lead to poorer matches between worker and employer, thus creating higher turnover (and more unemployment) in the long run.

   Second, because unemployed workers are now receiving less compensation from the government, those in jobs in which layoffs frequently occur will find them less attractive than they previously did. Employers who offer these jobs will have more difficulty attracting employees unless they raise wages (assuming workers have other job options). This compensating wage differential will act as a penalty for high layoff rates, and this penalty should induce firms to reduce layoffs to some extent. A reduced propensity to lay off workers, of course, should reduce the unemployment rate (other things being equal).

7. The level of unemployment is affected by flows into and out of the pool of unemployed workers. Restricting employers' ability to fire workers will reduce the flow of workers *into* the pool, thus tending to reduce unemployment.

However, because these restrictions increase the costs of hiring workers (the costs of firing them are a quasi-fixed cost of employment), firms will tend to reduce their *hiring* of labor. This reduction will slow the flows out of the unemployed pool, so one cannot predict the overall effect of the restrictions on the unemployment rate.

Problems

1. To make the calculations easier, we can drop the millions terms. The initial unemployment rate is $100 \times U/(U + E) = 100 \times 10/(10 + 120) = 7.69$ percent. The initial labor force participation rate is $100 \times (U + E)/(U + E + N) = 100 \times (10 + 120)/(10 + 120 + 70) = 65.0$ percent.

The new levels of the three measures (in millions) are as follows:

$U_1 = U_0 + EU + NU - UE - UN = 10 + 1.8 + 1.3 - 2.2 - 1.7 = 9.2$
$E_1 = E_0 + UE + NE - EU - EN = 120 + 2.2 + 4.5 - 1.8 - 3.0 = 121.9$
$N_1 = N_0 + EN + UN - NE - NU = 70 + 3.0 + 1.7 - 4.5 - 1.3 = 68.9$

The new rates are:

Unemployment rate $= 100 \times 9.2/(131.1) = 7.02$ percent
Labor force participation $= 100 \times 131.1/200 = 65.55$ percent

3. See the following figure.

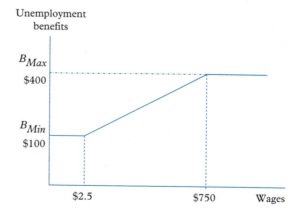

a. At wage = \$100, $B = 0.4(100) + 100 = \$140$, replacement rate = $140/100 = 1.4$
    At wage = \$200, $B = 0.4(200) + 100 = \$180$, replacement rate = $180/200 = 0.9$
    At wage = 1000, $B = 0.4(1000) + 100 = 500$, replacement rate = $500/1000 = 0.5$
b. When $B_{min} = \$100$, $W_{min} = \$2.5$
    When $B_{max} = 400$, $W_{max} = \$750$
5. The graph is as follows:

Experience - Rated UI Tax Rates

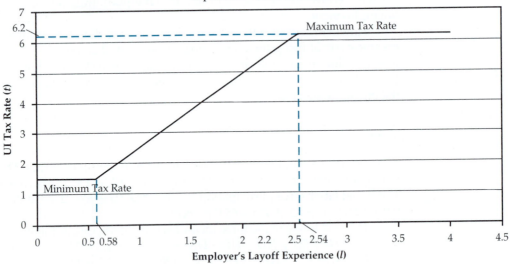

If the firm's layoff experience is below l_{min}, the firm pays the minimum tax rate. After the firm's layoff experience reaches the critical value of l_{min}, the firm's UI tax rate rises with increased layoff experience until it reaches the maximum tax rate.
To calculate the firm's critical value of layoff experience (l_{min}):
$$1.5 = .1 + 2.4\ l_{min} \rightarrow l_{min} = .58 \text{ percent}$$
To calculate the firm's ceiling value of layoff experience (l_{max}):
$$6.2 = .1 + 2.4\ l_{max} \rightarrow l_{max} = 2.54 \text{ percent}$$

Chapter 15

Review Questions

1. Increasing the investment tax credit reduces the price of capital and therefore has two possible effects on the demand for labor. If labor and capital are complements in production or are gross complements, then the tax credit will shift the labor demand curve to the right and tend to increase wages and employment. If, however, capital and labor are gross substitutes, then this tax credit could result in a decreased demand for labor.

We learned from chapter 4 that capital and unskilled labor are more likely to be substitutes in production than are skilled labor and capital; therefore, this investment tax credit is more likely to negatively affect the demand for unskilled labor than for skilled labor. If so, there will be more downward pressure on the wages of unskilled workers, and the resulting decline in the relative wages of the lowest-paid workers tends to widen the dispersion of earnings.

3. Forbidding employers to replace striking workers will have ambiguous effects on the dispersion of earnings. On the one hand, we know that forbidding striker replacement should increase the power of unions to raise the wages of their members, and we know that unions have historically raised the wages of less-skilled members relative to the wages of those who are more skilled. Thus, if union power is enhanced, the primary beneficiaries will be lower-skilled union workers, and this effect should tend to equalize the distribution of earnings.

On the other hand, we need to consider the effects on those who would have worked as replacements. We know that unions are more prevalent in large firms, which pay higher wages anyway, and we can suppose that workers who wish to work as replacements are attracted to these jobs because they can improve their earnings. By encouraging higher wages in large, unionized firms, forbidding striker replacement could cause a spillover effect that reduces wages in the nonunionized sector. Thus, prohibiting striker replacement may actually drive down wages paid to those now in the small-firm, nonunion sector and create a greater dispersion in earnings.

5. Increasing the subsidy guaranteed to those who do not work, but holding constant a nonzero effective wage rate, will clearly cause a reduction in labor supply. This reduction will take two forms: some who worked before may decide to withdraw from the labor force, and some who worked before may reduce their hours of work. These two forms of labor supply reduction have quite different effects on the distribution of *earnings*.

It is reasonable to suppose that the expected labor supply reductions will come mainly from workers with the lowest level of earnings. Thus, when labor force *withdrawal* takes place, those with the lowest earnings are leaving the labor force, and this *withdrawal* will tend to equalize the distribution of earnings (those at the lower end exit from the distribution).

Reduced hours of work among those who continue in the labor force, however, will have the opposite effect on the distribution of earnings if this labor supply response is also focused among those with the lowest level of earnings. Reductions in working hours will lower the earnings of these low-wage workers further, which will tend to widen the dispersion of earnings.

Therefore, while this increased generosity of the negative income tax program serves to equalize the distribution of *income* (which includes the subsidies), the labor supply responses can tend to either narrow or widen the dispersion of earnings.

7. Proposal "a" increases the cost of employing high-wage (skilled) labor and capital. This will have ambiguous effects on the demand curve for unskilled workers. On the one hand, it will tend to cause unskilled workers to be substituted for skilled workers and/or capital (assuming they are substitutes in production). On the other hand, the costs of production rise and the scale effect will tend to reduce both output and the demand for all workers (including the unskilled).

If the substitution effect dominates, the demand curve for the unskilled shifts to the right, tending to increase their employment and wage rate. If the scale effect dominates (or if the unskilled are complements in production with skilled labor and capital), then the demand curve for them shifts left, and their wage rate and employment level would decrease.

Proposal "b" cuts the cost of employing all labor, but the percentage decrease is greatest for the low-paid (unskilled). Thus, the proposal cuts the cost of unskilled labor relative to that of both capital and skilled labor. This will unambiguously shift the demand for unskilled labor to the right (keeping the employee wage on the vertical axis), because both the scale and the substitution effects work in the same direction. This will tend to increase both unskilled employment and the wages received by unskilled employees.

Proposal "b" is better for accomplishing the government's goal of improving the earnings of the unskilled, because the scale effect tends to increase, not reduce, the demand for their services.

Problems

1. (Appendix) First, order the students by income to find the poorest 20 percent, next poorest 20 percent, middle 20 percent, next richest 20 percent, and richest 20 percent (see the following table). Then, find the total income—in this case, $344,000. Divide the income in each 20 percent group by the total income to find its share of income. Finally, calculate the cumulative share of income.

Now graph this information, making sure that the cumulative share of income goes on the vertical axis and cumulative share of households goes on the horizontal axis (see the following figure). (An even more precise Lorenz curve can be graphed by breaking the data into tenths rather than fifths.)

To find the Gini coefficient, use the method outlined in the appendix to find the area below the Lorenz curve. This area equals .1 plus the area of the four rectangles whose bases are .2 and whose heights are the cumulative shares of income for the first four income groups. $Area = .1 + (.2 \times .128) + (.2 \times .302) + (.2 \times .494) + (.2 \times .703) = .1 + .3254 = .4254$. The Gini coefficient equals (0.5 − area under the Lorenz curve)/0.5 = $(0.5 - .4254)/0.5 = .1492$.

Name	Income	Share of Income	Cumulative Share of Income
		Bottom 20%	
Billy	$20,000	$44,000/$344,000 = .128	.128
Kasia	$24,000		
		Second 20%	
Rose	$29,000	$60,000/$344,000 = .174	.128 + .174 = .302
Charlie	$31,000		
		Middle 20%	
Yukiko	$32,000	$66,000/$344,000 = .192	.302 + .192 = .494
Nina	$34,000		
		Fourth 20%	
Thomas	$35,000	$72,000/$344,000 = .209	.494 + .209 = .703
Raul	$37,000		
		Top 20%	
Becky	$42,000	$102,000/$344,000 = .297	.703 + .297 = 1.000
Willis	$60,000		

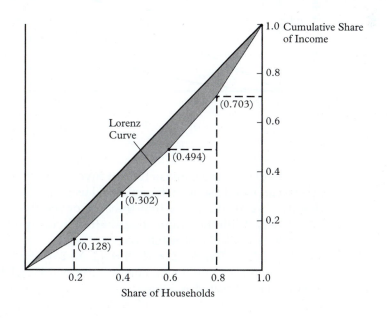

3. a.

Ratio of Earnings at Given Percentiles	1990	2005
90:10	1.53	1.41
90:50	1.24	1.22
50:10	1.23	1.16

b. All of the earnings ratios fell from 1990 to 2005. The fact that the fall in the 90:50 ratio was smaller than the fall in the 50:10 ratio indicates that the move toward equality was smaller at the upper end of the earnings distribution than at the lower end.

5.

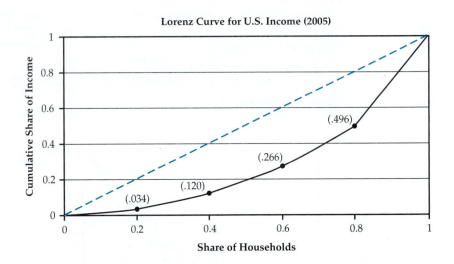

Calculating the Gini coefficient involves breaking the area under the Lorenz curve into a series of triangles and rectangles, as shown in the appendix (Figure 15A.3). We know that the area of the five triangles sums to 0.1 ($.2 \times 1 \times .5$). With the income distribution in this problem, the areas of the rectangles are calculated as follows:

$$(.2 \times .034) + (.2 \times .120) + (.2 \times .266) + (.2 \times .496) = .1832.$$

Thus, the area under the Lorenz curve is .2832 ($.1 + .1832$), and the Gini coefficient is calculated as follows:

$$(.5 - .2832)/.5 = .4336$$

Chapter 16

Review Questions

1. Comparative advantage is driven by the internal opportunity costs of producing the two goods—the trade-off that must be made in obtaining more of one good—not by differences in per-capita wealth or consumption. Thus, the population of B is irrelevant to the analysis.

3. The availability of cheaper foreign labor creates both a substitution and a scale effect. The substitution of foreign for American production workers clearly reduces employment in the United States, and the size of the employment loss depends on how easily it is to substitute foreign for American workers. The size of the substitution effect also depends in part on the elasticity of the labor supply curve of Americans in this industry. If the supply curve is elastic, Americans will readily leave the industry and their wages will not fall by much; if it is relatively inelastic, American wages will fall and this could make the substitution effect smaller.

   There will be a scale effect, however. As alarm systems fall in price, more Americans may buy them—increasing the demand for workers who are complements in production with those overseas: installers, sales people, and those who monitor and repair the systems. The scale effect will be larger if the demand for alarms is more elastic and if the share of total cost that is tied to production workers is larger.

5. As discussed in the text, the number of jobs in a society depends on how well supply and demand are equated in the labor market—not on a society's technology or its level of trade. Trade depends on comparative advantage, which in turn depends on the internal opportunity costs of producing goods and services (see Review Question 1).

7. The answer to this is similar to the answer to Review Question 4. Economic theory does suggest that by allowing greater specialization based on comparative advantage, reducing trade barriers will increase the overall consumption that is possible in the countries that trade. The goal of a society, however, is not to maximize consumption; it is to maximize the utility of individuals. If, as we discussed at the end of chapter 4, some policy change increased the income of the richest man in society by $1 billion but reduced the income of one million poor people by $500 each, the total income in society would rise by $500 million; however, the utility gains to the richest man may be close to nil, while the utility losses of the million poor people who lose $500 may be much larger. This $500 million gain in income would therefore be accompanied by an overall loss in utility. Given that we cannot measure utility, the only way we can find out if society has gained in utility levels is to see if the gainers (in this case, the richest man) would be willing to give $500 to each of the losers; if he is willing and makes the payments, then

the losers are held harmless—and there is a gainer without any losers (so the transaction would meet the Pareto criteria discussed in chapter 1).

Problems

1. a. In Country M, 60 million refrigerators would be given up in order to produce 50 million bicycles. The opportunity cost of each bicycle is 60/50, or 1.2, refrigerators. In Country N, 50 million refrigerators would be given up in order to produce 75 million bicycles. The opportunity cost of each bicycle is 50/75, or 0.67, refrigerators.

   In Country M, 50 million bicycles would have to be given up to produce 60 million refrigerators, so the opportunity cost of refrigerators is 50/60, or 0.83, bicycles. In Country N, 75 million bicycles would have to be given up to produce 50 million refrigerators, so the opportunity cost of refrigerators is 75/50, or 1.5, bicycles.

   b. Country N has a comparative advantage in bicycles because the opportunity cost of bicycles is lower in Country N. That is, fewer refrigerators would be given up for each bicycle produced.

   c. Yes, the two countries should trade. Country N should produce bicycles and Country M should produce refrigerators.

3. In the rich country, the marginal productivity of customer services representatives is

$$MP_L = 17 - .6L = 17 - .6(10) = 11.$$

In the poor country, the marginal productivity of customer services representatives is

$$MP_L = 11 - .8L = 11 - .8(5) = 7.$$

Comparing the ratio of wages to marginal productivity in the two countries:

Rich country: $W/MP_L = \$20/11 = \$1.82$ per unit
Poor country: $W/MP_L = \$10/7 = \$1.43$ per unit

In the poor country, the marginal cost of a unit of service is $1.43, while in the rich country it is $1.82 per unit. Thus, a firm in a rich country thinking of moving 1,000 jobs to the poor country could reduce costs by doing so. If it did move 1,000 jobs, MP_L in the rich country would rise to $17 - .6(9) = 11.6$. MP_L in the poor country would fall to $11 - .8(6) = 6.2$. So even with 1,000 jobs moved, the per-unit cost in the rich country (at $20/11.6 = 1.72$) is still above that in the poor country ($10/6.2 = 1.61$). Thus, the firm would want to consider moving more than 1,000 jobs to the poorer country.

Name Index

A

Abbott, Michael G., 375n
Abdulkadiroglu, Atila, 338n
Abowd, John M., 185, 299n, 303n, 399n, 415n, 486n, 490n
Abraham, Katharine G., 314n
Abraham, Steven E., 490n
Abramitzky, Ran, 357n
Abrams, Elliott, 363n
Abrams, Franklin S., 363n
Acemoglu, Daron, 124n, 177n, 575n
Acharya, Viral, 169
Adams, James D., 130n
Adams, Scott, 140n, 295n
Addison, John T., 124n, 138n, 479n, 507n, 515n
Aguiar, Mark, 562n
Aizer, Anna, 240n
Akerlof, George A., 338n, 401n, 542n, 555n
Akerman, Anders, 572n, 604n
Akke, Randall, 438n
Alchian, Armen, 97n
Allen, Steven G., 292n, 405n
Alston, Lee J., 417n
Altman, Morris, 417
Altman, Stuart H., 77
Altonji, Joseph G., 194n, 316n, 323n, 337n
Amin, Shanina, 245
Amin, Vikesh, 330n
Amuedo-Dorantes, Catalina, 246n
Anderson, David A., 303n
Anderson, James E., 606n
Anderson, Patricia M., 101n, 254n, 257n, 374n, 551n, 552n
Andersson, Henrik, 271n
Andreoni, James, 417
Angrist, Joshua D., 314n, 324n, 338n
Antecol, Heather, 359n
Arai, Mahmood, 463
Arkolakis, Costas, 596n
Artuc, Erhan, 603n
Ash, Michael, 511n
Ashenfelter, Orley, 56, 134n, 156n, 194n, 199, 299n, 303n, 328n, 330n, 338n, 341, 461n, 487n, 496n, 499n, 502n, 538n
Ashmore, David, 538n
Atkinson, Anthony B., 537n, 564n
Attfield, Clifford L. F., 557n
Auerbach, Alan, 219n
Austen-Smith, David, 315n

Autor, David H., 124n, 141n, 182, 218n, 575n, 576n, 577n, 578n, 581n, 601n, 602n, 604n
Averett, Susan, 553n
Aydemir, Abdurrahman, 369n
Azariadis, Costas, 548n

B

Baghai, Ramin, 169
Baicker, Katherine, 552, 609n, 610n, 611n
Baily, Martin, 548n
Baker, Bryan C., 361n
Baker, George, 183n, 389n, 390n, 400n, 408n
Baldwin, Marjorie, 428n, 447n
Ball, Laurence, 555n, 598n
Barkume, Anthony, 176n
Barnow, Burt S., 68n
Barrow, Lisa, 436n
Bartel, Ann P., 321n, 351n
Barth, Erling, 414n
Bartik, Timothy J., 104n
Bartling, Bjorn, 403n
Bassi, Laurie J., 177n, 321n
Basu, Kaushik, 245
Batchelder, Lily, 241n
Baumol, William J., 347n
Bawden, Lee, 386n
Bayard, Kimberly, 429n
Bazerman, Max H., 501n
Beach, Charles M., 375n
Becker, Brian E., 486n
Becker, Gary, 26n, 440n
Bedard, Kelly, 337n
Belfield, Clive R., 479n, 515n
Beller, Andrea H., 261n
Bellmann, Lutz, 124n, 543n
Belzer, Michael, 126, 491
Belzil, Christian, 532n, 539n
Bender, Keith A., 509n
Bender, Stefan, 538n
Benhabib, Jess, 347n
Bennett, Amanda, 557n
Berger, Mark C., 379n
Berlinski, Samuel, 154n
Berman, Eli, 355, 359n
Bernhardt, Dan, 411n
Bernhofen, Daniel M., 597
Bernstein, Jared, 175n
Bertola, Giuseppe, 510n
Bertrand, Marianne, 98n, 241n, 398n, 399n, 425n, 438n, 447n, 463
Betts, Julian R., 316n

Bewley, Truman F., 547n
Bhagwati, Jagdish, 602n
Bhaskar, V., 29n, 154n, 155n
Biddle, Jeff E., 204n, 261
Bils, Mark, 392n, 547n
Bingley, Paul, 246n
Bishop, John H., 104n, 169n, 170, 179, 179n
Bishop, Kelly, 217n
Black, Dan A., 295, 316n, 379n, 415n, 451n
Black, Sandra E., 445n, 511n
Blanchard, Olivier Jean, 541n, 542n
Blanchflower, David, 180n, 507n, 508n, 510n, 511n, 543n
Blanco, German, 341n
Blank, Rebecca, 181n, 222n
Blasi, Joseph, 398n
Blau, Francine D., 75n, 217n, 238n, 240n, 257n, 428n, 429n, 431n, 432n, 451n, 510n
Bleakley, Hoyt, 440n, 528n
Blien, Uwe, 543n
Blinder, Alan S., 396n, 449n, 603
Bloch, Farrell E., 377n
Bloemen, Hans G., 213n, 246n
Bloom, David, 502n
Blundell, Richard, 194n, 240n
Boal, William M., 510n
Bodenhorn, Howard, 553n
Bognanno, Michael L., 408n
Boisso, Dale, 428n
Boning, Brent, 398n
Bordo, Michael D., 552
Borjas, George, 168n, 355n, 358n, 359n, 369n, 439n, 575n, 604n
Bound, John, 315, 434n, 574n
Boustan, Leah, 357n
Bowen, William G., 327n
Bowlus, Audra J., 432n
Bowman, W. R., 181n
Bratsberg, Bernt, 359n
Brewer, Mike, 194n
Broman, Susan B., 496n
Bronars, Stephen G., 401n, 510n, 511n
Brown, Alessio J. G., 614n
Brown, Charles, 321n
Brown, Claire, 239n
Brown, Drusilla K., 607n
Brown, James N., 414n
Brown, John C., 597
Brown, Michelle, 510n
Brown, Robert W., 85
Brummund, Peter, 428n
Bryson, Alex, 507n, 508n

Buchmuller, Thomas C., 103, 509*n*
Budd, John W., 509*n*
Buffum, David, 448
Burfisher, Mary E., 602*n*
Burghardt, John, 342*n*
Burkhauser, Richard V., 117*n*, 138*n*, 139*n*
Burtless, Gary, 221*n*
Butcher, Kristin F., 373
Butler, Richard J., 428*n*, 447*n*
Byers, James F., 551*n*
Bythell, Duncan, 142

C

Cameron, Stephen V., 314*n*
Campbell, Carl M., III, 403*n*
Cappelli, Peter, 404*n*
Card, David, 117*n*, 137*n*, 181*n*, 321*n*, 328*n*, 359*n*, 368*n*, 369*n*, 370, 392, 436*n*, 461*n*, 475*n*, 491, 496*n*, 508*n*, 539*n*, 543*n*, 546*n*, 552*n*, 575*n*, 579*n*
Carling, Kenneth, 538*n*
Carmichael, H. Lorne, 387*n*, 404*n*
Carneiro, Pedro, 314*n*, 330*n*, 436*n*, 440*n*
Carpenter, Christopher S., 423*n*
Carpenter, Jeffrey, 409*n*
Carruth, Alan A., 147
Castillo, Marco, 417
Chandra, Amitabh, 434*n*
Chang, Yongsung, 392*n*, 547*n*
Chari, Anusha, 141*n*
Charles, Kerwin Kofi, 317*n*, 445*n*
Chaudhuri, Shubham, 603*n*
Chauvin, Keith, 404*n*
Chay, Kenneth Y., 463*n*
Chen, M. Keith, 313
Chen, Paul, 403*n*
Chen, Stacy H., 324*n*
Chen, Susan, 218*n*
Cherchye, Lauren, 240*n*
Chetty, Raj, 226*n*, 537*n*, 539*n*
Chiappori, Pierre-Andre, 240*n*
Chin, Aimee, 440*n*
Chirinko, Robert S., 121*n*
Chiswick, Barry R., 359*n*, 439*n*, 552*n*
Chou, Shin-Yi, 237
Christofides, Louis N., 546*n*
Chugh, Dolly, 438*n*
Ciccone, Antonio, 130*n*
Clark, Melissa A., 314*n*
Clark, Robert L., 405*n*
Clotfelter Charles T., 338*n*
Coffey, Bentley, 409*n*
Cohen-Goldner, Sarit, 370
Cole, Courtney C., 253*n*
Cole, Matthew A., 273*n*
Collins, William J., 338*n*, 353, 461*n*
Conte, Michael A., 396*n*
Cook, Philip J., 408*n*
Cornwall, Richard R., 463*n*
Cortes, Kalena, 379
Cortes, Patricia, 366*n*
Costa, Dora L., 174*n*, 357*n*
Costinot, Arnaud, 596*n*

Couch, Kenneth A., 117*n*, 139*n*, 528*n*
Courty, Pascal, 396*n*
Cox, James, 493*n*
Cramton, Peter C., 496*n*, 497, 497*n*
Crawford, David L., 321*n*
Crawford, Vincent P., 199, 501*n*
Croson, Rachel, 409*n*, 429*n*
Cuñat, Vicente, 604*n*
Currie, Janet, 423*n*
Cutler, David, 312*n*

D

Dahl, Gordon B., 502*n*
Daly, Mary C., 555*n*
Daniel, Christophe, 273*n*
Darity, William, Jr., 439
Davis, Steven J., 602*n*
Deere, Donald R., 510*n*, 511*n*
DeFreitas, Gregory, 373*n*
De La Rica, Sara, 475*n*
Del Bono, Emilia, 273*n*
DeLeire, Thomas, 281, 423*n*
DellaVigna, Stefano, 26*n*
Demsetz, Rebecca S., 488*n*
De Rock, Bram, 240*n*
Deschenes, Olivier, 538*n*
DeVaro, Jed, 429*n*
Devereux, Paul J., 546*n*
Devine, Theresa, 532*n*
DeVyver, Frank T., 69
Dickens, William T., 492*n*, 546*n*, 555*n*
Dickerson, A. P., 496*n*
DiNardo, John, 103, 507*n*, 509*n*, 581*n*
Disney, Richard, 253*n*
Dohmen, Thomas, 390, 394*n*
Dominitz, Jeff, 316*n*
Donald, Stephen, 254*n*
Donohue, John J., III, 463*n*, 464*n*
Doran, Kirk, 199
Dorn, David, 577*n*, 601*n*, 602*n*, 604*n*
Dorsey, Stuart, 379*n*
Drago, Robert, 400*n*
Dube, Arindrajit, 137*n*, 140*n*
Duflo, Ester, 461*n*
Duggan, Mark G., 218*n*
Dumond, J. Michael, 509*n*
Duncan, George, 509*n*
Dunne, Timothy, 510*n*
Durbin, David L., 220
Dustmann, Christian, 359*n*
Dynarski, Susan M., 338*n*

E

Edin, Per-Anders, 403*n*
Edmonds, Eric V., 245
Ehrenberg, Ronald, 98*n*, 194*n*, 243*n*, 251*n*, 301*n*, 375*n*, 376*n*, 386*n*, 458*n*, 469*n*, 470*n*, 471*n*
Eisenbrey, Ross, 175*n*
Eissa, Nada, 216, 226*n*
Elliott, Robert R. J., 273*n*
Ellwood, David T., 241*n*

Eren, Ozkan, 507*n*
Eriksson, Katherine, 357*n*
Ewing, Bradley T., 403*n*

F

Faberman, R. Jason, 602*n*
Fairlie, Robert W., 435*n*, 554*n*
Fairris, David, 417*n*
Falch, Torberg, 156*n*, 452*n*
Falk, Armin, 390, 394*n*
Famulari, Melissa, 401*n*
Farber, Henry, 156*n*, 488*n*, 489*n*, 501*n*, 502*n*, 504*n*, 519*n*, 523*n*, 538*n*
Fechter, Alan E., 77
Federman, Maya N., 364*n*
Feenstra, Robert C., 605*n*
Fehr, Ernst, 391*n*, 403*n*
Feldstein, Martin, 219
Ferber, Marianne A., 238*n*, 240*n*, 428*n*, 431*n*, 451*n*
Ferris, Ann E., 528*n*
Feynman, Richard T., 27
Feyrer, James, 241*n*
Fields, Gary S., 251*n*, 352*n*
Finegan, T. Aldrich, 246*n*
Fischer, Stanley, 403*n*
Fishelson, Gideon, 403*n*
Flaim, Paul, 527*n*
Flanagan, Robert, 492*n*, 547*n*
Flinn, Christopher J., 375*n*
Flores, Carlos A., 341*n*
Flores-Lagunes, Alfonso, 341*n*
Ford, Henry, 402
Fortin, Nicole M., 579*n*, 581*n*
Foster, Andrew D., 390
Fox, Jeremy T., 414*n*
Francesconi, Marco, 194*n*
Frank, Robert H., 242*n*, 408*n*, 414*n*
Frazis, Harley, 170*n*, 325*n*, 337*n*
Frederiksen, Anders, 376*n*
Freeman, Richard, 75*n*, 104*n*, 359*n*, 398*n*, 434*n*, 474*n*, 476*n*, 488*n*, 490*n*, 507*n*, 508*n*, 510*n*, 511*n*, 512*n*, 515, 515*n*, 569, 575*n*, 596*n*, 604*n*
Friedberg, Leora, 253*n*
Friedman, John, 226*n*
Frydman, Carola, 399*n*
Fryer, Roland G., Jr., 315*n*, 391*n*, 436*n*, 463
Fuhrer, Jeffrey C., 528*n*
Funk, Jonas P., 446*n*
Furtado, Delia, 366*n*, 367*n*

G

Galenson, David, 283
Galizzi, Monica, 375*n*
Gang, Ira N., 317*n*
Garfinkel, Irwin, 258*n*
Garvey, Gerald T., 400*n*
Gauthier-Loiselle, Marjolaine, 371*n*
Gelber, Alexander M., 238*n*
George, Peter, 439*n*

Gera, Surendra, 403*n*
Gibbons, Robert, 396*n*, 400*n*, 411*n*, 412*n*
Gill, Andrew M., 435*n*
Gilleskie, Donna B., 379*n*
Gittleman, Maury, 170*n*, 325*n*
Gleick, James, 347*n*
Gneezy, Uri, 409*n*, 429*n*
Godi, Gopi Shah, 253*n*
Goette, Lorenz, 391*n*, 546*n*
Goldberg, Pinelopi Koujianou, 605*n*, 614*n*
Golden, Miriam, 475*n*
Goldfarb, Robert S., 414*n*
Goldin, Claudia, 131*n*, 241*n*, 316*n*, 327*n*, 425*n*, 427, 552, 571
Gönsül, Füsun, 527*n*
Goos, Maarten, 577*n*
Gordon, David M., 453*n*
Gottschalk, Peter, 104*n*, 578*n*
Grafova, Irina B., 312*n*
Graham, John W., 261*n*
Gramm, Cynthia L., 497*n*
Grant, Darren, 508*n*
Greenaway, David, 596*n*
Greenberg, David H., 341*n*
Grenier, Gilles, 403*n*
Grogger, Jeffrey, 222*n*, 223*n*, 369*n*
Groot, Wim, 337*n*
Groshen, Erica L., 403*n*, 425*n*, 447*n*, 546*n*
Grossman, Michael, 237
Grossman, Sanford, 548*n*
Gruber, Jonathan, 103, 253*n*, 330*n*, 495*n*
Gu, Wulong, 498*n*
Guadalupe, Maria, 604*n*
Guilkey, David, 439
Gunderson, Morley, 497*n*
Gupta, Nabanita Datta, 426*n*
Guryan, Jonathan, 445*n*

H

Haber, Sheldon E., 414*n*
Haley, M. Ryan, 395*n*
Hall, Brian J., 399*n*
Hall, Robert E., 547*n*
Hallock, Kevin F., 447*n*, 528*n*
Haltiwanger, John C., 554*n*, 602*n*
Ham, John C., 194*n*, 248*n*
Hamermesh, Daniel S., 101*n*, 124, 124*n*, 130*n*, 204*n*, 237, 243*n*, 254*n*, 261, 270*n*, 437
Hamersma, Sasrah, 104*n*
Hamilton, Barton H., 396*n*
Hanes, Christopher, 546*n*
Hansen, Benjamin, 138*n*
Hansen, Bent, 68*n*
Hansen, W. Lee, 551*n*
Hanson, Gordon H., 357*n*, 361*n*, 368*n*, 369*n*, 372*n*, 601*n*, 602*n*, 604*n*, 605*n*, 607*n*
Hanushek, Eric A., 331*n*, 338*n*
Harrington, David E., 364*n*
Harrison, Alan, 496*n*
Harrison, Ann, 601*n*, 602*n*
Hart, Oliver, 548*n*
Hart, Robert A., 546*n*
Hartmann, Heidi L., 457*n*, 471*n*

Hayes, Kathy, 428*n*
Hecker, Daniel, 174*n*
Heckman, James J., 314*n*, 330*n*, 436*n*, 440*n*, 463*n*, 464*n*, 575*n*
Heim, Bradley T., 217*n*
Heisz, Andrew, 328*n*
Hellerstein, Judith K., 180*n*, 414*n*, 429*n*, 435*n*, 445*n*
Helper, Susan, 390*n*, 396*n*
Helpman, Elhanan, 572*n*, 604*n*
Henry, Peter Blair, 141*n*, 605*n*
Hersch, Joni, 241*n*, 283*n*
Heywood, John S., 509*n*, 510*n*
Hickman, Daniel C., 608*n*
Hicks, John, 120, 120*n*, 210*n*, 495*n*
Hight, Joseph, 323*n*
Hildreth, Andrew K. G., 402*n*
Hill, M. Anne, 471*n*
Hipple, Steven F., 194*n*
Hirsch, Barry T., 98*n*, 269*n*, 477, 478, 507*n*, 509*n*, 511*n*, 515*n*
Hirsch, Boris, 452*n*
Hirschberg, Joseph, 428*n*
Hirshleifer, Jack, 227, 305
Hobijn, Bart, 555*n*
Hock, Henrich, 366*n*, 367*n*
Hoefer, Michael, 361*n*
Hoffman, Saul D., 123*n*
Hogue, Carma, 527*n*
Holden, Steinar, 546*n*
Holmlund, Bertil, 538*n*
Holmstrom, Bengt, 183*n*, 408*n*
Holtz-Eakin, Douglas, 209
Holzer, Harry J., 446*n*, 461*n*, 464*n*, 546*n*
Horrigan, M., 325*n*
Hotchkiss, Julie L., 432*n*
Hoxby, Caroline M., 315*n*
Hoynes, Hilary, 181*n*, 226*n*
Hsieh, Chang-Tai, 605*n*
Hu, Wei-Yin, 261*n*
Huck, Steffen, 404*n*
Hunt, Jennifer, 371*n*
Hurst, Erik, 562*n*
Hussey, Andrew J., 330*n*
Hutchens, Robert, 408*n*, 412*n*, 414*n*, 496*n*
Hvide, Hans K., 409*n*
Hyslop, Dean, 502*n*, 546*n*

I

Ichino, Andrea, 426*n*
Ichniowski, Casey, 398*n*, 400*n*
Idson, Todd L., 415*n*
Ihlanfeldt, Keith R., 446*n*
Imai, Susumu, 248*n*
Imbens, Guido W., 206*n*, 229
Ioannides, Yannis M., 532*n*
Iranzo, Susana, 332*n*
Itskhoki, Oleg, 572*n*, 604*n*

J

Jacob, Brian A., 249
Jaeger, David A., 336*n*

James, John A., 546*n*
Jarrell, Stephen B., 432*n*
Jenkins, Clive, 143*n*
Joesch, Jutta M., 539*n*
Johnson, George, 493*n*, 496*n*, 499*n*, 574*n*
Johnson, Harry, 506*n*
Johnson, Richard W., 321*n*
Johnson, Rucker C., 436*n*, 447*n*
Johnson, Terry R., 539*n*
Johnson, William G., 428*n*
Joulfaian, David, 209
Jovanovic, Boyan, 376*n*
Joyce, Mary, 170*n*, 325*n*
Juhn, Chinhui, 191*n*, 433*n*
Juster, F. Thomas, 261

K

Kahn, Lawrence M., 75*n*, 169, 217*n*, 257*n*, 432*n*, 480, 508*n*, 510*n*
Kahn, Matthew E., 357*n*
Kahn, Shulamit, 458*n*, 546*n*
Kahneman, Daniel, 391*n*
Kain, John F., 338*n*
Kanazawa, Mark T., 446*n*
Kandel, Eugene, 397*n*
Kane, Thomas J., 336*n*, 338*n*
Kaplan, David S., 399*n*
Karoly, Lynn A., 222*n*
Katz, Harry, 474*n*, 475*n*, 519*n*, 523*n*
Katz, Lawrence F., 104*n*, 131*n*, 141*n*, 241*n*, 316*n*, 327*n*, 403*n*, 425*n*, 493*n*, 538*n*, 541*n*, 552, 571, 574*n*, 575*n*, 576*n*, 578*n*, 581*n*, 604*n*
Kaufman, Bruce E., 139*n*, 488*n*
Kawaguchi, Daiji, 548*n*
Keane, Michael P., 215*n*, 217*n*, 248*n*
Kearney, Melissa S., 578*n*, 581*n*
Keefe, Jeffrey, 477*n*
Kehoe, Timothy J., 596*n*
Keith, Kristen, 356*n*, 357*n*
Kerr, Clark, 474*n*
Kerr, William R., 371*n*
Kessel, Reuben, 97*n*
Kessler, Daniel P., 493*n*
Kiefer, Nicholas, 532*n*
Killingsworth, Mark, 243*n*, 458*n*, 471*n*
Kim, Moon-Kak, 429*n*
Kim, Sun-Bin, 547*n*
Kimko, Dennis D., 338*n*
Kimmel, Jean, 246*n*, 439*n*
Kinney, Eleanor D., 379*n*
Kleiner, Morris M., 390*n*, 396*n*, 488*n*, 495*n*, 511*n*
Klepinger, Daniel H., 539*n*
Kluve, Jochen, 609*n*, 611*n*, 613
Knetsch, Jack L., 391*n*
Kniesner, Thomas J., 273*n*, 287*n*, 295, 379*n*
Kochan, Thomas A., 477*n*
Koeniger, Winfried, 581*n*
Kolesnikova, Natalia, 316*n*
Konings, Jozef, 404*n*
Kosfeld, Michael, 391*n*
Kostiuk, Peter F., 269*n*
Kramarz, Francis, 185, 415*n*

Kranton, Rachel E., 338*n*
Kroft, Kory, 534, 537*n*, 538*n*
Krueger, Alan B., 117*n*, 137*n*, 141*n*, 180*n*,
    219*n*, 281*n*, 338*n*, 403*n*, 436*n*, 461*n*,
    488*n*, 489*n*, 495*n*, 537*n*, 538*n*, 575*n*, 576*n*
Kruse, Douglas, 398*n*
Krynski, Kathy J., 364*n*
Kugler, Adriana, 101*n*
Kugler, Maurice, 101*n*
Kuhn, Peter, 195*n*, 219*n*, 359*n*, 432*n*, 439*n*,
    498*n*, 537*n*, 552*n*
Kuziemko, Ilyana, 316*n*, 327*n*

L

Ladd, Helen F., 338*n*
Laing, Derek, 411*n*
Lalive, Rafael, 295
LaLonde, Robert J., 341*n*, 610*n*
LaLumia, Sara, 539*n*
Landers, Renée M., 410
Lang, Kevin, 101*n*, 339*n*, 359*n*, 375*n*, 433*n*,
    434*n*, 436*n*, 447*n*
Lange, Fabian, 449, 534
Lange, Peter, 475*n*
Laughlin, Teresa, 423*n*
Lavy, Victor, 409*n*, 429*n*
Lawrence, Robert Z., 604*n*
Lawson, Nicholas, 486*n*
Layard, Richard, 148*n*
Lazear, Edward P., 177*n*, 394*n*, 397*n*, 404*n*,
    407*n*, 414*n*, 425*n*, 488*n*, 545*n*
Leamer, Edward F., 604*n*
Lebow, David E., 55*n*
Lee, David S., 507*n*, 511*n*, 581*n*
Lefebvre, Pierre, 257*n*
Lehman, Jee-Yeon K., 433*n*, 434*n*, 447*n*
Leibbrandt, Andreas, 429*n*
Leigh, Andrew, 330*n*
Lemieux, Thomas, 321*n*, 490*n*, 508*n*, 546*n*,
    572*n*, 578*n*, 579*n*, 581*n*
Lengermann, Paul, 342*n*
Leonard, Jonathan S., 447*n*, 495*n*, 510*n*
Leonardi, Marco, 581*n*
Lester, T. William, 137*n*
Leuven, Edwin, 177*n*
Levine, David I., 447*n*
Levine, Phillip B., 253*n*, 254*n*, 257*n*, 552*n*
Levitt, Steven, 391*n*, 436*n*, 463
Levy, Frank, 563*n*
Levy, Helen, 281
Lewin, David, 423*n*, 477*n*
Lewis, H. G., 504*n*
Lewis, H. Gregg, 514–515
Lewis, John L., 94
Liebman, Jeffrey B., 253*n*, 399*n*
Lincoln, William F., 371*n*
Lindbeck, Assar, 512*n*, 547*n*
Lindley, Joanne K., 273*n*
Lindsay, C. M., 329*n*
Lipsky, David, 496*n*
List, John, 391*n*, 429*n*
Liu, Albert Yung-Hsu, 428*n*
Lleras-Muney, Adriana, 312*n*
Lochner, Lance, 575*n*

Loewenstein, Mark A., 177*n*
Long, Clarence D., 191, 192
Long, Richard J., 510*n*
Loury, Linda Datcher, 532*n*
Lowen, Aaron, 423*n*
Lozano, Fernando, 195*n*
Lubotsky, Darren, 358
Ludwig, Jens, 177*n*, 249
Lundberg, Shelly, 238*n*, 240*n*, 324*n*
Lundborg, Petter, 271*n*
Luoh, Ming-Ching, 317*n*
Luttmer, Erzo F. P., 253*n*
Lutz, Byron F., 379*n*
Lyle, David, 124*n*
Lynch, Lisa, 180*n*, 511*n*

M

McCall, Brian P., 509*n*
McConnell, Sheena, 342*n*, 496*n*
McCrary, Justin, 461*n*
McCulloch, Neil, 596*n*
McDermed, Ann A., 405*n*
McElroy, James C., 325*n*
McElroy, Marjorie B., 243*n*
Machin, Stephen, 154*n*
McKay, Andrew, 596*n*
McLaren, John, 603*n*
McLennan, Michele, 431*n*
MacLeod, W. Bentley, 546*n*, 572*n*
McMillan, Margaret, 601*n*, 602*n*
McNally, Sandra, 317*n*
Macpherson, David A., 477, 478, 507*n*,
    509*n*, 510*n*
McWilliams, Abagail, 356*n*, 357*n*
Madden, Janice F., 451*n*
Magnani, Elisabeth, 303*n*, 511*n*, 541*n*
Magnuson, Katherine, 314*n*
Malcomson, James M., 384*n*
Mallick, Debdulal, 121*n*
Maloney, M. T., 409*n*
Manchester, Colleen Flaherty, 177*n*
Mankiw, N. Gregory, 555*n*
Manning, Alan, 29*n*, 154*n*, 158*n*, 166*n*, 167*n*,
    429*n*, 453*n*, 458*n*, 577*n*
Manove, Michael, 436*n*
Manski, Charles F., 316*n*
Margo, Robert A., 353
Margolis, David N., 185
Marschke, Gerald, 396*n*
Marshall, Alfred, 120, 120*n*
Marston, Stephen T., 529*n*
Martins, Pedro S., 386*n*
Mas, Alexandre, 392, 397*n*, 495*n*, 511*n*
Maskin, Eric, 548*n*
Masterov, Dimitriy, 436*n*, 440*n*
Matsaganis, Manos, 101*n*
Matsudaira, Jordan, 156*n*
Matthews, Peter Hans, 409*n*
Mattila, J. Peter, 458*n*
Maurin, Eric, 317*n*
Mazumder, Bhashkar, 581
Medoff, James, 507*n*, 510*n*, 512*n*, 515*n*, 547*n*
Meghir, Costas, 240*n*
Mehay, Stephen L., 181*n*

Meng, Juanjuan, 199
Merkl, Christian, 614*n*
Merrigan, Philip, 257*n*
Messina, Julian, 546*n*
Meyer, Bruce D., 101*n*, 219*n*, 220, 374*n*,
    537*n*, 538*n*, 551*n*, 557, 565*n*
Meyer, Daniel R., 258*n*
Michael, Robert T., 471*n*
Michalopoulos, Charles, 341*n*
Micklewright, John, 537*n*
Mieszkowski, Peter, 506*n*
Mihaly, Kata, 217*n*
Milgrom, Paul, 400*n*
Miller, Paul W., 359*n*
Millward, Neil, 510*n*
Mincer, Jacob, 135*n*, 321*n*, 322*n*, 376*n*, 506*n*
Miskimin, Harry A., 69
Mitchell, Daniel, 423*n*
Mitchell, Joshua W., 238*n*
Mitchell, Olivia S., 251*n*
Modlin, George M., 69
Moffitt, Robert, 221*n*, 578*n*
Mok, Wallace K. C., 537*n*
Molloy, Raven, 352*n*
Moñarez, Paula, 274
Moncarz, Roger J., 603
Monger, Randall, 361*n*
Montgomery, Edward, 295*n*, 546*n*
Moore, Michael J., 271*n*
Moore, Robert L., 414*n*
Moore, William J., 71*n*
Moretti, Enrico, 303*n*, 332*n*, 392, 397*n*,
    426*n*, 553*n*, 565*n*
Morgan, Wyn, 596*n*
Morrall, John, III, 288*n*
Mortensen, Dale T., 154*n*, 161*n*, 532*n*
Mueller, Andreas, 537*n*, 538*n*
Muendler, Marc-Andreas, 572*n*, 604*n*
Mullainathan, Sendhil, 98*n*, 398*n*, 438*n*, 463
Murnane, Richard J., 314*n*, 563*n*
Murphy, Kevin J., 399*n*, 400*n*, 403*n*,
    411*n*, 412*n*
Murphy, Kevin M., 574*n*
Murray, John E., 397
Myers, Caitlin Knowles, 461*n*

N

Naidu, Suresh, 140*n*
Nalbantian, Haig R., 397*n*
Neal, Derek, 433*n*, 436*n*
Neckermann, Susanne, 391*n*
Needels, Karen, 535*n*
Nelson, Julie A., 239*n*
Neumann, George R., 497*n*
Neumark, David, 104*n*, 117*n*, 137*n*, 138*n*,
    139*n*, 140*n*, 180*n*, 242*n*, 321*n*, 408*n*,
    414*n*, 429*n*, 431*n*, 435*n*, 445*n*, 446*n*,
    455*n*, 461*n*, 508*n*
Newman, Robert J., 71*n*
Nicholson, Walter, 535*n*
Nickell, S., 98*n*
Nickell, Stephen, 75*n*, 569
Nickerson, Jack A., 396*n*
Noel, Brett J., 415*n*

North, Douglass C., 69
Notowidigdo, Matthew, 534, 537n, 538n
Nunziata, Luca, 581n

O

Oaxaca, Ronald L., 428n, 429n, 452n, 493n
O'Brien, Daniel M., 338n
Oettinger, Gerald, 215
O'Farrell, Brigid, 471n
Ohlsson, Henry, 269n
Ohtake, Fumio, 548n
Oi, Walter, 375n, 415n
Okun, Arthur, 34n, 557n
Olney, William W., 608n
Olsen, Reed Neil, 438n
Olson, Craig A., 295n
Olson, Keith W., 315
O'Neill, June, 428n, 432n
Oosterbeek, Hessel, 177n, 337n
Orazem, Peter F., 325n, 458n
Oreopoulos, Philip, 328n, 330n, 449, 463
Osili, Una Okonkwo, 372n
Osterman, Paul, 183n
Oswald, Andrew J., 147, 402n, 510n, 543n
Ottaviano, Gianmarco I. P., 369n
Owan, Hideo, 396n
Ozturk, Orgul Demet, 138n

P

Page, Marianne E., 336n
Panagariya, Arvind, 602n
Parent, Daniel, 546n, 572n
Pareto, Vilfredo, 29n
Parsons, Christopher A., 437
Parsons, Donald O., 375n, 377n
Paserman, M. Daniele, 370
Pathak, Parag A., 338n
Patrinos, Harry Anthony, 337
Pavcnik, Nina, 605n, 614n
Paxson, Christina H., 194n
Payne, James E., 403n
Pekkarinen, Tuomas, 395n
Peñaloza, Roberto V., 246n
Pencavel, John, 487n, 507n, 510n
Peoples, James, Jr., 445n, 508n
Peracchi, Franco, 215n
Peri, Giovanni, 130n, 332n, 367n, 369n, 371n
Perry, George L., 555n
Petrie, Ragan, 417
Phibbs, Ciaran S., 156n
Piatak, Jaclyn Schede, 68n
Piehl, Anne Morrison, 373
Pierce, Brooks, 562n
Piketty, Thomas, 564n
Pilarski, Adam M., 495n
Pinkston, Joshua C., 449
Pischke, Jörn-Steffen, 177n
Pitts, M. Melinda, 432n
Placzek, Dana W., 528n
Pleeter, Saul, 312n
Poitras, Marc, 271n
Polachek, Solomon W., 429n

Pollak, Robert A., 238n, 240n
Portugal, Pedro, 542n
Postlewaite, Andrew, 242n
Poterba, James M., 537n
Potter, Simon, 191n
Prendergast, Canice, 384n, 389n, 400n
Prentice, David, 511n
Preston, Ian, 359n
Price, Joseph, 437
Psacharopoulos, George, 337

Q

Quayes, Shakil, 245

R

Radwan, Samir, 68n
Raff, Daniel, 402
Ragan, James F., Jr., 447n
Ramos, Fernando A., 359n
Ransom, Michael R., 156n, 428n, 429n, 452n
Raphael, Steven, 369n, 507n
Rayack, Wendy L., 547n
Rebitzer, James B., 396n, 410, 415n, 417n, 451n
Redding, Stephen J., 572n, 604n
Reder, Melvin W., 488n, 497n
Rehavi, M. Marit, 609n, 610n, 611n
Reich, Michael, 137n, 140n, 453n
Reilly, Kevin T., 194n, 248n, 415n
Requena, Francisco, 371n
Rhoads, Steven E., 457n
Ribar, David C., 254n
Riddell, Chris, 219n, 395n, 537n, 552n
Riddell, W. Craig, 508n, 579n
Riley, John G., 387n
Rives, Janet M., 245
Rivkin, Steven G., 338n
Robins, Philip K., 258n, 341n
Robinson, Sherman, 602n
Rockoff, Jonah E., 338n
Rodríguez-Clare, Andrés, 596n
Rodrik, Dani, 614n
Rogerson, Richard, 238n
Romer, Christina D., 546n
Romer, David H., 546n
Rose, Elaina, 324n
Rosen, Harvey S., 209
Rosen, Sherwin, 274n, 299n, 348n, 425n
Rossenzweig, Mark R., 390
Rotemberg, Julio J., 392n
Rothstein, Jesse, 436n
Rouse, Cecilia Elena, 180n, 330n, 336n, 341, 427, 436n
Roy, Andrew D., 355n
Royalty, Anne Beeson, 376n
Rubin, Donald B., 206n, 229
Rucker, Ian, 602n
Rudd, Jeremy B., 55n
Ruhl, Kim J., 596n
Rupert, Peter, 272n
Ryan, Chris, 330n
Ryan, Paul, 342n

Ryoo, Jaewoo, 348n
Rytina, Nancy, 361n
Rzakhanov, Zaur, 355

S

Sabia, Joseph J., 138n, 139n
Sacerdote, Bruce I., 206n, 229, 241n
Sadoff, Sally, 391n
Saez, Emmanuel, 101n, 226n, 392, 564n
Saffer, Henry, 237
Sahin, Aysegul, 555n
Saidi, Farzad, 429n
Saint-Paul, Gilles, 75n
Saks, Raven E., 399n
Salvanes, Kjell G., 328n
Samuelson, Paul A., 168, 168n
Sandino, Tatiana, 399n
Sappington, David E., 389n
Sasson, Diego, 141n, 605n
Schady, Norbert, 245
Schaller, Bruce, 199
Schank, Thorsten, 124n, 452n
Schirm, John, 409n
Schkade, David, 281n
Schleifer, Andrei, 26n
Schmeider, Johannes F., 538n
Schmidt, Klaus M., 403n
Schnabel, Claus, 452n
Schnell, John F., 497n
Schochet, Peter Z., 342n
Schroeder, Larry D., 40n, 351n
Schultz, Theodore, 332n
Schumacher, Edward J., 269n
Schumann, Paul L., 301n
Schwartz, Aba, 354n
Schweitzer, Mark, 138n, 546n
Scott, Frank A., 379n
Seago, Jean Ann, 511n
Segal, Lewis M., 174
Seif, David G., 253n
Seiler, Eric, 395n
Seltzer, Andrew J., 137, 404n
Sexton, Edwin A., 438n
Shaw, Kathryn, 295n, 384n, 398n, 400n
Shearer, Bruce, 395n
Sherman, Barrie, 143n
Shintani, Mototsugu, 246n
Shoven, John B., 253n
Sicherman, Nachum, 194n
Sicilian, Paul, 423n
Siebert, W. S., 509n
Silber, Jacques, 428n
Silverstone, Brian, 557n
Simon, Herbert A., 384n
Sims, David P., 156n
Siniver, Erez, 359n
Sjoquist, David L., 40n
Skalli, Ali, 269n
Skidmore, Felicity, 386n
Slaughter, Matthew J., 490n, 604n
Slavov, Sita Nataraj, 253n
Sloane, Peter J., 509n
Sloof, Randolph, 177n
Slutsky, Evgeny, 210n

Smith, Adam, 273*n*
Smith, Christopher L., 352*n*
Smith, James P., 461*n*
Smith, Nina, 426*n*
Smith, Robert, 134*n*, 458*n*, 469*n*, 470*n*, 471*n*
Smith, Sarah, 253*n*
Smolensky, Eugene, 369*n*
Snower, Dennis J., 512*n*, 547*n*, 614*n*
Sofer, Catherine, 273*n*
Solberg, Eric, 423*n*
Solon, Gary, 581
Solow, Robert M., 401*n*, 449*n*
Song, Jae, 324*n*, 604*n*
Sopher, Barry, 498*n*
Sorensen, Elaine, 470*n*
Sparber, Chad, 367*n*
Spence, Michael, 182*n*, 333*n*
Sperling, Gene, 399*n*
Spetz, Joanne, 156*n*
Spilimbergo, Antonio, 372*n*
Spivey, Christy, 324*n*, 426*n*, 432*n*
Spletzer, James R., 177*n*, 323*n*, 545*n*
Spurr, Stephen J., 425*n*
Srinivasan, T. N., 602*n*
Stafford, Frank P., 261, 312*n*, 509*n*
Staiger, Douglas, 156*n*, 338*n*
Staisiunas, Justas, 553*n*
Stancanelli, Elena G. F., 213*n*
Stanley, T. D., 432*n*
Stanton, Christopher, 384*n*
Staudohar, Paul D., 474*n*
Stengos, Thanasis, 546*n*
Stephan, Paula E., 40*n*
Stephens, Melvin, Jr., 246*n*
Stern, Ariel Dora, 241*n*
Stern, Robert, 496*n*
Stevens, Margaret, 179*n*, 181*n*
Stewart, Mark, 496*n*
Stiglitz, Joseph, 403*n*, 608*n*, 614*n*
Stock, Wendy A., 408*n*, 455*n*
Strahan, Philip E., 445*n*
Stratton, Leslie S., 241*n*
Stroupe, Kevin T., 379*n*
Subramanian, Krishnamurthy, 169
Sueyoshi, Glenn J., 425*n*
Sulaman, Johan, 437
Sullivan, Daniel G., 174
Sullivan, James X., 565*n*
Summers, Lawrence, 402, 537*n*
Sundstrom, William A., 435*n*, 554*n*
Sutter, Daniel, 271*n*
Svaleryd, Helena, 445*n*
Svejnar, Jan, 396*n*, 485*n*
Swinton, Omari H., 330*n*

T

Taber, Christopher, 314*n*, 575*n*
Talley, Wayne K., 445*n*
Taubman, Paul, 414*n*
Taylor, Eric S., 400*n*
Taylor, Lowell, 316*n*, 410, 415*n*

Teixeira, Paulino, 124*n*
Tekin, Erdal, 257*n*
Tessada, Jose, 366*n*
Thaler, Richard H., 26*n*, 391*n*, 403*n*
Thierfelder, Karen, 602*n*
Thomas, Robert Paul, 69
Thompson, Jeffrey P., 138*n*
Thoursie, Peter Skogman, 463
To, Ted, 29*n*, 154*n*, 155*n*
Tobin, James, 554*n*
Toosi, Mitra, 422
Topel, Robert H., 352*n*, 403*n*, 551*n*
Tracy, Joseph S., 496*n*, 497, 497*n*, 498*n*,
    510*n*, 511*n*
Trefler, Daniel, 602*n*
Treiman, Donald J., 457*n*
Trejo, Stephen J., 176*n*, 359*n*
Tremblay, Carol Horton, 447*n*
Triplett, Jack E., 375*n*
Troske, Kenneth, 429*n*, 445*n*
Trutko, John, 68*n*
Tsakloglou, Panos, 101*n*
Tseng, Yi-Ping, 538*n*
Turner, Sarah, 315, 327*n*, 436*n*
Turunen, Jarkko, 546*n*
Tyler, John H., 400*n*

V

Vail, Leroy, 73
Vainiomaki, J., 98*n*
Valletta, Robert G., 103, 509*n*, 510*n*, 538*n*,
    555*n*
Vanderkamp, John, 359*n*
Van Der Klaauw, Wilbert, 218*n*
Van Klaveren, Chris, 177*n*
Van Wincoop, Eric, 606*n*
Vejsiu, Altin, 538*n*
Vella, Francis, 316*n*
Vermeulen, Frederic, 240*n*
Veum, Jonathan R., 180*n*
Vigdor, Jacob L., 338*n*
Viscusi, W. Kip, 220, 271*n*, 273*n*, 283*n*, 287*n*
Vlachos, Jonas, 445*n*
Von Wachter, Till, 328*n*, 538*n*
Voos, Paula B., 490*n*
Vytlacil, Edward J., 330*n*

W

Wachter, Michael L., 49*n*, 508*n*
Wadhwani, S., 98*n*
Waldfogel, Jane, 324*n*, 426*n*
Walker, Ian, 246*n*
Wallace, Brian, 404*n*
Wallerstein, Michael, 475*n*
Walsh, Patrick P., 404*n*
Wang, Yingchun, 390*n*, 396*n*
Wang, Zheng, 415*n*
Ward, Melanie E., 546*n*
Warner, John T., 312*n*

Wascher, William, 117*n*, 137*n*, 138*n*
Watts, Martin, 428*n*
Webb, Anthony, 253*n*
Weber, Andrea, 273*n*, 539*n*
Wei, Xiangdong, 509*n*
Weil, David, 134*n*
Weinberger, Catherine J., 432*n*
Weiss, Andrew, 337*n*, 403*n*, 542*n*, 547*n*
Weiss, Yoram, 24*n*, 403*n*
Welch, Finis, 215*n*, 461*n*
Welkum, Sherry K., 458*n*
Werbel. James D., 325*n*
West, Sarah, 198*n*
Whaples, Robert, 448
White, Eugene N., 552
White, Landeg, 73
Whitmore, Diane M., 338*n*
Wilde, Elizabeth Ty, 241*n*
Williams, Gordon C., 315*n*
Williams, Roberton, 198*n*
Winfrey, William, 439
Winkler, Anne E., 238*n*, 240*n*, 428*n*,
    431*n*, 451*n*
Winter-Ebmer, Rudolf, 415*n*
Winters, L. Alan, 596*n*
Wise, David A., 253*n*
Wittenburg, David C., 117*n*, 139*n*
Woessmann, Ludger, 331*n*
Wolf, Michael G., 603
Wolfers, Justice, 437
Wong, Pat, 258*n*
Woo, Keong T., 605*n*
Woock, Christopher, 273*n*, 287*n*
Wood, Adrian, 610*n*
Wozniak, Abigail, 352*n*
Wright, Benjamin, 603
Wright, Peter, 596*n*
Wright, Randall, 49*n*
Wunnava, Phanindra V., 463*n*

X

Xie, Jia, 372*n*

Y

Yates, Michael C., 437
Yellen, Janet, 401*n*, 403*n*, 542*n*
Yoon, Albert, 338*n*, 461*n*
Yuksel, Mutlu, 438*n*

Z

Zaidi, Mahmood, 423*n*
Zehnder, Christian, 391*n*
Ziegler, Philip, 69
Ziliak, James P., 273*n*, 287*n*
Zimmerman, David J., 315*n*
Zimmerman, Klaus F., 317*n*
Zweimuller, Josef, 415*n*

Subject Index

Note: Entries followed by *f*, *t*, and *n* refer to figures, tables, and notes, respectively.

A

Ability bias, 328–330, 340–341
Above-market wages, 70, 71–72, 71*f*, 75
Absolute value, 118, 205*n*
Active Labor Market Policies, 612–613
Actual average earnings, 430
Actual productivity, 185, 441–442, 512
Adaptability, 26
Adaptive expectations, 347–348
Added input, marginal expense of, 84–85
Added-worker effect, 243–244, 246
Adult civilian labor force, 49*f*
Adult labor, 129–130
Affirmative action, 459–460, 461, 463–464
AFL-CIO. *See* American Federation of Labor and Congress of Industrial Organizations (AFL/CIO)
African Americans
  earnings levels, 463–464
  migration of, to North, 353
Age
  college education and, 313
  earnings differential and, 423–424
  migration and, 352–353
  training decline with, 321–322
Age/earnings profiles, 321–322, 323, 325, 326*f*, 424
Aggregate labor demand, 545
Agricultural work incentives, 227
Airline industry, deregulation of, 490, 491
Airplane pilots, wage elasticity of demand for, 125, 127
Air traffic controllers' strike, 497
American Federation of Labor and Congress of Industrial Organizations (AFL/CIO), 478
American jobs, offshoring of, 601–605
Antidiscrimination programs, 454–464
Apparel industry, 142
Apprentice workers, 494
Arbitration
  contract zone, 500–501, 519–523
  conventional, 500
  effects of, 502
  final-offer, 500
  forms of, 500
  interest, 500
  persuading the arbitrator, 501–502
  threat of, 499–502
Armed Forces Qualification Test (AFQT), 436
Asian Americans, 422
Assumptions, 26, 28

B

Bargaining. *See* Collective bargaining
Bargaining protocols, 497–498
Behavior, positive economics and, 27
Behavioral skills, 314
Below-average pay, 65
Below-market wages, 72–73
Benefit-cost analysis, 286–288
Benefits. *See* Employee benefits
Bias, omitted variables, 43–46, 340
Big Mac per Hour of Work (BMPH) index, 56
Black Death, 69
Bonus plans, 393
Boom-and-bust cycles, 345
Border security, 349
Budget constraint, 204–206, 204*f*, 207*f*
  child support and, 258*f*
  household production and, 236
  retirement age and, 250–251
  with "spikes," 217–220, 218*f*
Bureau of Labor Statistics (BLS), 294–295

C

Calorie consumption, type of pay and, 390
Canada, foreign-born population in, 349
Canada-United States Free Trade Agreement, 602
Capital
  labor substitution, 141–142
  substitution, wages and, 94
  supply of, 61
Capital-intensive production, 59
Capital market, 58, 58*f*
  imperfections, 33
Capital prices, labor demand and, 61–62, 62*f*
Career compensation, 404
Career concerns, 410–412
Cheating
  discouraging, 386–387
  in groups, 397–398
Chief executive officers (CEOs), compensation of, 399

Asymmetric information, 386–388, 498, 548
Automation, 141–142
Average tendencies, 27
Average wage and quit-rate data, 39*t*, 44*t*

Child age, labor force participation rate and, 238–239, 239*t*
Child care
  hourly costs of, 256
  labor supply and, 254–261
  reducing fixed costs of, 255–256, 255*f*, 256*f*
  subsidies, 254–257
Child labor, 31, 245
Child support assurance, 257–259, 258*f*, 259*f*, 261
Cigarette smoking, 312–313
Civilian labor force, demographic groups, 422*t*
Civilian wages, 77
Civil Rights Act of 1964, Title VII of, 455–459
Class actions, 455
Coal mining wages, 94
Cobweb model, 345–348, 347*f*
Coefficient of variation, 564
Cognitive skills, 314
Collective bargaining, 473
  activities and tools of, 487–502
  arbitration and, 499–502, 519–523
  contract zone, 500–501, 519–523
  international comparison of, 473–475
  in public sector, 499–502
  threat of strikes and, 494–499
College education
  costs and benefits of, 310–311, 313–317
  demand for, 310–318
  earnings differentials from, 316–317
  as good investment, 328–342
  increased returns to, 569–570
  market responses to, 317–318
  mean earnings and, 570*t*
  signaling model and, 332–339
  women and, 325–327, 327*t*
College football stars, MRP of, 85
Collusion, 450, 453–454
Commissions, 393, 394
Comparable worth
  estimating earnings gaps, 468–471
  in practice, 457–458
  theory of, 456–457
  universities and, 458–459
Comparative advantage, 590–592, 593–594
Compensating wage differential, 268, 269–270, 394–395
  assumptions and predictions about, 270–272
  empirical tests for, 273

Compensating wage differential (*continued*)
    errors in variables problem, 294–295
    hedonic wage theory, 274–288
    indentured servitude and, 283
    job safety regulations and, 283–288
    layoffs and, 299–303
Compensation
    See also Pay; Wages
    aggregate, 23
    career, 404
    deferred, 288, 289
    delayed, 404–408
    effects of low, on worker satisfaction,
        392
    employee benefits, 53*n*, 170–172, 171*t*
    employee preferences, 393–395
    employer considerations, 395–400
    executive, 398–399
    fairness issues, 391–392, 401–402,
        416–417
    job tenure and, 412–414, 413*f*
    in large firms, 414–417
    merit raises, 399–400
    overview of, 393
    performance-based, 389–390
    piece-rate, 393–398, 411
    policies, 383
    productivity and, 384–385, 393–412
    targeting, 611, 613–614
    time-based, 390–391, 394, 399–400
    total, 57
    underpayment-overpayment, 404–408,
        406*f*
    union effects on, 508–509
    for workers, 269–270
Competitive model, 167–168
Consistency, 26
Construction unions, 493
Consumer Price Index (CPI), 54, 55–56,
    325, 565*n*
Consumers, effect of immigration on, 366
Consumption, 145
Consumption goods, 310
Contract curves, 485–486, 485*f*
Contract zone, 500–501, 519–523, 522*f*
Conventional arbitration, 500
Corner solution, 206*f*
Corporate scandals, 399
Cost minimization, 112–114, 112*f*, 114*f*
Costs
    of college education, 313–315
    hiring, 168–169, 170
    labor, 122–123, 152
    opportunity, 195, 196, 314, 607
    quasi-fixed, 168–172, 174
    training, 170
    worker mobility, 154–156, 165–167,
        180, 350
CPI. *See* Consumer Price Index (CPI)
Craft unions, 473, 494
Credentials, use of, 181–183
Crime, illegal immigrants and, 373
Cross-elasticities
    derived demand and, 128–130
    estimates relating to, 130–131

Cross-sectional data, 38
Cross-wage effect, 599
Cross-wage elasticity of demand,
    127–131, 600
    estimates relating to, 130–131
    laws of derived demand applied to,
        128–130
Crowding, 450–451, 450*f*
Cuban immigrants, 370
Current Population Survey (CPS), 526
Customer discrimination, 446
Cyclical unemployment, 545–551

D

Data
    cross-sectional, 38
    time-series, 38*n*
Deferred compensation, 288, 289
Deferred payments, 57
Defined benefit plans, 171
Defined contribution plans, 171
Delayed compensation, 404–408
Demand
    See also Labor demand
    changes in, 575–578
    for college education, 310–318
    cross-wage elasticity of, 127–131, 600
    derived, 120–122, 599
    for final product, 121
    price elasticity of, 121
    product, 121, 125, 140–141, 493,
        597–598
Demand curve
    See also Labor demand curve
    elastic, 118
    inelastic, 118
    market, 91, 96–97
    relative elasticities, 119*f*
    straight-line, 120
    unitary elastic, 118
Demand-deficient unemployment, 545–551
Demand schedule, labor, 59, 60*t*
Demographic changes, 421–422, 422*t*, 489
Demographics, unemployment and,
    554–555, 555*t*
Dependent variable, 39
Deregulation, 490, 491
Derived demand
    applying laws of, 125, 127, 128–130
    cross-elasticities and, 128–130
    Hicks-Marshall laws of, 120–122, 599
Dichotomous variable, 42
Diminishing marginal returns, 86
Diminishing marginal utility, 519
Direct expenses, 306
Discounting, 307
Discouraged-worker effect, 244, 246
Discouraged workers, 434
Discrimination
    See also Labor market discrimination;
        Wage discrimination
    customer, 446
    employee, 446–447
    employer, 441–445

racial, 432–438
statistical, 182–183, 447–449
Disparate impact, 455–456, 462
Disparate treatment, 455, 462
Distance, migration and, 354
Divorce laws, 329
Domestic content legislation, 493
Downsizing, 528
Dual-income households, 239–246
Dual labor markets, 451

E

Early childhood programs, 314
Earned income, 561
Earned Income Tax Credit (EITC), 224–226,
    225*f*, 610
Earnings, 56–57
    See also Income
    actual average, 430
    age/earnings profiles, 321–322
    alternative streams of, 310–311, 310*f*
    dispersion of, 566*t*, 570–572
    distribution, and international
        migration, 354–356
    distribution of, 562–565, 562*f*, 563*f*
    educational level and, 318–320, 319*f*,
        320*f*, 569–570, 570*t*
    within human-capital groups, 570–572
    immigrants, 357–359, 358*f*
    impact of college education on, 316–317
    inequality, 565–572
    instability, 578
    parents, as determinant of children's,
        580–581
    tenure and, 412–414
Earnings differences, 316–317
    age and, 423–424
    analyzing, 431–432
    between black and white Americans,
        432–438, 464
    education and, 423–424
    by ethnicity, 438–440
    by gender, 423–432
    hours and experience and, 424–426
    measured and unmeasured sources of,
        422–440
    occupation and, 424
    unexplained, 426
Earnings ratios, 567*t*, 570*t*, 572*t*
Economic analysis, 23
Economic mobility, 580–581
Economic models, 28–29
Economic rents, 73–74
Economic theory, 23
Education
    See also College education
    compulsory, 33
    early childhood, 314
    earnings differential and, 423–424
    estimating returns on, 340–341
    ethnicity and, 438
    as good investment, 328–342
    health status and, 312–313
    international comparisons of, 331

migration and, 353–354
premium to, 571
productivity and, 332
psychic costs of, 306, 314, 315, 327
returns to, 579
school quality and, 337–339
signaling model and, 332–339
social cost of, 331–332
as social investment, 331–339
socially optimal level of, 337
women and formal, 325–327
Educational groups, employment shares of, 574*t*
Educational level, average earnings and, 318–320, 319*f*, 320*f*
EEOC. *See* Equal Employment Opportunity Commission (EEOC)
Efficiency, 29
vs. equity, 33–34
Pareto, 29, 29*n*, 30, 483, 512
Efficiency wages, 402, 403–404
unemployment and, 542–544
wage curve and, 543–544, 544*f*
Efficient-contracts model, 483–486
Effort
distortion, 411
piece rates and, 411
sequencing of, 411–412
EITC. *See* Earned Income Tax Credit (EITC)
Elastic demand, curve, 118–119, 119*f*
Elasticities
See also Labor demand elasticities
along demand curve, 119*f*
relative demand, 119*f*
Employee benefits, 53*n*, 170–172, 171*t*
deferred compensation, 288, 289
employee preferences, 288–289
employer preferences, 290–292
hedonic wage theory and, 288–295
indifference curves, 289, 290*f*
joint determination of wages and, 292–295, 293*f*
payments in kind, 288, 289
union effects on, 508–509
Employee discrimination, 446–447
Employees
See also Workers
career concerns of, 410–412
commitment of, 401
effect of immigration on, 366–370
labor market frictions for, 153–168
labor supply preferences of, 193–194
matching employers and, 279–283
preferences of, 288–289, 393–395
safeguards for, 407
Employee turnover, 374–379
cyclical effects, 376
employer location and, 377
employer size and, 375–376
gender differences in, 376
wage effects, 374–375
Employer concession schedule, 496
Employer discrimination, 441–445
pay gaps under, 442–445

profit maximization and, 445
profits under, 442
Employer-funded maternity benefits, 102–103
Employer payroll taxes, 98–100
Employer resistance, to unions, 491–492
Employers
collusion by, 453–454
effect of immigration on, 366
labor market frictions for, 168–176
location of, 377
matching employees and, 279–283
safeguards for, 407
size, and turnover, 375–376
Employment
conditions of, 509
distribution by nonfarm sector, 52*f*
equilibrium level of, 68
full, 531*f*, 553–557
hours trade-off, 172–176
impact of minimum wage on, 117, 132–138
industrial distribution of, 52–53
levels of, 58
part-time, 324*t*, 425
regional shifts in, 490
subsidized, 101–104, 610
teenage, 130, 136–138, 165, 554
terms of, 58
total, 602–603
union effects on, 509–510
wages and, 59–60
Employment-at-will, 386*n*
Employment contracts, 385–386
Employment effects, of trade, 601–604
Employment levels, 159–160
Employment protection legislation, 169
Employment rate, 525
civilian, 525*t*
Employment ratios, 433–435
Employment relationship, 23
Employment services firms, 154
Employment subsidies, 100–104, 610
Employment-to-population ratios, 433
Equal Employment Opportunity Commission (EEOC), 455
Equal Pay Act of 1963, 454–455
Equilibrium differential, 268–269
Equilibrium disturbance, 67–69
Equity, 401–402
vs. efficiency, 33–34
Error term, 40
Ethnicity, earnings differences by, 438–440
Europe, foreign-born population in, 349
European active labor market policies, 612–613
Executive pay, 398–399
Expectations
adaptive, 347–348
rational, 348
Expected wages, 534
Experience rating, 550–551, 550*f*
Explanatory variable, 39–40
Externalities, 31, 33

F

Fair Labor Standards Act (1938), 173
Fairness, 391–392, 401–402, 416–417
Family incomes, 561, 564
Family migration, 356–357
Fast-food restaurants, 237
Federal antidiscrimination programs, 454–464
Female/male earnings ratios, 425*t*
Final-offer arbitration, 500
Firms
behavior of, 26
supply to, 64–65
Football players, downward-sloping demand curve for, 480
Forced labor, 73
Foregone earnings, 306
Foreign competition, 490
Foreign labor, 599–601
Formal employment contracts, 385
Free-rider problem, 32, 392, 397–398, 513
Frictional unemployment, 531–539
Full employment, 531*f*, 553–557
Furniture industry, 448

G

Gainsharing plans, 393
Garment workers, labor demand elasticities for, 125
Gasoline prices, 198, 198*n*
Gender, dispersion of earnings by, 566*t*
Gender differences
in earnings, 423–432
in employee turnover, 376
Gender discrimination
in labor market, 426–432
by symphony orchestras, 427
Geographic mobility, 351–374
G.I. Bill, 315
Gini coefficients, 586–588, 588*f*
Goals, 26
Going wage, 152
Government, as employer of last resort, 148, 610
Government job training programs, 339, 341–342
Government policy, normative economics and, 32–33
Government programs
to end discrimination, 454–464
to subsidize human capital investments, 608–609
Government regulations, on workplace safety, 283–288, 284*f*
Government subsidies
for employment, 100–104, 610
immigrants and, 372
Government unions, 476–477
Great Depression, 552
Great Migration, 353
Great Recession, 565
Grievance-arbitration process, 500

Gross complements, 95–96, 95*f*, 127–128, 130, 142
Gross substitutes, 95, 95*f*, 127–128, 130
Group incentives, 396–399
Group loyalty, 392
Group output, 394
Groups, motivation of individuals in, 391–392

H

Hamburg, Germany, 305
Hay Points, 468
Health insurance, 379
Health status, education and, 312–313
Hedonic wage theory
    behavioral insights, 282–283
    employee benefits and, 288–295
    employee considerations, 275–276
    employer considerations, 277–279
    job safety regulations and, 283–288
    risk of injury and, 274–288
Hedonism, 274*n*
Hicks' bargaining model, 495–498, 495*f*
Hicks-Marshall laws of derived demand, 120–122, 128–130, 599–600
Hidden unemployment, 246
Higher education. *See* College education
High school degree, 571
High-skilled workers, 572–573
Hiring costs, 168–169, 170, 174
Hiring investments, 181–186
    credentials, use of, 181–183
    internal labor markets, 183
    recouping, 185–186
Hiring subsidy programs, 101, 103
Hiroshima, 305
Hispanics, 439–440, 554
Hours of work, 172–176, 193–195
Household income, 588, 588*f*
Household production, 195
    budget constraint and, 236
    child care and, 254–261
    child labor and, 245
    income and substitution effects, 236
    joint labor supply decisions, 239–246
    labor supply model, 233–239
    vs. market productivity, 242*f*
    obesity and, 237
    women's role in, 324
Household work, time spent on, 234*t*, 235*f*
Housing subsidies, labor supply and, 249
Human capital
    acquisition of, 305–306
    components of, 305
    costs of, 306
    definition of, 304
    optimum acquisition of, 309*f*
    signaling or, 336–337
    wage rigidity and, 547
    war and, 305
Human-capital groups, earnings dispersion within, 570–572

Human capital investments, 304–344
    age and, 323
    basic model of, 306–309
    college education, 310–318
    divorce laws and, 329
    education, 328–342
    by political refugees, 378–379
    post-schooling training, 318–323, 325
    subsidizing, 608–609
    by women, 323–327
Hypotheses testing, 38–46

I

Ignorance, 30
Illegal immigration, 361–365, 372–374
Immigrants
    contributions of, 371–372
    earnings of, 357–359, 358*f*
    from Mexico, 362–363
    personal characteristics of, 352–354
    public subsidies and, 372
    taxes and, 372, 373–374
Immigration, 349
    See also Migration
    crime and, 373
    gainers and losers of, 365–374
    naive views of, 363–365
    net fiscal effects of, 372
    restrictions on, 349, 359–360, 360–361
    returns to, 357–359
    Spanish-speaking, 439–440
    unauthorized, 361–365, 372–374
    U.S. history of, 360–363, 360*t*
Immigration and Nationality Act, 361
Implicit employment contracts, 385–386
Imports
    increase in, 598
    restrictions on, 589
Incarceration rates, 373
Incentives
    for effort, 408–409
    group, 396–398, 398–399
    individual, 395–396
    promotion-related, 408–410
    work, 406
Income
    See also Earnings
    definition of, 57
    dispersion of, 561, 562–565
    earned, 561
    family, 561, 564
    household, 588, 588*f*
    household time and, 235*f*
    inequality, 562–581
    level of, 561, 564
    median, 564
    redistribution, 30
    unearned, 57, 206, 209, 561
    wealth and, 196
Income constraints, 203–205
Income effect
    child labor and, 245
    defining, 196–197
    empirical findings on, 214–217

household production and, 236
isolating, 208–212
labor/leisure choice and, 205–206
of lottery winnings, 228–229
overcoming, 197–198
size of, 212–213, 212*f*
wage increase, 198–199, 207–208, 209*f*, 211*f*
of welfare system, 221*f*
Income replacement programs, 217–220
Income support programs, 609–610
Income tax cuts, labor supply and, 216
Indentured servitude, 283
Independent variable, 39–40, 43
Index of dissimilarity, 428
Indifference curves, 200–203, 201*f*, 202*f*, 203*f*, 238, 258, 276*f*
    budget constraint and, 204*f*, 207*f*
    employee benefits, 289, 290*f*
Individual incentives, 395–396
Industrial mix, 489
Industrial unions, 473
Industries, 52–53
Inelastic demand curve, 118
Inequality
    differences in, across developed countries, 569
    Gini coefficients, 586–588
    Lorenz curves, 585–588, 586*f*
    measuring, 562–565, 585–588
    since 1980, 565–572
    underlying causes of, 572–581
Inferential analysis, 125, 127
Inflation, 55
Information asymmetries, 386–388, 498, 548
Inheritances, 209
Injury rates, 275
Injury risk
    estimating compensating wage differentials for, 294–295
    parenthood and, 281
    unknown, 286*f*
Inputs, 82
    complements in production, 96
    gross complements, 95, 95*f*, 127–128, 130
    gross substitutes, 95, 95*f*, 127–128, 130
    marginal expense of added, 84–85
    marginal income from additional unit of, 83–84
    substitutes in production, 95–96, 95*f*
Insider-outsider hypothesis, 547
Institutional forces, changes in, 579, 581
Institutional investors, 399
Insurance carriers, 154
Intelligence quotient (IQ), 330
Interdependent productivity, 243
Interest arbitration, 500
Internal labor markets, 183, 376
Internal migration, 356
Internal opportunity costs, 607
Internal rate of return, 308–309, 312
International Labor Organization (ILO), 245

International trade
    See also Trade
    employment effects of, 601–604
    incentives for, 592–596
    policy issues, 607–613
    product demand and, 597–598
    wage convergence and, 605–607
    wage effects of, 604–605
Investment decisions, present value and, 306–308
Isoexpenditure lines, 112–113
Isoprofit curves, 278–279, 278*f*, 280, 290–292, 292*f*, 483–484
    flatter slope, 290–291
    steeper slope, 291–292
    unitary slope, 290, 291*f*

J

Japan, openness to trade by, 597
Job choice
    assumptions and predictions about, 270–272
    parenthood and, 281
    utility maximization and, 271
    worker information and, 271–272
    worker mobility and, 272
Job injuries
    employee considerations, 275–276
    employer considerations, 277–279
    hedonic wage theory and, 274–288
    wages and, 276*f*
Job lock, 379
Job losses
    to offshoring, 601–604
    technological change and, 141–145
Job matching, 267–274
Job mobility. *See* Worker mobility
Job safety regulations, 283–288, 284*f*
Job search
    costs, 154–156, 165–167, 451–453, 452*f*
    model of, 532–533
    theory of, 532–535
    unemployment insurance and, 538–539
Job tenure, 166–167, 181, 412–414
Journeymen workers, 494

K

Knowledge and worker skills, investment in, 304, 305–306

L

Labor, 304–344
    adult, 129–130
    allocation of, 269
    child, 31, 245
    declining marginal productivity of, 110–111, 111*f*
    earnings of, 53–57
    forced, 73
    foreign, 599–601
    marginal expense of, 84–85, 157–158, 159*f*

marginal product of, 83, 86, 86*t*
marginal revenue of, 84
share of, in total costs, 122–123
skilled, 130–131, 367–368, 368*f*
substitution, 109–110
substitution of capital for, 141–142
supply, 58
unskilled, 130–131, 134–135, 141–142, 268
Labor contract, 24
Labor costs, 122–123
    variable, 152
Labor demand, 58, 59–63, 81–82
    aggregate, 545
    capital prices and, 61–62, 62*f*
    changes in, 60–62, 575–578, 600–601
    in competitive markets, 85–96
    effects of trade on, 596–605
    elasticity of, 600–601, 611
    employment subsidies and, 100–104
    firm-level, 62–63
    immigrant labor and, 366–368
    industry-level, 62–63
    long-run, 92–94, 111
    market-level, 62–63
    money wages and, 89–91, 90*f*
    multiple inputs and, 95–96
    net effect of, 601–605
    in noncompetitive markets, 96–98
    objections to marginal productivity theory of, 91–92
    payroll taxes and, 98–100
    profit maximization and, 82–85, 87–92
    real wages and, 87–89
    schedule, 59, 60*t*
    shifts in, 61–62, 61*f*
    short-run, 85–92, 88*f*, 110–111, 123
    unions and, 506
    for women and minorities, 443*f*
Labor demand curve, 59–60, 60*f*, 81
    elasticity of, 118–120, 119*f*, 366–367, 613–614
    estimating, 146–147
    graphical derivation of, 108–116
    inelastic, 613*f*
    long-run, 63
    movements along, 62
    payroll tax cuts and, 104*f*
    payroll taxes and, 99–100, 99*f*
    shifts in, 61–62, 67–68, 506
    short-run, 63
    union actions to alter, 492–494
Labor demand elasticities, 117–151
    cross-wage elasticity of demand, 127–131
    estimating, 146–147
    Hicks-Marshall laws of derived demand, 120–122
    inferential analysis of, 125, 127
    minimum wage laws and, 132–138
    own-wage elasticity of demand, 118–127
    policy application of, 131–140
    substitutability factors, 121–122
    technological change and, 140–148

Labor economics
    basic concepts, 24–34
    definition of, 24–25
Labor force, 190, 524
    demographic changes in, 421–422, 422*t*
    demographic composition of, 554–555
    new entrants to, 527
    reentrants, 527
    status of U.S. adult civilian population, 49*f*
    unemployment and, 49–52
    women in, 50*t*, 422, 489
Labor force participation
    hours of work, 193–195
    theory of decision to work, 195–217
    trends in, 190–195
Labor force participation rate, 50–51, 191–193
    age of children and, 238–239, 239*t*
    civilian, 525*t*
    definition of, 190
    of females, 191*t*, 193*t*, 247, 324*t*
    by gender, 50*t*
    of males, 192*t*, 193*t*, 247, 324*t*, 433–434
    by race and gender, 434*t*
Labor investments, 168–170
Labor/leisure choice, 199–214, 206*f*
    income and wage constraints on, 203–205
    income effect and, 205–206
    preferences, 200–203
    wage increase and, 207–212
Labor-Management Reporting and Disclosure Act, 476
Labor market, 24
    changes in, 52–53
    "cobweb" model of adjustment, 345–347
    crowding, 450–451, 450*f*
    demand and supply, 66*f*, 67*f*
    disequilibrium, 69–70
    dual, 451
    employment subsidies and, 100–104
    equilibrium, 67–69, 70*f*
    European policies, 612–613
    experience, 166
    flows, 50
    frictions in, 152–189
    internal, 183, 376
    monopsonistic, 156–168
    national, 48
    overview of, 47–57
    payroll taxes and, 98–100
    stock-flow model of, 526–531, 526*f*
    tightness, 376, 377*f*
    unions and, 472–518
    worker preferences and, 267–274
    workings of, 58–70, 58*f*
Labor market discrimination
    customer discrimination, 446
    definition of, 426
    employee discrimination, 446–447
    employer discrimination, 441–445
    by ethnicity, 438–440

Labor market discrimination (*continued*)
federal programs to end, 454–464
field experiments to identify, 462–463
gender-based, 426–432
noncompetitive models of, 450–454
occupational, 427–429
personal-prejudice models of, 441–447
racial, 432–438
sources of, 440
statistical, 447–449
theories of, 440–454
Labor market investments, 304
See also Human capital investments
Labor productivity, 179t, 181, 332
Labor supply, 63–65, 190
ballpark, 215
changes in, 573–575
child care and, 254–261
daily, 215
to firms, 64–65
household production and, 233–239
housing subsidies and, 249
income replacement programs and, 217–220
income tax cuts and, 216
joint decisions, 239–246
life cycle aspects of, 247–254
market supply, 63–64
to military, 73–74, 74f
of New York City taxi drivers, 199
in recessions, 243–246
schedule, 158t
wage increases and, 260–261
wages, 68–69
welfare programs and, 220–224
Labor supply curve
backward-bending, 199, 200f
to military, 73–74, 74f
monopsonistic firms and, 161–164, 162f
negatively sloped, 199
for paralegals, 64f
payroll taxes and, 100, 100f
positively sloped, 199
shifts in, 63–64, 68–69, 161–164
worker mobility costs and, 155f
Labor unions. *See* Unions
Laid off, 50
Landrum-Griffin Act, 476, 499
Language, investment behavior and, 313
Large firms, compensation in, 414–417
Law firms, rat race in, 410
Law of diminishing marginal returns, 86
Law of one price, 153–156, 606
Layoff experience, 550
Layoffs, 527–528
compensating wage differentials and, 299–303
effects of uncertain, 301–303
in nonunion firms, 547
relationship between wages and, 303
training investments and, 180–181
UI tax and, 551
Least squares regression analysis, 40

Leisure
choice between labor and, 199–214
hours, demand for, 195
opportunity cost of, 196
time spent on, 234t
Lewis, John L., 94
Life cycle
age/earnings profiles, 321–322
investment in training over the, 322f
labor supply and, 247–254
Lifetime earnings, impact of college education on, 316–317
Living wage laws, 139–140
Local unions, 478
Long run, labor demand in, 92–94, 111
Lorenz curves, 585–588, 586f, 587f
Lottery winners, 228–229
Low-skilled workers, 572–573
Luck, role of, in wages, 166

M

Magnitude, 118
Major League Baseball (MLB), umpires in, 437
Make-or-buy decisions, 590–592
Male earnings
by ancestry, 439t
female earnings as percentage of, 424t
Mandated wages, 162–164
Mandatory transactions, 29, 30
Manufacturing industry, weekly hours in, 194–195
Marginal expense, 84–85
Marginal expense of labor (MEL), 157–158, 159f, 161–164
Marginal income, from additional unit of input, 83–84
Marginal product, 83
Marginal product of labor (MPL), 83, 86t, 172
in car dealership, 170t
declining, 89, 110–111
ratio of wages to, 599, 606
Marginal rate of substitution, 202n
Marginal rate of technical substitution (MRTS), 109–110, 113–114
Marginal returns, diminishing, 86
Marginal revenue, 84
Marginal revenue (MR), 97
Marginal revenue product, 83, 84, 85, 97
Marginal revenue product of labor (MRPL), 89–91, 89f, 97, 159, 161–164
Mariel boatlift, 370
Market-clearing wage, 66–69, 73
Market demand curves, 91, 96–97
Market failure
externalities, 31
ignorance, 30
price distortion, 32
public goods, 32
transaction barriers, 31
Market supply, 63–64
curve, 64f
paralegals, 64f
Marshall, Alfred, 58

Masters of Business Administration (MBA) degrees, 425
Maternity benefits, 102–103
Median income, 564
Mediation, 500
Men
black/white earnings gap for, 432–433
labor force participation rate, 192t, 193t, 247, 324t, 433–434
labor supply decisions of, 215–216
occupational choice, risk, and, 281
Meritorious goods, 30
Merit raises, 399–400
Meta-analyses, 612–613
Method of least squares, 469
Mexico, immigrants from, 362–363
Miami, Cuban immigrants to, 370
Michigan furniture industry, 448
Migrants
See also Immigrants
personal characteristics of, 352–354
Migration
See also Immigration
of African Americans, 353
costs of, 354
direction of flows, 351–352
distribution of earnings and, 354–356
family, 356–357
internal, 356
international, 354–356
return, 359
returns on, 356–359
role of distance in, 354
time horizon and, 355
Military officers, pay levels and supply of, 76–77
Minimum wage, decline in real, 579, 581
Minimum wage laws, 34, 70, 131–140
employment effects of, 117, 132–138, 134f
history and description of, 131–132
illegal immigrants and, 364–365
intersectoral shifts in product demand and, 136
manufacturing, 132f
in monopsonistic conditions, 162–165, 163f
nominal vs. real wages, 133
noncompliance with, 134
poverty and, 138–139
uncovered sectors, 134–136, 135f
union support for, 493
Minorities, market demand for, as function of relative wages, 443f
Money wages, labor demand and, 89–91, 90f
Monopolies
employer discrimination in, 445
labor demand in, 96–98
product-market, 96–98, 157
profit maximization in, 96–97
wages in, 97–98
Monopoly-union model, 481–483, 482f
Monopsonistic conditions
competitive model and, 167–168
job search costs and, 165–167

minimum wage laws and, 162–165, 163*f*
profit maximization by, 157–161
shifts in supply curve and,
    161–164, 162*f*
wage policies, 160–161
Monopsonistic labor markets, 156–157
Monopsonistic power, 450
Moral hazard, 390
Mothers, labor force participation rate of,
    238–239, 239*t*
Mozambique, forced labor in colonial, 73
Multiple regression analysis, 42–43
Mutually advantageous, 29

N

NAFTA. *See* North American Free Trade
    Agreement (NAFTA)
National Football League (NFL), 85, 480
National Institute for Occupational Safety
    and Health (NIOSH), 294–295
National Labor Relations Act (NLRA),
    475, 491
National Labor Relations Board (NLRB),
    475, 491–492, 492*t*
Natural experiments, 216
Natural rate of unemployment, 553–554,
    555–557
Net wage rate
    positive, 224–226
    of zero, 220–224
New entrants, to labor force, 527
NFL. *See* National Football League (NFL)
NLRA. *See* National Labor Relations Act
    (NLRA)
NLRB. *See* National Labor Relations Board
    (NLRB)
Nominal wages, 53–55, 54*t*, 133,
    545–546
Noncomparable jobs, 65
Noncompetitive forces, 440
Noncompetitive models of discrimination,
    450–454
Nonhuman capital, 305
Nonpecuniary factors, 24
Normative economics, 29–32
    government policy and, 32–33
North American Free Trade Agreement
    (NAFTA), 493
Null hypothesis, 41

O

Obesity, household production model
    and, 237
Occupational discrimination, 427–429
Occupational groups, changes in share of
    employment for, 577–578, 577*t*
Occupational imbalances, in unemploy-
    ment rate, 539–540
Occupational Safety and Health Act,
    283–284
Occupational Safety and Health
    Administration (OSHA), 284–288
Occupational segregation, 427–429, 435

Occupations, 52–53
    earnings differential and, 424
OFCCO. *See* Office of Federal Contract
    Compliance Programs (OFCCP)
Offer curve, 281–282, 282*f*
Office of Federal Contract Compliance
    Programs (OFCCP), 459–460
Offshoring, 601–605
Omitted variables bias, 43–46, 340
On-the-job training, 318, 321–322, 322*f*, 325
    See also Training
Opportunistic behavior, 387
Opportunity costs, 195
    of college education, 314
    internal, 607
    of leisure, 196
OSHA. *See* Occupational Safety and Health
    Administration (OSHA)
Out-of-pocket expenses, 306
Output, 108
    group, 394
    optimal level of, 82–83
Output-based pay, 389–390, 393–398
Output effect, 60
Outsourcing, 590, 599–605
Overtaking age, 322*n*
Overtime
    hours, 173*f*
    pay premium, 173–175
    spreading the work and, 175
    total pay and, 175–176
Own-wage elasticity of demand, 118–127
    components of, 124*t*
    definition of, 118
    estimates of, 123–124
    Hicks-Marshall laws of derived
        demand, 120–122

P

Paid work, time spent on, 234*t*, 235*f*
Paralegals, supply and wages, 64–65
Parameters, 40
Parenthood, occupational choice, risk,
    and, 281
Parents, earnings of, as determinant of
    children's earnings, 580–581
Pareto efficiency, 29, 29*n*, 483, 512
Pareto-improving transactions, 30, 72, 374
Part-time employment, 324*t*, 425
Pay
    See also Compensation; Wages
    below-average, 65
    comparisons, 394–395
    executive, 398–399
    level of, 401–404
    merit, 399–400
    output-based, 389–390, 393–398
    sequencing of, 404
    time-based, 390–391, 394, 399–400
    between union and nonunion, 514–515
    variability of, 393–394
    yearly, 393–400
Pay for performance, 389–390, 393–394
Payments in kind, 57, 288, 289

Payroll subsidies, 100–104
Payroll taxes, 98–100, 171
    cuts in, 103–104
    immigrants and, 373–374
    unemployment insurance, 549–551
Peer effects, 315
Pension benefits, 250–254
Pension costs, 171
Pension plans, 379
Per capita wealth, 305
Perfect complements, 96
Performance-based pay, 389–390,
    393–394
Personal discount rates, 373
Personal prejudice, 440
    by customers, 446
    by employees, 446–447
    by employers, 441–445
Personal Responsibility and Work
    Opportunity Reconciliation Act
    (PRWORA), 222, 224
Physical model, of positive economics, 27
Piece-rate pay, 393–398, 411
Polarization hypothesis, 577–578
Political refugees, 378–379
Politicking, 400
Positive economics, 25–26
    behavior and, 27
    hedonic wage theory and, 282–283
    models, 26–29
    predictions, 26–29
Post-investment surplus, 185
Post-schooling training, 318–323
Post-training revenue, 176
Poverty, minimum wage and, 138–139
Predictions, 26–29
Preferences, 195, 196
    employee, 288–289, 393–395
    employer, 290–292
    household production and, 235–236
    labor/leisure choice and, 200–203
    worker, 267–274
Prejudgment, 440
Prejudice, 440, 441–447
Present-orientedness, 311–313
Present value
    concept of, 306–308
    investment returns using, 311–312
    of net benefits of mobility, 350–351
Prevailing wage, 493
Price distortion, 32
Price elasticity of demand, 121
Primary sector, 451
Product, marginal, 83
Product demand, 121, 125
    shifts in, 140–141, 493, 597–598
    trade and, 597–598
Production
    cost minimization in, 112–114, 112*f*, 114*f*
    geographic dispersion of, 589–590
    inputs are complements in, 96
    inputs are substitutes in, 95–96, 95*f*
    shifts in supply of alternative factors
        of, 599–601
Production function, 108–110

Production possibilities curve, 143–145,
144f, 593f, 594f
  with trade, 594–595
  without trade, 592–593
Production sharing, 589–590, 599–601
Productivity
  actual, 185, 441–452, 512
  appearance of, 400
  bargaining, 494
  basis of yearly pay and, 393–400
  career concerns and, 410–412
  compensation and, 384–385
  interdependent, 243
  level of pay and, 401–404
  range of worker, 384
  sequencing of pay and, 404–412
  union effects on, 510–511
  wage growth and, 179t
Product-market monopolies, 96–98, 157
Profit maximization, 26, 82–85
  employer discrimination and, 445
  employment/hours mix and, 172–173
  employment level for, 486
  executive pay and, 398
  labor demand and, 87–92
  in monopolies, 96–97
  under monopsonistic conditions,
    157–161
  wage and employment levels,
    159–160, 160f
Profits
  under employer discrimination, 442
  union effects on, 510–511
Profit-sharing plans, 393
Promotion tournaments, 408–410
PRWORA. *See* Personal Responsibility and
  Work Opportunity Reconciliation Act
  (PRWORA)
Psychic costs, 306, 314, 315, 327, 350, 353,
  354
Public goods, 32, 372
Public sector
  training, as social investment, 339,
    341–342
  unions, 476–477
Purchasing power, 53

Q

Quasi-fixed costs, 168–172, 174
Quit-rate data, average wage and, 39t, 44t
Quit rates
  by firm size, 375t
  labor market tightness and, 376, 377f
  wages and, 39f, 44f, 45f
Quitting, 50
Quota Law, 360–361
Quotas, import, 589

R

Racial discrimination, 432–438
Railroads, 274
Rank-and-file union members, 499
Rational expectations, 348

Rationality, 25–26
Reagan administration, air traffic
  controllers' strike and, 497–498
Real wages, 53–56, 54t, 133, 545–546
  labor demand and, 87–89
Recessions
  labor supply in, 243–246
  layoffs during, 180–181
Reemployment bonuses, 556–557
Reentrants, to labor force, 527
Reference groups, 391–392
Refugees, 378–379
Regional employment shifts, 490
Regional unemployment, 539–541
Regression analysis, 468–471
Relative wage advantage, 503, 507–508
Relative wages
  discriminatory employers, 444f
  nodiscriminatory employers, 444f
  women and minorities, 443f
Replacement rate, 536
Replacement workers, for strikers, 497
Reservation wage, 73, 213–214, 214f, 215,
  533–534, 533f
Reserve Officer Training Corps
  (ROTC), 77
Resource reallocation, 595–596
Retirement age, choice of, 249–254, 252f
Retirement plans, 171
Return migration, 359
Reverse discrimination, 460
Right-to-work laws, 476, 490
Risk aversion, 394, 520f, 521, 548
Risk-neutral party, 521–523, 522f
ROTC. *See* Reserve Officer Training Corps
  (ROTC)
Rough laborers, 363–365, 364f, 365f,
  366–367
Russian civil war, 227

S

Samuelson, Paul, 168
Scale effect, 59, 60, 61, 62–63, 94, 115f, 128
  alternative factors of production and,
    600
  influences on, 128–129
  long-run, 123
  minimum wage, 136
  short-run, 123, 124, 124t
  wage increase, 120
Scarcity, 25
Schooling. *See* Education
School quality, 337–339
Screening problem, 447–448, 449f
Seamless hosiery industry, minimum wage
  laws and, 137
Search-related monopsony, 451–453, 452f
Seasonal unemployment, 551–553
Secondary sector, 451
Self-enforcement, 387
Seniority, 456
Service jobs, 606–607
Shakers, 397
Shirking, 397–398

Short run, 85
  labor demand in, 85–92, 88f, 110–111, 123
Signaling
  benefits to workers of, 333f
  cautions about, 335–336
  discouraging cheating, 386–387
  human capital or, 336–337
  illustration of, 333–335
  lifetime benefits and costs of, 334f
  model, 332–333
Signals, 182–183
Simultaneity, 146–147
Skill-biased technological change, 575
Skilled labor, 130–131, 367–368, 368f
Skilled workers, 356, 577
Skills, dispersion of, 569
Slope, 205n, 278
Social insurance benefits, 217–220
Social investment
  education as, 331–339
  public sector training as, 339, 341–342
Social norms, 548–549
Social Security, 171, 171n, 373–374
  estimating benefits from, 250–254,
    251t
Social welfare
  potential increases in, 513–515
  potential reductions in, 512
Soviet Union, migration and, 355
Specialization of function, 240–241
Spillover effects, of unions, 503f, 504
Staffing requirements, 493–494
Standard deviation, 564
Standard error, 41
Statistical discrimination, 182–183,
  447–449
Statistical significance, 42
Steel gangs, 274
Stock-flow model, of labor market,
  526–531, 526f
Stock options, 399
Strategic Bombing Survey, 305
Strikers, permanent replacement of, 497
Strikes
  asymmetric information and, 498
  collective bargaining and, 494–499
  model of, 495–498, 495f
Structural unemployment, 539–544, 539f
Subcontracting, 494
Subsidized employment, 610
Subsidy programs, with positive net wage
  rates, 224–226
Substitutability factors, 121–122
Substitution, restrictions on, 493–494
Substitution effect, 59, 60, 61, 62–63, 94,
  114–115, 115f, 123–124, 124t, 127–128
  alternative factors of production and,
    599–600
  defining, 197
  empirical findings on, 214–217
  household production and, 236
  immigrant labor and, 367
  influences on, 129–130
  isolating, 208–212
  minimum wage, 136

overcoming, 197–198
wage increase, 120, 198–199, 207–208, 208*f*, 211*f*
of welfare system, 221*f*
when to work over lifetime and, 247–248
Supervision, of workers, 390–391
Supply
See also Labor supply
capital, 61
changes in, 573–575
of other factors, 122
Surplus
alternative divisions of, 388*f*
creation of, 387–388
Symphony orchestras, bias in selection of musicians by, 427
Synthetic cohorts, 378–379

T

Taft-Hartley Act, 476
Targeted Jobs Tax Credit (TJTC), 101, 103, 602
Tariffs, 589, 606
Tax credits, 101, 103, 224–226, 225*f*, 602, 610
Tax cuts, 216
Taxes
immigrants and, 372, 373–374
payroll, 98–100, 103–104, 171, 373–374
Technological change, 75, 595
labor demand elasticity and, 140–148
overall effects of, 142–145
shifts in demand and, 575–578
Teenage employment, 130, 136–138, 554
Teenage wages, 130, 130*n*, 136–138, 165
Telecommunications, 589
Temporary workers, 174, 182
Tenure
layoffs and, 181
wages and, 166–167, 412–414, 413*f*
Termination costs, 169
Threat effects, of unions, 504–505, 505*f*
Time, life-cycle allocation of, 247–248, 248*f*
Time-based pay, 390–391, 394, 399–400
Time horizons, migration and, 355
Time-series data, 38*n*
Title VII, 455–459
TJTC. *See* Targeted Jobs Tax Credit (TJTC)
Total compensation, 57
Total employment, 602–603
Trade
barriers to, 602
comparative advantage and, 590–592, 593–594
effects on demand for labor, 596–605
employment effects of, 601–604
growth effects of, 596, 597
incentives for, 592–596
between individuals, 590–592
product demand and, 597–598
production possibilities with, 594–595
reasons for, 590–596
resource reallocation and, 595–596
unemployment and, 595
wage effects of, 604–605

Trade Adjustment Assistance program, 608–609, 610, 611
Training
costs, 170
decision, 176–177
decline in, with age, 321–322
general, 177
internal labor market and, 183
investments in, 176–181
layoffs and, 180–181
on-the-job, 318, 321–322, 325
post-training wage increases and, 178–180
public sector, 339, 341–342
specific, 178
by temporary-help agencies, 182
types of, 177–178
women and, 325
Transaction barriers, 31
Trucking industry
deregulation of, 490, 491
union wages in, 126
t statistic, 41–42
Tuition costs, 313–314
Twin studies, on returns of education, 340–341

U

Umpires, 437
Unauthorized immigration, 361–362, 372–374
Underemployment, 535
Underpayment-overpayment compensation schemes, 404–408, 406*f*
Unearned income, 57, 206, 209, 561
Unemployment, 70, 524–560
definition of, 524
demand-deficient (cyclical), 545–551
demographic characteristics and, 554–555, 555*t*
duration of, 529–530
efficiency wages and, 542–544
employment protection legislation and, 169
frictional, 531–539
hidden, 246
incidence of, 529, 530
international comparison of, 530–531, 530*t*
international differences in, 74–75, 541–542
job search costs and, 167
labor force and, 49–52
long-term, 541–542
natural rate of, 553–554, 555–557
payroll tax cuts and, 104*f*
reemployment bonuses and, 556–557
rise in, 524
seasonal, 551–553
as self-perpetuating, 534
sources of, 527–528, 528*t*
structural, 539–544
trade and, 595
wages and, 75

wait, 135*n*, 505–506
for whites, 434–435
Unemployment benefits, 217–220
Unemployment insurance (UI), 171–172
benefits as function of previous earnings, 536*f*
effects of, 535–539
eligibility for, 538
experience rating, 550–551, 550*f*
extended, 609–610
financing, U.S., 549–551
job matches and, 538–539
payroll tax, 549–551
seasonal unemployment and, 552
unemployment and, 537–538
Unemployment levels, flow rates, 528–531
Unemployment rate, 51–52
for blacks, 434–435
civilian, 525*t*
civilian labor force, 51*f*
discouraged-worker effect and, 244
international comparison of, 530*t*
limitations of data, 525–526
measurement of, 524
occupational and regional differences, 539–541
by race and gender, 434*t*
technological change and, 75
Union leaders, 499
Union members, 499
Union membership, 477–479
declines in, 474–475, 477, 488–492, 579
demand and supply, 487–492, 487*f*
demographic changes and, 489
industrial mix and, 489
international comparison of, 474*t*
net benefits of, 488
as percentage of all workers, 477*f*
price of, 487–488
by selected characteristics, 478*t*
tastes for, 488
Union objectives, constraints on, 479–481
Union resistance curve, 496
Unions, 472–518
actions by, to alter labor demand curve, 492–494
collective bargaining by, 473, 487–502
competitive pressures on, 490–491
construction, 493
craft, 473, 494
definition of, 473
effects of, 502–515
efficient-contracts model of, 483–486
employer resistance to, 491–492
employment effects of, 509–510
goals of, 473, 479
government, 476–477
industrial, 473
international comparison of, 473–475
legal structure of, 475–479
local, 478
monopoly-union model, 481–483, 482*f*
normative analyses of, 511–515
political power of, 473
productivity and, 510–511

Unions, (*continued*)
  profits and, 510–511
  representation elections, 492*t*
  role of, 472
  shifts in labor demand and, 506
  social welfare and, 512–515
  spillover effects, 503*f*, 504
  strikes by, 494–499
  threat effects, 504–505, 505*f*
  total compensation effects, 508–509
  types of, 473
  wage effects, 503–509
  wage rigidity and, 547
  wait unemployment, 505–506
Union wages, 126
  gap between nonunion pay and,
    514–515
Unitary elastic demand curve, 118
United Mine Workers of America, 94
United States
  foreign-born population in, 349
  history of immigration in, 360–363
Univariate test, 38–42
Universities, comparable worth and,
  458–459
Unskilled labor, 130–131, 134–135, 141–142,
  268
Unskilled workers, 356
U.S. Army wages, 72–73
U.S. Department of Labor, 174
Utility, 200
Utility function
  for risk-averse party, 520*f*
  for risk-neutral party, 522*f*
Utility maximization, 26, 145, 148, 203, 235,
  267, 271, 308–309, 614

V

Variables
  dependent, 39
  dichotomous, 42–43
  independent, 39–40, 43
  omitted variables bias, 43–46
Veterans, educational attainment of, 315
Voluntary transactions, 29

W

Wage changes, unexpected, 248
Wage constraints, 203–205
Wage curve, 543–544, 544*f*
Wage determination, 383–420
Wage differences, 165–166
  explanations for, 184–185
Wage discrimination
  definition of, 426–427
  employer discrimination and, 442–445
  by gender, 423–432
  inferred, 430–431
  measurement, 429–430
  by race, 435–438
  search-related monopsony and,
    451–453, 452*f*

Wage effects
  of trade, 604–605
  of unions, 503–509
Wage gaps
  employer discrimination and, 442–445
  estimating comparable-worth, 468–471
  between union and nonunion pay,
    514–515
Wage increase
  income effect, 198–199, 207–208, 209*f*
  labor supply and, 260–261
  post-training, 178–180
  productivity and, 179*t*
  scale effect, 94, 115–116, 115*f*
  substitution effect, 94, 114–115, 115*f*,
    198–199, 207–208, 208*f*, 211*f*
Wage levels, 165–166
Wage rate, 53, 196
  downward-sloping function of, 81
  education levels and, 318–320
  employment effects of, 132–138
  labor demand elasticity and,
    118–127
  marginal expense of labor and,
    157–158, 159–160
Wage rigidity
  asymmetric information and, 548
  downward, 545–549
  human capital and, 547
  risk aversion and, 548
  social norms and, 548–549
  unions and, 547
  worker status and, 548–549
Wages
  See also Compensation; Pay
  above-market, 70, 71–72, 71*f*, 75
  below-market, 72–73
  Black Death and, 69
  capital substitution and, 94
  changes in, 59–60
  civilian, 77
  coal mining, 94
  compensating wage differential, 268,
    269–270
  convergence of, across countries,
    605–607
  determination of, 65–70
  earnings and, 56–57
  efficiency, 402, 403–404, 542–544
  elasticity of, 120–122
  employee turnover and, 374–375
  equilibrium differential, 268–269
  expected, 534
  immigrant labor and, 369–370
  income effect, 211*f*
  job tenure and, 166–167
  joint determination of benefits and,
    292–295, 293*f*
  labor demand and, 87–91
  labor market experience and, 166
  in large firms, 414–417
  living wage laws, 139–140
  luck and, 166
  mandated, 162–164

market-clearing, 66–69, 73
maternity benefits and, 102–103
military, 76–77
minimum, 34, 70, 131–140, 162–165,
  493, 579, 581
money, 89–91
in monopolies, 97–98
monopsonistic firms, 160–161
nominal, 53–55, 54*t*, 133, 545–546
nonmarket forces affecting, 70
overtime, 173–175
paralegals, 65*f*
prevailing, 493
quit rates and, 39*f*, 44*f*, 45*f*
ratio to marginal productivity, 599, 606
real, 53–56, 54*t*, 133, 545–546
relationship between earnings,
  compensation, income, and,
  57*f*
relationship between layoffs and, 303
reservation, 73, 213–214, 214*f*, 215,
  533–534, 533*f*
risk of injury and, 276*f*
teenage, 130, 130*n*, 136–138, 165
tenure and, 413*f*
unemployment and, 75
union, 126
work-incentive effects of, 195
Wage subsidies, 100–104
Wage takers, 65, 152
Wait unemployment, 135*n*, 505–506
War, human capital and, 305
Wartime food requisitions, 227
Wealth, 195, 196
  income and, 196
  per capita, 305
Welfare programs, 34, 220–224, 222*f*
  income and substitution effects of, 221*f*
  lifetime limits, 222–223
  nature of subsidies, 220–221
  reform, 222
  work requirements, 223–224, 224*f*
White male earnings, 422*f*
White workers, 421, 446–447
Women
  age/earnings profiles, 326*f*, 424
  child-rearing by, 324, 325
  college and university graduation
    rates, 327*t*
  earnings, as percentage of male
    earnings, 424*t*
  formal schooling and, 325–327
  human capital acquisition and,
    323–327
  job training and, 325
  in labor force, 50*t*, 422, 489
  labor force participation rate, 191*t*, 193*t*,
    247, 324*t*
  labor supply decisions of, 216–217
  market demand for, as function of
    relative wages, 443*f*
  occupational choice, risk, and, 281
Work, decision to, 195–217
Worker information, 271–272

Worker mobility, 349–382
  benefits of, 377, 379
  costs of, 154–156, 165–167, 180, 350
  determinants of, 350–351
  employee turnover, 374–379
  geographic, 351–374
  job choice and, 272
  role of, 350
Worker motivation
  career concerns and, 410–412
  compensation-sequencing schemes for, 404–408, 406f
  fairness and, 416–417
  promotion tournaments, 408–410
Worker preferences, 267–274
Worker productivity. *See* Productivity
Workers
  See also Employees
  apprentice, 494
  attracting better, 401
  demographics of, 421–422, 422t
  discouraged, 246, 434

  displaced by offshoring, 601–604, 606–613
  employment/hours trade-off, 172–176
  employment protection legislation and, 169
  high-skilled, 572–573
  hiring costs, 168–169, 170
  journeymen, 494
  low-skilled, 572–573
  motivation of, 385–393
  overpaid, 71–72
  skilled, 356, 577
  sorting, 405
  temporary, 174, 182
  termination costs, 169
  training costs, 170
  underpaid, 72–73
  unobserved heterogeneity in, 184–185
  unskilled, 356
  wage differences for, 184–185
Workers' compensation insurance, 171, 217–220

Worker sorting, 394
Worker status, 548–549
Work hours
  constrained, 300–301
  unconstrained choice of, 299–300, 300f
Work incentives, 406
Workplace-death statistics, 294–295
Workplace safety, 283–288, 284f
Workweeks, 193–195
World War II, 227, 305
World War II veterans, educational attainment of, 315

Y

Yearly net wage, 251
Yearly pay, productivity and, 393–400

Z

Zero net wage rate, 220–224
Zero profit, 277, 279f